THE ROUTLEDGE HANDBOOK OF EARLY MODERN KOREA

Korea is a historical region of prominence in the global political economy. Still, a comprehensive overview of its early modern era has yet to receive a book-length treatment in English. Comprising topical chapters written by 22 experts from 11 countries, *The Routledge Handbook of Early Modern Korea* presents an interdisciplinary survey of Korea's politics, society, economy, and culture from the founding of the Chosŏn state (1392–1897) to 1873 when its political leadership began preparing for treaty relations with Imperial Japan, the United States, and other Western nations.

Chosŏn mirrors shared historical patterns among literate sedentary societies of early modern Afro-Eurasia. Various long-term developments that shaped early modern Korea include the completion of centralized bureaucratic governance as codified in the State Administrative Code (Kyŏngguk taejŏn); the appearance of regular rural marketplaces facilitating transactions in an increasingly liberalized economy; continuity of an aristocracy (*yangban*) from the medieval period (Koryŏ: 918–1392); a decreasing correspondence between ascriptive status and socioeconomic class; and the state and the elite's growing interest in encyclopedic knowledge and its dissemination while their monopoly on knowledge production weakened.

This handbook provides historical context for readers wishing to know more than just the "Korea" that evokes K-pop or North Korea's nuclear weapons, while Hyundai, Samsung, and other South Korean brands have gained visibility in everyday life. Interested English-speaking scholars, educators, students, and the general public without access to the large body of Korean-language works on Chosŏn will find this book a valuable critical introduction to early modern Korea.

Eugene Y. Park is a professor in the Department of History at the University of Nevada, Reno. Author of seven books, including *Korea: A History* (2022), his scholarship focuses on East Asia, especially Korean politics and society from the fifteenth to the early twentieth century. Maintaining a comparative perspective and interested in periodizing global history, Park also enjoys readings and conversations in evolutionary biology, deep history, and population genetics. His current research topics include ancient animal symbolism and historical human-feline interactions. In 2016, Park co-chaired the organizing committee of the Eighth Biennial World Congress of Korean Studies.

The Routledge History Handbooks

The Routledge History Handbook of Central and Eastern Europe in the Twentieth Century
Volume 1: Challenges of Modernity
Edited by Włodzimierz Borodziej, Stanislav Holubec and Joachim von Puttkamer

The Routledge Handbook of the Mongols and Central-Eastern Europe
Edited by Alexander V. Maiorov and Roman Hautala

The Routledge Handbook of Medieval Rural Life
Edited by Miriam Müller

The Routledge Handbook of East Central and Eastern Europe in the Middle Ages, 500-1300
Edited by Florin Curta

The Routledge Handbook on Identity in Byzantium
Edited by Michael Edward Stewart, David Alan Parnell, and Conor Whately

The Routledge Handbook of Memory Activism
Edited by Yifat Gutman and Jenny Wüstenberg

The Routledge Handbook of Taxation in Medieval Europe
Edited by Denis Menjot, Mathieu Caesar, Florent Garnier and Pere Verdés Pijuan

The Routledge Handbook of the Byzantine City
From Justinian to Mehmet II (ca. 500 - ca.1500)
Edited by Nikolas Bakirtzis and Luca Zavagno

The Routledge Handbook of Byzantine Visual Culture in the Danube Regions, 1300–1600
Edited by Maria Alessia Rossi and Alice Isabella Sullivan

The Routledge Handbook of Gender and Sexuality in Byzantium
Edited by Mati Meyer and Charis Messis

The Routledge Handbook of Human-Animal Relations in the Byzantine World
Edited by Przemysław Marciniak and Tristan Schmidt

The Routledge Handbook of Early Modern Korea
Edited by Eugene Y. Park

For more information about this series, please visit: https://www.routledge.com/Routledge-History-Handbooks/book-series/RHISTHAND

THE ROUTLEDGE HANDBOOK OF EARLY MODERN KOREA

Edited by Eugene Y. Park

LONDON AND NEW YORK

Cover image credit: Yi Hyŏngnok, Ch'aekkŏri, nineteenth century, ten-fold screen, color on silk, 153.0 cm x 352.0 cm. Source and photo credit: National Museum of Korea.

First published 2025
by Routledge
4 Park Square, Milton Park, Abingdon, Oxon OX14 4RN

and by Routledge
605 Third Avenue, New York, NY 10158

Routledge is an imprint of the Taylor & Francis Group, an informa business

© 2025 selection and editorial matter, Eugene Y. Park; individual chapters, the contributors

The right of Eugene Y. Park to be identified as the author of the editorial material, and of the authors for their individual chapters, has been asserted in accordance with sections 77 and 78 of the Copyright, Designs and Patents Act 1988.

All rights reserved. No part of this book may be reprinted or reproduced or utilised in any form or by any electronic, mechanical, or other means, now known or hereafter invented, including photocopying and recording, or in any information storage or retrieval system, without permission in writing from the publishers.

Trademark notice: Product or corporate names may be trademarks or registered trademarks, and are used only for identification and explanation without intent to infringe.

British Library Cataloguing-in-Publication Data
A catalogue record for this book is available from the British Library

ISBN: 978-1-032-20062-0 (hbk)
ISBN: 978-1-032-20063-7 (pbk)
ISBN: 978-1-003-26205-3 (ebk)

DOI: 10.4324/9781003262053

Typeset in Times New Roman
by Deanta Global Publishing Services, Chennai, India

CONTENTS

List of tables	*viii*
List of figures	*ix*
List of contributors	*xii*
Acknowledgments	*xv*
Conventions	*xvi*
Maps	*xviii*

Introduction   1
Eugene Y. Park

PART I
Chosŏn in Time and Space   **11**

1   Korea and Early Modernity   13
    Sixiang Wang

2   Foreign Relations   28
    Kirk W. Larsen

3   Korea as "Little China" (*So Chunghwa*)   43
    Nataliya A. Chesnokova

4   Korea in Japan   58
    Rebekah Clements

Contents

PART II
The State, Power, and Resource   **73**

  5 Politics   75
     Christopher Lovins

  6 The Military   88
     Felix Siegmund

  7 Discontent   103
     Andrew David Jackson

  8 Economy   117
     Young-Jun Cho

PART III
Society and Identity   **131**

  9 Status and Class   133
     Eugene Y. Park

 10 Foreigners and the Descendants   150
     Adam Bohnet

 11 Gender   164
     Marion Eggert

PART IV
Philosophy and Religion   **179**

 12 Confucianism   181
     Isabelle Sancho

 13 Buddhism   197
     Juhn Y. Ahn

 14 Popular Religion   213
     Boudewijn Walraven

 15 Catholicism   227
     Franklin D. Rausch

Contents

PART V
Language, Learning, and Knowledge   **241**

16 Language   243
    Ross King

17 Education   260
    Diana Yuksel

18 Science and Technology   275
    Don Baker

PART VI
Creative Genres   **289**

19 Literature   291
    Gregory N. Evon

20 Visual Arts   305
    Yoonjung Seo

21 Performing Arts   323
    CedarBough T. Saeji

    Epilogue: Korea since 1873   339
    Mark E. Caprio

Index   *353*

vii

TABLES

F.1	Chosŏn monarchs	xix
16.1	Early Middle Korean chungch'ŏl Over-Spelling in Aspirates	249
21.1	Important performance-related texts and commissioning monarchs	326

FIGURES

1.1 Celestial globe and armillary clock by Chosŏn's court astronomer, Song
    Iyŏng, 1669. Both were set up at the Office of Special Counselors
    (Hongmun'gwan) for teaching astronomy and for measuring time. Source:
    Korea University Museum ... 19

2.1 Mandongmyo, Cheongcheon-myeon, Goesan-gun, Chungcheongbuk-do,
    Republic of Korea ... 37

3.1 Portrait of Song Siyŏl (1607–89), likely a copy of Kim Ch'angŏp's (1658–
    1721) undated copy of the original portrait (1680). A leading advocate
    of the Northern Expedition, Song became a central figure in the *So
    Chunghwa* ideology and the founding leader of the Patriarchs (Noron),
    who eventually achieved a paramount political position by the eighteenth
    century ... 49

4.1 Residents of Naeshirogawa in Korean dress ... 63

5.1 Draft portrait of Sejo, 1935, by Kim Ŭnho (1892–1979), 131.8 cm ×
    186.5 cm. Commissioned to paint portraits of two former emperors after
    Japan's annexation of Korea (1910), Kim also worked on copying then-
    extant official portraits of various Chosŏn kings, including an official
    portrait of Sejo from 1735, no longer extant ... 81

6.1 Portrait of Sin Hŏn at 61, 1870 ... 99

7.1 Portrait of Yŏngjo, 1900, 68 cm × 110 cm. Painted by Ch'ae Yongsin
    (1848–1941) and Cho Sŏkchin (1853–1920), this is a copy of the original
    work of 1744, no longer extant ... 109

9.1 A section in the *Origins of Descent Group* shows five Kyŏngju Kim lines
    unconnected, each descending from an individual surnamed Kim (金). In
    contrast, contemporary Kyŏngju Kim genealogies generally record various
    descent lines to King Kyŏngsun (r. 927–35), the last ruler of Silla ... 135

9.2 Local advisory bureau building in Koesan, Ch'ungch'ŏng Province, 1995
    restoration of the original construction, 1681 ... 141

Figures

9.3   *Fighting Males at a Kisaeng House* (*Yugwak chaengung*; early nineteenth century) by Sin Yunbok (1758–c. 1814), a *chungin* court painter descended from an illegitimate son of an early Chosŏn aristocrat. As a *kisaeng* holding a long smoking pipe watches, a *yangban* and a special martial arts officer (*muye pyŏlgam*), a military *chungin* running the *kisaeng* house, restrain a young man who lost the fight to the bare-chested man. The man on the far right is picking up the pieces of the loser's hat   144

9.4   Stele honoring Lady Miryang Pak of Hamyang, Kyŏngsang Province, as a chaste widow, erected in 1797. At 19, she married her husband, a local functionary, who soon fell ill and died. Upon completing the ritual mourning of three years for her husband, Lady Pak took her life   146

11.1   Depiction of Kyewŏrhyang, 1815. During the Imjin War, Kyewŏrhyang, who was a *kisaeng* in P'yŏngyang and a favorite concubine of a Korean military commander, helped him behead the Japanese military officer, whom she deceived with her charms and then took her own life. Deeming Kyewŏrhyang righteous, the people of P'yŏngyang prepared an image of her and made offerings to her spirit every year   170

12.1   Portrait of Yi Saek, 1654. Hŏ Ŭi (b. 1601) and Kim Myŏngguk (b. 1600) are said to have painted this version, copying the original portrait, no longer extant   186

12.2   Portrait of Chŏng Mongju, 1555. This is a copy of an earlier version no longer extant   187

12.3   Portrait of Pak Chiwŏn, early nineteenth century. This work by his grandson, Pak Chusu (1816–35), was likely based on an earlier version no longer extant   194

13.1   Hŭngch'ŏn-sa, Donam-dong, Seongbuk-gu, Seoul, Republic of Korea   200

13.2   Portrait of Hyujŏng, early or mid-eighteenth century, 106 cm × 76 cm   207

13.3   Portrait of Yujŏng, between 1610 and 1796, 122.9 cm × 78.8 cm   208

14.1   Female shaman performing a ritual. This depiction is by a late nineteenth-century artist, Kisan Kim Chun'gŭn   215

14.2   Blind exorcist (*p'ansu*) at work, as depicted by Kisan Kim Chun'gŭn   221

15.1   Portrait of Hŭngsŏn Taewŏn'gun painted by Yi Hanch'ŏl (b. 1808), 1869. Introduced to Catholicism by Martha Pak, the regent's wife, Lady Yŏhŭng Min (1818–98), would later receive baptism (1896)   237

16.1   Illustration for "Kaebaek Slices Off a Digit."   250

16.2   Text page for "Kaebaek Slices Off a Digit."   251

17.1   Looking out from the Tosan Academy's main hall, Chŏn'gyodang   268

18.1   Magic square. At the time, Koreans were not using Arabic numerals, which are shown here only for ready recognition by the readers of this chapter   280

19.1   Portrait of Kim Sisŭp, late seventeenth or early eighteen century, 71.8 cm × 48.1cm   294

20.1   *Gathering of Scholars at the Book Reading Hall*, c. 1531, hanging scroll, ink and light color on silk, 62.2 cm × 91.3 cm   307

Figures

20.2 Chŏng Sŏn, *After Rain at Mount Inwang*, 1751, hanging scroll, ink on paper, 79.2 cm × 138.2 cm — 308

20.3 Kim Hongdo, *Screen of Genre Scenes*, 1778, eight-fold screen, ink and light color on silk, each 90.9 cm × 42.7 cm — 309

20.4 Cho Chungmuk, Pak Kijun, Paek Ŭnbae, Pak Yonggi, Yu Suk, Yi Ch'angok, Pak Yonghun, An Kŏnyŏng, Cho Chaehŭng, and Sŏ Tup'yo, *Portrait of King T'aejo*, 1872, hanging scroll, color on silk, 150 cm × 218 cm — 310

20.5 Kang Sehwang, *Self Portrait,* 1782, hanging scroll, color on silk, 88.7 cm × 51.0 cm — 311

20.6 *King Chŏngjo's Visit to the Royal Tomb in Hwasŏng*, 1795–96, eight-fold screen, ink and color on silk, each panel 151.5 cm × 66.4 cm — 313

20.7 *The Banquet of the Queen Mother of the West,* 1800, eight-fold screen, ink and color on silk, each panel 145.0 × 54.0 cm — 314

20.8 Yi Hyŏngnok, *Ch'aekkŏri*, nineteenth century, ten-fold screen, color on silk, 153.0 cm × 352.0 cm — 315

20.9 *The Bhaisajyaguru Triad*, 1565, hanging scroll, gold on silk, 54.2 cm × 29.7 cm — 316

20.10 *The Porcelain Jar with Cloud and Dragon Design in Underglaze Cobalt Blue,* late eighteenth century, porcelain with cobalt-blue decoration, height 57.5 cm — 318

21.1 A screen painting of a royal court banquet with performers — 327

CONTRIBUTORS

Juhn Y. Ahn is an associate professor in the Department of Asian Languages and Cultures at the University of Michigan, Ann Arbor, MI. His research focuses on the economic history of Korea in Koryŏ and the cultural history of weather, empire, and wealth in early Chosŏn. Ahn is also interested in reading practices in Song China's Chan Buddhism.

Don Baker is a professor in the Department of Asian Studies at the University of British Columbia, Vancouver, Canada. His main research area is the last two centuries of Chosŏn history, particularly changes in philosophy, religion, and science. Baker is also the series editor of the three-volume *The Cambridge History of Korea* project, which is currently in progress.

Adam Bohnet is an associate professor in King's University College at the University of Western Ontario, London, Canada. His main research area is the social and cultural history of Chosŏn, especially foreign affairs and borderlands. Bohnet is also interested in global trade and cultural exchange networks from 1100 to 1800.

Mark E. Caprio is a professor emeritus in the Department of Intercultural Communication at Rikkyo University, Toshima, Japan. His research covers colonial Korea and the following years, especially pro-Japanese collaboration, Japan-based Korean repatriation, and Korean attitudes toward trusteeship. Caprio is also interested in ongoing Korean efforts to address the colonial legacy, their search for national sovereignty, and contemporary Korean–Japanese relations.

Nataliya A. Chesnokova is an associate professor at the Institute for Oriental and Classical Studies at HSE University, Moscow, Russia. Her area of research is premodern Korean history, especially identity construction and collective identity, legitimacy of power, and geomantic discourse.

Young-Jun Cho is an associate professor in the Department of Economics at Seoul National University, Seoul, South Korea. His main research area is the economy of Korea and East Asia before industrialization, especially late Chosŏn's royal finances and commerce in Hansŏng. Cho is also interested in paleography, which engages him with history and economics.

Contributors

Rebekah Clements is an ICREA Research Professor at the Autonomous University of Barcelona, Barcelona, Spain. She is a cultural historian of Japan, specializing in the Tokugawa period. Clements's research focuses on language, society, and the characteristics of Japanese early modernity, as understood in the broader context of East Asia.

Marion Eggert is a professor at the Korean Studies Institute, Ruhr University Bochum, Bochum, Germany. Her research focuses on the literary and intellectual history of mid-to-late Chosŏn, with eventual forays into colonial and South Korea. Eggert is a member of the Academia Europaea and served as president of the Association for Korean Studies in Europe (AKSE).

Gregory N. Evon is a senior lecturer in the School of Humanities and Languages at UNSW Sydney, Sydney, Australia. His research focuses on premodern and early modern Korean intellectual and religious history in its broader East Asian context. Evon has published on Korea's classical poetry and literary and intellectual history, often dealing with Buddhism.

Andrew David Jackson is an associate professor at Monash University's Korean Studies Research Hub, Melbourne, Australia. He is a researcher of Korean history with a particular focus on social unrest and rebellion and the development of film and cinematic spaces in North and South Korea.

Ross King is a professor in the Department of Asian Studies at the University of British Columbia, Vancouver, Canada. His research focuses on the cultural and social history of language, writing, and literary culture in Korea and the Sinographic Cosmopolis, with a particular interest in comparative histories of vernacularization. King serves as Editor-in-Chief of *Sungkyun Journal of East Asian Studies*.

Kirk W. Larsen is an associate professor in the Department of History at Brigham Young University, Provo, UT. His research focuses on East Asian foreign relations, especially Korea. Larsen has also published, presented, and commented on contemporary issues, including East Asian foreign relations, North Korea, nationalism and elections in South Korea, and Sino–Korean relations.

Christopher Lovins is an independent scholar. He publishes on political legitimacy, Korean slavery, evolutionary approaches to the humanities, and science fiction. Lovins's current book project is a comprehensive examination of slavery in premodern Korea.

Eugene Y. Park is a professor in the Department of History at the University of Nevada, Reno, NV. His main research area is the politics and society of Korea from the fifteenth to the early twentieth century, especially partisan identities, status mobility, and family history narratives. Park co-chaired the organizing committee for the 2016 World Congress of Korean Studies.

Franklin D. Rausch is a professor in the Department of History and Philosophy at Lander University, Greenwood, SC. His research focuses on Korean Catholicism, particularly the relationship between religion and violence. Rausch is also interested in historical memory and public history.

CedarBough T. Saeji is an assistant professor in the Department of Global Studies at Pusan National University, Busan, South Korea. She is a scholar of the presentation of Korean culture, including intangible cultural heritage and modern popular music. Saeji serves as vice-chair of the Committee on Korean Studies, Association for Asian Studies.

Contributors

Isabelle Sancho is a permanent researcher at the French National Center for Scientific Research and Center for Research on Korea at the School for Advanced Studies in the Social Sciences (EHESS), Paris, France. A specialist in Confucianism and translator of Literary Sinitic texts, she is interested in Korea's intellectual history, literary anthologies, and biographies before the late nineteenth century. Sancho is former director of the Center for Korean Studies at the EHESS.

Yoonjung Seo is an associate professor in the Department of Art History at Myongji University, Seoul, South Korea. Her research area is Korean art, especially Chosŏn court paintings from the eighteenth and nineteenth centuries. Additionally, Seo's work explores transcultural interactions in East Asian art, including artistic exchanges between China and Korea.

Felix Siegmund is a professor at the Korean Studies Institute of Ruhr University Bochum, Bochum, Germany. His main research areas are Korean and East Asian philology, Literary Sinitic, military writings and the history of Korea and China, and social history. Siegmund is also interested in Manchu translations, the history of stone fighting, and the history of the (sweet) potato.

Boudewijn Walraven is a professor emeritus at the Institute for Area Studies of Leiden University, Leiden, Netherlands. His research has focused on religious practices in the past and present, with a particular interest in the relations between the various religious traditions co-existing in Korea, such as shamanism, Confucianism, and Buddhism. He co-founded the online journal *Korean Histories*, collaborating with Remco Breuker and Koen De Ceuster.

Sixiang Wang is an associate professor in the Department of Asian Languages and Cultures at the University of California, Los Angeles, CA. He is a historian of Chosŏn Korea and early modern East Asia. Wang's research interests include comparative perspectives on early modern empires, the history of science and knowledge, and issues of language and writing in Korea's cultural and political history.

Diana Yuksel is an assistant professor in the Faculty of Foreign Languages and Literatures at the University of Bucharest, Bucharest, Romania. Her main research areas are premodern Korean literature and Confucianism, especially in the fifteenth and sixteenth centuries. Yuksel is the university's coordinator of the Korean Language and Literature Program.

ACKNOWLEDGMENTS

The present volume owes its inception to Routledge, which contacted Don Baker, the series editor for *The Cambridge History of Korea*. Explaining that *The Routledge Handbook of Early Modern Korea* will complement *The Cambridge History of Korea*'s Chosŏn dynasty volume already underway, Don advised Routledge to contact me. Upon submitting my proposal in May 2021, the subsequent feedback from anonymous reviewers helped me improve the overall framework for the project, which was under contract by August. I am grateful to Don, as well as Senior Editor Michael Greenwood of Routledge, for placing trust in me.

In the ensuing months, I was fortunate enough to secure the commitment of 21 scholars who ultimately contributed to this book. In May 2023, we presented our draft chapters for comments from one another during a contributor workshop in a hybrid synchronous format held at my institution, the University of Nevada, Reno (UNR). Funding the workshop was the Northeast Asia Council grant from the Association for Asian Studies, the Hilliard Endowment grant from UNR, and the Conference and Workshop Support Grant (AKS-2023-C007) from the Academy of Korean Studies. Then, in July 2024, a smaller group of contributing authors fine-tuned our revisions while participating as co-panelists at the Asian Studies Conference Japan in Tokyo. My participation in the conference would not have been possible without the Scholarly and Creative Activities Grant and the Research and Innovation Grant, both from UNR.

Since I found my new intellectual home at UNR in July 2020, many colleagues have extended friendship and support. In particular, I thank Greta de Jong, Dennis Dworkin, Elizabeth Raymond, Hugh Shapiro, and Chris von Nagy, who also gave an expert tour to the workshop participants for a stunning view of Lake Tahoe. Besides the privilege of daily rejuvenation from the Sierras, among countless other blessings are the inspiration and more that I receive from Seri and our children, Lauren and Harry, and all the joy our kitty, Clarabelle, has brought as a new family member.

CONVENTIONS

This book generally employs Pinyin, Revised Hepburn, and McCune–Reischauer systems to Romanize Chinese, Japanese, and Korean, respectively. Exceptions include such alternative spellings as "Seoul" (instead of Sŏul) that have become widely known and contemporary South Korean proper nouns using the Revised Romanization system. Whenever a Korean term in an alternative spelling appears for the first time, the McCune–Reischauer version follows inside parentheses. For the most part, English-language Wikipedia automatically converts McCune–Reischauer spelling of a search term—with or without diacritical marks and apostrophes—to that of South Korea's Revised Romanization spelling (for example, from Inch'ŏn to Incheon) unless the word has to do with North Korea which generally uses McCune–Reischauer without diacritical marks or apostrophes (for example, Pyongyang instead of P'yŏngyang). Regardless, all personal names except Western ones show the family name first if it is known. And while keeping Romanized East Asian terms to a minimum, existing English translations are used as much as possible.

In identifying historical political entities, this volume adopts the following conventions. The terms based on modern nation-states such as China, Japan, and Korea either stand in for geographical zones or describe a sense of political continuity tied to lines of monarchical transmission. Chinese and Korean regimes are rendered without the definite article "the": "Ming" rather than "the Ming" and "Chosŏn" rather than "the Chosŏn." They were proper names for states (*kukho*) rather than dynasties or ruling families (in the manner of, for example, the Stuarts, the Romanovs, the Ottomans, or the Safavids). After all, the official name of Chosŏn as documented in diplomatic documents at the state level is the "State of Chosŏn" (Chosŏn kuk), not the Chosŏn dynasty (Chosŏn wangjo), which is a modern construct that belies the fact that the royal branch of the Chŏnju Yi descent group was the ruling house. Accordingly, throughout the book, Chosŏn and the term "dynasty" refer to either this state or the court that ruled it.

To the extent readily searchable on the web, the text provides an individual's birth and death years and an entity's beginning and ending dates when first mentioned. All dates mentioned are according to the Gregorian calendar unless noted otherwise. According to the lunar calendar, which remained the standard in Korea until the government went solar on the seventeenth day of the eleventh lunar month of 1895, which became Gregorian New Year's Day 1896. Primary source citations use the format of "January 1, 1900" for Gregorian dates and "1800/1/1" (the first day of the first lunar month of 1800) for the lunar calendar—with "i" immediately preceding the month number to denote an intercalary lunar month. To the extent that they are more readily searchable,

xvi

Conventions

the text provides an individual's birth and death years when mentioned for the first time. The customary Korean age regards an individual as one *se* at birth, subsequently gaining a year on every lunar New Year's Day. Thus, according to Western practice, one's age in se is one or two years greater than one's age.

Aside from acronyms explained in the text or well known, the following abbreviations are used:

b.	born
BCE	before the Common Era
c.	circa
CE	Common Era
Ch.	Chinese
d.	died
fl.	*floruit*, flourished
Ja.	Japanese
Ko.	Korean
n.d.	no date
trad.	traditional date
+	or later

Notes and illustrations were kept to a minimum. For readability, all chapters employ in-text citations to refer to sources—except Ross King's more technical chapter on historical Korean linguistics, utilizing helpful footnotes.

MAP

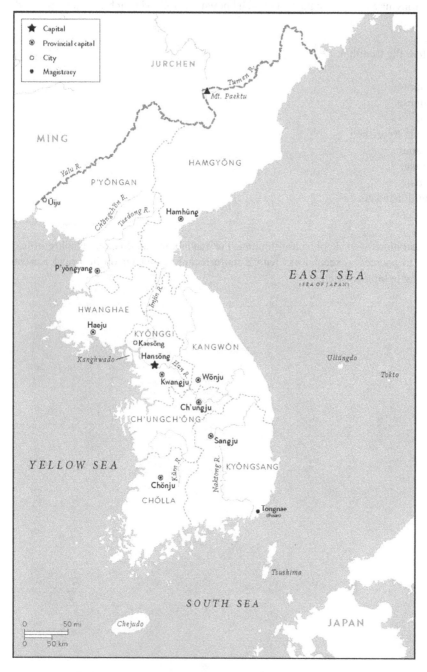

Map F.1 Major administrative centers and boundaries of Chosŏn, mid-fifteenth century. The capitals and boundaries, as shown, remained relatively unchanged until 1895.

Map

Table F.1 Choson monarchs

Monarch	Reign Years	Era Name (yŏnho)	Era Years	Relationship to Predecessor
T'aejo	1392–1398			Dynastic founder
Chŏngjong	1398–1400			Son
T'aejong	1400–1418			Younger brother
Sejong	1418–1450			Son
Munjong	1450–1452			Son
Tanjong	1452–1455			Son
Sejo	1455–1468			Uncle
Yejong	1468–1470			Son
Sŏngjong	1470–1495			Nephew
Yŏnsan Kun	1495–1506			Son
Chungjong	1506–1544			Younger brother
Injong	1544–1545			Son
Myŏngjong	1545–1567			Younger brother
Sŏnjo	1567–1608			Nephew
Kwanghae Kun	1608–1623			Son
Injo	1623–1649			Nephew
Hyojong	1649–1659			Son
Hyŏnjong	1659–1674			Son
Sukchong	1674–1720			Son
Kyŏngjong	1720–1724			Son
Yŏngjo	1724–1776			Younger brother
Chŏngjo	1776–1800			Grandson
Sunjo	1800–1834			Son
Hŏnjong	1834–1849			Grandson
Ch'ŏlchong	1849–1864			Second cousin once removed
Kojong	1864–1907			Second cousin once removed
		Kŏnyang	1896–1897	
		Kwangmu	1897–1907	
Sunjong	1907–1910	Yunghŭi	1907–1910	Son

Note: all are conventionally referred to by their respective temple names (*myoho*) except Yŏnsan Kun and Kwanghae Kun, who their officials deposed. Yŏnsan Kun is a princely title the successor Injo gave him after dethronement, whereas Kwanghae Kun is the princely title he had received before ascending the throne.

INTRODUCTION

Eugene Y. Park

This book highlights facets of early modern Korea from the founding of the State of Chosŏn (Chosŏn kuk; 1392–1897) to 1873, when its leadership began negotiating with forces of imperialism. "Chosŏn" (Ch. Chaoxian) is the modern Korean pronunciation of two Sinographs that together can mean "morning freshness." The fact that Korean history's first recorded polity is so named—referred to as Kojosŏn (Ancient Chosŏn; c. 350–108 BCE) in modern historiography—has engendered a widespread misperception that ancient Korea acquired a poetic name, the "land of morning freshness," or, as popularized by South Korea's tourist industry, the "land of morning calm" (*ach'im ŭi nara*). To the contrary, some two millennia ago, Chinese records began using the two Sinographs together for their sounds to approximate the pronunciation of a non-Chinese ethnonym or toponym to the northeast of China proper. Notwithstanding various speculative explanations, the meaning of Chosŏn is lost in the mists of time. Nonetheless, its aura of prestige spurred the successor to the State of Koryŏ (Koryŏ kuk; 918–1392)—which had established the Korean Peninsula's first united monarchy in 936—to assume the name Chosŏn. Following the propriety of "serving the great" (Ch. *shida*; Ko. *sadae*), Chosŏn's founder had the founding emperor of China's Ming dynasty (1368–1644) choose the name between two options (Wang 2023, 28–30).

Chosŏn ruled Korea during the "early modern era," a central concept in current discussions of world history. Historians interested in global interregional connections and shared patterns have utilized a four-part periodization in the past two decades. According to the paradigm, the classical era (antiquity; c. 600 BCE–c. 600 CE) saw the emergence of institutions and ideas, especially world religions, that laid the lasting foundation for polities, societies, and cultures thereafter. In the postclassical era (medieval period, including late antiquity; c. 600–c. 1450), the Indian Ocean world remained the epicenter in terms of the volume of movements of people, goods, and ideas (especially world religions), the standard of living, and the state of learning and technology. In the succeeding early modern era (c. 1450–c. 1850), the "rise of the West" shaped the Atlantic World and culminated with the Industrial Revolution, imperialism, and colonialism. In the following (late) modern era (since about 1850), industrialization spread to the rest of the world, increasingly centered around the Pacific Rim (Green 1995, 99–111; Belich, Darwin, and Wickham 2016, 3–22; Holmes and Standen 2018, 1–44). Reflecting this periodization, much throughout Afro-Eurasia, where writing systems played critical roles in legitimation and identity formation throughout history, the beginnings of reliable, patrilineal genealogies of aristocratic and middle-status (mainly professionals and big merchants) families as of 1900 mark the start of postclassical and early

DOI: 10.4324/9781003262053-1

The Routledge Handbook of Early Modern Korea

modern eras, respectively (Eberhard 1972, 27–29; Wagner 1975; Diamond 1997, 15–17, 176–91, 215–38; Yi Sugŏn 2003; Pohl 2016, 1–24). In stark contrast, how far back such a genealogy can be traced for anyone among the rest of the population depends on the availability of a modern nation-state's government records, such as household registers, tax rosters, and military conscription records.

Korean history is no exception. The reliable patrilineal genealogy of even the bona fide landed *yangban* ("two orders": civil and military officials), the aristocrats as of 1900—constituting less than two percent of the population and pursuing classical learning in Literary Sinitic (Classical Chinese)—goes back no farther than the turn of the tenth century, marking the division between Korea's classical and postclassical eras. For specialist *chungin* ("middle people"), who were state-employed experts in various fields, and local functionaries (*hyangni*), the fifteenth century is the limit, the beginning of Korea's early modern era during which Chosŏn ruled the peninsula. Transformative developments with human actors across status boundaries in Chosŏn amount to Korea's early modernity in a calendrical sense and global connections, if not in the early modernity's salient features.

As true elsewhere in early modern Afro-Eurasia, Chosŏn embodied continuities from Koryŏ, the postclassical state of Korea. Not only descended from Koryŏ's aristocracy, Chosŏn's *yangban* monopolized political power while holding the royal power in check (Haboush 1988, 14–19; Duncan 2000, 121–33). They sought to disseminate Confucian moral values among the general population, even devising a phonetic alphabet, Han'gŭl (Hangul; 1446), which was much easier to learn than Literary Sinitic, the lingua franca among East Asian elites. Confucian scholar-officials drawn from *yangban* ostensibly completed centralized bureaucratic governance with the court directly appointing all eight provincial governors and all of some 300 county magistrates. An increasing segment of the *yangban* population fell out of political power at the national level as partisan strife expanded and loyalties became hereditary (Jackson 2016, 16–20). In each county, landed local *yangban* with slaves (*nobi*) advised the magistrate through the local council (*hyanghoe*) on such matters as a tax levy. Gaining acceptance by the state and central officials as articulators of public opinion (*kongnon*) initially expected from high officials only, local *yangban* also used community compacts (*hyangyak*) to lord over commoners, most of whom were tenant farmers working *yangban*-owned land (Yi Tae-Jin 2007, 34–45; Kim Ingeol 2024, 31–48).

Also in line with other states of early modern Afro-Eurasia, Chosŏn coped with a fundamental transformation. In the late fifteenth century, regular rural marketplaces appeared and spread, especially bringing together farmers with surplus crops and profiteering merchants procuring tribute tax goods to the government (Palais 1996, 70–75; Kim Yong-sop 2005, 25; Yi Tae-Jin 2007, 102–05). In the eighteenth century, unfree labor began decreasing rapidly in an increasingly liberalized economy with a levy system requiring tax remittance as a village's collective responsibility (Palais 1996, 824–25, 1014–18; Kim Yong-sop 2005, 24; Deuchler 2015, 391–92). This system of tax levy allowed commoners of means to acquire such status trappings as court ranks and offices through grain donation and even take over local councils (Deuchler 2015, 388–89). For sure, the social base of public opinion became broader, but by the early nineteenth century, when centuries of sustained population growth and overcultivation were producing environmental disasters (Totman 2004, 123–60), consequent hardship forced struggling farmers to organize and speak out, in the name of public opinion, through people's assemblies (*minhoe*). In counties later in the century, such people's assemblies and local councils spearheaded riots and uprisings (Kim Ingeol 2024, 96–168).

Approaching Chosŏn in terms of early modernity is also an attempt to engage with a wide range of historiographical views, past and present. At one end of the spectrum is a decidedly negative

Introduction

view that squarely blames, among others, Chosŏn's royal house, officials, *yangban*, Confucianism, and subservience to China for losing national sovereignty to Imperial Japan (1868–1947) at the turn of the twentieth century. This perspective is a lingering legacy of Japanese colonial and Korean nationalist historiographies. Portraying historical Korea as stagnant and shaped by external forces, Social Darwinist apologists of Imperial Japan portrayed Chosŏn Korea as a land with its people needing progressive Japan's protection and guidance. In response, early twenty-century Korean nationalists found inspiration in ancient Korean history, for them rich in military feats and indigenous customs and supposedly pure and free from Chinese influence. In the 1930s, Korean Marxists sought to demonstrate that Chosŏn and Koryŏ maintained a feudal system. They intended to refute the colonial historiographical portrayal of Chosŏn as mired in the ancient slave society phase of socioeconomic development that the West and Japan ostensibly had gone through before feudalism and capitalism. In a departure, in the late twentieth century, a new scholarship—mainly in South Korea, Japan, and the West—began to understand Chosŏn "for what it is." While rejecting any global periodization scheme as Eurocentric or straightjacketing Korea's historical experience, the approach remained mindful of various theories based mainly on Western historical experience (Duncan 2000, 3–6; Park 2022, 3–6). In the past two decades, an increasing number of scholars have been researching Chosŏn in the context of early modernity as a calendrical concept and discursive tool for promoting a comparative dialogue on global connections.

Contributors to this volume subscribe to the notion of early modernity to varying degrees. Drawing from and addressing relevant studies, this book not only incorporates more-or-less traditional aspects of history such as politics, foreign relations, the military, social mobility, religion, philosophy, science, and technology but also engages relatively more recent debates on gender, language, literature, visual arts, and performing arts. Such approach should better meet the needs of scholars and students reading about Chosŏn from more diverse viewpoints than ever before. This book features 32 chapters grouped into six parts, followed by an epilogue.

Part I, "Chosŏn in Time and Space," begins with Chapter 1 by Sixiang Wang, who problematizes understanding Chosŏn as Korea's early modern. Wang notes two rival conventions in the historiography of Korea. A "short convention," which refers to precolonial Korea's Open Port Period (1876–1910) as early modern (*kŭndae*), is out of line in the sense that historians working on all other regions generally speak of the early modern era from the fifteen to the nineteenth century. A "long convention," which places Korea on the same temporal scale as other regions, raises the question of how to situate Korea within a larger story of global early modernity. The problem with "early modernity" as a Eurocentric concept is its presumption that history follows a universal trajectory as understood in liberal positivism and Marxist teleology, according to which each stage has distinct characteristics. While observing that the global early modern tropes of, among others, commerce, connection, and cosmopolitanism do not apply neatly to Chosŏn, Wang urges readers to view global periodization as a tool for drawing connections and making comparisons rather than a proxy for essentialization.

Interregional connections inform Chapter 2, in which Kirk W. Larsen characterizes early modern Korea's foreign relations as more dynamic and diverse than the turn of the twentieth-century caricature of Chosŏn as a "hermit kingdom" suggests. Larsen sees regional geopolitical, economic, and climatic trends, as well as the ideologies and decisions of Chosŏn rulers and officials, as structuring the foreign relations of Chosŏn despite its status as a "tributary" of "suzerain" China whether under the Ming dynasty or the succeeding Qing dynasty (1616–1912; self-renamed from Later Jin in 1636). Somewhat beyond the state's purview or control were the movements of people, willing or coerced, goods, and resources that possessed their logics and trajectories. While the number of foreign relations partners decreased to just China and Japan, Chosŏn Korea exhausted

3

The Routledge Handbook of Early Modern Korea

some vital natural resources that had been core foreign trade components. Ultimately, to Larsen, both trends shaped Chosŏn's initial response to imperialism in the late nineteenth century when the leadership rejected French, US, and Japanese demands for relations and trade.

Focusing on the ideological dimensions of Chosŏn's views toward others and itself, Chapter 3 by Nataliya A. Chesnokova turns to an early modern Korean self-identity, *So Chunghwa* ("Little China"). Commonly associated with late Chosŏn, *So Chunghwa*, to Chesnokova, is a self-identity asserted earlier by Koryŏ as an inheritor of Confucian morals and rituals of the Son of Heaven in a world of China proper's Song dynasty (960–1279) among equals. Koryŏ's submission to the Mongols and the subsequent Mongol overlordship (1259–1356) eclipsed the identity. It reappeared in the seventeenth century in Chosŏn upon its capitulation to the Manchus, who conquered Ming China. As Chosŏn saw Manchus as barbarians with no legitimate claim to be *hua* ("civilization") or the inheritor of *tianxia* ("all-under-heaven"), the re-emerged *So Chunghwa* concept shaped Chosŏn's politics and culture, bolstering royal legitimacy and a more centralized state in the eighteenth century. In the following century, *So Chunghwa* restrained Chosŏn from a more flexible response to imperialism before suffering modern nationalists' condemnation of it as *sadae chuŭi* ("toadyism," "flunkeyism").

Turning to Chosŏn's other "barbarian" neighbor, in Chapter 4, Rebekah Clements considers how Japan perceived Korea—as "Chōsen" (Ko. Chosŏn) or "Korai" (Ko. Koryŏ)—from the fourteenth to the nineteenth century. Unlike the Korean Peninsula, where the State of Chosŏn ruled throughout the subject period, the Japanese Archipelago underwent three major regime transitions, from the Ashikaga shogunate (1336–1573), to the Tokugawa shogunate (1603–1868), to Imperial Japan. Clements highlights how Chosŏn Korea received attention in various areas of Japan's cultural life, from art to philosophy and literature, and among sundry polities across the archipelago, from urbanites in Edo to regional towns and coastal communities. The way people in Japan learned of Korea was similarly diverse, including material objects such as ceramics, books, and paintings, as well as word of mouth, diplomatic encounters, and war. Such interactions and understandings shaped Japan's cultural identity as distinct from Korea's in the early modern world, Clements concludes.

Covering internal matters of Chosŏn, Part II, "The State, Power, and Resource," features three chapters, beginning with Chapter 5 on Chosŏn's politics by Christopher Lovins. While recognizing that Chosŏn was a centralized early modern monarchy, Lovins emphasizes that the king ruled according to Neo-Confucian norms and in consultation with *yangban*. As hereditary elites, the *yangban* dominated politics and society both in and outside the capital, Hansŏng (present-day Seoul). After attempts at royal absolutism failed in the early sixteenth century, factional strife among central officials produced competing political associations (*pungdang*) by the mid-seventeenth century—each with its ideological orientations, political agendas, regional base, and inter-generational loyalties. At the same time, an increasingly liberalized economy of late Chosŏn produced nonelites of means who began taking over local councils in the eighteenth century. Lovins concludes that despite the widening social base of those articulating public opinion, the relative rigidity of Chosŏn's political system at the center prevented more prepared, effective responses—whether diplomatic or military—to challenges of imperialism in the nineteenth century.

More than just addressing Chosŏn's seemingly chronic problem of inadequate military capability, Felix Siegmund provides a critical overview of the kingdom's military and military literature in Chapter 6. Siegmund begins with a reminder that as Chosŏn fought wars with the Jurchens–Manchus in the north and with the Japanese in the south, its fighting techniques and military organization changed considerably over some five centuries of the state's existence. Much of the military comprised troops who could be professional soldiers or conscripts, whereas the military's

Introduction

top leadership consisted of *yangban* military officials, typically those who passed the military examination (*mukwa*). Apart from fighting and patrol duties, the military's rank-and-file, led by noncommissioned officers of *chungin* status, served as a labor battalion for state projects and engaged in various economic activities. In contrast, elites, military men or not, advanced theories and instructions in a large body of military literature, comprising treatises grounded in earlier Chinese works and adapted to conditions in Chosŏn. Although such works covered an impressively wide range of topics, Siegmund leaves no doubt in any reader's mind that they explored little beyond the knowledge base of East Asia.

Of course, non-state actors can challenge the state's monopoly on the use of force, and Andrew David Jackson's Chapter 7 addresses expressions of discontent as a central theme in Chosŏn's politics of royal legitimacy. According to Confucian principles, a king must act in the interests of his subjects, and the people have the right to rebel against unjust governance. Chosŏn angered the population, particularly excessive taxation, periods of food scarcity, and overall sociopolitical inequity. In early Chosŏn, the northern region experienced unrest shaped by environmental challenges, distance from the center, ethnically diverse communities, and discriminatory treatment by the center. In the seventeenth and eighteenth centuries, a complex combination of partisan strife and shifting allegiances over the issue of the Ming–Qing transition in China intensified political contention and even engendered rebellions led by *yangban*. Nonelites, too, used ritualized protests to express anger over official abuses and other sociopolitical problems. Then, in the nineteenth century, the predatory state controlled by an oligarchy and rampant corruption that exacerbated hardship on the population elicited larger, more violent, and organized responses.

Albeit decreasing, the critical role played by the state in shaping lives in early modern Korea receives a broad overview in Chapter 8, in which Young-Jun Cho considers Chosŏn's economy as reflecting the characteristics of a centralized state. The state's role as the prime economic agent relied on its tax system assessing and collecting the land tax, supplemented by taxes from commerce and manufacturing. Chosŏn's revenue base shows that agriculture was the core industry, with commerce and handicraft manufacturing playing secondary roles. Given agriculture's central place in the government's management of its economy, the land was the critical factor in production. The state exercised ownership in theory and practice, but private ownership increased over time. In the framework of state finances and land tenure, Cho understands agricultural production as the link between the two while approaching manufacturing, commerce, and monetary finances as the economy's secondary sectors. Instead of presenting an institutional narrative, Cho utilizes quantitative data to assess Chosŏn's economic reality, long-term economic changes, and living standards.

Exploring facets of interpersonal relations, Part III, "Society and Identity," begins with Chapter 9 by Eugene Y. Park, who portrays Chosŏn as an early modern society in which the correspondence between ascriptive status and socioeconomic class decreased. Among *yangban*, hereditary elites directly descended from Koryŏ's aristocracy, the capital *yangban* increasingly monopolized political power at the national level. As a progressively liberalized economy produced wealthy commoners and gradually replaced slave labor with wage labor, local *yangban* even lost ground to wealthy commoners, on whom county magistrates and *yangban* alike relied to meet the government's tax quota. Marriages between *yangban* males and wealthy commoner females and between self-sufficient slave males and commoner females became more common. All the same, Park notes clear limits of upward social mobility in Chosŏn. Among the *chungin* broadly defined, those culturally refined and well-to-do among the illegitimate sons (*sŏŏl*) of *yangban*, state-employed experts in various fields, and northern regional elites struggled to overcome the glass ceiling in the central bureaucracy.

The Routledge Handbook of Early Modern Korea

Introducing the dimension of ethnicity in Chosŏn, in Chapter 10, Adam Bohnet highlights the varied experiences of foreign migrants and their descendants as government policies shaped. Before the Imjin War (East Asian War; 1592–98), foreigners living in Chosŏn were those the state formally settled, traders at ports, and individuals stranded or trespassing. The war and the ensuing decades of tumultuous Ming–Qing transition brought more outsiders, especially refugees. Among various institutional mechanisms Chosŏn employed to manage them was *hyanghwa* ("turn toward edification") status, which assumed that foreigners sought moral transformation under the Chosŏn king and provided protection and benefits to Chinese, Japanese, and Jurchen settlers. Bohnet argues that in the 1750s, Ming loyalist ritualism restricted the status to those of Chinese ancestry since treating them as representatives of fallen Ming sanctified Chosŏn as the sole inheritor of Ming traditions. Few foreigners entered late Chosŏn until the late nineteenth century, but *hyanghwa* continued to denote the Ming migrants' descendants.

The discussion of the state, individuals, identities, and relationships in Chosŏn continues with Marion Eggert's Chapter 11, which reflects on gendered social roles, gender relations, and sexuality. According to Eggert, the Chosŏn state sought to strengthen the patrilineal family line with norms and laws that upheld female chastity (*yŏl*) and excluded women from public life and private inheritance. Actual social practice, however, could not entirely separate the male and female spheres of life or suppress the female agency that these norms and laws theoretically entailed. Constraints and contradictions of Chosŏn's hereditary status system allowed female activity in the economic and cultural spheres. Also providing some insights into sexual mores, including homosexuality and transgender, Eggert finds that visions of ideal love relationships and perfect femininity in literary works reveal a surprisingly equitable appreciation of female capacities and sexual desires. A gender ideology that assumed female subordination saw little need for further legitimation through the ascription of natural differences between the sexes, Eggert concludes.

Concerned with the dynamism of ideas and their manifestations in Chosŏn, Part IV, "Philosophy and Religion," begins with Isabelle Sancho's Chapter 12, which approaches Confucianism as a plurisecular intellectual tradition of multiple dimensions. Above all, Sancho rejects the conventional view of Confucianism as the dominant, uniform ideology that affected—and potentially explains—all aspects of Chosŏn's politics, society, and culture. Instead, the material context in which the people applied and adapted Confucianism for evolving historical circumstances shaped the Confucian tradition. Accordingly, Sancho gives considerable attention to elucidating the origins and history of Confucianism before focusing on the "project" developed by Confucian scholar-officials for the Chosŏn state and society. The project's implementation process produced anthropological and cultural shifts. Sancho finds what amounted to Chosŏn Confucianism as a complex, multifaceted phenomenon best addressed through an interdisciplinary approach bridging, among others, philosophy, anthropology, sociology, prosopographies, and cultural history.

Although the Confucian state and its elite proprietors stripped Buddhism of state sponsorship, in Chapter 13, Juhn Y. Ahn demonstrates that Buddhism flourished despite falling victim to early Chosŏn's ambitious state-building project. Bent on increasing its control of resources, the new state sought to restrict the flow of people, land, and movable wealth into the Buddhist establishment. Also, Confucian scholar-officials striving to rid statecraft of Buddhist influence, especially its role in the royal cult, led efforts to subordinate Buddhism and the royal house to an independent civil bureaucracy. Gradually losing the public role it had played for centuries, Buddhism nonetheless thrived outside the boundaries of state authority as Buddhist ritualism and scholasticism continued to develop, influenced by the Buddhist revival in late Ming China. Also, the Imjin War and the Ming–Qing transition presented new opportunities for further growth. The leadership of such celebrated monks as Hyujŏng (1520–1604), Sŏnsu (1543–1615), and Yujŏng (1544–1610)

Introduction

launched a monastic revival and gave birth to a new state-supported Buddhist establishment far cry from a marginalized religion, as Ahn explains.

Including Buddhism, the difficulty of demarcating the confines of popular religion frames Boudewijn Walraven's discussion of religious ideas and practices among Chosŏn's ordinary people in Chapter 14. Walraven defines popular religion as forms of religiosity that do not depend on a formal organizational structure and a corpus of written canonical texts while primarily addressing the exigencies of daily life, including concerns related to death and the well-being of the dead. Often from the lower classes, shamans engaged in a religious career based on highly personal experiences, acted as approachable mediators between the world of humans and the unseen forces of the universe and assumed a central place in the religious life of the people of Chosŏn. All the same, a considerable amount of widespread religious practice did not involve shamans. The elite looked askance at shaman practices but sometimes felt the need for intervention in moments of crisis offered by the shamans, whose rituals and practices incorporated Buddhist elements. As Walraven concludes, shaman prayers and songs overall affirmed Confucian social ethics.

Further enriching Chosŏn's spiritual life was Catholicism, which Koreans—unlike those colonized by Catholic nations—espoused on their own accord, as discussed in Chapter 15 by Franklin D. Rausch. When Catholic ideas began circulating among *yangban* intellectuals in the seventeenth century, they suffered rejection by the state and the mainstream aristocracy as a false teaching (*sahak*). In the late eighteenth century, however, some scholars began to take the Catholic faith seriously and to help build Chosŏn's own Catholic Church that would include people of all social strata. At their invitation, foreign missionaries, particularly from France, devoted themselves to shepherding the community and performed the sacraments at the core of the Catholic faith while seeking to establish an indigenous priesthood. In the nineteenth century, Koreans, as well as French and Chinese Catholics who had secretly entered Chosŏn as missionaries, suffered martyrdom during brutal government persecutions. Rausch concludes that the experience spurred the development of an otherworldly church focused on suffering in this world and bliss in the afterlife.

Including Catholicism, Part V, "Language, Learning, and Knowledge," surveys the vehicles, methods, and contents they entailed, beginning with Chapter 16 by Ross King on the Korean language. King illustrates some characteristic linguistic features of Early Modern Korean (phonological, grammatical, lexical orthographic) through seven short annotated excerpts from representative texts from the early seventeenth to the late nineteenth centuries. Despite the usefulness of applying language-internal criteria as traditional historical linguistics requires, the concepts of "modernity" and "early modern" as relevant to linguistic change and the historical periodization of the Korean language also embody the fundamental problem of "disconnect" between the notion of modernity in Korean historical linguistics and such other fields of Korean Studies as history and literature. Accordingly, King asks how else linguists could define "(Early) Modern Korean" as the consequences of applying language-external criteria (sociolinguistic criteria) to periodizing Korean linguistic history and applicability, if at all, of "linguistic modernity" to Chosŏn.

Regardless, the Korean language in Chosŏn was a powerful discursive tool in education, as discussed in Chapter 17 by Diana Yuksel. Using a syncretic approach, Yuksel examines the historical development of Chosŏn's educational institutions, beginning with an overview of Confucian education and its core ideas on teaching and learning, as well as surveying influential understandings of the purpose of education and the role of scholars. Confucian education embodied dual aspects: one, the purpose of self-cultivation for individuals, and two, the social aim of creating a public servant. Surveying both dimensions as reflected in the works of iconic scholars, Yuksel also critiques various approaches to the notion of "study" (*hak*) and the methods it implied, the importance of educational institutions and the transformations they underwent, and the fundamental texts that formed the core of formal education. In assessing the role of formal education, Yuksel highlights two unique aspects of Chosŏn's political institutions: the official recognition of Confucian moral training through the royal lectures and the tradition of remonstrance, which was a privilege and duty of Confucian scholars.

Exploring more empirical realms of knowledge production, in Chapter 18, Don Baker views Chosŏn's science and technology as early modern for their analytical, experimental approaches. Astronomers predicted celestial movements by using mathematical formulae to extrapolate from phenomena they carefully observed in the sky. Cartographers depicted what they had learned about geography on sheets of paper. Physicians diagnosed diseases and prescribed appropriate treatments. Evidence suggests creativity in Chosŏn's science and technology. Technicians of King Sejong (r. 1418–50) constructed possibly the most advanced astronomical observatory of its time. In the seventeenth century, Hŏ Chun (1539–1615) wrote a treatise on traditional East Asian medicine unrivaled in comprehensive coverage. In the nineteenth century, Kim Chŏngho (1804?–1866?) produced an astonishingly accurate, detailed map of Korea. Baker concludes that Chosŏn's efforts to understand the natural world for centuries accomplished much before Western science and technology began supplanting most traditional approaches to mathematics, astronomy, geography, and medicine.

Surveying arts and literature in early modern Korea, Part VI, "Creative Genres," begins with Gregory N. Evon's Chapter 19, which traces historical developments that shaped Chosŏn's literature. By the founding of Chosŏn, Koreans had mastered Chinese literary styles and had a literary history stretching back a millennium. Also, the invention of Han'gŭl in the mid-fifteenth century enabled the full development of vernacular literature. Even so, Chinese models remained dominant and served as the basis of literary production and thought among elites—mostly *yangban* but, in late Chosŏn, also *chungin*. Consequently, works in Literary Sinitic and vernacular formats underwent a parallel development. Accordingly, Evon examines the historical and conceptual factors that shaped literature's development in Chosŏn, considering elite and popular practices, commercialization, and the intersection of politics and cultural prestige. The vernacular works grew in popularity in late Chosŏn but were nowhere near replacing forms in Literary Sinitic as "national literature" until the turn of the twentieth century.

Introducing creative genres in visual arts, in Chapter 20, Yoonjung Suh explores how the Chosŏn state and elites' adoption of Neo-Confucianism as the ruling ideology and dominant social philosophy transformed artistic tastes, practices, and production. Six key themes stand out in the history of Chosŏn's visual art: (1) the evolution of the artistic style of landscape painting, including the emergence of "true-view" (*chin'gyŏng*) painting, (2) the court paintings for state rituals and events, (3) the development of genre painting, (4) Buddhist art under royal patronage, (5) the aesthetics and technical development of porcelains, and (6) royal palace architecture and landscaping. In providing a critical, historical overview of visual art and its sociopolitical, cultural, and religious contexts, Suh analyzes selected examples of painting, calligraphy, ceramics, Buddhist painting and sculpture, and architecture. The breadth of Chosŏn's artistic achievements reflects Korea's transcultural encounters with its neighboring countries and the West, Suh observes.

A full range of creative genres in performing arts, too, offer lively vignettes of life in Chosŏn, as discussed in Chapter 21 by CedarBough T. Saeji, who surveys performances that catered to the royal court, the elite, and nonelites. All Koreans watched and listened to music created for Confucian, Buddhist, or shamanic rituals. Still, they also appreciated non-ritual music performed by professionals, dabbling elites, and "participatory mutual enjoyment" among ordinary people.

Introduction

Confucianism, in particular, made a strong impact. For example, once the Confucian state began supporting the mask dance (*t'alch'um*) dramas, its budget concerns and the conservatism of *yangban* laid off many performers. Those who somehow continued to perform did so in ways that articulated the concerns of ordinary people. Meanwhile, performers reduced *p'ansori* (story-telling singing accompanied by a drummer) epics from 12 to 5, keeping only those most acceptable to the elite. Saeji's overview of performing arts thus shows that while elite and popular cultures co-existed, they also influenced each other and produced a middle ground—as common elsewhere in the early modern world.

Weaving a colorful tapestry portraying Chosŏn, this book ends with not so much a "conclusion" as reflections on what lay ahead for Korea and its people once Chosŏn began to engage with the forces of imperialism. In "Epilogue: Korea since 1873," Mark E. Caprio provides an overview of Korea's modern odyssey, highlighting abortive efforts to build a modern nation-state (1873–1910), the Japanese colonial rule (1910–45), the US–Soviet partition and occupation of Korea (1945–48), the establishment of the US-supported Republic of Korea (South Korea; since 1948) and the Soviet-supported Democratic People's Republic of Korea (North Korea; since 1948), and the evolution of the two mutually antagonistic Koreas into a significant player in the global politics, economy, and culture and an isolated, impoverished totalitarian state struggling for survival, respectively. As Caprio discusses, external forces have engendered many aspects of Korea's modernity, whereas others had roots in Chosŏn—hence its position as the early modern era in Korean history.

References

Belich, James, John Darwin, and Chris Wickham. 2016. "Introduction: The Prospect of Global History." In *The Prospect of Global History*, edited by James Belich, John Darwin, Margaret Frenz, and Chris Wickham, 3–22. Oxford University Press.

Deuchler, Martina. 2015. *Under the Ancestors' Eyes: Kinship, Status, and Locality in Premodern Korea*. Harvard University Asia Center.

Diamond, Jared. 1997. *Guns, Germs, and Steel: The Fate of Human Societies*. W. W. Norton.

Duncan, John B. 2000. *The Origins of the Chosŏn Dynasty*. University of Washington Press.

Eberhard, Wolfram. 1972. "Chinese Genealogies as a Source for the Study of Chinese Society." In *Studies in Asian Genealogy*, edited by Spencer J. Palmer, 27–37. Brigham Young University Press.

Green, William A. 1995. "Periodizing World History." *History and Theory* 34, no. 2, theme issue 34, "World Historians and Their Critics" (May): 99–111.

Haboush, JaHyun Kim. 1988. *A Heritage of Kings: One Man's Monarchy in the Confucian World*. Columbia University Press.

Holmes, Catherine, and Naomi Standen. 2018. "Introduction: Towards a Global Middle Ages." *Past & Present* 238, issue supplement 13 (November), "The Global Middle Ages": 1–44.

Jackson, Andrew David. 2016. *The 1728 Musin Rebellion: Politics and Plotting in Eighteenth-Century Korea*. University of Hawai'i Press.

Kim Ingeol. 2024. *Politics of Public Opinion: Local Councils and People's Assemblies in Korea, 1567–1894*. Translated by Eugene Y. Park. Brill.

Kim Yong-sop. 2005. "The Two Courses of Agrarian Reform in Korea's Modernization." In *Landlords, Peasants and Intellectuals in Modern Korea*, edited by Pang Kie-chung and Michael D. Shin, 21–52. East Asia Program, Cornell University.

Palais, James B. 1996. *Confucian Statecraft and Korean Institutions: Yu Hyŏngwŏn and the Late Chosŏn Dynasty*. University of Washington Press.

Park, Eugene Y. 2022. *Korea: A History*. Stanford University Press.

Pohl, Walter. 2016. "Introduction: Meanings of Community in Medieval Eurasia." In *Meanings of Community across Medieval Eurasia: Comparative Approaches*, edited by Eirik Hovden, Christina Lutter, and Walter Pohl, 1–24. Brill.

Totman, Conrad. 2004. *Pre-Industrial Korea and Japan in Environmental Perspective*. Brill.

Wagner, Anthony. 1975. *Pedigree and Progress: Essays in the Genealogical Interpretation of History*. Phillimore.

Wang, Sixiang. 2023. *Boundless Winds of Empire: Rhetoric and Ritual in Early Chosŏn Diplomacy with Ming China*. Columbia University Press.

Yi Sugŏn. 2003. *Han'guk ŭi sŏngssi wa chokpo*. Sŏul taehakkyo ch'ulp'an munhwawŏn.

Yi Tae-Jin. 2007. *The Dynamics of Confucianism and Modernization in Korean History*. East Asia Program, Cornell University.

PART I

Chosŏn in Time and Space

1
KOREA AND EARLY MODERNITY

Sixiang Wang

Two incompatible notions of "early modern" are used to periodize Korean history. A "short" convention covering the 1870s to 1910s (for example, Hwang 2015, 1–14; Yuh 2019) describes the period before Japanese colonial rule (1910–45). This convention views "modernity" as a host of institutions associated with the West, including "industrialism, nationalism, the nation-state, [and] the capitalist world-system," and "early modern" as the period when they first spread to Korea (Shin and Michael Robinson 1999, 9–11; Gluck 2011, 676–78; Karlsson 2013, 190). The "short" convention is at odds with how "early modern" usually appears in world history. Book-ended by the years 1300 and 1800, a "long" convention used by, the *Journal of Early Modern History*, points to the period of globalization between the Mongol conquests and "the onset of industrialization in the West" ("Journal of Early Modern History" n.d.).

The rival understandings of "early modernity" are more than just two arbitrary conventions. They represent distinct approaches to connecting Korea's past with world history. If the "short" convention emphasizes Western "impact" as a watershed moment in Korean history, the "long" convention suggests deep "evolutionary processes" leading to a European ideal of modernity (Kishimoto 2005, 6–7). Both adopt a teleological view of history as "progress" towards that ideal. Long embedded in the modern social sciences, this teleology stands on the conceit that, by using European economic, cultural, or social developments as a benchmark, one can create a typology of historical stages to identify how far society has "progressed" towards modernity (Chakrabarty 2007; Popper 2013, 5–9, 242–402).

Teleology and typology turn the question of Korea's path to "modernity" into the master paradigm of Korean history. This chapter will show how this question has created problems for placing Korea under the rule of the Chosŏn state (1392–1897) on the same "calendar" as the early modern world. It also suggests that some of these problems can be avoided if Korean history could be aligned with early modernity through the notion of "connected histories." This essay aims to orient the reader to the historiography of early modern Korea and invite the reader to use Korea's case to reflect critically on how global history is written.

DOI: 10.4324/9781003262053-3

The Routledge Handbook of Early Modern Korea

Periodization and the Historiography of Chosŏn Korea

A Korean historian writing in Korean can count on a professional academic community numbering in the thousands. They can also turn to a general public invested in a shared national past. On the other hand, scholars writing about Korean history in English face a different situation. The field of Korean history is small, and knowledgeable interlocutors are few. Housed in general history departments or interdisciplinary Asian studies departments, the typical "Western" scholar must address interdisciplinary or comparative concerns to find a wider audience. As a result, engaging the priorities and trends of other area fields becomes an everyday, professional necessity.

These pressures explain why synchronizing Korea's early modernity to its conventional usage in global history, roughly 1300–1800, makes sense. Not doing so "risks relegating Korea to ... [a] backwater outside the mainstream of world history" (Duncan 2019). Nevertheless, this "long" usage has only recently found advocates in English-language scholarship. As recently as 2013, "early modern Korea" still pointed only to the late nineteenth century in the English-language historiography (Karlsson 2013, 188–90).

Conventions in contemporary South Korean historiography parallel this dilemma. In one prevailing convention, the Korean term *kŭndae* corresponds to the "short" early modern, whereas *kŭnse* coincides with the "long" early modern. This convention, however, did not arise from a long-standing consensus. Instead, it amalgamated different historiographical approaches. The "short" view traces back to a 1950s usage in which the terms *kŭndae* and *kŭnse* were used interchangeably to describe the late nineteenth century. In contrast, the "long" application of *kŭnse* to roughly the Chosŏn period tracks with even earlier propositions dating to the colonial period (Cho Kijun 1970, 8–9). In contrast to these earlier conventions, where *kŭnse* and *kŭndae* were two alternatives to what came after the "medieval" period, *chungse* in Korean, the current South Korean convention treats *kŭnse* and *kŭndae* as two distinct periods, with the latter immediately following the former.

These possible referents for "early modern" in Korean help explain why two rival conventions still exist in English. Behind them are wider historiographical and political stakes, which *On Periodizing Korean History* (*Han'guksa sidae kubun ron* 1970) sought to clarify by reconciling them. It advocated a new "nationalist" and "materialist" periodization to counteract Japanese colonialist historiography that cast Korea as incapable of self-rule and, therefore, ineligible for national sovereignty. To do so, *On Periodizing Korean History* needed to refute the idea that Japanese colonial rule (1910–45) enabled Korean progress and modernization (Cho Kijun 1970, 1).

With the urgency of decolonization, *On Periodizing Korean History* charted a historical trajectory based on internal Korean socioeconomic dynamics rather than one punctuated by external, foreign influence (Cho Kijun 1970, 7; Palais 1995, 410–14). This challenge to the idea of a stagnant precolonial Korea still reproduced the underlying logic of the colonial narrative. After all, it still assumed that history progressed through distinct and recognizable stages—a signature element of Marxist historicism (Oh 2018, 10, 145–58, 170–75). In the colonialist narrative, Korea lacked a "feudal stage" altogether. In contrast, the new so-called "internal development theory" (*Naejaejŏk palchŏn non*) described a distinct "Korean feudal period" (the Chosŏn period) characterized by "endogenous development of capitalist relations and production"—the "sprouts of capitalism" that would have prepared the ground for Korean modernity without Japanese intervention. This theory, which enjoyed its heyday in the 1980s, was later challenged by the scholars of the Naksŏngdae School. Holding a more "pessimistic" view of late Chosŏn economic and social institutions, they instead concluded that Korea could not have developed capitalism "without an outside shock" (Miller 2010, 5–8).

Korea and Early Modernity

In other words, the debate revolved around where Korea fit on a "developmental curve from feudalism to capitalism" (Jun, Lewis, and Kang Han-Rog 2008, 244–55; Karlsson 2013, 196). Calling the Chosŏn period "early modern" therefore implied it "[displayed] certain qualities of modernity" without being fully modern. This framing immediately raises the problems of teleology and typology. First, it assumes the inevitability of "modernity" along this trajectory. Second, it raises the question of what historical phenomena should count as indicative of "modernity." This "Weberian approach" assumed that social theories derived from the European experience could readily apply to other parts of the world (Karlsson 2013, 188).

To be sure, these problems have also preoccupied historians of Korea's East Asian neighbors. The Korean use of *kŭnse* as the "long" early modern corresponds temporally to Japanese sinologist Naito Konan's use of "early modernity" or, in Japanese, *kinsei* for Chinese history in 1922. This usage expanded the scope of Marxist-inspired historical periodization from economic concerns to cultural and social developments. The epochal shifts it charted were intended to be comparable, for instance, to transformative moments in European history such as the Renaissance (Kishimoto 2005, 2).

If East Asia historians agree that the concept of "early modernity" is Eurocentric, they have not converged on a single solution to the problem. One vein of scholarship disarmed European superiority by challenging its empirical basis. They show how China or Japan had surpassed European benchmarks of "advancement" by proving more adept at fiscal centralization or bureaucratic governance than their European counterparts (Wong 2002, 455–65). In this logic, Eurocentric narratives are invalid because they ignore East Asia's successes, not because of the narratives' flawed premises. Since this way of "debunk[ing]" Asian backwardness still held up European experiences as a benchmark, it still treats alternative Asian trajectories as "functional equivalents to European changes." Even if serious historians and sociologists have largely abandoned the European triumphalism behind ideas of modernization since the 1990s, an imagined, "idealized European trajectory of change" persists as a comparative touchstone for Asian historical experiences (Wong 1993, 27; Goldstone 1998, 245–51). So long as attempts to discard European models retain their "teleological development scenario," it remains an open question whether non-European history can be periodized meaningfully (Kishimoto 2005, 7; Struve 2004, 29–33).

Though unresolved, this decades-long debate has nevertheless enabled historians to speak of China under the Ming dynasty (1368–1644) and the succeeding Qing dynasty (1616–1912; Later Jin until 1636), as well as Japan under the Tokugawa shogunate (1603–1868), as "early modern" without much hand-wringing. However, many Anglophone historians of Chosŏn Korea still hesitate to adopt the term "early modern" as a mere convention, partly because the same debate has not yielded the same fruit. Meanwhile, scholars are also wary of reproducing the Eurocentric paradigms and retracing the old colonialist and nationalist debate, even though adopting the "early modern" label for Chosŏn would facilitate communication with colleagues working on other parts of the early modern world.

What, then, is to be done about this seeming impasse? If treating Chosŏn Korea as "early modern" entails checking off boxes in a list of Eurocentric benchmarks, the conclusion will always be that Chosŏn fits in some ways and not in others. So rather than evaluate how well Korea "fits," this chapter will focus on where Chosŏn stood apart from the "early modern" pattern. These include cases of divergence, where a situation looks analogous to developments elsewhere in the early modern world but does not follow the same trajectory; and cases of disconnection, where Chosŏn seems to link up firmly with wider, regional, or global currents, only to disengage. Exploring these cases will show how the expectation that Chosŏn Korea might follow "early modern" trajectories often leads to the misrecognition of important phenomena.

15

The Routledge Handbook of Early Modern Korea

Convergences and Divergences

A typical early modern society is expected to have state centralization, burgeoning trade, an emerging national identity, and advancement in science and technology. They may also be accompanied by urbanization, population growth, print culture, and increasing upward social mobility. On each of these counts, Chosŏn gives plenty of grist for the mill while also breaking the mold (Duncan 2019; Pomeranz 2013). All the same, if these expectations exist because of teleological and typological assumptions about progress, then "an overemphasis on modernity.... "risk[s] marginalizing significant topics that fall outside of the definition of 'modern' life" (Stephens 2019, 109–16).

Economic Development

Chosŏn's economic conditions do not seem "early modern." Unlike the mercantile Venetians, the Dutch, or the Portuguese in the same period, Chosŏn did not sponsor sea-borne merchants. Nor did Korea's agrarian economy, characterized by modest domestic commerce and reliance on slave (*nobi*) labor, germinate "sprouts of capitalism" comparable in density to Japanese inter-domain commerce or Chinese market towns in the eighteenth century (Miller 2010, 8–10). Meanwhile, the low intensity of urbanization (unlike Tokugawa daimyo who lived inside administrative settlements, Chosŏn elites, *yangban*, preferred to live outside) provided Chosŏn little in the way of a bustling urban culture (Deuchler 2015, 102–03).

However, if Chosŏn's political economy is extricated from these expectations, the same phenomena might be interpreted differently. Rather than a sign of "backwardness," the Chosŏn state's economic policies point to a common challenge of squaring fiscal goals with avowed ideology—one hardly unique to Chosŏn in the early modern world. Slavery, which persisted in Chosŏn until 1894 and was seen as a marker of underdevelopment, was a widespread feature of the global economy. Attention to local, rural patterns also reveals complex economic institutions. The dearth of state-issued currency did not mean local economies ran on "barter" but instead a complex intertwining of social debts, obligations, and economic activity. The private journals of rural *yangban* recorded social favors alongside their ledgers of debt and exchange. In the meantime, their mutual aid associations, *kye*, could function as endowments, propertied shares, or contracts (Stephens 2019).

State, Civil Society, and Public Sphere

These examples are mentioned not as proof of Chosŏn Korea's economic or fiscal precocity but as signposts for the analytical blind spots of the "early modern" approach. Another example is Chosŏn's bureaucracy. The Chosŏn state kept meticulous records, produced paperwork, and formalized a legal system. These processes might seem to fit the usual story of global, early modern administrative, and state centralization, but a closer inspection reveals other patterns. Local *yangban* increasingly acted as brokers of local resources, whether natural or human, for central authorities. This mechanism calls into question whether "centralization" indeed describes how the state bureaucracy relates to local society (John S. Lee 2019).

Rather, perhaps Chosŏn was on the path to acquiring a different facet of political modernity: a "civil society" outside formal state control. The 1990s saw a debate over the applicability of philosopher Jürgen Habermas's (b. 1929) notion of civil society to the history of Asia. For Chosŏn, the debate surrounded the Confucian private academies (*sŏwŏn*) that first appeared in the sixteenth century. As they became sites for learning and political organization, local elites could discuss matters of national significance and participate in a "public sphere" without holding office or having direct ties to the state (Huang 1993; Haboush 1994; Hejtmanek 2013).

This angle challenged the colonial period stereotype of Chosŏn's political culture as one mired in factionalism. No longer evidence of stagnation, the revised view suggests a dynamic political culture accompanied by expanding "collective activism." These developments might even be seen as anticipating the mass politics of the twentieth century, whether manifested in the anti-colonial March First Movement of 1919 or the South Korean pro-democratic and *minjung* movements in the 1970s and '80s (Hein Cho 1997; Hwisang Cho 2020, 176–81, 185–93). Nevertheless, direct lines of continuity are hard to draw. Even scholars who see private academies in Chosŏn in terms of "nascent civil society" refrain from concluding that they were part of a modernizing social-political transformation analogous to the bourgeois "civil society" of Habermas (Duncan 2002; Koo 2007). But if an emerging "civil society" is typical of global "early modernity," why does the Chosŏn version of this story stop before the modern period? Either the typology, the teleology, or Chosŏn is broken.

Nationalism

The same problem affects another hallmark of modernity: the nation-state. The colonial historiography used the supposed absence of Korean national consciousness before the nineteenth century to justify Japan's colonization of Korea; inversely, Korean intellectuals and activists who resisted colonialism, insisting on the timeless presence of Korean national identity, pressed for Korea's continued existence in the concert of nations. Neither the "modernist" view, which sees nationalism as a recent Western import, nor the "primordialist" view, which assumes the "nation has always existed from time immemorial," have much to say about how identity functioned in the past (Haboush 2016, 10–14; Em 2013). For these reasons, "proto-nationalism" captures how Korea's identity in Koryŏ (918–1392) and the succeeding Chosŏn incorporated many requisite ingredients for a nation-state: common language, shared history, and political affiliation. Nevertheless, elite identification with "Chinese" Sinitic or Confucian civilization and the presence of status distinctions precluded a truly "nationalist" identity (Duncan 1998).

In contrast, Korean invocations of the political community during the Imjin War (East Asian War 1592–97) arguably is an emerging "discourse of the nation." In this existential crisis, the discourse imagined a political and ethnic identity cutting across all segments of Chosŏn society (Haboush 2016, 10, 39–51). This discourse, however, did not necessarily link up with modern articulations of Korean identity. The constitutional debates between the Chosŏn statesmen Sŏng Siyŏl (1607–89) and Yun Hyu (1617–80) reveal other parameters of Korean identity. Their central disagreement was how to define it against wider Confucian civilizational horizons after the fall of the Ming Chinese empire (Haboush 1999, 80–81, 89).

Rather than a national discourse, this latter mode engaged with culturalist identity markers. Nevertheless, Chosŏn elites could adapt this admixture of Sinocentric ideology and political legitimacy based on Ming loyalism for various agendas. The admixture could even serve "nationalist" functions by asserting Korean cultural superiority and legitimacy against the Manchu Qing rulers of China in the seventeenth and eighteenth centuries (Bohnet 2020, 5–9). Indeed, investment in a Sinitic imperial tradition remained relevant even after Chosŏn broke from Qing domination after the First Sino–Japanese War (1894–95). When King Kojong (r. 1864–1907; emperor from 1897) assumed the imperial title and inaugurated the Empire of Korea (Ko. Taehan cheguk, "Great Han Empire"; 1897–1910), he was asserting the nation's equality vis-à-vis the Empire of Japan (Ja. Dai Nippon teikoku, "Great Nippon Empire") and the Empire of China (Ch. Daqing diguo, "Great

Qing Empire"). Simultaneously, Kojong's courtiers traced the new Korean imperium through a line of inheritance from Ming China, one that harkened back to the sage kings of Chinese antiquity (*Kojong sillok* 1897/10/10 entry 6, 1897/10/11 entry 3). Although this culturalist mode was politically defunct after Japan colonized Korea, it existed alongside ethnonational articulations of Korean identity at the turn of the nineteenth century (Schmid 2002, 172–98).

Korean identity did not develop along a single line towards an arbitrary threshold in the twentieth century when it suddenly became "national." Instead, nation, whether as consciousness, ideology, or discourse, ebbed and flowed. Perhaps what made the turn of the seventeenth and twentieth centuries conducive to national forms of identity was the degree and intensity of outside threats amid regional diplomatic instability. Nationalism understood this way had more to do with how Koreans related to the outside world than the culmination of a predetermined trajectory.

Scientific Progress

If the formation of national identity is not linear, viewing its onset as emblematic of any historical stage makes little sense. Indeed, even in the eighteenth century, Chosŏn intellectuals took an antiquarian interest in Korea's past (Schmid 2002, 176–79). Along with a growing interest in empirical learning, which extended to technology and natural knowledge, these trends have been lumped under a catch-all term, Practical Learning (Sirhak), to serve as evidence for Chosŏn Korea's progress towards "modernity." In this regard, the story of Chosŏn knowledge and science confronts analogous historiographical problems to Korean economic and political history.

At work is an approach to the history of science and knowledge that highlights Korean achievements to parallel global scientific progress. The resulting account of Korean science becomes a search for precursors or parallels to Western innovation, with particular attention placed on the genius of individual thinkers or scientists. These might include talented engineers such as Chang Yŏngsil (1390?–1450?) or the polymath Hong Taeyong (1731–83) (Jeon 2011, 153–56, 394–402). Chosŏn's astronomy occupies a privileged position because it connects to the story of the West's "Scientific Revolution" (Figure 1.1). After all, the shift from Ptolemaic astronomy to a Copernican heliocentric model is the classic example of a paradigm shift that made the Scientific Revolution possible (Kuhn 1962, 68–69).

Under this approach, the central question becomes: why did Chosŏn not undergo the intellectual and social changes that supposedly accompanied the Scientific Revolution in European early modernity? Blame is often placed at the foot of a conservative Neo-Confucian ideology. Its followers play the role of Aristotlean-trained church fathers in Europe who supposedly prevented progress in the natural sciences. In contrast, Practical Learning scholars of the seventeenth and eighteenth centuries are lionized as the vanguard of modern science. Like in the search for sprouts of capitalism, the accounting of villains and heroes of science treats a stereotyped view of European historical progress as the touchstone for evaluating Korean achievements.

Here and elsewhere, the assumption of a predetermined trajectory (teleology) has structured historical inquiry, and a related problem also applies to the history of technology. In the traditional narratives of European early modernity, Johannes Gutenberg's (d. 1468) printing press (1454) heralded the Reformation and the Enlightenment. The pivotal role ascribed to this technology has, in turn, inspired scholars to consider an analogous role for printing technology in East Asia. Although Korea did not import the mechanical printing press until the nineteenth century, printing itself had long been widespread. In Chosŏn, woodblock printing and metallic movable type technology served private and government publication needs. Earlier, Koryŏ had produced the first extant book printed by metallic movable type, the *Chikchi* (1377). However, with the promise of

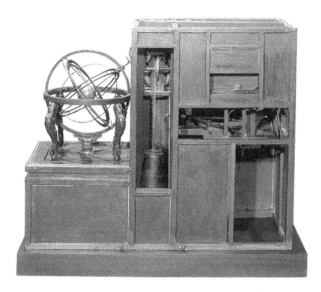

Figure 1.1 Celestial globe and armillary clock by Chosŏn's court astronomer, Song Iyŏng, 1669. Both were set up at the Office of Special Counselors (Hongmun'gwan) for teaching astronomy and for measuring time. Source: Korea University Museum. Photo credit: Korean Heritage Service.

Gutenberg's press in mind, scholars have often been disappointed that Korea's precocious print culture did not instigate revolutionary processes or supplant its manuscript culture (Si Nae Park 2022, 19–21). Here, again, is the problem of expectation: a Eurocentric template drives the analytical question. Falling to the wayside is the relationship between print technology and Korean society.

The "Middle People"

Analogs, parallels, and convergences exist between Chosŏn and other early modern societies. However, as bats and birds fly only thanks to convergent evolution, not all historical similarities are evidence of shared historical mechanisms (Fitzgerald 2023). One such example is the emergence of the *chungin* (parsed "middle people" by dint of etymological accident), who were below *yangban* but above commoners in social status. The identity of this group was tied to employment in the state's professional bureaucracy. Usually relegated to specialist roles in astronomy, medicine, linguistics, law, or painting, their growing prominence has been treated as a harbinger of "modernity," in part because of the roles prominent *chungin* played in the late nineteenth century (Hwang 2004, 106–60). *Chungin*, particularly those who served as diplomatic interpreters (*yŏkkwan*), are also credited with being a vector of knowledge about the outside world. Their artistic counterparts, court painters (*hwawŏn*), have also been lauded for adapting Western perspective into their genre paintings, engaging in new modes of individual subjectivity, depicting Chosŏn's encounters with the world beyond Korea, and bringing Korea's vernacular culture into focus (Sunglim Kim 2018).

The common thread in the above narratives is how the *chungin* represents a more forward-looking element of Chosŏn society. The emergence of new status groups such as *chungin* tempts their misrecognition as something akin to an emerging bourgeois or middle class, a key concept to Marxist and later modernization theories of development. The same phenomena above could also

The Routledge Handbook of Early Modern Korea

be reframed in terms of secondary elite emulation, a process that has less to do with modernity and more with the status dynamics of late Chosŏn's evolving social order (Eugene Y. Park 2014, 4–6, 48–70). If one presumes a modernization teleology, the story of the *chungin* also risks being shoehorned into a predetermined narrative, leaving the actual dynamics of Chosŏn society under-explored (Eugene Y. Park 2013).

Korea is not China, Japan, or Europe, and divergences are to be expected. But when these divergences are treated as examples of Korean "failure," history writing becomes an exercise in "why not?" Why did King Sejong's (r. 1418–50) astronomical reforms not lead to a scientific revolution? Why did print technology not produce a Korean Enlightenment? Why did Korean economic development not amount to capitalism (Karlsson 2013, 195–97)? The discourse of failure—failure to awaken as a nation, failure to leave behind China, failure to be like Japan, and failure to modernize like the West—continues an old colonialist line of inquiry and reproduces the developmental concerns of Cold War Area Studies in the United States. It assumes that barriers to modernization, once identified, could be extirpated from Korea's traditional culture to make way for Korea's national development (Oh 2018, 39–47, 54–79, 113–22, 133–37, 149–50; Miller 2010, 5–6).

At the same time, efforts to repudiate the narrative of failure by unearthing sprouts of capitalism only reproduced its teleological assumptions. Benchmarked to European (and, to a lesser degree, Chinese and Japanese) experience, "early modernity" expects similar patterns to follow analogous trajectories. But what if historians treated Korean divergences not as failures but as distinct historical experiences worthy of investigation in their own right. In that case, one might wonder whether the expected trajectories are even valid in the first place. Particular relationships between certain phenomena—economic development and urbanization; increasing state centralization and development of national identity; astronomical innovation and scientific revolution—are not universal but potential subjects of investigation and demonstration.

Connections and Disconnections

There is also an implicit reason for the widespread investment in the idea of Korean modernity. Whether in Marxist historiography in both the capitalist and socialist blocs or American modernization theory during the Cold War, modernity is a shorthand for the material, intellectual, and sociocultural conditions for some "emancipatory project." Modernity, across political ideologies, implies a triumph over forms of oppression or at least "successful resistance" against bigotry, servitude, and tyranny (Chakrabarty 2011, 668–69; Woodside 2006, 18). Finding early modernity in Korean history is to identify the origins of Korea's material and social progress, however defined. In other words, by "What is early modern Korea?" one also asks implicitly, "What counts as progress?" The underlying question remains whether Korea possessed an autonomous and culturally specific path to modernity, however defined (Yuh 2010).

Answering these questions has not always entailed rigorous engagement with the Hegelian, Marxist, or Weberian ideas behind them. Instead, they manifest as conventions of analysis that see significance in past phenomena only if tied to vague notions of progress (Palais 1996, 3–4, 16–17). These questions ultimately limit the range of historical inquiry by funneling attention towards a sense of teleology, but they have the advantage of integrating Korea's past into broader historical conversations. Given Korean history's relatively marginal position in the Western academy, historians of Chosŏn are anxious about disconnection, which generates pressure to conform to existing terminology and follow prevailing trends, even if not readily appropriate to Korea's history (Karlsson 2013, 186–87). Whether Korean early modernity can be conceived without presuming the universality of Eurocentric teleology remains a conundrum.

To circumvent this issue, scholars working on other regions of early modern East Asia have adopted two strategies. The first is to accept "early modern" as pointing to broad, contemporaneous similarities—cosmopolitanism, maritime trade, urbanization, and booming consumer culture in Qing China—as common "early modern" patterns, even if they "did not culminate in modernity" (Rawski 2004, 207–11) This framing avoids the problem of teleology. Still, leaving those particular Eurocentric benchmarks in place also indirectly excludes Chosŏn Korea from the conversation. The second strategy is to focus on concrete connections and linkages. Rather than a "Weberian model of modernization" or a "European paradigm or universal model of development," early modernity instead points to a "particular configuration of global relationships." In the case of Tokugawa Japan, "new modes of navigation, finance, and weaponry in the fifteenth century" connecting the globe in new ways engendered apparent convergences and parallels. They were not necessarily the outcomes of a presumably universal developmental trajectory (Wigen 1995, 2–4, 7).

This turn to "connected history" has helped overturn the old stereotype of an "isolated" Tokugawa Japan (Walker 1996). Revisiting once-overlooked transnational circuits of exchange will likely produce fruitful insights for Chosŏn Korea. Nevertheless, to completely overwrite the old story of an isolationist Korea (Chosŏn as the "Hermit Kingdom") with one emphasizing interconnection is a tall order. Scholars still face empirical challenges when including Chosŏn Korea in a connected global history. Even so, treating "early modernity" as a shorthand for the circulations of global connection provides a fruitful opportunity to use Korea's global links to interrogate critical elements of this paradigm of historiography.

Connected Histories

A classic example of "connected history," the concurrence of millenarian movements across Eurasia suggested far-flung linkages (Subrahmanyam 1997, 738–54). In Korea, too, such disruptions rode wider regional and global currents. The Red Turban invasions of 1359–60 that weakened Koryŏ began as such a movement in the wake of widespread societal collapse in China (David M. Robinson 2019, 130–59). From 1861 to 1894, the Tonghak ("Eastern Learning") movement propagated thanks to the messianic promises of a Christianity-inspired salvationist cosmology. As the proximate cause of the First Sino–Japanese War, the movement triggered a regional geopolitical realignment and set the stage for the Kabo Reform (1894–96) (Kallander 2013).

On the other hand, the cultural scripts of insurrection had as much to do with outside connections as these scripts did with indigenous templates for voicing grievance. They drew upon vernacular tropes of prophecy and epochal renewal common in prohibited insurrectionist texts. Indeed, the early nineteenth-century rebellions that shook Chosŏn, such as the Hong Kyŏngnae rebellion (1812), had distinctly local causes, one rooted in social discontent over the hereditary status system, not inspiration by foreign ideology or socioeconomic transformation in the Marxist vein (Sun Joo Kim 2007, 89–104, 170–73).

Nor did interconnection produce the same results everywhere at the same time. For instance, the Korean and Japanese timelines are desynchronized. Two phases of European maritime expansion bookend Japanese "early modernity" (1550–1876). The fifteenth and sixteenth centuries saw Japan's integration into the early modern world system spurred on by the oceanic trade of Europe's "Age of Discovery." In contrast, Chosŏn Korea never extended direct maritime contacts: no Korean equivalent of Japanese Red Seal Ships or the Ming eunuch Zheng He's (1371–1433) treasure fleet. The Ming merchant pirates Wang Zhi (1501–60) and Zheng Zhilong (1604–61) are reminiscent of earlier Korea's Chang Pogo (d. 846), who dominated the Yellow Sea and the East

China Sea, but by the fourteenth century, Korean maritime activity was restricted to its immediate littoral (Lewis 2003).

Cosmopolitan Circulations

To write Korea into "early modernity" requires a different imperial encounter: Koryŏ's integration into the Mongol empire (1206–1368). Eurasian trends deeply affected Korea during what was arguably the most cosmopolitan period of Korean history before the modern era, whereas Japan, by repelling the Mongol invasions (1274, 1281), was less connected. Tibetan Buddhists and Muslim merchants traveled to Korea, while Koryŏ elites adopted Mongol court culture (Sorenson 1993; David M. Robinson 2009, 98–129). Knowledge of Korea spread as far as western Europe, just as awareness of Africa and Europe entered Korean geographical knowledge, represented in the famous 1402 Kangnido map (Ledyard 1991).

However, this cosmopolitanism, at least from the point of view of early Chosŏn elites, was not something to be relished. Foreign trade disrupted state coffers and reduced the tax base, while the enlistment of Koreans into the Mongol invasions of Japan proved ruinous. The period of Mongol rule (1259–1356) was blamed for corrupting state and religious institutions, while the Koryŏ king's eagerness to patronize outsiders upended the traditional social order (Juhn Y. Ahn 2018, 55–58, 91–104; Deuchler 2015, 41–51). After the founding of Chosŏn, the vestiges of an earlier, cosmopolitan era faded away. For instance, a small Muslim minority was forced to assimilate in 1427, while Chosŏn pursued Confucianization that tried to root out Mongol cultural practices, even though their influence on vocabulary, dress, food, and elite pastimes such as the royal hunt lingered (Bohnet 2020, 24–53; Kallander 2023, 72–86).

Perhaps the most stunning legacy of this cosmopolitan period was the fifteenth-century Chosŏn court's scientific achievements. Best represented by Sejong's astronomical and linguistic projects (notably the invention of Han'gŭl (Hangul), the Korean alphabet), they drew upon a range of international inspirations, mathematical techniques used by Muslim calendar makers, and alphabetic script systems devised by Tibetan monks (Eun Hee Lee 2015; Ledyard 1997). The projects were the fruits of Korea's thirteenth and fourteenth-century exposure to circuits of knowledge exchange made possible by Pax Mongolica. In this regard, the relationship between innovation and circulation also figures into the later development of Practical Learning. It emerged with the growing extent and intensity of Chosŏn Korea's engagement with another phase of globalization after the seventeenth century, even though it did not come with the kind of cosmopolitanism that characterized late Koryŏ (Kanghun Ahn 2018, 163–67).

Early Modern Disconnections

The collapse of the Mongol empire also impacted Korea and Japan differently, explaining in part Chosŏn's reluctant interaction with the wider maritime world. Social and economic collapse led to rampant piracy in the Yellow Sea and the Korean-Japanese littoral in the late fourteenth and early fifteenth centuries. Pirate raids disrupted tax shipments in Korea and led many communities to move further inland. To address the problem, Chosŏn pursued diplomacy with local Japanese rulers and the Ashikaga shogunate (1336–1573). It also dispatched a fleet to attack the pirate base of Tsushima in 1396 and 1419 (Shapinsky 2014). Chosŏn settled on a tally system, which restricted Japanese traders to the treaty port in Pusan. In the fifteenth and sixteenth centuries, visitors also included those who claimed to be from the Ryukyu Kingdom (1429–1879), though they stopped coming after the Imjin War (Kenneth R. Robinson 2000).

Korea and Early Modernity

The Imjin War placed Chosŏn in the crucible of regional realignments, of which European maritime expansion was one element. Chosŏn's links to this process were, however, tenuous. Chosŏn did not open treaty ports for seafaring Europeans as the Japanese did in Nagasaki. Even Chinese ships were barred from Korean shores. Save for occasional castaways (and a few priests accompanying the Japanese invaders during the Imjin War), the Chosŏn state had no direct contact with Europeans. Likewise, few Koreans (except those attached to embassies to China and Japan) traveled abroad, although some, who were captured or otherwise displaced by the war, found themselves in Japan, Vietnam, and even Europe (Ledyard 1971). These limited and sporadic contacts were enough to spark imagination and reflection. Stories such as the *Tale of Ch'oe Chŏk* (*Ch'oe Chŏk chŏn*; 1621) were likely inspired by actual Korean accounts of travel to Vietnam and Japan, while Pak Chiwŏn's satirical *Tale of Master Hŏ* (*Hŏ saeng chŏn*; late eighteenth century) reflected fascination about an international economy ruled by mercantile acumen (Pettid, Evon, and Chan Eung Park 2018, 132–61; Peter H. Lee 1981).

Ideas and goods still flowed into Chosŏn Korea. The first Korean converts to Catholicism encountered the religion through imported books rather than through missionaries (Baker 2017, 59–82). Chosŏn Korea was also a conduit in the global circulation of silver specie, which by the eighteenth century flowed to Korea from Japan via Tsushima and helped fund Chosŏn tribute missions to Qing China. The 600,000 or so *yang* of silver flowing into Qing from Chosŏn has been evaluated at around 1.8 percent to 5.5 percent of Chosŏn's total agricultural production—enough to sustain a modest import market for foreign goods (Kwon Nae-Hyun 2015, 168–74). Nevertheless, it would not be until the late nineteenth century, when Chosŏn began signing open port treaties, that significant numbers of foreign merchants resided and traded in Korea—a phenomenon not seen since late Koryŏ.

The increased circulation of people and goods promoted technological convergence and cultural cosmopolitanism. An iconic early modern technology, firearms became critical for the military power of the "gunpowder empires," and Chosŏn Korea, too, witnessed a boom in firearms production. Chosŏn gunmakers relied on preexisting technology in Korea and reverse-engineered Chinese, Japanese, and European techniques. Not everything fits the "early modern" story of the "fluid movement of knowledge and technology." On the surface, Korean gunpowder suggests inter-regional technology transfer, but closer examination reveals something quite different. Although Korean techniques of making gunpowder resembled European and Chinese methods, imported knowledge misled Chosŏn artisans to believe that they could extract niter from seawater; eventually, they discovered a working formula only through systematic experimentation—a long-standing tradition of Chosŏn state manufactories. Therefore, the resulting convergence had more to do with the technology's inherent physical and material proprieties (Kang 2022, 20–21). At least the story of Korean gunpowder, which shows the role of *disconnection* rather than connectivity, doubles as a reminder that all societies existed within material limitations.

This attention to physical materiality, borne out by recent research in human–natural intersections, also offers other ways to link Korea with global rhythms. On a macrohistorical level, periods of intense social, economic, and political change coincide with global climate patterns. Meanwhile, environmental approaches enable comparisons of Chosŏn's state forestry administration in the context of lumber scarcity with what occurred in early modern Venice or Japan (John S. Lee 2018). The spread of new farming techniques and New World crops is an important part of the story, even if tubers such as potatoes did not have the same nutritional impact in Korea as elsewhere (Siegmund 2011). From the perspective of energy consumption and production, the notion of "advanced organic societies" can also explain the features of early modernity. Chosŏn, like other advanced organic societies, confronted insurmountable natural resource constraints.

What ultimately made modernity as commonly understood possible was the global transition to inorganic fuel sources, namely fossil fuels such as coal and later petroleum (Goldstone 1998), a process that began in the nineteenth century and spread to Korea with the construction of the capital Hansŏng's (present-day Seoul) first coal-powered electrical plant in 1899.

Final Thoughts

What historical inquiries would suit a specific Korean context while remaining broadly accessible to a wider English-speaking scholarly audience? Framing Korean history in terms of a march to "modernity" renders it legible but beholden to the standards of others. Pointing out Chosŏn's divergences from global patterns risks turning them into Korea-specific idiosyncrasies. In both cases, Korean history remains consigned to the margins.

At the heart of the Korean "early modernity" question is what theory of history is best for engaging Korea's past with the rest of the world. At a minimum, "early modern" can be understood as a calendrical term of convenience. Alternatively, the term can still be used productively to invite questions about global convergences and circulations. As used in this book, Korea's "early modern period" was punctuated by three phases of globalization: the rise of the Mongol empire in the thirteenth century, the expansion of the maritime world in the sixteenth and seventeenth centuries, and finally, the global transition to industrial modernity in the nineteenth and twentieth centuries. In the first and third phases, the Korean Peninsula was subsumed under a larger imperial order, first the Mongols and later under Japanese colonial rule.

These two imperial bookends might hold more than an accident of political history. Observing similarities between the period of Mongol rule and the later Japanese colonial period, Remco Breuker has argued that "many of the characteristics now exclusively defined as modern" are often "found in clusters" at different historical periods. In this view, industrialization, though "our modernity's most visible ingredient," is no longer the "essential" criterion for modernity. Instead, modernity is a condition that uproots once-stable foundations while also "provoking the need to re-establish or re-root society" in a new sense of order. Spurred on by precisely the kinds of "political, cultural, and economic integration" made possible by imperialism or globalization, "modernity" in this respect is not a strictly nineteenth or twentieth-century phenomenon but something that can be "found, lost, and presumably regained" (Breuker 2007, 47).

By describing Mongol rule as an earlier iteration of colonial modernity, Breuker does not treat modernity as a fixed stage of history but as a contingent result of interconnection and integration. If modernity momentarily clusters together discrete phenomena, similarities across time and place need not imply movement in a common trajectory. In that respect, Chosŏn Korea's divergence from "early modern" expectations should be treated neither as points of failure nor evidence of uniqueness. Instead, these divergences are opportunities to interrogate the connection between different parcels in the larger package of modernity.

The main lesson here is to see early modernity as not so much as a historical stage but rather as a heuristic tool for engaging in historiographical dialogue. The challenge, though, is to ensure a true conversation. The discussion should provide feedback on historiographical trends of the moment and reveal their underlying assumptions, not just apply exogenous models to Korea's early modern past. Instead of making an empirical case for what in Chosŏn Korea should count as early modern according to ultimately arbitrary benchmarks, scholars could do just as well to use Korea's past to question and reinvestigate early modernity. Rather than merely asking why Korea is different, historians might also reflect on why other early modern regions were not more like Korea.

References

Ahn, Juhn Y. 2018. *Buddhas and Ancestors: Religion and Wealth in Fourteenth-Century Korea*. University of Washington Press.

Ahn, Kanghun. 2018. "Beyond the Discourse of Practical Learning: Rethinking Chosŏn Intellectual History in a Broader Context." *Seoul Journal of Korean Studies* 31, no. 2: 141–67.

Baker, Don. 2017. *Catholics and Anti-Catholicism in Chosŏn Korea*. Edited by Franklin D. Rausch. University of Hawai'i Press.

Bohnet, Adam. 2020. *Turning Toward Edification: Foreigners in Chosŏn Korea*. University of Hawai'i Press.

Breuker, Remco E. 2007. "Colonial Modernities in the 14th Century: Empire as the Harbinger of Modernity." In *Korea in the Middle: Korean Studies and Area Studies, Essays in Honour of Boudewijn Walraven*, 45–66. CNWS Publications.

Chakrabarty, Dipesh. 2007. *Provincializing Europe: Postcolonial Thought and Historical Difference*. New edition. Princeton University Press.

Chakrabarty, Dipesh. 2011. "The Muddle of Modernity." *American Historical Review* 116, no. 3: 663–75.

Cho, Hein. 1997. "The Historical Origin of Civil Society in Korea." *Korea Journal* 37, no. 2: 24–41.

Cho, Hwisang. 2020. *The Power of the Brush: Epistolary Practices in Chosŏn Korea*. University of Washington Press.

Cho Kijun. 1970. *Han'guksa sidae kubun ron*. Ŭryu munhwasa.

Deuchler, Martina. 2015. *Under the Ancestors' Eyes: Kinship, Status, and Locality in Premodern Korea*. Harvard University Asia Center.

Duncan, John B. 1998. "Proto-Nationalism in Premodern Korea." In *Perspectives on Korea*, edited by Duk-Soo Park and Sang-Oak Lee, 198–221. Wild Peony.

Duncan, John B. 2002. "The Problematic Modernity of Confucianism: The Question of 'Civil Society' in Chosŏn Dynasty Korea." In *Korean Society: Civil Society, Democracy and the State*, edited by Charles K. Armstrong, 33–52. Routledge.

Duncan, John B. 2019. "Change and Continuity between Koryŏ and Chosŏn: A View from California." UCLA Korean History and Culture Digital Museum. https://koreanhistory.humspace.ucla.edu/items/show/46.

Em, Henry. 2013. *The Great Enterprise: Sovereignty and Historiography in Modern Korea*. Duke University Press.

Fitzgerald, Devin. 2023. "Birds and Bats." Blog. Books and the Early Modern World: The Research of Devin Fitzgerald. March 21. https://devinfitz.com/birds-and-bats/.

Gluck, Carol. 2011. "The End of Elsewhere: Writing Modernity Now." *American Historical Review* 116, no. 3: 676–87.

Goldstone, Jack A. 1998. "The Problem of the 'Early Modern' World." *Journal of the Economic and Social History of the Orient* 41, no. 3: 249–84.

Haboush, JaHyun Kim. 1994. "Academies and Civil Society in Chosŏn Korea." In *La société civile face à l'État: dans les traditions chinoise, japonaise, coréenne et vietnamienne*, edited by Léon Vandermeersch, 383–92. École Française d'Extrême-Orient.

Haboush, JaHyun Kim. 1999. "Constructing the Center: The Ritual Controversy and the Search for a New Identity in Seventeenth Century Korea." In *Culture and the State in Late Chosŏn Korea*, edited by JaHyun Kim Haboush and Martina Deuchler, 46–90. Harvard University Asia Center.

Haboush, JaHyun Kim. 2016. *The Great East Asian War of 1592 and the Birth of the Korean Nation*. Edited by William Joseph Haboush and Jisoo M. Kim. Columbia University Press.

Hejtmanek, Milan. 2013. "The Elusive Path to Sagehood: Origins of the Confucian Academy System in Chosŏn Korea." *Seoul Journal of Korean Studies* 26, no. 2: 233–68.

Huang, Philip C. C. 1993. "'Public Sphere'/'Civil Society' in China? The Third Realm between State and Society." *Modern China* 19, no. 2: 216–40.

Hwang, Kyung Moon. 2004. *Beyond Birth: Social Status in the Emergence of Modern Korea*. Harvard University Asia Center.

Hwang, Kyung Moon. 2015. *Rationalizing Korea: The Rise of the Modern State, 1894–1945*. University of California Press.

Jeon, Sang-Woon. 2011. *A History of Korean Science and Technology*. NUS Press.

"Journal of Early Modern History." n.d. Brill. Accessed February 21, 2023. https://brill.com/view/journals/jemh/jemh-overview.xml.

Jun Seong Ho, James B. Lewis, and Kang Han-Rog. 2008. "Korean Expansion and Decline from the Seventeenth to the Nineteenth Century: A View Suggested by Adam Smith." *Journal of Economic History* 68, no. 1: 244–82.

Kallander, George L. 2013. *Salvation through Dissent: Tonghak Heterodoxy and Early Modern Korea.* University of Hawai'i Press.

Kallander, George L. 2023. *Human–Animal Relations and the Hunt in Korea and Northeast Asia.* Edinburgh University Press.

Kang, Hyeok Hweon. 2022. "Cooking Niter, Prototyping Nature: Saltpeter and Artisanal Experiment in Korea, 1592–1635." *Isis* 113, no. 1: 1–21.

Karlsson, Anders. 2013. "Recent Western-European Historical Studies on 'Pre-Modern' Korea and the Issue of 'Modernity' Revisited." *International Journal of Korean History* 18, no. 1: 185–202.

Kim, Sun Joo. 2007. *Marginality and Subversion in Korea: The Hong Kyŏngnae Rebellion of 1812.* University of Washington Press.

Kim, Sunglim. 2018. *Flowering Plums and Curio Cabinets: The Culture of Objects in Late Chosŏn Korean Art.* University of Washington Press.

Kishimoto Mio. 2005. "Chinese History and the Concept of 'Early Modernities.'" Paper presented at the conference, "The Early Modern World," University of Chicago, June 3. http://earlymodernworld.uchicago.edu/kishimoto.pdf.

Kojong sillok. In *Chosŏn wangjo sillok.* Available at: https://sillok.history.go.kr/main/main.do.

Koo, Jeong-Woo. 2007. "The Origins of the Public Sphere and Civil Society: Private Academies and Petitions in Korea, 1506–1800." *Social Science History* 31, no. 3: 381–409.

Kuhn, Thomas S. 1962. *The Structure of Scientific Revolutions.* University of Chicago Press.

Kwon, Nae-Hyun. 2015. "Chosŏn Korea's Trade with Qing China and the Circulation of Silver." *Acta Koreana* 18, no. 1: 163–85.

Ledyard, Gari. 1971. *The Dutch Come to Korea: An Account of the Life of the First Westerners in Korea (1653–1666).* Royal Asiatic Society, Korea Branch.

Ledyard, Gari. 1991. "The Kangnido: A Korean World Map, 1402." In *Circa 1492: Art in the Age of Exploration,* edited by Jay Levenson, 329–33. Yale University Press.

Ledyard, Gari. 1997. "The International Linguistic Background of the Correct Sounds for the Instruction of the People." In *The Korean Alphabet: Its History and Structure,* edited by Young-Key Kim-Renaud, 31–88. University of Hawai'i Press.

Lee, Eun Hee. 2015. "Korean Astronomical Calendar, Chiljeongsan." In *Handbook of Archaeoastronomy and Ethnoastronomy,* edited by Clive L. N. Ruggles, 2157–62. Springer.

Lee, John S. 2018. "Postwar Pines: The Military and the Expansion of State Forests in Post-Imjin Korea, 1598–1684." *Journal of Asian Studies* 77, no. 2: 319–32.

Lee, John S. 2019. "The Rise of the Brokered State: Situating Administrative Expansion in Chosŏn Korea." *Seoul Journal of Korean Studies* 32, no. 1: 81–108.

Lee, Peter H., ed. 1981. *Anthology of Korean Literature: From Early Times to the Nineteenth Century.* University of Hawai'i Press.

Lewis, James B. 2003. *Frontier Contact Between Chosŏn Korea and Tokugawa Japan.* Routledge.

Miller, Owen. 2010. "The Idea of Stagnation in Korean Historiography from Fukuda Tokuzō to the New Right." *Korean Histories* 2, no. 1: 3–12.

Oh, Sangmee. 2018. "From Colonial to International: American Knowledge Construction of Korean History, 1880s–1960s." Ph.D. dissertation, University of California, Los Angeles.

Palais, James B. 1995. "A Search for Korean Uniqueness." *Harvard Journal of Asiatic Studies* 55, no. 2: 409–25.

Palais, James B. 1996. *Confucian Statecraft and Korean Institutions: Yu Hyŏngwŏn and the Late Chosŏn Dynasty.* University of Washington Press.

Park, Eugene Y. 2013. "Old Status Trappings in a New World: The 'Middle People' (*Chungin*) and Genealogies in Modern Korea." *Journal of Family History* 38, no. 2: 166–87.

Park, Eugene Y. 2014. *A Family of No Prominence: The Descendants of Pak Tŏkhwa and the Birth of Modern Korea.* Stanford University Press.

Park, Si Nae. 2022. "Manuscript, Not Print, in the Book World of Chosŏn Korea (1392–1910)." In *The Routledge Companion to Korean Literature,* edited by Heekyoung Cho, 19–38. Routledge.

Pettid, Michael J., Gregory N. Evon, and Chan E. Park, eds. 2018. *Premodern Korean Literary Prose: An Anthology.* Columbia University Press.

Pomeranz, Kenneth. 2013. "Teleology, Discontinuity and World History: Periodization and Some Creation Myths of Modernity." *Asian Review of World Histories* 1, no. 2: 189–226.

Popper, Karl. 2013. *The Open Society and Its Enemies*. Princeton University Press.

Rawski, Evelyn S. 2004. "The Qing Formation and the Early Modern Period." In *The Qing Formation in World-Historical Time*, edited by Lynn A. Struve, 207–35. Harvard University Asia Center.

Robinson, David M. 2009. *Empire's Twilight: Northeast Asia under the Mongols*. Harvard University Asia Center.

Robinson, David M. 2019. *In the Shadow of the Mongol Empire: Ming China and Eurasia*. Cambridge University Press.

Robinson, Kenneth R. 2000. "Centering the King of Chosŏn." *Journal of Asian Studies* 59, no. 1: 33–54.

Schmid, Andre. 2002. *Korea between Empires, 1895–1919*. Columbia University Press.

Shapinsky, Peter D. 2014. *Lords of the Sea: Pirates, Violence, and Commerce in Late Medieval Japan*. Center for Japanese Studies, University of Michigan.

Shin, Gi-Wook, and Michael Robinson, eds. 1999. *Colonial Modernity in Korea*. Harvard University Asia Center.

Siegmund, Felix. 2011. "Tubers in a Grain Culture: The Introduction of Sweet and White Potatoes to Chosŏn Korea and Its Cultural Implications." *Korean Histories* 2, no. 2: 59–74.

Sorenson, Henrik H. 1993. "Lamaism in Korea during the Late Koryŏ Dynasty." *Korea Journal* 33, no. 3: 67–81.

Stephens, Holly. 2019. "Three Reforming Regimes? Modernity and the Fiscal State in Modern Korean History." *Seoul Journal of Korean Studies* 32, no. 1: 109–46.

Struve, Lynn A., ed. 2004. *The Qing Formation in World-Historical Time*. Harvard University Asia Center.

Subrahmanyam, Sanjay. 1997. "Connected Histories: Notes towards a Reconfiguration of Early Modern Eurasia." *Modern Asian Studies* 31, no. 3: 735–62.

Walker, Brett L. 1996. "Reappraising the 'Sakoku' Paradigm: The Ezo Trade and the Extension of Tokugawa Political Space into Hokkaidō." *Journal of Asian History* 30, no. 2: 169–92.

Wigen, Kären. 1995. "Mapping Early Modernity: Geographical Meditations on a Comparative Concept." *Early Modern Japan: An Interdisciplinary Journal* 5, no. 2: 1–13.

Wong, R. Bin. 1993. "Great Expectations: The 'Public Sphere' and the Search for Modern Times in Chinese History." *Chūgoku shigaku* 3: 7–50.

Wong, R. Bin. 2002. "The Search for European Differences and Domination in the Early Modern World: A View from Asia." *American Historical Review* 107, no. 2: 447–69.

Woodside, Alexander. 2006. *Lost Modernities: China, Vietnam, Korea, and the Hazards of World History*. Harvard University Press.

Yuh, Leighanne. 2010. "The Historiography of Korea in the United States." *International Journal of Korean History* 15, no. 2: 127–44.

Yuh, Leighanne. 2019. "Loyalty to the King and Love for Country: Confucian Traditions, Western-Style Learning, and the Evolution of Early Modern Korean Education, 1895–1910." *Sungkyun Journal of East Asian Studies* 19, no. 2: 189–212.

2
FOREIGN RELATIONS

Kirk W. Larsen

The foreign relations of Korea ruled by the Chosŏn state (1392–1897) manifest dynamism and diversity. They belie the persistent turn of the twentieth-century caricature of Chosŏn as a "hermit kingdom." Two broad trends in Chosŏn's foreign relations reflect its early modern identity: one, the gradual reduction in the number of relations partners, largely a result of state-building and consolidation throughout eastern Eurasia; and two, the impact of sustained population growth on the availability of natural resources and the carrying capacity of the Korean Peninsula's ecosystems.

Chosŏn replaced its predecessor, the Koryŏ state (918–1392), amidst geopolitical and climatic turmoil. By the mid-fourteenth century, the Mongols, who had subjugated Koryŏ in the mid-thirteenth century and ruled over much of Eurasia, were retreating in Asia, abandoning most of their territory south of the steppes. Breaking free from Mongol control, Koryŏ faced Red Turban invasions and continual Wakō ("Japanese pirate") raids. Supplanting the Mongol Yuan dynasty (1271–1368), the Ming dynasty (1368–1644) as the new ruler of China proper wielded nominal power in Liaodong, the region bordering the northwestern Korean Peninsula and was home to Jurchens and others. Much of the Japanese Archipelago was in a similar condition, with the Ashikaga shogunate (1336–1573) exercising limited control over the many islands and peoples closest to Korea.

The Little Ice Age (c. 1300–c. 1850) contributed to this regional instability. Globally, intense political turmoil, famine, epidemics, and declines in state revenue marked periods of unusually cold temperatures. The late-fourteenth-century nadir of temperatures corresponds with geopolitical shifts in Northeast Asia, including Yi Sŏnggye's (1335–1408; King T'aejo, r. 1392–98) overthrow of Koryŏ and the founding of Chosŏn. Early Chosŏn coped with unusually heavy rains and other extreme weather conditions, adding to its challenges. T'aejo and his immediate successors sought to increase their legitimacy by acknowledging Ming suzerainty over Chosŏn as a "tributary" state, expanding and solidifying territorial claims, and developing its relations with neighboring Jurchens, Japanese, and others as "tributaries."

In the Mongol Empire's Shadow, 1392–1521

Early Chosŏn stabilized its relations with Ming. T'aejo sent emissaries to the Ming founder, the Hongwu emperor (r. 1368–98), to seek investiture. Hongwu ultimately acknowledged the new kingdom, even helping to select its name, Chosŏn. Subsequently, both Ming and Chosŏn experi-

Foreign Relations

enced civil turmoil. Once the dust settled, some Chosŏn monarchs sought close cooperation with Ming. Others, including King Sejong (r. 1418–50) and King Sejo (r. 1455–68), forged a more independent path. Sejo was particularly confident, dismissing Ming's presumption that "their tongues alone" could bring the "Four Barbarians" (*siyi*) into submission (Sixiang Wang 2023, 188–95).

Chosŏn consistently participated in the Ming-centered "tribute system." Key elements included acceptance of hierarchy with Ming as the superior, the regular dispatch of envoy missions to Ming, Ming emperors granting of investiture to Chosŏn kings, and the use of the Ming calendar. Chosŏn kings never seriously contemplated not accepting Ming investiture. Nonetheless, describing Chosŏn's relations with Ming as "serving the great" (Ko. *sadae*; Ch. *shida*) belies that the relationship was not a top-down imposition of Chinese power and ideas. Rather, the two co-constructed the relationship with Koreans exercising considerable agency. Indeed, after Hongwu refused to grant full legitimacy to T'aejo, subsequent Ming emperors rather consistently sanctioned every royal succession in Chosŏn, almost regardless of circumstances.

The continuing legacies of Mongol rule influenced the Chosŏn–Ming relationship. Not only did Hongwu propose a marriage alliance between the two states, Chosŏn sent royal princes as emissaries and later sought for some royal princes to be able to study in China. Ming demanded tribute—horses, gold, and silver—in amounts of more than a symbolic significance. Echoing Mongol practices, Ming also sought human tribute, girls to serve in the imperial harem, and boys to serve as eunuchs in the imperial court. Some of the former became favored consorts of several Ming rulers, including the Hongwu, Yongle (r. 1402–24), and Xuande (r. 1425–35) emperors. Tribute boys sometimes became prominent eunuch officials, often used for diplomatic purposes, not least with Korea. Some gained a reputation for arrogance and repeated and resented demands for extra gifts. Others provided advice and intelligence to their Chosŏn hosts and sought opportunities to show proper filial obeisance to their natal families. Ming also requested Chosŏn's assistance for joint military expeditions in Liaodong in 1449, 1467, and 1479. Chosŏn's reactions to these requests varied with Sejong hesitating, Sejo eagerly complying (not least because he had already contemplated sending troops north on his own), and King Sŏngjong (r. 1468–95) minimally cooperating. As the early sixteenth century smoothed many of the roughest edges of these Mongol-influenced practices, the Chosŏn–Ming relationship began to approximate the tributary ideal—even though relations were never solely tributary.

Early Chosŏn aggressively defended its territorial claims and projected its power far beyond. To secure northern Korea, in 1434–43, Chosŏn constructed an array of defensive fortifications, including the "Six Garrison Fortresses" (Yukchin) near the Tumen (Ko. Tuman) River as well as the "Four Outposts" (Sagun) in the northern salient of the Yalu (Ko. Amnok) River near Mount Paektu (Ch. Changbai). The Four Outposts were later abandoned, but Chosŏn's territorial consolidation during this period marked "the farthest point north reached" by a Korean state since Koguryŏ (37 BCE, trad.–668 CE) (Ledyard 1994, 290), not counting its successor state, Parhae (698–926).

Early Chosŏn rulers worried about the Mongols and the possibility of their resurgence. This fear was strongest during the Tumu Crisis (1449) when the Mongols under Esen Khan (r. 1453–54) captured Ming's Zhengtong emperor (r. 1435–49) and reached the outskirts of the Ming capital, Beijing. Fears were similar in 1515–16 when the Dayan Khan (r. 1480–1517) neared Beijing and in 1550 when Altan Khan (r. 1571–82) did likewise. Some Mongol leaders approached the Chosŏn court for validation and support. These overtures were never seriously entertained, but some Chosŏn sources indicate the recognition of a regional order in which there were at least two emperors, one Ming and one Mongol.

The Routledge Handbook of Early Modern Korea

Ostensibly the suzerain of Chosŏn, Ming, too, stirred fear in early Chosŏn. At times, the mercurial Hongwu threatened military action against Chosŏn. Nonetheless, he sought to soothe his empire's neighbors by claiming he had learned lessons from Sui dynasty (581–618) China under Emperor Yang (r. 604–18), whose attacks against Koguryŏ were spectacular failures. Hongwu placed Chosŏn on a list of countries not to be invaded, but any reassurance this might have been to Chosŏn was likely shattered in 1407 when Yongle invaded Vietnam—also on the list.

Another source of threat from the north came from the Jurchens in Liaodong. Jurchens often attacked Chosŏn envoy missions traveling—with hundreds of escorting troops—through the borderlands between Chosŏn and Ming. Also, Jurchens attacked Chosŏn at least 131 times between 1392 and 1627. For its part, Chosŏn launched at least 15 military expeditions north of the Yalu and Tumen Rivers during the same period. Chosŏn's military actions sometimes created tension with Ming, especially if any target of Chosŏn had received Ming titles. Chosŏn's capture and execution of a Jurchen chieftain in 1459 resulted in Ming dispatching an envoy to Chosŏn to investigate and remind Chosŏn not to meddle in "imperial affairs." Chosŏn contested Ming jurisdiction, insisting that the chieftain was a person of Chosŏn and refused to hand over his wife, who was allegedly of Korean descent (Sixiang Wang 2023, 113–17).

The *Songs of Flying Dragons* (*Yongbi ŏch'ŏn ka*), a mid-fifteenth-century paean to T'aejo, narrates how his charisma led Jurchen leaders to submit voluntarily, even before the arrival of his envoy. This exaggerated account hints at Chosŏn's practice of sending royal envoys to Jurchen chieftains. These envoys were ordered to prostrate in the direction of the Chosŏn king. Around 675 Jurchen leaders received Chosŏn titles and access to Chosŏn territory, with over a thousand envoy missions to Hansŏng (present-day Seoul) from 1395 to 1554. Some Jurchens forged identities for privileges. Although Chosŏn officials grumbled about imposters, denying access risked raids. The enlistment of Jurchen into a Chosŏn-centered order saw its greatest success from 1482 to 1541, resulting in fewer incursions, though minor clashes persisted.

Chosŏn implemented a multifaceted policy to address southern neighbors, especially the Wakō. Recognizing their threat, early Chosŏn rulers undertook military expeditions against their base, Tsushima (1396–97, 1419), and employed diplomacy to integrate Japanese entities into their international order. Diplomatic efforts targeted the Ashikaga shogunate, which reciprocated eagerly, indicating the relationship's importance. From 1404 to 1589, the shogunate sent over sixty envoys to Chosŏn, while Chosŏn reciprocated twelve times. Chosŏn also engaged local actors such as the Kyushu *tandai* (regional administrators appointed by the shogunate), western Honshu's Ōuchi clan, and Tsushima's Sō clan. Diplomatic goals included repatriating Korean captives, curbing Wakō raids, ensuring envoy mission safety, and facilitating trade (Choi 2014, 264).

Chosŏn managed various Japanese actors with titles, stipends, and permissions to visit Korea for trade and diplomacy. Japanese groups responded with alacrity, sending 4,632 missions from 1392 to 1504. They usually entered Korea through one of the "Three Ports" (Samp'o): Che (present-day Chinhae), Pusan, and Yŏm (present-day Ulsan). Some received permission to reside in and trade at each port's "Japan House" (Ko. *Waegwan;* Ja. *Wakan*). Chosŏn often restricted Japanese access to the Three Ports in response to riots, pirate raids, or other disturbances but generally restored it after a few years, especially in the case of Pusan. Some Japanese journeyed overland to Hansŏng, where they would participate in rituals displaying their acceptance of the Chosŏn-centered order and secured more trade opportunities.

Deception and forgery influenced Korea-Japan relations. Following the 1419 Chosŏn attack on Tsushima, Korean records emphasized victory and Tsushima's submission as a Chosŏn vassal. In 1420, however, Chosŏn envoy Song Hŭigyŏng (1376–1446) discovered that the "submitting" Japanese envoy was an imposter and that Tsushima rulers had not submitted (Kenneth R.

Foreign Relations

Robinson 2006, 45–46). Diplomatic efforts created ambiguity, with Tsushima being part of Chosŏn in Korean records but not in Japanese documents. The Sō clan of Tsushima utilized this ambiguity, managing diplomatic and commercial interactions between Koreans and Japanese, issuing travel permits for Japanese diplomats and traders bound for Korea.

Many other Japanese actors approached Korea under pretenses. They purportedly represented the "king of Japan" (a fictitious entity), the Ashikaga shogunate, various "pirate lords," the king of Ryukyu, and a mysterious place, "Jiubian." The ubiquity of faked seals, forged genealogies, and invented identities led some Chosŏn officials to conclude that "Japanese have many deceptions and their words lack credibility" (Kenneth R. Robinson 1999, 75). While Chosŏn occasionally attempted to unmask and expel imposters, it typically accepted them, hoping that doing so would reduce piracy.

By the end of the fifteenth century, Chosŏn had successfully created a Korea-centered order that structured its interactions with most non-Ming neighbors. Chosŏn hid the extent of these interactions from Ming, requiring the Jurchens to travel to Hansŏng via different routes than Ming envoys and forcing Japanese delegations to stop before entering Hansŏng if a Ming mission was present. Chosŏn often praised foreign visitors to their faces but sometimes spoke of them as barbarian or beastly behind their backs. Those who approached Korea did so for their reasons, often contesting and co-constructing relations rather than submitting to Korea's putatively superior power and civilization. The growing Japanese population in the Three Ports, described by one Chosŏn official as "a malignant tumor in the stomach," was also a cause for concern (Etsuko Hae-Jin Kang 1997, 79). In 1510, the Chosŏn court's attempts to further limit trade and residence incited widespread rioting by the Japanese at the Three Ports. Normal relations were restored in 1512, drastically reducing the number of ships allowed yearly.

Japanese riots and pirate raids, Jurchen incursions, or the seemingly never-ending flow of forgeries and imposters would occasionally cause Chosŏn to cut off its relations with the offending neighbor. However, relations were usually quickly restored, not least because of the potential for profit from the circulation of goods and people. The fifteenth century saw the official movement of people on the peninsula as Sejong resettled agricultural colonists from the south to the northeast. Unofficially, numerous Koreans were also present north of the Yalu and Tumen Rivers. Perhaps three out of ten people in Liaodong under Ming control were Korean; they spoke Korean and were "no different from the people of P'yŏngan Province" (Hasegawa 2020, 481–82). The court was aware that Liaodong's lower tax and corvée obligations might pull more Koreans across the rivers and repeatedly announced prohibitions on border crossing. Behind closed doors, some officials lamented that these prohibitions were routinely ignored.

Many Koreans were present in the Japanese Archipelago and Ryukyu, too, often due to shipwrecks or Wakō raids. Pirates regarded people as valuable commodities, making them "one variety of the slave trade" in the region (Smits 2019, 49). The Wakō often used repatriating Koreans to gain more opportunities to trade, but many captives never returned. A Sejong-era account of Japan reported, "At any port where our ship stopped, we could find our people who would come to talk to us. However, their owners prevented them from coming near our ship" (Seoh 1969, 38). Chosŏn also repatriated foreigners found in Korea and presented captured Wakō to Beijing.

Goods and resources flowed through the region, each with their logic that the various states involved could seek to channel but never entirely control or stop. In early Chosŏn, Ming requested horses by the thousands. The Jianwen emperor's (r. 1398–1402) need for horses in his civil conflict with his uncle likely prompted Ming to grant full investiture to King T'aejong (r. 1400–18), the first time a Chosŏn monarch received it from Ming. The demands for extra horses declined as the fifteenth century wore on, but horses remained on lists of tributary gifts until nearly the end of Ming.

Early Ming also demanded large amounts of gold and silver. Chosŏn pleas for leniency fell upon deaf ears until 1430 when the Xuande emperor allowed substitutes for specie. Repeated attempts to enforce sumptuary laws and other restrictions on the conspicuous use of silver either for trade or ornamentation often used the fear of the return of the hated specie tribute demands as justification. Despite claims regarding the difficulty of procuring silver, Chosŏn envoys and merchants seemed to possess plenty of it. Ironically, the successful removal of silver from the tribute list reduced silver's price in Korea, making it an even more attractive commodity to export to China. At the time, Japan had few sources of domestic silver, save Tsushima. Therefore, Korean silver was exported to the Japanese Archipelago as well.

Wild ginseng gathered from forested mountainsides, including northern Korea, was particularly valued in East Asia. A regular item on tributary gift lists, wild ginseng was presented as diplomatic gifts by Chosŏn envoys traveling to Japan. Interestingly, the amount of ginseng Chosŏn sent to kings of Ryukyu (in 1431, 1462, 1467, and 1471) exceeded the official amounts sent to either China or Japan. During this period, ginseng as a trade commodity accounted for as much as twenty percent of Korean exports to Japan.

Furs—squirrel and sable—and, to a lesser extent, skins—tiger, leopard, and Eurasian lynx— also occupied an important role in Chosŏn commerce and culture. The domestic production and consumption of furs and skins and their exchange abroad (along with ginseng) connected Chosŏn to a "northern silk road" that linked together the various peoples of Afro-Eurasia (Schlesinger 2017, 131). Chosŏn attempted to limit the export of these items, often for the same reasons as silver exports, but those involved in transactions routinely circumvented or ignored them.

Buddhist scriptures were a much sought-after item for many Japanese and Ryukyuans. They made more than one hundred requests between 1388 and the mid-sixteenth century. Ashikaga shoguns made the requests most often, and the Chosŏn court granted roughly half of them. Japanese and Ryukyuan merchants also did a thriving business in Southeast Asian goods such as sapanwood, pepper, cinnabar, and water buffalo horns.

Korea in a Globalizing World, 1521–1624

Cooler temperatures of the Little Ice Age persisted in Northeast Asia through most of the sixteenth century but not at the extremes of the late-fourteenth century. Indeed, Chosŏn's population boomed, perhaps reaching the ten million milestone as early as 1511. Temperatures dipped in the 1590s and again in a several-decade span in the mid-seventeenth century. During this time, all polities in the region experienced "sharp climatic fluctuations, severe agricultural problems, and significant political unrest" (Atwell 2001, 32).

In the sixteenth century, Ming China's late-fifteenth-century shift from confidently projecting its power onto the steppe and ocean to a "grim-faced defensive crouch" continued (Dardess 2019, 328) while Japan suffered incessant warfare. Piracy increased in numbers not seen since the late fourteenth century. Despite the longstanding Ming maritime ban, population growth, increasing commercialization, and the beginnings of globalization spurred greater circulation of people, goods, and resources. Such globalization peaked in the early 1570s with the founding of Manila, the arrival of the first Portuguese ships in Nagasaki, the lifting of the Ming maritime ban, and the establishment of bustling entrepôts across Northeast and Southeast Asia.

For Korea, the shadow of the Mongol empire would significantly fade in 1521 when the last Korean-born Ming eunuch envoys visited Chosŏn. Many feared a revival of demands for human tribute by the Zhengde emperor (r. 1505–21), but none came. Similarly, until the seventeenth century, Ming never resumed demands for gold, silver, or horses more than the minimal numbers on tributary gift lists or called for joint military expeditions beyond Chosŏn's borders. On both sides, Confucian literati replaced royal princes and eunuchs as the chief agents of diplomacy. Assisting them were interpreters, clerks, and other members of the complex institutional apparatus for dispatching and receiving envoy missions. Envoys wrote and exchanged poetry and waxed eloquently about the virtue of "serving the great" and of Chosŏn as a "country of propriety and righteousness." This conveyed a sense of timeless continuity in Sino–Korean relations that belied the increasingly downplayed, if not forgotten, difficulties of the fifteenth century.

Internal political imperatives also brought Chosŏn and Ming closer together. In Chosŏn, officials enthroned King Chungjong (r. 1506–44) with a coup dethroning his elder half-brother King Yŏnsan Kun (r. 1495–1506). When Chungjong immediately sought Ming investiture, his officials hid the usurpation and Yŏnsan Kun's death, which soon followed. A combination of "poetry diplomacy," gift giving, and mediation by Korean-born Ming eunuchs resulted in Ming recognition of Chungjong (David M. Robinson 1999, 39). Still, for decades, the Chosŏn court would awkwardly receive Ming gifts on behalf of the long-dead "retired king." In Ming, the Jiajing emperor (r. 1521–67), embroiled in his own legitimacy struggles, welcomed Chosŏn's demonstrations of loyalty. Receiving unprompted support from the "country of propriety and righteousness" at a time when even many Ming provinces failed to send supportive congratulatory messages was important to Jiajing, who would sometimes personally receive Chosŏn envoys as well as hold special banquets for them.

Chinese and Korean literati envoys wrote poetry to and about each other and the righteousness of the Chosŏn–Ming relationship. Ming envoys visited the alleged grave of semi-legendary Kija (r. 1126, trad.–1082 BCE, trad.), the Shang dynasty (c. 1600–c. 1045 BCE) prince whom Koreans had come to revere as the transmitter of civilization to Korea; the shrine to the "filial daughter of Kwaksan"; and other carefully curated and managed sites of Korea's adherence to civilization and propriety (Sixiang Wang 2012). Chosŏn elites reveled in stories of Ming recognition of Chosŏn's lofty culture, as when a famed Ming calligrapher requested one hundred couplets describing P'yŏngyang—where Kija supposedly ruled—and was amazed when a Chosŏn scholar produced them in short order, declaring that "Korea is indeed the land of the Superior Man!" (Gale and Rutt 1972, 270).

In contrast, Chosŏn's relatively peaceful interactions with the Jurchens changed in the 1540s, with new groupings requiring continuous intelligence gathering, diplomacy, and occasionally military action. The sixteenth century also witnessed the increasing use of the classification *pŏnho* ("subordinate barbarians") to describe some Jurchen groups who had received titles and stipends from Chosŏn and who were "neither fully within Chosŏn authority nor completely outside of it" (Bohnet 2020, 45). Some rebelled, including Nit'anggae (1583), which was only quelled by large, hastily mobilized Korean armies. As of 1591, Chosŏn population registers recorded some 42,000 *pŏnho*.

Chosŏn's interactions with the Japanese Archipelago were simpler in the sixteenth century. Previous foreign relations partners, such as the Kyushu *tandai* and the Ōuchi clan, faded from the scene. The Sō family in Tsushima increasingly became the only conduit for trade and diplomacy between Korea and Japan. An upsurge in piracy in the mid-sixteenth century led to another break in all interactions between Korea and Japan until the "Agreement of 1547," negotiated with an imposter king of Japan, repaired relations.

After more than a century of warfare, one of Japan's "Great Unifiers," Toyotomi Hideyoshi (1537–98), launched a massive invasion of Korea, commencing the Imjin War (East Asian War; 1592–98). In 1590, Chosŏn sent its first delegation to the archipelago's central authority in 147 years, primarily to gather intelligence about Hideyoshi. Of the two differing reports he received,

The Routledge Handbook of Early Modern Korea

the one that minimized the Japanese threat and recommended no preparations for a potential attack persuaded King Sŏnjo (r. 1567–1608). The war threatened Chosŏn's very existence. Initially, Japanese troops raced north, reaching Hansŏng in 19 days. One Japanese column reached the Tumen River. At the same time, another pursued the fleeing Sŏnjo toward the Yalu River, only to be slowed near P'yŏngyang by an advance contingent of Ming forces sent to assist Chosŏn. The Japanese withdrew to fortifications in southern Korea, and Japanese and Ming commanders held largely ineffective negotiations. In 1597, a new major offensive saw some initial success, but successful Korean and Chinese counterattacks and Hideoyshi's death prompted the Japanese to withdraw.

Ming officials and subsequent Chinese historians have portrayed the Ming intervention in Chosŏn as the expected actions of a benevolent suzerain, assisting its vassal in times of emergency. In reality, Ming leaders questioned the sincerity of Chosŏn's calls for help and the utility of intervening. Often, the behaviors of Ming commanders in Korea were so arrogant that Sŏnjo briefly "resigned" from his royal position in protest. Many Koreans formed militias, "righteous armies" (*ŭibyŏng*), often at considerable sacrifice.

Postwar Chosŏn focused on recovery from the immense devastation. As early as 1599, Japan's Tokugawa Ieyasu (1543–1616) reached out to Chosŏn to normalize relations. The steady repatriation of some Korean prisoners, as well as the dispatch of two Japanese who allegedly desecrated Chosŏn royal tombs during the war, served to restore relations. A series of forged letters, most created at the behest of the Tsushima Sō family, facilitated re-establishment of normal relations in 1609. Aside from one Japanese mission permitted to travel to Hansŏng in 1629, Chosŏn restricted Japanese presence to the single Japan House near Pusan.

The main dynamic of Korean–Japanese relations in the postwar period remained commercial. In contrast to older descriptions of Japan as a "closed country" (*sakoku*), its Tokugawa shogunate (1603–1868), founded by Ieyasu, did not so much prohibit foreign trade as seek to control it more. Hence, the shogunate was both eager to normalize relations with Chosŏn and willing to look the other way vis-à-vis Tsushima's forged documents. In 1635, the shogunate punished the Yanagawa clan, which they held responsible for the forgeries, and stationed Zen monks on Tsushima to oversee future communication. The measure, however, had little impact on Tokugawa–Chosŏn relations or Tsushima's role in facilitating them.

In the meantime, the climate stresses of the early seventeenth century held Ming back from responding more effectively to the menace of the Jianzhou Jurchens. Led by the shrewd and ambitious leader and the founder of Later Jin (1616–1912; self-renamed to Qing, 1636), Nurhaci (r. 1616–26), the Jianzhou Jurchens conquered or integrated other Jurchen groups in Manchuria enriched by its ginseng and furs but somewhat hit hard by poor harvests. A key moment was the Later Jin victory at the Battle of Sarhu in 1619. Chosŏn heeded the Ming call for troops by sending thirteen thousand soldiers, mostly musketeers. Some acquitted themselves admirably on the battlefield, but most were unable to escape the ruin that surrounded them as the charging Jurchen cavalry killed an estimated 50,000 Chosŏn and Ming troops.

Despite its victory, Later Jin would likely not have been able to conquer China proper without the advent of unprecedented cold weather. The decades of the 1630s and 1640s were some of the coldest on record in Asia and devastated much of Ming's most productive agricultural regions. The adverse weather conditions also affected the Jurchens, prompting two Chosŏn invasions. The first, in 1627, ended when King Injo (r. 1623–49) agreed to "brotherly relations" and copious tribute. Frustrated by what he saw as Chosŏn intransigence, Nurhaci's successor, Hong Taiji (r. 1636–43), personally led an army into Chosŏn in 1637. Injo sought protection in Namhan fort near Hansŏng but surrendered after a siege of 45 days. Hong Taiji demanded complete submission, requiring Injo to kowtow nine times. The Manchus (self-renamed from Jurchens, 1635) would end Ming rule in northern and central China proper (1644).

Economic and commercial changes accompanied the geopolitical shifts. Ming's use of silver as currency made the metal's value in China the highest globally, pulling silver into China regardless of any attempts to restrict its circulation. Whether by legal trade or smuggling, Korean silver, often obtained from Japan, flowed into China. In return, Chinese silks and Korean or Manchurian ginseng passed through Korean hands into Japan. The massive influx of Japanese silver lowered its price in Korea: by 1542, the value of a piece of silver had dropped from four bolts of cotton cloth to half a bolt. Not only fearing the renewal of Ming demands for tribute silver, Chosŏn officials lamented the foreign luxury goods in Korea, even base people consuming them. Furs, particularly sable, were popular, eliciting similarly futile attempts to restrict circulation and consumption. When local sources of coats (mostly in the north) were nearly exhausted, Korean merchants looked across the rivers to the Jurchens and sponsored the exchange of iron tools and cows for the ever-popular fashion items.

The increased circulation of goods spurred the movements of people. In the sixteenth century, a growing number of "pirates" appeared on Korea's shores. Although often depicted as Japanese, some spoke Korean, whereas others hailed from China. In 1546–47 alone, the Chosŏn authorities returned some one thousand seafarers from Fujian to Ming. These numbers, surely only a fraction of the total interactions along Korea's coasts, attest to the massive volume of regional travels and exchanges.

The Imjin War led to increased migration. The Japanese used some captured Koreans as bargaining tools to re-establish relations with Chosŏn, selling others as slaves. Many Koreans assimilated into Japanese society, especially in Nagasaki. Portuguese merchants who bought Koreans as slaves transported them across East Asia, Manila, Macao, Goa, Italy, and Latin America. Records show over 7,000 Koreans were transferred to various places. Conversely, at least 10,000 Japanese remained in Korea after the war, with skilled individuals in demand, some gaining recognition like Kim Ch'ungsŏn (former name Sayaga; 1571–1642), who aided in suppressing Yi Kwal's (1587–1624) rebellion in 1624. Ming deserters also settled in Korea in substantial numbers.

"Simplified" Relations, 1644–1850

After taking Beijing (1644), Manchu Qing crushed Ming resistance by 1662 and eliminated other challengers. The cooler temperatures accompanying Qing's rise would continue throughout the seventeenth century, with Chosŏn particularly hard hit in 1670 and again at the end of the century. The Little Ice Age waned in the eighteenth century, but the human impact on the environment—as growing populations depleted resources and strained carrying capacity—produced even more devastating effects. All the same, the Qing conquest and Russian expansion eliminated the pluralism that once characterized power dynamics in Liaodong and the steppes. This left Chosŏn with only Qing as the polity to treat on the Northeast Asian mainland. In Japan, the Tokugawa shogunate and its Tsushima representatives became Chosŏn's primary foreign relations partners.

Qing consciously "followed the model of Chosŏn" (Ch. *zhao Chaoxian zhi li*) in structuring its relations with Annam, Ryukyu, Siam, and others (Yuanchong Wang 2018, 72). Qing emperors reveled in Chosŏn's ever-consistent dispatch of envoy missions and careful use of the Qing calendar as clear evidence of Qing inheriting the Mandate of Heaven from Ming. Ostentatious empire-bolstering ceremonies such as the celebration of the Qianlong emperor's (r. 1735–96) eightieth birthday (1790) required the presence of Chosŏn representatives: his court postponed the ceremony until the travel-delayed Chosŏn delegation finally arrived in at Qianlong's mountain resort in Rehe (Jehol; present-day Chengde).

Early Qing–Chosŏn relations resembled earlier Ming–Chosŏn and Yuan–Koryŏ interactions. Qing demanded and kept hostages, including royal princes. Early demands for tribute—gold, silver, rice, and tea—were often more than ceremonial. Chosŏn sent several women to the Qing regent Dorgon (1612–50). Chosŏn also heeded Qing calls for joint military expeditions, most notably in 1654 and 1658 when Korean musketeers distinguished themselves in victories against Russian Cossacks. Not unlike the Ming Hongwu emperor, the Qing Kangxi emperor (r. 1661–1722) criticized the wording contained in Chosŏn communications. In one case, Kangxi fined the Chosŏn king 10,000 *liang* of silver for the offending letters.

Many in Chosŏn hoped that the Revolt of the Three Feudatories (1673–81) would topple Qing, though some worried about the rebels' suggestion that Kangxi could conquer Chosŏn if he retreated to Manchuria. Ultimately, Qing's quelling of the revolt and the eradication of Dongning (1661–83), the Ming loyalist regime of Taiwan, showcased Qing's durability. Over time, Qing and Chosŏn smoothed some of the rough edges of their relationship. No longer demanding hostages, Qing returned many Chosŏn captives. The calls for joint military expeditions ceased after 1658. Demands for tribute gold ended in 1692 and for silver in 1711. The tribute rice required was reduced in 1647 and again in 1728.

Climate-related phenomena continued to shape the Qing–Chosŏn relationship. In 1670, a cold summer destroyed much of the harvest and led King Hyŏnjong (r. 1659–74) to consider petitioning Qing for aid, and his decision to heed anti-Manchu voices at court and not ask for help probably cost a million lives in Korea. Even more devastating were the years of famine, beginning in 1695. Losing up to one-third of its population, a desperate Chosŏn finally sought aid, which Qing provided with some 900 tons of rice. The resource did not eliminate the anti-Qing sentiments in Chosŏn but improved the Qing–Chosŏn relations.

State consolidation and border demarcation played a role in the relationship. From its founding, Chosŏn and its counterpart in China, whether Ming or Qing, generally accepted the Yalu and Tumen Rivers as Chosŏn's northern border. In 1711, Kangxi dispatched the Manchu official Mukedeng (1644–1735) to survey and demarcate the border at the headwaters of the two rivers on Mount Paektu. Chosŏn resisted Mukedeng's efforts at every juncture, presenting him with inaccurate maps of Chosŏn. Ultimately, the indefatigable Qing representative prevailed, commemorating his success with a stone stele near the top of Paektu.

As a stabilized relationship continued during the eighteenth and much of the nineteenth century, Chosŏn regularly dispatched envoys Qing, averaging two missions a year. Qing envoys visited Chosŏn occasionally, usually to grant investiture to a new Chosŏn king. Chosŏn used the Qing calendar, at least in its correspondence with Qing. All seemed consistent with a "tributary" relationship in which Chosŏn "served the great" and Qing "fostered the small" (Ch. *zixiao*). Beneath the proper ceremonial interactions lingered resentment of and even condescension toward Qing. The Chosŏn scholar-official O Toil (1645–1703) was not alone when he lamented how the fall of the Ming meant that the "high level of civility, music, and culture of the Middle Kingdom has fallen deep into the rotten and nauseating filth of dogs and pigs" (J. P. Park 2018, 5).

Ming loyalism took root. In 1703, the Chosŏn elite established Mandongmyo, a shrine commemorating Ming's Wanli emperor (r. 1572–1620), who sent military aid during the Imjin War, and Chongzhen emperor (r. 1627–44), who committed suicide as the last Ming monarch to rule from Beijing (Figure 2.1). Chosŏn kings, too, established a shrine, the Altar of Great Requital (Taebodan), in the following year. Other shrines in Hansŏng and P'yŏngyang honored Ming generals and the general-turned-deity Guan Yu (d. 220). The use of the Ming calendar in private writings

Figure 2.1 Mandongmyo, Cheongcheon-myeon, Goesan-gun, Chungcheongbuk-do, Republic of Korea. Photo credit: Korean Heritage Service.

and Chosŏn envoys wearing Ming-style clothing embodied pro-Ming sentiments. Notably, envoys such as Kim Ch'angŏp (1658–1722) and Kim Ch'angjip (1648–1722) hurriedly had to rewrite their Qing visit diary after Kangxi expressed curiosity about it, which happened to contain references to the Manchus as "barbarians" (*hu*).

After 1644, Chosŏn Korea's limited foreign policy options heightened the importance of envoy missions. They provided intelligence about Qing China and the wider world, enabling direct interactions with foreigners such as Vietnamese and Europeans. Envoys documented their journeys in *Records of Visits to Beijing* (*Yŏnhaeng nok*), detailing geography, commerce, society, and interactions. Initially, some lamented China's decline under Manchu rule, but in the eighteenth century, admiration for Qing stability and innovations grew. Influential figures like Hong Taeyong (1731–83), Pak Chiwŏn (1737–1805), and Pak Chega (1750–1805) advocated adopting Qing ideas through Northern Learning (Pukhak). King Chŏngjo (r. 1776–1800) emulated Qing practices, undertaking public tours influenced by Qianlong and constructing Hwasŏng, inspired by China's military stronghold, Shanhaiguan.

Chosŏn Korea maintained diplomatic relations with Tokugawa Japan, aiming to benefit from commercial exchanges while preserving limited contact. Chosŏn sent envoys to congratulate new shoguns, with six visits to Edo after 1644 and a final 1811 mission reaching Tsushima. These missions, comprising over 500 members, were celebrated along their route, drawing crowds of local Japanese eager to witness the procession or request artworks. Interaction with Japanese elites either elevated the esteem for the Korean delegation or reinforced existing beliefs about Korean superiority. Some Japanese left these encounters convinced that Chosŏn was subservient, lacking military strength and cultural parity, highlighting the complex dynamics between the two nations during this period (J. P. Park 2018, 200).

In Chosŏn, the Japan House, first in Tumo and then after 1678 in Ch'oryang (both near Pusan), was the one location officially designated for interaction between Japanese and Koreans. Although the number of Japanese was restricted, they often ignored these limitations. At least 19 times from 1626 to 1824, the Japanese left the Japan House in sizable numbers to protest living conditions or official restrictions. Chosŏn officials were especially concerned about restricting interactions between Japanese men and Korean women. Those who engaged in or facilitated such relations could suffer beheading.

The Japan House influenced the economy and society of Pusan and beyond. Up to 50 counties in Kyŏngsang Province had to provide foodstuffs or other resources earmarked for accommodating Japanese visitors in Pusan. A perennial complaint was that the cost of hosting the Japanese amounted to half of the entire revenue of the province. However, more recent calculations put the number at a lower but substantial fourteen percent. The scale of illegal interaction and exchange was even larger. Japanese culture also influenced Kyŏngsang, with observers noting the ubiquity of Japanese folding fans, paper, clothing, food, and swords among Koreans.

Between 1644 and 1850, migration in Northeast Asia exceeded official boundaries. Jurchen pŏnho responded to Manchus' calls, leaving Chosŏn to join the Manchu state. Some moved south, integrating into Kyŏnggi Province, marrying Koreans, and blending into local society (Bohnet 2020, 93). Nonetheless, some exploited their *hyanghwain* ("foreigners turning toward edification") status for generations. During the tumultuous Ming–Qing transition, Chosŏn treated Liaodong refugees, ostensibly Ming migrants, no differently from "submitting" Jurchens or Japanese. Still, many descendants of Han Chinese migrants leveraged Ming ties, gaining positions as royal guards or keepers of Ming loyalist edifices. Victorious Manchus established markets where Koreans captured during Chosŏn invasions could be redeemed. Some Koreans willingly joined the Manchus, contributing to their diverse population and evolving Manchu identity, later joining Manchu banners.

Despite the hardening of identities and borders, Koreans continued crossing the rivers, seeking ginseng, wood, and other resources. Most went unrecorded, but some fought with local Qing inhabitants, sometimes killing them and stealing their ginseng. Promises of food, clothing, or land lured other Koreans across the border, only to be enslaved by local Manchus, who, in turn, handed over some such captives to Qing authorities, offering rewards for seizing border crossers.

Despite official prohibitions, travel and trade between Korea and Japan persisted. More than 10,000 Koreans "drifted" to Japan between 1599 and 1888, with the actual numbers likely higher due to undetected cases. The official narrative of accidental sailors masked intentional travel and trade interactions. Japanese individuals, especially from Tsushima, manipulated sanctioned repatriation processes to travel to Pusan more frequently than regulations allowed. Repatriation ceremonies involved expressions of vassalage; special envoys staying at the Japan House for up to 55 days likely engaged in illicit trade, highlighting the continuous and often covert connections between the two countries, contrary to official accounts.

Goods and resources circulated through official, private, and illegal channels. Envoys, especially interpreters, profited from missions to China, engaging in diplomatic communication and clandestine trade. They traded items such as ginseng and silver, importing luxury goods, books, ceramics, and more to Korea. Interpreters also procured Chinese silks for Japan, exchanging them for Japanese silver at a significant markup. Recorded exchanges represent only a fraction of actual trade, leading interpreters to amass wealth and even become fictional characters due to their extravagant lifestyles.

Military escorts, grooms, carters, porters, and merchants eagerly sought to join envoy missions, often under pretenses. They participated in various exchanges on the long journey from the Chosŏn border city Ŭiju to Beijing and back. Many coped with rampant graft, corruption, and banditry along the envoy mission path. Local jurisdictions, including Ŭiju, Kaesŏng, and Kanghwa, had permission to engage in trade of their own (more often in Shenyang or Zhamen than Beijing), ostensibly to help defray the costs of hosting visiting Qing delegations. A 1686 report of an envoy mission's more than one thousand "additional horses," far more than the officially stipulated ten, offers a glimpse of the extent of these interactions. The amount of silver exported through these channels was more than five percent of Korea's total rice production at its peak.

In the late seventeenth century, Korea and Japan had a thriving trade facilitated by Tsushima, where Japanese silver was exchanged for Chinese silks and Korean ginseng. The Tokugawa shogunate issued "Special Mint Silver" coins specifically for Korean trade. Silver exports to Korea often surpassed those to Nagasaki, but by the century's end, regional trade declined as Japan and Korea exhausted their silver mines. China's demand for silver stabilized in the mid-eighteenth century, reducing profits for exporters (Flynn and Lee 2013, 140–41). The last shipment of Japanese silver reached Pusan in 1752. Japan briefly replaced silver with copper, but copper exports also dwindled, remaining significant until the mid-nineteenth century.

The reduction in available silver hurt merchants, interpreters, and government officials who often lent silver to them. In the late eighteenth century, the Chosŏn government experimented with granting licenses to import Chinese winter hats, a popular item at the time, for a fixed fee. Visiting a Chinese hat factory, one Chosŏn envoy lamented that "we send half of our Korean silver to be used up in these shops" (Ledyard 1982, 88). The hat-licensing system briefly helped stave off financial ruin but collapsed as domestic demand did not support the number of licenses issued. While hats were a short-lived fad, Korean consumers demonstrated a more longstanding penchant to acquire many things Chinese, not unlike the simultaneous *Chinoiserie* fad that was sweeping across Europe. In 1789, Chŏngjo castigated the "poseurs" who would "drink tea and burn incense" and conspicuously display their Chinese "miniature screens, brush holders, chairs, tables, bronze vessels, wine cups, and jugs." (J. P. Park 2018, 162–63).

Korean ginseng once played a significant role in diplomacy and trade. The ginseng the 1720 envoy presented in Japan amounted to nearly half of the average annual amount of ginseng sold in Japan. However, wild ginseng in Korea was foraged to extinction. This, coupled with competition from American ginseng beginning in the 1740s and a Japanese shift toward domestic cultivation, sharply reduced the availability and appeal of Korea's largest and most valuable non-silver commodity.

Korea increasingly relied on cotton textiles, paper, brushes, inkstones, cattle, and marine products as exports. The development of a Japanese domestic silk industry removed a key element in Korea's trade with both China and Japan. Also, fur-bearing animals were overhunted and dwindled as an element in regional trade. Moreover, over-extraction and Japanese competition thwarted even the once-promising possibility of exporting sea cucumber. Diseases such as rinderpest periodically ravaged the cattle population and further reduced its utility as a reliable trade good, although temporarily increasing available hides for sale. By the nineteenth century, the commodities and resources that once circulated in vast amounts—silver, ginseng, furs—and even some of their replacements were removed from the economic equation.

As the resources that once drove interactions among the various peoples of Northeast Asia declined, so did the motivation to maintain the frequency of interactions. The Tsushima Sō clan increasingly relied on Tokugawa subsidies to survive. Nonetheless, even as Tsushima's living standards declined, the islanders did not resort to piracy like their ancestors once did. Trade, both official and illicit, continued to accompany envoy missions to Qing. The goods offered as official tribute, however, shifted over the *longue durée* of Qing–Chosŏn relations from silver to ginseng to paper and animal and marine products. Markets on the Qing–Chosŏn border survived, though increasingly featuring the half-hearted exchange of cattle, paper, salt, and other necessities for animal skins and shoddy blue cotton cloth.

The Routledge Handbook of Early Modern Korea

The reduction in the available resources utilized in trade resulted from the growing population with its attendant overhunting, over-foraging, crowding out of natural habitats, and deforestation. What followed was a vicious cycle of droughts, floods, rebellions, and disease; a concomitant reduction in agricultural productivity, grain reserves, sharecropping rents, and even the stature of males registered as soldiers; and a shift from commercialization to subsistence. A common perception among nineteenth-century Westerners that Chosŏn was a poor country with nothing to trade reflected longer-term resource exhaustion and regional trading shifts.

Early Modern Korea, East Asia, and the West

Chosŏn's foreign relations expanded in the nineteenth century as Western powers sought trade and diplomatic ties. Long before, though, Jesuit Gregorio de Cespedes, in 1593, accompanied invading Christian Japanese troops to Korea, thus becoming the first known Westerner to do so. In the seventeenth century, two groups of Dutch sailors arrived: in 1627, Jans Janse Weltevree (1595–1653+) and his two shipmates; and in 1653, Hendrik Hamel (1630–92+) and 35 other shipwrecked crew members. Hamel's account was perhaps the only first-person report on Korea available in Europe at the time. Koreans occasionally appeared in European art, such as Peter Paul Rubens's (1577–1640) sketch, *Man in Korean Costume* (1617), though whether the subject was Antonio Corea, a slave taken by an Italian slave trader, or perhaps a different, Chinese, person remains uncertain.

Western maps of the time began to demonstrate a growing awareness of Korea, if not always an accurate appreciation of its topography. Some of the earliest Western maps to depict Korea portrayed it as an island. Later maps conveyed a more precise sense of Chosŏn's geography but often contained little specific detail beyond its peninsular nature. Present in many Western maps was the designation "King-Ki-Tao" (Kyŏnggi Province) as the capital city of Chosŏn, a mistaken feature that would persist well into the nineteenth century.

As a hostage of the Manchus, Injo's son Prince Sohyŏn (1612–45) had extensive interactions with the Jesuit Priest Johann Adam Schall von Bell (1591–1666). Upon his return to Korea (1644), Sohyŏn brought books, scientific instruments, and even a statue of Jesus Christ. Interactions between Chosŏn envoys and Catholics in Beijing continued through the eighteenth and nineteenth centuries. Many Korean visitors showed keen interest in Western painting techniques, astronomical and other scientific instruments, and all kinds of forbidden literature.

Indeed, some became interested in Christianity. Yi Sŭnghŭn (1756–1801), the son of a Chosŏn envoy, received baptism while in Beijing (1784). He and others brought back Catholic literature, which they shared with family and friends, soon creating a thriving Catholic community. Foreign priests, first from China (1795) and then from France (1831), helped organize Korean believers and increase their numbers. A visceral rejection of Catholic doctrines and a suspicion that believers were forerunners to Western invasions prompted a series of state-led persecutions, most prominently in 1801, 1839, and 1866. Reinforcing the perception of Christianity as the vanguard of Western aggression was the infamous 1801 "silk letter" of the Korean Catholic Hwang Sayŏng (1775–1801), who appealed to Western powers to send military forces to protect Korean Catholics. The Western response to these persecutions, as well as the more general later-nineteenth-century pursuit of diplomatic and commercial relations with Korea, would once again dramatically increase the number of Korea's foreign relations partners.

Final Thoughts

Many studies of "modern" foreign or international relations appear to accept the notion that "modern," "Western," and "Westphalian" are interchangeable. According to the idea, treaties, embassies, diplomatic representatives, and the acceptance of an order of sovereign and equal nation-states are core characteristics of this "modern" international order that Korea entered only late and under duress—when Meiji Japan (1868–1912) using gunboat diplomacy became the first country to impose an unequal treaty on Chosŏn Korea (1876) (Hsü 1960; Woong Joe Kang 2005; Alyssa M. Park 2019, 51). Such an understanding ignores that the international order implemented in much of the world in the nineteenth and early twentieth centuries was far from Westphalian. Instead, it comprised congeries of empires and a host of less than fully sovereign imperial structures such as protectorates and mandates, all mediated by treaties not worth the paper showing them.

That Chosŏn Korea was reluctant to embrace this new order until the 1870s redounds to its credit as a proud and impressively durable early modern polity. Indeed, Korea stands out as one of the last independent polities to succumb to the era of "High Imperialism" when, arguably, only Morocco and Ethiopia fell later. The Chosŏn state's longevity owed much to statesmen's flexible and pragmatic foreign policy decisions and usually nameless travelers and traders who grappled with climatic, environmental, and geopolitical challenges and changes.

References

Atwell, William. 2001. "Volcanism, and Short-Term Climatic Change in East Asian and World History, c. 1200–1699." *Journal of World History* 12, no. 1 (Spring): 29–98.

Bohnet, Adam. 2020. *Turning Toward Edification: Foreigners in Chosŏn Korea*. University of Hawai'i Press.

Choi Byonghyon. 2014. *The Annals of King T'aejo: Founder of Korea's Chosŏn Dynasty*. Harvard University Press.

Dardess, John. 2019. *More Than the Great Wall: The Northern Frontier and Ming National Security, 1368–1644*. Rowman and Littlefield.

Flynn, Dennis O., and Marie A. Lee. 2013. "East Asian Trade before/after 1590s Occupation of Korea: Modeling Imports and Exports in Global Context." *Asian Review of World Histories* 1, no. 1 (January): 117–49.

Gale, James Scarth, and Richard Rutt. 1972. *History of the Korean People*. Royal Asiatic Society, Korea Branch.

Hasegawa, Masato. 2020. "War Commerce, and Tributary Relations in the Sino–Korean Borderland of the Late Sixteenth Century." In *The Ming World*, edited by Kenneth M. Swope, 481–99. Routledge.

Hsü, Immanuel. 1960. *China's Entrance into the Family of Nations: The Diplomatic Phase, 1858–1880*. Harvard University Press.

Kang, Etsuko Hae-Jin. 1997. *Diplomacy and Ideology in Japanese–Korean Relations: From the Fifteenth to the Eighteenth Century*. St. Martin's Press, Inc.

Kang, Woong Joe. 2005. *The Korean Struggle for International Identity in the Foreground of the Shufeldt Negotiation, 1866-1882*. University Press of America.

Ledyard, Gari. 1982. "Hong Taeyong and His 'Peking Memoir.'" *Korean Studies* 6: 63–103.

Ledyard, Gari. 1994. "Cartography in Korea." In *The History of Cartography*, volume 2, part 2, *Cartography in the Traditional East and Southeast Asian Societies*, edited by J. B. Harley and David Woodward, 235–345. University of Chicago Press.

Park, Alyssa M. 2019. *Sovereignty Experiments: Korean Migrants and the Building of Borders in Northeast Asia, 1860–1945*. Cornell University Press.

Park, J. P. 2018. *A New Middle Kingdom: Painting and Cultural Politics in Late Chosŏn Korea (1700–1850)*. University of Washington Press.

Robinson, David M. 1999. "Korean Lobbying at the Ming Court: King Chunjong's Usurpation of 1506: A Research Note." *Ming Studies* 41, no. 1: 37–53.

Robinson, Kenneth R. 1999. "The Imposter Branch of the Hatakeyama Family and Japanese–Chosŏn Korea Court Relations, 1455–1580s." *Ajia bunka kenkyū* 25, no. 3: 67–87.

Robinson, Kenneth R. 2006. "An Island's Place in History: Tsushima in Japan and in Chosŏn, 1392–1592." *Korean Studies* 30: 40–66.

Schlesinger, Jonathan. 2017. *A World Trimmed with Fur: Wild Things, Pristine Places, and the Natural Fringes of Qing Rule*. Stanford University Press.

Seoh, M. S. 1969. "A Brief Documentary Survey of Japanese Pirate Activities in Korea in the 13th–15th Centuries." *Journal of Korean Studies* 1, no. 1 (July–December): 23–39.

Smits, Gregory. 2019. *Maritime Ryukyu, 1050–1650*. University of Hawai'i Press.

Wang, Sixiang. 2012. "The Filial Daughter of Kwaksan: Finger Severing, Confucian Virtues, and Envoy Poetry in Early Chosŏn." *Seoul Journal of Korean Studies* 25, no. 2 (December): 175–212.

Wang, Sixiang. 2023. *Boundless Winds of Empire: Rhetoric and Ritual in Early Chosŏn Diplomacy with Ming China*. Columbia University Press.

Wang, Yuanchong. 2018. *Remaking the Chinese Empire: Manchu–Korean Relations, 1616–1911*. Cornell University Press.

3
KOREA AS "LITTLE CHINA" (*SO CHUNGHWA*)

Nataliya A. Chesnokova

The setting in many contemporary South Korean historical dramas is the Chosŏn state (1392–1897). The public has become familiar with ideas, institutions, and artifacts supposedly representing Chosŏn. Admiring Chosŏn arts and literature, some may dream about wearing *hanbok*, the traditional clothing of Korea, and pacing along the Han River in the kingdom's capital, Hansŏng (present-day Seoul). Not so many would question the meanings of the clothing's designs and colors, Chosŏn society's strict adherence to Confucian norms or the importance of preserving the established traditions in Chosŏn.

This chapter argues that the continuity of *sadae* (Ch. *shida*; "serving the great") vis-à-vis Korean relations and the emerging notion of Chosŏn as *So Chunghwa* ("Little China") shaped Korea's self-identity in the seventeenth and eighteenth centuries. The discussion below explores one of the most controversial, if not emotionally charged, topics in Korean history and culture. The subject demands addressing an ideologically complex question. The main difficulty is that the world has changed. Since the late nineteenth century, Korea has undergone a modern transformation that rejected ideas such as *sadae* and *So Chunghwa*, which were important in late Chosŏn. An observation by James B. Palais is thought-provoking: "[C]ultural borrowing does not reduce a nation to a cipher. Korea is no more a replica of China than Spain or France of Rome despite their indebtedness to Rome for the source of their language and culture" (Palais 1995, 413). This chapter discusses how Chosŏn Korea's efforts toward autonomy capitalized on Sinocentric understandings of China as the civilized realm, *chunghwa* (Ch. *zhonghua*; "central efflorescence").

So Chunghwa: The Concept

A logical starting point for understanding *So Chunghwa* is to consider what *sadae* meant in Chosŏn Korea's worldview and relations with China. Deriving from early China's Mencius (372–289 BCE)—who laid the foundation for the mainstream interpretation of teachings of Confucius (c. 551–c. 479 BCE)—*sadae* describes a reciprocal hierarchical relationship between a superior and a subordinate. In Korea, Silla (57 BCE, trad.–935 CE) approached its relations with China's Tang dynasty (618–907) in the seventh century in terms of *sadae*, but it was Chosŏn which applied the concept more fully and consistently in its diplomacy, beginning with Ming dynasty (1368–1644) China. Much throughout history, in the Sinocentric worldview, the "great" (*dae*) in *sadae* referred

DOI: 10.4324/9781003262053-5

to the "Central State" (Ch. Zhongguo; Ko. Chungguk) in the sense of the hegemon of China proper's Central Plains (Ch. Zhongyuan; Ko. Chungwŏn).

Modern scholars disagree on the historical manifestations of *sadae* in rhetoric and practice. Western scholars in Korean Studies tend to explain interstate relations informed by *sadae* as a "tributary system." Such an interpretation aims to point out the similarities between European and Asian world systems, and some scholars criticize this approach. For Nianshen Song, for example, the explanation "overlooks the fundamental difference of sociopolitical background" between East Asian and Western worldviews, as the term "tributary" comes from the imperial Roman historical setting, which was fundamentally different from the Chinese one. Instead, he prefers to speak of *zongfan* ("royals holding feudal benefices") or *chaogong* (Ko. *chogong*; "tribute") relations (Song 2012, 156–57), although *zongfan*, too, is a modern neologism (Sixiang Wang 2023, 291n40). More fundamentally, these terms reflect the Chinese evaluation of diplomatic relations with neighbors. The relationships China maintained with others were hierarchical. All the same, scholars argue that *zongfan* relations were closer to the patriarchal family approach. In contrast, *chogong* relations emphasized the role of ritual and moral authority of the Chinese state. Given that Chosŏn began to identify itself as a loyal "inner subordinate" (*naebok*) of Ming in the early sixteenth century (Yuanchong Wang 2019, 146), "tributary system" seems too narrow for describing the Chosŏn–Ming relations.

The Sinocentric worldview supposes a highly hierarchical system where the civilized realm, *zhonghua*, is ruled by the Son of Heaven and is surrounded by others who are less civilized. More practically, the master of Central Plains has a right to control and educate them. This type of "we–they" distinction, according to which *zhonghua* spreads its influence to benefit the less civilized others, is the dichotomy of *hua* (Ko. *hwa*; "civilized") and *yi* (Ko. *i*; "barbarian"). For Chosŏn, the Sinocentric worldview was a critical factor that shaped politics and culture. Sinocentrism as such not only centered Ming but also allowed Ming to legitimate Chosŏn as a new state of Korea, founded by Yi Sŏnggye (King T'aejo; r. 1392–98) through usurpation and overthrowing the Koryŏ state (918–1392). Subsequently, the people of Chosŏn "viewed the world through the prism of Sinocentrism" (Bae 2008, 73). Nonetheless, the ideology alone cannot explain the Chosŏn–Ming relations. For example, the two states initially pursued conflicting economic interests along the Sino–Korean border. The ever-suspicious Ming also made demands on Chosŏn's trade policies that were not in Chosŏn's interest. Nor did Ming encourage Chosŏn to build up its navy, even though Chosŏn continued to deal with the Wakō, the pirates based on the Japanese Archipelago at the time.

Chosŏn gauged the level of the "civilization" according to the preservation of Confucian traditions. The more Confucian a state, the more civilized it was. Accordingly, Chosŏn saw itself as the co-equal of the Central State while viewing others as barbarians who must recognize Chinese superiority. Building a diplomatic pyramid with China on the top, Chosŏn upheld the Sinocentric ideology in interacting with other neighboring groups, such as the Jurchens and the Japanese (Robinson 2000). This practice was supposed to demonstrate "the construction of a multilayered hierarchy" (Kim 2017, 31). Being in its own smaller yet as civilized as the Central State, Chosŏn used the term *kyorin* ("neighborly relations") in exchanges with other states, emphasizing Chosŏn's superiority.

Such a worldview reflected Confucian norms and moral values, influencing Korea's philosophy and ideology that produced the notion of *So Chunghwa*. This term implied that as Little China, Korea successfully preserved Confucian traditions and educated its people accordingly. If China, as the Central State, for some reason, could not fulfill its duties as a civilized state, Korea should be the leader of a new hierarchy. In this setting, Korea becomes the new Central State if a non-Han

*Korea as "Little China" (*So Chunghwa*)*

Central State fails to be the role model for surrounding barbarians yearning for knowledge and harmony.

In Korea, the *So Chunghwa* concept emerged in the thirteenth century when Koryŏ submitted to the Mongol Yuan dynasty (1271–1368), the first of two non-Han states to conquer the entire China proper. However, even before the Mongol conquest, Koryŏ elites had been subscribing to a worldview positioning their king as a Son of Heaven (Breuker 2010). At the same time, the Song dynasty (960–1279) of China proper remained one among relative equals such as the Khitan Liao dynasty (916–1125) and the Jurchen Jin dynasty (1115–1234)—each a Son of Heaven (Ch. *Tianzi*; Ko. *Ch'ŏnja*; Breuker 2003). Thus, as the Mongol conquest of China proper appeared a matter of time, Korean intellectuals were ready to proclaim that Koryŏ, with its Confucian norms and rituals, was uniquely qualified to replace the Central State in a new world order. The pursuit of this aspiration, however, did not last long. Not only did Koryŏ formally capitulate to the Mongols, but the latter's suppression of dissent and the emergence of a symbiotic relationship between Yuan and Koryŏ elites kept any notion of elevating Koryŏ above Yuan unfeasible for a century of the latter's suzerainty over Koryŏ. Four centuries later, the *So Chunghwa* concept resurfaced in Chosŏn's political and cultural circles, this time due to the Manchu (self-renamed from Jurchens, 1635) conquest of the Central State, and the phenomenon is the focus of the following discussion.

Historical Context and Interpretive Framework

At the beginning of the seventeenth century, following the devastating Imjin War (East Asian War; 1592–98), Chosŏn was not alone in facing a general crisis. Ming, which had sent more than 50,000 troops to aid Chosŏn during the war, suffered a general decline in the morale of government leadership torn by partisan strife, a deflation following a sudden drop in the supply of Spanish silver, a revenue shortage, accelerating breakdown of military organization, crop failures, famines, and rebellions. In the meantime, the Jurchens under Nurhaci (fouding khan of Later Jin; r. 1616–26) grew rapidly in power during the Imjin War. Capitalizing on Ming's troubles, Nurhaci founded the Qing dynasty (1616–1912; self-renamed from Later Jin in 1636), which would not only replace Ming but also create a vast empire larger than present-day China, Mongolia, and Taiwan combined in the seventeenth–eighteenth centuries. For Chosŏn, steeped in a Sinocentric worldview stronger than ever, the "barbarian" Manchu conquest of Ming, the subject of Chosŏn's *sadae*, was a moral outrage of a subordinate attacking the superior.

Chosŏn's relations with Ming and Qing changed due to internal and external factors. The court of King Sŏnjo (r. 1567–1608) coped with the war's aftermath, pursuing recovery for Chosŏn with taxable registered land just one-fifth level before the war. His successor, King Kwanghae Kun (r. 1608–23), born the second son, mothered by a concubine, had demonstrated leadership during the war, but the birth of Sŏnjo's only legitimate son, Yŏngch'ang Taegun (1606–14), just before Kwanghae Kun's accession fueled deadly partisan struggles and human tragedies at court—including the murder of Yŏngch'ang. Also, Ming's request for military aid in fighting against Later Jin tested Kwanghae Kun's policy of neutrality vis-à-vis the expanding war between Ming and Later Jin. Mounting pressures of Ming and his pro-Ming officials compelled him to dispatch some 13,000 troops, more than half of whom perished during the Battle of Sarhu (1619) before the rest surrendered to Nurhaci, who was aware of Kwanghae Kun's reluctance to aid Ming, subsequently released the captives, and Chosŏn stayed out of any further involvement in the Ming–Later Jin war while still complying to Ming's request for provisions. Before long, however, a coup by one of the main political parties, the Westerners (Sŏin), who were pro-Ming and anti-Later Jin, removed Kwanghae Kun and elevated his nephew and Sŏnjo's grandson, King Injo (r. 1623–49). Whether

The Routledge Handbook of Early Modern Korea

the partisan struggle or Kwanghae Kun's policy of neutrality was more decisive in his fall from power is debatable (Song 2012, 161).

The unequivocally pro-Ming, anti-Later Jin policy of Injo's court commenced the Chŏngmyo War (1627). Chosŏn's expressed pro-Ming sentiments and severing all ties with Later Jin gave Nurhaci's son and successor, Hong Taiji (r. 1636–43), a pretext to attack Chosŏn. Besides expressing outrage at the absence of Chosŏn representatives at his father's funeral, Hong Taiji noted that Chosŏn did not express gratitude for his father's release of Chosŏn prisoners of war even after they had fought against him in 1619 and that Chosŏn allowed Ming troops to use its territory to conduct military operations against Later Jin, despite the repeated requests to stop. During the Chŏngmyo War, Chosŏn was able to hold the invaders in Hwanghae Province but unable to repel them. Later Jin withdrew its troops when Chosŏn agreed to a fraternal relationship with Later Jin as the elder brother.

The ensuing diplomacy came under a severe new challenge when Hong Taiji made gestures as the new, self-proclaimed Son of Heaven. In 1635, he changed his people's ethnonym from Jurchens to Manchus. The following year, Hong Taiji renamed his state from Later Jin to Qing and elevated his position from khan to emperor. Furthermore, he demanded *sadae* from Chosŏn, thus pressing it to transfer its allegiance from Ming to Qing as the Central State. Although the Chosŏn court debated what to do, in May 1636, it sent an envoy to the ceremony of Hong Taiji's self-elevation as the emperor of Qing. Probably still attempting to preserve the integrity of Ming as the subject of Chosŏn's *sadae*, the envoy delegation made a series of protocol missteps.

The incident sparked a protracted political crisis, giving Hong Taiji a pretext to attack Chosŏn and commence the Pyŏngja War (1637). Among the most likely reasons for invading Chosŏn again were "the economic goal of protecting ginseng profits from Korean intruders and the political goal of enhancing the position of the Qing state as a contender for control of Liaodong" (Kim 2017, 46). The situation did not allow turning back for Chosŏn, and Injo declared war against Qing. On January 3, 1637, Qing troops led by Hong Taiji entered Chosŏn. Reaching Hansŏng in just five days, several days later, the army surrounded Injo and his court holding out at the Namhan fort, defended by 14,000 troops with provisions for 50 days. With provisions just enough for five days left, on February 24, Injo came out of the fort and surrendered.

The capitulation reshaped Chosŏn's *chogong* relations with the Central State. Above all, Chosŏn had to transfer its loyal obedience and concomitant *sadae* duties and obligations from Ming to Qing. The more immediate consequence was for Chosŏn to erect a monument, "Stele to the Merits and Virtues of the Great Qing Emperor" (Taech'ŏng hwangje kongdŏkpi; 1639), to demonstrate his power and to emphasize Chosŏn's subordination to its people. Also, Injo had to send his two eldest sons, Prince Sohyŏn (1612–45) and Pongnim Taegun (future King Hyojong; r. 1649–59), to the Qing capital Mukden (present-day Shenyang) as hostages. More fundamentally, according to the new relationship, every Chosŏn king had to receive an investiture with the royal seal, submit tribute, dispatch envoys for designated days and occasions, send dignitaries to meet and escort Qing envoys, contribute troops when requested, turn away fugitives fleeing Qing, and refrain from building fortifications.

Qing politico-economic discourse incorporated Chosŏn into the empire just as Ming had done (Yuanchong Wang 2019, 150), but Chosŏn resented Manchus as barbarians. As Qing demanded *sadae* obligation, a strong anti-Qing sentiment spread in Chosŏn. Even after Qing suppressed the Southern Ming (1644–62) resistance, Chosŏn still adhered to the Confucian worldview that recognized a hierarchy of states headed by Chosŏn and bolstered its royal legitimacy. In such a setting, an anamnesis of Koryŏ as Little China made Chosŏn doing likewise only too logical.

Understanding how Chosŏn reimagined its position in the world can benefit from the concept of a "universal state" explained by Arnold J. Toynbee (1889–1975). In his multi-volume tome, *A*

Study of History (1934–61), Toynbee traced world civilizations' development and decay through distinct stages, namely genesis, growth, the time of troubles, universal state, and disintegration. He analyzed Korea as a part of "Far Eastern civilization" and in connection with China, highlighting the cementing effect of Confucianism.

According to Toynbee, universal states "arise after, and not before, the breakdowns of the civilizations to whose bodies social they bring political unity." Such universal states are "Indian Summers," masking autumn and presaging winter. They are also the products of dominant minorities, that is, "of once creative minorities that have lost their creative power." Moreover, the universal states "are expressions of a rally and a particularly notable one in a process of disintegration that works itself out in successive pulsations of lapse-and-rally followed by relapse." The universal states are "symptoms of social disintegration, yet at the same time, they are attempts to check this disintegration and to defy it" (Toynbee 1954, 3–4). All the same, Toynbee emphasizes that the destinies of the universal states vary, and he devises an algorithm of variants. Typically, an alien society intrudes into a nearly collapsing state, compelling the besieged elite to establish a universal state. To preserve the collapsing state's original values, elites aim to either repel an alien aggressor or constrain the aggressor to provide the collapsing state with institutions unfeasible earlier in times of prosperity.

Toynbee considers various possibilities regarding the further development of a universal state. Some such states cooperate with alien intruders and establish new social institutions. According to Toynbee, if an alien civilization breaks into an indigenous universal state before the complete exhaustion of the social rally inaugurated by the formation of the universal state, the remaining impulse to create a universal state in the body of the disintegrated society is powerful enough to constrain the aggressor to provide an alien substitute for the damaged indigenous institutions. Such a universal state may cooperate and even await centuries until it finds an opportunity to expel the aggressor and re-establish the overthrown indigenous universal state. Another possibility is that an alien civilization breaks into an indigenous universal state *after* the full exhaustion of the social rally inaugurated by the universal state's formation. The remaining impulse is powerful enough to restore the prostate indigenous "universal state." In the third possibility, an indigenous universal state has reached its term of existence and gives way to a social interregnum. Such a state's social impulse is powerful enough to revive the state and maintain its institutional "mummy case." The Chinese civilization, on the eve of the Manchu conquests, was suffering a slow death and ultimately relied on a "barbarian invader to shoulder the burden of preserving an institution which he might have been expected to destroy" (Toynbee 1954, 5–6). Viewing the universal state as a phase in the process of social disintegration, he describes the phenomenon as a logical outcome in the life of civilizations.

From this perspective, the *So Chunghwa* case embodies two distinct phases. At first, the indigenous state was Ming instead of Chosŏn. Due to political and ideological reasons, Chosŏn did not avoid confronting the Manchus in the 1630s. As the inheritor of Confucianism and Sinocentrism, Chosŏn responded to the Qing conquest of the Central State by embracing the position of *So Chunghwa*. The "barbarian" Qing invasion of the "civilized" Ming and the latter's destruction produced an impulse among seventeenth-century Chosŏn intellectuals to remember the thirteenth-century Koryŏ experience and proclaim their state as the lone preserver of Confucianism, or the "Way" (Ch. *Dao*; Ko. *To*). The *So Chunghwa* already was a self-identity for Chosŏn's social and ideological norms before wars with the Manchus. What made Chosŏn's *So Chunghwa* identity more durable than the thirteenth-century antecedent was Confucian literati's insistence on *sadae* towards Ming for its military aid during the Imjin War. Despite the destruction of Ming, Chosŏn's ruling elites in general and the royal legitimacy in particular relied on Confucianism and Sinocentrism.

The Routledge Handbook of Early Modern Korea

Evolving into a "universal state," in theory, Chosŏn's stance toward Qing could have been bona fide cooperation, confrontation, or simply taking no action—awaiting an opportunity. These are references to cases one and two explained above. Forced into *chogong* relations with Qing upon capitulation, Chosŏn chose the third course. Especially after sending his sons as hostages to Mukden and without adequate military resources, Injo refrained from any anti-Qing action—duly performing *sadae* toward the victor.

Under Injo's successor Hyojong, the Chosŏn state and elites formally manifested the universal state but could realize it only through cultural expressions. Hyojong ascended the throne after returning from Shyenyang and upon Sohyŏn's death soon thereafter in suspicious circumstances—with his wife executed and his sons banished subsequently. During his captivity in Mukden, Sohyŏn became acquainted with Western knowledge and Catholicism and harbored a more accommodating attitude toward Qing. As king, he likely would have pursued cooperation with Qing, a prospect detested by Injo, if not motivating the father or his supporters to destroy Sohyŏn and his family.

Succeeding Injo, Hyojong exhibited a strong anti-Qing attitude and secretly undertook preparation for the Northern Expedition (Pukpŏl) to attack the Manchu state (Figure 3.1). Logical in Toynbee's conception of a universal state with an impulse to prove its might to an aggressor, Hyojong's project was not feasible against Qing's continuing military successes and territorial expansion that showed no sign of slowing. Also, Qing and Russia were having border disputes at the time, and twice, upon Qing's requests, Chosŏn had to contribute troops to Qing campaigns against Russians (1654, 1658). The occasions gave Chosŏn a glimpse of knowledge about a new northern neighbor but prevented attacking Qing. Upon Hyojong's death, Chosŏn effectively abandoned the project.

Regardless, as Ming legitimated Chosŏn founded by Yi Sŏnggye and ruled by his heirs, the Chosŏn court continued to dwell in the cultural realm of Ming China. The six public offices, the system of ranks, and the laws were identical to Ming's except for relatively minor differences (for example, the grounds for the death penalty). Despite Qing's unchallengeable position as the master of eastern Eurasia by the eighteenth century, Chosŏn was unwavering and systematic in its pro-Ming course. An anecdote mentioned by a Protestant missionary James Scarth Gale (1863–1937) in his article on Chosŏn's capital, "Han-Yang (Seoul)," (1902, 20) is revealing:

> It was forever after a violently haunted house, a sort of chamber of horrors, was this Nam-pyul-kung. A tower had been built beside it called Myung-sul-lu [明雪樓]. [T]he three characters [mean] "Mings," "wash away," "tower," a memorial expressive of Korea's sorrow at the fall of the Mings. When the embassy from the Ch'ungs, or present Manchu dynasty, first came, the government took good care not to honor them by entertaining them in the Ta-pyung-kwan, where the Ming ambassadors had been feted, but put them up in the haunted Nam-pyul-kung,where the Myung-sul Tower was. "What on earth is this?" asked the ambassador and his party. "Myung-sul-lu! Is this some sort of memorial to the hated Mings?" "By no means," said the Korean government, "it has no reference to the Mings at all. It means simply "Bright-snow Tower."

In the latter half of the seventeenth century, symptoms of stagnation, potential decay, and looming social changes grew strong upon the collapse of Ming, the external source of Chosŏn's legitimacy. The triumph of the Manchu Qing empire frightened Chosŏn, where the *Record of Chŏng Kam* (*Chŏng Kam rok*) and similar others prophesized the Yi royal house's doom. The throne sought to recreate the source of legitimacy by relying on the memory of Ming and proclaim-

Figure 3.1 Portrait of Song Siyŏl (1607–89), likely a copy of Kim Ch'angŏp's (1658–1721) undated copy of the original portrait (1680). A leading advocate of the Northern Expedition, Song became a central figure in the *So Chunghwa* ideology and the founding leader of the Patriarchs (Noron), who eventually achieved a paramount political position by the eighteenth century. Source: Uirimji History Museum, Jecheon, Chungcheongbuk-do, Republic of Korea. Photo credit: Korean Heritage Service.

ing Chosŏn as the new Central State, but such efforts were not enough. Chosŏn society needed something more potent as a new source of stability and hope. It needed a new ideology centered on Chosŏn.

Metamorphosis of *So Chunghwa* in the Seventeenth and Eighteenth Centuries

Chosŏn as *So Chunghwa*, in the seventeenth and eighteenth centuries, virtually engaged in cultural sabotage of Qing superiority. Despite the *chogong* relations with Qing, Chosŏn's object of sincere respect remained Ming. As Ming no longer ruled the Central Plains, Chosŏn kings continued their veneration through such symbols of power as calendar, royal seals, rituals in honor of Ming emperors, and erecting commemorative buildings in memory of Chosŏn's pro-Ming scholars and officials.

Chosŏn's *chogong* relations with Qing revived the *So Chunghwa* concept, but how long it lasted is debatable. Depending on the scholar, the end date varies from the first half of the eighteenth century to the late nineteenth century (Chan 2017, 136). Regardless, what is clear is that

The Routledge Handbook of Early Modern Korea

the Chosŏn ruling elite, whose legitimacy and prosperity depended on the *hua–yi* (Ko. *hwa–i*) dichotomy, invoked *So Chunghwa*.

A feature of the *hua–yi* dichotomy and *chogong* relations that Qing demanded was Chosŏn's symbolic subordination in time and space, controlled by the Qing emperor as the ruler of all-under-heaven, the Son of Heaven. Qing preferred to describe Chosŏn as a province in imperial discourse on the ideological level but without seeking to gain control over Chosŏn territory (Yuanchong Wang 2019, 135). In practice, Chosŏn had to provide Qing with a map of Chosŏn upon request, accept Qing currency, and use the official calendar issued by the Qing court—all amounting to a ubiquitous confirmation of unequal relations in the diplomatic hierarchy. Accordingly, any change in the usage of symbols in the *chogong* relations had implications for Chosŏn's *So Chunghwa* ideology, including its transformation and endpoint. Historians studying the ideology then must pay attention to the demonstration and discussions of, among others, Chosŏn obtaining and using a calendar of the "superior," providing up-to-date information about the territory of the "subordinate," and acknowledging a hierarchy in diplomatic relations in a system of ranks, titles, and other indicators.

Time: The Calendar

One of the many responsibilities of the Chosŏn king as the mediator between Heaven and humanity was to provide a calendar to his people. In the *chogong* relations, the Chosŏn monarch had to obtain and use a calendar issued by his "superior," initially the Ming emperor, then the Qing emperor. After all, a Chosŏn king could not rule time without permission from the Qing emperor who ruled the Central State. Indeed, the Central State forbade other countries from devising their own calendars. Any daring to do so risked punishment for violating *chogong* relations.

Nonetheless, in 1653, during Hyojong's reign, the Chosŏn court secretly began to calculate its calendar despite a new calendar issued by Qing each year. The idea of such a symbolic rejection of Qing authority first surfaced in 1645, during Injo's reign, when his head of the Bureau of Astronomy and Meteorology, Kim Yuk (1580–1658), proposed adopting Western techniques of measuring time in devising Chosŏn's calendar. In his memorial to the throne, Kim Yuk explained:

> China changed to Western methods of calendrical calculation between 1636 and 1637. Next year the official calendar we receive from China will certainly be quite different from the one we use here in Korea. If the new calendar is really as accurate as reported, we should abandon our old ways of calendrical calculation and accept the new.
>
> *(Ch'oe et al. 2001, 119)*

Kim Yuk pointed out the differences between Sinitic and European technologies in favor of the latter. He was correct in that the European time measurement methods that Jesuits brought to China differed from the earlier Chinese and Korean methods. In his memorial, Kim Yuk focused not only on the science behind a new calendar but also expressed unwillingness to use the Qing calendar without knowing how it worked, and the only way to find out was to steal the technologies. Accordingly, his memorial proposed to send one or two astronomers on the next *chogong* mission to Beijing to secure "some copies of the latest ephemerides and examine the methods behind them closely, obtaining explanations of difficult and questionable points before returning," so they "will be able to deduce the underlying principles of the Western calendar and will know how to apply them" (Ch'oe et al. 2001, 120). Of course, an interest in the new scientific methods did not mean respect for or admiration towards Qing, especially if risking punishment. Nevertheless, Chosŏn secretly dispatched its astronomers to obtain new knowledge and began to devise its calendar upon their return.

For assessing possible consequences Chosŏn's action faced if discovered by Qing, the letter by a Korean Catholic, Alexander Hwang Sayŏng (1755–1801), addressing Bishop Alexandre de Gouvea (1751–1808) in Beijing is revealing. In the letter, written on silk, Hwang Sayŏng appealed for help for desperate Korean Catholics who were being arrested and executed by the Chosŏn government. He even proposed what the bishop should urge Qing to do:

> China must find some legitimate grounds for seizing control of Korea. If Korea has violated the terms of its relationship with China as a subordinate state, then such transgressions could be used as an excuse for carrying out this plan. In fact, the Korean state has secretly engaged in many activities that violate this relationship and is fearful lest China learn of them. For instance, Korea has promulgated its own calendar and minted its own currency. This is common knowledge in the Chinese court, but no one has raised such issues officially. If it were to be investigated thoroughly, it would be sufficient to prove that Korea was in violation of its tributary status.
>
> *(Baker 2017, 198)*

The Chosŏn authorities apprehended Hwang Sayŏng and executed him for treason. For sure, the incident shows that the Chosŏn king, officials, and scholars understood the danger of "cultural disobedience" to Qing.

Simultaneously, the Chosŏn court and elites continued various pro-Ming and anti-Qing gestures in internal cultural politics. While performing its obligations to Qing per the *chogong* relations, in Chosŏn, the government went about as if nothing changed with Chosŏn's capitulation to Qing in 1637. Above all, the king and his officials continued to don Ming-style court dresses and Korean-style hairstyles with a top knot that Qing allowed them to keep. Also, Chosŏn elites continued to reckon years according to the reign of the Chongzhen emperor (r. 1627–44), the last Ming Son of Heaven to reign from Beijing. Chongzhen remained the "honorable and auspicious" era name in the blessed memory of the emperor, which the Chosŏn scholar Pak Chiwŏn (1737–1805), in his famous work *Jehol Diary* (*Yŏrha ilgi*), explained as follows:

> Our country uses the reign title Chongzhen because Imperial Ming is Chinese. China's rulers acknowledged our nationhood from the beginning, and we became a sovereign country. In the seventeenth year of Chongzhen [1644], Emperor Zhuanglie [Chongzhen emperor] died for his country and Ming fell. It has been over one hundred and thirty years since the fall of Ming, but our country still uses the reign title Chongzhen. The Manchurians invaded China, displaced the Ming government and enforced the Qing system. But this eastern land of ours, with its several thousand *ri* extending at that time even across the Yalu River, preserved the Ming government's standards. This meant that the Ming court still existed in the east, over the river. Though we were not powerful enough to drive the Manchurians out of China, purge them and resurrect the old imperial house, we at least preserved the Chinese way by respectfully using the reign title of the former rulers.
>
> *(Choe-Wall 2010, 1–2)*

As a universal state conceptualized by Toynbee, Chosŏn continued to perform *sadae* toward Ming, even after the latter's fall. How Chosŏn used not force but the language of rituals in its *chogong* relations with Qing aligns with the second type of response to an intrusion, as discussed

The Routledge Handbook of Early Modern Korea

by Toynbee: cooperating with the intruder while awaiting an opportunity to win over the aggressor and to re-establish the overthrown indigenous universal state.

Space: The Seal

The seal that the king of Chosŏn had to obtain from the emperor of the Central State to confirm their legitimacy illustrates the flip sides of Chosŏn's *chogong* relations with Qing in the seventeenth and eighteenth centuries. Qing and Chosŏn used two types of seals. From Qing, Chosŏn always received an *-in* type seal that legitimated a Chosŏn king's reign, and the seal was of lower class than *-sae* type seals reserved for Qing emperor's edicts. Internally, however, Chosŏn classified the *-in* seal as *-sae* seal, thus regarding it as the most important seal in the kingdom. Before entering into the *chogong* relations with Qing in 1637, Chosŏn had received three seals from Ming. Chosŏn obtained its first seal from the Central State in 1401, during the reign of King T'aejong (r. 1400–18), when the initially rocky Chosŏn–Ming relations stabilized. The inscription on the seal's surface read, "Seal of the King of Chosŏn" (Chosŏn kugwang chi in). From Qing, too, Chosŏn received seals on three occasions, but the conventions and politics of seals changed. The inscription on the first one (1637) was in Manchu rather than Literary Sinitic (Classical Chinese), whereas the seals of 1653 and 1776 used both Manchu and Literary Sinitic. All the same, during King Sukchong's reign (1674–1720), someone in Chosŏn discovered an old Ming seal, and subsequent accessions of Chosŏn kings utilized it (Sŏng 2008, 90). Used strictly for internal protocols, this ritual did not affect Chosŏn's relations with Qing.

Space, National Unity, and *So Chunghwa* in the Seventeenth and Eighteenth Centuries

The Chosŏn monarchy maintained a dualism of the expressed observance towards no longer existing Ming and formal diplomatic relations with Qing to protect the state inspired by the notion of *So Chunghwa*. While performing *sadae* toward Qing, Chosŏn elites invoked geography, history, and Confucianism in explaining how Chosŏn had the right to inherit the Central State. In the expanding discourse, an increasingly prominent figure cited was ancient China's Shang dynasty (c. 1600–c. 1045 BCE) prince, Kija (Ch. Jizi), who is said to have fled to Korea where he ruled as a marquis of Chosŏn upon enfeoffment by the founder of the succeeding Zhou dynasty (c. 1046–256 BCE). As such, Kija connected Korean and Chinese histories. Well before the Ming–Qing transition, Chosŏn scholars focused on the figure of Kija upon the founding of Chosŏn. For the first time in Korean history, in the late fourteenth century, state-sponsored rituals honored both Tan'gun and Kija as the first Korean ruler who had received his Mandate of Heaven and the sage who brought civilization to Korea, respectively (Han 1985, 358). Since the fourteenth century, details on Kija and his rule varied relatively little, and overall, he remained a cultural bridge between China and Korea and the source of Korea's true Confucian rituals. In the chapter on P'yŏngan Province in *Ecological Guide to Korea* (*T'aengni chi*; 1751), its author Yi Chunghwan (1690–1756) highlights Kija as follows:

> This was the land where Kija held his fiefdom. … Thanks to Kija, of all the territories of the Nine Eastern Tribes, this area developed its civilization first. It was the capital for one thousand years under the Ki family…. There remain traces of the grid-pattern land division system of Kija's state and of Kija's tomb.
>
> *(Yoon 2018, 39)*

*Korea as "Little China" (*So Chunghwa*)*

Yi Chunghwan also compares Kija's tomb and shrine in P'yŏngyang, P'yŏngan Province, with the Confucius shrine in China, emphasizing how Koreans are grateful to Kija and his deeds (Yoon 2018, 39). Such an invocation of Kija in late Chosŏn not only celebrated a connection between particular Korean and Chinese dynasties but also, more fundamentally, an enduring, deep connection between Korea and China stretching back nearly three millennia to early times.

All the same, Chosŏn scholars in geography advanced the theory of *Paektu-taegan* ("Great Paektu Trunk"), through which they articulated the notion of ethnic unity of all people on the Korean Peninsula. According to the theory, all mountains on the peninsula originate from Mount Paektu (Ch. Changbai) and are connected. Chosŏn scholars credited a famous Buddhist monk, Tosŏn (826–98), with the theory, but such an understanding of the mountains likely emerged only after the rise of Qing. Also, until the twentieth century, Korean cartographers located Mount Paektu beyond the northern border (Song 2016, 158). Explaining that the peninsula's mountain ranges are all connected to Mount Paektu, Chosŏn intellectuals of the seventeenth and eighteenth centuries claimed that initially, Paektu was on Korean soil and, therefore, the mountain belonged to Chosŏn. Contributing to the *Paektu-taegan* theory were new understandings of indigenous scholarship in Korean geography, especially among Practical Learning (Sirhak) scholars, as well as the idea of *So Chunghwa*. The theory's growing popularity in the latter part of the eighteenth century reflected their belief in the importance of the Chosŏn people's unity for strengthening the state.

The emergence and spread of the *Paektu-taegan* theory exemplifies Gustave Le Bon's theory about the development of ideas by elites and their subsequent dissemination among the masses. At first, anxiety about the northern part of the kingdom appeared at the Chosŏn court due to Qing's field investigation in 1685. The concern grew only when the Kangxi emperor (r. 1661–1722) initiated an exploration of the area surrounding Mount Paektu in 1711 to clarify the border between Qing and Chosŏn. In this context, Chosŏn's interest in its northern border reached a high level in the late seventeenth century. It persisted much throughout the eighteenth century before declining in the nineteenth century.

The Ming–Qing transition affected Chosŏn and Qing's understanding of their shared border. Before the Qing conquest of China proper, Chinese maps generally marked the frontier between Chosŏn and Jurchen territories with a line along the Changbaishan Ridge (as it was called in China) to the northeast of the Korean Peninsula. The frontier region, as such, embraced Mount Paektu to the north and extended westward up to the line of fortification known as Willow Palisade, located north of the eastern Great Wall. Subsequently, Qing declared the region around Mount Paektu a restricted zone due to its proximity to the Manchu ancestral homeland.

Qing's interest in the Mount Paektu region and the Yalu River basin was manifold. Above all, the Qing state desired to delineate the contours of the empire for military defense, protecting national resources, and enhancing the empire's stature. Also, mapping the region emphasized the Central State's new rulers, Manchus, as distinct from Han Chinese (Kim 2017, 50–52). Given the importance of Mount Paektu as the sacred birthplace of the Manchu court, "[t]hrough occupation of the land, ritual practices and cultural accretion, the Qing court marked the landscape of the Northeast in manners that elevated it on par with the landscapes of China proper, creating a Qing landscape with the Manchu emperor at its center" (Whiteman 2013, 38).

The Chosŏn–Qing boundary remained undefined even after two expeditions led by the Qing court's Mukedeng (1664–1735) aiming to resolve the border issue (1712). Qing relied on Mukedeng's survey and viewed Chosŏn as subordinate, whereas Chosŏn—with its *So Chunghwa* identity and lingering anti-Manchu sentiment—did not assent. Subsequently, the Qianlong emperor (r. 1735–96) strongly re-emphasized the importance of Mount Paektu as the sacred land for the Manchu people. In the meantime, during the reign of King Yŏngjo (r. 1724–76), Chosŏn scholars often discussed

53

The Routledge Handbook of Early Modern Korea

the *Paektu-taegan* theory in various writings. Based on ideological and economic considerations, the Chosŏn state and elites' political interest in the northern frontier and the Chosŏn–Qing border dispute encouraged scholarly interest in the region, if not inspiring national consciousness.

Chosŏn literati showed a keen interest in Mount Paektu's place in Korean history and culture. Among them, Yi Chunghwan introduced the idea of connected mountain ranges. Describing the phenomenon without a term for it, in his *Ecological Guide to Korea*, Yi Chunghwan connected Mount Paektu to China's sacred Mount Kunlun. This connection was significant in terms of politics and geomancy. In *Miscellany of Sŏngho* (*Sŏngho sasŏl*; 1760), his great-uncle and famous Practice Learning scholar, Yi Ik (pen name Sŏngho; 1681–1763), gave these ranges a name—the *Paektu-taegan*—and a short, systematic description. This theory subsequently became popular among Chosŏn scholars, inspiring many followers.

Yŏngjo's court rode on the momentum. In 1761, the minister of rites proposed a new name for Mount Paektu, Pugak ("Northern Peak"), reasoning: "[T]here are no rivers or mountains that do not originate from Paektusan. This mountain is surely the origin of our country" (Kim 2017, 71). Indeed, in 1768, the court officially renamed Paektu Pugak, enshrining the designation with the first government-sanctioned ritual for the mountain. Two years later, another official, Sin Kyŏngjun (1712–81), completed *Description of Mountain Ranges* (*San'gyŏng p'yo*; 1770), not only providing a detailed account of the peninsula's mountains but also explaining how they are interconnected.

In the eighteenth century, the discourse on Mount Paektu unfolding in both Chosŏn and Qing spurred Chosŏn scholars to find new ways to argue that the mountain belonged to Chosŏn. As they made their case in terms of, among others, geomancy and rituals, the *So Chunghwa* assumed a prominent role in both Chosŏn royal rhetoric and the "we–they" dichotomy. The argument emphasized the importance of the Mount Paektu region as it was connected through geomancy to Mount Kunlun, the sacred Chinese mountain. Accordingly, in philosophical and geomantic rhetoric, the same flow of qi (Ko. *ki*) that previously supported Ming filled Mount Paektu—hence the notion that Chosŏn was the heir to Ming, the vanquished Central State.

By the end of the century, under King Chŏngjo (r. 1776–1800), the *Paektu taegan* theory was powerful enough to explain the importance of the region's history. As both the Chosŏn state and ruling elite closely associated Mount Paektu with the Yi royal house, the mountain's historical and cultural role for the people of Chosŏn was now beyond any doubt.

The Twilight Era, 1800–73

The *So Chunghwa* concept that arose as a masquerade of disrespect towards Qing China strongly influenced the Korean mentality in the early modern era. In light of Toynbee's study, the evolution of Chosŏn as a "universal state" entailed three stages. First, Chosŏn sought to avenge its humiliation through the Northern Expedition, only to abandon the project after contributing troops to Qing campaigns against Russians. Subsequently, the Chosŏn court focused on preserving established Confucian rituals. All the same, Chosŏn abandoned bona fide *sadae* rituals (although nominally performed vis-à-vis Qing) and asserted its legitimacy as the Central State, if not *So Chunghwa*. Furthermore, in the latter part of the eighteenth century, some Chosŏn scholars showed interest in the West through the body of knowledge they accessed through Qing. Mostly Practical Learning intellectuals, such scholars pursued a new vision of Chosŏn without compromising its distinct culture and history.

Upon Chŏngjo's death, Chosŏn, as the universal state, collapsed mainly due to internal political circumstances. Chosŏn faced a range of challenges. Foremost among them were the concentration of political power in the oligarchy of consort families and spreading government corruption as a series of monarchs ascended the throne either as a minor or unprepared: Kings Sunjo (r. 1800–34), Hŏnjong (r. 1834–49), Ch'ŏlchong (r. 1849–64), and Kojong (r. 1864–1907; emperor from 1897). Also, the growing number of Catholics and increasing frequency of appearance of Western ships were symptomatic of social unrest in Chosŏn as well as its vulnerable international position in the world of imperialism. The Chosŏn state and its leadership saw Catholicism as a dangerous "false learning" (*sahak*), challenging the ideology of *So Chunghwa* based on Confucianism and thus demanding eradication.

Accordingly, Chosŏn's oligarchy saw it was in its interest to maintain good relations with Qing. As beleaguered as Qing was by unequal treaties imposed by Britain and other great powers following the First Opium War (1839–42), Chosŏn as self-declared *So Chunghwa* nonetheless sought Qing's protection if and when needed. Indeed, when dealing with French and American incursions (1866, 1871), Chosŏn, led by Hŭngsŏn Taewŏn'gun (1821–98), who wielded power during the minority of his son Kojong (1864–73), directed both France and the United States to Qing as having the final say on Chosŏn's foreign policy. However, when attacked, his government fiercely resisted the aggressors, deemed "ocean barbarians" (*Yangi*). While honoring the memory of Ming, Chosŏn as its successor—and *So Chunghwa*—went through the motions of *sadae* toward Qing as the "superior state" (*sangguk*). From 1637 to 1894, the stance was intact and "absolutely reasonable based on Confucian doctrines and the usual practice in Joseon–China history" (Chan 2017, 136).

Final Thoughts

The turn of the twentieth century was when Korea reconsidered its attitude toward China. Upon commencing his personal rule, Kojong pursued a policy of engagement that soon entailed establishing treaty relations with Japan (1876), the United States (1882), Germany (1882), Britain (1883), and Russia (1884), among others. Kojong sought a balance of power among various powers interested in the region, where ascendant Japan sought to expand its influence vis-à-vis Qing China. Qing military interventions Chosŏn's internal disturbances (1882, 1884) tightened Qing's control of Chosŏn as a de facto protectorate before the conclusion of the First Sino–Japanese War (1894–95) with Japan's victory terminated centuries of *chogong* relations between Qing and Chosŏn.

Russia, however, quickly replaced China as Japan's rival in the region, and the relative balance of power lasting not even a decade (1895–1904) encouraged Kojong to Chosŏn's complete autonomy. With Russia holding Japan in check, the Chosŏn monarch symbolically and officially upgraded the status of his country to the Empire of Korea (Taehan cheguk; 1897–1910), thus asserting its equality with the Empire of China (Daqing diguo) and the Empire of Japan (Dai Nippon teikoku). Long gone were the centuries of Chosŏn's *So Chunghwa* identity or *sadae* toward Qing.

Japan's victory over Russia in the Russo–Japanese War (1904–05) paved the way for Japan's colonization of Korea. Still, the latter's nonetheless growing spirit of independence reshaped attitudes toward Korea's past relations with China. By the early twentieth century, the *sadae* concept central in Chosŏn's Sinocentric worldview had become a symbol of historical Korea's dependence, if not subservience, to China. Modern Korea's understanding and denigration of *sadae* gave rise to a new concept and term, *sadae chuŭi* ("*sadae*-ism"), effectively meaning "toadyism" or "flunkeyism." As such, *sadae chuŭi* condemned long-lasting relations between Chosŏn Korea and Ming–Qing China as Korea's humiliation and oppression by a foreign power claiming to be the universal ruler before suffering humiliation by forces of imperialism. As vigorously criticized by

The Routledge Handbook of Early Modern Korea

such Korean intellectuals as Sin Ch'aeho (1880–1936) and Ch'oe Namsŏn (1890–1957), the allegedly pernicious effect of *sadae chuŭi* on Chosŏn occupied a central position in nationalistic Korean discourse during the Japanese colonial rule (1910–45) and thereafter, both North and South Korea (Schmid 2002, 61–64, 133–36, 263–66).

In the past three decades, a growing body of scholarship in Korean history has revisited the concept of *So Chunghwa* as not so much a shameful relic of the past as an ideal making a lasting impact. Not only did the political decisions of Chosŏn monarchs and officialdom mindful of *So Chunghwa* chart the development of late Chosŏn as an early modern Korean state, but the notion of *So Chunghwa* influenced its esthetics and episteme. In the context of *So Chunghwa* self-identity, the *Paektu-taegan* theory, for example, became popular during what arguably corresponds to Chosŏn's third phase of its evolution as a "universal state" and focused on the kingdom's borders, ethnos, and ancestor, Tan-gun. All became symbols crucial for modern Korean identity by the twentieth century. Furthermore, in North Korea, since the Sino–Soviet rift following the death of Joseph Stalin (1878–1953), the *sadae chuŭi* became the prima facie antithesis of the *juche* (*chuch'e*) asserting North Korea's self-reliance. From the repercussions of *So Chunghwa* to this day, it should be evident that the notion was not about Korea's subservience to or aping China. Instead, *So Chunghwa* as an ideal inspired a visionary universal state ready to preserve Confucianism as the Way that fundamentally asserted Korea's uniqueness in the early modern world.

References

Bae, Woosung. 2008. "Joseon Maps and East Asia." *Korea Journal* 48, no. 1 (March): 46–79.

Baker, Don. 2017. *Catholics and Anti-Catholicism in Chosŏn Korea*. University of Hawai'i Press.

Breuker, Remco E. 2003. "Koryŏ as an Independent Realm: The Emperor's Clothes?" *Korean Studies* 27, no. 1: 48–84.

Breuker, Remco E. 2010. *Establishing a Pluralist Society in Medieval Korea, 918–1170: History, Ideology and Identity in the Koryŏ Dynasty*. Brill.

Ch'oe, Yŏngho, Peter H. Lee, and Wm. Theodore de Bary, eds. 2001. *Sources of Korean Tradition*. Volume 2, *From the Sixteenth to the Twentieth Centuries*. Columbia University Press.

Chan, Robert Kong. 2017. *Korea–China Relations in History and Contemporary Implications*. Springer Publishing.

Choe-Wall, Yang Hi. 2010. *The Jehol Diary: Yŏrha Ilgi of Pak Chiwŏn (1737–1805)*. Global Oriental.

Gale, James S. 1902. "Han-Yang (Seoul)." *Transaction of the Royal Asiatic Society, Korea Branch* II, Part II: 1–43.

Han, Young-woo. 1985. "Kija worship in the Koryŏ and Early Yi Dynasties: A Cultural Symbol in the Relationship Between Korea and China." In *The Rise of Neo-Confucianism in Korea*, edited by Wm. Theodore de Bary and JaHyun Kim Haboush, 348–74. Columbia University Press.

Kim, Seonmin. 2017. *Ginseng and Borderland: Territorial Boundaries and Political Relations Between Qing China and Chosŏn Korea, 1636–1912*. University of California Press.

Palais, James B. 1995. "A Search for Korean Uniqueness." *Harvard Journal of Asiatic Studies* 55, no. 2 (December): 409–25.

Robinson, Kenneth R. 2000. "Centering the King of Chosŏn: Aspects of Korean Maritime Diplomacy, 1392–1592." *Journal of Asian Studies* 59, no. 1 (February): 109–25.

Schmid, Andre. 2002. *Korea Between Empires, 1895–1919*. Columbia University Press.

Sŏng In'gŭn. 2008. "Chosŏn sidae wa Taehan cheguk ki kuksae ŭi pyŏnhwasang." *Yŏksa wa sirhak* 36: 85–112.

Song, Nianshen. 2012. "'Tributary' from a Multilateral and Multilayered Perspective." *The Chinese Journal of International Politics* 5, no. 2: 155–82.

Song, Nianshen. 2016. "Imagined Territory: Paektusan in Late Chosŏn Maps and Writings." *Studies in the History of Gardens and Designed Landscapes* 37, no. 2: 157–73.

Toynbee, Arnold. 1954. *A Study of History*. Volume VII, *Universal Churches*. Oxford University Press.

Wang, Sixiang. 2023. *Boundless Winds of Empire: Rhetoric and Ritual in Early Chosŏn Diplomacy with Ming China*. Columbia University Press.

Wang, Yuanchong. 2019. "Provincializing Korea: The Construction of the Chinese Empire in the Borderland and the Rise of the Modern Chinese State." *T'oung Pao* 105, no. 1–2 (June): 128–82.

Whiteman, Stephen. 2013. "Kangxi's Auspicious Empire: Rhetorics of Geographic Integration in the Early Qing." In *Chinese History in Geographical Perspective*, edited by Yongtao Du and Jeff Kyong-McClain, 33–54. Lexington Books.

Yoon, Inshil Choe. 2018. *A Place to Live: A New Translation of Yi Chung-Hwan's T'aengniji, the Korean Classic for Choosing Settlements*. University of Hawai'i Press.

4

KOREA IN JAPAN

Rebekah Clements

From the importation of written texts during the fifth century to the popularity of K-drama in the twentieth, the states of the Korean Peninsula and those of the Japanese Archipelago have maintained contact over two millennia. This chapter examines knowledge of and attitudes towards Korea in Japan from the founding of Korea's Chosŏn state (1392–1897) to 1873, when King Kojong (r. 1864–1907; emperor from 1897) began to rule in person and made diplomatic overtures to Japan seeking a new relationship. This period of nearly 500 years saw great change in the Japanese Archipelago and, likewise, in its relations with Korea. At the level of the state, the "medieval" Ashikaga shogunate (1336–1573) gave way to the fragmentary Warring States (Ja. *Sengoku*) period (1467–1568) and the Azuchi-Momoyama period (1568–1600), which saw Oda Nobunaga and Toyotomi Hideyoshi's unification efforts. What followed was the "early modern" Tokugawa shogunate (1603–1868) and, finally, the Meiji Restoration of 1868, which ushered in the beginnings of Japan's modern parliamentary system. From the sixteenth to the nineteenth century, Japan underwent the development of a market economy, improved transport and communication systems, and a commercial print industry. Regime change across the centuries affected the nature of the Japan–Korea relationship at a state level; economic and social developments entailed a variety of ever-changing fields in which people in Japan consumed Korean products and formed artistic and intellectual images of Korea.

The idea of "Korea" or of "Japan" as cohesive national collectives in the modern sense was still in the early stages of development for much of this time (Anderson 2006; Burns 2003). Likewise, a Japanese public sphere of discourse—a shared domain of social life in Japan where public opinion was formed—was only beginning, as the commercial print industry took hold in the seventeenth and eighteenth centuries, followed by the Meiji period (1868–1912) efforts in national education and literacy (Habermas 1992; Berry 2007). Indeed, rather than being a monolithic concept, "Korea" was known by several terms in Japan during the fourteenth through nineteenth centuries. The main ones were "Chōsen," which is the Japanese pronunciation of Chosŏn, and "Kōrai," a Japanese approximation of Koryŏ (918–1392).

With the above factors in consideration, this chapter surveys Korea in different areas of Japanese cultural life and among different polities across the Japanese Archipelago. Art, philosophy, and literature, among others, attracted producers and consumers, from urbanites in Edo (present-day Tokyo), where the Tokugawa shogunate was headquartered, to regional towns and coastal communities. The means by which people in Japan learned of Korea were similarly diverse, including

DOI: 10.4324/9781003262053-6

material objects such as ceramics, books, and paintings, as well as word of mouth, diplomatic encounters, and war.

Diplomacy, Trade, and War

Japan arguably had closer state-level relations with Korea than any other country throughout its premodern and early modern history (Etsuko Hae-Jin Kang 1997, 2). This is largely due to the close geographical proximity between Korea and Japan. The four main islands of the Japanese Archipelago arch southwestwards from Hokkaido in the northeast to Kyushu in the southwest. Kyushu is the closest of the four islands to the Korean Peninsula and has historically had close relations with Korea, lying roughly 200 kilometers off the southeast corner of the peninsula, across the narrow waters of the Korea Strait (Totman 2014, 7–8). Even closer is the small Japanese island of Tsushima, which sits in the Korea Strait, almost equidistant between the two land masses, and has long served as an intermediary in diplomacy and trade (Lewis 2003).

Long durée Japan–Korean interactions from the fourteenth to the nineteenth century feature ebbs and flows in the cordiality of relations and the intensity of trade—official and unofficial—between the two states. These relations and trade, and the Japanese communities involved, were, in turn, important contexts in which ideas of Korea emerged, in which Korean goods were traded, and in which Korean technology circulated. In the fourteenth century, relations between Muromachi Japan (so named after the district where the Ashikaga shogunate was headquartered) and early Chosŏn Korea formally resumed after a period of no contact that began in the tenth century. Shogun Ashikaga Yoshimitsu (r. 1369–94) accepted Ming dynasty (1368–1644) China's suzerainty and the title of "King of Japan" to legitimize his government and to bring Japan once again within the orbit of the East Asian tributary system, where the Chinese emperor symbolically invested non-Chinese monarchs with the right to rule in exchange for sending tribute missions to the Chinese court (Saeyoung Park 2017). In 1404, Yoshimitsu sent an embassy to Korea using his Chinese title. Within this context, Japanese diplomatic perception of Korea positioned Korea and Japan on an equal footing in the East Asian world order as coequal vassals of Ming China (Etsuko Hae-Jin Kang 1997, 18; Elisonas 1991, 242).

After the last dispatch of a Chosŏn Korean mission to Muromachi Japan in 1443, formal relations between the two states deteriorated due to Japan's growing domestic disorder and financial difficulties in hosting the embassies. The shogunate no longer wanted to receive Korean missions. Still, a Confucian scholar, Kiyohara Naritada (1409–67), argued that relations with Korea should be maintained because the ancient Japanese empress, Jingū (r. 201, trad.–269, trad.), had conquered one of Korea's Three Kingdoms, Silla (57 BCE, trad.–935 CE). Therefore, it was the will of the (Japanese) gods. Drawing upon Jingū's mythical conquest of Silla placed Korea within a Japan-centered nativist framework that was to be later echoed both in Toyotomi Hideyoshi's dealings with Chosŏn and in the writings of Tokugawa intellectuals (Etsuko Hae-Jin Kang 1997, 87).

The Ashikaga shoguns, however, did not have a monopoly on Japan–Korea relations as their authority was precarious and did not extend to the western *shugo* daimyo, who were military governors of large territories appointed by the shogunate. The limitation resulted in "pluralistic relations" and diverse views of Korea across the archipelago (Etsuko Hae-Jin Kang 1997, 27–28). As daimyo and powerful merchants from the western parts of Japan engaged in trade with Korea during the Muromachi period, regional differences in the development of markets meant that different products were sought from and associated with Korea. For example, daimyo from southern Kyushyu wanted cotton and linens; the islands of Tsushima, Iki, and Matsuura required imports of rice and beans; and daimyo from the Kinai region and the Ouchi family demanded luxury goods and copies of the *Tripitaka Koreana*, the oldest extant version of the Buddhist canon written in Sinographs. Elites across East Asia sought copies as a form of political legitimization (Robinson 2001).

Moreover, these daimyo and merchants were the rulers of the shores and islands that harbored bands of raiding seafarers known as Wakō ("Japanese pirates")—originally petty military families from the coasts and islands in Kyushu and later included bands of Chinese merchants who used armed force to maintain their hold in international trade—that attacked the Korean coasts (Shapinsky 2014). This led to them having closer diplomatic and trade relations with Chosŏn. In response to Wakō raids, Koreans attacked Tsushima in 1389 (David C. Kang 2010, 118), but from around 1396, there was a move towards using incentives and rewards as well as force as Chosŏn began granting official Korean titles with stipends to residents of Japan who assisted with repatriating Korean captives of the Wakō.

By 1418, the Korean court was also issuing copper seals to their allies for trade (David C. Kang 2010, 118; Elisonas 1991, 240–45). Among the most important regional powers who had close ties with Korea as a result were the Ōuchi daimyo family who were influential in Japan's Inland Sea (Conlan 2024); Kyushu's Ōtomo family who were military governors (*shogoshiki*) of Bungo Province; the Munakata, rulers of Chikuzen Province and patrons of the seafarers of Ōshima; the warriors constituting the Matsuura-tō, which was a group of military families; and most importantly, the Sō family who were the preeminent power on Tsushima, where the pirates mustered before attacking Korea less than 30 nautical miles away (Elisonas 1991, 243). The Sō family's relationship with the Korean state became stronger in the 1420s when Chosŏn began allowing a limited number of licensed Japanese ships each year for trade. Agreements in the 1440s and 1510s permitted the Sō to sponsor vessels and verify the documents of all Korea-bound Japanese vessels—both lucrative operations for the Sō (Elisonas 1991, 244). Pluralistic relations between Japanese powerholders and Korea continued during the domestic warfare and political fluidity of Japan's sixteenth century (the Warring States period). This instability, combined with urbanization, economic change, and social mobility, began "to stimulate an interlude of ninety years of unprecedented freedom for 'private persons' and regional lords to engage in foreign trade and private diplomacy more untrammeled than in any other period of the Japanese past" (Toby 1984, xiii; Shapinsky 2014).

Later, the range of channels through which Japan communicated with Korea narrowed in the 1580s, as Toyotomi Hideyoshi (1536–98) took over from Oda Nobunaga (1534–82), continuing Nobunaga's unification of the country and creation of a central authority (Ronald P. Toby 1984, xiii). In contrast to Yoshimitsu, who had used diplomatic language that portrayed Chosŏn and Japan as equals in the fifteenth century, Hideyoshi's first message to the Koreans in 1587 demanded that they submit to him by sending a tribute mission. Throughout the letter, Hideyoshi referred to himself using the honorific Chinese character *zhèn* (Ja. *chin*; Ko. *chim*), a term reserved for the emperor in Beijing (Hawley 2005, 77–79). In fact, the Sō had already toned down the letter, as they wished to avoid conflict with Chosŏn and to preserve their lucrative trade connections. A second letter, delivered to the Koreans by Tsushima daimyo, Sō Yoshitoshi (1568–1615), in 1588, was similar in tone, demanding passage through Korea so that Hideyoshi might conquer Ming China (Hawley 2005, 80–81). Similarly, Hideyoshi interpreted a goodwill mission by the Chosŏn court in 1590 as a "tribute" mission and a sign of Korean submission to him (Etsuko Hae-Jin Kang 1997, 89). By the time it became apparent that this was not the case, and Sō Yoshitoshi's final overture to the Chosŏn court met with no response, Hideyoshi and his vassals in western Japan began to prepare for war (Hawley 2005, 88–89; Swope 2009, 61).

In justification for the war against Chosŏn, Hideyoshi framed Korea as a wayward Japanese territory. Before launching the war, he drew upon the authority of the Japanese emperor and, in particular, the legendary Jingū empress's expedition to Silla. This involved Hideyoshi visiting the shrines of Jingū and her husband, Emperor Chūai (r. 192, trad.–200, trad.), in the fourth lunar month of 1592 while preparing to launch his first invasion. Hideyoshi was thus locating his attempt to conquer Korea within a Japanese nativist framework (Etsuko Hae-Jin Kang 1997, 101). During the ensuring Imjin War (East Asian War; 1592–98), he referred to his campaign as a "chastisement" (Ja. *seibatsu*) of Korea, using a term he had employed domestically during "*seibatsu*" campaigns in Shikoku, Kyushu, and Odawara in his efforts to unify the country (Lewis 2015, 260).

Consistent with his authoritarian rhetoric, in the first campaign of the war, launched in 1592 "to force Korea to serve [Japan]" (Hur 2022, 25), Hideyoshi gave signs of intending to establish benevolent rulership on the peninsula once the Chosŏn king had been chastised. Accordingly, he issued a code of conduct to the Japanese troops, encouraging them to refrain from violence, raping, and looting. During the negotiations amidst the war, Hideyoshi's insistence on refusing to treat Chosŏn as a foreign territory outside his domain of control was a factor in the breakdown of the talks with the Ming (Sajima 2015). In the second campaign, launched in 1597 after negotiations broke down acrimoniously at the end of 1596, Hideyoshi ordered that heads and noses be severed to punish the Korean populace for defying him (Hur 2023). These body parts were interred in an "ear mound" on the grounds of the Hōkō-ji temple he had founded in Kyoto. Hideyoshi commissioned an elaborate spirit pacification ceremony to be held there in 1597.

In the period following Hideyoshi's death and the end of the Imjin War, the Tokugawa shogunate secured a centralized power and exercised an increasing monopoly over Japanese economic and diplomatic contact with other states, including Korea (Toby 1984; Etsuko Hae-Jin Kang 1997, 137). At the same time, Japan and Korea normalized their relationship following the repatriation of thousands of Korean prisoners. Korean embassies to Edo resumed, leading to amicable relations between Japanese and Korean intellectuals and cultural exchanges. The interactions also increased the visibility of "Korea" on the highways of Japan and the streets of the shogunal city of Edo as the large and impressive embassy retinues wound their way across the country (Toby 1984). Twelve such embassies sent by Chosŏn to Japan during the Tokugawa period were minutely choreographed spectacles, attracting the attention of hundreds of thousands of onlookers. The embassies became a major trope in Japanese art of the eighteenth century, as discussed below, were depicted in maps, and were incorporated into popular culture through *karako odori* (*Tōjin odori*) folk dances and kabuki theatre (Gonnami 1998, 11; Doyoung Park 2013, 8).

Despite the resumption of apparently good relations, the Tokugawa period nonetheless saw a clash of diplomatic ideologies between Tokugawa Japan and Chosŏn Korea as each state laid claim to be the center of civilization in East Asia in the wake of Ming China's fall to the "barbaric" Jurchens (self-renamed Manchus in 1635) who founded the Qing dynasty (1616–1912; Later Jin until 1636). As discussed below, the embassy visits became sites for contesting each state's claim to superiority in sinological knowledge, painting, poetic composition, and calligraphy.

Art

The close geographical, diplomatic, and economic ties between Japan and Korea in history have meant that Korean art has played a significant role in the history of art in Japan since the earliest written records began. For example, much of the extant corpus of Koryŏ Buddhist painting survives only in Japan. Over time, however, as the Korean origin of these paintings was forgotten in Japan, they came to bear attributions to Chinese professional painters of the Ningbo region instead (Lippit 2005). During the period covered by this chapter, three main genres of Japanese art recognized "Korea": ceramics, ink painting associated with Korean embassy visits, and popular woodblock illustrations of the embassies. Together, these examples show the presence of Korea at all levels of society.

In early modern Japan, Korean ceramics had been enjoying appreciation for centuries, beginning with refined Koryŏ celadons that began reaching Japan in the twelfth century (Pollard 2020, 23–24). In the sixteenth century, a vogue for the rough beauty of Chosŏn *buncheong* (*punch'ŏng*) ceramics emerged in Japan's tea ceremony community. The most influential Japanese tea master of the sixteenth century, Sen no Rikyū (1522–91), redefined the tea ceremony, simplifying it and developing the rustic aesthetic for which the way of tea is now known. Yamanoue no Sōji (1544–90), a disciple of Sen no Rikyū, recorded this new trend for rustic simplicity and noted the importance of Korean pieces: "Chinese teabowls are out of fashion, Korean (Kōrai), Seto, and 'just-fired' Raku teabowls are popular today" (Tokyo National Museum 2017, 175). The rustic Korean bowls, many of which were not originally intended to be used as tea utensils, were known as *Kōrai chawan* ("Koryŏ teabowls") in Japanese. Many characteristics of *Kōrai chawan* were copied by and influenced styles in Japan (Lee 2011).

Upon normalization of Japan–Korea relations following the Imjin War, Korea again exported tea bowls to Japan. From the 1640s, these were produced within the Japan House (Waegwan), where Tsushima officials in Korea resided, rather than directly purchased from kilns elsewhere in Korea. The tea bowls made in Korea for the Japanese market were sold in Edo, Kyoto, and Osaka. Eventually, the fashions of the Japanese tea ceremony changed and moved towards an appreciation for Japanese rather than Korean aesthetics. However, some tea ceremony lineages, such as the Sen House, continued to value Korean aesthetics (Hur 2015; Watanabe 2007; Katayama 2012).

The Japanese interest in Korean ceramics also resulted in the Japanese who lived in inland Japan—beyond the coastal communities who had traded with Korea in the past—coming into direct contact with communities of Koreans. During the Imjin War, potters and their families were among the many Chosŏn Koreans taken to Japan (Sousa 2019). The potters were settled in daimyo domains in Kyushu, where they founded kilns and ceramic industries, many of which remain today (Cort 1986; Maske 1994, 2011; Hur 2015). Small numbers of Korean potters had already been active in northern Kyushu beforehand. Still, the mass arrival of Korean potters in Kyushu and Western Honshu during and shortly after the Imjin War fundamentally altered the nature of ceramic production in southwestern Japan. The region became one of the major production centers for ceramics in Japan (Cort 1986).

Varying combinations of archaeological and documentary evidence suggest that the following ceramic wares had their origins in Korean potters in Japan: Arita, Karatsu, Mikawachi (Hirado), Hasami, Satsuma, Agano, Hagi, and Takatori (Cort 1986; Maske 2011; Lee 2014, 51). According to legend, Yi Samp'yŏng (Ja. Ri Sanpei; d. 1655), a Korean immigrant potter, discovered porcelain stone for the first time in Japan and founded the porcelain industry in Arita. In fact, besides Koreans, the Chinese, too, evidently contributed to establishing porcelain manufacture in Hizen (Rousmaniere 2012; Lee 2014, 123).

Most Korean potters who founded ceramic traditions in Japan assimilated into Japanese society in the seventeenth century, but one community, settled in the village of Naeshirogawa in Satsuma, retained elements of its Chosŏn Korean identity throughout the Tokugawa period (Figure 4.1). The Naeshirogawa kilns produced the distinctive "Black Satsuma" (*kurosatsuma*) and later the "White Satsuma" (*shirosatsuma*) wares for which the area is still famous. Although the exact size of Naeshirogawa's contribution to the Satsuma economy is unknown, the Shimazu family of daimyo recognized the importance of the Naeshirogawa ceramics industry and put measures in place to protect the village community, including gifts of land rights, proclamations against harming the Koreans, financial aid in times of difficulty, and the building of wells (Clements 2022).

Figure 4.1 Residents of Naeshirogawa in Korean dress. Source: *Sangoku meishō zue* [Illustrations of famous sites in Three Provinces] (Yamamoto Morihide 1905), volume 8; reprint of the 1844 original. Photo credit: National Diet Library of Japan.

The Satsuma domain administration promulgated regulations to protect the villagers' Korean identity as "*Chōsenjin*"— "people from Chosŏn." In 1676, the domain prohibited the Koreans from marrying outside the village, and from 1695, they could not use Japanese names. Probably designed to preserve specialized knowledge of ceramic production, the extramural marriage prohibition was a regulation seen in other Satsuma villages with such specialized occupations as mining and fishing. The order to preserve Korean names may also be seen in this light, but likely, it was also intended to preserve the village's Korean identity. When the daimyo of Satsuma stayed in Naeshirogawa on their travels to and from Edo, the visit featured public banquets, ritual gift exchanges, Korean dance and music performances, and displays of local ceramic wares. The Shimazu family who ruled Satsuma evidently utilized such occasions as a public display of their international stature—by displaying the carefully preserved "Koreanness" of the Naeshirogawa villagers and their descendants (Clements 2022, 145–46).

In addition to ceramic encounters, the Korean embassies that visited Japan during the Muromachi and Tokugawa periods proved to be a source of artistic contact between the two states. As the embassies traveled north-eastwards from Tsushima to Edo and back again over several months, each rest point presented an opportunity for interactions between the Koreans and hordes of eager locals (Clements 2019). Although interpreters traveled with the embassies, meetings between the Koreans and Japanese—literati and Buddhist monks—usually involved an exchange of Chinese writing, both prose and poetry. The meetings were opportunities to display both sides' erudition, calligraphic skill, poetry, and painterly abilities, and the stakes were high. King Sŏnjo of Chosŏn (r. 1567–1608) ordered that the most talented poets be chosen as the officials charged with receiving Japanese visitors to Korea. "If the talents of our men do not match theirs at times of exchange, we will be ridiculed in that country," he reasoned (Clements 2019, 297). While attending poetry parties hosted by Japanese monks, the Korean envoys and their aids composed poetry, and the painters who accompanied the mission provided ink and brush illustrations. An early extant example is *Banana Tree under Night Rain* (*P'ach'o yaudo*), executed in 1410 at a welcome party for the Korean ambassador Yang Su (fl. 1404–12) held at Nanzen-ji temple (Ahn 1997, 198). During the Tokugawa period, Korean paintings of the Southern School (Ch. *Nanzonghua*, Ja. *Nanga*, Ko. *Namjonghwa*) seem to have been particularly influential in such exchanges during Korean embassy visits to Japan (Jungmann 2004). Japanese painters of the Southern School sought advice from the Korean painters who accompanied the embassies because they perceived the Korean Southern School as faithfully based on the Southern School of literati painting that emerged in Ming China.

The colorful spectacles of the embassies themselves proved to be a source of artistic inspiration in Japan (Toby 1986; Lewis 2010). Over one hundred paintings, prints, and illustrated pamphlets depicting the Korean processions are extant, produced by artists among the spectators watching the processions in the metropolises of Edo and Osaka and along the route from Kyushu. (Ryukyuan embassies, similarly, are the subject of nearly one hundred other works.) Some works were commissioned by social and political elites and were painted by leading artists—including Kanō Tan'yū's (1602–74) *Tōshōsa engi emaki,* which depicts the 1636 embassy's approach to the Tōshōgu Shrine dedicated to Tokugawa Ieyasu (1543–1616), the founder of the Tokugawa Shogunate. His son and the third Tokugawa shogun, Tokugawa Iemitsu (r. 1623–51), commissioned the painting as part of a series of shrine-building projects designed to consolidate a ritual platform for the posthumous veneration of Ieyasu (Gerhart 2004). Other artworks testify to the popular appeal of the Korean embassies, such as the single-sheet woodblock prints by Hishikawa Moronobu (1618–94) and Katsushika Hokusai (1760–1849), which were produced in large numbers for commercial sale. Although it is unknown precisely how profitable such sales were, publishers counted on a large market for these prints and pamphlets, numbering in the tens of thousands of copies (Toby 1986, 420).

Books

Books published by the commercial print industry and other forms of literature became another conduit for knowledge about Korea to spread in Japan during the Imjin War and in the centuries that followed. The Imjin War was depicted in various Japanese works, including soldiers' memoirs, military tales, novels, poetry, folk songs, and the theater (Murai 2015; Choi 2015). Particularly prolific was a genre of military tales now known as *Chōsen gunki monogatari* (military tales from Korea). Many of these works immortalized the story of a Japanese general, Katō Kiyomasa (1562–1611), killing a tiger in Korea during the war. Not native to the Japanese Archipelago, tigers were endemic to the Korean Peninsula and had long been associated with Korea in Japan. The story of Kiyomasa's tiger hunt was one of a long line of tales in Japanese literature in which a Japanese hero traveled to the Korean Peninsula and killed a tiger, a display of martial valor supposedly unmatched by the locals (Kim et al. 2023). Other fictionalized Japanese accounts of the Imjin War depicted Korean generals. The famous playwright Chikamatsu Monzaemon (1653–1724) based his character "Mokuso Hangan" on the magistrate (Ko. *moksa*) of Chinju, who commanded the Chosŏn forces at the First Battle for Chinju (1592) during which the Japanese suffered a resounding defeat. The magistrate was also featured in a play by Nanboku Tsuruya (1755–1859), who portrayed Mokuso as a Korean wizard harboring a grudge against Japan (Choi 2015, 350). A Korean account of the war, *Chingbirok* (*The Book of Corrections*) by Yu Sŏngnyong (1542–1607), was published in Kyōto in 1695. The Japanese printing of *Chingbirok* introduced Japanese readers to Korean accounts of the war and the Korean naval hero, Admiral Yi Sunsin (1545–1598). Extracts from *Chingbirok* were later included in works from the *Chōsen gunki monogatari* genre (Choi 349).

The reprinting of *Chingbirok* in Japan typified many Korean books that became the source of information about Korea in Japan after they had either been reprinted in Japan or circulated in their original copies after being acquired from Korea. Due to its close geographical proximity to China and role as an exemplary vassal state, Korea attracted Japanese scholars as an authoritative source of knowledge about Chinese philosophy, law, medicine, and literature in Japan for centuries. Accordingly, they sought Korean books written in Literary Sinitic and copies of Chinese books that could be obtained via Korea. The flow of books from Korea to Japan during the period covered by this chapter may be broadly divided into two sections, from the founding of Chosŏn until the Imjin War and from the Imjin War onwards. This division exists because, first, during the Imjin War, significant numbers of Korean books and movable type printing presses were taken to Japan, and second, because the subsequent Tokugawa period saw an increase in literacy and the commercial print industry, which increased the demand for and circulation of books, including those from Korea.

The flow of books from Korea to Japan was intermittent during the Muromachi period before the Imjin War, and most were copies of Buddhist canons (Robinson 2001; Kornicki 2015). According to Chosŏn's veritable records (*sillok*), in 1394, two years after the founding of Chosŏn, the military commander of Kyushu, Imagawa Ryōshun (b. 1326), sent a messenger requesting a copy of the *Tripitaka*. The only books mentioned in the sources for the next two decades are copies of the Tripitaka and occasionally the *Great Sutra of the Perfection of Wisdom* (Sk. *Mahdprajhdparamita-sutra*). The fourth Ashikaga shogun, Ashikaga Yoshimochi (r. 1394–1423), also sought copies of the Korean *Tripitaka*, referring to his embassy to Chosŏn as a "Sutra Request Envoy" (*seikyōshi*) (Lippit 2005, 197). The first record of books other than religious texts is dated 1416 when an envoy from somebody claiming to be a local ruler in Japan came with gifts and requested "books." This occurred again in 1418 and 1423. Imported Korean books may have been reprinted in Japan during this period as woodblock facsimiles (Ja. *kabusebori, fukkoku*), but the evidence is inconclusive (Kornicki 2015, 591–92).

In contrast to the relative scarcity of Korean books in Japan before the Imjin War, many books were among the booty taken by Hideyoshi's armies during the conflict. A letter written by the monk Ankokuji Eiji (c.1538–1600) to his home temple and over a dozen other temples and individuals in 1592 reported that he would "load books—both Buddhist and non-Buddhist—and various treasures on board ship(s) and send them to each of you" (Kornicki 2013b, 74). Kornicki surmises that at this stage of the war, before the capture of Chosŏn's capital, Hansŏng (present-day Seoul), the books and treasures taken were from the *sago* (historical record office) at Sŏngju and government offices in Pusan, both in southwestern Korea. Apart from Eiji's letter, no other contemporary evidence of book looting has come to light in Japanese sources. Still, a well-known later account describes how one of Hideyoshi's senior medics, Manase Shōrin (1565–1611), received Korean medical texts as a gift from Ukita Hideie (1573–1655), one of Hideyoshi's generals. Of the 242 medical and Confucian books listed as having been in Shōrin's possession, most likely came into his possession in the 1590s after the Imjin War (Kornicki 2013b, 75).

During the war, metallic movable types for printing books in classical Chinese were also looted, taken from the Printing Office (*Sŏjŏkwŏn*), established by the Korean court in 1392. The booty was

The Routledge Handbook of Early Modern Korea

presented to Emperor Go-Yōzei (r. 1586–1611) and used to print a copy of the *Xiao jing* (*Classic of Filial Piety*) in 1593. In Japan, printing mostly relied on woodblocks carved page by page rather than reusable movable types. In 1597, in the postface to a work printed in Japan with movable type, a monk who had been present at Hideyoshi's headquarters acknowledged that typography in Japan had come from Korea. For about five decades following the arrival of Korean print, the use of movable type was extensive in Japan for producing books known as *kokatsujiban* (old movable-type editions) (Kornicki 1998, 128–30).

Many books still extant in Japan date back to the Imjin War, including texts owned by prominent intellectuals and even the Tokugawa shoguns. For example, the prominent Confucian scholar Fujiwara Seika (1561–1618) owned a copy of Kwon Kŭn's (1352–1409) *Introduction to Confucian Learning* (*Iphak tosŏl*) that came to him as a result of the war. Likewise, Seika's most famous pupil, Hayashi Razan (1583–1657), also owned looted Korean books. Inspired by Korean vernacular translations and commentaries (*ŏnhae*) of Literary Sinitic texts, he produced vernacular Japanese translations and commentaries (Kornicki 2013a). Looking beyond the literati, Ieyasu, the founder of the Tokugawa Shogunate, most likely owned a large collection of looted books from Korea. Ieyasu presumably acquired whatever he had as gifts or by confiscating them since he did not participate in the Imjin War directly. After his death, most of Ieyasu's books were distributed to the three powerful collateral Tokugawa houses of Mito, Kii, and Owari—all branches of the Tokugawa family that could provide a shogunal heir if a ruling shogun from the main branch died without a son. Only the Owari collection survives intact, and it has a large number of Korean editions, which "can only have been part of the loot from Korea" (Kornicki 2013b, 77).

Philosophy and Medicine

The impact Korean books taken to Japan had upon the Japanese intellectual world in the centuries after the Imjin War remains the subject of scholarly debate. For some time, many pointed to the sudden availability of Korean copies of Neo-Confucian texts as a result of the war in explaining the rise of Neo-Confucianism in early seventeenth-century Japan (Boot 2013, 98–99). More recent research suggests, though, that the interest of Neo-Confucianism in Japan predates the Imjin War and that reading and dissemination of the looted books were more gradual (Boot 2013, 107). Scholars now attribute the rise of Neo-Confucianism in Tokugawa Japan to other factors: a growing specialization in Neo-Confucianism within the powerful Chinese philological (*Kangaku*) movement, the diffusion of Neo-Confucianism among the general population as an important part of moral education (Boot 2013), and the emergence of the Way of Heaven (*tendō*) as a syncretic tradition that became an independent popular religious tradition in Japan (Paramore 2016, 42). All the same, there is evidence that prominent Japanese Confucian scholars read Korean editions of the Chinese classics and were influenced by them, as discussed above in the cases of Fujiwara Seika and Hayashi Razan. They also sought out Korean scholars in Japan from the time of the Imjin War onwards, taking advantage of these encounters to ask for information about Confucianism, Chinese literature, medicine, and pharmacology and to receive endorsements from the Koreans as evidence of their expertise in the Chinese tradition (Boot 2013).

The most famous Korean scholar taken to Japan during the Imjin War was Kang Hang (1567–1618), a scholar-bureaucrat working for the Chosŏn government. He was captured together with his family by Japanese forces off the coast of Chŏlla Province in the ninth month of 1597. They were held by Tōdō Takatora (1556–1630) in Ōzu, in Shikoku, for about ten months before being moved to Osaka in the ninth month of 1598, and then moved to Fushimi, from which they escaped to Korea, arriving in the fifth month of 1600. During his time in Japan, Kang Hang sent a series of letters and reports back to Korea, circulated in manuscript and later published as *The Record of a Shepherd* (Haboush and Robinson 2013). *The Record of a Shepherd* describes several meetings between Kang Hang and Fujiwara Seika. Japanese documents also record their interactions, including exchanges of letters (Haboush and Robinson 2013, 19, 85; Boot 2013, 14–35).

The 12 embassies from Chosŏn Korea to Tokugawa Japan were likewise opportunities for Japanese scholars and, on occasion, the general public to interact with Korean visitors (Clements 2019). Without a common spoken language, such interactions utilized interpreters or written communication in classical Chinese (Ko. *Hanmun*, Ja. *Kanbun*) (Li et al. 2022). For example, "brush talk" with Korean physicians who traveled in the embassy entourages was a rare opportunity for Japanese physicians to discuss medical topics with other East Asian medics in person rather than relying on information gleaned from imported books (Trambaiolo 2014). These encounters also provided opportunities for both sides to demonstrate their erudition. Hayashi Razan is known to have asked numerous questions of the Korean envoys, which were designed to impress them with his erudition rather than to receive an answer (Boot 2013, 116). Exchanges of poetry were similarly fraught, and skill in Chinese poetry was an important selection criterion when choosing the literati who would accompany the embassies. The shogun's Confucian teacher Arai Hakuseki's (1657–1725) first poetry collection, *Tōjō shishū* (Collected poems on crafting sentiment), contained a foreword by a Korean secretary of mission. This endorsement enabled Hakuseki to enter a prestigious Confucian academy and launch his career (Clements 2019, 297). Such displays of erudition became increasingly important from the mid-seventeenth century onwards as debates raged in Korea and Japan about who was the rightful inheritor of the mantle of civilization following the fall of Ming to Qing "barbarians" and a newfound confidence in Japanese superiority over China (Nakai 1980).

The schools of thought that emerged in Tokugawa Japan also witnessed new debates about ancient history, including a school of thought that suggested a significant Korean influence on ancient Japan (Cho 2022). This brought them into conflict with the contemporary Japanese Kokugaku school, which emphasized the traditional understanding that the origins of Japanese culture were entirely indigenous to the archipelago (Teeuwen 2006). A prominent proponent of Korea as the origin of Japanese culture was Tō Teikan (1732–97), who reinterpreted legends from the Age of the Gods (*kamiyo*), which were contained in the *Kojiki* (*Records of Ancient Matters*; early eighth century) and the *Nihon shoki* (*Chronicles of Japan*; 720). Teikan argued that it was the god Susanoo rather than the sun goddess Amaterasu, who was the leading protagonist of ancient Japan, and that Susanoo had imported Japanese customs and civilization from Korea. This drew the ire of Kokugaku scholars, such as Motoori Norinaga (1730–1801), who rejected Teikan's theories in an angry letter written in defense of the conventional, Amaterasu-centered account of Japanese history, casting Japan as independent and autochthonous in its origins. In this way, Korea became an important element in how scholars of ancient Japanese texts analyzed the history of ancient Japan (Cho 2022, 8–9).

Nineteenth-Century Politics

The years between 1867 and 1873, which bring this chapter to a close, witnessed major changes in the East Asian international order, the Japanese political system, and Japan's relationship with Korea. With Japan under increasing pressure from Western "gunboat diplomacy" to open its markets to trade with European and US powers, the Tokugawa shogunate became a casualty of domestic power struggles between factions for and against greater foreign contact (Gordon 2003, 56–60). The shogunate formally ended in November 1867, when the fifteenth shogun, Tokugawa

The Routledge Handbook of Early Modern Korea

Yoshinobu (r. 1866–68), resigned, ostensibly placing authority in the hands of the young Meiji emperor (r. 1867–1912). Shortly thereafter, in January 1868, the Boshin War (1868–69) began. The combined forces of Chōshū and Satsuma domains defeated Yoshinobu's army, seized Tokugawa lands, and placed them under the control of the new Meiji government. This ushered in a period of almost half a century during which Meiji government officials debated what form the new Japanese state should take in matters ranging from the constitution, education, the postal service, transport, and foreign policy, including Korea (Jansen 1989).

The newly established Meiji government sent a credential letter to the Chosŏn court. In a repetition of Toyotomi Hideyoshi's letters, the tone of the Meiji letter implied that the Korean ruler was a subordinate of the Japanese emperor, which prompted the Korean authorities to reject it. Known as the "Credential Letter Incident" (Ko. Sŏgye sakkŏn), this turned the peaceful Korea–Japan relationship into one of mutual antagonism (Han 2023, 258). In the autumn of 1873, King Kojong of Chosŏn proclaimed his direct rule and immediately took actions to restore his country's relations with Japan, only to elicit resistance in Japan. By then, there was mounting pressure on the Meiji government, both from within and without, to punish the Koreans for refusing to accept the credential letter containing official greetings of the Meiji emperor and acknowledge the change from shogunal to imperial rule. Also, Korea's restrictions on the small Japanese merchant community confined to a walled enclosure outside of Pusan fueled resentment (Mayo 1972, 798). While the Iwakura Mission from the Japanese government was abroad in 1873, Saigō Takamori (1828–77), a samurai leader from Satsuma, pushed for the caretaker government to plan an invasion of Korea.

Drawing upon Hideyoshi and Empress Jingū's invasions for inspiration, Saigō's plan precipitated a series of debates in the Meiji government, known as the *seikanron* ("Korea expedition debate"), using the term Hideyoshi had employed to describe his intention to chastise Korea for refusing to submit. The memory of Hideyoshi's invasions had never gone away. Earlier, during the 1860s, images of Katō Kiyomasa's tiger hunting expedition had resurfaced in the popular print industry, this time with the tiger contorted into the shape of the Korean Peninsula as the Japanese hero, Kiyomasa, stabbed the threatening Korean menace (Seeley and Skabelund 2015, 487–88). Proponents of Saigō's Korea expedition claimed that failure to avenge Korea's treatment of Japan and its representatives would weaken Japan's international standing and leave the nation vulnerable to attack (Mayo 1972, 812). However, when the representatives of the Iwakura Mission returned to Japan in 1873, they did so with a more realistic understanding of international politics and Japan's vulnerability in the face of Western imperialism. Including Iwakura Tomomi (1825–83) and Ōkubo Toshimichi (1830–78), members of the mission persuaded other officials of the government to concentrate on strengthening Japan's domestic development and not impoverishing the Japanese population with a war, which would risk civil strife (Mayo 1972, 812–13). Accordingly, the question of military action against Korea was shelved until 1876, when Japanese gunboat diplomacy forced the Treaty of Kanghwado on Korea.

Final Thoughts

Thus, we can see that during the fourteenth to the nineteenth centuries, Korea, known by its early-modern Japanese approximations, "Chōsen" and "Kōrai," was present in Japanese art, philosophy, and literature, as well as being geopolitically significant among different polities across the Japanese Archipelago. Evidence for this may be found in the extant traces of trade in physical objects, such as Korean books, ceramics, and paintings in Japan today, as well as in diplomatic documents and the writings of intellectuals.

With the Meiji Revolution and the incremental establishment of a centralized Japanese state, the plurality of conduits through which Japan–Korea relations took place diminished as the Meiji government centralized the conduct of international relations. Although the question of military action against Korea was shelved in 1873, the Meiji Government later used force to enact the Treaty of Kanghwado (1876), opening three Korean ports to the Japanese for trade and giving Japan extraterritorial jurisdiction in Korea. This began a new era for what Korea meant in Japan, as Japan's "trajectory to empire" subsequently severed Korea's traditional ties to China, eventually turning Korea into a Japanese colony (Gordon 2003, 115).

References

Ahn, Hwi-Joon. 1997. "Korean Influence on Japanese Ink Paintings of the Muromachi Period." *Korea Journal* 37, no. 4 (December): 195–220.

Anderson, Benedict. 2006. *Imagined Communities: Reflections on the Origin and Spread of Nationalism.* Revised edition. Verso.

Berry, Mary Elizabeth. 2007. *Japan in Print: Information and Nation in the Early Modern Period.* University of California Press.

Boot, W. J. 2013. *The Adoption and Adaptation of Neo-Confucianism in Japan: The Role of Fujiwara Seika and Hayashi Razan.* Version 3.0. Publisher unknown. http://www.ngjs.nl/files/artikelen/Boot_W_J_The _Adoption_and_Adaptation_of_Neo_Confucianism_in_Japan_v3.pdf, accessed April 29, 2024.

Burns, Susan L. 2003. *Before the Nation: Kokugaku and the Imagining of Community in Early Modern Japan.* Duke University Press.

Cho, Ilsoo. 2022. "Korea in the *Kamiyo*: Locating Korea in the Age of the Gods Narratives in Early Modern Japan." *Japanese Journal of Religious Studies* 49, no. 1: 1–20.

Choi, Gwan. 2015. "The Imjin Waeran in Korean and Japanese Literature." In *The East Asian War, 1592– 1598: International Relations, Violence, and Memory*, edited by James B. Lewis, 340–56. Routledge.

Clements, Rebekah. 2019. "Brush Talk as the 'Lingua Franca' of Diplomacy in Japanese–Korean Encounters, c. 1600–1868." *Historical Journal* 62, no. 2: 289–309.

Clements, Rebekah. 2022. "Alternate Attendance Parades in the Japanese Domain of Satsuma, Seventeenth to Eighteenth Centuries: Pottery, Power and Foreign Spectacle." *Transactions of the Royal Historical Society* 32: 135–58.

Conlan, Thomas D. 2024. *Kings in All but Name: The Lost History of Ouchi Rule in Japan, 1350–1569.* Oxford University Press.

Cort, Louise Allison. 1986. "Korean Influences in Japanese Ceramics: The Impact of the Teabowl Wars of 1592–1598." In *Ceramics and Civilization*, Volume II, "Technology and Style," edited by Prudence M. Rice, 331–62. American Ceramic Society.

Elisonas, Jurgis. 1991. "The Inseparable Trinity: Japan's Relations with China and Korea." In *The Cambridge History of Japan*, Volume 4, *Early Modern Japan*, edited by John Whitney Hall and James L. McClain, 235–300. Cambridge University Press.

Gerhart, Karen M. 2004. "Visions of the Dead: Kano Tan'yū's Paintings of Tokugawa Iemitsu's Dreams." *Monumenta Nipponica* 59, no. 1: 1–34.

Gonnami, Tsuneharu. 1998. "Images of Foreigners in Edo Period Maps and Prints." *Journal of East Asian Libraries* 1998, no. 116: 5–18.

Gordon, Andrew. 2003. *A Modern History of Japan: From Tokugawa Times to the Present.* Oxford University Press.

Habermas, Jürgen. 1992. *The Structural Transformation of the Public Sphere: An Inquiry into a Category of Bourgeois Society.* Translated by Thomas Burger and Frederick Lawrence. MIT Press.

Haboush, JaHyun Kim, and Kenneth R. Robinson. 2013. *A Korean War Captive in Japan, 1597–1600: The Writings of Kang Hang.* Columbia University Press.

Han, Sean S. 2023. "Informal Diplomacy in Chosŏn Korea and New Engagement with the West and Westernized Japan, 1873–1876." *Modern Asian Studies* 57, no. 1 (January): 252–82.

Hawley, Samuel. 2005. *The Imjin War: Japan's Sixteenth Century Invasion of Korea and Attempt to Conquer China.* Institute of East Asian Studies, University of California.

Hur, Nam-lin. 2015. "Korean Tea Bowls (Kōrai Chawan) and Japanese Wabicha: A Story of Acculturation in Premodern Northeast Asia." *Korean Studies* 39: 1–22.

Hur, Nam-lin. 2022. "Japan's Invasions of Korea in 1592–1598 and the Hideyoshi Regime." In *The Tokugawa World*, edited by Garry P. Leupp and De-min Tao, 23–45. Routledge.

Hur, Nam-lin. 2023. "Atrocity and Genocide in Japan's Invasion of Korea, 1592–1598." In *The Cambridge World History of Genocide*. Volume II, *Genocide in the Indigenous, Early Modern and Imperial Worlds, from c.1535 to World War One*, edited by Ned Blackhawk, Ben Kiernan, Benjamin Madley, and Rebe Taylor, 118–38. Cambridge University Press.

Jansen, Marius B. 1989. "The Meiji Restoration." In *The Cambridge History of Japan*, Volume 5, *The Nineteenth Century*, edited by Marius B. Jansen, 308–66. Cambridge University Press.

Jungmann, Burglind. 2004. *Painters as Envoys: Korean Inspiration in Eighteenth-Century Japanese Nanga*. Princeton University Press.

Kang, David C. 2010. *East Asia before the West: Five Centuries of Trade and Tribute*. Columbia University Press.

Kang, Etsuko Hae-Jin. 1997. *Diplomacy and Ideology in Japanese-Korean Relations: From the Fifteenth to the Eighteenth Century*. Macmillan.

Katayama, Mabi. 2012. "Korean Tea Bowls and the Tea Ceremony." In *Korean Art in the Freer and Sackler Galleries*, edited by The Freer and Sackler Galleries, 24–29. Smithsonian Institution Press.

Kim, Hyosook, Rebekah Clements, and Mina Rhyu. 2023. "A Genealogy of Tiger Nationalism in Korea: Post-Colonial Discourse, Ch'oe Namsŏn and the Seoul Olympics." *International Journal of Asian Studies* 20, no. 2: 555–74.

Kornicki, Peter. 1998. *The Book in Japan: A Cultural History from the Beginnings to the Nineteenth Century*. Brill.

Kornicki, Peter. 2013a. "Hayashi Razan's Vernacular Translations and Commentaries." In *On Translation History*, Volume III, *Towards a History of Translating*, edited by Lawrence Wong, 189–212. Hong Kong University Press.

Kornicki, Peter. 2013b. "Korean Books in Japan: From the 1590s to the End of the Edo Period." *Journal of the American Oriental Society* 133, no. 1: 71–92.

Kornicki, Peter. 2015. "Korean Books in Japan before Hideyoshi's Invasion." *Journal of the American Oriental Society* 135, no. 3: 587–93.

Lee, Soyoung. 2011. "Beyond the Original: Buncheong Idioms in Japan, 1500–1900, and Contemporary Revivals." In *Korean Buncheong Ceramics from Leeum, Samsung Museum of Art*, edited by Soyoung Lee and Seung-chang Jeon, 95–155. Metropolitan Museum of Art.

Lee, Soyoung. 2014. *Interregional Reception and Invention in Korean and Japanese Ceramics, 1400–1800*. Columbia University Press.

Lewis, James B. 2003. *Frontier Contact between Chosŏn Korea and Tokugawa Japan*. Routledge Curzon.

Lewis, James B. 2010. "A Scroll of the 1748 Korean Embassy to Japan Preserved in the British Museum." *Acta Koreana* 13, no. 1: 53–89.

Lewis, James B. 2015. "International Relations and the Imjin War." In *The East Asian War, 1592–1598: International Relations, Violence, and Memory*, edited by James B. Lewis, 256–73. Routledge.

Li, David C. S., Reijiro Aoyama, and Tak-sum Wong. 2022. *Brush Conversation in the Sinographic Cosmopolis: Interactional Cross-Border Communication Using Literary Sinitic in Early Modern East Asia*. Routledge.

Lippit, Yukio. 2005. "Goryeo Buddhist Painting in an Interregional Context." *Ars Orientalis* 35: 192–232.

Maske, Andrew L. 1994. "The Continental Origins of Taketori Ware: The Introduction of Korean Potters and Technology to Japan Through the Invasions of 1592–1598." *Transactions of the Asiatic Society of Japan* 9 (fourth series): 43–61.

Maske, Andrew L. 2011. *Potters and Patrons in Edo Period Japan : Takatori Ware and the Kuroda Domain*. Ashgate.

Mayo, Marlene J. 1972. "The Korean Crisis of 1873 and Early Meiji Foreign Policy." *Journal of Asian Studies* 31, no. 4 (August): 793–819.

Murai, Shōsuke. 2015. "Post-War Domain Source Material on Hideyoshi's Invasion of Korea: The Wartime Memoirs of Shimazu Soldiers." In *The East Asian War, 1592–1598: International Relations, Violence, and Memory*, edited by James B. Lewis, 108–19. Routledge.

Nakai, Kate Wildman. 1980. "The Naturalization of Confucianism in Tokugawa Japan: The Problem of Sinocentrism." *Harvard Journal of Asiatic Studies* 40, no. 1: 157–99.

Paramore, Kiri. 2016. *Japanese Confucianism: A Cultural History*. Cambridge University Press.

Park, Doyoung. 2013. "A New Perspective on the Korean Embassy (Chōsen Tsūshinshi): The View from the Intellectuals in Tokugawa Japan." *Studies on Asia* 3, no. 1: 6–24.

Park, Saeyoung. 2017. "Long Live the Tributary System! The Future of Studying East Asian Foreign Relations." *Harvard Journal of Asiatic Studies* 77, no. 1: 1–20.

Pollard, Clare. 2020. "Tradition, Modernity, and National Identity: Celadon Production at the Makuzu Ceramic Workshop 1870–1916." In *Ceramics and Modernity in Japan*, edited by Meghen Jones and Louise Allison Cort, 21–39. Routledge.

Robinson, Kenneth R. 2001. "Treated As Treasures: The Circulation of Sutras in Maritime Northeast Asia, from 1388 to the Mid-Sixteenth Century." *East Asian History* 21: 33–54.

Rousmaniere, Nicole Coolidge. 2012. *Vessels of Influence: China and the Birth of Porcelain in Medieval and Early Modern Japan*. Bloomsbury Academic.

Sajima, Akiko. 2015. "Hideyoshi's View of Chosŏn Korea and Japan–Ming Negotiations." In *The East Asian War, 1592–1598: International Relations, Violence, and Memory*, edited by James B. Lewis, 93–107. Routledge.

Seeley, Joseph, and Aaron Skabelund. 2015. "Tigers—Real and Imagined—in Korea's Physical and Cultural Landscape." *Environmental History* 20, no. 3 (July): 475–503.

Shapinsky, Peter D. 2014. *Lords of the Sea: Pirates, Violence, and Commerce in Late Medieval Japan*. University of Michigan Press.

Sousa, Lúcio de. 2019. *The Portuguese Slave Trade in Early Modern Japan: Merchants, Jesuits and Japanese, Chinese, and Korean Slaves*. Brill.

Swope, Kenneth. 2009. *A Dragon's Head and a Serpent's Tail: Ming China and the First Great East Asian War, 1592–1598*. University of Oklahoma Press.

Teeuwen, Mark. 2006. "Kokugaku vs. Nativism." *Monumenta Nipponica* 61, no. 2: 227–42.

Toby, Ronald P. 1984. *State and Diplomacy in Early Modern Japan: Asia in the Development of the Tokugawa Bakufu*. Princeton University Press.

Toby, Ronald P. 1986. "Carnival of the Aliens. Korean Embassies in Edo-Period Art and Popular Culture." *Monumenta Nipponica* 41, no. 4: 415–56.

Tokyo National Museum. 2017. *Chanoyu: The Arts of Tea Ceremony, The Essence of Japan*. NHK Promotions.

Totman, Conrad D. 2014. *Japan: An Environmental History*. I. B. Tauris.

Trambaiolo, Daniel. 2014. "Diplomatic Journeys and Medical Brush Talks: Eighteenth-Century Dialogues between Korean and Japanese Medicine." In *Motion and Knowledge in the Changing Early Modern World*, edited by Ofer Gal and Yi Zheng, 93–113. Springer.

Watanabe, Takeshi. 2007. "From Korea to Japan and Back Again: One Hundred Years of Japanese Tea Culture through Five Bowls, 1550–1650." *Yale University Art Gallery Bulletin 2007: Japanese Art at Yale*: 82–99.

Yamamoto Morihide. 1905. *Sangoku meishō zue*. Volume 8. Reprint of the 1844 original.

PART II

The State, Power, and Resource

5

POLITICS

Christopher Lovins

Korea, ruled by the state of Chosŏn (1392–1897), was a relatively centralized early modern monarchy divided into eight provinces and approximately 300 counties. The king ruled primarily by reading reports and recommendations submitted by government officials and other politically influential figures, discussing them with appropriate officials, and issuing decrees in response. Chosŏn politics featured negotiations involving the monarch, current and past officials, influential figures outside the government, and the norms and mores of Zhu Xi's Neo-Confucianism as interpreted by the aristocracy, the *yangban* comprising patrilineal descent groups tracing as far back as the late ninth century. The top *yangban* lineages based in the capital, Hansŏng (present-day Seoul), and its surrounding area wielded political power that brought them into cooperation and conflict with the throne. Inherited status tracing back to illustrious ancestors, ownership of land and slaves (*nobi*), regionalism, and freedom from excessive central interference in local affairs limited the central government's ability to implement its will. All the same, the aristocracy needed the throne to legitimate its position. Above all, much of aristocratic prestige was derived from office holding in the central bureaucracy, even though the *yangban* status itself was ascriptive. Also, the Neo-Confucian ideology that buttressed its privileges required a monarch with at least a nominal presence and influence in court politics.

Throughout Chosŏn's history, its political system enjoyed relative security from foreign military threats. From the kingdom's founding in 1392 up to 1873, Chosŏn dealt with three major conflicts: the Imjin War (East Asian War; 1592–98) against the Japanese, the Chŏngmyo War (1627) against the Jurchens (subsequently self-renamed Manchus, 1635), and the Pyŏngja War (1637) against the Manchus. As devastating as these wars were, they account for less than two decades out of almost five centuries of Chosŏn rule. This relative stability allowed the central aristocracy's proprietorship of the political system, in contrast to contemporary China under the Ming dynasty (1368–1644) or the succeeding Qing dynasty (1616–1912; Later Jin until 1636). Earlier in China, the aristocratic-bureaucratic hybrid elite of the Tang dynasty (618–907) had changed to the bureaucratic gentry of the Song dynasty (960–1279)—with their elite status becoming dependent on service in Ming's autocratic imperial government. Fueling the transition was a growing market economy, foreign trade, and urbanization—the trends notably absent from Chosŏn until the eighteenth century. Thus, Chosŏn Korea resembled early modern European monarchies with powerful

DOI: 10.4324/9781003262053-8

75

The Routledge Handbook of Early Modern Korea

and dominant aristocracies tracing back to the medieval period than the sprawling multiethnic empire of Ming or Qing China.

The King

The *yangban* aristocracy expected the monarch to rule according to Neo-Confucian norms as they understood them and in consultation with his most respected high officials. Accordingly, such officials were his allies when implementing any policy other officials or non-government political actors opposed. Like the aristocracy of early modern Europe, a Chosŏn *yangban* family's aristocratic status was ascriptive, tracing as far back as the late ninth century without any illegitimate child (*sŏŏl*) in the intervening generations. Ideally, however, the status had to be reinforced from time to time through examination degrees, court rank titles (*p'umgye*), and offices. Anyone who aspired to attain higher, politically significant positions in government had to pass the civil examination (*munkwa*), which tested a candidate's ability to apply his knowledge of Confucian classics in writing a policy essay following prescribed conventions. The prestige conferred by success in the civil examinations gave the *yangban* aristocracy a stake in the monarchy, even when most *yangban* were no longer passing an examination or holding an office by the eighteenth century.

Theoretically, the Chosŏn king had the exclusive right to appoint and dismiss officials. Above all, the royal house—the membership in which the state limited to "royal kin" (*chongch'in*) who were Chŏnju Yi males no more than four generations patrilineally removed from a king—was the wealthiest in the realm. The aristocrats could never significantly restrain the monarch's use of the Royal Treasury (Naesusa). Short of insisting that the king be frugal, the *yangban* could do little to limit the king's spending. Nor were they able, at least in the first half or so of Chosŏn's history, to prevent the king's creation of merit subjects (*kongsin*). Honored and rewarded for supporting the king's accession or other vital political role, they received titles, tax-exempt land, and slaves from the state. Even more outspoken social critics such as Yu Hyŏngwŏn (1622–73) did not advocate abolishing the practice of elevating merit subjects, merely limiting them. Kings could also use secret inspectors (*amhaeng ŏsa*), who traveled incognito to investigate local corruption cases. The king's backing, however, could only do so much to protect the inspectors, so they had to be careful when accusing an influential official from a powerful lineage. Even if dismissed, such figures were unlikely to remain out of office long.

Thus, the king of Chosŏn always remained at the center of the political system, even if he could not quite dominate his officials as did many Ming or Qing emperors. In theory, as long as the monarch was an adult of sound mind and body and was not deemed a tyrant, he could not be deposed, as emperors of Japan had been for centuries. In contrast, no official, regardless of his position or power base, could remain in power after losing the royal favor, as shown by the fates of some influential figures: Cho Kwangjo (1482–1520) in the sixteenth century, Song Siyŏl (1607–89) in the seventeenth, and Hong Kugyŏng (1748–81) in the eighteenth century. All reached the apex of political power when they enjoyed the king's support, only to suffer death upon losing it.

The Officials

The king's officials were the landowning, slave-holding *yangban* who dominated Chosŏn politics and society as hereditary elites. Though *yangban* was not a legally defined class, the state punished the members more lightly than others, who owed respect and obedience to *yangban*. The language of politics was Literary Sinitic, the written language that originated in ancient China and had become the cosmopolitan language of China, Japan, Korea, and Vietnam's elites, none of whom *spoke* a Sinitic language except those in China. Chosŏn officialdom comprised civil and military branches, each with ranks and an examination system. Although of equal standing in theory, the civil branch was far more respected and influential than the military, a difference further accentuated by the growing nonelite participation in the increasingly frequent, larger-scale military examinations (*mukwa*) from the sixteenth century. By the seventeenth century, the officeholding *yangban* lineages based in Hansŏng and its vicinity were divided into distinctly civil and military elite families (Eugene Y. Park 2007, 1–14).

The central bureaucracy comprised nine ranks (*p'um*), each subdivided into "senior" (*chŏng*) and "junior" (*chong*) levels. The highest organ of the government was the State Council (Ŭijŏngbu), whose three senior officials held the senior first rank. Officially playing only an advisory body, by the second half of the fifteenth century, the State Council had become the most powerful organ because it had to approve any action taken by the next highest government bodies, the Six Ministries (Yukcho): Personnel, Rites, Taxation, Military, Punishments, and Public Works. The Ministry of Rites (Yejo) and the Ministry of War (Pyŏngjo) administered the civil and military examinations, respectively. Although headed by officials of lower rank than the Six Ministries, the critical voice of the Censorate (Taegan) became sacrosanct in the late fifteenth century. It remained so up to the eighteenth century. Charged with policing the other officials for immoral conduct and accusing them accordingly, censors tended to be younger officials of scholarly reputation and moral probity—supposedly making them more ideologically pure and free from politicking. Unlike in Ming or Qing China, in Chosŏn Korea, even the monarch's conduct was subject to criticism, though, in practice, censors usually attacked the high officials to avoid accusations of *lèse majesté*. The censorial voice checked royal power and pushed the high officials into defending him. All the same, the higher officials shaped the careers of lower officials through performance reviews and recommendations to higher offices. By doing so, high officials could ensure that lower officials would be careful in performing their duties from their otherwise inviolate censorial offices.

Outside the capital, governors of all eight provinces and magistrates of the approximately three hundred counties appointed by the central government received assistance from unpaid, hereditary local functionaries (*hyangni*). Their service was critical, as a county magistrate had more work to do than what resources allowed. Also, the Law of Avoidance (*sangp'ije*) intended to prevent a conflict of interest prohibited an official from serving in his home locale. This meant newly arrived magistrates were unfamiliar with local conditions. Also, especially for a *yangban* from a distinguished family, magistracy was not so much a coveted appointment as a de facto demotion since the posting removed the appointee from the capital, the site of national politics. Thus, magistrates were generally more interested in finding their way back to Hansŏng than diligently learning anything about the locality they were serving. Furthermore, most magistrates did not serve into the third year, which was the allowed term limit. While the extent of corruption fluctuated among magistrates and other officials in Chosŏn's political system dominated by *yangban*, the vast majority appear to have striven to enforce the law, administer justice, and rationally perform their required tasks.

Local Government

Before the founding of Chosŏn, Korea had long had a tradition of relative independence from strong central authority. Even in Chosŏn, provincial governors oversaw county magistrates, who depended on local functionaries, who no longer received government salaries. With their assistance, a magistrate appointed by the king served for about two years. Most county governments functioned as a microcosm of the central government. The county magistrate served in the king's position, issuing decisions and ultimately responsible for whatever happened in his county. As

Chosŏn had no separation of powers, the magistrate was the chief executive, criminal investigator, judge, and military commander. He had two missions: to raise and send the required taxes to the capital and to keep order. Like the king in Hansŏng, the magistrate received assistance from local functionaries who served as working-level administrative staff—analogs to the capital's *chungin* ("middle people"), who were government-employed specialists in various fields. Each county also maintained a military office that handled security matters in a way analogous to modern police.

The most critical organ in local administration was the county-level local council (*hyanghoe*), dominated by the county elites. Its predecessor, the local agency (*yuhyangso*), was abolished, only to be reestablished repeatedly during the fifteenth century as the new state's center negotiated its relations with local areas. By the sixteenth century, the local council was firmly a part of county government, as it was the parent organization of the local advisory bureau (*hyangch'ŏng*) that the magistrate consulted in administering the county (Yi 2007, 41–47). The local council admitted new members to serve in the local advisory bureau from among its membership, which was strictly controlled; only a man of a prominent *yangban* lineage might be added to its registry, the local council roster (*hyangan*). The local council's primary purpose was to look out for the interests of the county's leading lineages, whose members were on the roster. As such, the council remained a fixed feature of local government in most counties until the end of the nineteenth century. Alongside local affairs were concerns with what was happening in the capital and other provinces, as many lineages had extended family in Hansŏng and elsewhere, thus linking the Chosŏn elite throughout the country. The local advisory bureau likewise offered an avenue of Confucian public service for many *yangban* who passed the examination but never held a central government post (Kawashima 1980, 114–23).

Mirroring the king and his relationship with central officialdom, the county magistrate governed in close consultation with the local advisory bureau (whose members, probably not coincidentally, also served two-year terms). The local council also held the power to administer "local punishment" (*hyangbŏl*) against the community members. The most severe punishment was permanent expulsion from the community, including punishment for anyone maintaining contact with those so expelled. The government recognized *hyangbŏl* as equivalent to discipline by the magistrate—not surprising given that local councilors might be from lineages as illustrious as the magistrates'. In 1624, however, concerns about the severity of *hyangbŏl* and abuse of the power prompted a royal edict prohibiting it. The court wrote further bans into the law code. Like many Chosŏn laws, the prohibitions merely reduced rather than eliminated the practice (Jungwon Kim 2022). Chosŏn then got the local elite to work with the magistrate and enforce his decisions. In this way, approximately 300 county magistrates could govern a country of 12 million people.

Public Opinion

At the heart of the negotiation between the throne and the officialdom—and likewise of legitimacy in Chosŏn—was "public opinion" (*kongnon*). Kings were expected to listen to the concerns and advice *of* the people, though not, crucially, *from* the people. That is, while the court was obligated to heed the people's concerns, the elite mediated them in articulating the public opinion, which political players considered "right" because it was widely held as the truths of the Confucian sages plain for all to see. All the same, public opinion could also be understood in the sense of unchanging rightness. Public opinion was allegedly the view of the people, but the pool of those whom the political establishment regarded as legitimate articulators broadened gradually over time from high officials (at the beginning of Chosŏn). The opinion base came to include the Censorate (late fifteenth century), Confucian students (sixteenth century), the rank-and-file *yangban* (seventeenth century), wealthy commoners (eighteenth century), and commoners as a whole (nineteenth century). The inclusion of the last two groups entailed changing local council membership in the eighteenth century and the emergence of people's assemblies (*minhoe*) in the nineteenth century (Kim Ingeol 2024, 23–35, 51–62).

Even when the pool was restricted to elites, they did not canvas themselves to determine their collective opinion on various matters. Instead, whatever a person or group described as "public opinion" was whatever they believed was or should be widely held, and it was left to the king to judge whose view was indeed public opinion. This meant that discussions determining public opinion were more like lawyers (the officials) arguing a case before a judge (the king). Accordingly, claims of overwhelming majority or high numbers of support for a given opinion were exaggerated rhetoric, not the result of nationwide or even countywide surveys. What mattered was not the precise number of individuals supporting this or that policy but who embodied a public spirit and moral worth, sometimes allowing even the king to claim his own opinion as "the public opinion." Because the literati voiced their positions before a royal decision, it was difficult for them to challenge it. Public opinion was thus less a weapon of the *yangban* against royal tyranny than a balanced system that brought the king and *yangban* together.

An Overview of Chosŏn Political History

Before the founding of Chosŏn, its founder, King T'aejo (Yi Sŏnggye; r. 1392–98), turned against the preceding state of Koryŏ (918–1392) to escape the trap in which he found himself caught when given command of an army to attack the ascendant Ming. At first, unable to ignore a royal command, he recognized that defeating Ming was unlikely. Either outcome meant a likely death sentence, so Yi Sŏnggye turned his army around, seized the capital, and deposed the king (1388). When he finally took the throne, the new Chosŏn state upheld Confucianism as the official ideology, but this did not immediately marginalize Buddhism, which had enjoyed the Koryŏ state's patronage. The "Confucian transformation" took up most of the fifteenth century (Deuchler 1992, 3–27). Indeed, T'aejo's apologists justified the founding of Chosŏn not only with Confucian rhetoric but also with Buddhism, geomancy, and even his military prowess (Baker 2013, 157–60). Moving the capital to Hansŏng for its geomantic merits as advocated by his Buddhist advisor, T'aejo aligned his kingdom with Ming, offering its emperor two options for naming his new state; the emperor chose Chosŏn. It was also T'aejo who created the first merit subjects.

T'aejo's sons competed to become his heir. When the most capable and ambitious among them, the fifth son Yi Pangwŏn (1367–1422), heard that T'aejo planned to make his youngest son his heir, Pangwŏn had the boy and his brother from the same mother killed. Traumatized, T'aejo abdicated in 1398 in favor of his eldest surviving son and retired to a Buddhist monastery. For his part, Pangwŏn became the power behind his brother's throne for two years before being challenged by yet another brother, T'aejo's fourth son, leading to clashes between their respective armies on the streets of Hansŏng. Pangwŏn won the contest, exiled his rebellious brother, and forced his puppet king to abdicate. Posthumously known as King T'aejong (r. 1400–18), he began shifting government support away from Buddhism, closing monasteries in the capital and returning monks to secular life (Buswell 1999, 138–39). Having used a private army (*sabyŏng*) to secure his accession, T'aejong promptly abolished all private armies. He responded to opposition, actual or potential, with brute force during the first half of his reign. Still, in the second half, he became more willing to negotiate with his ministers and consult them in significant policy decisions, an attitude more aligned with Confucian governance (Park Hong-Kyu 2006, 213–18). T'aejong also eased this transition by making supporters into merit subjects. Rather than a single prime minister, T'aejong established the State Council to replace the high Koryŏ institutions. Yet even this weaker organization was too restrictive for T'aejong. He eventually bypassed the State Council, had reports from the Six Ministries sent directly to him, and gave them instructions in return. While his successor reestablished the State Council's position above the Six Ministries, it never wielded the power of the analogous Koryŏ institutions earlier. Even the power the State Council did have began declining in the seventeenth century.

T'aejong abdicated in favor of his third son, King Sejong (r. 1418–50), though he continued to wield power as the retired king (*sangwang*) until his death (1422). A gifted Confucian scholar rather than a military man like his father and grandfather, Sejong continued his father's policy of disestablishing Buddhism by seizing monastic assets and limiting the number of monks while resisting officials' calls to suppress the religion harder. His reign saw advancements in knowledge and technology, particularly in agriculture. Alongside his cultural achievements lay his successful expansion of Chosŏn power against Jurchens in the northeast. Following up his military success with resettlement efforts, Sejong secured Korea's northeastern portion of the border with Manchuria, essentially establishing the present-day boundaries of Korea. His most far-reaching achievement was the creation of Han'gŭl (Hangul), a native system for writing the Korean language still used throughout Korea today. Rejected by the *yangban* elite in favor of the prestigious Literary Sinitic, Han'gŭl survived through the centuries on the pens of elite women and nonelites. Elite men were schooled in Han'gŭl, even if they refused to use it in public documents; instead, they wrote in Han'gŭl in private documents to write Korean words that did not derive from Sinographs and to correspond with their female relatives.

Sejong was succeeded in 1450 by his eldest son following Confucian practice, Chosŏn's first proper royal succession. The new king died after less than two years of rule, and again, the throne passed to his son, a boy of 12. Yet the increasing Confucianization of Korea was not strong enough to restrain the boy's ambitious uncle and Sejong's second son, King Sejo (r. 1455–68), who seized the throne from his nephew (Figure 5.1). Two years later, Sejo discovered a plot to restore the boy to the throne and executed the plotters and his hapless nephew, who was probably unaware of the scheme. Sejo proved an able ruler who ordered the compilation of the Great Code of Administration (Kyŏngguk taejŏn), based on the Great Ming Code (Da Ming lu). With amendments and revisions, the Great Code of Administration served as the basis of Chosŏn's law. Sejo did not usurp the throne to become a figurehead. Like his grandfather, T'aejong, Sejo bypassed the State Council and ruled more directly. He also encouraged using Han'gŭl to swipe at the prestige of the yangban while bolstering royal legitimacy by championing his father Sejong's achievement. Also, in the pursuit of the former—and also undoubtedly due to Confucian ministers' opposition to his usurpation—Sejo encouraged a Buddhist revival. These efforts did not carry into the reigns of his immediate successors, with his grandson, King Sŏngjong (r. 1470–95), reigning over an even more Confucian court than Sejong had. Sŏngjong completed the publication of the Great Code of Administration, strengthened the censorial organs of the government—doing more than any other early Chosŏn king to render sacrosanct their duty to criticize—and instituted the law banning illegitimate sons from holding office against the consensus of his officials, siding instead with the more zealous Confucian minority.

Sŏngjong's Confucianization of the court was put to the test by King Yŏnsan Kun (r. 1494–1506), his son by Deposed Consort Yun (1455–82), who had been put to death for, among other crimes, poisoning people and striking the king. Yŏnsan Kun first came into deadly conflict with his officials in 1498 when one of them wrote a criticism of Sejo's usurpation. Since Yŏnsan Kun's royal legitimacy was traced back to Sejo, he initiated the first "literati purges" (*sahwa*). Yŏnsan Kun set off a second, bloodier purge in 1504 when he learned the details of his mother's death. A

Figure 5.1 Draft portrait of Sejo, 1935, by Kim Ŭnho (1892–1979), 131.8 cm × 186.5 cm. Commissioned to paint portraits of two former emperors after Japan's annexation of Korea (1910), Kim also worked on copying then-extant official portraits of various Chosŏn kings, including an official portrait of Sejo from 1735, no longer extant. Source and photo credit: National Palace Museum of Korea.

toddler when she died, Yŏnsan Kun had grown up ignorant of the sordid details and was enraged to discover that certain officials had pressured Sŏngjong into executing her. Yŏnsan Kun took revenge against those he deemed responsible. The excesses of this purge pushed his remaining officials into action—deposing and exiling him in 1506 (Wagner 1974, 51–69). Before the year's end, he and his sons were dead at their respective sites of banishment.

Yŏnsan Kun is one of two Chosŏn monarchs to be overthrown, not by an ambitious relative but by his officials. Neither received a posthumous name (*siho*) befitting a king that includes a Sinograph for "progenitor" (*cho*) or "ancestor" (*chong*), instead referred to as a "prince" (*kun*). Also, official histories were termed "daily records" (*ilgi*) rather than "veritable records" (*sillok*), as were the accounts of other Chosŏn rulers. Yŏnsan Kun went down in Korean history as one of the worst monarchs: a tyrant who punished good Confucian officials on a whim. Of course, modern-day historians cannot overlook the fact that the recorded instances of Yŏnsan Kun's erratic behavior were written entirely by the victims of his purges and those who overthrew him—immediately urging the new king to kill Yŏnsan Kun's sons, all minors. Accordingly, historians have approached with a degree of skepticism the more outlandish claims the official histories of his reign made, including executing an official for looking directly at him during a lecture and exiling the Minister of Rites for spilling a drink the king had poured. All the same, credible are the accounts

The Routledge Handbook of Early Modern Korea

of other alleged crimes, such as abolishing the royal lecture (*kyŏngyŏn*)—in which the king and his officials read together and discuss various classical texts in ways gaining insights on matters of the state—and attacking centers of aristocratic power through confiscating the properties of the most powerful officials. After all, Yŏnsan Kun ascended the throne, surrounded by a large group of wealthy, powerful officials to whom the throne was indebted since Sejo's usurpation.

The coup leaders replaced Yŏnsan Kun with his half-brother King Chungjong (r. 1506–44), a thoroughly schooled Confucian who played one faction after another to strengthen his position. Seeking to free himself from his minders, Chungjong found an ally in Cho Kwangjo (1482–1519), a leading figure of the Sarim ("rusticated literati"), who, as more reform-minded Neo-Confucian scholars, found many merit subjects unworthy of the honor, not to mention all the land and slaves they had received. A true Neo-Confucian believer, Cho advocated merit over status and sought to replace the examination system with recommendations (*ch'ŏn'gŏ*) for official appointments. Chungjong enacted many reforms before growing tired of his endless moralizing lectures and uncompromising stance. Chungjong allowed Cho's enemies to frame him for treason and stage the third literati purge (1519), thus ridding the government of Cho and his Sarim allies (Wagner 1974, 70–120).

Subsequently, as Chungjong continued to play one group against another, he rehabilitated Cho, whom later kings and literati venerated as a martyr. In continuation of the trend that began during Sŏngjong's reign, the Censorate role in the government and in shaping public opinion continued to expand during Chungjong's reign, partly due to Cho's influence. Still, the maternal kin of the king's two legitimate sons jockeyed for position. Upon the accession of his son and successor, King Injong (r. 1544–45), the Sarim regained power with the support of Injong's maternal kin—only to be cast out again when the maternal kin of his half-brother and successor, King Myŏngjong (r. 1545–67) purged them (1545). As the young king's mother and dowager, Queen Munjŏng (1501–65), wielded power, her brothers and their supporters dominated the political scene. Upon her death, Myŏngjong asserted himself, reinstating the Sarim during his short personal rule.

King Sŏnjo's reign (1567–1608) is especially notable for the emergence of increasingly hereditary political factions that would turn into institutionalized political parties, as discussed below, and the Imjin War. The conflict devastated the Korean Peninsula: the population and arable land did not return to prewar levels for a hundred years. Despite the destruction, as well as the initially poor performance of government armies and Sŏnjo's ignominious flight from the capital shortly after the war began, the Chosŏn state did not collapse. Chosŏn's survival owed much to the Ming military aid, Admiral Yi Sunsin's (1545–98) naval victories, the "righteous army" (*ŭibyŏng*) militias organized and led by local *yangban* landlords, and the Buddhist monk militias. Aside from a new military unit that utilized semi-professional troops of commoners (including slaves manumitted for their service) trained as musketeers, archers, or sworders, the postwar political leadership introduced no significant change.

Sŏnjo's son and successor, King Kwanghae Kun (r. 1608–23), was an able ruler who instituted the Uniform Land Tax Law (Taedongpŏp) intended to rationalize tax levy in line with an increasingly commercialized economy. However, his troubles at home and abroad did not allow him to reach his full potential as monarch. The son of a royal concubine, Kwanghae Kun had long been Sŏnjo's heir apparent and was a proven leader, but his position came under threat when Sŏnjo's queen gave birth to his only legitimate son. Ultimately, Kwanghae Kun ascended the throne because this new, legitimate half-brother was still a toddler. The brother remained a threat to the new king's position. Upon mounting pressure from the Great Northerner (Taebuk) faction, which had supported Kwanghae Kun's accession, he killed the half-brother and turned the boy's mother into a commoner (1613). Internationally, Kwanghae Kun navigated the delicate balance

Politics

between the declining but still powerful Ming—to whom Chosŏn elites felt loyalty for its military aid in the Imjin War—and the rising Jurchens. Pro-Ming figures at the court, mostly the Westerner (Sŏin) party, had their way, deposing and exiling Kwanghae Kun (1623).

The Westerners placed Kwanghae Kun's nephew, King Injo, on the throne (r. 1623–49). Owing his throne to the Westerners and lacking a strong desire to rule in the first place, Injo was unable to resist their openly anti-Jurchen policy, and Chosŏn paid the price with the Chŏngmyo War and the Pyŏngja War, which ended only with capitulation. Injo was forced to kowtow to the victorious Qing emperor and transfer Chosŏn's allegiance from Ming to Qing. Though less devastating than the Imjin War, the outcome of the Pyŏngja War fueled a lingering, widespread resentment toward the Manchus as well as viewing Chosŏn as "Little China" (*So Chunghwa*), in effect, the heir of the vanquished Ming (Kye 2011). Injo's son and successor, King Hyojong (r. 1649–59), had to live in the Qing capital as a hostage before ascending the throne, and he capitalized on the anti-Manchu sentiment to prepare Chosŏn for an invasion of Qing, an enterprise which never materialized, and his son and successor, King Hyŏnjong (r. 1659–74), abandoned the preparation.

The reign of King Sukchong (r. 1674–1720), who succeeded his father Hyŏnjong, produced much bloodshed comparable to Kwanghae Kun's reign. Sukchong sought to contain partisan struggles by playing one off against another with an unintended consequence: his crown prince, King Kyŏngjong (r. 1720–24)—who was supported by minority parties, the Disciples (Soron) and the Southerners (Namin), had no son, and suffered from poor health—was a transition figure before the throne went to his half-brother, King Yŏngjo (r. 1724–76), supported by the majority party, the Patriarchs. Yŏngjo was the longest-reigning Chosŏn monarch and one of the most dedicated to ruling justly—projecting himself as a sage king above the partisan fray and somewhat equalizing the military tax burden on commoners. Before doing so, the king had to suppress a rebellion soon after his succession and a groundless accusation of poisoning his predecessor (Jackson 2016). Subsequently, Yŏngjo sought to end the partisan conflict with his Policy of Impartiality (T'angp'yŏngch'aek). Although somewhat successful in curtailing partisan violence, Yŏngjo's relationship with his son and heir, Prince Sado (1735–62), was fraught with tension and partisan intrigue. The mentally unstable prince engaged in unacceptable behaviors, including murdering palace servants. Eventually, Yŏngjo put him to death to eliminate the threat to dynastic survival he would have posed were he to ascend the throne (Haboush 1988, chapter 5).

The throne then passed to the son of Sado, King Chŏngjo (r. 1776–1800), a diligent, scholarly monarch determined to avoid his father's fate. Regarding himself as the teacher of his officials, Chŏngjo stressed the centrality of his kingship and instituted several reforms to create an ideal Confucian society. In addition to his ideological struggle for expanded royal power, Chŏngjo took practical steps to achieve it. He lifted restrictions on the content of direct petitions to the throne to give nonelites a channel to bring problems to his attention. This measure also expanded central control over the populace. He established the Kyujanggak, which was not only a royal library but also offered an alternative path into government service for illegitimate sons of *yangban* otherwise locked out of officialdom. Chŏngjo also ordered the construction of a city wall near Suwŏn, Hwasŏng ("Illustrious Fortress"), and stationed a newly created military unit, the Robust and Brave Division (Changyongyŏng), ostensibly to guard the nearby tomb of his father he frequently visited—thus using filial piety as a pretext to venture outside Hansŏng, which had become rare for a monarch after early Chosŏn. The Division's real purpose was to militarily strengthen the king's hand against his officials. The Hwasŏng city wall was the most technologically advanced in Chosŏn and was far larger than necessary to protect a tomb. He steadily increased the troop strength of the Robust and Brave Division at the expense of units of the regular capital armies. He placed it under the command of the governor of Kyŏnggi—an office to which Chŏngjo con-

The Routledge Handbook of Early Modern Korea

sistently appointed a confidant—and a segment of the Division guarded the king even outside Hwasŏng. Chŏngjo's approach to kingship took a great deal of effort. He gave personal attention to thousands of memorials and other documents dealing with government business, to say nothing of writing and reading thousands of individual letters that nevertheless carried policy implications. It is little wonder that, given the time he lived in, Chŏngjo took ill and died at the relatively young age of 47 (Lovins 2019, 149–59).

His death left a power vacuum at the center filled by an oligarchy of consort families. His son and successor, King Sunjo (r. 1800–34), was just 11 when he ascended the throne and was not in a position to resist his father's detractors who abolished the Division and abandoned the Hwasŏng project. In officialdom, they purged Chŏngjo's supporters from the state apparatus. For over six decades, the powerful aristocratic families kept the throne weak—occupied a series of kings, either a minor or unprepared—and married one of their daughters to the current or future king to exercise power through their status as the royal in-law. Rather than the generational blood-letting of intense partisan strife, the consort family oligarchy saw relatively bloodless power shifts among the most powerful aristocratic families. Moreover, the Chosŏn government they dominated continued to perform such fundamental functions as taking disaster relief measures and administering justice (Karlsson 2007, 86). The government was able to put down the Hong Kyŏngnae Rebellion in 1812 in the northwest and punished corrupt officials who had ignited riots in Chinju and dozens of other counties in 1862 in southern and central Korea.

Indeed, Chosŏn's political system did not experience a fundamental challenge until the arrival of imperialism. In 1864, the Hŭngsŏn Taewŏn'gun (1821–98), father of the child-king Kojong (r. 1864–1907; emperor from 1897), took the reins of power in his son's name. The Taewŏn'gun sought to reform and strengthen the country centered around enhancing the dignity of the royal house, ending corruption, and improving government finances (Palais 1975, 1–22). He rejected the West and Japan's demands for relations and trade, launched the largest-ever persecution of Catholic Christians (1866), and repelled incursions by France (1866) and the United States (1871). His policy alienated the conservative Defend Orthodoxy–Reject Heterodoxy (Wijŏng ch'ŏksa) group and the pro-Western Enlightenment Party (Kaehwadang), and pressures from both forced him to relinquish power—with Kojong beginning to rule in person (1873).

From Factions to Political Parties

A prominent feature of Chosŏn politics from the late sixteenth century is the emergence of factionalism, which eventually produced institutionalized, lasting political parties. Clearly defined by Sŏnjo's reign, initially, factions did not necessarily coalesce around individual leaders or disagreement over policies but, instead, were political ties that bound kin groups. As the winning factions became entrenched and more stable, partisan strife touched every aspect of Chosŏn's political and intellectual development for over 200 years. Partisan conflicts arose from disputes over ideological and substantive policy matters that led to significant intellectual developments and, in some cases, even directly to reform (Haboush 1999, 46–90; Deuchler 1999, 91–133).

The first clearly defined, more lasting factions arose in 1575 during Sŏnjo's reign due to a dispute between the queen's brother Sim Ŭigyŏm (1535–87) and Kim Hyowŏn (1542–90) over control of appointments to the crucial positions, the section chiefs (Chŏngnang) and assistant section chiefs (Chwarang) of the Ministry of Personnel (Ijo). The two sides in this dispute came to be known as Easterners (Tongin; Kim Hyowŏn lived in the eastern part of Hansŏng) and Westerners (Sim Ŭigyŏm lived in the western part). All subsequent political associations traced their history to one of these two: later in Sŏnjo's reign, the Easterners split into Northerners (Pugin) and

Politics

Southerners, and the Northerners soon split into Great Northerners and Lesser Northerners (Han 2015, 25). During Sukchong's reign, the Westerners broke into Patriarchs and Disciples.

Several means perpetuated factions and parties. Each operated its private academies (*sŏwŏn*), teaching their interpretations of Confucianism that included commentaries by prominent members (Ch'oe 1999, 41–45). Surrounding and obeying them were students who performed rituals to sages—all of the same factional or partisan allegiance. Once factions had become more stable, lasting political parties after the accession of Injo, *yangban* tended to marry within the party. At times, though, an inter-factional marriage was sought to bring the two factions together as allies. When the Westerners staged a coup enthroning Injo, they effectively destroyed the hardline Great Northerners (who had instigated murdering Kwanghae Kun's half-brothers and deposed the queen mother) and formed a de facto coalition government with the Southerners. Most of the more moderate Lesser Northerners joined the Southerners, though some kept their Northerner identity until the end of Chosŏn.

By the mid-seventeenth century, partisan politics embodied personal animosities and policy differences over a particular moral dimension as understood in Neo-Confucianism, as exemplified by the two rounds of Rites Controversy. When Hyojong died (1659), officials debated the proper mourning period and garments for his still-living stepmother and queen dowager. The Westerner party, led by Song Siyŏl, argued for a mourning period of just one year—instead of the three years required for mourning a son—as Hyojong was not Injo's eldest son, whereas the Southerner party, led by Hŏ Mok (1596–1682), contended that since Hyojong had succeeded Injo (after Injo's eldest son's death), he was effectively the eldest son (heir) and thus duty-bound to three-year mourning. Yun Hyu (1617–80), another Southerner, went further, arguing that Hyŏnjong must mourn for three years, as he had been king (royal heir) and, therefore, the birth order was irrelevant. To do otherwise, said Yun, would cast doubt on Hyojong's royal legitimacy and, consequently, the legitimacy of Hyojong's only son and heir apparent. When Hyojong's widow died (1674), the Second Rites Controversy arose. Since a wife had to be mourned according to her husband's status, Hyojong's legitimacy was again at issue.

Song Siyŏl, Hŏ Mok, and Yun Hyu were passionate about their positions. Song approached the Rites Controversies as more than power plays. To him, they represented moments in which Chosŏn had to choose between holding fast to the true Way (Dao), as explicated by Zhu Xi, or casting it aside for political expediency. Indeed, considering Song's close relationship with the deceased Hyojong (as reflected in a private meeting without the presence of the court historians, a severe breach of protocol), he must have been reluctant to take any step that might impugn Hyojong's legitimacy. All the same, Song could not accept the arguments of Hŏ or Yun since both relied on a commentary not validated by Song China's Zhu Xi (1130–1200), whose interpretations of the classics the mainstream Neo-Confucians of Chosŏn deemed orthodox. For Yun's part, the monarchy was separate and distinct from ordinary *yangban*; hence, the rules applied to the latter did not apply to the former. Yun reasoned that since the "Eastern State" (*Tongguk*; Korea) was now the custodian of civilization after the fall of Ming, Chosŏn could make its own decisions and was not bound by Zhu Xi's ideas. Far from being naked power struggles or even policy issues taken with calculus divorced from feeling, these controversies were deeply felt, tremendously important, and based on comprehensive worldviews and legitimate intellectual interpretation. Song's view carried the day at first, but eventually, Sukchong decided Song's argument did impugn his father Hyŏnjong's legitimacy and had him executed.

Final Thoughts

As political players rose and fell from power amidst partisan struggle, they criticized those in power, giving rise to fruitful criticism of the system and its foundational ideology, orthodox Neo-

The Routledge Handbook of Early Modern Korea

Confucianism. Disputes such as that between Yun Hyu and Song Siyŏl over the authority of Zhu Xi stemmed from well-thought-out and erudite philosophical positions, not mere personal dislike. These positions, in turn, set the stage for later discussion of such concrete policy issues as the relationship between the throne and the bureaucracy. For example, Pak Sedang (1629–1703) condemned the Neo-Confucian orthodoxy's estrangement from everyday life while his Disciples party was out of power vis-à-vis Song Siyŏl's Patriarchs party. Such out-of-power scholars had much to write about their concerns with statecraft, arguing that the welfare of the people was being neglected in favor of metaphysical speculation. During Chŏngjo's reign, the Southerner party, exemplified by Chŏng Yagyong (1762–1836), advocated a more activist king, an argument that met a sympathetic ear from Chŏngjo as he pursued reforms to strengthen the kingship (Lovins 2019, 37–40).

After decades of oligarchic reaction against Chŏngjo's reforms, as well as the Taewŏn'gun's efforts to restore the state's power centered around the royal house, Chosŏn Korea found itself in new waters—struggling to strengthen itself as a modern nation-state vis-à-vis pressures of imperialism and colonialism. Having learned from how Western powers had earlier imposed unequal treaties, in 1876, Meiji Japan (1868–1912) used its own display of force to demand and secure such an arrangement with Korea, the Treaty of Kanghwado. No longer a mostly insulated phenomenon, Chosŏn politics was fully integrated into a vortex of international relations involving great powers, among which Japan, China, and Russia were especially eager to influence, if not control, Korea.

References

Baker, Don. 2013. "Rhetoric, Ritual, and Political Legitimacy: Justifying Yi Seong-gye's Ascension to the Throne." *Korea Journal* 53, no. 4: 141–67.

Buswell, Robert E., Jr. 1999. "Buddhism Under Confucian Domination: The Synthetic Vision of Sŏsan Hyujŏng." In *Culture and the State in Late Chosŏn Korea*, edited by JaHyun Kim Haboush and Martina Deuchler, 134–59. Harvard University Asia Center.

Ch'oe, Yŏng-ho. 1999. "Private Academies and the State in Late Chosŏn Korea." In *Culture and the State in Late Chosŏn Korea*, edited by JaHyun Kim Haboush and Martina Deuchler, 15–45. Harvard University Asia Center.

Deuchler, Martina. 1992. *The Confucian Transformation of Korea: A Study of Society and Ideology*. Council on East Asian Studies, Harvard University.

Deuchler, Martina. 1999. "Despoilers of the Way – Insulters of the Sages: Controversies over the Classics in Seventeenth-Century Korea." In *Culture and the State in Late Chosŏn Korea*, edited by JaHyun Kim Haboush and Martina Deuchler, 91–133. Harvard University Asia Center.

Haboush, JaHyun Kim. 1988. *A Heritage of Kings: One Man's Monarchy in the Confucian World*. Columbia University Press.

Haboush, JaHyun Kim. 1999. "Constructing the Center: The Ritual Controversy and the Search for a New Identity in Seventeenth-Century Korea." In *Culture and the State in Late Chosŏn Korea*, edited by JaHyun Kim Haboush and Martina Deuchler, 46–90. Harvard University Asia Center.

Han Moon Jong. 2015. "Korea's Pre-War Domestic Situation and Relations with Japan." In *The East Asian War, 1592–1598: International Relations, Violence, and Memory*, edited by James B. Lewis, 22–41. Routledge.

Jackson, Andrew David. 2016. *The 1728 Musin Rebellion: Politics and Plotting in Eighteenth-Century Korea*. University of Hawai'i Press.

Karlsson, Anders. 2007. "Royal Compassion and Disaster Relief in Chosŏn Korea." *Seoul Journal of Korean Studies* 20, no. 1: 71–98.

Kawashima, Fujiya. 1980. "The Local Gentry Association in Mid-Yi Dynasty Korea: A Preliminary Study of the Ch'angnyŏng Hyangan, 1600–1838." *Journal of Korean Studies* 2: 113–37.

Kim Ingeol. 2024. *Politics of Public Opinion: Local Councils and People's Assemblies in Korea, 1567–1894*. Translated by Eugene Y. Park. Brill.

Politics

Kim, Jungwon. 2022. "Inscribing Grievances, Litigation, and Local Community in Eighteenth-Century Korea." *Journal of Asian Studies* 81, no. 2: 289–303.

Kye Sŭngbŏm. 2011. *Chŏngjidoen sigan: Chosŏn sidae ŭi Taebodan kwa kŭndae ŭi munt'ŏk*. Sŏgang taehakkyo ch'ulp'anbu.

Lovins, Christopher. 2019. *King Chŏngjo: An Enlightened Despot in Early Modern Korea*. State University of New York Press.

Palais, James B. 1975. *Politics and Policy in Traditional Korea*. Council on East Asian Studies, Harvard University Press.

Park, Eugene Y. 2007. *Between Dreams and Reality: The Military Examination in Late Chosŏn Korea, 1600–1894*. Harvard University Asia Center.

Park Hong-Kyu. 2006. "King Taejong as a Statesman: From Power to Authority." *Korea Journal* 46, no. 4: 192–222.

Wagner, Edward Willett. 1974. *The Literati Purges: Political Conflict in Early Yi Korea*. East Asian Research Center, Harvard University Press.

Yi Tae-Jin. 2007. *Confucianization and Modernization in Korean History*. East Asia Program, Cornell University.

6

THE MILITARY

Felix Siegmund

The military history of the Chosŏn state (1392–1897) arguably comprises early and late periods. A commonly cited watershed event is the Imjin War (East Asian War; 1592–98), which devastated Korea and destroyed most records and documents. Accordingly, many more sources are available for late Chosŏn. During half a millennium of Chosŏn rule, Korea fought wars with the Japanese, Jurchens, Manchus, and, toward the end, with Western military forces. As was the case for the preceding Koryŏ state (918–1392), Chosŏn's navy had to fight the Wakō ("Japanese pirates"), who often operated on an organized military scale. In addition to these external threats, the Chosŏn army dealt with numerous rebellions of varying scale. As a peninsula situated east of China's Liaodong Peninsula and surrounded by water on three sides, Chosŏn Korea naturally had a strong interest in naval defenses and maintaining a strong navy. While the army was trained and equipped mainly to deal with threats coming from the north—Mongols and Jurchens in early Chosŏn and Manchus in the seventeenth century—the navy kept the role of defense against threats from the sea, which mostly meant threats from the south, especially from the Japanese Archipelago.

Understanding the Chosŏn military thought and organization can benefit from an overview of Korea's earlier military history, beginning with the Three Kingdoms period. The term "Three Kingdoms" in the Korean context refers to the states of Koguryŏ (37 BCE, trad.–668 CE), Paekche (18 BCE, trad.–660 CE), and Silla (57 BCE, trad.–935 CE). All three emerged from earlier tribal structures and evolved into more centralized aristocratic kingdoms around the first, third, and fourth century CE, respectively. Allied with China's Tang dynasty (618–907), Silla conquered Paekche and Koguryŏ, ultimately establishing its rule over the southern two-thirds of the Korean Peninsula by 676. Arguably, Silla's victory was a war of unification if one were to disregard Koguryŏ's successor state, Parhae (698–926), as a part of Korean history.

The Three Kingdoms maintained an aristocratic army system (Lee 1975, 2). Nobles who commanded units that consisted of their kin and clan members led armies. In Silla, semi-permanent units grouped into six divisions constituted the army. Also, the garrison troops of Silla fortresses made up distinct units, often, in fact, private armies (*sabyŏng*) of powerful aristocrats. Moreover, these fortress garrisons pursued economic activities, primarily agriculture. In the late sixth century, the Silla army began to incorporate troops of defeated peoples into separate units (Lee 1975, 8–11). During this period, the Hwarang ("flower youths") warriors formed a Buddhist-influenced aristocratic order that performed military duties and participated in combats. As such, the Hwarang

88   DOI: 10.4324/9781003262053-9

The Military

might have been an elite unit of the army, but their exact function, role, and subsequent history are unclear (Tikhonov 1998). What is certain, though, is that in the ninth century, the military might of the local strongmen (*hojok*), including some members of Silla nobility, with their private armies increased. Such local elites became a decisive factor in the power struggle that led to the disintegration of Silla and the rise of the new Koryŏ state. They formed the core of what was to become the new elite in Koryŏ's professional military class system (Lee 1975, 14–15).

In a departure from its predecessor, Koryŏ's army operated on a professional military class (*kunban*) system (Lee 1975, 2, 15). King T'aejo (Wang Kŏn; r. 918–43), the founder of Koryŏ, emerged victorious from the turmoil of the final decades of Silla. The centralizing Koryŏ state recorded the standing army soldiers in special registers, and the status became hereditary. Registered soldiers received land allotments and retainers to farm that land (Lee 1975, 15–16). Also, commoners could volunteer or be conscripted, primarily for provincial units. In contrast, the capital units drew from professional and hereditary soldiers. This system allowed social mobility: some soldiers rose through the ranks, even becoming military officials. Such an attainment made an official and his more immediate male family members eligible for offices (Lee 1975, 18–20). Aside from upward social mobility, Koryŏ soldiers were subject to corvée. In late Koryŏ, even the elite central army units were not exempt, perhaps due to increased corruption and other problems plaguing the state's military land allocation (Lee 1975, 21).

As its army evolved, so did Koryŏ's relations with various Tungusic and Mongol peoples who had been allies and enemies of the states on the Korean Peninsula since the beginning of written history. A struggle for control of Manchuria escalated into wars between Koryŏ and its northern neighbors. In the tenth and eleventh centuries, Koryŏ fought a series of wars with the Khitan Liao dynasty (916–1125), which controlled Inner Mongolia and Northeast China until they agreed to peace in 1022. At the end of the eleventh century, Koryŏ dealt with the increasing Jurchen threat as their leader founded the Jin dynasty (1115–1234) and went on to conquer Liao. This time, however, Koryŏ acquiesced to the new power's demand for ritual submission rather than to fight any war.

In the meantime, the military's declining prestige and spreading discontent as unfair practices and corruption led to a military coup in 1170, followed by a series of military strongmen wielding power through figurehead kings (1170–1270). The military leaders relied on their private armies, which began to replace the regular army and strong lord–retainer relationships. Thus, ostensibly, the king still exercised military command. However, throughout the military rule, loyalty to the Ubong Ch'oe as the ruling military family (1196–1258) and loyalty to various private army leaders held the overall military organization together. The widespread usage and the chaotic structure of private armies weakened the state and public order, with some private armies assuming gang-like characteristics (Lee 1975, 23).

When faced with invasions by the largest empire in world history to that point, the Mongol empire, Koryŏ's military strongmen kept their private armies intact, instead choosing to field the less effective government troops. In 1215, when the Mongols entered Koryŏ territory to pursue the Khitans who had revolted against Jin, Koryŏ cooperated in a successful joint operation that defeated the Khitans. Seeing themselves as Koryŏ's benefactors, Mongols imposed a list of demands before commencing a series of six invasions (1231–58) when assailants in Koryŏ dress killed Mongol envoys returning from Koryŏ. After a generation of warfare, the Mongol Yuan dynasty (1271–1368) and Koryŏ agreed to peace under harsh conditions for Koryŏ—amounting to its subjugation as Yuan's vassal state.

In 1270, when the last military strongman fell from power (the Ch'oe house rule had ended in 1258), most private armies were disbanded, and the old order returned. Since the old system of

89

central and provincial units had suffered neglect when military rulers favored their private armies, the late Koryŏ state attempted to reconstruct the earlier system of professional military class—an effort only partially successful. In particular, Koryŏ found it difficult to mobilize soldiers when facing Yuan's demand for troops. The government attempted a system in which farmers were to serve as self-sufficient soldiers and to be mobilized when needed. The effective abolition of the earlier professional military class led to the peasant–soldier system (Lee 1975, 25).

While Koryŏ struggled to reorganize the military, the Wakō, based mainly in Japan's Tsushima and Kyushu, constantly threatened the coastal regions. In the thirteenth century, the Wakō began raiding the shore, each time going away only when Koryŏ responded with sufficient troop strength. The Wakō mainly pursued pillage, sometimes taking residents as well, and frequent raids depopulated some parts of Korea. Koryŏ's effort to end the raids through diplomacy with Japan failed, as the latter was decentralized and militarized by then. Recognizing that military force was the only way to contain the Wakō raids, in the 1360s, Koryŏ began fielding increasingly effective armies— equipped with cannons by the 1370s, when the tide of conflict shifted in favor of Koryŏ. A leading commander was the future founder of Chosŏn, Yi Sŏnggye (King T'aejo; r. 1392–98).

The turmoil of the power transition in China from the Yuan to the new Ming dynasty (1368–1644) put Yi Sŏnggye in the position of effecting the dynastic change in Korea. In 1388, when the Koryŏ court decided to attack Ming China upon the latter's overbearing demand for territories Koryŏ had recovered from Yuan, Yi Sŏnggye refused to attack Ming. Taking the Koryŏ capital instead, he consolidated his paramount position by eliminating one adversarial group after another before taking the throne in 1392. Subsequently, he renamed the kingdom "Chosŏn" after consulting with Ming.

The Leadership

Chosŏn military leaders came from the hereditary aristocracy, the *yangban* ("two orders") carried over from Koryŏ. When Yi Sŏnggye rose to prominence in the final decades of Koryŏ, he was among many military commanders from the northeast who were joining the capital aristocracy. By then, the term *yangban*, which had earlier denoted civil officials (*munban*) and military officials (*muban*)—both earlier hailing from families of central officials, hereditary functionaries, and even commoners—had become synonymous with the aristocracy. Increasingly, through the mid- and late Koryŏ periods, *yangban* denoted not just those who were central officials but also their immediate relatives and descendants—all typically residing in the capital. The Koryŏ–Chosŏn regime change effectively marked the end of a trickling stream of nonelites joining the *yangban* aristocracy by then.

The Chosŏn state continued Koryŏ's notion of recruiting officials through the government service examinations ostensibly open to most free males. Unlike Koryŏ, which was unable to institute a lasting military examination system due to opposition from the civil aristocracy, Chosŏn succeeded—establishing the military examination (*mukwa*) in 1402 when King T'aejong (r. 1400–18) abolished and incorporated private armies (*sabyŏng*) into a centralized military organization. As true with the civil examination (*munkwa*), the military examination was open to all except the lowborn (*ch'ŏnmin*), most of whom were enslaved people (*nobi*), and others that the state deemed morally disqualified in person, such as criminals, or in birth—including the sons mothered by concubines or remarried women. Thus, besides the aristocracy, commoners were eligible to compete in the examination system and had a shot at pursuing a career as an official, especially in the military branch. After all, in contrast to the civil examination centered around a candidate's ability to apply his knowledge of the required texts in writing an essay following prescribed conventions, the military examination tested a range of weaponry skills (mostly a wide variety of archery), many involving horsemanship, as well as a demonstrated knowledge of the military classics and other texts. Civil or military, the average age of Chosŏn examination passers was in the early thirties. This figure suggests that devoting oneself to preparing for passing the examination was beyond the means of most other than bona fide *yangban* (Park 2007, 26–28, 38–47).

All the same, opportunities for social mobility for those from more modest backgrounds were somewhat greater in the military branch since the Chosŏn elite held it in low regard compared to the civil branch. Although a military man himself, the Chosŏn founder, Yi Sŏnggye, ruled as the first among equals, heeding the advice of high-level civil officials—Confucian scholar-officials. Especially from the sixteenth century, Chosŏn monarchs emphasized the role of the civil branch even more heavily while keeping the military branch effectively subordinated to it. A contributing factor was that throughout the Chosŏn period, practical achievements and direct appointments allowed military men to rise through the ranks—something nearly impossible in the civil branch. Although late Chosŏn kings generally neglected military affairs, King Chŏngjo (r. 1776–1800), for example, sponsored military books and other projects, especially those concerning fighting techniques.

Apart from the problem of deep-seated bias against military men, which often resulted in a neglect of military offices and military affairs in general, Chosŏn politics from the late sixteenth century on suffered from increasingly violent partisan conflict. Various political associations, each with its regional base and agenda, struggled over issues to the effect that the party triumphant not only purged the members of the losing party from officialdom (punishments ranging from dismissal to banishment to execution), but the winner subsequently split into two mutually antagonistic parties over a new issue: often the extent of punishment for the losing partisans. The late Chosŏn partisan politics continued to limit the functionality of the state, at least until the mid-eighteenth century when the Patriarchs (Noron) achieved a paramount position. Such a disorderly state of official affairs naturally had a strong negative influence on the functioning and the readiness of the military, which, much through the Chosŏn period, the state and its aristocratic proprietors tended to utilize not so much for defense against a foreign power as internal political turmoil.

Security Threats, External and Internal

While duly performing tributary obligations to Ming China, from time to time, early Chosŏn Korea clashed with the Jurchens, the ancestors of Manchus, who, too, submitted tributes to Ming. As intermittent Jurchen raids continued, in the fifteenth century, Chosŏn expanded and gradually strengthened its control of northeastern Korea that Koryŏ had conquered from the Jurchens. Chosŏn pursued an active, sometimes brutal, policy of military subjugation and the subsequent displacement and re-settlement of the Jurchen population, as well as offering incentives to the Jurchens to settle peacefully in Chosŏn territory and colonizing the northeast with farmers from southern Korea. By the end of the century, the present-day northeastern boundary of North Korea along the Tuman (Ch. Tumen) River, separating the country from China and Russia, had become at least the nominal northeastern boundary between Chosŏn and the Jurchens. Jurchen raids increased in frequency and intensity in the late sixteenth century, when Japan, too, reunified by Toyotomi Hideyoshi (1537–98), posed a renewed threat.

The Imjin War, sparked by a massive Japanese invasion in May 1592, features prominently in Chosŏn military history (Swope 2009). Variously known as the Hideyoshi Invasion, the Sino–Japanese–Korean War, the East Asian War, or the Great East Asian War in Anglophone studies on the conflict, the Imjin War saw the initial occupation of much of Korea by the Japanese before

Ming China dispatched an army commanded by the competent and successful general Li Rusong (1549–98). In the following year, a collaborative effort of Ming and Chosŏn armies—the latter quickly growing in troop strength after perhaps no more than 8,000 battleworthy troops initially suffered defeats—drove back the Japanese, and the conflict developed into a slow war of attrition, without either side able to overwhelm the other. At the same time, the Japanese locked down in southern Korea. While lower-intensity warfare continued, negotiations between Ming China and Japan failed due to their respective bargaining positions so far apart. Japan renewed a full-scale offensive in 1597, but making no lasting gain, its troops withdrew upon Hideyoshi's order, issued just before his death. During the war, military action by Chosŏn forces comprised increasingly effective operations by the army, often aided by militias (*ŭibyŏng*; "righteous armies") led by local *yangban* (aristocrat) leaders, and by the navy, which, under the command of Admiral Yi Sunsin (1545–98), prevailed over the Japanese counterpart in every engagement except one draw. The Chosŏn navy's success prevented the Japanese navy from extending its sea lane into the Yellow Sea to provide logistical support to the Japanese land forces' operations further north in Korea. The joint Ming–Chosŏn armies ultimately pressured the demoralized Japanese to pull back upon their dying leader's order.

The Imjin War was a watershed not just in Chosŏn military history but also in both the history and historiography of Chosŏn. To begin with, the sheer horrors and destructions of the war impacted Chosŏn's politics, society, economy, and culture in such ways that many older studies, including some Western-language works, use the war to divide the Chosŏn period into early and late periods. For example, the productivity of taxable land measured in *kyŏl* ("stacks") immediately after the war was only a fifth of the pre-war level. Not only did the Imjin War leave Chosŏn Korea and Ming China weakened, facilitating the Manchu subjugation of Korea and conquest of China, but the conflict also accelerated the emergence of Korean national consciousness (Lewis 2015; Haboush 2016).

Indeed, the Jurchens grew in power in the late sixteenth century before they adopted a new ethnonym, Manchu, in 1635. Under Nurhaci (1559–1626), who founded the Qing dynasty (1616–1912; Later Jin until 1636), the Jurchens became independent from Ming and built their military forces. King Kwanghae Kun (r. 1608–23) was realistic in his assessment of the Jurchen threat, in contrast to many of his officials, who insisted on aiding Ming, and Chosŏn tried to remain neutral. Even after Chosŏn eventually succumbed to the Ming demand for military aid against the Jurchens (1618), Kwanghae Kun instructed the commander, Kang Hongnip (1560–1627), to surrender to the Jurchens as soon as possible. He did so after being drawn into a battle, during which the Chosŏn army lost about 8,000 out of 15,000 troops before surrendering to Nurhaci. Recognizing Chosŏn's reluctant involvement, he released the Koreans. Kwanghae Kun maintained the status quo, but the politics changed dramatically when the Westerner (Sŏin) party staged a coup, overthrew him, and elevated his nephew, King Injo (r. 1623–49). The new monarch and his court adopted a confrontational stance against the Jurchens.

While Chosŏn–Jurchen relations deteriorated, Injo's court also had to deal with internal turmoil. Despite his role in Injo's enthronement, a general, Yi Kwal (1587–1624), received relatively modest rewards—to his resentment—before being posted in the northern frontier to organize a defense against the Jurchens. Moreover, his political enemies at the court accused him of plotting treason. The accusation likely was wrongful, but Yi Kwal resisted his arrest and staged an open rebellion in March 1624. Marching to the capital, Hansŏng (present-day Seoul), he defeated the government troops, took the city, and installed a new king. However, early in the following month, loyalist troops recaptured Hansŏng and killed Yi Kwal.

Despite the outcome, the rebellion not only exposed the internal weakness of the Chosŏn state, but the Jurchens capitalized on the turmoil to launch an attack against Chosŏn. Succeeding Nurhaci,

The Military

his son Hong Taiji (r. 1626–43) discontinued diplomatic engagement with Chosŏn, renamed his people and his state to Manchu and Qing, respectively, and expanded his war efforts against Ming. Branding Injo usurper, Hong Taiji invaded Chosŏn in 1627 and 1637. The second invasion secured Chosŏn's capitulation and transfer of its loyalty as a tributary state from Ming to Qing.

This experience informed military rhetoric and practice in Chosŏn for over two centuries. Qing took the Ming capital, Beijing, in 1644, though loyalists in South China resisted until 1662. For Chosŏn, the Ming–Qing transition in China meant the loss of its long-standing suzerain and submission to a powerful new state, which the Chosŏn elite viewed as barbaric. Accordingly, Injo's son and successor, King Hyojong (r. 1649–59), and the Westerner party supporting him advocated revenge and active support of Ming loyalists in China through a "Northern Expedition" (*Pukpŏl*), which remained a significant part of official Chosŏn discourse well into the eighteenth century. No military action against Qing materialized, but the Northern Expedition as a rhetoric inspired military thoughts, writings, planning, and continuing partisan strife at the court.

Motivated by such strife, the Musin Rebellion (1728) under the leadership of Yi Injwa (1695–1728) unsuccessfully challenged King Yŏngjo (r. 1724–76). Yi Injwa accused Yŏngjo—supported by the Patriarchs, who constituted one of the two parties resulting from the division of Westerners—of killing his predecessor to ascend the throne. Receiving support from extremists among Disciples (Soron), the Westerners' other successor party, and Southerners (Namin), the rebels were able to take many counties and a fortified outpost. Although suppressed in just three weeks, the Musin Rebellion demonstrated the late Chosŏn military defense system's lack of readiness and inefficiency (Jackson 2016).

In contrast to the Musin Rebellion, engendered by a partisan struggle at the court, the Hong Kyŏngnae Rebellion (1812) tapped into widespread discontent among a marginalized regional elite. Sparking the rebellion was what the residents of P'yŏngan Province perceived as heavy taxation, discriminatory treatment by capital elites, and possibly a belief in favorable omens. A geomancer who had failed in repeated attempts to pass the government service examination, the leader, Hong Kyŏngnae (1780–1812), and his troops gained control of many counties in northwestern P'yŏngan before internal quarrels hampered their efforts to advance southward. Four months into the rebellion, Hong Kyŏngnae died in battle, the government troops massacred his followers, and the captives subsequently executed numbered in the thousands. Even though unsuccessful, the Hong Kyŏngnae Rebellion was the first serious challenge—within Chosŏn—against the establishment by the marginalized. It inspired a series of counter-measures by the state against corruption and dissent (Kim 2007). The military system was not immune to such problems.

Military Organization

The military system underwent significant changes during the half a millennium of Chosŏn rule. Whereas some are poorly documented, others are clear on paper—though in many cases, whether or how implemented is unclear. Also, the state formed several military agencies on an ad-hoc basis before adapting them to changing circumstances as needed. Accordingly, the character of military organization in practice quite different from what was in the documents can be difficult to understand. The following is an overview of the Chosŏn military system to 1873 and some notable agencies.

After the founding of Chosŏn, significant political figures continued to command private armies until King T'aejong abolished them and placed the troops under the central government's control. Comprising land combat troops, marines, and labor battalions, the new Chosŏn military organization system divided Korea into five military districts (Center, North, South, East, and West), each of which maintained military units under the central bureaucracy's control. By the mid-fifteenth century, the capital army consisted of the Five Guards (Owi), each comprising professional soldiers—including royal guard units stationed at royal palaces and essential state institutions. The most important troops among them were the "armored soldiers" (*kapsa*), recruited through various martial skill tests. Including the armored soldiers, various units among the Five Guards were "in essence a police force rather than a national defense army." Instead, national defense was the task of the regional forces primarily comprising farmer soldiers (Lee 1975, 27–28). Each province had its own army and navy commands, all decentralized. Among them were various special task units, such as border guards and tiger hunters.

The early Chosŏn state continued the late Koryŏ system of the self-sufficient army of farmer soldiers grouped into mutually supporting militia units based on the Tang Chinese *fubing* system. Most soldiers served in garrisons, and when stationed at a military camp or garrison, soldiers were supposed to farm. Only a minority of the troops provided actual military service, as the majority pursued farming to support active-duty soldiers (Lee 1975, 29–30). This arrangement ostensibly provided sustenance, so additional food costs would be low. The more ambitious models even intended military farming to produce a surplus that could be used to finance other state projects. Specialists among the soldiers also engaged in handicrafts to manufacture tools and weapons. Such arrangements supplemented the goods produced for the military under village contracts. The sale of some of the goods the military produced generated additional funds. Nonetheless, the military organization as a whole was a considerable burden on state finances, as expenses for food, clothes, weapons, and fortifications were high—aside from the salaried positions that tended to be sinecures for elites.

Only a relatively small part of the ostensibly self-supported army comprised professional soldiers in permanent units. The military capability of the rest, the farmer-soldier militias, deteriorated in the sixteenth century. In theory, militia units should undergo training and serve as garrison troops, but soldiers were often absent. Beginning in the late fifteenth century, by which Jurchen and Wakō threats had long subsided, Chosŏn Korea, *yangban* generally shunned military obligations by taking advantage of exemptions granted to scholars in preparation for the government service examination. More importantly, tax reforms in the sixteenth century allowed draft-worthy nonelites to secure exemption from military service by submitting military cloth (*kunp'o*) tax and pressured farmers to avoid corvée, shifting this burden to farmer soldiers. Even though corvée was a duty separate from military service under Chosŏn law, the state even used active-duty soldiers for public projects. For farmers, such military corvée became a leading factor in their deteriorating living conditions, resulting in vagrancy and banditry. The Border Defense Council (Pibyŏnsa), set up in 1510 in response to Japanese riots and raids on southern shores, rose to importance in the mid-sixteenth century as a central military planning agency. The council, however, could do little about the overall woeful state of the military, which significantly contributed to the poor performance of Chosŏn's army at the beginning of the Imjin War (Lee 1975, 30–31).

The vulnerability as exposed forced the court to pursue a rapid series of reforms that amounted to streamlining the by-then defunct peasant–soldier system to a hired-solider system (Lee 1975, 2–3). Even though unsystematic, fragmentary in nature, and only partially implemented, these reforms proved decisive for the reorganization of the Chosŏn army for nearly three centuries—until the arrival of Western imperialism in the late nineteenth century. For the most part, the late Chosŏn military employed a semiprofessional army, as the state continued to draft soldiers into militias while utilizing the professional army for other tasks.

The most important feature of these reforms was the recruitment of new-style, paid professional soldiers assigned to the Military Training Agency (Hullyŏn togam). Established in 1593 during the Imjin War, the directorate implemented new organization and training techniques based on the principles developed by a Ming Chinese general Qi Jiguang (1528–88), and the directorate troops emerged as the core of the expanding semiprofessional army of late Chosŏn. The soldiers under the directorate's command were salaried and equipped with muskets and other early modern fire-arms. In effect, they became a model of reform for the rest of the army (Park 2006, 6–7). Not all reforms underwent full implementation, but those put in practice were closely observed—at least in part meeting the state's need for permanent, better-equipped, professional forces.

Underpinning the creation and maintenance of the Military Training Agency was a militia sys-tem of *sogo* army ostensibly conscripting males across status boundaries. Designed in response to the crisis of the Imjin War, the system suffered from many exceptions, and the military service register (*kunjŏk*) was far from a comprehensive record of all non-disabled males. Nonetheless, the *sogo* army was a meaningful first step toward establishing a universal militia system as a founda-tion for national defense. During the war, in 1594, the government required men from all social status groups—*yangban*, commoners, and enslaved people—to enlist for militia units. However, *yangban* and commoners were allowed to send their slaves as substitutes. Militia soldiers received regular training designed according to a system Qi Jiguang laid out in his manual, *New Treatise on Military Efficiency* (*Jixiao xinshu*; 1584), and its later Korean adaptation, *Instructions in Military Study* (*Pyŏnghak chinam*; 1787). The system featured soldiers trained as specialists in one of the three skills (*samsu*)—musketeers (*p'osu*), archers (*sasu*), and close-combat specialists (*salsu*; "killers")—so that the army could employ more effective, mutually supported, combined-arms tactics. The new system was not fully effective as the degree to which local authorities recruited and trained soldiers varied. Nonetheless, the *sogo* army improved the old system, and after the Imjin War, the government retained the system's basic structure. After Chosŏn capitulated to Qing, the *sogo* army underwent further improvement, with military specialists providing improved train-ing and civil officials performing only administrative functions.

Interest in the militia system declined once military tensions in East Asia eased by the late sev-enteenth century with the Qing conquest of China proper. From the outset, *yangban* had always found a way to avoid military service, and Yŏngjo's court also changed the system to exclude com-moners. By the late eighteenth century, the militia comprised only slaves, who mostly performed corvée with virtually no military training. In the nineteenth century, "militia" became synonymous with corvée.

Even the semiprofessional troop units suffered from corruption and mismanagement of tax rev-enue collection and allocation—all chronic problems throughout the late Chosŏn period. Attempts to bring order into the chaos ultimately failed, including Yŏngjo's reforms of 1750, which halved the military cloth levy on taxpayers by shifting much of the burden to formerly exempt, wealthy commoners while *yangban* remained exempt. Aside from the notoriously faulty and corrupt tax system, introducing other taxes seems to have contributed to the failure.

While various problems with the management of the military organization persisted in the absence of external military threats, partisan politics at the court drove military reorganization, entailing the establishment of new military units. For example, in 1626, Injo formed the Royal Defense Command (Suŏch'ŏng) to facilitate the Namhan Fortress's construction and to garrison it. The unit comprised about 1,500 soldiers, and the government gradually expanded and reorganized it to include cavalry and elite guard units. Likewise, the late Chosŏn government strengthened the "palace army" (*kŭmgun*) as a royal guard meant to maintain the safety of the king, who typically appointed a member of the dominant political party in command of the unit. Originating in Koryŏ, the unit had grown from a small guard of around 300 men in the fifteenth century to a more for-midable military force of about 1,200 men in the seventeenth century. In late Chosŏn, the palace

The Routledge Handbook of Early Modern Korea

army underwent much change, but protecting the king in and outside the royal palaces remained its primary duty. The palace army ostensibly recruited only the top tiers of military examination passers, but in reality, the unit drew from military examination graduates as a whole.

The politicization of the military organization centered around the throne and partisan interests culminated with Chŏngjo's Robust Brave Division (Changyongyŏng). In 1793, Chŏngjo, who arguably ruled as the most powerful Chosŏn monarch since officialdom had deposed despotic King Yŏnsan Kun (r. 1495–1506), established the Robust Brave Division in his ongoing efforts to strengthen his position vis-à-vis the Faction of Principle (Pyŏkp'a), among the paramount Patriarchs, as they continued to challenge Chŏngjo's royal legitimacy. The monarch limited recruitment for the Robust Brave Division to mostly military examination passers and garrisoned the division in Hwasŏng, which he developed as the kingdom's future capital in place of Hansŏng, where the Faction of Principle *yangban* families were entrenched. Upon his death, a series of monarchs ascended the throne as minor or unprepared (1800–64), and the court dominated by a few powerful royal consort families undid his measures, including the Robust Brave Division (abolished in 1802). In fact, with the end of partisan strife, military reorganization, too, more or less ceased. Nonetheless, many, especially those affiliated with marginalized parties, continued to explore new ideas on military technology and tactics.

Military Technology, Tactics, and Texts

The Chosŏn state and scholars alike were interested in military matters, albeit the level of interest fluctuated. They likely wrote about warfare and tactics based on experience and relevant earlier Chinese works such as *Sunzi's Military Method* (*The Art of War*; *Sunzi bingfa*). No pre-Chosŏn Korean military text is extant, but in Koryŏ, elites read and wrote military texts (Chŏng 2004, 37f). Continuing the tradition, Chosŏn reformers explored old and new ideas on military organization, economy, and politics. Among the so-called Practical Learning (Sirhak) scholars, sundry aspects of military technology attracted much attention. All the same, the official commemorative texts of the "ritual protocols" (*ŭigwe*) type commissioned by the court bear witness to the high prestige that some military events enjoyed. For example, the 1743 *Grand Ritual Protocols* (*Taesarye ŭigwe*) describes the ritual archery contest reinstalled by Yŏngjo (Chŏng 2008, 23–36). The 1801 *Hwasŏng City Wall Construction Protocols* (*Hwasŏng sŏngyŏk ŭigwe*) describes Chŏngjo's new capital project in detail (Chŏng 2004, 324–36; Pölking 2017). For a better understanding of the post-Imjin War military texts of Chosŏn, first, an overview of its military installations, technology, and tactics is in order.

Chosŏn's military system maintained an elaborate network of communication lines. Constituting its backbone were chains of beacon fires that enabled relaying any urgent matter from the kingdom's shore or northern border to Hansŏng. Also, a messenger system allowed a rapid transmission of written messages nationwide. Along the way, each relay station provided the necessary dispatchers, support personnel, horses, and other resources to keep the system operating. Not purely military facilities, such relay stations also provided lodging for traveling officials and transmitted non-military information to elites.

Another vital aspect of Chosŏn's military system featured "mountain fortresses" (*sansŏng*), usually on hilltops. Fortresses were supposed to function as strong points where the population could take refuge and from where defense and counter-attacks could be organized against an enemy force, whether rebels or foreign invaders. For example, during the Pyŏngja War (1637), 13,000 troops manned the Namhan Fortress with provision for 50 days. Surrounded by a sea of Qing army, though, all attempts to break the siege failed, and the court capitulated to Qing with just five days' worth of food left.

For battles on land and at seas alike, an essential element of Chosŏn military technology was gunpowder weaponry. First produced in the late fourteenth century by Ch'oe Musŏn (1325–95), the majority of early gunpowder weapons were of heavy artillery type, mainly cannons, supplemented by less important "fire carts" (*hwach'a*), early multiple rocket launchers. Handguns, too, saw deployment, but their role was relatively minor. The use of the European-style muskets introduced in the late sixteenth century spread quickly during the Imjin War when the Japanese musketeers initially terrorized and overwhelmed Korean troops. As new weapons, the muskets became the most important infantry weapon for Chosŏn—even becoming a required component of a comprehensive military examination (distinct from simpler ones emphasizing archery).

Firearms contributed to Chosŏn's adoption of heavier armament for warships. Most commonly deployed were "plank-structure ships" (*p'anoksŏn*), each built as squarish, not particularly agile but sturdy platforms for gunnery and with high walls to provide an advantage in close combat. A specialized warship, of which the navy seems to have produced only a limited number, was the "turtle ship" (*kusŏn, kwisŏn, kŏbuksŏn*). As assault vessels, turtle ships were fully covered to attack enemy ships and to protect the crew from close combat with the Japanese, generally recognized as expert sworders. Scholars debate whether turtle ships were steel-plated and were an early form of dreadnought (Bak 1977). Also, their actual combat value is not clear, but regardless, turtle ships are an important symbol of national pride in contemporary Korea, North and South.

All the same, archers and close-quarters fighters retained their traditional prominence much throughout Chosŏn's history. Much of the weaponry component of a comprehensive military examination continued to test a candidate's skills in a wide range of archery types but no sword-wielding. Like bows and arrows, close combat weapons per se changed little during Chosŏn's history. However, the deployment method of sworders underwent modification thanks to Qi Jiguang's organizational and training techniques featuring a mix of musketeers, archers, and close-combat specialists, as discussed above. Adopting Japanese weapons and fighting methods during the Imjin War also influenced sword-fighting.

Encompassing material and tactical concerns, knowledge of military literature was useful for individuals and the state. Above all, the continuing appreciation for literary knowledge in Chinese civilization inspired the production of texts important in Korean literary discourse. Such Sino–Korean continuity was especially true for texts understood as part of a direct lineage to Chinese antiquity, including the military texts. Accordingly, the king and his officials discussed such works in ways that presented an opportunity to enter and manipulate the Chosŏn elite's discourse on a full range of topics. Some monarchs, such as Chŏngjo, were interested in military affairs and would listen to military text authors. As Chinese texts played an important role, they provided models that formed a substantial part of late Chosŏn military literature (Siegmund 2018).

The consequences of the lack of the Chosŏn army's preparedness, as exposed during the Imjin War, spurred a radical change based on Qi Jiguang's military techniques, as discussed above. His ideas influenced late Chosŏn military thought through two works: the *New Treatise on Military Efficiency*, introduced to Korea in 1593 or earlier (Chŏng 2004, 219, 2008, 108), and the *Record of Military Training* (*Lianbing shiji*; 1571), introduced in the sixteenth or seventeenth century. As presented in both works, Qi Jiguang's system emphasized squads with mixed weapons and mutually supporting units. Deploying such troops required an efficient organization and special training in weaponry and inter-unit coordination. The system also demanded incorporating support from ranged weapons—bows and firearms—into fighting tactics. For various reasons, a direct application of the system to Korea proved impracticable.

Instead, Qi Jiguang's ideas wielded a lasting influence through shortened Chosŏn adaptions, especially the most successful one, the *Instructions in Military Study* mentioned above. Enjoying

The Routledge Handbook of Early Modern Korea

popularity, the text appeared in many editions difficult to date. Various editions of the *Instructions in Military Study* had become so convoluted that in 1787, Chŏngjo's court saw the need to produce an official version (Chŏng 2004, 219–20). The work comprises five chapters explaining command words and signals, training methods, formations, and the organization of infantry, cavalry, and war-wagon units. Reflecting overall successful applicability, the *Instructions in Military Study* remained an authoritative text providing an essential basis for military training and organization until the nineteenth century.

Adaptations of Qi Jiguang's works appeared, all of the more limited influence. These texts include the *Abridged New Treatise on Military Efficiency* (*Kihyo sinsŏ chŏryo*; completed by 1602) (Chŏng 2008, 81–91); Han Hyosun's (1543–1621) *Exposition on Formations* (*Chinsŏl*; 1603), which drew from the *New Treatise on Military Efficiency* but also incorporated ideas from other military treatises (Chŏng 2008, 92–107); the *Record of Protocols* (*Holgi*; 1652) by Ming refugee in Korea, Li Yuan (Ko. Yi Wŏn) (Chŏng 2008, 125–37); Ch'oe Suk's (1646–1708) *Formation Methods in Korean Vernacular* (*Chinpŏp ŏnhae*; 1693) (Chŏng 2008, 138–49); the *Extended Meaning of Instructions in Military Study* (*Pyŏnghak chinam yŏnŭi*; 1798) by Yi Sangjŏng (Chŏng 2004, 232–40); and the *Mastery of Military Study* (*Pyŏnghak t'ong*; 1785), compiled on Chŏngjo's order and at least partially based on the *Instructions in Military Study* (Chŏng 2004, 198–211). Readapting Qi Jiguang's *Record of Military Training*, Han Kyo's (1556–1627) *Instructions in Military Training* (*Yŏnbyŏng chinam*; 1612) introduced fighting techniques for the combined use of infantry, cavalry, and war wagons—all meant to counter to the Jurchen cavalry at the time (Chŏng 2008, 108–24). Some texts explicated the *Instructions in Military Study*, such as aforementioned Ch'oe Suk's *Instructions in Military Study in Korean Vernacular* (*Pyŏnghak chinam ŏnhae*; 1684) (Chŏng 2008, 438–47), Kim Sŏngok's (fl. eighteenth century) *Annotated Instructions in Military Study* (*Pyŏnghak chinam chusŏk*), which is partly in Korean (Chŏng 2008, 425–37), and the *Annotated Instructions in Military Study* (*Pyŏnghak chinam chuhae*) (Chŏng 2008, 448–62).

Outside the Qi Jiguang tradition, various post–Imjin War texts of Chosŏn provided a multifaceted exposition of military affairs. Among them, the *Essentials of Marching Formations* (*Haenggun suji*; 1679) by Minister of War Kim Sŏkchu (1634–84) consists of outtakes from Song dynasty (960–1279) China's *Complete Essentials for the Military Classics* (*Wujing zongyao*; c. 1040–44). Recognizing that additional knowledge of military theory was necessary, Kim Sŏkchu intended the work to supplement the *Instructions in Military Study* (Chŏng 2004, 385–95). Published seven decades later, the *Updated Illustrated Exposition on Military Training and Tactics* (*Sok pyŏngjang tosŏl*; 1749) was a revision of the earlier *Illustrated Exposition on Military Training and Tactics* (*Pyŏngjang tosŏl*; 1492), reflecting the changes Chosŏn's military organization had undergone since the fifteenth century. Providing an overview of military organization, command structure, and formations, the text includes relevant diagrams (*to*) (Chŏng 2004, 186–88). A generation later, a more forward-looking work, the *Echoes amidst Winds and Springs* (*P'ungch'ŏn yuhyang*; 1778), by a military man, Song Kyubin (1696–1778), advocated a military reform. Arguing mostly by historical analogy, the text urged a wholesale change encompassing, among others, fortifications, organization, tactics, armament, and logistics (Chŏng 2008, 279–96). A late text of encyclopedic character is the *Essentials of Military Texts* (*Yungsŏ ch'waryo*; 1867), generally attributed to Sin Hŏn (1810–84), an erudite military aristocrat (Figure 6.1). He summarized a wealth of information from Chinese and Korean military texts, including most aspects of military affairs. Sin's work also features many illustrations, maps, and diagrams (Park 2007, 139–40; Chŏng 2008, 309–23).

Other post–Imjin War Chosŏn military texts focused on a particular topic, such as military equipment. The *Secrets of New Weaponry* (*Sin'gi pigyŏl*; 1603) by Han Hyosun is a manual on firearms and their usage. The text includes a description of new-style muskets, which played

Figure 6.1 Portrait of Sin Hŏn at 61, 1870. Source: Korea University Museum. Photo credit: Eggmoon via Wikimedia Commons.

a prominent role during the Imjin War (Chŏng 2004, 243–56). Another firearms manual is the *Fire Arms Methods in Korean Vernacular* (*Hwap'osik ŏnhae*; 1635), which describes the loading and firing of various types of guns (Chŏng 2004, 267–82). Compiled in the same year, the *New Transmission of Gunpower Preparation Methods in Korean Vernacular* (*Sinjŏn chach'wi yŏmch'o pang ŏnhae*; 1635) offers an overview of sundry aspects of gunpowder preparation (Chŏng 2004, 284–93). Published some six decades later, the *New Transmission of Gunpowder Preparation Methods* (*Sinjŏn chach'o pang*; 1698) by Kim Chinam (1654–1718), a polymath interpreter, describes improved techniques of production (Chŏng 2004, 294–306). Published a century later in the aftermath of the Hong Kyŏngnae rebellion, in which the government troops did not perform well, the *Required Preparations for Military Division Commanders* (*Yungwŏn p'ilbi*; 1813)

The Routledge Handbook of Early Modern Korea

by Pak Chonggyŏng (1765–1817) explains weapon use, especially firearms of all sizes (Chŏng 2008, 217–38). The *Illustrated Exposition on Equipment of Armament of the Training Directorate* (*Hun'guk sinjo kun'gi tosŏl*; c. 1869) and the Illustrated *Exposition on Equipment of the Military Training Agency* (*Hun'guk sinjo kigye tosŏl*; c. 1871) review the various types of weapons, primarily firearms, produced in the eighteenth and nineteenth centuries by the Directorate (Chŏng 2008, 239–65).

Mindful of those wielding weapons, many post-Imjin War military texts of Chosŏn discussed fighting techniques. The oldest extant Korean manual of its kind, the *Lineages of Martial Art* (*Muye chebo*; 1598) by the aforementioned Han Kyo, described fighting techniques against the Japanese. Taking much of its materials from Qi Jiguang's *New Treatise on Military Efficiency* (Chŏng 2004, 339–50; Pratt 2000), the *Lineages of Martial Art* inspired subsequent revisions. Compiled by Ch'oe Kinam (1559–1619) a little over a decade later, the *Revised Lineages of Martial Art in Translation* (*Muye chebo pŏnyŏk sokchip*; 1610) featured a description of additional fighting techniques and also included unarmed fighting techniques (Chŏng 2004, 351–61). Then, nearly two centuries later, Chŏngjo commissioned the last revision, the *Comprehensive Illustrated Manual of Martial Arts (Muye tobo t'ongji*; 1790), which included and further explained cavalry fighting techniques (Chŏng 2004, 362–82).

Some post–Imjin military texts of Chosŏn dealt with physical installations connected to fighting techniques, especially the construction and organization of fortifications. Commissioned by Chŏngjo, the *Study of Fortification Systems* (*Sŏngje ko*; 1794) quotes extensively from such Ming Chinese sources as Qi Jiguang's *New Treatise on Military Efficiency* and Mao Yuanyi's (1594–1640?) *Treatise on Armament Technology* (*Wubei Zhi*; 1621) (Chŏng 2004, 311–23). In comparison, the *Discussion of People's Fortifications* (*Minbo ŭi*; 1812) by a celebrated polymath, Chŏng Yagyong (1762–1836), is a more political text, describing an ideal system of military organization in which fortifications relying on organization and mobilization of well-prepared general population feature prominently (Chŏng 2004, 471–89). Some five decades later, the aforementioned Sin Hŏn authored *Collected Explanations of People's Fortifications* (*Minbo chipsŏl*; 1867). Concerned about the arrival of Western imperialism in East Asia by then, Sin Hŏn proposed a system of defensive fortifications—fully mobilizing a well-prepared population—to counter this threat (Chŏng 2004, 490–501). Similar texts also published in the late nineteenth century include *New Compact on People's Fortifications* (*Minbo sinyak*) and the *New Edition on People's Fortifications* (*Minbo sinp'yŏn*) by Chu Hŭisang (1831–87) (Chŏng 2004, 505–07, 508–11).

All the same, the military's prominent personnel and their indispensable companions, horses, received ample coverage by various late Chosŏn military texts. Among them, the *Biographies of Famed Korean Generals* (*Haedong myŏngjang chŏn*; 1794) by Hong Yangho (1724–1802) is a record of 55 exemplary military commanders from the Three Kingdoms period to the seventeenth century (Chŏng 2004, 458–67). The text is based on Chinese models of biographies of generals, such as the *Biography of Hundred Generals* (*Baijiang zhuan*) by Zhang Yu of Song dynasty China. In contrast, the *Comprehensive Essentials on the Military Examination* (*Mukwa ch'ongyo*; 1810) by Im Inmuk (fl. 1789–1810) provides detailed information on the organization of military state examinations (Chŏng 2008, 49–63). Regardless of rank, Chosŏn military men valued horses. The hippological treatise, the *Collected Essentials of the Classic of Hippology in Korean Vernacular* (*Magyŏng ch'ojip ŏnhae*; 1630s), by Yi Sŏ (1580–1637) draws from a Ming work, the *Encyclopedic Classic of Hippology* (*Majing daquan*; 1608), providing information on various aspects of horse breeding and care (Chŏng 2008, 167–81).

The Military

Final Thoughts

Early Chosŏn had little trouble with military preparedness. After a brief period of tension, Chosŏn–Ming relations stabilized, with Chosŏn accepting the role of a loyal tributary under the protection and guidance of the suzerain Ming state. Also, no serious external threat threatened Chosŏn. The military personnel were constantly engaged in border-guard duties, so the Wakō were relatively easy to keep in check. Moreover, Chosŏn acted aggressively towards its northern neighbors, attacking the Jurchens, conquering their lands, and incorporating them into the kingdom.

From the late fifteenth century, when a real external threat vanished, military preparedness eroded. Initially suffering annihilation by the invading Japanese, Chosŏn barely survived the Imjin War thanks to the Ming intervention. Two subsequent invasions by the Jurchens, who renamed themselves Manchu and went on to conquer Ming China, again exposed the Chosŏn military's weaknesses.

Despite the military reforms initiated during the Imjin War and any lessons Chosŏn should have drawn from the turn of the seventeenth-century conflicts, its military remained weak. Above all, maintaining a sizable standing army, a partly standing army, or an army of any sort proved financially burdensome to a state that relied on a clunky tax-collection system. Perhaps unsurprisingly, the more than two centuries of peace once Chosŏn normalized relations with Qing China and Tokugawa Japan (1603–1868) gave the Chosŏn state little incentive to maintain anything more than an army strong enough to suppress an internal disturbance. As a result, the army remained understaffed, minimally equipped, and poorly paid. Chronic corruption and poor leadership were among the reasons for this lack of funding and the irregularities in the system.

Ultimately, the late Chosŏn military system, likely no more than 30,000 combat-worthy troops, crumbled away in the late nineteenth century as Korea weathered the pressures of imperialism. Confronted with Western military forces and the modernizing military of Meiji Japan (1868–1912), Chosŏn's military underwent modernization, beginning with some 80 troops comprising the Special Skills Force (Pyŏlgigun) formed in 1881. By 1904, the accelerating military reform was maintaining the Imperial Korean Army of some 28,000 soldiers trained in modern weapons and tactics, but this was not enough. Japan fielded more than 200,000 troops at the onset of the Russo–Japanese War (1904–5)—immediately occupying Korea, turning it into a protectorate (1905), and disbanding the Imperial Korean Army (1907).

References

Bak, Hae-ill. 1977. "A Short Note on the Iron-clad Turtle-boats of Admiral Yi Sun-sin." *Korea Journal* 17, no. 1: 34–39.

Chŏng Haeŭn. 2004. *Han'guk chŏnt'ong pyŏngsŏ ŭi ihae*. Kukpangbu Kunsa p'yŏnch'an yŏn'guwŏn.

Chŏng Haeŭn. 2008. *Han'guk chŏnt'ong pyŏngsŏ ŭi ihae*. Volume II. Kukpangbu Kunsa p'yŏnch'an yŏn'guwŏn.

Haboush, JaHyun Kim. 2016. *The Great East Asian War and the Birth of the Korean Nation*. Edited by William J. Haboush and Jisoo M. Kim. Columbia University Press.

Jackson, Andrew David. 2016. *The 1728 Musin Rebellion: Politics and Plotting in Eighteenth-Century Korea*. University of Hawai'i Press.

Kim, Sun Joo. 2007. *Marginality and Subversion in Korea: The Hong Kyŏngnae Rebellion*. University of Washington Press.

Lee, Kibaek. 1975. "Korea: The Military Tradition." In *The Traditional Culture and Society of Korea, Thought and Institutions: Papers of the International Conference on Traditional Korean Culture and Society*, edited by Hugh H. W. Kang, 1–42. Center for Korean Studies, University of Hawai'i.

Lewis, James B., ed. 2015. *The East Asian War, 1592–1598: International Relations, Violence, and Memory*. Routledge.

Park, Eugene Y. 2006. "War and Peace in Premodern Korea: Institutional and Ideological Dimensions." In *The Military and South Korean Society*, edited by Young-Key Kim-Renaud, R. Richard Grinker, and Kirk W. Larsen, 1–13. Sigur Center for Asian Studies, George Washington University.

Park, Eugene Y. 2007. *Between Dreams and Reality: The Military Examination in Late Chosŏn Korea, 1600–1894*. Harvard University Asia Center.

Pölking, Florian. 2017. "The Status of the Hwaseong seongyeok uigwe in the History of Architectural Knowledge: Documentation, Innovation, Tradition." *Han'guk kwahaksa hakhoeji* 39, no. 2: 257–91.

Pratt, Andrew. 2000. "Change and Continuity in Chosŏn Military Techniques During the Later Chosŏn Period." *Papers of the British Association for Korean Studies* 7: 31–48.

Siegmund, Felix. 2018. *Theorie und Praxis militärischen Wissens zwischen China und Korea im langen 17. Jahrhundert: Qi Jiguangs militärische Schriften und die nordöstliche Grenzregion*. Harrassowitz.

Swope, Kenneth M. 2009. *A Dragon's Head and a Serpent's Tail: Ming China and the First Great East Asian War, 1592–1598*. University of Oklahoma Press.

Tikhonov, Vladimir. 1998. "*Hwawang* Organization: Its Functions and Ethics." *Korea Journal* (Summer): 318–38.

7

DISCONTENT

Andrew David Jackson

Popular discontent occupies a central place in the core Confucian political notions that the founders of the Chosŏn state (1392–1897) used to justify their rule.[1] Yi Sŏnggye (1335–1408; King T'aejo, r. 1392–98) legitimized his seizure of power with the notion of the Mandate of Heaven (*ch'ŏnmyŏng*), which dictated that kings should be men of virtue who set a moral example. Upon accession, T'aejo ordered: "Capture the hearts of the people so that they should not rise up against them" (Choi 2014, 363). According to Confucian notions, rulers should act in the interests of their subjects, and the people had the right to rebel against unjust governance (Dillon 1998, 209). Alleging that immoral and unscrupulous men had dominated the Koryŏ state (918–1392) in its final years, T'aejo felt obligated to take the throne to restore social and political harmony (Duncan 2000, 3). Chosŏn's monarchs were mindful of the philosophical justification for their rule. Anger about injustice and corruption was the death knell for Koryŏ, and discontent could just as easily help bring down Chosŏn, ruler as the recipient of the Mandate of Heaven.

This chapter investigates the causes of discontent and how the people responded to anger in early modern Korea. Discussions of elites' and nonelites' discontent focus on political dissent rather than artistic protest or everyday resistance (Korea Historical Research Association 2005, 130). During certain periods, protests, social unrest (such as banditry), and organized rebellions intensified, producing the geographical fault lines where dissent was most severe. Several assumptions guide this chapter. Above all, discontent is never the sole cause of contention. Other variables, such as the geopolitical context and regional and community solidarities, influence anger (Goldstone 2014). Also, discontent elicits not a uniform response but rather an assortment of reactions that customary, political, and ecological variables condition. Moreover, a common binary of *chŏngbyŏn* (coup) versus *millan* ("popular uprising") defies the complexity of expressions of discontent in Chosŏn. The binary distinguishes *chŏngbyŏn*, as a product of power struggle within the ruling class, from a *millan* as the bottom-up expression of discontent from disenfranchised masses (*minjung*) aimed at transforming society. In reality, though, both involved the broad participation of large sections of society. Accordingly, a fuller understanding of discontent and dissent requires examining both elite-led attempts at power and popular uprisings.

A lot of things angered the population in Chosŏn, particularly excessive taxation, periods of food scarcity, and social and political discrimination. Life for rural farmers was particularly challenging, exacerbated by periodic crop failures and natural disasters (Sang Kwon Han 2014, 181).

DOI: 10.4324/9781003262053-10

The Routledge Handbook of Early Modern Korea

Another persistent source of anger amongst the impoverished was taxation. Three forms of taxation overburdened commoners—a land tax, conscripted labor, and a household tax (paid in locally produced goods) (Palais 1996, 47; Korea Historical Research Association 2005, 100; Sung Woo Kim 2014, 61). Evidence of the systematic problems is manifest in the frequent attempts to reform the taxation system, beginning with King Sejong's (r. 1418–50) land tax reduction from ten to five percent of the harvest (Ki-baik Lee 1984, 184, 203). Such efforts typically did little to alleviate their hardships (Korea Historical Research Association 2005, 101). Corruption within the tax system was endemic and worsened the situation for many. Officials frequently embezzled goods they rejected as tax payments, ostensibly for inferior quality (Sung Woo Kim 2014, 65). Ultimately, taxpayers had to submit additional items to replace those officials had stolen. In 1723, the Ch'ungch'ŏng Province governor estimated that the average taxpayer was being assessed four times the amount of tax they could bear (Haboush 1988, 102–05).

In addition to financial hardships, social discrimination impacted the lives of Koreans. *Paekchŏng* (outcasts), legally commoners but socially the "lowborn," suffered cradle-to-grave prejudices because of their work in socially denigrated occupations. Among them were butchers, tanners, leatherworkers, and gravediggers (Sang Kwon Han 2014, 181). However, it was not just the lowborns who suffered from social prejudices. In Chosŏn, as in late imperial China, officeholding in the central government was the key to power, bringing recognition, authority, and wealth, and a preoccupation with gaining and maintaining social status was widespread (Kuhn 1970, 8–9; Deuchler 1997, 303–04). Discriminatory practices blocked the route to officeholding for certain groups, including illegitimate sons (*sŏŏl*) of *yangban* fathers. Because their mother was a commoner or a lowborn, laws and social conventions denied them the full benefits of *yangban* status (Deuchler 1997, 302; Lovins 2014, 5). Thus, in terms of contention, economic hardship and social and political discrimination certainly did not afflict Koreans equally at all times or in all areas of the peninsula.

Challengers from the North, 1392–1583

In early Chosŏn, the northern regions of Korea showed the clearest indications of anger and social volatility. The instability and discontent in the north were rooted in its geopolitical transformations during the Koryŏ–Chosŏn transition, a time of upheaval in East Asia, if not the entire post-Mongol Eurasia. Rebellions broke out in China against the Mongol Yuan dynasty (1271–1368). The collapse of Mongol power and the rise of the Ming dynasty (1368–1644) impacted the Koryŏ court, which split into pro-Yuan and pro-Ming factions. Ming–Yuan clashes (1368–88) also occurred in Manchuria, creating instability in the northern border regions of Koryŏ (Duncan 2000, 175). T'aejo, who had ascended the throne from his family base in northeastern Korea, attempted to consolidate his control over the entire Korean Peninsula by incorporating the lands stretching up to the Tumen (Ko. Tuman) River into a greater Chosŏn. Strategically, this was a vital area of the country since it bordered Korea's most important regional neighbor and trading partner, Ming China. T'aejo, however, faced strong resistance from the Jurchens, who frequently raided this area. Ultimately, the Chosŏn founder could not "pacify" the region, not only because the security challenges the Jurchens posed were too formidable but also because he faced internal court conspiracies (Choi 2014, 231, 831–45). Assertion of central authority over the area was left up to his successors, including Sejong, to achieve.

Sejong followed a three-pronged carrot-and-stick strategy to keep the northern regions under control. Launching military campaigns against the Jurchens, he established garrison forts to pacify the population, mobilized local farmers to construct fortifications, and restricted the move-

Discontent

ment of the Jurchens to exert further central control (Robinson 1992, 100). At the same time, the king incentivized open trading relations with the Jurchens to win them over through profit. Those Jurchens who pledged allegiance to the throne received court ranks and offices (Ki-baik Lee 1984, 191). Sejong also established a colonization policy by settling Koreans from southern provinces in borderland areas. Finally, the authorities encouraged intermarriage between Koreans and Jurchen to blur cultural and ethnic identities that they saw as obstacles to stability and friendlier relations.

An unintended consequence of attempts to exert greater centralized control over the area was growing discontent amongst northern elites and nonelites. Concerned that the breakdowns in security resulted from the inefficient implementation of central policy by local administrators, King Sejo (r. 1455–68) reduced the number of locally recruited officials and dispatched more replacements directly from the capital Hansŏng (present-day Seoul) to govern the area. The center's distrust of indigenous officeholders fed into broader prejudices against northern elites, and over time, discrimination would intensify against men from the provinces of the north. Central and southern *yangban*, who monopolized court positions in early Chosŏn, considered northerners less erudite, if not uncivilized.

People who migrated to the north from southern provinces were often reluctant to do so and were frequently coerced (Choi 2014, 554). To improve security by controlling the movements of commoners, Sejo introduced the *hop'ae* ("household tally"; identification tag) system. This disadvantaged ordinary people but also incensed elites, who believed the *hop'ae* system directly threatened their interests because it meant they had less control over commoners. The tax burden was particularly problematic in parts of the north, such as Hwanghae Province, with less arable land than other parts of the Korean Peninsula. Despite the lower crop productivity, the tax extraction remained high as centrally appointed local officials sought revenue to meet the region's greater security needs. Nor did such indirect taxation as corvée or mandatory military service arouse less resentment. In certain areas, particularly those bordering Ming China and the Jurchens, officials required farmers to perform sentry duty and construct fortifications, thus taking time away from them from tending their plots (Sang Kwon Han 2014, 182–83). Unable to meet these tax or corvée burdens, struggling farmers fled their land (Sung Woo Kim 2014, 64). Thus, efforts at pacification, which continued through the reigns of Kings T'aejong (r. 1400–18) and Sejong, partly exacerbated the conditions of many commoners and frustrated the local elite. Northern frontier regions remained the Achilles' heel of early Chosŏn security.

With smoldering dissent, the early Chosŏn north became the site of significant challenges to central rule—either led by or at least involving the Jurchens. In 1402, Cho Saŭi (d. 1402), the magistrate of Anbyŏn, mobilized his local troops against the throne and achieved some initial success by defeating government troops dispatched from the capital. In 1453, a military commander from the region, Yi Chingok (1399–1453), mobilized forces, including Jurchen tribes, against central authority. Yi declared the founding of a new state and seized territory before the government troops snuffed out his challenge. In 1467, another local official, Yi Siae (d. 1467), followed in the footsteps of Cho Saŭi and Yi Chingok by mobilizing a combination of royal troops and farmer conscripts before suppression in three months. Yi Siae, too, sought out Jurchen support. All these rebellions were launched by officials ostensibly dissatisfied with their rank. The rebel leaders were in positions that allowed them to mobilize their troops against the throne. It is rather unlikely that they took their cues from Yi Sŏnggye's seizure of power. Evidently, they took advantage of their geography and popular local grievances to rally a rebel army against central state authority. These rebels drew on the support of local agricultural colonists from the south, angered by the excessive taxation demands (Ki-baik Lee 1984, 184). The challengers also received the support of the Jurchens, laying bare the limits of central authority. The distance from Hansŏng meant the

The Routledge Handbook of Early Modern Korea

rebels could amass material and men in a relatively short period and use them until the central government's suppression forces could be sent to crush the threat. The rebellions established a tactical and geographical precedent that would reappear throughout Chosŏn's history. In subsequent attempts at power, rebel-turned-officials used their state resources (weapons and conscripted troops) against the central authority.

A further challenge to security in the north came from the activities of local bandits. Perhaps the most well-known was Im Kkŏkchŏng (d. 1562), who pursued his marauding activities between 1559–62 in northern Hwanghae Province (Ki-baik Lee 1984, 203–04). Using guerilla tactics well-suited to mountainous areas, he launched hit-and-run raids in small groups of eight to ten on local officials and then melted in with the population. Remote local administrative positions were often lightly defended but proved to be an abundant source of material—weapons and tax payments. Legends arose about Im—about how he robbed and murdered corrupt officials and redistributed their wealth to the poor. Im, a former paekchŏng, has captured the imagination of Marxist historians and the Korean public, North and South, who have imagined Im, along with the fictional Hong Kiltong, as "righteous bandits" (*ŭijŏk*). The concept is controversial in historiography since scholars differ over whether banditry should be understood as principled resistance or a rational response to predatory states. Regardless, the actions of Im's band are significant for understanding discontent in early modern Korea. Im's bandits made certain areas of Hwanghae virtual no-go areas for government troops for three years. Since Im's forces largely comprised poor farmers who abandoned their plots to escape state-enforced extraction, the strength and duration of their banditry is a barometer of the widespread discontent in the region. Although Im provided a significant security scare for the court, his forces were eventually overwhelmed (Sang Kwon Han 2014, 181–88).

For almost two centuries, the north remained a security headache for the central government. Discontented local officials and bandit leaders used the widespread resentment among farmers and a disenfranchised Jurchen population to form their armies. The region's remoteness also proved advantageous for challengers. Eventually, a combination of the center's assimilation policy and economic incentives improved relations with the Jurchens and helped stabilize the area (Robinson 1992, 110). The Jurchen Nit'anggae's rebellion in 1583 was the last of the major conflicts between central authority and the early Chosŏn north (Ki-baik Lee 1984, 190–91). The locus of conflict shifted to the court and the southern provinces of Korea.

Mid-Chosŏn Geopolitical Changes and Political Turmoil, 1583–1728

A complex combination of factionalism at court and shifting allegiances over the protracted Ming–Qing transition (1616–44) intensified political contention in mid-Chosŏn Korea. The factional conflict began to exclude an increasing segment of the *yangban* population from officialdom—a process that soon turned into a primary source of discontent amongst ruling elites. The ostensible start of factionalism was the 1574 dispute over official appointments in the reign of King Sŏnjo (1567–1608). From that moment on, factions—assuming their names from the location of their leaders' residences in the capital—essentially operated as "political associations on a quest for power" (Haboush 1988, 119). These organizations dominated the court because of merciless competition from an increasing number of qualified candidates for an effectively fixed number of governmental positions (Haboush 1988, 91). Within the cutthroat atmosphere of officialdom, factions protected their supporter's interests by helping them gain office. Gaining their authority in court by supporting the king in policy disputes, factions adopted positions based on moral positions. They

Discontent

regarded policy compromise with rivals not as a pragmatic solution to preserve harmony and serve the court's interests but rather as an unforgivable betrayal of ideological positions.

A new source of contention within the court arose over loyalty to the declining Ming. During the reign of King Kwanghae Kun (r. 1608–23), Chosŏn was drawn into the conflict erupting in China. A beleaguered Ming suzerain called on its Chosŏn vassal to help defend Beijing, the imperial capital, against the ascendant Jurchens. Earlier, during the Imjin War (East Asian War; 1592–98), Ming had protected Chosŏn from the invading Japanese. Kwanghae Kun, backed by the Northerner (Pugin) faction, adopted a pragmatic, non-committal approach when faced with the conflict of two mighty neighbors to maintain Chosŏn sovereignty (Ki-baik Lee 1984, 215). Kwanghae Kun's strategy of appeasing both Ming and the Jurchens was deeply unpopular with many Chosŏn literati who regarded the Jurchens (self-renamed Manchus in 1635) as barbarian marauders. Ming loyalist elites associated with the Westerner (Sŏin) party saw themselves as guardians of civilization, and their rejection of the Jurchen-founded Later Jin dynasty (1616–1912; self-renamed Qing in 1636) was a source of ideological purity. Pro-Ming factional forces overthrew Kwanghae Kun in a coup and elevated King Injo (r. 1623–49).

The capitulation of Injo's court to Qing (1637) forced Chosŏn to transfer its loyalty as a vassal from Ming to Qing, thus acknowledging the latter as the new masters of the Sinitic world order. Subsequently, Injo trod a careful path between not appearing to insult the powerful Qing while at the same time retaining a pro-Ming stance in Chosŏn so as not to upset influential anti-Qing groups among his subjects. Anti-Qing sentiment was not limited to ruling Chosŏn elites but was more widespread, partly because of rusticated literati (*sallim*) who were locally influential (Sunah Lee 2008, 16–17). The recent experience of two cataclysmic punitive invasions by Qing forces intensified animosity towards the new rulers of China (Ki-baik Lee 1984, 215).

A perusal of the 25 meritorious subject (*kongsin*) titles awarded over the first 350 years of Chosŏn's history reveals that nine of these, almost 40 percent, were granted between 1613 and 1644 (Pratt and Rutt 1999, 284). Many were given by monarchs to subjects who defended them against conspiracies. Between 1623 and 1646, officials made no fewer than seven large-scale attempts to overthrow reigning monarchs, and most, if not all, stemmed from factional interests. These included the rebellions of Yi Kwal (1624), Yi In'gŏ (1627), Yi Hyorip (1628), and Sim Kiwŏn (1644)—all led by officials who had once fought for Injo during his seizure of power and had received high offices as rewards. Yet, they subsequently turned against their former benefactor. Historians have emphasized that, in most cases, the primary motivation was dissatisfaction with their rank. These power attempts were also wrapped up in the complex geopolitical realities of the Ming–Qing transition, in which the court trod a careful path between unofficially embracing the popular sentiment of revering Ming and rejecting Qing while cooperating fully with the Qing rulers (Sunah Lee 2008, 8–9). A representative case was the 1646 An Iksin Rebellion—one of the most significant challenges to central authority during the political instability that followed the 1623 coup that had overthrown Kwanghae Kun and elevated Injo.

An Iksin's Rebellion is closely linked to the 1644 attempt to overthrow Injo by a pro-Ming loyalist, Sim Kiwŏn. Sim had actively supported Injo's accession and fought loyally for the throne during subsequent challenges against Injo. Sim controlled significant military resources as a high official, especially in Ch'ungch'ŏng Province. Eventually, however, he split from the monarch, asserting that the court should adopt a more aggressively anti-Qing stance. In 1644, Qing finally took the Ming capital, Beijing, which generated unrest in Chosŏn. Among others, alleged sightings of Ming ships in coastal areas gave ordinary people the impression of further incursions from the Chinese mainland (Sunah Lee 2008, 8–9). Sim used the sightings as the pretext to mobilize troops, claiming that he was preparing to suppress outbreaks of disorder. He planned to challenge

The Routledge Handbook of Early Modern Korea

the throne and elevate Injo's brother. Sim's plot was swiftly betrayed, his organization unraveled, and the prime plotters were tried and executed.

An Iksin's rebellion flared two years after Sim's attempt at power was suppressed, but the two events share key organizational features. An's conspiracy, too, took shape among disgruntled capital-based elites who attempted to mobilize an army to overthrow the court, replacing it with a more aggressively pro-Ming leadership that would assist in overthrowing Qing (Sunah Lee 2008, 9). In both cases, rebels attacked what they deemed Injo's ideological illegitimacy—arguing that the monarch spurned loyalty to Ming by kowtowing to the barbarian Qing. Indeed, rebels used the same terms that Injo had used to seize power in 1623. The leaders of both rebellions also secured the participation of many military officials. Challengers succeeded in capturing territory and mobilizing arms, troops, and supplies but ultimately suffered defeat (Palais 1996, 93–94; Jackson 2016, 24). Subsequently, Kim Sik's (1620–51) rebellion in 1651 and Hŏ Kyŏn's (1646–80) rebellion in 1680 used the fifth columnist strategy.

The leaders of the Ak Iksin Rebellion secured local assistance for their ventures with the understanding that Ming forces would render support with experienced generals. Local ties ensured that rebel leaders gained significant backing in Ch'ungch'ŏng Province. For instance, the rebels mobilized the support of military officials in Kongju, Ch'ungch'ŏng. The involvement of insurgents within the area was a particular concern for the court since Ch'ungch'ŏng had produced significant challenges to Injo's authority. Many rebel troops were poor farmers who had joined the rebellion because they had heard leaders were mobilizing an army to attack Qing. Such a motive indicates broader popular agreement with the anti-Qing feeling of court elites (Sunah Lee 2008, 9–12).

The suppression of An Iksin's rebellion heralded a period during which Chosŏn society experienced greater instability. The Qing takeover of the Kingdom of Tungning (1661–83), a Taiwan-based Ming-loyalist regime, snuffed out the hopes within Chosŏn for a Ming restoration, and the Chosŏn court grudgingly resigned itself to a Qing-dominated world order (Palais 1996, 104). By then, Chosŏn had more or less recovered from the catastrophic devastation of the Imjin War, and relative economic prosperity in the provinces and new taxation methods enacted in 1708 lightened the financial burden on peasants (Ki-baik Lee 1984, 224). More widespread use of new agricultural techniques such as double cropping, wet-field cultivation, and fertilizer improved crop yields (Kuentae Kim 2014, 37–40). With this greater prosperity, the locus of discontent and contention shifted to court and centered around factionalism.

Eighteenth-Century Discontent and Court Politics

By King Yŏngjo's reign (1724–76), the dynamics of Chosŏn court politics had evolved to feature a particularly stubborn form of political contention (Figure 7.1). The original factionalism of the turn of the seventeenth century had turned into a bitter partisan strife featuring deeply entrenched, lasting political parties rather than more ephemeral, less stable factions of Sŏnjo and Kwanghae Kun's reigns. Especially at the beginning of Yŏngjo's rule, court politics was a zero-sum game in which political associations aimed to maximize their control over the court's decision-making processes while excluding rivals (Jackson 2016, 18). A great deal was at stake for the winners or losers in contention over power; the losers suffered exclusion from officialdom—capital and provincial offices alike—for the rest of their lives. For example, no Southerner (Namin) held high office for nearly a century after 1694 (Lovins 2014, 3). Officials forced from power and their descendants entrenched themselves in the provinces as local *yangban*. Certain partisans frequently associated with particular areas: the Southerners dominated Kyŏngsang Province as a whole (surviving Northerners in their original stronghold of southern Kyŏngsang switched over to Southerners

108

Discontent

Figure 7.1 Portrait of Yŏngjo, 1900, 68 cm × 110 cm. Painted by Ch'ae Yongsin (1848–1941) and Cho Sŏkchin (1853–1920), this is a copy of the original work of 1744, no longer extant. Source and photo credit: National Palace Museum of Korea.

after Kwanghae Kun was deposed), whereas their rivals—the Patriarchs (Noron) split Kyŏnggi Province, close to the capital, with Southerners. Outside the capital, private academies (*sŏwŏn*) turned into centers of partisan rural powerbases, and for disempowered groups, these areas became seething sites of resentment (Ch'oe 1999, 42). Members of a party out of power made it their goal to return to power as soon as possible.

Intense conflict erupted between 1674 and 1800 over the succession of King Sukchong (r. 1674–1720), an issue exacerbated by the lack of clear guidelines for selecting the heir apparent. Two opposing forces, the Extreme Disciples (Chunso) and Southerners, supported his oldest son, King Kyŏngjong (r. 1720–24), whereas the Moderate Disciples (Wanso) and the Patriarchs supported his half-brother Yŏngjo. The animosity generated by the purges resulting from the clash eventually led to Yi Injwa's Rebellion (1728). Rebels associated with the Extreme Disciples and Southerners attempted to seize power by replacing Yŏngjo with royal kin more sympathetic to them. During a three-week military campaign, belligerents faced each other in bloody conflict.

The rebellion was the most well-organized assault on court authority in a century and the largest of the eighteenth century (Jackson 2016, 4). It also helped shape the subsequent rule of Yŏngjo and his grandson, King Chŏngjo (r. 1776–1800), both of whom prioritized suppressing the deleterious effects of partisan strife.

The long-term disenfranchisement of elites associated with a losing party was the primary grievance uniting the elite rebels. Leaders also attempted to tap into wider grievances and mobilize nonelites by equating wider socioeconomic problems with a ruler they deemed illegitimate. Before the Yi Injwa Rebellion, in the preceding year (1727), a widespread famine had caused great dislocation in the southern provinces (Haboush 1988, 136–39). The rebels primarily comprised *yangban* like Yi Injwa associated with the Extreme Disciples and Southerners in their Kyŏngsang and Chŏlla strongholds. Many were from single-surname villages. As such, they were *yangban* communities effectively disenfranchised during partisan strife (Jackson 2016, 45). The rebels also included supporters within the government, including the provincial army commander (Pyŏngma chŏltosa) of P'yŏngan and the Palace Guard commander (Kŭmgun Pyŏlchang). Rebels mobilized a sizeable army; estimates vary, but one provincial rebel force numbered up to 1,000 men (Jackson 2016, 99). Nonelite rebels included personal servants and slaves of leaders, farmers recruited in occupied territories, and other commoners. The resulting rebel forces were a cross-section of local society.

The rebels took 12 county seats in three provinces, including Ch'ŏngju in Ch'ungch'ŏng Province. The rebel officials tried turning their troops against the court to seize power like plotters who had elevated Injo and rebelled during his reign. Yi Injwa and his followers portrayed themselves as defenders of the Chosŏn state, righteous adherents of Confucian morality, and Kyŏngjong loyalists who would overthrow the usurper (Jackson 2016, 41).

Ritualized Protest and Greater Popular Unrest, 1729–1873

Reeling from the rebellion in shock, Yŏngjo spent the remainder of his long reign attempting to subdue the worst excesses of partisan conflict and prevent violence. This effort as a policy continued during the reign of his grandson and successor, Chŏngjo. Their campaigns certainly did not prevent parties and factions from exerting influence over the political process, and the discontent so engendered persisted. Instead of resorting to armed violence, partisan supporters, elites in general, and nonelites engaged in more ritualized forms of protest. Commoners and non-officeholding *yangban* used various methods to express their grievance over official abuses and other sociopolitical problems; these ranged from officially permitted written remonstrations steeped in Confucian custom to unsanctioned and forbidden protests. Recorded instances of such action increased in the eighteenth century, reflecting both Yŏngjo and Chŏngjo's efforts to present themselves as sage monarchs listening to the grievances of their subjects (Haboush 1988, 10, 86). The non-violent and ritualistic qualities linked these demonstrations of disapproval.

One primary method for elites to protest perceived abuses or injustices was through the memorial system—delivering epistles written by individuals or groups expressing concerns about political issues and a decline in Confucian morality. Joint memorials, in particular, were a powerful method of expressing political concerns. For example, the 1792 memorial signed by 10,000 Southerners affirmed their oft-questioned loyalty to Chŏngjo and called for the punishment of the Patriarchs they claimed had connived in the killing of the king's father, Prince Sado (1735–62), by Yŏngjo—a tragedy which cast a shadow over Chŏngjo's royal legitimacy (Haboush 1988; Cho 2009, 56–57). Before long, though, Chŏngjo placed restrictions on the production of memorials to

Discontent

the effect that their authors could be investigated for memorials deemed to challenge the authority of the throne (Cho 2009, 57).

Subjects could also resort to two forms of petition to the king while he was on a royal procession, thus gaining access to a monarch normally off-limits to all but a few family members and officials. A petition to the throne (*sangŏn*) was the delivery of a written document outlining a particular grievance directly to the king. A gong-beating petition (*kyŏkchaeng*) was an oral appeal to the king made after the ringing of a large gong (*ching*) or a small flat gong (*kkwaenggwari*). To monopolize political authority, most Chosŏn monarchs and high officials restricted the scope of petitions to issues of Confucian propriety (Han Sang-kwon 2000, 231–33), but the petitions system changed during Chŏngjo's reign. Given those who questioned his royal legitimacy as the son of disgraced Sado, Chŏngjo was keen on portraying himself as a sage ruler concerned with the conditions of his subjects. Chŏng was, therefore, willing to loosen restrictions governing petitions, allowing a greater range of people to participate in the petitioning process over a wider array of issues (Cho 2009, 58). Rather than complaints over systematic failings or abuses, most of the 4,500 petitions the court received were about local disputes over burials or appeals over aspects of Confucian ritual, such as the right to adopt a son or perform ancestral rites on someone's behalf. Around a quarter of the petitions were complaints over excessive taxation or other financial abuses by local officials or powerful elites (Han Sang-kwon 2000). Despite Chŏngjo's relaxation of restrictions, considerable barriers continued to limit access to this form of protest. Not only the ritualized and ceremonial aspects of the petition system but also the requirement for petitioners to be present during the king's procession made this form of raising grievances inaccessible to all but a fraction of the population.

Other forms of protest were not delivered via official channels of redress, and as such, they were unauthorized and illegal expressions of discontent. Examples are the spreading of malicious rumors about the magistrate (*waŏn*); the attacking of the county office (*pŏmgwan*); the theft of the county office board representing royal authority (*t'up'ae*); the delivery of petitions condemning the misrule of magistrates (*hosong*); the criticism of local officials (*tanhyang*); and the distribution of leaflets critical of the magistrate's rule (*t'usŏ*) (Karlsson 2006, 209). As evident in the nomenclature, these forms of protest targeted local abuses of power. Especially as such abuses worsened in the nineteenth century, remonstrants responded by spreading rumors about the magistrate deemed perpetrator. Many of these forms of remonstrance—even those that were unauthorized and illegal—contained ceremonial and ritualistic elements. Especially common in rural areas, they were symbolic attacks on the paraphernalia of the state to criticize local rule by targeting individual officials (Yi Ihwa 1994). Protesters were careful not to attack the legitimacy of the throne itself. This approach had a greater chance of securing more serious consideration by removing the king and his court from culpability. In other words, the protesters found fault not in the ruling political system but in the localized implementation of policy.

Chosŏn officials also recorded other forms of unauthorized protest in which participants attacked the royal legitimacy. Two examples are the posting of seditious posters (*kwesŏ*) and the illegal singing of subversive songs in public areas such as marketplaces (Ki-baik Lee 1984, 253; Haboush 1988, 141–42). The unlawful character of these protests means that the authorship is unclear, and the content is often unknown. Official historians frequently replaced treasonous allegations against incumbent kings with expressions such as "words I could not bear to hear" (Jackson 2016). Officials feared that by revealing allegations against the throne, they could be accused of committing *lèse-majesté*. Chosŏn records document many forms of ritualized protest, official and unauthorized, which became particularly prevalent in the nineteenth century (Karlsson 2006, 209). Such ritualized remonstrance has attracted less interest among historians, as they tend

The Routledge Handbook of Early Modern Korea

to see these protests as a sideshow to the main rebellions of late Chosŏn. Regardless, various forms of ritualized remonstrance provide evidence of the increasing resistance of struggling farmers (Han Sang-kwon 2000, 228).

Food scarcity was a main source of anger during the eighteenth and nineteenth centuries. Commoners in rural and urban areas alike frequently faced food shortages. Following severe famines in 1732–34 and 1812–13, the 1833 famine sparked major rice riots in Hansŏng, which was often shielded from the worst effects of food scarcity because it was the seat of government (Haboush 1988, 136–39, 141–42). In addition, sudden price increases in essential foodstuffs like rice during shortages heightened discontent amongst the rural and urban poor (Uk Lee 2014, 90–92). Burdened by excessive taxation and faced with food scarcity, many farmers voted with their feet, fled their villages, and took to mountainous regions out of reach of the authorities to get by as slash-and-burn farmers (*hwajŏnmin*) (Ki-baik Lee 1984, 253). Other peasants joined gangs of brigands in the way of Im KKŏkjong. They operated in mountainous areas, robbed travelers, and plundered the houses of the wealthy (Korea Historical Research Association 2005, 130).

The direct cause of food scarcity was ecological events, but the actions of an increasingly dysfunctional government exacerbated these problems. Amidst general disarray in the governing process, corruption spread among officials operating in the state fiscal organizations, leading to decreased revenue despite increasing extraction from commoners (Ki-baik Lee 1984, 248–49). Economic challenges prompted state ministries to seek new ways to make up shortfalls left from standard sources of tax income, bringing the center into conflict with local society. Over the nineteenth century, the scale and intensity of contention gradually increased. Predatory central state behavior elicited more violent, organized responses, and the participation of farmers in these events grew common.

The 1812 Hong Kyŏngnae Rebellion

The first large-scale outbreak of violence in the nineteenth century was Hong Kyŏngnae's (1780–1812) rebellion, occurring between the twelfth month of 1811 (January 1812) and the fourth month of 1812 (May 1812) in the northwest, P'yŏngan Province. The rebellion was an armed assault on central authority by groups of disenfranchised provincial elites (Karlsson 2006, 218). Even more territory fell to the rebels than during Yi Injwa's rebellion, making the 1812 rebellion the most significant challenge faced by the Chosŏn state (Sun Joo Kim 2009, 144, 147).

The rebellion was a region's response to endemic discrimination against local elites and a struggle over economic resources. The central *yangban* aristocracy saw the northwestern regional elites as militaristic and lacking in scholarship. Although their examination success increased dramatically in late Chosŏn (Wagner 1977, 23–26; Park 2007, 109–14), a glass ceiling withheld prestigious, significant posts—civil and military—from them. Stymied, many northwestern elites turned to trade (Sun Joo Kim 2007a, 9–10, 35, 57; Karlsson 2006, 218). With less arable land for crop cultivation than the southeastern and southwestern provinces and situated close to Qing China, northwesterners developed a lucrative cross-border trade in handicrafts. The production, transport, and exchange of manufactured goods allowed elites to maintain their wealth and benefited the entire local community (Karlsson 2000, 228). The increasing intrusion of the court into the financial affairs of P'yŏngan Province challenged the economic agency of regional communities (Karlsson 2006, 218). Until late Chosŏn, the trade generated enough revenue to satisfy local elites and the court. However, when the central government faced severe fiscal challenges and mass starvation in the southern provinces, it attempted to alleviate the famine by extracting more from the cross-border trade (Karlsson 2000, 219). This critical shift

112

Discontent

in the control over economic resources led to smoldering resentment over discrimination to tip over into an open rebellion.

Leading the challenge was Hong Kyŏngnae, a charismatic, educated individual. Failing to pass the licentiate examination (*samasi*)—required for enrolling in the Confucian Academy (Sŏnggyun'gwan), where students prepared for the civil examination (*munkwa*) to serve in government—he became a wandering geomancer (*chisa*), spending several years building up support for insurrection. The emerging leadership comprised intellectuals, merchants, men with military backgrounds, and county functionaries (*hyangni*). The insurgents had a sizeable number of supporters: the central government had to field 8,000 troops to quell the rebellion, and afterward, the authorities executed 1,917 rebels (Karlsson 2006, 224–28).

Solidarity formed among disenfranchised groups within P'yŏngan. Reflecting a strong regional sentiment and sense of autonomy fuelled by resentment toward discrimination, solidarity is evident in rebel manifestos (Karlsson 2000, 237; Sun Joo Kim 2007a, 9–10, 35, 57, 2009, 144). Common economic interests also linked local elites, county functionaries, merchants, and farmers who formed the main rebel forces (Karlsson 2000, 228). Using local administrative structures to mobilize troops, leaders—including rebel officials—also lured commoners into the rebellion through promises of lucrative opportunities in mining operations. Fed meat and alcohol, potential recruits received cash advances on their future mining work, generally deemed a temporary occupation and a quick way to earn cash. At times, some had to be threatened before being led off to fight for the rebels (Karlsson 2000, 116–61). The rebel manifestos claimed insurgents were attempting to mobilize an army in the north that would "save the people" (*anmin*). They complained of the corruption of court officials and called for the restoration of a more just central rule. Thus, the rebels did not proclaim any emancipatory ideology (Sun Joo Kim 2009, 147).

The 1862 Chinju Rebellion

Half a century later, in 1862, an uprising occurred in Chinju in Kyŏngsang Province when large groups of locals attacked and killed municipal officials. The court dispatched troops to suppress the violence, but the events at Chinju sparked more than 70 copycat uprisings across the southern part of the peninsula and even further north. Collectively dubbed the "Chinju Rebellion," in the geographical distribution of violence, the uprisings were the most severe outbreaks of political violence until that point in Chosŏn's history (Sun Joo Kim 2007b, 993).

Ostensibly, Chinju residents rebelled against the corruption of oppressive Provincial Army Commander Paek Naksin (1814–87) and local functionaries, but the causes were more complex. The background to the outbreak of violence was the longer-term conflict between the court and local society arising from the central government's attempts to make up for financial deficits by seeking additional tax revenues through an excessive levy on land (Karlsson 2000, 219; Sun Joo Kim 2007b, 1001). A primary reason behind the local government's fiscal worries was the grain loan (*hwan'gok*) system originally designed to aid needy farmers but abused by provincial government offices to raise funds. As officials lent out grain reserves at high interest, the default rate was high, and the system was subject to widespread abuse. Officials benefited from territorial price variations caused by shortages and gluts in grain supply, selling at high rates, buying cheaply, and embezzling profits. The grain loan system was inherently flawed and increased popular anger (Sun Joo Kim 2007b, 1001–04).

The scale of the 1862 Chinju Rebellion was far greater than in 1646, 1728, or 1811, involving tens of thousands of Chinju inhabitants and other county residents fighting state authority (Karlsson 2006, 224). People from diverse levels of society joined the rebellion, including educated local elites and large landowners who assumed leadership roles. Ordinary farmers were involved in greater numbers, but the participation of those of social standing fuelled the rebellion's rapid growth. The leadership recruited kin groups, single-surname villages, lineage associations, and work organizations (Sun Joo Kim 2007b, 1007–11). Among the rebels, the wood gatherers mobilized via collaborative community labor groups (*ture*), which performed corvée from villages (Karlsson 2006, 232).

Severe violence erupted on one of the periodic market days in the area (Sun Joo Kim 2007b, 1009). Rebels attacked county offices and the houses of the wealthy and powerful who had supported the new land tax; they destroyed documents, killed 15 local functionaries, wounded hundreds, and torched over a thousand homes (Karlsson 2006, 224–25). What began as a tax riot revealed deeper tensions between the center and the locals (Sun Joo Kim 2007b, 994). The complexity of the rebellion embodied both spontaneous and more determined acts of violence. On the one hand, the insurgent attacks appeared random and indiscriminate; on the other, some aspects of their behavior were targeted and planned. For example, the rebels selected market days to launch their protest—when the venue was likely busy, and insurgents could mobilize more supporters for their cause.

Economic changes deeply impacted landowners; for this reason, even some prominent *yangban* coordinated the rebellion and demanded the abolition of the land tax. To generate support, rebel leaders used the local administration and lineage organizations to mobilize farmers and other nonelites to protest the taxes (Sun Joo Kim 2007b, 1007–21; Karlsson 2006, 232). Large landowners also organized the participants through the county local council (*hyanghoe*), which, as true in most counties throughout Korea, used to be dominated by local *yangban* until the eighteenth century when wealthy local commoners began taking over (Kim Ingeol 2024, 87–95). Council meetings decided whether to target local officials for punishment (Karlsson 2006, 231). The Chinju Rebellion featured no attempt to make a broader movement, overthrow the Chosŏn state, or advance any underlying ideology (Sun Joo Kim 2007b, 1020).

Final Thoughts

Early modern Korea's unrest, protests, and armed rebellions reflect elements of fundamental sociopolitical continuity and change. The ultimate causes of discontent remained consistent throughout Chosŏn's history. Exacerbating subsistence crises were recurrent administrative corruption, malpractice, and incompetence that could inflame communities and ignite violent protests. Also, regional fault lines that emerged at the beginning of Chosŏn remained consistent for centuries. The mountainous terrain of the north made the food supply of the local population more prone to ecological crises. The status discrimination, presence of ethnically diverse communities, and distance from the controlling hand of the central court made the region prone to unrest. Korea's north thus mirrors patterns amongst parts of contemporary China, where ecological vulnerability and administrative fragility led to more frequent occurrences of historical unrest. Protest and political violence became a feature of the collective memory of communities and potential weapons in the armory of responses to the predation of central bureaucracies (Perry 1980, 258–62).

Korea's north remained prone to rebellion in the early modern era, but it was neither in continuous revolt nor the sole site of unrest. The locus of contention shifted from the northern border areas to the court and then to the agriculturally rich regions in the south. These shifts reflect the changing character of the discontent afflicting the society—from mid-Chosŏn political conflict in the central bureaucracy to provincial resistance against the center's intrusion and extraction of local resources. Another significant change is the increasing scale of regional protests in the

Discontent

nineteenth century. Dwarfing previous outbursts of unrest, both the Hong Kyŏngnae Rebellion of 1812 and the Chinju Rebellion of 1862 also reveal a growing collaboration between elites and nonelites. The contention was not so much based on status as on community-organized attempts to right wrongs.

The transformation of contention in Chosŏn Korea generally reflects the trajectory of rebellion elsewhere in the early modern world. For example, the peasant uprisings (*ikki*) of Tokugawa Japan (1603–1868) swelled in size and intensity as the nineteenth century progressed (Borton 1968, 1–2, 16). The defensive and backward-looking nature of Chosŏn rebellions was also common to insurrections in other parts of the early modern world. In nineteenth-century China, rebels yearning for a more "just society" contained a "traditionalist ethos unsuited to modern revolution" (Perry 1980, 148). During Tokugawa peasant uprisings, rebels "invoked the status quo and appealed to the duly constituted authorities" (White 1995, 108). English popular unrest mobilized rebels demanding a return to "past experience and traditional arrangements" (Stevenson 1979, 317). The political rebellion in Chosŏn Korea is not exceptional but comparable to contention elsewhere in the early modern world for pursuing a rectification of the system, not its destruction.

Note

1 This work was supported by the Core University Program for Korean Studies through the Ministry of Education of the Republic of Korea and the Korean Studies Promotion Service of the Academy of Korean Studies (AKS-2023-OLU-2250001).

References

Borton, Hugh. 1968. *Peasant Uprisings in Japan of the Tokugawa Period.* Paragon.
Ch'oe, Yŏng-ho. 1999. "Private Academies and the State in Late Chosŏn Korea." In *Culture and the State in Late Chosŏn Korea*, edited by JaHyun Kim Haboush and Martina Deuchler, 15–45. Harvard University Asia Center.
Cho, Hwisang. 2009. "Joint Memorials: Scholars' Channel of Communication to the Throne." In *Epistolary Korea: Letters in the Communicative Space of the Chosŏn, 1392–1910*, edited by JaHyun Kim Haboush, 56–67. Columbia University Press.
Choi Byonghyon. 2014. *The Annals of King T'aejo: Founder of Korea's Chosŏn Dynasty*. Harvard University Press.
Deuchler, Martina. 1997. "Social and Economic Developments in Eighteenth-Century Korea." In *The Last Stand of Asian Autonomies: Responses to Modernity in the Diverse States of Southeast Asia and Korea, 1750–1900*, edited by Anthony Reid, 299–320. Palgrave.
Dillon, Michael. 1998. *China: A Cultural and Historical Dictionary*. Curzon.
Duncan, John. 2000. *The Origins of the Chosŏn Dynasty*. University of Washington Press.
Goldstone, Jack. 2014. *Revolutions: A Very Short Introduction*. Oxford University Press.
Haboush, JaHyun Kim. 1988. *A Heritage of Kings: One Man's Monarchy in the Confucian World*. Columbia University Press.
Han Sang-kwon [Sang Kwon Han]. 2000. "Social Problems and the Active Use of Petitions during the Reign of King Chŏngjo." *Korea Journal* 40, no. 4 (Winter): 227–46.
Han, Sang Kwon [Han Sang-kwon]. 2014. "The Rebellion of Im Ggeokjeong." In *Everyday Life in Joseon-Era Korea: Economy and Society*, edited by Michael D. Shin, 181–88. Global Oriental.
Jackson, Andrew David. 2016. *The 1728 Musin Rebellion: Politics and Plotting in Eighteenth-Century Korea*. University of Hawai'i Press.
Karlsson, Anders. 2000. "The Hong Kyŏngnae Rebellion 1811–1812: Conflict between Central Power and Local Society in 19th-Century Korea." Ph.D. dissertation, Stockholm University.
Karlsson, Anders. 2006. "Central Power, Local Society, and Rural Unrest in Nineteenth-Century Korea: An Attempt at Comparative Local History." *Sungkyun Journal of East Asian Studies* 6, no. 2: 207–38.

Kim Ingeol. 2024. *Politics of Public Opinion: Local Councils and People's Assemblies in Korea, 1567–1894.* Translated by Eugene Y. Park. Brill.

Kim, Kuentae. 2014. "Farming in the Joseon Period." In *Everyday Life in Joseon-Era Korea: Economy and Society*, edited by Michael D. Shin, 37–46. Global Oriental.

Kim, Sun Joo. 2007a. *Marginality and Subversion in Korea: The Hong Kyŏngnae Rebellion of 1812.* University of Washington Press.

Kim, Sun Joo. 2007b. "Taxes, the Local Elite, and the Rural Populace in the Chinju Uprising of 1862." *Journal of Asian Studies* 66, no. 4 (November): 993–1027.

Kim, Sun Joo. 2009. "Manifestos During the Hong Kyŏngnae Rebellion of 1812." In *Epistolary Korea: Letters in the Communicative Space of the Chosŏn, 1392–1910*, edited by JaHyun Kim Haboush, 141–51. Columbia University Press.

Kim, Sung Woo. 2014. "The Tax Burden of the Peasantry." In *Everyday Life in Joseon-Era Korea: Economy and Society*, edited by Michael D. Shin, 61–69. Global Oriental.

Korea Historical Research Association. 2005. *A History of Korea.* Translated by Joshua Van Lieu. Saffron Books.

Kuhn, Philip A. 1970. *Rebellion and its Enemies in Late Imperial China: Militarization and Social Structure, 1796–1864.* Harvard University Press.

Lee, Ki-baik. 1984. *A New History of Korea.* Translated by Edward W. Wagner with Edward J. Shultz. Harvard University Press.

Lee, Sunah. 2008. "Sim Kiwŏn's Revolt and the Return of Im Kyŏngŏp." *International Journal of Korean History* 12, no. 1: 1–24.

Lee, Uk. 2014. "The Merchants of Seoul." In *Everyday Life in Joseon-Era Korea: Economy and Society*, edited by Michael D. Shin, 83–92. Global Oriental.

Lovins, Christopher. 2014. "Testing the Limits: King Chŏngjo and Royal Power in Late Chosŏn." Ph.D. dissertation, University of British Columbia.

Palais, James B. 1996. *Confucian Statecraft and Korean Institutions: Yu Hyŏngwŏn and the Late Chosŏn Dynasty.* University of Washington Press.

Park, Eugene Y. 2007. *Between Dreams and Reality: The Military Examination in Late Chosŏn Korea, 1600–1894.* Harvard University Asia Center.

Perry, Elizabeth J. 1980. *Rebels and Revolutionaries in North China, 1845–1945.* Stanford University Press.

Pratt, Keith, and Richard Rutt. 1999. *Korea: A Historical and Cultural Dictionary.* Curzon.

Robinson, Kenneth R. 1992. "From Raiders to Traders: Border Security and Border Control in Early Chosŏn, 1392–1450." *Korean Studies* 16: 94–115.

Stevenson, John. 1979. *Popular Disturbances in England, 1700–1832.* Longman.

Wagner, Edward W. 1977. "The Civil Examination Process as Social Leaven: The Case of the Northern Provinces in the Yi Dynasty." *Korea Journal* 17 (January): 22–27.

White, James W. 1995. *Ikki: Social Conflict and Political Protest in Early Modern Japan.* Cornell University Press.

Yi Ihwa. 1994. *Chosŏn hugi ŭi chŏngch'i sasang kwa sahoe pyŏndong.* Han'gilsa.

8

ECONOMY

Young-Jun Cho

This chapter explores the economy of early modern Korea up to 1873 when the Chosŏn state (1392–1897) began to examine the possibility of entering into treaty relations with various countries. For Chosŏn, which lasted more than 500 years, opening its ports following the first treaty (1876) would mark a milestone in its economic history. It signaled a transition from a closed economy restricting foreign trade to an open economy integrated into global capitalism. Therefore, the Korean economy before and after the post-1873 policy shift differed not only in terms of everyday life but also in terms of institutions. Even the pre-1873 economic history of Chosŏn defies any easy explanation in one fell swoop, given the span of nearly five centuries. Highlighting the impact of the Imjin War (East Asian War; 1592–98), many scholars group the fifteenth and sixteenth centuries as early Chosŏn and the seventeenth, eighteenth, and nineteenth centuries as late Chosŏn. However, this approach is not ideal because it emphasizes discontinuities over longer-term trends.

Understanding the longue durée history of Chosŏn's economy has presented challenges. Until recently, scholars approached Chosŏn's economic history primarily through institutional or policy history. Nevertheless, of course, institutions and policies articulate only the ideals of the government as led by the monarch and officialdom. Thus, they do not necessarily reflect the actual living conditions of the people or how they changed. More recent studies have achieved two breakthroughs in addressing these limitations. One is introducing the quantitative history approach, which largely relies on collecting and organizing numeric information that can be estimated, detecting certain patterns from these data, or performing econometric analysis. Moreover, two, the application of the microhistory approach, according to which scholars attempt to adjust the perspective of the historical narrative by searching elsewhere for more specific information not found in official sources.

Reflecting these approaches, the overall organization of the chapter is topical rather than chronological. The relative weight of coverage in terms of early versus late Chosŏn varies among sections. Nonetheless, the sections connect in ways that contribute to a better understanding of Chosŏn's economy. For example, we examine the population as producers and consumers and how state revenue is received and redistributed. Afterward, we consider land, a key variable in production, and the commodity price. After reviewing Chosŏn's status system and slavery, the discussion turns to wages and stature to assess living standards, followed by commerce, money, and finance, which operate behind the scenes of the real economy.

DOI: 10.4324/9781003262053-11

The Routledge Handbook of Early Modern Korea

Population

Unlike the predecessor state of Koryŏ (918–1392), Chosŏn posted a magistrate to every county of the kingdom to maintain centralized control over all land and people. While the management of human resources became tighter, the state's presence in everyone's life varied widely. The government recorded information about residents in household registers (*hojŏk*), updated triennially. Although voluminous and often referred to as "big ledgers," these registers came nowhere near including the information on every person living in the country. As a result, information on approximately one-third of the population for the entire history of Chosŏn is likely missing.

An alternative source that can compensate for the incompleteness of household registers is a family record (*chokpo*), a written genealogy. As private individuals compiled such genealogies to record a descent line comprising its apical ancestor and his direct descendants, they had no reason to edit these records arbitrarily. Even so, family records, too, are problematic for population history research. First, genealogies rarely contain information on commoners (*yangin*) or slaves (*nobi*) because most compilers were *yangban* (aristocrats) or *chungin* (especially government-employed, capital-resident specialists in various fields). Therefore, genealogies do not reflect data for the entire population. Second, a preponderance of extant genealogies includes contents forged by later generations. Especially between the late nineteenth century, when the government officially abolished the status system in 1894, and the mid-twentieth century, when the Korean War accelerated the demise of traditionally kin-based rural communities, Koreans rushed to acquire written genealogies—thus claiming descent from royals and aristocrats. Third, the compilation of genealogies was much less frequent than household registers. Whereas the state funded household register compilation, individual families that compiled genealogies often found associated expenses beyond their means.

Since some information is missing from the household register, presumably, the census focused on those who owed taxes to the state. According to this assumption, the primary purpose of the census was to identify individuals paying their poll tax. Unlike other forms of tax, remittance of a poll tax was via corvée, performed by an individual mobilized to work for a certain period, and military service, which the individual provided through an army or navy unit. Given that the state imposed these obligations on males aged 16 to 60, the main subject of taxation comprised adult males.

These observations highlight three characteristics of human resource control by the Chosŏn state. First, the state could not readily identify those under 16. In general, young children did not even have a given name on the household register, given the high infant mortality. Second, the state viewed only some females as bearing formal obligations to the state (for example, government-registered female entertainers, *kwan'gi*), and thus not having a more accurate record of the female population did not pose a significant problem for the state. Accordingly, the omission of females from household registers is disproportionately greater than males. Third, household registers left out a disproportionately large number of slaves since the state did not require them to remit taxes or serve in the military. The government had little incentive to diligently estimate their number for the costly triennial project of updating household registers.

Although the dearth of data poses a challenge in tracing the population change in Chosŏn, some general trends are clear. The early Chosŏn state grew in its centralized power and wielded greater population control. It also implemented innovations such as more effective land clearance for cultivation and overcoming fallowing that sustained population growth. However, the Imjin War inflicted heavy casualties in the late sixteenth century, and after a plunge, the growth resumed only in the late seventeenth century. Then, in the nineteenth century, the population recorded on household registers decreased. According to one explanation, such natural disasters as droughts and epidemics in the early nineteenth century, cumulative effects of the poor living standards during the seventeenth and eighteenth centuries, and any combination thereof contributed. According to another explanation, in the nineteenth century, the government may have experienced increased difficulties with census taking as an oligarchy of royal consort families at the expense of royal authority fanned corruption among local officials—thereby compromising the state's control over human resources. Apart from the decrease in the overall population, the number of vagrants uprooted in rural communities increased during the century. Indeed, household registers document those leaving their residence locales following the collapse of their farming businesses. These trends suggest a rupture in rural collectives centered around kin groups, highlighting the overall instability of Chosŏn society and its lack of a social safety net at the time (Yi Yŏnghun and Cho Yŏngjun 2005).

State Finance

More recent research on Chosŏn suggests that dominant forms of integration varied through the kingdom's history. For example, in early Chosŏn, the "gift economy" prevailed in the *yangban*-dominated society. In contrast, in late Chosŏn, redistribution was the dominant form of integration, with an exchange, the market, as the secondary form (Yi Hŏnch'ang 2010). The dominance of redistribution highlights the critical role of state finance at the time.

References that provide a realistic picture of the public finances of Chosŏn are rare. Chosŏn's public finance system reflected the basic tax law of Tang dynasty (618–907) China. King Sejong (r. 1418–50) sought to create a tax system unique to Chosŏn through the tribute tax (*kongnap*) system, but it was ineffective in securing adequate tax revenues. As a result, land surveys remained largely ineffective in producing accurate assessments, and the state had to maintain an effective tax rate at a surprisingly low level. No government record from late Chosŏn provides any detail about the fiscal revenues and expenditures; generally, time-series datasets are unavailable. However, such scarcity of data does not mean that the government did not keep tabs on its accounts; instead, only some are extant, including account books for some fiscal years, presently housed in Kyujanggak, the royal archive established by King Chŏngjo (r. 1776–1800). In the absence of more complete data, a good proxy for fiscal revenues derives from a document, *Record of Land Tax Assessment* (*T'akchi chŏnbu ko*; 1796), which records taxable and tax-exempt lands and also tax cuts depending on the weather conditions for each year. The total area of cultivated land and the breakdown of tax cuts enable the estimation of the state's overall fiscal budget and the year-to-year changes in the budgetary revenue, respectively.

Annual data on the Chosŏn state's budget or settlement are unavailable. Still, the reign-by-reign veritable records (*sillok*) provide a partial, yearly record of how much the government stockpiled in its warehouses. The earliest inventory records date back to the reign of Chŏngjo, from 1776 to 1884. The government's inventory for each year is not meaningful in and of itself, but whether the inventory increased or decreased from one year to the next is of interest to economic historians. An increase and a decrease suggest revenue surplus and deficit, respectively.

Interpreting the total stock of goods held by the government in a way meaningful for economic historians demands unit conversion to a single metric, either in a quantity of rice or in monetary value. Some studies have used prices from a specific period (for example, the government's officially fixed price around 1807–08) and converted them to the value of rice for the entire period. Using rice rather than cash for the conversion avoids the additional step of converting nominal variables to real variables. All the same, using a fixed price from a particular period may not

The Routledge Handbook of Early Modern Korea

reflect any inflation. For example, the graph presented by Kim Chaeho (2008, 11) shows a spike in inventories in 1867. This spike is evident in the graphs showing the data series of the value calculated in coins and the graphs charting the value in rice. These graphs give a false impression of a surge in actual inventories. Since the government issued the Hundred-Cash Coin (*Tangbaek chŏn*; 1866–67), the figures from the period should be excluded from conversion to real variables. The rice price in 1867 needs to be applied rather than retroactively applying the rice price of 1807.

Apart from inflation, since price change varies among commodities, quantity, inventory, and distribution changes require consideration. Ideally, all commodity values should be converted to yearly prices based on market prices, but such conversions are difficult. Research on Chosŏn's economic history typically collects information on commodity prices in the southern provinces but not the capital, Hansŏng (present-day Seoul), where government offices were located. Therefore, as presented in many studies, these prices do not represent the entire country.

With these issues considered, some trends regarding the central government's year-end inventory become clear. The late eighteenth and early nineteenth centuries saw fluctuations in stock, but it remained relatively stable. Then, a steady downward trend continued from the 1810s until the 1870s, when government finances recovered. In other words, the government's finances steadily deteriorated throughout the century.

The royal finances fared no better. Extant royal accounting records from the late eighteenth to the early twentieth century provide a detailed look at how the royal house financed the more personal needs of its members not covered by government funds (Cho 2016). As government finances deteriorated, the royal treasury, too, could not avoid accumulating deficits. The government and the royal house responded to the fiscal crisis by shifting the burden to the private sector. Government redistribution was supposed to revitalize the private sector, but the institution intended to serve this purpose, the state granary system offering the gran loan (*hwan'gok*) to needy farmers, was no longer functioning properly.

Agriculture

Primary industries, of which agriculture played a central role, accounted for much of economic production before the Industrial Revolution. For the most part, the industry was limited to household handicrafts, commerce had yet to develop to the point of national market integration, and services were considered secondary. In this sense, the economic history of the pre–Industrial Revolution era is agricultural. Agricultural production requires three inputs: land, labor, and capital. Given that the concepts of labor and capital are difficult to delineate for a pre-capitalist economy, the land was the decisive factor of production. Accordingly, an overview of the land tenure system is essential for understanding the structure and changes in agriculture.

Based on the concept of royal land, in theory, the state owned all land in Chosŏn. The Rank Land Law (*Kwajŏn pŏp*; 1391–1466), adopted just before the Koryŏ–Chosŏn, was designed to distribute the right of taxation on state-owned land among government officials, including "merit subjects" (*kongsin*), who were honored and rewarded for rendering extraordinary service to the state. This system was built on the experience of late Koryŏ when the farmland increasingly took on characteristics of private control and ultimately contributed to the fall of Koryŏ. At the time, expanding private ownership of land meant that the state's material and human resources decreased, which also meant the weakening of royal power. In the process of strengthening the state's control over land, the early Chosŏn state replaced the rank land (*kwajŏn*) with office land (*chikchŏn*; 1466) and instituted a new system, according to which the "government collects, government disburses" (*kwansu kwan'gŭp*; 1470). Both systems were discontinued by the mid-sixteenth century. The notion that the government managed all land persisted, but the state's ownership was only legal and formal. Private individuals exercised de facto rights.

In the early years of the rank-land system, the state prohibited land transactions among private individuals, but by the late fifteenth century, when the Great Code for State Administration (Kyŏngguk taejŏn; 1471) was in place, the government effectively began to permit free transactions with sales contract documents notarized by the state. In late Chosŏn, the notarization process disappeared, meaning a transaction between two parties was private—no longer backed by law vis-à-vis any third party. Such lack of legal backing for land transactions persisted until the 1910s after Japan annexed Korea (1910) and introduced the real-estate registration system.

The freedom of land transactions led to the growth of large landholdings. Since the landowners could not cultivate large plots of land, the slaves owned by the landlords performed the necessary labor. Annual year-round cultivation was one spreading development in early Chosŏn that facilitated land aggregation. A government-compiled manual, *Straight Talk on Farming* (*Nongsa chiksŏl*; 1429), disseminated improved methods and increased agricultural productivity. Meanwhile, the improvements in irrigation facilities led to the spread of rice paddy farming. Also, the seedling transplanting technique reduced the labor required for weeding. Moreover, the spreading use of oxen for deeper plowing improved dry-field farming.

As labor productivity increased, the average plot size decreased mainly due to the practice of divided inheritance. The improved farming techniques, especially among those owning smaller plots, pushed individual farmers toward more intensive cultivation. Small-scale farmers were not necessarily self-cultivators but rather those who cultivated relatively small plots.

In terms of ownership, the large landowners grew their businesses by lending their land to tenant farmers and collecting rent. The rent was usually half of the harvest: sharecropping (*pyŏngjak*). In place since the fifteenth century, sharecropping became the general norm only by the nineteenth century. Unlike the serfs of medieval manors in Europe, tenant farmers, who constituted most of Chosŏn's population, were owed no non-economic obligations to any feudal lord or landlord. As the sharecropping system evolved, the conversion of rent remittance to fixed-amount payment (similar to *fermage* in medieval and early modern France) became widespread—with in-kind payment giving way to cash.

During the dominance of the 50-percent flat rate system, a decrease in the amount of land meant decreased productivity per unit of land. Long-term analyses of harvest records from various regions show a consistent downward trend in land productivity from the seventeenth to the nineteenth century—a pattern not reversed until the 1880s (Yi Yŏnghun 2012). Land productivity declined for many reasons, including the degradation of forests due to indiscriminate logging for firewood, difficulty with seedling transplantation due to the deterioration of irrigation facilities, and a shortage of manure due to poor fertilizing technology.

Chosŏn's land sale documents, which reflect these challenges, contain information on the location and area of the land for the transaction and its price. For example, the price of rice paddy—converted into a real variable by economic historians—remained largely stable in the eighteenth century but gradually dropped in the nineteenth century (Yi Yŏnghun 2004), probably due to decreased land productivity.

Prices

A uniform price for any given commodity in Chosŏn is inconceivable because the price is as good as the market, though Chosŏn did not have a market economy. To begin with, the government had a significant role in determining prices. Also, the lack of market integration made establishing the law of one price difficult. Therefore, understanding specific prices does not necessarily allow explaining general prices.

The most notable among the prices determined by the Chosŏn government is the tribute price (*kongga*). The enactment of the Uniform Land Tax Law (Taedong pŏp; 1608), which was in effect in seven out of eight provinces by 1708, replaced the procurement of goods by tribute merchants (*kongin*) with taxpayers remitting rice and set the per-item prices in detail. Taxpayers submitted the tributes to the tribute merchants and Hansŏng's licensed shops (*sijŏn*), responsible for supplying government agencies with various commodities. The tribute prices were not so much a single set of prices for individual items as a hierarchy that varied by season and for other reasons. For example, the government usually fixed tribute prices over an extended period. In contrast to price fluctuations reflecting market or prevailing prices, tribute prices remained relatively stable for centuries, as the government tended to set tribute prices well above the market price—a price that factored in a premium of some sort (Yi Hŏnch'ang and Cho Yŏngjun 2008). However, even when market prices suddenly changed and produced inflation, the tribute price remained fixed. Eventually, market prices far surpassed fixed tribute prices. By the mid-nineteenth century, the market price and tribute price trends were reversed.

As the market price surpassed the tribute price, tribute merchants exhausted their financial sources, leading to their demise. However, under the oligarchy of royal consort families in the nineteenth century, the market prices did not rise above the tribute prices even as the state's coffers dwindled. The tribute system was rigid, and the government could not make necessary adjustments. The system would effectively collapse when Chosŏn began opening its ports (1876)—followed by its abolition during the Kabo Reform (1894–96).

Diaries are an essential source of information on prices in the freely traded private market. Several diaries by elites contain record prices, and economic historians are gaining access to more such diaries. Of course, an individual tends to keep a diary for an extended period, and the entries follow a regular format—often focusing on a particular topic. An author mentioning prices typically recorded them every five days, implying that these prices were taken at a local marketplace (*changsi*). Chosŏn had about 1,000 marketplaces nationwide, each occurring every five days. A marketplace was a trading center and a meeting and communication hub.

Typically, slaves bought or sold things at the marketplace on behalf of their owners, whereas the latter kept a diary of the transactions. Given that various items were purchased and sold for each trip to the marketplace, the price information for most commodities lacks long-term consistency. Nonetheless, since diary authors recorded rice more regularly than other commodities, fluctuations in rice price provide sufficient data for constructing a long-term time series. Moreover, given that it was the most common transaction commodity in rural areas, rice is a representative indicator of economic changes during Chosŏn's history. Since these records were not subject to an audit, not all information is reliable.

The account books of mutual assistance societies (*kye*) and local institutions are additional sources of price information. Most kin groups assembled regularly and tracked essential items for their meetings and rituals. In a type of account book, "finance record" (*yonghagi*), kin-group mutual assistance societies noted the quantity of each item used and its corresponding unit cost and value. Whereas diaries stop with the author's death, members of a mutual assistance society could continuously update their financial records, regardless of an individual record keeper's death. Therefore, the price time series from such finance records are generally longer than those from diaries. Account books maintained by such local institutions as private academies (*sŏwŏn*) are similar to those of kinship-based mutual assistance societies in that they, too, record the prices of commodities at regularly scheduled events.

Economy

Research in the economic history of Chosŏn has made steady gains in understanding price fluctuation. Pioneering studies on the commodity prices in Chosŏn present a time series of rice prices utilizing individual diaries, finance records, and private academy account books. As information on the pricing of various commodities became available, subsequent studies established a price index. These indicators show slow yet steady inflation in the eighteenth and nineteenth centuries, followed by rapid inflation in the mid-nineteenth century (Yi Yŏnghun 2004). More recent studies have shown that commodities prices may be extracted from royal account books (Cho 2016), which provide pricing data for just Hansŏng—in contrast to older studies that primarily relied on data from southern provinces. In addition, the prices in royal account books cover a wide range of commodities sold in the capital. Since Hansŏng was a logistical hub then, these sources are more valuable than others that only record the prices of a few daily essentials sold at local marketplaces.

Slavery

Chosŏn society was centered around a de facto caste system of the hereditary status hierarchy, at the bottom of which were chattel slaves. To begin with, their physical features were not different from those of a commoner. In contrast, slaves in ancient Rome, the early modern Middle East, or the pre-1865 American South were of a different ethnicity or race from their owners. All the same, as generally true in other historical societies using unfree labor, the slave status in Chosŏn was hereditary. A child typically was born a slave if either one of the parents was a slave—or at least if the mother was a slave. Such matrilineal rule of slave status inheritance applied even to the offspring of a *yangban* father and a female slave. Given this practice, the slave population increased to somewhere between 30 to 40 percent of the total population from the Koryŏ–Chosŏn regime change until the sixteenth century. Given its large population of slaves, such scholars as James B. Palais have described Chosŏn as a slave society (1995, 414–18).

Slave owners not only could inherit slaves but also bought and sold them. Transaction documents include information on the price of a slave in addition to their name, age, place of birth, and parents. Using these records allows for aggregating the price of slaves for price comparison across periods and regions. Females were generally more expensive than males because the offspring of female slaves also belonged to their owners. All the same, commoners selling themselves to become slaves of others was widespread (Kim Chaeho 2005). Although self-enslavement lowered their position on the status hierarchy, they reaped financial benefits. However, the frequency of these incidents decreased over time, thereby limiting any further increase in the already large slave population.

Chosŏn slaves fell under three distinct categories. Among them, "tribute-submitting" slaves (*napkong nobi*) lived far away from their owners' residences, in stark contrast to household slaves (*kasa nobi*), who lived with their owners, and agricultural slaves (*nonggyŏng nobi*) who worked directly for their masters. Often dispersed across the country, tribute-submitting slaves lived in more remote places. As such, they owned properties and pursued their agricultural activities. For the most part, their existence was similar to that of an ordinary commoner, except that each year, they had to remit a tribute to their masters.

Many slaves sought to improve their positions. Slaves with property could use the money they saved to free themselves through "grain submission" (*napsok*) to their owners.

Including those suffering inhumane treatment by their owners, other slaves frequently attempted to run away and start a new life in a remote location. Many successfully evaded capture since discerning whether someone was a slave or a commoner based on appearance was impossible. Such runaway slaves often went unpunished, unlike China's runaway servants branded with black ink

The Routledge Handbook of Early Modern Korea

or Japan's *burakumin* ("hamlet people"), who were outcastes of socially denigrated occupations. As more slaves ran away or paid their way out of enslavement, the status hierarchy premised on unfree labor became increasingly unstable.

Slavery as a whole began to break down in the seventeenth century, and by the late eighteenth century, the number of slaves on household registries had drastically dropped. As their population decreased, former slaves without surnames began acquiring one. At least initially, they selected their surnames in such ways as to avoid offending *yangban*. A former slave, as a commoner, could also acquire a high court rank title through grain submission as the financially strapped government institutionalized the practice in late Chosŏn. These trends marked the beginning of a new era in which, in many locales, the majority of the male population was being recorded on household registers as "young scholars" (*yuhak*) if living and as "students" (*haksaeng*) if deceased.

The demise of Chosŏn Korea's slavery was slow. The use of slaves by the government and the royal courts ended in 1801, whereas private slavery would not be abolished until 1894. The latter was not so much a government-led initiative as a result of the dwindling slave population since the mid-nineteenth century. The official abolition of slavery did not mean everyone could suddenly become self-sufficient. On the contrary, many former slaves continued to work for their former owners. Rural areas, in particular, still had excess labor or an idle labor force willing to work for minimal compensation. This situation would not change until Korea's industrialization and urbanization in the twentieth century.

Wages

Agricultural management in Chosŏn was variegated, featuring four distinct types. In one type, entailing the owner's management via slave laborers, the landlord provided housing and food to the slaves, who, in turn, farmed at their master's command. In the second type, landed or independent farming, the landowners or farmers worked their properties, consumed their products, and stored or sold the excess at the market. The third type, the landlord-tenant relationship, involved farmers who lent their services to landlords and submitted a part of the harvest as rent. The fourth type, capitalist management, involved land owners paying others wages for their labor.

Wage payments were not unique to agricultural management. For example, an individual could use an annual salary (*segyŏng*) to hire others to assist with household chores. Another common form of wage was fees the state paid to artisans as needed by the government or the royal house. Many distinct types of salaries existed during Chosŏn's history. However, their exact forms and varieties are largely unknown as it was still relatively uncommon for people to hire others in exchange for wages.

Despite all the recorded instances of people hiring others for their labor, long-term records of their wages are rare. Nevertheless, economic historians are eager to gather information on wages because labor supply and demand determine wages if these concepts apply to Chosŏn's economy. Above all, salary changes can serve as an indicator of labor market changes. Also, inflation-adjusted wages or real wages measure living standards, given that actual earnings can measure purchasing power.

During the busy season in rural areas, farming villages typically hired day laborers (*ilgo*). Records of wages paid in these cases show that rural real wages remained nearly constant through the mid-nineteenth century and then decreased in the late nineteenth century, which may suggest a decline in living standards due to the economic crisis at the time (An Pyŏngjik and Yi Yŏnghun 2001). However, substantiating this assumption is difficult due to insufficient data. This is not to argue that the real wages in Chosŏn do not provide a sufficient proxy for living conditions. Instead,

Economy

as noted above, the existence of a labor market was secondary, and thus, real wages cannot be a significant indicator.

A comparative historical assessment reveals that the real worth of wages in Chosŏn Korea during the first half of the nineteenth century—in terms of rice price—was not much lower than that paid at the time in Tokugawa Japan (1603–1868) or Qing dynasty (1616–1912; self-renamed from Later Jin in 1636) China, both more commercialized than Korea (Yi Taegŭn et al. 2005). Nonetheless, a more accurate comparison should consider that the rice sold in these countries had different qualities.

Fortunately, wage data for Hansŏng and rural areas are available from the government and royal rituals (*ŭigwe*). In the case of Hansŏng, the government or the royal family paid the highest wages, and they remained relatively steady over time (Yi Yŏnghun 2004). Wages in the public sector were slightly higher than those paid in the private sector. After all, as those working for the government or the royal house had been their employees for lengthy periods, they received a premium as a token of appreciation for their public service. Therefore, using government records as the sole source of wage data for Hansŏng is problematic. The data from these records are more ritualistic or symbolic than a reflection of the real market or prices.

Stature

GDP (Gross Domestic Product) per capita is a widely used quantitative measure of living standards, but estimating GDP per capita for Chosŏn Korea is difficult. After all, both the population and production of Chosŏn remain in the realm of guesswork. Also, government-kept statistical data only date to 1910, and thus, calculating Chosŏn's GDP per capita is impossible. Without the GDP per capita, economic historians must rely on proxies for living standards. For other historical regions, scholars have employed real wage, consumption expenditure, and human stature, that is, height measurement, as proxies. Still, as noted above, sufficient statistical data on actual salaries in Chosŏn are precious little. Instead, researchers must look elsewhere for relevant information; height is one alternative recently gaining scholarly attention.

Height data for Chosŏn are available from various sources, among which the most extensive come from military registers (*kunjŏk*). The oldest extant military register dates to the Imjin War, and thus, the source allows estimating the average height of an adult male born in the mid-sixteenth century. Several military registers from the seventeenth century have survived, even more so from the eighteenth and nineteenth centuries. Perhaps reflecting a declining state of military preparedness during more than two centuries of peace in late Chosŏn, the eighteenth- and nineteenth-century military registers are not as detailed as the earlier ones. Height data are missing.

No method filled the height data gaps for the eighteenth and nineteenth centuries until more recent studies used autopsy reports (*kŏman*) to assess height in the late nineteenth century. These reports provide height data for individuals born in the mid-nineteenth century. A longitudinal time series of height data from the sixteenth to the nineteenth centuries is now available thanks to a combination of autopsy and military records. The data show that the average height of men declined during the period (Cho Yŏngjun and Ch'a Myŏngsu 2012). This finding is consistent with earlier studies' conclusions that land productivity and wages declined over time.

Studies in physical anthropology have examined skeletal remains, but the number of samples is limited. Based on approximately 100 skeletal remains datable to Chosŏn, researchers estimated that an adult male in Chosŏn had an average height of around 162 centimeters (Shin et al. 2012). This finding has several limitations. First, the height measured from human bones is not precise, and the margin of estimation error is unclear. Second, an individual's remains do not necessarily

The Routledge Handbook of Early Modern Korea

allow for an accurate determination of when the person lived. Carbon isotope dating allows a large margin of error for the birth year. Third, a sample of 100 skeletal remains cannot sufficiently represent Chosŏn's population over five centuries. Fourth, the location where the skeleton was discovered may not be the same as the locale where the individual was born or raised. After all, the person may have moved from a home locale. As these limitations make using skeletal data to estimate height a complex challenge, any insights gained can only supplement other findings.

Commerce

Chosŏn Korea maintained a de facto occupational hierarchy recognizing "four peoples" (*samin*): scholars, farmers, craftspeople, and merchants. Whereas deeming agriculture the most important industry, the state and the ruling elite denigrated commerce as the lowest form of industry. Commerce itself had a four-tiered hierarchy. At the bottom were the rural markets where ordinary commodities were bought and sold. Above them was the port (*p'ogu*) commerce that linked these markets. Higher up the hierarchy was the Hansŏng market, the logistics hub of the country and the focal point in the domestic market. At the top was international trade, in which Qing China and Tokugawa Japan were the only partners.

Rural marketplaces opened and closed periodically, and only a few merchants sold their goods full-time. Unlike urban marketplaces that had existed for a millennium before Chosŏn, rural marketplaces appeared only after the founding of Chosŏn. The lag was most likely due to low agricultural productivity and, thus, a limited need for daily transactions based on surplus goods. More numerous than storekeepers, peddlers did not have a permanent storefront; instead, they sold their wares from a temporary location. Since a marketplace was empty on its non-market days, peddlers traveled accordingly among various marketplaces to meet their customers, effectively connecting market networks.

Whereas peddlers generally moved items overland using wrapping cloths and traditional Korean A-frames, many remote areas also engaged in port trade. Each port had coastal trade brokers who provided board and lodging for merchant sailors, consigning and selling their products and handling financial transactions. Local ports were bustling, with the Han River ports seeing the most activity. Along the commercial routes to Hansŏng, those along Map'o and Yongsan along the Kyŏnggang ("Capital's River")—the Han River stretch under the jurisdiction of the Hansŏng City government— played the most significant role. As such, the Kyŏnggang became a vital conduit for logistics from all across the country. Coastal trade brokers along the river operated and managed the logistics of ships coming from southern provinces. They maintained a significant monopoly on products by controlling various commercial vessels.

In the logistics centered around Hansŏng, government warehouses and licensed shops (*sijŏn*) were two key actors. Since early Chosŏn, the merchants operating licensed shops enjoyed the exclusive right to procure goods for the government or the royal family. Over time, they became more organized and managed with membership criteria. Among the considerations for licensed shop membership were acquisition, withdrawal, rewards, and punishments. As such, licensed shop communities numbered over 100, each dedicated to a particular commodity. In addition, the state prohibited any non-licensed commercial activity (Cho Young-Jun and Lee Hun-Chang 2015). Licensed shop communities performed assigned obligations of procurement and service to the state in proportion to the privilege of monopolizing a commodity. Their duties included repairing government or royal buildings, painting walls, and weaving ceremonial mats.

For the most part, licensed merchants continually coped with excessive expropriation by the state, payment delays for the products delivered, and market infringement by non-licensed mer-

Economy

chants. Unlicensed merchants continued to proliferate to the point where the government had no choice but to allow them to operate freely. Consequently, by the end of the eighteenth century, most licensed shop merchants, except those selling essential commodities, lost their monopoly. The guild privileges of the six (or eight) major licensed shops would last until the Kabo Reform, but their role in the market decreased well before the abolition. In addition to treaty port openings and inflation, the non-payment and late payment of government and royal bills would be the last straw for these merchants.

Externally, the Chosŏn state restricted international trade, permitting only minimal trading activity with Qing China and Tokugawa Japan. Before creating permanent trading offices (*husi*), interpreters accompanying the royal envoy on their visits to Beijing conducted much of the trade. Silk and silk thread were major imports from China, while ginseng and leather were the key exports until the middle of the seventeenth century. As a relay trade, imported silk was exported to Japan, and payments to China used Japanese silver.

International trade stopped growing in the late eighteenth century, by which Qing China and Tokugawa Japan traded directly rather than routing through Chosŏn Korea. As a result, foreign trade probably accounted for less than two percent of Chosŏn's GDP over the long term. The fundamental reason for international trade's minuscule role in the economy reflects its worldview and identity as a relatively insulated tributary of China. Chosŏn's commerce system based on importing handicraft products and exporting agricultural products also played a role.

Money and Finance

Money was relatively limited in Chosŏn's economy until the seventeenth century. In early Chosŏn, high-value and routine transactions used various means. Specifically, high-value purchases utilized cotton cloth, whereas daily trading relied on rice. Silver ingots were also used in these transactions, albeit rare. In addition, the early Chosŏn government introduced paper money (*chŏhwa*) but failed to circulate it among the public. The use of cotton cloth and rice in trading continued as further attempts to introduce the use of coins in these transactions were unsuccessful until the late seventeenth century when copper coins known as Ever-Normal Circulating Treasure (*Sangp'yŏng t'ongbo*) enjoyed wide circulation. The Ever-Normal Circulating Treasure remained the official currency for nearly two centuries. During the period, money remained centered around One-Cash Coin (*Tangil chŏn*) and Two-Cash Coin (*Tangi chŏn*). The Hundred-Cash Coin and Five-Cash Coin (*Tango chŏn*) were not issued until the late nineteenth century.

The government's primary concern as the issuer of the Ever-Normal Circulating Treasure was its inability to control the money supply as wanted. Given its unstable supply of copper from mining, the government eventually exhausted raw materials for producing the currency, and periods of currency scarcity, "coin drought" (*chŏnhwang*), became frequent. To address this shortage, the government started importing copper from Tokugawa Japan. As a result, identifying the clear long-term trend with Chosŏn's money stock is difficult, and only a rough estimate using the amount of money issued is available (Yi Hŏnch'ang 1999). However, this approach fails to consider the extent of melting down and reminting money, private entities using copper to mint illegal coins, and the illegal minting of low-quality coins. As an alternative, estimating the amount of money in circulation requires considering copper imports.

The primary function of money in Chosŏn was to serve as a medium of exchange, and its spreading use had lasting repercussions. Several records of real estate transactions, including those for land and homes, show a clear shift in payment methods from cotton cloth or silver ingots to copper coins. However, the older practice continued even when copper coins or Ever-Normal

The Routledge Handbook of Early Modern Korea

Circulating Treasure became common. To begin with, the use of a currency lowered transaction costs. Although taxes in mountain regions or remote areas generally required payment in rice, the government sometimes allowed people to pay their taxes in copper coins.

The increased use of copper coins fanned usury. A farmer secured a loan when the rice price was high, in other words, when the copper coin's value was low, and repaid the loan when the rice price was low, that is when the copper coin's value was high. However, since the interest rate for the loan calculated in copper coin remained at fifty percent, the borrower's burden increased manifold. These changes seem to have facilitated fund accumulation. Even for landlords with large stretches of land across the country, having their tenants pay with cash (*kŭmnap*) rather than rice became a regular practice.

As the demand for copper coins increased while the scarcity of copper persisted, the government gradually shrank the coin size, decreasing their actual value vis-à-vis the face value, contributing to inflation. Inflation became more severe in the mid-nineteenth century when the government issued the Hundred-Cash Coin to commemorate the reconstruction of Kyŏngbok Palace (1865–68). The new coin became a symbol of bad money in Chosŏn: the face value was 100 times greater than that of the Ever-Normal Circulating Treasure, but the material value was just five or six times greater, leading to skyrocketing prices. However, the Hundred-Cash Coin was only issued for roughly a year in Hansŏng, and thus, it had no long-term detrimental consequences. This was in contrast to the long-term negative impact of the Five-Cash Coin, another bad money that the government would issue in the 1880s following the opening of treaty ports.

Final Thoughts

In early modern Korea, Chosŏn was a centralized state with an economy where the government played a prominent role. Consequently, tax collection formed the foundation of a nationwide network of transactions, whereas commercial distribution was of secondary concern for the state. Nonetheless, over time, the more logistically burdensome, direct exchange of commodities, as typical in early Chosŏn, gave way to the spreading use of rice as de facto currency and coins as a means of exchange.

Chosŏn's tax system certainly reflects these long-term trends. Most of the government's revenue came from land taxes, whereas commercial taxes accounted for a small portion. This suggests that agriculture was the primary industry, whereas trade and handicrafts played relatively minor roles. Since economic life depended primarily on agriculture, land was the most important factor in production. The state exercised nominal land ownership in the monarch's name, but private individuals maintained de facto ownership. This dual ownership increasingly lost its relevance by late Chosŏn, but private owners could not entirely dismiss the notion of state ownership of land.

This chapter's overview of Chosŏn's economy focused on state finance and land ownership, with agricultural output as a bridge between the two and the secondary areas: commerce, money, and finance. The above discussion described these variables while examining the quantitative indicators and institutional elements. This approach connected empirical inquiries and assessing economic realities, including various financial organizations and systems. How economic conditions and living standards changed over time was considered in this context. Of course, a comparative historical analysis is difficult without quantitative indicators. Accordingly, future studies of Chosŏn's economic history should give more weight to generating time series in investigating long-term trends and producing estimates.

Economy

References

An Pyŏngjik and Yi Yŏnghun, eds. 2001. *Matchil ŭi nongmindŭl: Han'guk kŭnse ch'ollak saenghwalsa*. Ilchogak.

Cho Yŏngjun [Cho Young-Jun; Young-Jun Cho]. 2016. *Chosŏn hugi wangsil chaejŏng kwa Sŏul sangŏp*. Somyong ch'ulp'an.

Cho Yŏngjun [Cho Young-Jun; Young-Jun Cho] and Ch'a Myŏngsu. 2012. "Chosŏn chung-hugi ŭi sinjang ch'use, 1547–1882." *Kyŏngje sahak* 53: 3–37.

Cho Young-Jun [Cho Yŏngjun; Young-Jun Cho] and Lee Hun-Chang [Yi Honch'ang]. 2015. "Seoul Merchant Communities in Late Chosŏn Korea." In *Merchant Communities in Asia, 1600–1980*, edited by Lin Yu-ju and Madeleine Zelin, 29–51. Routledge.

Kim Chaeho. 2005. "Chamae nobi wa in'gan e taehan chaesankwŏn, 1750–1905." *Kyŏngje sahak* 38: 3–39.

Kim Chaeho. 2008. "Chosŏn hugi chungang chaejŏng kwa tongjŏn: *Puyŏk silch'ong* ŭl chungsim ŭro." *Kyŏngje sahak* 44: 3–46.

Palais, James B. 1995. "A Search for Korean Uniqueness." *Harvard Journal of Asiatic Studies* 55, no. 2 (December): 409–25.

Shin, Dong Hoon, Chang Seok Oh, Yi-Suk Kim, and Young-il Hwang. 2012. "Ancient-to-Modern Secular Changes in Korean Stature." *American Journal of Physical Anthropology* 147, no. 3: 433–42.

Yi Hŏnch'ang [Lee Hun-Chang]. 1999. "1678–1865 nyŏn'gan hwap'ye ryang kwa hwap'ye kach'i ŭi ch'ui." *Kyŏngje sahak* 27: 3–45.

Yi Hŏnch'ang [Lee Hun-Chang], ed. 2010. *Chosŏn hugi chaejŏng kwa sijang: kyŏngje ch'ejeron ŭi chŏpkŭn*. Sŏul taehakkyo ch'ulp'an munhwawŏn.

Yi Hŏnch'ang [Lee Hun-Chang] and Cho Yŏngjun [Cho Young-Jun; Young-Jun Cho]. 2008. "Chosŏn hugi kongka ŭi ch'egye wa ch'ui." *Han'guksa yŏn'gu* 142: 203–49.

Yi Taegŭn, Pak It'aek, Pak Kiju, Kim Chaeho, Yi Hŏnch'ang [Lee Hun-Chang], Yi Yŏnghun, Yi Myŏnghwi, Chang Siwŏn, Kim Nangnyŏn, Chu Ikchong, Ch'oe Sango, Yi Sangch'ŏl, Pak Yŏnggu, Sin Changsŏp, Pak Tŏkche, and Kim Sŏkchin. 2005. *Saeroun Han'guk kyŏngje palchŏnsa: Chosŏn hugi esŏ 20 segi kodo sŏngjang kkaji*. Nanam ch'ulp'an.

Yi Yŏnghun, ed. 2004. *Suryang kyŏngjesa ro tasi pon Chosŏn hugi*. Sŏul taehakkyo ch'ulp'anbu.

Yi Yŏnghun. 2012. "17 segi huban–20 segi chŏnban sudojak t'oji saengsan ŭi changgi ch'use." *Kyŏngje nonjip* 51, no. 2: 411–60.

Yi Yŏnghun and Cho Yŏngjun [Cho Young-Jun; Young-Jun Cho]. 2005. "18–19 segi nongga ŭi kagye kyesŭng ŭi ch'ui: Kyŏngsang-do Tansŏng-hyŏn Pŏmmurya-myŏn hojŏk esŏ." *Kyŏngje sahak* 39: 3–25.

PART III

Society and Identity

9
STATUS AND CLASS

Eugene Y. Park

Chosŏn was an early modern society. Hereditary elites rooted in postclassical (medieval) Korea continued to wield supreme power while the socioeconomic positions of nonelites improved. As true in literate sedentary societies elsewhere in Afro-Eurasia, Chosŏn's aristocracy comprised families descended from postclassical regional elites, in the Korean case, the turn of the tenth-century local strongmen (*hojok*) and their local functionary (*hyangni*) descendants. Among them, those who entered Koryŏ's officialdom (918–1392) became *yangban* ("two orders") that comprised civil and military officials (*munban* and *muban*). By the beginning of Chosŏn, the *yangban* became a hereditary elite, *sajok* ("scholarly families"), and birth defined the membership. While the Chosŏn *yangban,* as aristocrats, continued to maintain power at the royal court, the positions of many *chungin* ("middle people"), commoners (*yangin*), and the "lowborn" (*ch'ŏnmin*) improved. Correspondence between ascriptive status categories as such and traditionally recognized occupational categories as scholars (*sa*), farmers (*nong*), artisans (*kong*), and merchants (*sang*) grew weak. Reflecting this change, the participation base of shapers of the officially recognized "public opinion" (*kongnon*), which legitimated deliberations, expanded. The pool evolved from a small group of senior officials in early Chosŏn to include mid-level remonstrance officials, local *yangban*, and Confucian students (*yusaeng*) in mid-Chosŏn to accommodate ordinary commoners in the nineteenth century. Also, aristocratic male–wealthy nonaristocratic female marriages in local society and male slave–female commoner marriages became more common.

This chapter critiques and builds on relevant previous studies in articulating the above argument on Chosŏn's status hierarchy and mobility. According to the Japanese colonial historiography (1910–45), which portrayed Korean history as "stagnant," Chosŏn was a pre-feudal society—unlike the early modern West or Tokugawa Japan (1603–1868) that had ostensibly undergone the phase before achieving capitalism. While noting the concentration of political power at the national level in an increasingly small segment of the aristocracy, beginning in the 1930s, Korean scholarship influenced by Marxism sought to demonstrate a feudal society, if not sprouts of capitalism, in Chosŏn. Since the 1970s, some scholars in and outside Korea have emphasized the overall stability and continuity of Chosŏn society as dominated by Confucian *yangban*. Song Chunho, for example, stressed that *yangban* identity, values, customs, and networks not only persisted throughout Chosŏn's history but even continued into the twentieth century until the Korean War (Song Chunho 1987). In contrast, others have highlighted a broadening

DOI: 10.4324/9781003262053-13

The Routledge Handbook of Early Modern Korea

socioeconomic base of political participation, especially in local society. For example, Ch'oe Yuno views the seventeenth and eighteenth centuries as a transition when the medieval land tenure system based on private ownership monopolized by *yangban* disintegrated. In a more liberalized economy, in which managerial agriculture and commercial transactions assumed greater importance, a new socioeconomic divide emerged between landlords and peasants, replacing the medieval *yangban*-nonelite divide (Ch'oe 2006). The two seemingly opposing viewpoints have been merging in the last two decades. Studies have shown continuity and change are not mutually exclusive trends for understanding Chosŏn or any other historical society.

Mindful of relevant interpretive approaches, this chapter divides the social history of early modern Korea into three phases, each covered by a section. The tripartite division reflects major sociopolitical transitions at both national and local levels. In early Chosŏn (1392–1567), opportunities for political advancement were available to the aristocracy as a whole. The members, *yangban*, wielded power as proprietors of a centralizing state. However, intensifying internal strife split the political establishment into two groups: the reformist Sarim ("rusticated literati"), who articulated Neo-Confucian moral rhetoric, and the Hun'gu ("meritorious old [elite]"), who were generally capital region-based high officials content with status quo. Also, the aristocracy's avoidance of tax and military obligations weakened the state while overburdening other taxpayers. In the mid-Chosŏn period (1567–1724), the triumphant Sarim political rhetoric of moral governance underwent a series of internal divisions through institutionalized partisan politics that purged losers. While local *yangban* enjoyed elite standing at the county level, state-employed technical specialist *chungin* in the capital emerged as an expert class. Then, in late Chosŏn (1724–1873), the capital aristocracy monopolized political power at the court while the local *yangban* hegemony eroded. County magistrates empowered by stronger monarchs of the eighteenth century co-opted influential local nonelites. Likewise, the technical specialist *chungin* and northern regional elites continued accumulating sociocultural capital despite a political glass ceiling. Along with illegitimate sons of *yangban*, they struggled to overcome the barrier. This chapter ends with a summation and a reflection on what lay ahead for Korea beyond 1873.

Aristocracy, *Chungin*, Commoners, and the Lowborn, 1392–1567

The Chosŏn state institutionalized a social hierarchy of four status groups. Among the population, which grew from roughly 7.5 million in 1392 to perhaps 15 million in 1567, the highest status group, *yangban*—who generally corresponded to "scholars" traditionally recognized in East Asia as most prestigious—had become a hereditary aristocracy by the beginning of Chosŏn. Such *yangban* constituted no more than two percent of the population, as true elsewhere in sedentary societies throughout early modern Afro-Eurasia. Just below the aristocracy was a heterogenous status group, the *chungin* broadly defined: the narrow-definition *chungin*, who were state-employed technical specialists; capital functionaries (*kyŏng ajŏn*); local functionaries (*hyangni*); noncommissioned military officers (*kun'gyo, changgyo*); the illegitimate children (*sŏ*) of *yangban* males by commoner concubines (*yangch'ŏp*); and regional elites of northern Korea, especially P'yŏngan and Hamgyŏng Provinces (Cho 1999, 68–72). Not recognized as social peers by the *yangban*, the *chungin* nonetheless viewed themselves as scholars and held offices (Han 1997, 85–92). Below them were the rest of the free population, the commoners (*yangin, yangmin*)—primarily farmers but also an increasing number of artisans and merchants. At the bottom of the status hierarchy was an unfree population, the lowborn, who performed various duties. Most were chattel slaves (*nobi*) owned by a private individual or the state, but some were *kisaeng*: professional female entertainers registered with the government. An offspring of parents not of the same social status generally inherited the lower status.

A binary of the *yangban* (or *pan*) and the "ordinary" (*sang*) set the aristocracy apart from the rest. A closed status group that no longer admitted a newcomer, *yangban* comprised civil and military officials of Koryŏ aristocratic descent. In a seventeenth-century genealogy of *yangban* families, *Origins of Descent Groups* (*Ssijok wŏllyu*), for the most part, the author, who was an aristocratic civil official, Cho Chongun (1607–83), views a reliable continuous patrilineal genealogy of an aristocratic descent group as going no further back than an early Koryŏ local strongman or functionary. He records various descent lines of shared surname and ancestral seat (*pon'gwan*) for most descent groups without connecting them to a common founding ancestor—as later genealogies would do (Figure 9.1). The *yangban*, a closed status group with origins in Koryŏ, also included their kin mothered by a woman of *yangban* status. As such, the Chosŏn aristocracy was a continuation of the Koryŏ elite. Some did not survive the political turmoil of the Koryŏ–Chosŏn transition. Such a case, however, typically had more to do with a relatively small number of male members as new, potential officeholders compared to other families (Duncan 2000). In possession of land and slaves, Chosŏn *yangban* sought official careers through the government service examination (*kwagŏ*), protection appointment ("shadow privilege"; *ŭmsŏ*), or recommendation (*ch'ŏn'gŏ*). From childhood on, aristocratic males could devote themselves to studies focused on texts in literature (*mun*), history (*sa*), and philosophy (*ch'ŏl*) while pursuing the arts of prose, poetry, and calligraphy. Supporting an aristocratic lifestyle were various institutionalized privileges sanctioned by the state. *Yangban* enjoyed exemption from tax and corvée obligations because they served the state as scholars and officials. In the late fifteenth century, exemption from active-duty military service became increasingly common.

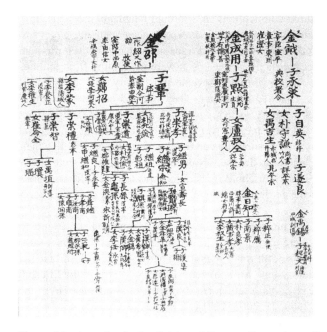

Figure 9.1 A section in the *Origins of Descent Group* shows five Kyŏngju Kim lines unconnected, each descending from an individual surnamed Kim (金). In contrast, contemporary Kyŏngju Kim genealogies generally record various descent lines to King Kyŏngsun (r. 927–35), the last ruler of Silla. Source: *Ssijok wŏllyu*; reprint by Pogyŏng munhwasa, 1991. Photo credit: Eugene Y. Park.

The Routledge Handbook of Early Modern Korea

The aristocracy sought to exclude others while defending its interests and wielding political power. In the fifteenth century, some nonaristocrats of talent passed the prestigious civil examination (*munkwa*) and even attained civil offices. *Yangban* officials, however, scrutinized such an appointee to the effect of ending his official career. A case in point is Chang Yŏngsil (fl. 1423–38), the son of a Chinese émigré and a Korean *kisaeng*. A technician who devised various astronomical devices as clepsydras, Chang enjoyed the patronage of Kings T'aejong (r. 1400–18) and Sejong (r. 1418–50)—until the latter's sedan chair that Chang crafted broke. Casting the incident as lesemajesty, the State Tribunal (Ŭigŭmbu) sought to have Chang punished with 80 strokes of flogging and stripped of his office. Although Sejong commuted his sentence, Chang no longer appears in any historical record thereafter (*Sejong sillok* 1433/9/16, entry 3; 1434/7/1, entry 4; 1438/1/7, entry 3; 1442/3/16, entry 2; 1442/4/27, entry 2; 1442/5/3, entry 2).

Below the aristocracy but above the commoners were *chungin,* who married among themselves and thus constituted a closed status group. In a late nineteenth-century genealogy of lineages that produced technical specialists and capital-based noncommissioned military officers, *Records of Surname Origins* (*Sŏngwŏllok*) by Yi Ch'anghyŏn (1850–1921), the earliest recorded figure in each case is someone who lived in early Chosŏn. Typically, the first or two generations of individuals have no degree, court rank, or office indicated. Much smaller in number are the lineages that are offshoots of a *yangban* family. The geographical treatise (*chiriji*) section of the *Veritable Records of King Sejong* records each county's local functionary surnames. Barred from the civil and military examinations (*mukwa*), some such illegitimate sons nonetheless obtained lower-level military offices or technical specialist positions.

Although denigrated by the aristocracy, technical specialist *chungin* held their ground as their services were essential to the state. The most highly regarded were those who passed the technical examination (*chapkwa*), which featured competitions in a foreign language, medicine, law, astronomy, and accounting. Among technical specialists, interpreters accompanying envoys to China or Japan even enjoyed profits from officially approved trade accompanying each mission. Including such interpreters, technical specialists of early Chosŏn were not hailing from families monopolizing such positions as would be true by the early seventeenth century.

In contrast, local functionary duties remained hereditary. They wielded considerable influence, as centrally appointed magistrates—almost always *yangban*—were neither familiar with local conditions nor served a long term. All the same, the *yangban* who relocated from the capital and established themselves as landed local elites subordinated the functionaries who, unlike their Koryŏ predecessors, no longer received land from the state. Nonetheless, as agents of state power performing such duties as tax collection and household registration updates, local functionaries could be at odds with local *yangban* and the general population, especially during economic hardship (Yi Hunsang 1990).

As true with southern local *yangban*, lineages of P'yŏngan and Hamgyŏng, emerging as regional elites by the sixteenth century, were transplants. The aristocracy, however, did not view them as their peers. After all, early Chosŏn's north was a region that had been Koryŏ's militarized border zones with garrisons before a century-long Mongol control (1258–1356). In the fifteenth century, the Chosŏn state promoted the region's resettlement by agricultural colonists from the south (Wagner 1977, 23; Kang Sŏkhwa 2000, 21, 2002, 12–14).

Commoners constituted the majority of the population. Most were free cultivators, but the segment of the population working as handcrafters and merchants increased. Commoners were legally eligible to take the government service examinations, but most were illiterate. Thus, devoting themselves to years of intensive study in preparation for the examination was not feasible for most. Responsible for land tax, local tribute, corvée, and military service, all of which were

136

Status and Class

burdensome, they struggled to survive. Handcrafters worked for government or private clients, whereas market merchants and peddlers performed transactions under government regulation. As the early Chosŏn economic policy prioritized agriculture while restricting commerce, merchants remained inferior to farmers in social status. Early Chosŏn also treated some commoners who performed certain arduous, socially denigrated duties as de facto lowborn. They included marines (*sugun*), government office runners (*saryŏng*), State Tribunal security guards (*najang*), beacon fire station guards (*pongsugun*), post station staff (*yŏngni*), and tax transport guards (*chogun*). Before the late fifteenth century, Korea's occasional military campaigns against pirates, the Wakō, or domestic rebellions offered opportunities for actions of military merit. Such an opportunity could result in an office or a court rank for a commoner. However, the attainment did not enable him to become a *yangban*. As most commoners struggled to perform various obligations to the state, many resorted to banditry in times of hardship—some even robbing goods transported to the central government or *yangban*. Among them, Im Kkŏkchŏng (1504–62), who was active in Hwanghae and Kyŏnggi Provinces during the reign of King Myŏngjong (r. 1545–67), reportedly took from the rich and gave to the poor before being captured and executed (*Myŏngjong sillok* 1559/3/27, entry 2; 1562/1/8, entry 1).

Below commoners in status were the lowborn. As descendants of those enslaved as war prisoners or state criminals throughout history, most were chattel slaves. They were transferable as commodities through a financial transaction, inheritance, or gift exchange. As was true in Koryŏ, a resident slave (*solgŏ nobi*) lived and worked in a private household or at a government office. An out-resident slave (*oegŏ nobi*), who managed the owner's property elsewhere, typically a landholding, resided onsite and periodically remitted "personal tribute" (*sin'gong*) to the owner. After decades of debate on the legal status of an offspring of a mixed commoner–lowborn union, the court's application of the Great Code of Administration (Kyŏngguk taejŏn; promulgated in 1471) was such that such a child generally inherited the lowborn status (Palais 1996, 221–25). The lowborn also included *kisaeng*, who were professional female entertainers. Some *kisaeng* were former government slaves. The most highly regarded by their clients were those well-versed in prose, poetry, and painting. In principle, the government allowed only aristocratic officials to hire *kisaeng* for special occasions rather than going to *kisaeng* houses (*kibang*). In reality, besides officials, royals and ordinary *yangban* patronized such venues.

Except for the lowborn, more or less everyone bore a patrilineally inherited surname linked to an ancestral seat. For *yangban* and local functionaries, as well as technical specialists descended from *yangban* or local functionaries, the identifiers together ostensibly indicated the locale of patrilineal ancestors of the tenth century—when autonomous local strongmen from Silla–Koryŏ transition became hereditary local functionaries (Yi Sugŏn 2003, 26–28). In the fifteenth century, the locally based descendants of *yangban* who took up residence in a particular county outside the capital began organizing themselves into lineages as cohesive social collectives. Mostly commoners, the rest of the population of status higher than the lowborn had surnames, but they generally lacked knowledge of their ancestors based on sustained genealogical record keeping. For many, one's residence functioned as an ancestral seat for household registers maintained and updated triennially by the state (Park 2013, 172).

Indeed, among those of the same surname and ancestral seat, social status varied, covering a full spectrum of status categories. A case in point is any Chŏnju Yi patrilineally descended from a Chosŏn king. Unlike in Koryŏ, when the definition of a royal entitled to privileges and constraints changed over time (Kim Kidŏk 1993, 8–21), the Chosŏn state set the definition in Sejong's reign and subsequently abided by it for nearly five centuries. Legal status as a male "royal kin" (*chongch'in*) only applied to a Chŏnju Yi no more than four generations removed

The Routledge Handbook of Early Modern Korea

from a monarch through direct male descent, that is up to great-great-grandsons. Generally barred from competing in the government service examination or holding an office, a royal received guaranteed living support. The privilege was even extended to his children by a concubine—commoner or lowborn—as long as they were no more than four generations removed from the most recent royal ancestor. Reflecting these practices are various editions of government-compiled royal Chŏnju Yi genealogies, beginning with the mid-seventeenth-century compilation known today as the *Records of the Royal House of the Chosŏn Dynasty* (*Chosŏn wangjo sŏnwŏllok*). As evident in these sources, beyond the four-generation limit, a Chŏnju Yi of royal descent was no different from the general aristocracy in that an offspring of a *yangban* male and a concubine was not a bona fide *yangban*. Thus, in theory and practice, a fifth-generation patrilineal descendant of a Chosŏn king, male or female, could be a commoner or lowborn, depending on the concubine mother's status.

The basis for a shared patrilineal descent that shaped a socially meaningful collective shifted from an ancestral seat to a socially recognized male of prominence, a prominent ancestor (*hyŏnjo*). As such, county-based lineages emerged in the provinces in the sixteenth century as elite social groups enjoying a degree of autonomy from the state. An increasing number of aristocrats left Hansŏng for a provincial locale as victims of political turmoil or economic security through in-laws, if not for both reasons. From the mid-fifteenth century to the mid-sixteenth century, such incidents as the coup (1453) of future King Sejo (r. 1455–68) against the protectors of his nephew in the minority, King Tanjong (r. 1452–55), and the Literati Purges (1498, 1504, 1519, and 1545) drove surviving victims and immediate kin to take up residence in the provinces, especially in the two southernmost provinces, Chŏlla and Kyŏngsang, both agriculturally productive. Kyŏngsang was also the early epicenter of Nature and Principle Learning, that is Neo-Confucianism. Despite its patriarchal and patrilineal tendencies, ancient uxorilocal marriage customs persisted. Not only did newlyweds reside with the wife's parents for years, but many stayed permanently, especially if the in-laws were more affluent. Typically, the custom laid the foundation for subsequent successes of the descendants as members of a local elite lineage (Deuchler 2015, 97–101).

Emerging *yangban* lineages shared some defining characteristics. Above all, *yangban* males were members of a lineage, a patrilineally defined kin group descended from a founding ancestor (*iphyangjo*; "ancestor who first entered the locale")—typically a prominent official or scholar, if not both. For generations, the members resided in the county where the founding ancestors had first settled. Also, such lineage members formed a pool of candidates eligible for election to the local council (*hyanghoe*) by its incumbent members. A potential member had to be from a family of previous local councilors (*hyangwŏn*), not only through his father but also his mother and in-laws. Recorded in the local council roster (*hyangan*), updated whenever new members were elected, the councilors advised the centrally appointed magistrate. Institutionalizing such a relationship was Sejong's revival (1428) of local agencies (*yuhyangso*), staffed by local council officers and local functionaries, and the capital agency (*kyŏngjaeso*) of late Koryŏ that his father T'aejong had abolished (1406) as a part of his centralization effort to strengthen local control through magistrates (Yi Tae-Jin 2010, 37–38). Furthermore, the Sarim pursued social reform guided by Nature and Principle Learning through "moral transformation by education" (*kyohwa*) at individual and community levels. Especially after the Literati Purges, local *yangban*, among whom were surviving Sarim victims, devised and implemented community compacts (*hyangyak*), which enforced a *yangban*-dominated local social order (Kawashima 2002, 40–42). Reflecting so much at stake for a local elite lineage, a compilation of genealogy (*chokpo*) intended to record all members sharing the same surname and ancestral seat emerged as a custom. In practical terms, those recorded were mostly bona fide *yangban* (Song Ch'ansik 1999, 55–57).

Status and Class

Local elites even secured a presence in politics of public opinion that initially featured only the high officials at the court. The Sarim began to assert themselves as a cohesive political force in the reign of King Sŏngjong (r. 1469–95) through the Censorate (Taegan) with its role of remonstrance. This development engaged politics of public opinion with an increasingly more comprehensive range of moral discourse on realizing the "principles of heaven" (*ch'ŏlli*), by which all phenomena ultimately operate. In more practical terms, this meant the politics that sought to realize the ideal Confucian society. In the reign of King Chungjong (r. 1506–45), the politics of public opinion also began to deal with the articulations of Confucian Academy students. Subsequently, in the ensuing decades, provincial *yangban* too began to secure participation as they solidified their local elite positions through such institutions as local councils and community compacts (Kim Ingeol 2024, 52–54).

Inspiring the new, *yangban*-dominated local social order were the Sarim, guided by Neo-Confucianism. The Sarim actively promoted *Elementary Learning* (*Sohak*; Ch. *Xiaoxue*), a textbook for the young written by the Neo-Confucian philosopher Zhu Xi (1130–1200) of Song dynasty (960–1279) China. The Chosŏn aristocracy regarded it as the introductory text on morality and rituals. Accordingly, the local elite devised a community compact in one county after another, which a reformist Sarim scholar-official, Cho Kwangjo (1482–1520), introduced during Chungjong's reign. Highlighting mutual aid organizations and activities, Cho and other Sarim imbued community compacts with Confucian ethics. Guiding them were the Three Bonds (the relationships of subject to ruler, child to parents, and husband and wife) and the Five Moral Imperatives (the morality informing the relationships of subject to ruler, child to parents, husband and wife, younger brother to elder brother, and friend to friend). In doing so, the Sarim sought moral transformation of the entire community through education and rituals. Simultaneously, community compacts performed functions of local autonomy, such as maintaining public safety and social order, especially after the devastating Imjin War (East Asian War; 1592–98), when local *yangban* lineages exercised leadership in rebuilding their communities.

While lineages as patrilineally organized social collectives emerged, uxorilocal marriage customs persisted well into the sixteenth century. Above all, as true in the past for some millennium, newlywed couples resided at the wife's natal home. Also, while a new law gave the eldest legitimate son (*chŏk changja*) an additional fifth of the inheritance from the parents to cover the cost of his ancestral ritual duties, other children, sons and daughters alike, received an equal share of the remainder of the estate, as was customary, dating back to Koryŏ (Deuchler 2015, 151). Furthermore, siblings could take turns performing or sharing responsibilities for ancestral rites, rather than the eldest legitimate son having to assume all the duties. Accordingly, for an aristocratic male without a legitimate son, an illegitimate son could become the fully vested heir (*sŭngjung ch'ŏpcha*; "concubine's son continuing the line"), or the eldest legitimate daughter's legitimate son could perform ancestral rites. Reflecting such customs, the oldest extant genealogy, the Andong Kwŏn genealogy of 1476, and the next oldest, the Munhwa Yu genealogy of 1565, each records direct descendants of an apex figure to the effect that about 70 percent of those recorded are not a Kwŏn or a Yu respectively.

All the same, the sixteenth century was a transition period in terms of kinship customs among elites. The 1565 Munhwa Yu genealogy records some cases of adoption—of either a patrilineal nephew or of a cousin's legitimate son—to continue the line of a male without a legitimate son. In contrast, the earlier 1476 Andong Kwŏn genealogy records none (Peterson 1996, 7). By the mid-sixteenth century, more doctrinaire Neo-Confucian scholar-officials' pursuit of ideal patriarchy by devising new laws that emphasized filial piety and chaste widowhood was well underway. After decades of debate, the Great Code of Administration prohibited a widow's remarriage. Moreover, it barred illegitimate sons and the sons and grandsons of remarried women from the civil and military examinations. In the same context, the state made provisions for recognizing and honoring filial sons and daughters (*hyoja*, *hyonyŏ*) and chaste wives (*yŏlnyŏ*)—even disseminating stories about them with books printed in Han'gŭl (Hangul), the Korean phonetic alphabet, for nonelites and women (Oh 2013, 128–90). Although a husband could have only one wife by law, he could maintain concubines. Consequently, the population of commoners and the lowborn of recent *yangban* descent rapidly increased.

The Center and Stabilization of Local Society, 1567–1724

Mid-Chosŏn Korea experienced remarkable population growth, fueled by a continuing expansion in agricultural output. Reflecting a significant dip due to the Imjin War, the Chŏngmyo War (1627), and the Pyŏngja War (1637), as of 1678, the total population increased to about 10 to 12 million. By then, the long-term growth since the fourteenth century had resumed. Shaping the upward trajectory were improved efficiencies in predominantly agricultural production that drove commercialization, urbanization, and diversification in material goods. More Koreans moved to towns and cities, while most still lived in villages in the larger river basins: some close to major rivers, others deep in interior valleys. Korea had no urban center comparable in population to China's metropolises or Japan's Edo—each with at least one million residents. Chosŏn Korea's capital, Hansŏng, had less than 200,000 (Totman 2004, 132–34, 137–38).

At the top of the social hierarchy, the mid-Chosŏn *yangban* bifurcated into those residing in the capital region, who remained active in the central political arena, and the rest, who became purely local elites. The *yangban* likely constituted less than two percent of the population, as in other early modern, sedentary, literate Afro-Eurasian societies. As such, the *yangban* became also divided in terms of partisan loyalty as institutionalized political parties, each with a distinct socio-regional base and intellectual orientation, emerged in the reign of King Sŏnjo (r. 1567–1608). Partisan politics, as such, set forth a winner-take-all process wherein the victor purged the loser, and the victor subsequently subdivided into new, mutually antagonistic parties. Moreover, as partisan identities crystalized by the mid-seventeenth century, the segment of the overall *yangban* population fully participating in national politics decreased to the extent that landed aristocrats of a county outside western central Korea wielded power as local elites only.

At the end of the sixteenth century, virtually every rural county had some leading *yangban* lineages, each claiming descent from a renowned scholar or official who had first moved to the county. For the most part, no longer producing an examination graduate, not to mention an officeholder, such *yangban* as local council officers advised the magistrate through the local advisory bureau (*hyangch'ŏng*), which was the new name for the earlier local agency (Figure 9.2). Producing council members, local aristocrats diligently recorded the councilors in a local council roster. At the same time, the elite lorded over the population with community compacts and private Confucian academies (*sŏwŏn*). Besides honoring Confucian worthies from prominent lineages, academies increasingly brought the local political leadership to weigh in on court politics through debates, memorials, and group petitions to the throne (Yŏng-ho Ch'oe 1999, 41–45). Such *yangban* lineages played a leading role in rebuilding local society amidst the devastations of the mid-Chosŏn wars. The effort fundamentally sought to reaffirm a social hierarchy guided by Confucian moral rhetoric as local *yangban* articulated. As the typical natural village had decreased in size by the mid-seventeenth century, the villages controlled by *yangban* enjoyed considerable autonomy. Constituting a closed status group, aristocrats compiled increasingly voluminous family genealogies intended to record all members of a descent group sharing the same surname and ances-

Figure 9.2 Local advisory bureau building in Koesan, Ch'ungch'ŏng Province, 1995 restoration of the original construction, 1681. Photo credit: County of Goesan (Koesan), Chungcheongbuk-do, Republic of Korea.

tral seat. Still, the coverage remained more or less limited to *yangban* members (Song Ch'ansik 1999, 56–57). Besides such genealogies, as well as ancestral gravesites and family shrines, local aristocrats maintained marriage ties among themselves. However, occasional adoptions involving distantly related local and capital *yangban* descent lines of the same surname and ancestral seat continued into the eighteenth century (Park 2007, 123–25).

As local *yangban* could abuse their power and engage in extortion, commoners used various means to hold their ground. Especially important to the ordinary farmers' survival strategy was *ture* (or *nonggye*), which were collaborative community labor groups, and incense associations (*hyangdo*), which, as before in Koryŏ and earlier, remained village collectives with shared Buddhist and popular religious rituals. Often overburdened by the state and bullied by *yangban*, farmers relied on *ture* and incense associations for such occasions as a community member's death in particular and in times of hardship in general. In the late seventeenth century, when the labor-intensive farming technology of rice seedling transfer began to spread, *ture* assumed even greater importance. The trend left incense associations with more solely funeral-related responsibilities, including pallbearing.

Most nonelites struggled to make ends meet, but a small yet growing number improved their positions. When Jurchen raids became more frequent and intense in the late sixteenth century, increasingly frequent, larger-scale military examinations began to recruit candidates from more diverse social backgrounds. The subsequent wars accelerated this trend, offering advancement opportunities for those performing acts of military merit. The commoners who did so mainly received court ranks or offices, whereas meritorious slaves won manumission (Park 2007, 53–58). In the postwar era, the financially strapped government instituted a system granting court ranks and offices to grain donors, often by issuing blank appointment certificates (*kongmyŏngch'ŏp*). Before long, such state-sanctioned status trappings became more widely available to illegitimate sons of *yangban*, commoners, and even former slaves (Park

The Routledge Handbook of Early Modern Korea

2007, 128–32, 2008a, 747–48). Furthermore, as economic factors defined social relations more than traditional ascriptive status did, male slave–female commoner marriages increased (Hejtmanek 2011, 142). In the seventeenth century, the legal status of an offspring of a mixed commoner–lowborn union—which the Great Code of Administration had more or less declared to be lowborn—began to change back and forth between commoner and lowborn, depending on the policies of the political party in power until 1731 when matrifilial practice prevailed (Palais 1996, 247–48; Hejtmanek 2011, 142).

Albeit rejected as social peers by *yangban*, in mid-Chosŏn, technical specialist *chungin* of Hansŏng and the regional elites of P'yŏngan and Hamgyŏng began to enjoy some upward social mobility. In the seventeenth century, the capital *chungin* formed a closed-status group of state-employed experts who married, adopted heirs, and kept genealogical records. The *chungin* of Hansŏng comprised interpreters, physicians, jurists, astronomers, accountants, calligraphers, musicians, administrative functionaries, and noncommissioned military officers. They typically hailed from families descended from commoners who had made their way up by 1600. Others were descendants of illegitimate children of aristocrats (Han 1997, 92–95; Kim Tuhŏn 2013, 150–70; Park 2014, 14–16). Likewise, northern regional elites generally descended from commoners who had migrated from the south in early Chosŏn. By the seventeenth century, their strong socio-economic position allowed them to begin securing even the coveted civil examination degrees (Wagner 1977, 23–24). Increasingly claiming *yangban* descent through patently false early or mid-Chosŏn connecting links, the elites of P'yŏngan and Hamgyŏng too married, adopted heirs, and kept genealogical records all among themselves (Park 2008b). The northern elites came to differ little from the southern local *yangban* in overall sociocultural capital (Sun Joo Kim 2007), aside from problematic genealogical claims.

Geographically based lineages as patrilineally organized kin groups thrived among *yangban*, and others increasingly emulated the model, which entailed some associated trends. Above all, the rotation of ancestral ritual duty (*pongsa*) among siblings, regardless of sex, gave way to the deceased's eldest legitimate son performing the duty. Earlier, if the deceased male had no heir, his legitimate daughter's legitimate son could perform the duty, as mentioned, but by the seventeenth century, the deceased's adopted son performing the duty had become common (Peterson 1996, 160). Reflecting the status barrier between legitimate and illegitimate children, a male of entirely legitimate-son descent could only adopt a male of the next generation born as a legitimate son. A corollary to the practice among *yangban* and *chungin* was that an illegitimate son married such a female counterpart, for whom an alternative was to become a concubine of a male born as a legiti-mate son (Deuchler 1992, 270–73). Accompanying the change was the emergence of the concept of lineage heir (*chongson*), according to which transmission of the ancestral ritual duty continued through the eldest legitimate sons. Since the duty demanded economic resources, the earlier prac-tice of more equitable inheritance among siblings regardless of sex gave way to primogeniture geared toward preventing fragmentation of family land and other resources among descendants over time (Deuchler 2015, 155, 267).

The consequences were manifold. By the eighteenth century, uxorilocal marriage had given way to virilocal marriage. Per the new practice, a daughter no longer received a meaningful inher-itance but a one-time dowry when married. And a newlywed took up permanent residence with the husband's family (Deuchler 1992, 227–29). Reflecting these new trends, as descent group popula-tions continued to grow, increasingly more voluminous genealogies, stopping the coverage of the descendants through daughters after three generations became the norm. As shaped by *yangban*, new customs gradually spread among the rest of the population emulating the aristocracy, espe-cially among those whose socioeconomic positions improved.

Status and Class

Accelerating Status Mobility, 1724–1873

The earlier general correspondence between the four status categories and the four occupational categories grew weak as various socioeconomic changes unfolded. Above all, Korea's population growth slowed as Chosŏn encountered constraints concerning population density, urban settlement, elite lifestyles, and the ordinary people's hardship. The population fluctuated erratically in the 10 to 14 million range from about 1700 to 1864. The capital's population surpassed and stabilized at around 200,000 in the eighteenth century, reflecting the demographic stability before the late nineteenth century. Elsewhere, smaller towns likely stopped growing or even declined. Not only did the Chosŏn state's revenue base cease to expand, increasing artisanal output, such as cloth manufacturing, migrated into the hinterland, closer to raw materials and lower-cost land and labor. Geographical mobility probably intensified. Changes in agriculture practice and rural social organization created new needs and possibilities that spurred those seeking work. Generally, nonelites in urban areas also faced greater exposure to disease and other harms. By contrast, the de facto one-party rule at the court kept most local aristocrats away from Hansŏng (Totman 2004, 116–17). Some even cultivated their land, if not struggling to survive as tenant farmers. By the mid-nineteenth century, *yangban*, *chungin*, commoners, and the lowborn could find themselves in any of the four occupational groups: scholars, farmers, artisans, and merchants.

Among various determinants of a socioeconomic class, patrilineal lineage as a social organization earlier limited to the aristocracy spread across status boundaries. By the eighteenth century, single-surname or lineage villages had sprung up throughout the country, many with their prominent ancestors honored at a local private academy or a lineage shrine. A woman could not own property, and daughters lost the right of inheritance. Especially among *yangban*, a couple took residence at the husband's natal home upon the wedding. Only occasionally, the wife visited hers. While lower-class women continued to enjoy more freedom in such regard, the state honored them, as well as lower-class men, regardless of social status, for a manifest cardinal Confucian virtue. As the performance of ancestral rites by the eldest legitimate son became the norm, such a son received the lion's share of inheritance as the lineage heir. Since an illegitimate son was ineligible for heirship, a father without a legitimate son adopted a brother's or a patrilineal cousin's legitimate son, even if only distantly related.

Furthermore, posthumous adoptions also became common. Accordingly, becoming widespread was the compilation of genealogy as a record of membership in a patrilineal descent group, a belief that all those with the same surname and ancestral seat are of common descent, and tracing a descent group's ancestry as far back as early Korea or to China. In this context, genealogies began to connect, one way or another, various descent lines of shared surname and ancestral seat. Also, a descent group changing its ancestral seat to that best known for the given surname became common (Yi Sugŏn 2003, 318–27). All the same, membership in a particular lineage associated with a locale continued to define social identity, especially among *yangban*.

The spreading lineage consciousness across the traditional status boundaries reflects improving positions of some nonelites, such as aristocratic men's illegitimate sons and specialist *chungin*. Kings Yŏngjo (r. 1724–76) and King Chŏngjo (r. 1776–1800) sought to appoint and promote more such individuals. Illegitimate sons of *yangban* men successfully petitioned the court to remove restrictions on their access to certain prestigious offices reserved for bona fide aristocrats. Their efforts encouraged specialist *chungin* to do likewise, although ultimately failing to achieve the goal (Kim Yangsu 1999, 227–33; Park 2014, 48). Among the specialist *chungin*, many of whom amassed wealth through their expertise in various areas, interpreters became exceptionally knowledgeable about the world beyond East Asia and understood the ramifications of Western imperialism. Since their duties were vital in diplomacy, interpreters assumed an expanding role in introducing new knowledge from the West through China (Kim Yangsu 1999, 237–46). Interpreters and other state-employed experts profited from official international trade and involved themselves in expanding private trade of all forms. Likewise, other capital residents with ties to the court profited from agriculture and commerce, including officeholders across status boundaries, noncommissioned military officers, capital functionaries, and commoners (Figure 9.3). Rising from commoner status, capital functionaries even gained cultural capital that put many on par with *yangban* in such areas as the classics, prose, and poetry (Cho Sŏngyun 1999, 86–88).

Indeed, many commoners became well-to-do and gained political clout thanks to various factors. Some commoners became affluent by acquiring cultivated plots and improving farm management. In Hansŏng, booming commerce and larger-scale construction projects fueled the demand for skilled laborers. As late as 1800, they enjoyed a living standard comparable to that of their counterparts in China and Western Europe, the most affluent parts of the world (Jun, Lewis, and Kang Han-Rog 2008). Mindful of nonelites of means, in the eighteenth century, Yŏngjo and Chŏngjo's Policy of Impartiality sought the people's opinions to enhance royal legitimacy against the Patriarchs' (Noron) de facto one-party rule. Once the government's tax levy began heeding the public opinion of elites and nonelites alike, wealthy commoners backed by magistrates secured local council memberships. Collaborating with the state power centered around the magistrate and local functionaries, in most counties, such commoners' growing presence in local councils compelled the bona fide *yangban* stopped updating local council rosters by the early nineteenth century. As local council membership became diverse, the scope of the members' action too expanded, although the state continued to manipulate their advice for effective tax collection. The space for new public opinion that could narrow the gap between *yangban* and the rest remained confined. However, Chŏngjo's efforts to seek feedback from his subjects across status boundaries invigorated the official petition (*chŏngso*) system, which provided a new site for public opinion (Kim Ingeol 2024, 56–60).

Figure 9.3 Fighting Males at a Kisaeng House (*Yugwak chaengung*; early nineteenth century) by Sin Yunbok (1758–c. 1814), a *chungin* court painter descended from an illegitimate son of an early Chosŏn aristocrat. As a *kisaeng* holding a long smoking pipe watches, a *yangban* and a special martial arts officer (*muye pyŏlgam*), a military *chungin* running the *kisaeng* house, restrain a young man who lost the fight to the bare-chested man. The man on the far right is picking up the pieces of the loser's hat. Source and photo credit: Kansong Art Museum.

Status and Class

Although not accepted as social peers by the old aristocracy, new elites effectively weakened the correspondence between traditional status categories and socioeconomic classes. As the government not only continued to grant court ranks and offices to grain donors, often through blank appointment certificates, but also sold local council memberships, the upwardly mobile used status trappings to gain exemption from military service and other obligations to the state—all privileges formerly monopolized by *yangban*. Besides, many wealthy commoners, along with specialist capital *chungin* and northern regional elites, attained a level of education and cultural sophistication comparable to *yangban*. In particular, keen on securing social recognition as an equal to *yangban*, an increasing number of expert *chungin*, functionaries, northern regional elites, merchants, crafters, and wealthy farmers pursued literary activities formerly monopolized by the aristocracy (Yi Hunsang 1990; Kim Yangsu 1999, 237–46). Indeed, in late Chosŏn, three northern provinces—Hamgyŏng, P'yŏngan, and Hwanghae—were more successful than the south (except for the capital) in civil examination success (Wagner 1977). Likewise, Kaesŏng, formerly Koryŏ's the capital, which had become a merchant city barred from government service examinations until the sixteenth century, enjoyed a dramatic increase in the success of its native sons, especially in licentiate (*saengwŏn-chinsa*) examinations (Peterson 1979).

In the meantime, the overall socioeconomic position of slaves improved to the extent that in the late eighteenth century, the unfree population began decreasing rapidly for various reasons. The ruling Patriarchs generally sought to increase the tax-paying commoner population. In fact, in 1731, the government began treating the offspring of a slave father and a commoner mother as a commoner. This practice had been the case only for the offspring of a commoner father and a slave mother. Also, grain donations and military merit continued to lead to manumission if not court ranks or offices (Park 2007, 53–56, 128–32). Moreover, increasingly, slaves ran away from their owners and became farmhands, slash-and-burn farmers, wage laborers, or peddlers. This phenomenon overburdened the remaining government slaves with personal tribute obligations, which compelled them to run away. Stopgap measures by the state, such as reducing the amount of tribute and attempting to round up the runaways, could not turn the tide. As maintaining public slaves (*kong nobi*) became financially less viable, the government converted them from paid service slaves to tribute-paying out-resident slaves. By the late eighteenth century, even collecting personal tribute from them had become unfeasible. Finally, in 1801, the court of Chŏngjo's son and successor, King Sunjo (r. 1800–34), manumitted all of some 66,000 slaves attached to government offices in Hansŏng (Palais 1996, 249–52, 257–61). Compared to public slaves and ordinary farmers, private slaves (*sa nobi*) were more vulnerable to cruel treatment, and the number of those running away continued to increase. Rather than spending money searching for or catching runaways, their owners found it financially more sensible to hire wage laborers.

Reflecting waves of socioeconomic change, a new form of public opinion emerged from below in the nineteenth century even though politics of public opinion at the court ceased thanks to consort family oligarchy (Han'guk yŏksa yŏn'guhoe 1990, 1.165, 193). Alienated local *yangban* and the more affluent commoners collaborated through local councils in canvassing and articulating popular opinion across status boundaries. Not only did local councils undergo a fundamental transformation, but people's assemblies (*minhoe*) that arose brought nonelites together for deliberation. Such local councils and people's assemblies constituted a new arena of public opinion, no longer monopolized by *yangban*. Unable to lord over an entire county's general population with a community compact, *yangban* lineages settled for a neighborhood compact (*tongyak*) or kin group solidarity among themselves. The state and its proprietors, *yangban*, generally found the demands of new local councils and their extension, the people's assemblies, unacceptable. Both types of deliberative bodies marshaled local public opinion that increasingly took issues with the state's tax

Figure 9.4 Stele honoring Lady Miryang Pak of Hamyang, Kyŏngsang Province, as a chaste widow, erected in 1797. At 19, she married her husband, a local functionary, who soon fell ill and died. Upon completing the ritual mourning of three years for her husband, Lady Pak took her life. Photo credit: Korean Heritage Service.

policies as implemented through magistrates. Local councils and people's assemblies alike pushed the limits of the official petition system through group actions, even defying their magistrates representing the king. Such local councils and people's assemblies even sparked "popular uprisings" (*millan*) in 1862 in dozens of counties throughout Korea, forcing many magistrates to flee their posts (Kim Ingeol 2024, 57–58, 61–62, 119–68).

The erosion of the yangban hegemony in local society also transformed marriage, a social institution bringing together two families of equal standing. Marriages between the *yangban* families, who used to dominate local councils, and the nouveau riche, who had begun to secure memberships in such bodies in the eighteenth century, became more common. By the nineteenth century, the latter had acquired the various cultural trappings that the old aristocracy had used to monopolize power, including Confucian education, proper rituals, ancestral shrines, lineage graves, and published genealogies. More than ever, the state honored non-*yangban* exemplars of cardinal Confucian virtues (Figure 9.4). All the same, old status distinctions persisted in considerations of marriage. An illegitimate daughter of a *yangban* father still married an illegitimate son of a *yangban* male or became the concubine of a *yangban* man, and specialist *chungin* mirrored the custom. Many non-*yangban* parents made their daughters concubines of males of higher social status rather than marry them to men of their status. Such customs would continue well into the twentieth century in the context of overall socioeconomic change that provided more advancement opportunities for nonelites.

Final Thoughts

As surveyed, the social history of Chosŏn Korea reflects general patterns shared among literate, sedentary societies of early modern Afro-Eurasia. Wielding political power was an aristocracy rooted in the postclassical era, the *yangban*. Although the hereditary elite continued to dominate politics at the national level throughout the early modern era, such nonelites as *chungin* and commoners gained wealth, cultural sophistication, and local political power. Moreover, the population of those unfree began to decrease as they became commoners. To reflect on early modern Korea's

Status and Class

status hierarchy and mobility, as well as what lay ahead, a summation of significant developments discussed is in order.

In Chosŏn, the general correspondence between its status hierarchy (of *yangban*, *chungin*, commoners, and the lowborn) and occupational groups grew weak. Among the *yangban* as articulators of public opinion, tumultuous partisan politics cast losing party after another out of power. Such aristocrats replaced hereditary local functionaries, who continued to perform duties as intermediaries among the state and the population, as new local elites. All the same, the politics of public opinion dominated earlier by senior officials came to include not only mid-level Censorate officials, Confucian students, and local aristocrats but also affluent commoners. While the throne increased contacts with the ordinary people, magistrates collaborated with nouveau riche through local councils previously controlled by *yangban*. In the meantime, the lowborn population began to decrease as a more liberalized, commercialized economy presented opportunities to merchants, artisans, and wage laborers—initially for those contracted with the government but gradually for others. Furthermore, Hansŏng's state-employed technical specialists and illegitimate sons of *yangban* secured access to offices formerly reserved for bona fide *yangban*. Accommodating all these changes was a new kinship culture in which patrilineally organized lineages became widespread among *yangban*, followed by others. The core principle was patrilineal succession through a legitimate son, biological or adopted. As reflected in increasingly voluminous genealogies, the custom further marginalized younger sons, daughters, and illegitimate children.

Accelerating changes in the late nineteenth century amounted to a break in Korea's history of social status and class. Today, neither the Chosŏn monarchy nor the *yangban* aristocracy exists. In South Korea, descent group organizations (*chongch'inhoe*, *hwasuhoe*) continue to uphold a notion of patrilineal lineage and even influence election candidates, but it is hardly a central part of everyday life for most Koreans. As discussed, Kim Ingeol (Kim In'gŏl) traces the roots of modern Korean democracy to Chosŏn politics of public opinion. Also, Yi Tae-Jin (Yi T'aejin) has argued that the Confucian royal rhetoric of "people as foundation" (*minbon*) expanded to articulate *min'guk* ("people's state"; republic) in the eighteenth century (298–300). However, Korean historiography more commonly cites imperialism and colonialism in explaining the demise of Chosŏn social practices and engendering such notions as equality and republicanism. Depending on the viewpoint, the Japanese occupation either hindered the development or facilitated it.

Regardless, Korea's early modern transformations with status hierarchy and mobility prepared the ground for social movements of expanding scope and diversity. In particular, the Kabo Reform (1894–96) led by the Enlightenment Party (c. 1874–96) heeded a demand for change, spreading among the Tonghak ("Eastern Learning") and others. The reform abolished the government service examinations, slavery, childhood marriages, and guilt by association through kinship, as well as affirming the rights of widows to remarry. Also, the Kabo government attempted to institutionalize local councils via its Articles of Regulation on Local Councils (Hyanghoe chogyu) as bodies for garnering popular opinion. As the governing leadership deemed the general populace ignorant, the local councils, as stipulated, could not allow sufficient roles for people's assemblies. The new government of the Empire of Korea (1897–1910) even resurrected the Articles of Regulation on Community Compacts (Hyangyak changjŏng) from centuries earlier (Kim Ingeol 2024, 178). Nonetheless, the tradition of local councils and people's assemblies rendered strength to an ever-widening range of reform movements. Under the subsequent Japanese occupation, Korea's continuing social transformation rooted in Chosŏn fueled the March First Movement of 1919, the Provisional Government of the Republic of Korea (1919–48), and a broad spectrum of anti-Japanese armed resistance—ultimately contributing to the establishment of both South and North Korean states in 1948.

The Routledge Handbook of Early Modern Korea

References

Cho Sŏngyun. 1999. "Chosŏn hugi sahoe pyŏndong kwa haengjŏngjik chungin." In *Han'guk kŭndae ihaenggi chungin yŏn'gu*, edited by Yŏnse taehakkyo kukhak yŏn'guwŏn, 61–90. Tosŏ ch'ulp'an Sinsŏwŏn.

Ch'oe, Yŏng-ho. 1999. "Private Academies and the State in Late Chosŏn Korea." In *Culture and the State in Late Chosŏn Korea*, edited by JaHyun Kim Haboush and Martina Deuchler, 15–45. Harvard University Asia Center.

Ch'oe Yuno. 2006. *Chosŏn hugi t'oji soyukwŏn ŭi paltal kwa chijuje*. Hyean.

Chosŏn wangjo sillok. Available at: https://sillok.history.go.kr/main/main.do

Chosŏn wangjo sŏnwŏllok. 1992. Reprint. 10 vols. Minch'ang munhwasa.

Deuchler, Martina. 1992. *The Confucian Transformation of Korea: A Study of Society and Ideology*. Council on East Asian Studies, Harvard University.

Deuchler, Martina. 2015. *Under the Ancestors' Eyes: Kinship, Status, and Locality in Premodern Korea*. Harvard University Asia Center.

Duncan, John B. 2000. *The Origins of the Chosŏn Dynasty*. University of Washington Press.

Han Yŏngu. 1997. *Chosŏn sidae sinbunsa yŏn'gu*. Chimmundang.

Han'guk yŏksa yŏn'guhoe. 1990. *Chosŏn chŏngch'isa, 1800–1863*. 2 vols. Ch'ŏngnyŏnsa.

Hejtmanek, Milan. 2011. "Devalued Bodies, Revalued Status: Confucianism and the Plight of Female Slaves in Late Chosŏn Korea." In *Women and Confucianism in Chosŏn Korea: New Perspectives*, edited by Youngmin Kim and Michael J. Pettid, 137–49. State University of New York Press.

Jun Seong-Ho, James B. Lewis, and Kang Han-Rog. 2008. "Korean Expansion and Decline from the Seventeenth to the Nineteenth Century: A View Suggested by Adam Smith." *Journal of Economic History* 68, no. 1 (March): 244–82.

Kang Sŏkhwa. 2000. *Chosŏn hugi Hamgyŏng-do wa pukpang yŏngt'o ŭisik*. Kyŏngsewŏn.

Kawashima, Fujiya. 2002. *What is Yangban? A Legacy for Modern Korea*. Institute for Modern Korean Studies, Yonsei University.

Kim Ingeol. 2024. *Politics of Public Opinion: Local Councils and People's Assemblies in Korea, 1567–1894*. Translated by Eugene Y. Park. Brill.

Kim Kidŏk. 1993. "Koryŏ sigi wangsil ŭi kusŏng kwa kŭnch'inhon." *Kuksagwan nonch'ong* 49: 1–25.

Kim, Sun Joo. 2007. *Marginality and Subversion in Korea: The Hong Kyŏngnae Rebellion of 1812*. University of Washington Press.

Kim Tuhŏn 2013. *Chosŏn sidae kisuljik chungin sinbun yŏn'gu*. Kyŏngin munhwasa.

Kim Yangsu 1999. "Chosŏn hugi sahoe pyŏndong kwa chŏnmunjik chungin ŭi hwaltong: yŏkkwan, ŭigwan, ŭmyanggwan, yulgwan, sanwŏn, hwawŏn, agin tŭng kwa kwallyŏnhayŏ." In *Han'guk kŭndae ihaenggi chungin yŏn'gu*, edited by Yŏnse taehakkyo kukhak yŏn'guwŏn, 171–298. Tosŏ ch'ulp'an Sinsŏwon.

Myŏngjong sillok. In *Chosŏn wangjo sillok*.

O Such'ang. 2002. *Chosŏn hugi P'yŏngan-do sahoe palchŏn yŏn'gu*. Ilchogak.

Oh, Young Kyun. 2013. *Engraving Virtue: The Printing History of a Premodern Korean Moral Primer*. Brill.

Palais, James B. 1996. *Confucian Statecraft and Korean Institutions: Yu Hyŏngwŏn and the Late Chosŏn Dynasty*. University of Washington Press.

Park, Eugene Y. 2007. *Between Dreams and Reality: The Military Examination in Late Chosŏn Korea, 1600–1894*. Harvard University Asia Center.

Park, Eugene Y. 2008a. "Status and 'Defunct' Offices in Early Modern Korea: The Case of Five Guards Generals (Owijang), 1864–1910." *Journal of Social History* 41, no. 3 (Spring): 737–57.

Park, Eugene Y. 2008b. "Imagined Connections in Early Modern Korea, 1600–1894: Representations of Northern Elite Miryang Pak Lineages in Genealogies." *Seoul Journal of Korean Studies* 21, no. 1 (June): 1–27.

Park, Eugene Y. 2013. "Old Status Trappings in a New World: The 'Middle People' (Chungin) and Genealogies in Modern Korea." *Journal of Family History* 38, no. 2.

Park, Eugene Y. 2014. *A Family of No Prominence: The Descendants of Pak Tŏkhwa and the Birth of Modern Korea*. Stanford University Press.

Peterson, Mark. 1979. "Hyangban and Merchant in Kaesŏng." *Korea Journal* 19 (October): 4–18.

Peterson, Mark. 1996. *Korean Adoption and Inheritance: Case Studies in the Creation of a Classic Confucian Society*. East Asia Program, Cornell University.

Sejong sillok. In *Chosŏn wangjo sillok*.

Song Ch'ansik. 1999. "Chokpo ŭi kanhaeng." *Han'guksa simin kangjwa* 24 (February): 50–66.

Song Chunho. 1987. *Chosŏn sahoesa yŏn'gu: Chosŏn sahoe ŭi kujo wa sŏngkyŏk mit kŭ pyŏnch'ŏn e kwanhan yŏn'gu*. Ilchogak.

Ssijok wŏllyu. 1991. By Cho Chongun. Reprint. Pogyŏng munhwasa.

Totman, Conrad. 2004. *Pre-industrial Korea and Japan in Environmental Perspective*. Brill.

Wagner, Edward W. 1977. "The Civil Examination Process as Social Leaven: The Case of the Northern Provinces in the Yi Dynasty." *Korea Journal* 17, no. 1 (January): 22–27.

Yi Hunsang. 1990. *Chosŏn hugi ŭi hyangni*. Ilchogak.

Yi Sugŏn. 2003. *Han'guk ŭi sŏngssi wa chokpo*. Sŏul taehakkyo ch'ulp'an munhwawŏn.

Yi Tae-Jin. 2010. *The Dynamics of Confucianism and Modernization in Korean History*. East Asia Program, Cornell University.

10

FOREIGNERS AND THE DESCENDANTS

Adam Bohnet

Korea under the rule of the Chosŏn state (1392–1897) was the last Northeast Asian state the gunships of imperialism forced open, and for this reason, Western Missionaries referred to it as the "Hermit Kingdom" (Dittrich 2016, 3–4), a phrase that, although inaccurate, continues to shape popular understandings of Chosŏn. Colonizing Korea, Japanese propaganda described Chosŏn as a closed, stagnant Sinocentric backwater (Schmid 2002, 61–64). Subsequently, scholarship in North and South Korea emphasized Korea's racial and ethnic homogeneity (Hyun 2019). Since the 1990s, South Korea's increased stature in the global political economy and growing immigrant population considerably weakened the nationalist narrative while fostering more research establishing Korea's multicultural past, contradicting many of the established narratives emphasizing Chosŏn's supposed isolationism and ethnic homogeneity (Kyung-koo Han 2007; Lie 2014, 3–22).

The Chosŏn state succeeded a collapsing Koryŏ state (918–1392) that had been, only a few decades before, deeply integrated into the multiethnic, Mongolian-dominated empire under the Yuan dynasty (1271–1368), based in Daidu (present-day Beijing). Many Yuan officials established themselves in Koryŏ during the period of Yuan dominance (Yun 2002), while the Yuan empire governed large regions of Korea, notably Ssangsŏng in northeastern Korea and T'amna on the island of Chejudo, as separate policies, and maintained a distinct apparatus for governing the large numbers of Koreans forcibly resettled in Liaodong during the Mongol invasions of the thirteenth century: Koreans, Mongols, Jurchens, Chinese, and others who shared these spaces (David M. Robinson 2009, 28–34; Nakano 2013; David M. Robinson 2022, 238–43). Chosŏn's founder, Yi Sŏnggye (King T'aejo, r. 1392–98), was himself from one of these multiethnic spaces. His father was from a Korean military family based in Ssangsŏng who shifted their loyalties to King Kongmin (r. 1351–74) of Koryŏ when Koryŏ seized Ssangsŏng in 1356 (David M. Robinson 2009, 127–28). Yi Sŏnggye spent his early career as a general serving Koryŏ before seizing control of the state in 1388 and establishing himself as monarch of the new Chosŏn state in 1392. Both as general and monarch, he enjoyed support from the Jurchens of his home region and attracted and accommodated others from diverse backgrounds, including refugees from the collapsing Yuan empire (Clark 1982, 24–27; Brose 2013, 188–91).

Indeed, as this chapter argues, early Chosŏn sought after peoples on its borders in continuing the Koryŏ policy for settling outsiders in its territory. During the Imjin War (East Asian War; 1592–98) against Japan and the warfare of China's transition from the Ming dynasty (1368–1644)

150

DOI: 10.4324/9781003262053-14

Foreigners and the Descendants

to the Manchu Qing dynasty (1616–1912; Later Jin until 1636), Chosŏn faced the challenge of absorbing refugees and deserters. Despite the political and social problems caused by this large influx of often armed refugees, the Chosŏn state maintained its traditional means for settling them on its territory. By the mid-seventeenth century, the consolidation of the Tokugawa shogunate (1603–1868) in Japan and the Qing empire in China stemmed the tide of migrants, effectively ending Chosŏn's active support for migration. Migrants' descendants, however, continued to play important social and ritual roles in the Chosŏn state. Also, not only did some legitimate migrants still manage to establish themselves in Chosŏn territory, but even "illegitimate" migrants, such as border-crossers, castaways, and Catholic missionaries, were able to enter via networks in Chosŏn that were open to them.

Migrants and Foreigners in Early Chosŏn

Once the migrants from China established themselves during the Koryŏ–Chosŏn transition, very few Chinese migrated to Chosŏn nearly two centuries following T'aejo's reign. A joint decision of Ming and Chosŏn closed the Yellow Sea, effectively ending regular visits from Chinese traders. Of those who remained in Chosŏn, many appear in the geography section (*Chiriji*) of the *Veritable Records of King Sejong* (*Sejong sillok*) as those receiving "royally granted surnames" (*sasŏng*). In many cases, though, the recorded migrants to Chosŏn kept their original surnames and only "received" ancestral seats. For example, the geography section of the *Veritable Records of King Sejong* notes the family of Sŏl Changsu (1341–99), a Uighur migrant from Yuan China, as a family from Kyŏngju. Administratively, Chosŏn assigned migrants to a special, protected, but not prestigious, tax category, generally called *hyanghwain* ("foreigners turning toward edification") status. Recipients of this status received Korean-style surnames, wives, agricultural implements, and tax exemptions for a set period (Duncan 2000, 104–09; Bohnet 2020, 41–43). In practice, the exemption tended to become permanent or near-permanent, and people with this status dominated certain regions such as Hamgyŏng Province (Bohnet 2020, 43–45).

The Korean monarch's ostensibly transformative, civilizing influence on "inferior" peoples rationalized *hyanghwa* status (Kyung-koo Han 2007, 15–22), but it also applied, to some extent, even to Chinese migrants (Bohnet 2020, 42). Usually categorized as "civilized" within the "civilized-barbarian" dichotomy, some migrants of Chinese origin settled in Chosŏn by the mid-fifteenth century. Ordinary Koreans, Chinese border-crossers, and tax-avoiders from both sides formed multiethnic communities on the Yellow Sea islands and north of the Yalu (Ko. Amnok) River. However, there was no legal migration of Chinese to Korea (Liu 2023).

Most foreigners in Chosŏn were Jurchens from the northern frontier and Japanese and Ryukyuans from the maritime south. Late Koryŏ had suffered constant raids from the Japanese Archipelago torn by chaos and wars. Yi Sŏnggye had gained power partly through military success in suppressing the raiders and bringing security to the southern provinces. Early Chosŏn pacified Japanese raiders by settling them in Chosŏn's territory (Kenneth R. Robinson 1992, 103–04). In contrast, Jurchens had closely associated with Koryŏ before the Mongol conquest (Breuker 2011, 201–04). For example, Jurchens and Koreans had been inhabiting Yi Sŏnggye's family power base in northeastern Koryŏ. As mentioned, many of his earlier supporters were Jurchens; one notable figure, Yi Chiran (1331–1402), became a military ally and merit subject (Clark 1982, 24–27).

Like the Japanese Archipelago, the Jurchen world was politically fragmented in the wake of the Yuan collapse; well into the fifteenth century, the Chosŏn court was sure to clearly distinguish the "local" (*t'och'ak*) Jurchens of Hamgyŏng Province, the Jianzhou Jurchens from the region of the upper Yalu and Tumen, the Odoli Jurchens who settled in Hoeryŏng and vicinity in the upper

151

Tumen (Ko. Tuman), and the Hulun Udeha Jurchens from northeast of the Tumen River (Woodruff 1987, 125; Kenneth R. Robinson 1992, 97–101). Relations with the Jurchens were significant enough to the early Chosŏn court that it was willing to compete against the Ming for the loyalty of Jurchen potentates—including Möngke Temür (Mengtemu; 1370–1433), who was an early ally of Yi Sŏnggye who settled in the region of Hoeryŏng, only to be later lured, over the objections of the Chosŏn court, into the Ming sphere of influence, and settled in the Ming commandery of Jianzhou. Chosŏn did not lose interest in him. By 1423, Möngke Temür had once more decamped to Hoeryŏng and Chosŏn's sphere of interest (Kenneth R. Robinson 1992, 98–100; Clark 1998, 283–88).

Although Chosŏn utilized military means against raiders on both frontiers, military successes soon proved insufficient. In the south, diplomacy was limited as Japan's Ashikaga shogunate (1336–1573) could not control the Japanese raiders based in western Honshu and Kyushu. In the north, Ming China established a commandery in Liaodong, keeping the Jurchens divided, and was suspicious of Chosŏn's interests in the region. Accordingly, the Chosŏn court pursued relationships with individual potentates—Jurchen allies to its north and Japanese leaders in Kyushu and western Honshu—to supplement both military means and traditional diplomacy. This strategy involved granting titles to key Japanese or Jurchen leaders, often in reward for repatriating Korean captives. These titles enabled them to submit a tribute to the capital, Hansŏng (present-day Seoul), and also bestowed trade privileges. Japanese, Ryukyuans, and Jurchens greatly valued such an arrangement, so many falsified their identities to participate in the system (Kenneth R. Robinson 2013, 341–47).

This was not a purely practical transaction, either for the Chosŏn court or for the border potentates. Ideologically, Chosŏn's tributary system played a crucial role in asserting the superior authority and transformative power of Chosŏn's monarch. The very act of presenting tribute brought envoys from the port of entry to Hansŏng by established routes—with each stage of travel involving ceremonial occasions that integrated them into a world order centered around Chosŏn (Kenneth R. Robinson 2000, 110–12, 2013, 342–46). In early Chosŏn, Cho Chun (1346–1405) described T'aejo in such a way that submission of Ryukyuan, Japanese, and Jurchen rulers revealed the Chosŏn founder's sage virtue, which Ryukyuan kings would even declare themselves vassals of the Chosŏn court (Choi 2014, 220, 233). Such imperial rhetoric continued during the reigns of his successors; in 1442, King Sejong (r. 1418–50) sent an envoy to admonish the Orankhai, who were then raiding Chosŏn's borders, noting that they had "surrendered and paid allegiance" to Chosŏn "since ancient times," and upbraiding them for so "falling from virtue" as to launch raids on Chosŏn (*The Veritable Records of King Sejong* 1442/10/8 entry 3).

Chosŏn's policies concerning migrants and envoys did not assume a clear "ethnic" distinction between Koreans and non-Koreans on Chosŏn's frontiers. This was, to some extent, a reflection of preexisting reality—the so-called Japanese raiders, for instance, had, in fact, diverse origins from among the peoples of the "Inner Sea" and included people from Korea (Smits 2018, 39–42). In the south, Chosŏn increasingly passed the task of administering the arrival of Japanese at Korean points over to the governor of Tsushima, an island nearly equidistant between Kyushu and Chosŏn's Kyŏngsang Province (Kenneth R. Robinson 1992, 106–07). Legally and rhetorically, Chosŏn treated Tsushima as historical Korean territory and part of Kyŏngsang Province, although, in practice, it was outside Chosŏn's direct control (Kenneth R. Robinson 2006; Chong 2010, 31–33). In the north, Chosŏn had no choice but to maintain control after establishing a series of fortifications south of the Tumen River. As Ming suspicions made active diplomacy more difficult, Chosŏn cultivated Jurchen communities—known first as Jurchens in the vicinity of the fortresses and then as Pŏnho ("Fence Jurchens" or "Vassal Jurchens")—to act as intermediaries

Foreigners and the Descendants

between Jurchen groups beyond the Tumen River and the Chosŏn court (Bohnet 2020, 38–39). Beyond formal institutions, culturally and socially, smaller polities linked to Chosŏn would often assimilate Korean cultural markers into their own identities. For example, the Ōuchi family of western Honshu lobbied to have its status as descendants of Paekche kings confirmed by the Chosŏn court (Kenneth R. Robinson 1992, 102, 2016, 92; Stiller 2021, 12–13).

The socioeconomic relationships further confused matters. Jurchens became accustomed to serving as guards in Hansŏng and often received Korean wives. Also, Pŏnho on the northern border, as tribute providers from outside Chosŏn, and *hyanghwain* (or submitting foreigners from within Chosŏn) were not supposed to interact. In practice, people regularly crossed that boundary (Bohnet 2020, 48–49). Not all foreigners residing on Chosŏn soil were present with even the veneer of legality, as Japanese and Jurchens entered Chosŏn with little restriction. The area around Mount Paektu (Ch. Changbai) in the north was largely uncontrolled, while in the south, in the Three Ports (Samp'o) established initially to allow Japanese merchants to conduct trade, the supposedly visiting merchants tended to establish permanent residence, resulting in the swelling of the Japanese population of the ports far over the small number of legal households. The court's attempts to suppress this practice resulted in a massive revolt in 1510, after which enforcement of the regulations became stricter (Lewis 2005, 195).

The Impact of Mid-Chosŏn Warfare

All changed with a series of mid-Chosŏn wars, beginning in 1592, upon a massive attack by the Japanese, setting off the Imjin War. With about 159,000 troops, battled-hardened, and many armed with arquebuses, the invasion swept across the Korean Peninsula before being pushed back by an alliance of at least 84,000 Chosŏn troops and the intervening 48,000 Ming troops. Many Koreans left the peninsula, forcibly or freely, whereas some Japanese and Ming soldiers stayed behind and settled in Chosŏn. After the Imjin War, new confederacies formed in the Jurchen regions to Chosŏn's north, notably including one led by Nurhaci (r. 1616–26) of Jianzhou across the Yalu River from P'yŏngan Province (Elliott 2001, 47–56). This caused considerable troubles for the Pŏnho on Chosŏn's northern frontier, as Nurhaci, claiming authority over Chosŏn's Pŏnho, demanded their "repatriation" to Jianzhou—only to see many fleeing to Hansŏng and southern provinces to avoid assimilation. Their flight left Chosŏn's northern frontier regions empty (Bohnet 2020, 79–82; Yuh and Jang 2023, 52). In 1618, Nurhaci began to attack Ming's Liaodong, ultimately gaining control over much of the region. Although many Liaodong Chinese accommodated themselves to Manchu rule (Crossley 1999, 90–99), a significant number fled to Chosŏn, with some, under a Ming general Mao Wenlong (1576–1629), establishing a military base in Kado, an island off the west coast of P'yŏngan Province. Chosŏn accounts from this period describe how the refugee population from Liaodong overwhelmed the local Korean population of northern P'yŏngan (Liu 2019, 243–301).

The significant increase in the population of foreigners and unattached men created challenges for the Chosŏn court in adapting its established systems for resettling migrants. At first, this challenge was daunting when dealing with Japanese defectors. When the Imjin War commenced, widespread anger toward the Japanese onslaught and the perceived treachery of Tsushima militated against the acceptance of migrants. However, as a Korean taken captive to Japan, Kang Hang (1567–1618) wrote, unquestionably, encouraging the defection of the Japanese was beneficial to Chosŏn. The defectors could bring military skills much needed by Chosŏn after the disasters of the first year of the war, notably in using arquebuses, which, initially, few in Chosŏn could use adeptly. More than simply killing soldiers, encouraging Japanese soldiers to defect capitalized on their low morale (Haboush and Kenneth R. Robinson 2013, 65).

The Routledge Handbook of Early Modern Korea

Encouraging defection fit well with the ideology involved in Chosŏn's earlier relationship with the Japanese—the notion that the power of Chosŏn king's sage virtue secured the submission of foreigners. Kang Hang, a student of the philosopher Yi Hwang (pen name T'oegye; 1502–71), represented this well when he claimed that the Japanese, used from youth to harsh and inhumane laws of Japan, found Chosŏn more civilized (Haboush and Kenneth R. Robinson 2013, 65). Defection became central to the representation of Japanese in other sources, including the most famous among defectors, Sayaga (1571–1642), later known by his adopted Korean name Kim Ch'ungsŏn. Based on later sources, much of the available information concerning him lacks credibility. Kim likely submitted some time after Japan's 1597 offensive, though later accounts depict him as planning to defect even before 1592. Subsequently, he served Chosŏn commendably against the Japanese, domestic rebels (1624), and Later Jin (1627). Along with other defecting Japanese officers and soldiers, he received the surname Kim and the ancestral seat Kimhae and served in a special cavalry brigade. Later accounts described Kim as having submitted to the Chosŏn court because of his profound admiration for Chosŏn civilization (Fujiwara 2014).

The widespread flight of Jurchens from Chosŏn's northern border to its interior provinces raised a somewhat different set of issues. Unrest among Jurchens in northern Hamgyŏng preceded the Imjin War, rising to a dangerous level with the Nit'anggae Revolt (1583). The unrest worsened during the war when the Korean settlers of northern Hamgyŏng, hardly loyal to the center, rose in revolt. Jurchens, notably residents of the fortified town of Yŏksu north of the Tumen River, also rose, and the Chosŏn troops were able to suppress them with difficulty. Despite these troubles, Chosŏn valued its connection with the frontier region's Pŏnho Jurchens and was concerned by Nurhaci's policy of removing them from the Tumen River region. Many Jurchens unwilling to be assimilated into Nurhaci's new khanate, Later Jin, fled south and typically re-established themselves in fishing villages as submitting foreigners (Bohnet 2020, 82–85).

By contrast, Ming defectors and then Liaodong refugees lacked the long-established connection to the Chosŏn court that made Jurchens, and to a lesser extent, Japanese, welcome subjects. In the case of the Ming military, they were generally unwelcome as many were insubordinate and troublesome—seeing themselves as defecting from Chosŏn's suzerain and ally. Exceptions were those, such as Japanese defectors, bringing valuable skills and abilities in weaponry, medicine, and geomancy—in which Chosŏn saw Ming as superior. Ming soldiers defected for various reasons, including conflict with officers, sickness, existing social ties to Chosŏn, or any combination. The massive flight of Liaodongese from Nurhaci was even more destabilizing due to the scale and the further political complications they introduced.

To begin with, many had illicit connections with Later Jin—and in fact, Chosŏn did not clearly distinguish them from the Manchu in the first place (Liu 2019, 256–57). Moreover, many were organized militarily by the Ming general Mao Wenlong, who, based partly on Chosŏn territory, acted in many ways without attention to the Ming court, made substantial financial demands on Chosŏn, and pursued private diplomacy with Later Jin, which consistently demanded "repatriation" of Chosŏn's Jurchen subjects and Liaodongese refugees, as well as fugitive Koreans (Mengheng Lee 2018, 16–21). These demands for repatriation became part of the pretext for both Later Jin and Qing, as Later Jin self-renamed, to invade Chosŏn, setting off the Chŏngmyo War (1627) and the Pyŏngja War (1637). Chosŏn's surrender to Qing in 1637 did not bring these demands to an end, at least not initially—Inggudai and Mafuta, the Qing officials in charge of much of the invasion, made specific demands for the repatriation of both "Jurchen people who fled" to Chosŏn and of Chinese refugees from Liaodong in their communications to the Chosŏn court in 1637 (Bohnet 2020, 83–84, 139). Even when Chosŏn sought to comply, the porosity of ethnic categories complicated its actions. For instance, distinguishing Jurchens from non-Jurchens within the formerly

Foreigners and the Descendants

mixed region of northern Hamgyŏng was exceptionally difficult. People would manipulate their identities. For example, a ginseng poacher from northern Hamgyŏng claimed to be Jurchen to avoid punishment for border crossing (Bohnet 2020, 101–02).

Many migrants did establish themselves securely in Chosŏn society. With some Chinese migrants, our sources reveal some aspects of the process whereby they became established. For instance, Du Shizhong, a deserter from the Ming military during the Imjin War, settled in Taegu, where he married a commoner (*yangin*) Chosŏn woman, according to extant household registers and genealogical records (Sangwoo Han 2021, 251–65). Du's profession marked him as more marginal, as he became especially known for geomancy—expertise that, even if pursued by a professional employed by the state, placed one in the ranks of specialist *chungin* ("middle people"), whose social status was below *yangban* (Bohnet 2020, 180). Nonetheless, Du gained meaningful connections to *yangban*. Yi Sibal (1569–1626), for instance, wrote two poems about him, one referring entirely to Du's expertise in geomancy and describing him as a Daoist wonderworker and the other praising him as a migrant (*Pyŏgo yugo* 2.25a):

The sage desired to live among the barbarians
and you have now fled, coming here.
Kija, granted control over Chosŏn, left good customs,
So why would you think of returning home?

Yi Sibal's poem compared Du Shizhong to Confucius, described in the *Analects* as wanting to live among the "Nine Yi" (*The Analects* 2014, 137), a passage many assumed referred to Kija (Ch. Jizi) who, according to legend, was the sage uncle of the wicked last king of China's Shang dynasty (c. 1600–c. 1045 BCE) and was enfeoffed as Marquis of Chaoxian (Ch. Chaoxian hou; Ko. Chosŏn hu) by the king of the succeeding Zhou dynasty (c. 1046–256 BCE). Chosŏn elites accepted and understood this story as relating that Kija founded a new line of rulers of Old Chosŏn (Kojosŏn; 2333, trad.–108 BCE)—or Kija Chosŏn (c. 1045, trad.–194 BCE)—in present-day Pyongyang and transmitted proper rites from China (Han Young-woo 1985). In other words, Yi praised a deserter from the Ming military for his decision to come to a land of proper Confucian virtue.

By no means were all responses to Ming deserters so positive. Shi Wenyong (d. 1623), a Ming soldier with geomantic talents who stayed in Chosŏn pleading illness, became the subject of conflict at court. The route of the conflict was Chŏng Inhong (1535–1623)—a prominent Confucian scholar and a prominent leader of a "righteous army" (*ŭibyŏng*) militia against the Japanese during the Imjin War—had enabled Shi's desertion. Critics argued that Chŏng, by sheltering Ming fugitive soldiers, was encouraging the collapse of social order itself by encouraging subordinates to rebel against superiors. The critics also argued that Chŏng had forced the daughter of a woman, whom the Japanese had abducted, to marry Shi—something, they argued, was utterly shameful, as even the humblest of Koreans considered it shameful to marry a foreigner. Strictly speaking, of course, this was not true: the early Chosŏn court had encouraged the marriage of Koreans with foreigners. In any case, defenders of Shi Wenyong articulated a different perspective, emphasizing that Chŏng's ancestors had been refugees from Song dynasty (960–1279) China and that his desire to help a "home-town friend" motivated his decision to help Ming deserters such as Shi. At first, Chŏng's allies had the day. During the reign of King Kwanghae Kun (r. 1608–23), the court employed Shi as a geomancer for rebuilding Kyŏngbok Palace. In contrast to Du Shizhong, who earned mentions locally or privately, Shi gained official employment in the Chosŏn court as a geomancer. However, after Kwanghae Kun's overthrow, the succeeding court of King Injo (r. 1623–49) executed him (Bohnet 2020, 66–72).

The Routledge Handbook of Early Modern Korea

Most Ming deserters and refugees from Liaodong received much less notice, if at all. Most were of obscure backgrounds. Kang Shijue (1602–85) is an intriguing example of a once-marginal refugee who later attracted official attention. We know a great deal about him because, unusually so, he left a self-account and was also the subject of detailed biographies written by prominent officials while he was still alive. According to these accounts, Kang followed his father (whom he describes as a man of elite background, although the veracity of this description cannot be confirmed) to the Battle of Sarhu, which he survived. After participating in the rear-guard struggle by Ming remnants against Later Jin and even suffering capture, he escaped to Chosŏn via Mamp'o on the Yalu River (1625). Subsequently, Kang relocated multiple times within northern Korea, first wandering widely around P'yŏngan Province, then crossing over to Hamhŭng in Hamgyŏng Province before traveling northward. He finally settled in a community called Togon—meaning "river crossing" in Manchu. Kang eventually married a *kisaeng* (professional female entertainer) based in a post-station in the region. He seems to have had no contact with any formal government organ until the 1660s when he encountered a prominent high official, Pak Sedang (1629–1703). Earlier, Kang must have been among the thieving Liaodong refugees eliciting hostile comments from Chosŏn officials at the time. By the 1660s, however, after years of being outside of state authority, he gained a new role, thanks to his connection to central elites, as an intermediary for the Chosŏn court in northern Hamgyŏng, resulting in improved social status for his descendants, and in particular, their freedom from the burdens of base status (Bohnet 2020, 116–18).

When Chosŏn submitted to Qing and terminated its relationship with Ming in 1637, most Chosŏn elites maintained a largely ineffectual attitude of loyalty to Ming in private. The sentiment persisted even after the Qing conquest of Southern Ming (1644–62). The consolidation of the Qing empire and the Tokugawa shogunate eliminated the sources of migration to Chosŏn. Smaller migrant groups continued to settle in Chosŏn as the frontiers remained not fully controlled, and the court's institutions for administering the migrants' descendants retained their functions. Nonetheless, the era of large-scale migration to Chosŏn was over.

In 1644, when Qing armies successfully advanced into northern China, their attention shifted entirely toward China proper, and maintaining close control over Chosŏn was no longer essential. Accordingly, Qing not only dropped all further demands for repatriations but also sent the Chosŏn princes back with several Chinese—notably, the "Nine Righteous Scholars" (*Kuŭisa*), who accompanied one of the two princes who ascended the throne, King Hyojong (r. 1649–59). Later accounts described these individuals as exemplary anti-Qing activists from elite backgrounds, an image not in accord with the few surviving contemporary records (Kimura 2017, 63–66). Extant sources indicate that the nine men settled in Hansŏng, where other Ming migrants with military ability joined them, ultimately forming the Han Ivory Troops (*Hanin abyŏng*), an army unit (Seunghyun Han 2018, 178–79).

Another group of foreigners, the famous Hendrick Hamel (1630–92), a member of the Dutch East India Company (1602–1799), and his crew also joined the unit. Shipwrecked at Chejudo in southern Korea and apprehended by the Chosŏn authorities, the castaways eventually met another Dutch castaway, Jan Jansz Weltevree (1595–1653+), a likely former pirate who, too, had suffered shipwreck in Korea in 1627. Within Chosŏn, the Dutch received much the same treatment as other foreigners with assumed military skills. Initially, the authorities housed Hamel and his crewmates with an army unit of Ming Chinese refugees. The tense geopolitical environment of the seventeenth century meant that Chosŏn was unwilling to repatriate the Dutch via Qing China or Tokugawa Japan. After Hamel and his company failed to enlist the Qing envoy's help with escape, the authorities scattered them in small garrisons around the country. Their sojourn ended with a

Foreigners and the Descendants

successful escape to Nagasaki, Japan, from which they eventually returned home (Ledyard 1971, 45–47, 51–52, 59–97).

Throughout the seventeenth century, the tense geopolitics of East Asia constrained Chosŏn's migration policy. The reunification of Japan under the Tokugawa shogunate ended migration from Japan (other than the return of Korean captives in the decades following the Tokugawa victory). However, Nagasaki became a vital port not only for a small number of Dutch ships but also for many Chinese ships that, until 1683, were generally associated with Ming loyalists in coastal Fujian and Taiwan. Even more so than with the Dutch, Chosŏn's interactions with such Chinese ships were highly cautious when they ran aground on Korean shores. Sending them to Japan was dangerous, as some were Catholics, and Japan asserted the extraterritorial right to punish Catholics wherever they were found (Roux 2014, 121–30).

Nearly all of them, moreover, had some association with the Southern Ming regime of southern China and Dongning (1661–83), a Taiwan-based Ming loyalist regime, and what to do with them was a dilemma to Chosŏn. Sending them to Beijing meant certain deaths for Ming loyalists, but allowing them to stay in Chosŏn was risky, not only because of potential reprisals from the Qing empire should it imagine that Chosŏn had changed its loyalties but also dangerous entanglements with what to Chosŏn were the piratical and illegitimate regimes of Maritime China. In 1667, when a ship from Taiwan, carrying a document using the calendar of the Yongli emperor (r. 1646–62) of Southern Ming, landed on Chejudo, Chosŏn had to repatriate the ship to Qing since the latter learned its presence. The Chosŏn court never had reliable contact with the Yongli emperor, and even after its diplomatic missions to Beijing learned of his capture and execution by Qing troops in 1662, the reliability of such reports remained uncertain. Thus, the Chosŏn court's betrayal of those some deemed connected with China's legitimate emperor became a major political scandal. Consequently, the Chosŏn court set a precedent whereby, if possible, local officials would send these ships onward without burdening the court with a report (Bohnet 2016, 12–13).

Informal contact with foreigners continued, and Chosŏn's relationships with the broader world differed from the frontiers (Lewis 2005, 9–16). The usual practice in early Chosŏn was to reduce conflict on its borders by emptying the border regions of the population—a practice that Chosŏn had pursued in the island archipelago to the southwest and, after the expulsion of the Pŏnho by Qing, in the northern border regions as well. In the seventeenth century, however, Chosŏn's approach shifted to encouraging settlement in border regions increasingly organized as constituent elements of the Chosŏn state proper (Kang 2008, 82–85; Bohnet 2016, 19–20). Accordingly, in 1711, a joint inquiry by Chosŏn and Qing determined the source of the Tumen River and thus clarified the northeastern border (Kim 2017, 52–75). Some people still crossed the Chosŏn–Qing border, but more extensive institutions controlled and policed these crossings. In the northwest, merchants accompanying Chosŏn diplomatic missions to Beijing could travel freely across the Yalu River to engage in trade during each mission (Kwon 2015, 168–69). Koreans also crossed the border for economic activities like ginseng digging and encountered Chinese traders illegally entering the region where the Qing state banned their settlement (Kim 2017, 77–92).

On the maritime frontier, Japanese and Korean fishermen regularly appeared on each other's shores, some traveling with families, and many were "deliberately drifting" (Hoon Lee 2006, 84–85). Chosŏn government's control of the Japan House (Ko. *Waegwan*) in Pusan steadily became tighter (Lewis 2005, 177–209). Nonetheless, clashes in the island Ullŭngdo between subordinates of key daimyo, who had received the right to exploit the island's resources, and Korean fisherman, who asserted Chosŏn's and their proper claim to Ullŭngdo, culminated with an extraordinary moment of An Yongbok (fl. 1693–97) traveling illicitly to Japan to appeal to the shogun directly. Consequently, the shogun, weary of undesirable entanglements, banned further exploitation of

Ullŭngdo by the Japanese. In contrast, the Chosŏn court asserted its control over the island (and performed regular patrols) but banned access by anyone else (Hoon Lee 1997, 401–18)

Others continued to arrive on Chosŏn's shores. The islands off the southwestern coast, which only came under consistent Chosŏn administration in the late seventeenth century, continued to see the arrival of Chinese castaways. No longer politically troublesome after the fall of the Ming-loyalist Dongning to Qing (1683), the Chosŏn court could now repatriate arrivals with limited bureaucratic fuss. The problem was that the islanders were not necessarily hostile to foreigners or interested in cooperating with the repatriation. In many cases, Chinese castaways spent considerable time in the southwestern islands unreported (Bohnet 2016, 19–22). In fact, not only people but even Buddhist texts arrived on Chosŏn's southwest coast (Jorgensen 2020, 171–88).

While migration declined considerably after 1644, Chosŏn continued administering foreigners and their descendants with the same submitting-foreigner category used earlier. Held by all people of foreign descent, including Chinese, Dutch, Japanese, and Jurchens, the submitting foreign status had become hereditary by the late seventeenth. As true earlier, holders of submitting-foreigner status were exempt from most personal taxes, though still responsible for a tribute to the Ministry of Rites (Yejo). Those who were settled in coastal villages submitted the tribute in fish (Bohnet 2020, 128–29).

Protected status though the status was, it was not a particularly desirable one. Late seventeenth and early eighteenth-century records abound with references to local officials eager to meet the tax collection quota, ignoring the protections provided by the submitting-foreigner status. Suffering double taxation, people of submitting-foreigner status complained, as did the Ministry of Rites, which worried that abusive taxation of a significant revenue source might ultimately result in the loss of this revenue source. A small minority of people of foreign status secured significant, generally middling, social status. For instance, the Nine Righteous Scholars' descendants had been enrolled in the Han Ivory Troop based in the capital but did not enjoy a prominent position. Existing records reveal, moreover, that just like submitting foreigners who were Jurchens, members of the Han Ivory Troop were required to submit fish as a tribute to the Ministry of Rites (Bohnet 2020, 123–32).

Continuities and Disruptions in Late Chosŏn

While the Chosŏn state's relationship with the Qing empire and the Tokugawa shogunate facilitated the repatriation of castaways, foreigners continued to arrive and establish themselves in Korea. The most famous cases involved the Catholic missionaries, French and Chinese, who operated in Chosŏn in the nineteenth century. The Roman Catholic Church entered Chosŏn through Jesuit writings in Literary Sinitic among elites in the seventeenth and eighteenth centuries and contacts between Chosŏn envoys with European Catholic missionaries in Beijing during diplomatic missions (Roux 2016). By the late eighteenth century, a small, indigenous Catholic community was growing in Chosŏn. The Korean converts finally received someone to hold mass with the arrival of a Chinese priest, Father James Zhou Wenmo (1752–1801), followed by French priests beginning in the 1830s and the first Korean priest, Andrew Kim Taegŏn (1821–46). The budding Catholic community grew significantly in the nineteenth century despite bloody persecutions.

A considerable body of scholarship on the Catholic Church of nineteenth-century Chosŏn focuses on the persecutions, reflecting martyrdom's vital role in Catholic doctrine. Indeed, the first martyrologies were written by Catholic missionaries in Chosŏn, such as Marie-Nicolas-Antoine Daveluy (1818–66), when Chosŏn still proscribed the Catholicism (Finch 2015, 677). Viewed differently, though, the development of the small Catholic Church also reflects the porosity of

Foreigners and the Descendants

Chosŏn's borders and the ease with which local society could accept outsiders. The first foreign missionary, Father James, took advantage of Chosŏn merchants' freedom to travel between the Yalu River and Beijing during a tribute mission. In contrast, other missionaries entered through the coast, for instance, taking advantage of Chinese fishermen catching sea cucumbers off the Korean coast. Except during periods of active persecution, the missionaries in Chosŏn could survive for considerable lengths of time, thanks to a welcoming community sheltering them and evidently broader acquiescence beyond the nascent Korean Catholic community. Bishop Marie-Nicolas-Antoine Daveluy survived unmolested in various locales in southern Korea between 1845 and 1866. A more extreme case was Bishop Siméon François Berneux (1814–66), who established himself in Hansŏng between 1856 and 1866, where he could have hardly avoided being noticed by numerous people. He even communicated directly with high officials close to the Hŭngsŏn Taewon'gun (1821–98)—who wielded power during the minority of his son, King Kojong (r. 1864–1907; emperor from 1897), until 1873—to secure support from upper echelons of political leadership. This attempt to meddle in Chosŏn politics resulted in disaster for the tiny Catholic community in Chosŏn when it became the initial cause of Chosŏn's final and harshest anti-Catholic persecution (1866–73) (Seo 2007, 325–33).

This persecution, in turn, set off a series of interventions by European and Japanese gunboats that, ultimately, resulted in Korea being forced open to the broader capitalist world. A new community of foreigners—now protected by European, Japanese, and Qing gunships—formed in port cities and Chosŏn's capital. These foreign communities, however, came with the advantages of passports and consular representation in the Chosŏn court. They were no longer organized through the *hyanghwa* category or represented as receiving moral edification from the Chosŏn monarch. Indeed, Korea entered a new era in its history of migrants (Dittrich 2016; Sinwoo Lee 2016).

In the meantime, the rise of Ming loyalist ritualism attracted new interest in the descendants of Ming refugees. In 1704, King Sukchong (r. 1674–1720) decided—with little hope of a Ming revival—to pursue the commemoration of fallen Ming on an altar in the palace complex, the Altar of Great Requital (Taebodan). The initial commemoration honored only the Wanli emperor, who had sent troops to aid Chosŏn during the Imjin War. Under King Yŏngjo (r. 1724–76), the court added more Ming emperors for commemoration at this shrine: the Hongwu emperor (r. 1368–98), the Ming founder, and the Chongzhen emperor (r. 1627–44), whose suicide in 1644 marked the end of the Ming rule in northern China proper. Performed rites effectively conferred upon Chosŏn the status of the true heir to the Ming tradition (Haboush 2017, 121–28; Kye 2014).

Such official ritualization of Chosŏn's claimed inheritance also affected the state's treatment of those submitting foreigners who could trace their ancestry to Ming refugees. For instance, in the 1750s, Yŏngjo expressed shock at the classification of the descendants of refugees from Ming as "submitting foreigners" (*hyanghwain*), along with the descendants of Jurchens and Japanese. Considering this categorization—which marked them as recipients of the edification of the Chosŏn monarch—unsuited to the representatives of Ming, Yŏngjo ordered their recategorization, first as "Chinese" (*Hwain*) and then as "Imperial Subjects" (*Hwangjoin*). They were to enjoy advantages in the government service examinations, especially the military examination (*mukwa*). He also encouraged their participation in the recently established Ming loyalist shrine, the Altar of Great Requital. Yŏngjo's successor, King Chŏngjo (1776–1800), furthered this process. He reorganized the military units to which Ming migrants and their descendants were assigned—from the déclassé Han Ivory Troops to the much more dignified Han Brigades (*Hallyŏ*). Chŏngjo also created a position within the Han Brigades, the Guards of the Altar of Great Requital (*Taebodan sujikkwan*), which performed specific ritual duties for the Altar (Seunghyun Han 2018, 178–79). Both monarchs also granted Ming migrants privileged access to examinations held in consort with Ming

159

The Routledge Handbook of Early Modern Korea

Loyalist rituals. Chosŏn monarchs used their patronage of the descendants of Ming migrants to strengthen their royal authority and status as Confucian rulers (Seunghyun Han 2022, 10). On the other hand, being identified as a person of Ming migrant ancestry could transform the individual's social status. For instance, by law, some were "lowborn" (*ch'ŏnmin*) in status, as were all slaves and *kisaeng*, due to descent from a Ming migrant or migrant-descent male and a Korean lowborn female, but being identified as a Ming migrant's descendant could result in manumission (Bohnet 2020, 117).

The problem was that identifying someone as a descendant of a Ming migrant was not easy, and a positive identification was to the monarch's political interest. Some, like the descendants of Kang Shijue of Musan, who was well documented while still alive, had maintained a continuous connection to their distinguished ancestors. The origins of many, though, were obscure. For instance, Ma Shunshang (fl. 1627), a Ming migrant who arrived in Chosŏn after the Battle of Sarhu, appeared in private writings of a famous Chosŏn scholar-official Kim Yuk (1580–1658) before vanishing from history. Chŏngjo's order to search for Ma's descendants (1800) located some who claimed descent, the veracity of which is uncertain (Bohnet 2020, 178–80). In fact, many, such as the alleged descendants of a Ming official during the Imjin War, Shi Xing (1538–99), came forth with highly doubtful accounts full of impossible claims. Despite ample doubts expressed by high officials, Chŏngjo insisted that the claim of descent from Shi was legitimate and ordered a search for supporting evidence. In the case of the Nongsŏ Yi, descended from Ming generals Li Rusong (1549–98) and Li Rumei (fl. 1596), a branch based in Kanghwado was relatively well documented. In contrast, two others were obscure and possibly fraudulent. The ideological importance of Nongsŏ Yi to Yŏngjo and Chŏngjo was such that they often ignored the well-founded doubts of their officials when considering the claims of Nongsŏ Yi and similar others (Bohnet 2020, 151–59).

Creating a ritually significant community of Ming migrants under Yŏngjo and Chŏngjo engendered a new social grouping centered around certain shrines. Both their ritual participation and the significance of the examinations associated with the monarchs' involvement in the Altar of Great Requital rituals decreased in the nineteenth century when an oligarchy of consort families eclipsed royal power during a series of kings either a minor or utterly unprepared ascended the throne. Consequently, the cultivation of this royally created social status became dependent on the active assertions of Ming migrant descendants. Building on court-commissioned biographies of their ancestors from the eighteenth century, they began to produce such biographies on their own and established shrines under their control to supplement the declining status of the Altar of Great Requital. For instance, in 1818, Wang Tŏkku (1788–1863), a descendant of a Ming migrant, wrote his account of the Nine Righteous Officials and other Ming migrants in a text that, in many ways, brought the already embellished court-sponsored biographical tradition to a new level (Bohnet 2020, 178–79). In 1831, furthermore, he and a relative established the Temporary Shrine of Great Succession (*Taet'ong haengmyo*) at a location in Kap'yŏng, Kyŏnggi Province, where a mid-Chosŏn Ming loyalist, Hŏ Kyŏk (1608–89+), had carved the Chongzhen emperor's calligraphy in a rock. Wang Tŏkku's shrine, however, hosted rituals specifically for Ming's founder, the Hongwu emperor, whom they praised for restoring the distinction between civilization and barbarians (Seunghyun Han 2018, 188–94).

In late Chosŏn, a growing number of descent groups, such as the T'aean Yi, constructed false claims of descent from prominent Chinese ancestors in their genealogies to assert a higher social status (Kenneth R. Robinson 2008). Although evidence often substantiated the Chinese ancestors of descent groups with Ming migrant ancestry, in other respects, they were essentially indistinguishable from other Koreans, aside from their institutional connection to Chosŏn's official Ming loyalism. Still, a Ming loyalist identity was important enough to them that genealogies show that

Foreigners and the Descendants

beginning in the early nineteenth century, many descendants of the Nine Righteous Scholars began to practice endogamy with others of Ming migrant descent (Seunghyun Han 2018, 185–87). Even after such endogamy had declined by the late nineteenth century, many Ming migrant descent groups, notably those associated with the Temporary Shrine of Great Succession, continued to emphasize their Ming loyalism at least until the 1990s (Mason 1991).

Final Thoughts

Well before South Korea's history textbooks stopped asserting ethnic homogeneity in the new millennium, South Korean, Japanese, and English-speaking scholars were writing about early Chosŏn's ethnic diversity, especially concerning frontier contact with the Japanese and Jurchens. Since then, a sizable body of scholarship has established the presence and the importance of those connected to Yuan and the people of Jurchen or Japanese origin in early Chosŏn. This research has highlighted their ideological significance to the early Chosŏn monarchy, their capacity as vital conduits for trade, and their crucial role in frontier defense. Far from rejecting all outsiders, early Chosŏn adapted Koryŏ bureaucratic tools for settling outsiders in its territory. Chosŏn further adopted these tools during the Imjin War and the wars of the Ming–Qing transition (1616–44), when large numbers of Japanese, Jurchens, and Chinese refugees and deserters arrived.

After 1644, with few exceptions, Chosŏn did not receive new legal migrants other than a few Dutch and Portuguese castaways. Driving this change was the disappearance of the small frontier polities that had existed since early Chosŏn, the establishment of a regularized repatriation process between Chosŏn and, on the other hand, Qing China and Tokugawa Japan, and Chosŏn's relative isolation from a major global trade route. Catholic missionaries from China and France—whom the Chosŏn court suspected of political subversion—suffered violent persecution during the nineteenth century. Even then, notably, the authorities left many key figures unmolested for more than a decade, even though their presence must indeed have been widely known.

In its self-perception, Chosŏn did not pursue ethnic homogeneity. Long after active migration had ceased, the Chosŏn state continued to organize the descendants of migrants according to the same bureaucratic categories that early Chosŏn had used for migrants. Also, in the 1750s, the state began actively honoring the descendants of Ming migrants, integrating them into court rituals to make their continued foreignness central to Chosŏn's self-perception and royal legitimacy. Of course, by the 1750s, few Ming migrant descendants would have spoken Chinese, and almost certainly in ancestry, each such individual was substantially Korean on the female side. In daily life, they hardly differed from an increasing number of descent groups claiming largely spurious Chinese ancestors from Song China or earlier. The proliferation of such claims demands reconsidering the notion of Chosŏn as a homogenous, autarchic state.

References

The Analects. 2014. By Confucius. Translated by Annping Chin. Penguin Books.

Bohnet, Adam. 2016. "Lies, Rumours and Sino-Korean Relations: The Pseudo-Fujianese Incident of 1687." *Acta Koreana* 19, no. 2: 1–29.

Bohnet, Adam. 2020. *Turning toward Edification: Foreigners in Chosŏn Korea.* University of Hawaiʻi Press.

Breuker, Remco. 2011. "Narratives of Inauthenticity, Impurity, and Disorder. Or: How Forgeries, Half-Castes, and Hooligans Shaped Pre-Modern Korean History." *Sungkyun Journal of East Asian Studies* 11, no. 2: 183–208.

Brose, Michael C. 2013. "Neo-Confucian Uyghur Semuren in Koryŏ and Chosŏn Korean Society and Politics." In *Eurasian Influences on Yuan China*, edited by Morris Rossabi, 178–99. Institute of Southeast Asian Studies.

The Routledge Handbook of Early Modern Korea

Choi Byonghyon. 2014. *The Annals of King T'aejo: Founder of Korea's Chosŏn Dynasty.* Harvard University Press.

Chong, Daham. 2010. "Making Chosŏn's Own Tributaries: Dynamics between the Ming-Centered World Order and a Chosŏn-Centered Regional Order in the East Asian Periphery." *International Journal of Korean History* 15, no. 1: 29–63.

Clark, Donald N. 1982. "Chosŏn's Founding Fathers: A Study of Merit Subjects in the Early Yi Dynasty." *Korean Studies* 6, no. 1: 17–40.

Clark, Donald N. 1988. "Sino–Korean Tributary Relations under the Ming." In *The Cambridge History of China.* Volume 8, *The Ming Dynasty*, Part 2, edited by Denis C. Twitchett and Frederick W. Mote, 272–300. Cambridge University Press.

Crossley, Pamela Kyle. 1999. *A Translucent Mirror: History and Identity in Qing Imperial Ideology.* University of California Press.

Dittrich, Klaus. 2016. "Europeans and Americans in Korea, 1882–1910: A Bourgeois and Translocal Community." *Itinerario* 40, no. 1: 3–28.

Duncan, John B. 2000. "Hyanghwain: Migration and Assimilation in Chosŏn Korea." *Acta Koreana* 3, no. 1: 99–113.

Elliott, Mark C. 2001. *The Manchu Way : The Eight Banners and Ethnic Identity in Late Imperial China.* Stanford University Press.

Finch, Andrew. 2015. "The 'Blood of the Martyrs' and the Growth of Catholicism in Late Chosŏn Korea." *Historical Research: The Bulletin of the Institute of Historical Research* 88: 674–92.

Fujiwara Takao. 2014. "Sayak'a (Kim Ch'ungsŏn) ŭi t'uhang yoin kwa sigi ŭi yunsaek munje." *Chosŏnsa yŏn'gu* 23: 83–116.

Haboush, JaHyun Kim. 2017. "Contesting Chinese Time, Nationalizing Temporal Space: Temporal Inscription in Late Chosŏn Korea." In *Time, Temporality, and Imperial Transition*, edited by Lynn A. Struve, 115–41. University of Hawai'i Press.

Haboush, JaHyu Kim, and Kenneth R. Robinson. 2013. *A Korean War Captive in Japan, 1597–1600: The Writings of Kang Hang.* Columbia University Press.

Han, Kyung-koo. 2007. "The Archaeology of the Ethnically Homogeneous Nation-State and Multiculturalism in Korea." *Korea Journal* 47, no. 4: 8–31.

Han, Sangwoo. 2021. "The Marriage Market for Immigrant Families in Chosŏn Korea after the Imjin War: Women, Integration, and Cultural Capital." *International Journal of Asian Studies* 18, no. 2: 247–69.

Han, Seunghyun. 2018. "Ming Loyalist Families and the Changing Meanings of Chojong'am in Early Nineteenth-Century Chosŏn." *Acta Koreana* 21, no. 1: 169–203.

Han, Seunghyun. 2022. "The Mangbaerye Examinations: Ming Loyalist Court Rituals and Royal Authority in Eighteenth-and Nineteenth-Century Chosŏn." *Journal of Korean Studies* 27, no. 1: 3–36.

Han, Young-woo. 1985. "Kija Worship in the Koryŏ and Early Yi Dynasties: A Cultural Symbol in the Relationship Between Korea and China." In *The Rise of Neo-Confucianism in Korea*, edited by Wm. Theodore de Bary and JaHyun Kim Haboush, 349–74. Columbia University Press.

Hyun, Jaehwan. 2019. "Racializing Chōsenjin: Science and Biological Speculations in Colonial Korea." *East Asian Science, Technology and Society* 13 no. 4: 489–510.

Jorgensen, John. 2020. "Infiltrating the Hermit Kingdom: The Penetration of Chinese Buddhist Texts into Seventeenth Century Korea." *Foguang xuebao* (*Fo Guang Journal of Buddhist Studies*) 2: 153–210.

Kang, Seok Hwa. 2008. "Frontier Maps from the Late Joseon Period and the Joseon People's Perceptions of the Northern Territory." *Korea Journal* 48, no.1: 80–105.

Kim, Seonmin. 2017. *Ginseng and Borderland.* University of California Press.

Kimura Taku. 2017. "Chōsen kōki ni okeru kyūgisi seiritsu no keii taimin giriron no tenkai ni sokusite." *Tōyō bunka kenkyū* 19: 63–94.

Kwon, Nae-Hyun. 2015. "Chosŏn Korea's Trade with Qing China and the Circulation of Silver." *Acta Koreana* 18, no. 1: 163–85.

Kye, Seung B. 2014. "The Altar of Great Gratitude: A Korean Memory of Ming China under Manchu Dominance, 1704–1894." *Journal of Korean Religions* 5, no. 2: 71–88.

Ledyard, Gari. 1971. *The Dutch Come to Korea.* Royal Asiatic Society, Korea Branch.

Lee, Hoon. 1997."Dispute over Territorial Ownership of Tokdo in the Late Chosŏn Period" *Korea Observer* 28, no. 3: 389–421.

Lee, Hoon. 2006. "The Repatriation of Castaways in Chosŏn Korea–Japan Relations, 1599–1888." *Korean Studies* 30: 67–90.

Foreigners and the Descendants

Lee, Meng Heng. 2018. "Ukanju and the Changing Political Order of Northeastern Asia in the 17th Century." *International Journal of Korean History* 23, no. 1: 5–25.

Lee, Sinwoo. 2016. "Blurring Boundaries: Mixed Residence, Extraterritoriality, and Citizenship in Seoul, 1876–1910." *Journal of Korean Studies* 21, no. 1: 71–100.

Lewis, James B. 2005. *Frontier Contact between Chosŏn Korea and Tokugawa Japan*. Routledge.

Lie, John. 2014. "Introduction: Multiethnic Korea." In *Multiethnic Korea? Multiculturalism, Migration, and Peoplehood Diversity in Contemporary South Korea*, edited by John Lie, 59–78. Institute of East Asian Studies.

Liu, Jing. 2019. "Beyond the Land: Maritime Interactions, Border Control, and Regional Powers between China and Korea, 1500–1637." Ph.D. dissertation, Syracuse University.

Liu, Jing. 2023. "Beyond Categories and Boundaries: Transmarine Mobility and Coastal Governance of Northeast Asia in the Sixteenth Century." *Journal of the Royal Asiatic Society* 33, no. 1: 133–54.

Mason, David. 1991. "The Samhyang paehyang Sacrificial Ceremony for Three Emperors: Korea's Link to the Ming Dynasty." *Korea Journal* 31 no. 3: 117–36.

Nakano Kota. 2013. "Ssangsŏng Ch'onggwanbu as the Border between Koryŏ and Yuan Dynasty." *International Journal of Korean History* 18, no. 1: 93–120.

Pyŏgo yugo. Collected writings of Yi Sibal. Available at: db.itkc.or.kr.

Robinson, David M. 2009. *Empire's Twilight: Northeast Asia under the Mongols*. Harvard University Asia Center.

Robinson, David M. 2022. *Korea and the Fall of the Mongol Empire : Alliance, Upheaval, and the Rise of a New East Asian Order*. Cambridge University Press.

Robinson, Kenneth R. 1992. "From Raiders to Traders: Border Security and Border Control in Early Chosŏn, 1392–1450." *Korean Studies* 16: 94–115.

Robinson, Kenneth R. 2000. "Centering the King of Chosŏn: Aspects of Korean Maritime Diplomacy, 1392–1592" *Journal of Asian Studies* 59, no. 1: 109–25.

Robinson, Kenneth R. 2006. "An Island's Place in History: Tsushima in Japan and in Chosŏn, 1392–1592." *Korean Studies* 30: 40–66.

Robinson, Kenneth R. 2008. "The Chinese Ancestors in a Korean Descent Group's Genealogies." *Journal of Korean Studies* 13, no. 1: 89–114.

Robinson, Kenneth R. 2013. "Organizing Japanese and Jurchens in Tribute Systems in Early Chosŏn Korea." *Journal of East Asian Studies* 13, no. 2: 337–60.

Robinson, Kenneth R. 2016. "Pak Tonji and the Vagaries of Government Service in Koryŏ and Chosŏn, 1360–1412." *Korean Studies* 40, no. 1: 78–118.

Roux, Pierre-Emmanuel. 2014. "The Prohibited Sect of Yaso: Catholicism in Diplomatic and Cultural Encounters between Edo Japan and Chosŏn Korea (17th to 19th Century)." In *Space and Location in Circulation of Knowledge (1400–1800): Korea and Beyond*, edited by Marion Eggert, Felix Siegmund, and Dennis Würthner, 119–40. Peter Lang GmbH.

Roux, Pierre-Emmanuel. 2016. "The Catholic Experience of Chosŏn Envoys in Beijing: A Contact Zone and the Circulation of Religious Knowledge in the Eighteenth Century." *Acta Koreana* 19, no. 1: 9–44.

Schmid, Andre. 2002. *Korea Between Empires, 1895–1919*. Columbia University Press.

Sejong sillok. In *Chosŏn wangjo sillok*. Available at: https://sillok.history.go.kr/main/main.do.

Seo, Jongtae. 2007. "The Western Missionaries and the Persecution of 1866." In *Sŏng Tori sinbu wa son'gol*, edited by Youn Minku, 321–52. Kippŭn sosik.

Smits, Gregory. 2018. *Maritime Ryukyu, 1050–1650*. University of Hawai'i Press.

Stiller, Maya. 2021. "Precious Items Piling up Like Mountains: Buddhist Art Production via Fundraising Campaigns in Late Koryŏ Korea (918–1392)." *Religions* 12, no. 10: 885.

Veritable Records of King Sejong. Available at: http://esillok.history.go.kr/.

Woodruff, Phillip. 1987. "Status and Lineage among the Jurchens of the Korean Northeast in the Mid-fifteenth Century." *Central and Inner Asian Studies* 1: 117–54.

Yuh, Leighanne, and Jungsoo Jang. 2023. "A Reinterpretation of Chosŏn–Qing Foreign Relations through an Analysis of Chosŏn and Later Jin Bilateral Relations." *Sungkyun Journal of East Asian Studies* 23, no. 1: 49–71.

Yun, Peter. 2002. "Mongols and Western Asians in the Late Koryŏ Ruling Stratum." *International Journal of Korean History* 3, no. 1: 51–69.

11
GENDER

Marion Eggert

How gender played out in early modern Korea ruled by the Chosŏn state (1392–1897) is a meaningful inquiry since understanding much of the social and ideological structuring of Chosŏn society is feasible with gender and sexuality as a starting point. Yet, providing clear-cut answers to even such basic questions as whether the social position of women deteriorated or improved in Chosŏn is difficult. It is generally accepted that Confucian norms and laws heavily regulated gender relations and sexuality, but the scope of the efficacy of laws and norms in shaping actual behaviors in daily life was at least as limited in this sphere of social life as in others. Further factors, such as economic necessities or developments in the literary field, had their own validating power.

Thus, scholarship on gender relations in Chosŏn has often pointed out the impossibility of overcoming seeming contradictions. Some have highlighted apparent discrepancies in how women of Chosŏn seemed to both gain and lose agency (Haboush 2002, 221). Others have noted inconsistencies in the scholarly description of Chosŏn as undergoing increasingly rigid Confucianization or as producing new trends (Youngmin Kim and Pettid 2011, 1). Accordingly, this chapter cannot deliver a fully streamlined account of Chosŏn's gender relations or scholarship on the subject nor provide a comprehensive, diachronic narrative. Instead, the following discussion aims to give an overview of the most important aspects of the topic, enriched with some illustrations through primary sources.

Norms and Laws

The Chosŏn state's builders conceived the social order centered around the patriarchal family, structured around gender relations. The sincerity with which the new state committed to Confucianism as state ideology led to scrutinizing indigenous Korean customs regarding their compatibility with Confucian doctrines, rituals, and laws. Family structure, though, embodied one blatant divergence: as true elsewhere in the early modern world, Korea had a strong tradition of bilaterality, that is, the equal importance of maternal and paternal family lines for the inheritance of both wealth and status, whereas Confucianism reflected Chinese patrilineal traditions.

In early Chosŏn, much legislative effort went into fostering the emergence of clearly delineated patrilineal kin groups. To this end, the officials enacting new laws, above all, outlawed plural marriage, common in Chosŏn's predecessor state, Koryŏ (918–1392), so that men could take only

164

DOI: 10.4324/9781003262053-15

Gender

one legal wife, even while being allowed to keep as many concubines ("secondary wives"; *ch'ŏp*) as they could afford. Enforcement of the law not only utilized harsh punishments of perpetrators but also barred the offspring of concubines from taking the government service examinations, thus effectively excluding them from office. Similarly, and through the same measures, the state outlawed the remarriage of widows. It made remarried women's offspring ineligible for the government service examinations—all to ensure that women and their offspring remained attached to a single, patrilineal family. New measures taken also targeted the old custom of uxorilocal marriage. The practice persisted until the mid-Chosŏn period, at least during the first years of marriage before wives would move in with their husbands' families. At the same time, the wives could no longer inherit land from their natal families. This change weakened their economic autonomy. Ritual rules derived from the Chinese classics excluded women from the ancestral rites, relegating them symbolically as well to the fringes of the descent group. Conversely, the notion of wives being members of their husbands' families made divorce virtually unthinkable, at least among elites. In theory, divorcing a wife was allowed on seven grounds, including the failure to bear an heir; even then, certain conditions, such as the wife having no one else to rely on, did not allow divorce. Since the head of the patriarchal household made such decisions, husbands likely had as little say in this matter as wives, especially if they were residing with the husband's parents (CCHKW 1976, 100).

Efforts to safeguard the purity of the patrilineal bloodline engendered an obsession with female chastity. The remarriage ban became so broad that even women bereft of their bridegrooms before the wedding were not supposed to marry into another family. Suicide was deemed an honorable escape from the predicament for young women who no longer belonged to their natal families yet might be considered an economic burden by their deceased bridegrooms' families.

The early Chosŏn state promulgated laws and edicts to ensure sex segregation. Limiting women's mobility outside the house first entailed outlawing their visits to shrines and monasteries (activities perceived as an opportunity for sexual license). Further regulations followed, restricting elite women to the house altogether—with few exceptions such as specific holidays or the nighttime when they were allowed to move about, albeit fully covered. Those traveling had to do so in closed palanquins. With the application of the rule from the Confucian *Book of Rites* (*Liji*) that males and females should be separated from age seven, domestic space, too, had to be divided into the "inner" and "outer" chambers, two parts of the house (or estate) separated by a wall. Guests could only enter the outer part; generally, women were not to speak to males outside the household except for close relatives. Many of these rules applied to, or could be upheld by, the *yangban* only. Thus, the death penalty for adulteresses, introduced much later, applied only to *yangban* women (Jisoo Kim 2015, 14).

All the same, the rationale behind this set of rules—the utmost importance of female chastity—spread even among the general population over time. For example, the remarriage of widows became so ill-reputed that among commoners, being kidnapped by a man became the only means for a widow to remarry without loss of reputation. For the honor of such families, untainted female morality sufficed. For *yangban*, however, having been submitted to physical force did nothing to alleviate their defilement in case of their contact with males outside the family. Accordingly, for example, *yangban* families refused to take back daughters-in-law abducted by Manchus during the Pyŏngja War (1637) when they were finally able to return (Pak 2008, 199). While the court decided against a right to divorce such women, the contempt they had to suffer revives in the derogatory term *hwanyangnyŏn* in the sense of "loose females" derived from the term coined for these "women returning home" (*hwanhyangnyŏ*) (Lee Bae-Yong 2008, 38).

The Routledge Handbook of Early Modern Korea

Legal stipulations manifested and reinforced a clear gender hierarchy, with females harming males more severely punished than vice versa. The general, deep-seated conception of the gender hierarchy drew an analogy to the relationship between sovereign and minister or master and slave (*nobi*). For example, literati males addressing the monarch in poetry—especially when expressing their longing for recognition as loyal subjects—frequently impersonated female voices. This normative order privileging males over females cited yin-yang (*ŭm-yang*) thought and Confucian tenets of social hierarchy.

Confucian and Daoist Chinese thought held the notion of nature and cosmos embodying the complementary natural forces, yin and yang. Originally the shadowy and the bright side of a hill, yin and yang came to correlate with a female and male principle. Indeed, intellectuals rarely questioned the yin–yang pair as the basis of a more comprehensive system of correlative natural philosophy. From this perspective, the forces of yin and yang permeate all natural phenomena, wax and wane in turns, and are both indispensable—as their balance maintains a state of harmony. In that sense, yin–yang thought can potentially alleviate gender hierarchy, and Daoist thought can attach positive value to the yin force and everything connected to it, especially the generative power of the womb and the quiet, self-sustained force of water. All the same, such appreciation of the yin force was a conscious inversion of general values: identification of yang with the sky, light, warmth, dryness and yin with the earth, darkness, cold, and moisture rationalized a clear distinction in "high" and "low" seamlessly translating into social terms. Yin-yang thought fostered the ideal of a mutually beneficial and supportive relationship between the male and the female sphere. Yin–yang dualism also reinforced gender segregation by naturalizing the dichotomy of inner (yin) and outer (yang) spaces and duties.

On rare occasions, yin–yang thought even worked in favor of women. During severe droughts, the court sometimes released palace ladies (Lee Bae-Yong 2008, 68). Both Lee and CCHKW (1976, 126) opine that this was an attempt to appease court women's discontent. However, the entry from the veritable records (*sillok*) referenced by the latter study does not fully support this view. In 1684, the official Kim Suhang (1629–89) observed: "From olden times, droughts were brought about by various reasons, but often they result from the stopping-up and accumulation of the female force" (*Sukchong sillok* 1684/7/5 entry 2). Although the words translated here as "stopping-up and accumulation" (*ulchŏk*) can be read in a psychological way as "pent-up frustration," "the accumulation of excessive female qi in one place" seems to be a more straightforward reading of the passage. Although the sexual frustration of court ladies may have played a role in this imagery, freeing them was not intended as a humanistic act: Kim Suhang recommended expelling those not of good use as a measure of cutting costs.

Nevertheless, such (horizontal) harmony could only accrue through accepting the (vertical) hierarchy that puts men above women in a clearly defined power relationship. In theory, women were confined to the domestic sphere and did not need higher learning, but their moral education was paramount. Accordingly, the early Chosŏn state and its elite proprietors began disseminating texts to educate the populace, including women, in the basics of Confucian ethics and their duties. Initially compiled in Literary Sinitic (Classical Chinese), *Illustrated Guide to the Virtues of the Three Bonds* (*Samgang haengsil to*; 1432)—a book propagating the virtuous conduct of subjects towards rulers, sons towards fathers, and women towards their husbands (and the latter's families) through illustrated moral anecdotes—was later translated into Korean to facilitate dissemination among the general population (Deuchler 2003, 146). Other works targeted women even more specifically, seeking to make them internalize their subordinated position. For example, the Confucian primer *Elementary Learning* (Ch. *Xiaoxue*; Ko. *Sohak*) compiled by the revered Zhu Xi (1130–1200) of Song dynasty (960–1279) China and first reprinted by the Chosŏn state in

1407 saw editions customized for a female audience. Other morality books for women featured biographies of exemplary women or compilations of Confucian sayings on female virtue (Kim Kyŏngnam 2021). Among the books for the moral instruction of women that enjoyed circulation throughout Chosŏn's history were works by female authors, starting with *Instructions for the Inner Chambers* (*Naehun*), drawing from Chinese sources and compiled in 1475 by King Sŏngjong's (r. 1470–95) mother, Queen Sohye (1437–1504).

The mounting pressure on women to adapt their conduct to Confucian rules increased the perceived need for women's moral education, which furthered female submissiveness, yet also provided women with at least a minimum education. As objects of moral teachings, women were simultaneously instated as autonomous moral subjects who could decide for or against living a virtuous life and even exhibit superiority over men in moral terms (Koh 2008, 358; Haboush 2003, 287, 298). In this sense, social critic Ch'oe Han'gi (1803–79), writing towards the end of Chosŏn, could say: "In teaching them to serve well those above [that is, the parents] and to rear well those below [that is, the children], in accordance with the unfolding of life in the family, the education of women is no different from that of men" ("Yŏja kyo," *Injŏng* 11).

As paragons of Confucian morality, women could even earn honor for their families. After all, in special cases of upholding chastity against extreme adversity, the government might erect an arch of honor (*chŏngnyŏ*) for her in front of her house or village. She might even enter the memory of posterity by her virtuous deeds becoming part of the written record. In all these cases, however, exerting moral agency meant submitting to a social order that excluded women from many life choices. For some, it meant death, but most chose survival.

Social Life

What was the actual reach of the norms and laws concerning gender relations? Enforcement of the law was far from uniform, and the Confucianization of Chosŏn society was a drawn-out process continuing to the late seventeenth century for the elite and reaching lower strata of society even later (Deuchler 1992; Deuchler 2015). As soon as the Confucian order was ostensibly in place, it came under challenge. Nonetheless, Western visitors in the late nineteenth century described a society marked by gender segregation and female subordination. The normative order certainly shaped social reality, though the latter could never fully correspond to the normative ideals.

Female Economic Activity

Even though the public, in both spatial and political sense, excluded women by segregating the "inner" and "outer" worlds, they could exercise agency in the economic sphere. A *yangban* wife of a head of household would have far-reaching obligations in overseeing the work of the servants, tenants, and slaves. Having everything ready for the all-important ancestor rituals and the guests' feast was another of her primary duties. This meant that she lived within an extended social network. A diary kept by such *yangban* woman, Lady Kigye Yu—who married into the Andong Kim lineage of Hongsŏng, Ch'ungch'ŏng Province—over one and a half years in 1849–51 reveals that during this time, she met with 253 persons and hosted a total of 188 for at least one meal (Kim Hyŏnsuk 2018, 194–200). In her case, management of household affairs entailed directly supervising 43 slaves. The responsibility entailed distributing the chores, deciding about work and rest periods (for example, rest for an ill servant and a free day for slaves), reviewing the results, and hiring a wet nurse for the infant of a slave woman deceased after childbirth (Kim Hyŏnsuk 2018, 68–70). As Lady Yu had to visit the slaves who worked from their quarters, her duty as a household manager afforded her some mobility outside her compartments. Economic necessity trumped

The Routledge Handbook of Early Modern Korea

Confucian decorum even in an affluent elite household, and this held all the more true in times of hardship when even respectable *yangban* women might be forced to attempt to make money as small vendors at the market (Lee Bae-Yong 2008, 56).

For women of lower social status, engaging in agriculture and selling (or bartering) their goods at the markets was commonplace. Outside the house, many females worked as sewists. Women across status boundaries participated in cloth production by spinning and weaving, though embroidering was mainly an elite occupation. Cloth being a main exchange item and tax currency, textile production was an essential female contribution to the household economy (Kim Kyŏngmi 2012); it was also a modest one, performed inside the women's quarters. Stories abound of hardworking women of noble but poor families who sustained their family's livelihood and brought up their children thanks to their needlework (Pettid 2010, 30–37). An exceptional case was the female divers of the island Chejudo, who harvested seafood from the sea-bed and often were the main breadwinners of their families. Literati from the mainland who visited (or, more often, were banished to) the island took note of them with much appreciation, though not without a tinge of exoticism.

Further instances of "women in professions" include court ladies (*kungnyŏ, kungin, nain*), *ŭinyŏ* (female healers), *kisaeng* (female entertainers), shamans (*mudang*), and Buddhist nuns. "Court ladies" were the women brought into the court at a young age—typically commoners—as potential sexual partners for the king (and, to some extent, the princes) and as attendants for the royal family and the king's concubines. A ranking system similar to that of male officials—ranging from "senior first" to "junior ninth" rank—regulated the hierarchy among the court ladies and the tasks to which they were put. Ranks one to four were reserved for the king's concubines on the receiving end of service, and ranks five to nine for serving duties. These tasks ranged from secretarial duties and messenger service to silk-worm raising and menial work such as fetching buckets of water. As the number of court women increased—from a two-digit number in the beginnings to around a hundred in Sŏngjong's reign, 230 in Sukchong's reign (1674–1720), and over 600 in Yŏngjo's reign (1724–76) (Hong 2004, 252–23)—their hopes of winning the king's favors and becoming a royal concubine dwindled. At the same time, working duties per female diminished so that half-day shifts became common rather than all-day work (CCHKW 1976, 127). Those assigned as attendants to members of the royal family had the chance to receive a literary education. Given the more stable livelihood they enjoyed, their position was enviable enough, notwithstanding their being deprived of family life, that a law was in place that stipulated harsh punishments for women attempting to become court ladies on their own accord (Hong 2004, 257).

Including some knowledge of Literary Sinitic, education was also necessary for the training of *ŭinyŏ*, needed to treat women of high status. First established for the needs of the female members of the royal family, the institution of *ŭinyŏ* was soon extended to the countryside as well. Selected among nonelites (mostly from slave families attached to central and local offices) between 9 and 14 years of age and mainly trained to assist male physicians by checking the symptoms of female patients, even in this subordinate function, they could not do without some understanding of the rationales of the medical art, which was to a considerable degree based on cosmological ideas such as yin–yang and five phases thought. Specifically, the *ŭinyŏ* received training with texts in acupuncture, pulse-taking, midwifery, and medicinal herbs; in late Chosŏn, some became renowned specialists in one of these arts (Yi Misuk 2012, 174–81). However, rather than being respected for their knowledge, *ŭinyŏ* tended to be grouped with *kisaeng*. Oft cited reason is King Yŏnsan Kun's (r. 1495–1506) misuse of *ŭinyŏ* by ordering them to entertain at banquets (CCHKW 1976, 138; Yi Misuk 2012, 189–91), but that this perception persisted was probably mostly due to both the physical nature of the duties performed by *ŭinyŏ* and the relatively high degree of mobility outside the house demanded of them. In an ironic twist, the *ŭinyŏ* system, which had come into existence because of the demands of strict gender segregation, allowed a certain degree of transgression of gender boundaries to those "lowborn" (*ch'ŏnmin*) women chosen to fill their ranks.

The obvious example of women living beyond at least some of the gender norms was the *kisaeng*, who belonged to the lowborn status group, as did slaves. The early Chosŏn state selected *kisaeng* from the lowborn for training in performing arts at the court or the provincial government offices. As their trade became hereditary with time, *kisaeng* increasingly stood out from ordinary government slaves, though not in terms of status (Park 2015, 5–6). At court and provincial offices, *kisaeng* were, first and foremost, performative artists enriching festivities of all kinds with song, dance, and instrumental music. The higher-ranking among them also acquired literacy—even in Literary Sinitic—to engage in elegant poetry exchanges. *Kisaeng* had to provide sexual services to envoys (in the capital and along the embassy routes), traveling officials (at all provincial headquarters), and county magistrates. Stories of legendary *kisaeng* such as Hwang Chini (1506–67), an elusive figure around whom a dense web of narrative has been spun from the seventeenth century onward, have created an image of *kisaeng* having control of their sexual favors, but this is hardly true. Certainly, flirtation was part of the entertainment that guests at a banquet expected. In that sense, the entertainers had a certain leeway for devoting special attention to individual men and may thus have possessed a modicum of agency concerning their liaisons. As the lowborn, however, *kisaeng* ultimately could not refuse the demands of those exerting governmental authority over them. Without a say, they could be given away as gifts or taken as concubines by high officials. The seeming sexual liberty of a *kisaeng* and the comparatively non-secluded life she could live "made modern readers regard her as a predecessor of the purported liberated modern woman" yet "were indeed the source of her degradation in Chosŏn society" (Park 2015, 22).

Nonetheless, their life in (semi-) public space allowed some *kisaeng* to occupy a place as historical agents in collective memory. For a long time, popular imagination has remained captive to the stories of two *kisaeng*, Chu Non'gae (1574–93), better known as Non'gae, and Kyewŏrhyang (d. 1592), both of whom, during the Imjin War (East Asian War; 1592–98), gave their lives in killing Japanese generals—Non'gae by throwing herself off a cliff while clinging to her victim during a dance. Both stories, transmitted through anecdotal rather than official historiography, may be spurious, but their circulation in late Chosŏn illustrates the ascription of historical agency to *kisaeng* (Figure 11.1). A less-known but better-documented case is the *kisaeng* Kim Mandŏk (1739–1812), from Chejudo, who came to fame during King Chŏngjo's reign (1776–1800). According to Ch'ae Chegong (1720–99), one of Chŏngjo's prominent officials, Mandŏk became a *kisaeng* after losing her parents early. However, in her early twenties, she was taken off the register. From then on, she lived unmarried as a successful merchant. When a famine hit Chejudo in 1795, Mandŏk spent her amassed fortune on alleviating the suffering of other islanders. Upon hearing this, Chŏngjo granted her wish to tour Mount Kŭmgang and see the capital, Hansŏng (present-day Seoul), where she became the head *ŭinyŏ*. During her half a year in Hansŏng, Mandŏk became an attraction for the officials and literati. According to Ch'ae Chaegong, he forbade her "womanlike" tears at the farewell meeting, citing that her achievements surpassed most men's ("Mandŏk chŏn," *Pŏnam chip* 55). In words and deeds, many at court treated Mandŏk as traversing the threshold between the male and female worlds—no doubt due to her former existence as a *kisaeng*.

Cultural Activities by Women

At least the higher-ranking *kisaeng*, albeit subjected to servitude, could gain visibility as artists in their own right—not only in song and dance but also as poets or, in some cases, painters. For all

Figure 11.1 Depiction of Kyewŏrhyang, 1815. During the Imjin War, Kyewŏrhyang, who was a *kisaeng* in P'yŏngyang and a favorite concubine of a Korean military commander, helped him behead the Japanese military officer, whom she deceived with her charms and then took her own life. Deeming Kyewŏrhyang righteous, the people of P'yŏngyang prepared an image of her and made offerings to her spirit every year. Source and photo credit: National Folk Museum of Korea.

other women, this was more difficult, given the restrictions on the public appearance of women of non-slave status. Nevertheless, female contributions to the cultural sphere—in other words, to symbolic communication—continued even after Confucian rules of gender segregation had attained a firm grip on society. The most important cultural activity of Chosŏn women was the most overlooked until recently: embroidery and other creative needlework, such as the produc-

Gender

tion of *pojagi*, colorful wrapping cloths used for both mundane and ceremonial purposes. Often stitched together from patches, these cloths now draw recognition as an art form, given their "bold color combinations, innovative patterns, and fine needlework" (Horlyck 2017, 236).

Embroidery was also a mode of artistic expression for women, and they trained early in the genre (Sunglim Kim 2016, 208). By combining colors and motifs through embroidery, women could express symbolic meaning in a condensed manner, creating their own tool of communication. An embroidery album produced by an Andong Kim woman, concubine of Kang Hangnyŏn (1585–1647)—on a piece of red silk which her father-in-law Kang Ch'ŏm (1557–1611) had received as gift from the emperor during a mission to Ming dynasty (1368–1644) China in 1605—was treasured for generations by her family and applauded in several literati texts not only for its extraordinary craft but also for its "uniquely elaborated meaning" (Kim Kiwan 2022, 406–10; Yi Ik's (1681–1763) "Preface to the Embroidery Album kept by Recorder Kang's Family" (Sŏ Kang Chubu ka chang such'ŏp) includes the phrasing, "her employment of meaning was uniquely painstaking" (*yongŭi tokko*), but Kim Kiwan seems to understand *yongŭi* as referring only to Lady Kim's sense of purpose and therefore argues that Yi Ik ignored the "contents" of the embroidery— even though literary criticism before the turn of the twentieth century often used *yongŭi* to indicate auctorial intent). Regardless, as apparent from the example, women used embroidery to decorate clothing and to create stand-alone works of art, such as hanging scrolls or windscreens. In stitching poems or calligraphy on textiles, women could, in certain ways, participate in the literary pursuits of men. Yet, embroidery's symbolic and formal language—rather regulated and statuary—provided limited space for creativity.

Some educated women also found the means and leisure to paint. About 17 female artists are known from historical records (Horlyck 2017, 233). Even fewer in number are those to whom extant works can be positively attributed. This is true even with the most famous female artist before the twentieth century, Lady P'yŏngsan Sin (studio name Saimdang; 1504–51), celebrated mother of the eminent philosopher-statesman Yi I (pen name Yulgok; 1536–84). Surviving paintings ascribed to her, none of which can be proven authentic, mainly depict grass, flowers, birds, and insects—yet the earliest records about her speak of landscapes and grapes as her main subjects (Jungmann 2018, 51). Sin Saimdang is an example of a female painter of such renown that legends overgrew the facts of her life. Chosŏn's polite society did not universally accept women's engagement in the genre, perceived as an encroachment on the male domain (Horlyck 2017, 42). Further, the more self-expressive and the more easily detachable from house and family an art form, the more subject to doubt was female participation in it.

While painting was tolerated, women practicing the literary arts, to which both these criteria applied best, were under particular suspicion. The historical archive abounds with injunctions against women wielding the brush, or at least against their products leaving the family precincts. However, as literacy and literary pursuits were all-pervasive in *yangban* society, women could not always be prevented from using these means of self-expression. Thus, beyond shaping the growing market for book sales and lending in late Chosŏn by their taste as readers, women used a wide range of writing genres. The dissemination of the Korean alphabet, Han'gŭl (Hangul), facilitated the trend, especially from the sixteenth century. The medium made household lists and letter-writing in the vernacular commonplace among elite families, thus opening a venue for legitimate female literacy (Cho 2020, 20–25). Some women did even more. In beautifully flowing vernacular prose, Lady Nam (studio name Ŭiyudang; 1727–1823) recorded outings she undertook with her husband's special permission when she had accompanied him to his post far away in the northeast, Hamhŭng. More widespread among *yangban* women, especially in Kyŏngsang Province, was the

The Routledge Handbook of Early Modern Korea

composition of long poetry (*kasa*), some narrative, others exhortative. The latter often addressed daughters about to leave for their in-law families.

In contrast, not even *yangban* families taught Literary Sinitic to women, but their brothers and cousins' home education offered opportunities for quick-witted girls to pick up at least a modicum. In some exceptional cases, girls received classical training by indulging family members. Such was the case with Sin Saimdang, who is well-known for her superior learning. Another outstanding example from the sixteenth century is Hŏ Ch'ohŭi (pen name Nansŏrhŏn; 1563–89), who wrote excellent *hansi* (poetry in Literary Sinitic), with topics ranging from political concerns to grief about the early death of her children to her aspirations for transcendence of the constricted life as woman, often expressed in Daoist terms. Thanks to her brother Hŏ Kyun (1569–1618), who carried her collection along on an embassy mission, her poetry became known in Ming China, where a print edition came out in 1606. Chosŏn literati viewed the modest fame she gained in China with discomfort, as they felt the public circulation of a woman's poetry violated their claim to chastity. Therefore, women who became publicly known for their *hansi* poetry tended to either come from families that took great pride in their literary achievements, as was the case with Hŏ Nansŏrhŏn or with Lady Andong Kim (studio name Hoyŏnjae; 1681–1722) (Lee Hai-soon 2005, 45), or did not have to defend *yangban* status even while enjoying high privileges—such as the small group of nineteenth-century women who formed Three-Lake Pavillion Poetry Society (Samhojŏng sisa): all of them were either former *kisaeng* or illegitimate daughters of *yangban* (aristocratic) men who were now married as concubines to high officials. One poetry club member, Lady Kim (studio name Kŭmwŏn; b. 1817), also wrote a lengthy prose account about travels of her earlier life, some presumably conducted alone and in men's clothing.

Some women engaged in more scholarly writing as well. Such works include recipe books, which often centered on wine and dining necessary for conducting ceremonies and entertaining guests and sometimes—as in the case of the *Encyclopedia of Women's Daily Life* (*Kyuhap ch'ongsŏ*; 1809) authored by Lady Chŏnju Yi (studio name Pinghŏgak; 1759–1824)—developed into veritable encyclopedias. Others, in rare cases, feature philosophical writings in the Neo-Confucian tradition, as seen in the collected "extant writings" (*yugo*) of Lady P'ungch'ŏn Im (studio name Yunjidang; 1721–93) (Yi Hyesun 2007, 83–145) Dissemination of these kinds of writing was rare; instead, they were handed down as cherished heritage within each author's family.

The situation was different with works of vernacular narrative fiction that circulated anonymously. Women may have authored some, especially the genre of kinship novels that tell the story of a family over generations. However, arguably the most noteworthy extant work of prose by a female is non-fictional, offering an astounding psychological realism akin to the modern novel: *The Memoirs of Lady Hyegyŏng* (*Hanjungnok*). Lady Hyegyŏng-gung Hong (1735–1816) wrote this memoir about her court life as the wife of the troubled Prince Sado (1735–62), whom his father ultimately ordered to die. The memoir can be regarded as the most outstanding example of vernacular literature from premodern times (Haboush 2013). Likely, many works by female writers remain unknown due to the dominant ideology restricting their circulation. Nonetheless, in direct and indirect ways, women were an active force in cultural production for centuries in Chosŏn.

Sexuality, Homosexuality, Transgender

Neo-Confucianism did not regard the sexual drive as intrinsically problematic but, instead, as a natural part of the mysterious working of yin and yang. Yet, like all personal desires, sexuality had to be reined in and regulated to prevent interference with social obligations and propriety. As in all

Gender

patriarchal societies, social practices—if not the theory—conceded more legitimacy to the sexual desire of men than of women. Nonetheless, elders supervised and restricted even male sexuality. In some *yangban* households, parents regulated when the young married couple could spend the night together. During the two-year (nominally three) mourning period for a parent, men were to remain abstinent; a child born to them was considered disgraceful. Otherwise, chastity was not a male virtue. Since procreation was the obligation of any filial son, a celibate life was not deemed meritorious.

Although the Chosŏn state did not outlaw homosexuality, the notion that it was socially acceptable and that modern prejudices resulted from Western or Christian influences is not warranted either. Rather, male homosexual activity was looked down upon, whereas female homosexuality was outright condemned. Understanding homosexuality not as part of the personality but as an improper overflow of sexual desire fuelled aversion, but it was not regarded as "unnatural" in itself.

Records of female homosexuality are scarce, and the apparent absence of any special term makes discovering sources difficult. The term *taesik* ("face-to-face meal"), commonly used in its literal meaning, also served as a euphemism for (and is even lexicalized today as) a "couple-like relationship between palace ladies." Conspicuous examples found in the records stem from the fifteenth century. Among them are references to the second wife of Sejong's son and crown prince, King Munjong (r. 1450–52), Lady Haŭm Pong (fl. 1429–36), who is said to have admitted to her lesbian leanings, and a prince's wife, who, as part of an intrigue, was accused of the attempt to seduce younger court ladies. Both cases illustrate that, while not subject to judiciary action, the state regarded homosexual activity by the court ladies as utterly depraved or, as Sejong labeled them, "extremely dirty." Such an attitude towards female homosexuality seems to have changed little during the remainder of Chosŏn's history (Kang Munjong 2015, 17–23).

In contrast, attitudes towards male homosexuality seem more lenient, reflecting the greater acceptance of male sexual desire, and more subject to change. Extant sources suggest that, especially in early Chosŏn, male homosexuality was quite acceptable. Such references are typically found in miscellanies, including an anecdote in *Yongjae's Collection of Stories* (*Yongjae ch'onghwa*; first printed 1525) by Sŏng Hyŏn (pen name Yongjae; 1439–1504). According to the account, an amorous official who "loved to frolic with friends" would drunkenly go after a "beautiful boy" serving his host (*Yongjae ch'onghwa* 9). The amusement this tale was meant to arouse is over the official's inability to control his desire, not so much at his homoerotic target. Likewise, according to a high official Pak Tongnyang's (1569–1639) memoirs on the Imjin War, his friend and a successful military official, Yi Taenyŏn (b. 1564), fell deeply in love with young Chŏng Ch'ungsin (1576–1636) due to the latter's courage, beauty, and eloquence and kept him so close that "people spoke of Chŏng as his concubine" ("Imjin chapsa ha," *Kijae sach'o*). This text gives no impression of wishing to scandalize the relationship or speaking ill of either individual. Whatever implied message the observation carries would rather be a statement on Yi Taenyŏn's virility.

Towards the end of Chosŏn, references to homosexuality became almost exclusively derogatory in tone (Young-Gwan Kim and Hahn 2006, 61). In the latter part of the nineteenth century, Yi Kyugyŏng (1788–1856), in his "Exposition on the [Sexual] Preference for Men" (Namch'ong pyŏnjŭng sŏl) (Oju yŏnmun changjŏn san'go, Insa p'yŏn il [1]), traced records of male homosexuality throughout Chinese history before turning to early modern Japan:

The Japanese customs are similar. From the king and the nobility down to rich merchants and prominent families, all spend much on keeping male companions with them night and

The Routledge Handbook of Early Modern Korea

day. There are even instances of murder out of jealousy. Dutch dwellings in Nagasaki also keep male prostitutes, in the same way as the Japanese custom. What kind of beautiful custom is this that it is so widespread all over the world? In Korea, only the hoodlums of the gutters and the ugly-behaved monks do such things with each other.

In another entry of his encyclopedic work, Yi Kyugyŏng relates that cases of intersexuality "are heard about from time to time," more than he can record. The two cases he does record include the famous "affair" of Sabangji (fl. 1463). As a female and going about as a sewist, Sabangji was found to possess a penis and have had intercourse with multiple women. In the contemporaneous case of a "young boy" attached to the house of Kim Igyo (1764–1832), the former "was equipped with both male and female organs" and "used both," according to "Exposition of Two Bodies, Yin and Yang" (Ŭmyang ich'e pyŏnjŭngsŏl) by Yi (*Oju yŏnmun changjŏn san'go*, Insa p'yŏn il [1]). In the quoted sources, the attitude towards these phenomena ranges from "this throws the human way into disorder" to "such is the variability of the working of nature." In general, however, the tone of the anecdotes conveys curiosity or fascination rather than abhorrence or rejection. Instead, articulations of cultural anxiety concerned the involuntary celibacy of court ladies and their male complement, the palace eunuchs, whose services were indispensable but whose situation, as discussed in the case of the court ladies, was deemed going against nature and thus as a potential source of disaster.

Literary Configurations of Gender and Gender Relations

Discussing gendered social roles and gender relations in early modern Korea would be incomplete without considering their treatment in literature. Non-fictional and fictional narratives yield some insights, albeit with some limitations. Relevant non-fictional accounts, mostly commemorative literature, tend to over-emphasize gender-related societal expectations of propriety, whereas fictional texts may bear little resemblance to social realities. All the same, authors of non-fictional writings could not wholly disregard real-life emotions and experiences. On the same token, fictional works may mirror, engender, or reinforce emotions in ways that can, in turn, impact real life and at least afford insights into what may have been deemed desirable, even if divorced from reality.

Perfect Femininity

Commemorative texts such as funeral orations or biographies written about mothers, sisters, wives, or daughters afford a view of how writers conceived perfect womanhood. Of course, such eulogies mainly dwell on such expected virtues as decorum, selflessness, filial piety (especially lauded when directed towards the parents-in-law), a quiet, soft-spoken demeanor, and patience; women naturally received praises for fulfilling the gender norms and ungrudgingly fitting into their social roles. At least at times, however, such compliance was valued as a sign, not of submissiveness but of good judgment and subordinate to the cardinal virtues such as filial piety and family loyalty. Thus, O Wŏn (1700–40), a civil official from a prominent *yangban* family, relates how his wife used to serve her parents-in-law with a lively, humorous attitude instead of dignified silence. When he reprimanded her, she convinced him that her demeanors helped lighten the elders' mood (Im 2003, 304).

By their prescribed role of supporting their husbands, wives regularly received praise for the good advice and even moral guidance they provided to the latter and their sons. To begin with, since women usually married slightly younger husbands, and since marriages occurred when both were in their teens, the couples' relationships tended to start with a gap in maturity in favor of the wives. The undisputed role that female wisdom played for the family's prosperity and status contrasted to some degree with the norm that "being without talent is a virtue in women." This conflict found resolution in the eulogies boasting their female family members' knowledge, education, and intelligence while claiming that their learning sought to acquire moral knowledge—albeit due to the respectable women's virtuous reclusiveness, their talents remained hidden from the world. A prominent Neo-Confucian scholar, Kwŏn Sangha (1641–1721), articulated such a view when praising his nephew's wife ("Chongjabu Yuin Yi-ssi myojimyŏng," *Hansujae sŏnsaeng munjip* 30; Kim Miran 2016, 58–59):

> She told her husband: "As I have grown up in secluded chambers, I have not been able to accrue any knowledge, but now, as I have married into a family of great significance, how can I [without such knowledge] serve our elders?" Thereupon, she read the *Elementary Learning* and the *Instructions for the Inner Chambers* and excerpted [from other books] chaste and filial words and deeds to use them as examples. However, she did not deign to look at poetry or vernacular literature. She did not want to brag about knowing how to read, so she did not let others know.

The female quest for knowledge being established as a potential virtue enabled Chosŏn literati to tell the world about their womenfolk's intellectual pursuits and achievements. Time and again, women received praise for their love for reading, their great intelligence, and their powers of memory from early childhood. Also ample are records of girls impressing others with their mathematical abilities, poetic talents, and even their unusual comprehension of Chinese phonology (Kim Miran 2016, 57–65). Often, such records compare women's intellectual qualities positively to men's. This leads to the wish, uttered especially by fathers such as Kang Paengnyŏn (1603–81), a prominent scholar-official of moral probity, that the girl with all her qualities and talents would have been born a male ("Mangnyŏ Nam-nang Ikhun ch'ŏ chemun," *Sŏlbong yugo* 24): "I often told you it was a pity you were born into this body. Had you been a man, you would have uplifted our family affairs. To be born a woman was already your bad luck. Moreover, it was your ill fate to be born into our poor family." Another father, Sim Saju (1691–1757), who was especially diligent when serving as a magistrate, describes his sharp-witted daughter as a soul companion ("Che mangnyŏ O-ssi pu mun," *Hansongjae chip* 3):

> Your words and deeds were always as reasonable as this. I once sighed: "If you had been born a man, I would have no worries." Your mother, who was at my side, smiled and said: "If all the wise women would turn into men, then men would have to do without wise wives." You and I both laughed. I was often ill and suffered from age early on, so I had little interaction with friends. Instead, I often discussed with you the qualities of men of the past and present to hear your opinions. … This seemed enough for me to enjoy my life for my remaining years.

Beyond normative theory, literary texts show that the qualities of an ideal woman that Chosŏn men propagated through their commemorative texts included intellectual and cultural brilliance, sharp judgment, resolution, and strength of purpose (Kim Miran 2016, 118–27).

Love Relationships

Except for humorous anecdotes, non-fictional prose records rarely touch upon romantic feelings or physical companionship, for which fictional literature is the best available source, albeit idealized.

The Routledge Handbook of Early Modern Korea

Unlike non-fictional genres, fictional narratives may depend on intertextual influences and must be interpreted carefully. Yet, even motifs that have immigrated from beyond the country's borders, if reproduced by authors and welcomed by readers, will have something to tell about the latter's desires and fantasies. Especially revealing are the most highly acclaimed love-related fiction of Chosŏn times: Kim Sisŭp's (1435–93) five classical tales constituting *New Stories of the Golden Turtle* (*Kŭmo sinhwa*); Kim Manjung's (1637–92) novel, *A Nine-Cloud Dream* (*Kuunmong*); and the anonymous multi-version *Tale of Ch'unhyang* (*Ch'unhyang chŏn*; eighteenth century). Despite the differences in plot, language of creation, genre, circulation, and target audience, these works share three conspicuous commonalities in depicting love relationships.

First, fictional literary texts depict marriages as love relationships brought about by mutual attraction, although fate tends to play a role behind the scenes. A furtive glance at a face behind a window or a half-hidden figure, or a sound of music or a poem, can kindle the passion upon which protagonists become a couple. Although the result of a momentary impression, these unions are binding for life, with male and female lovers remaining faithful to each other. In the *New Stories of the Golden Turtle*, the male protagonists forego a mundane life for their short-lived supernatural encounters. Ch'unhyang, in the eponymous story, stubbornly keeps her vows of fidelity in the face of brutal force before her lover marries her against all social odds. The allegorically motivated plot of *A Nine-Cloud Dream* allows the male protagonist, Yang Soyu, to gain two wives and six concubines. Nevertheless, he shows applaudable fidelity, defending his prior betrothal against the emperor's demands that he take his daughter as his wife—the conflict ultimately resolved by the emperor's special permission for Yang Soyu to have two wives. Even if his love is toward more than one woman, all relationships are stable, lasting for a whole life and beyond.

Second, these literary love relationships pair men and women who may be of different social status backgrounds yet are personally on eye level, both in beauty and talent. The female protagonists are invariably on par with their male counterparts in poetic skills, classical knowledge, intellectual resources, and moral maturity. Yang Soyu's lovers not only help him along his way, partly through their heroic deeds, but they also frequently outwit him. In addition to serving the reader's amusement, these scenes intensify the impression of not hierarchical but rather complementary relationships between the male and female protagonists. The idealized relationships in fictional narratives thus mirror the appraisal of female talent in commemorative texts.

Third, unlike non-fictional texts, fiction—including anecdotal literature and some vernacular poetry—acknowledges female sexual desire to varying extents. This theme is especially pronounced in the seventeenth-century *Tale of Unyŏng* (*Unyŏng chŏn*), a story about a palace lady who falls in love with another man and follows her desire. Although this unavoidably leads to a tragic ending, the sympathy of the narrative voice is clearly with the sexually deprived, desirous woman.

Final Thoughts

Literary texts ranging from personal memoirs to narrative fiction to poetry deconstructed and, at times, overwrote the normative gender order in Chosŏn. They provide insights into this order's grey zones, if not inner contradictions. Precisely due to their unsettling indeterminacy, the grey zones forcefully attracted literary attention in Chosŏn. A glaring example is the fascination exuded by the *kisaeng*, who not only provided a focus for erotic fantasies but also—at least as importantly—by default crossed over from the female sphere into the male sphere through their non-domestic lives. Highlighting this ambiguity of both representing femininity in terms of physical attraction and sharing male activities were the sword-dance *kisaeng*, dressed in military costumes, who

Gender

performed in Ŭiju at the Sino–Korean border at least from the early eighteenth century onwards (Park 2015, 143–45). Cross-dressing—both of females as males and the other way round—is also a frequent motif in fictional narratives. Its entertainment value can partly be ascribed to a fascination with gender fluidity, which can be witnessed "in the commensurate distribution of beauty, education, and refinement among male and female protagonists of the lineage novel" (Chizhova 2021, 131). In different ways, the rather common case of male literati speaking in a female voice to express their "love" for the monarch employed fluidity.

The literary representations of gender express not only a certain longing for life opportunities beyond the rigid patriarchal gender norms. They also reflect the conceptualization of hierarchy between the sexes as naturally given to such a degree that the notion did not need much legitimation in ascribing natural abilities—or the lack thereof—to either sex. This may have been one of the reasons Korean women, once liberated from the force of such a naturalized hierarchy, have become less captives of a traditional ideology of natural divergence in talent than many counterparts elsewhere, including the contemporary West. In this sense, the rigidity of Chosŏn's gender order arguably lies at the roots of its own demise.

References

CCHKW. See Committee for the Compilation of the History of Korean Women.

Chizhova, Ksenia. 2021. *Kinship Novels of Early Modern Korea: Between Genealogical Time and the Domestic Everyday*. Columbia University Press.

Cho, Hwisang. 2020. *The Power of the Brush: Epistolary Practices in Chosŏn Korea*. University of Washington Press.

Committee for the Compilation of the History of Korean Women. 1976. *Women of Korea: A History from Ancient Times to 1945*. Edited and translated by Yung-Chung Kim. Ewha Womans University Press.

Deuchler, Martina. 1992. *The Confucian Transformation of Korea: A Study of Society and Ideology*. Council on East Asian Studies, Harvard University.

Deuchler, Martina. 2003. "Propagating Female Virtues in Chosŏn Korea." In *Women and Confucian Cultures in Premodern China, Korea, and Japan*, edited by Dorothy Ko, JaHyun Kim Haboush, and Joan Piggott, 142–69. University of California Press.

Deuchler, Martina. 2015. *Under the Ancestors' Eyes: Kinship, Status, and Locality in Premodern Korea*. Harvard University Asia Center.

Haboush, JaHyun Kim. 2002. "Gender and the Politics of Language in Chosŏn Korea." In *Rethinking Confucianism: Past and Present in China, Japan, Korea, and Vietnam*, edited by Benjamin A. Elman, John B. Duncan, and Herman Ooms, 220–57. UCLA Asian Pacific Monograph Series.

Haboush, JaHyun Kim. 2003. "Versions and Subversions: Patriarchy and Polygamy in Korean Narratives." In *Women and Confucian Cultures in Premodern China, Korea, and Japan*, edited by Dorothy Ko, JaHyun Kim Haboush, and Joan Piggott, 279–304. University of California Press.

Haboush, JaHyun Kim. 2013. *The Memoirs of Lady Hyegyŏng: The Autobiographical Writings of a Crown Princess of Eighteenth-Century Korea*. University of California Press.

Hansongjae chip. Collected works of Sim Saju. Available at: https://db.itkc.or.kr.

Hong Sunmin. 2004. "Chosŏn sidae kungnyŏ ŭi wisang." *Yŏksa pip'yŏng* 58: 241–67.

Horlyck, Charlotte. 2017. "Questioning Women's Place in the Canon of Korean Art History." In *Gender, Continuity, and the Shaping of Modernity in the Arts of East Asia, 16th–20th Centuries*, edited by Kristen L. Chiem and Lara C. W. Blanchard, 224–50. Brill.

Im Yugyŏng. 2003. "O Wŏn: Noron pŏryŏlch'ŭng ŭi yŏsŏng insik." In *Uri Hanmunhaksa ŭi yŏsŏng insik*, edited by Yi Hyesun, 302–23. Chimmundang.

Injŏng. By Ch'oe Han'gi. Available at: https://db.itkc.or.kr/.

Jungmann, Burglind. 2018. "Changing Notions of 'Feminine Spaces' in Chosŏn-Dynasty Korea: The Forged Image of Sin Saimdang (1504–1511)." *Archives of Asian Art* 68, no. 1: 47–66.

Kang Munjong. 2015. "Chŏnt'ong sidae tongsŏngae yŏn'gu." *Yŏngju ŏmun* 30: 5–37.

Kijae sach'o. Draft history by Pak Tongnyang. In *Taedong yasŭng*, volume 13, 30–92. Available at: https://db.itkc.or.kr.

Kim, Hye-Kyung. 2016. "The Dream of Sagehood: A Re-Examination of Queen Sohae's Naehoon." In *The Bloomsbury Research Handbook of Chinese Philosophy and Gender*, edited by Ann A. Pang-White, 89–108. Bloomsbury Academic.

Kim Hyŏnsuk. 2018. *Chosŏn ŭi yŏsŏng: kagyebu rŭl ssŭda*. Kyŏngin munhwasa.

Kim, Jisoo M. 2015. *The Emotions of Justice: Gender, Status, and Legal Performance in Chosŏn Korea*. University of Washington Press.

Kim Kiwan. 2022. "Yŏsŏng ŭi hwamok, chasu: chasu chebal ro pon Chosŏn sidae yŏsŏng munje." *Uri ŏmun yŏn'gu* 74: 399–434.

Kim Kyŏngmi. 2012. "Chosŏn hugi yŏsŏng ŭi nodong kwa kyŏngje hwaltong: 18–19 segi yangban yŏsŏng ŭl chungsim ŭro." *Han'guk yŏsŏnghak* 28, no. 4: 85–117.

Kim Kyŏngnam. 2021. "Chosŏn sidae yŏja kyohunsŏ (yŏhunsŏ) ŭi yuhyŏng kwa ŭimi." *Munhwa wa yunghap* 43, no. 3: 753–74.

Kim Miran. 2016. *Chosŏn sidae yangban'ga yŏsŏng ŭi chŏn'gimun yŏn'gu*. P'yŏngminsa.

Kim, Sunglim. 2016. "Defining a Woman: The Painting of Sin Saimdang." In *Women, Gender and Art in Asia, c. 1500–1900*, edited by Melia Belli Bose, 201–28. Routledge.

Kim, Young-Gwan, and Sook-Ja Hahn. 2006. "Homosexuality in Ancient and Modern Korea." *Culture, Health & Sexuality* 8, no. 1: 59–65.

Kim, Youngmin, and Michael J. Pettid, eds. 2011. *Women and Confucianism in Chosŏn Korea: New Perspectives*. State University of New York Press.

Koh, Eunkang. 2008. "Gender Issues and Confucian Scriptures: Is Confucianism Incompatible with Gender Equality in South Korea?" *Bulletin of the School of Oriental and African Studies* 71, no. 2: 345–62.

Lee Bae-yong. 2008. *Women in Korean History*. Translated by Lee Kyong-hee. Ewha Womans University Press.

Lee Hai-soon. 2005. *The Poetic World of Classic Korean Women Writers*. Ewha Womans University Press.

Oju yŏnmun changjŏn san'go. Miscellanea by Yi Kyugyŏng. Available at: https://db.itkc.or.kr.

Pak Chu. 2008. *Chosŏn sidae ŭi yŏsŏng kwa Yugyo munhwa*. Kukhak charyowŏn.

Park, Hyun Suk. 2015. "The Government Courtesan: Status, Gender, and Performance in Late Chosŏn Korea." Ph.D. dissertation, University of Chicago.

Pettid, Michael J. 2010. "Working Women in Chosŏn Korea: An Exploration of Women's Economic Activities in a Patriarchal Society." *Journal of Global Initiatives: Policy, Pedagogy, Perspectives* 5, no. 2: 24–44.

Pŏnam chip. Collected works of Ch'ae Chegong. Available at: https://db.itkc.or.kr.

Sŏlbong yugo. Collected works of Kang Paengnyŏn. Available at: https://db.itkc.or.kr.

Sukchong sillok. In *Chosŏn wangjo sillok*. Available at: https://sillok.history.go.kr/main/main.do.

Yi Hyesun. 2007. *Chosŏnjo hugi yŏsŏng chisŏngsa*. Ihwa yŏja taehakkyo ch'ulp'anbu.

Yi Misuk. 2012. "Chosŏn sidae ŭinyŏ ŭi yŏkhal." *Han'guk sasang kwa munhwa* 61: 169–203.

Yongjae ch'onghwa. Miscellanea by Sŏng Hyŏn. In *Taedong yasŭng*, volume 1. Available at: https://db.itkc.or.kr.

PART IV

Philosophy and Religion

12

CONFUCIANISM

Isabelle Sancho

Probably introduced to Korea a millennium before the founding of the Chosŏn state (1392–1897), Confucianism designates the teaching of "Confucius" (c. 551–c. 479 BCE), the Latinized form of *Kong fuzi* ("Master Kong"). Confucius was neither a god nor a prophet. Nor was he the founder of a religion in the sense of a social institution organized around a clergy and a theology or a worship centered on one spiritual leader. His followers would rather claim to be part of his "school" (Ch. *jia*; Ko. *ka*), a term encompassing the meanings of family, household, and philosophical school. As such, Confucians constituted one school among many others in early China. It was mainly defined as a scholarly tradition characterized by expertise in texts and rituals, a preponderance of which the Chosŏn state and elites would value in reverence to Confucius. As an impoverished scholar of probable noble ancestry, Confucius was a specialist in the rituals and textual legacy of the early centuries of Zhou dynasty (c. 1046–256 BCE) China. He lived in the Spring and Autumn period (770–481 BCE), when the power and authority of Zhou was eroding. Spending his life trying to secure employment as a political advisor to one of the hegemon rulers and, later in life, teaching, Confucius attracted numerous disciples. Hailing from diverse backgrounds, they would forge the "school of expert-scholars" (Ch. *rujia;* Ko. *yuga*), the Confucian school in Western languages.

The Confucian school expanded over the centuries, represented and disseminated by many prominent figures. Among them, Mencius (372–289 BCE) and Xunzi (c. 310–238+ BCE) were brilliant political advisors and experts in persuasion at a time of intense, raging philosophical debates. As the Chinese model of empire emerged at the turn of the second century BCE, Confucius's intellectual legacy underwent institutionalization. The process also produced various Confucian lineages that progressively built on what was perceived as the Confucian tradition while elaborating on different—and sometimes diverging—philosophical approaches and exegetical methods. Sometimes called a "king without a throne" (*suwang*), Confucius became a semi-legendary figure and even an icon embodying the essence of Chinese civilization (*hua, zhonghua*). He has been revered with a form of piety nourishing various ritual and religious practices. Although Confucius was not a religious founder, his teaching did not exclude spirituality or belief in supernatural entities—be they called "spirits," "ghosts," or "Heaven." Historically, Confucianism has involved a religious and spiritual sensitivity for its practitioners and exegetes.

Many writings from preimperial China include testimonies of the words and deeds of Confucius. Still, the *Analects*, a vivid collection of sayings compiled by his disciples in a dialogic

DOI: 10.4324/9781003262053-17

181

form, preserves his core teaching. Two key concepts are fundamental: Humaneness (Humanity or Benevolence; Ch. *ren*; Ko. *in*) and Learning (Ch. *xue*; Ko. *hak*). Humaneness points to the social dimension of the human condition while highlighting the internal attitude of the individual toward their fellow humans. This inner disposition encompasses sympathy and empathy, as well as a moral exigence resembling the Golden Rule shared by many moral traditions: treat others with the same dignity and gravity as oneself. The Confucian moral injunction consists of perfecting the ability to know men and cultivating clear-sightedness by practicing virtue through the performance of rites (Ch. *li*; Ko. *ye*) in an ethical process, Learning.

In Confucianism, learning is the process through which an individual may become genuinely human. Above all, learning entails practicing the rites. The term designates ritual practices, such as ceremonies and sacrifices, and the spirit of ancient rituals that the practice of rituals and ritualized behaviors should recapture and embody. As concrete exercises in moral training, rites appeal to inner reverence, attention, faithfulness, and self-mastery. They emphasize the constrained and morally aestheticized formal expression that every human interaction should assume in daily life. Such an interaction involves a human bond that an individual experiences by living with others in an organized society. These experiences are summarized in the Five Bonds (Ch. *wulun*; Ko. *oryun*), which are metonymical of all possible human interactions: the relations between a prince and a minister, a father and a son, an elder brother and a younger brother, a husband and a wife, and between friends. The aim of practicing rites is to become aware and learn by experience—through various and repeated configurations—how the ritualized outer display of the self corresponds with an inner, innate sense of sincerity and commitment to others that define a shared understanding of humanity. To act ritually means to perform ancient rituals in both form and spirit in daily life.

As documented in a group of texts subsequently known as the Confucian classics, Confucius presented himself as the transmitter of the wise rule coming down from antiquity. These texts, the exact number of which varied throughout history, are commonly grouped as the Five Classics: the *Classic of Poetry* (or *Book of Odes*; *Shijing*), the *Book of Documents* (*Shujing*), the *Book of Rites* (*Liji*), the *Book of Changes* (*Yijing*), and the *Spring and Autumn Annals* (*Chunqiu*). Concise or even curt in style, they provide moral, political, institutional, literary, historical, and cosmological principles and present esthetical and stylistic norms. Regarded as enclosing the ultimate wisdom of human civilization, the canonicity of the Five Classics lies in their being, paradoxically, open texts: only reading with commentary reveals their meaning. With Confucius considered the first editor, compiler, and exegete of the Five Classics, much of the Confucian tradition involved studying and further reflecting on them. The Five Classics and their many conflicting commentaries constituted the core curriculum for government service examinations in later times. They contributed to the theoretical foundations of the institutions of imperial China. Eventually, various polities in Korea and elsewhere emulated and adopted this system as a civilizational model.

For some two millennia, East Asians have conceptualized, renewed, and defended Confucianism for appeals of its political philosophy, holistic nature, and ideological ambition. In essence, Confucianism arguably is a civilizational project scholar-officials defined. This select group generally comprised highly educated male elites who, although formulating policy and exerting sociopolitical influence, seldom sought to seize supreme power. Confucius redefined the "superior person" (Ch. *junzi*; Ko. *kunja*) as noble, not so much in birth as morality. This definition gave rise to political thinking praising moral persuasion over brute force. Sharing a sense of pursuing a higher mission, the Way (Dao; Ko. *to*), scholar-officials retained the position of controlling both the ruler and the ordinary people. The rigorous moral path scholar-officials pursued morally entitled them to decide whether to serve in officialdom or retire to dedicate themselves to Learning. In this sense, Confucianism as an ideology was challenging and liberating—a combination of salient characteristics arguably befitting an early modern society.

Neo-Confucianism: Main Characteristics

Confucianism in China underwent significant changes in its doctrine and usage. Coexisting for over a millennium with Buddhism and Daoism that attained philosophical sophistication and impregnated elite and popular cultures, Confucianism tended towards either standardization or hybridization. During the transition between the Tang dynasty (618–907) and the Song dynasty (960–1279), the evolution of Confucianism generated doubts among some scholars who came to reflect on what Confucianism should be. Defending a supposedly genuine version of Confucianism before Buddhism's introduction to China, they focused on the writings of Confucius and his direct disciples. Going against the currents of the time, they advocated a return to the real sources of Chinese civilization as they saw.

The Confucian tradition reinvented in Song China incorporated many novelties. They include a considerable augmentation and new exegesis of the canonical corpus, a renewed conceptual toolkit to question Buddhist metaphysical speculations, a stronger emphasis on Confucian ritualism, and a new sense of identity for literati, many of whom turned themselves into keepers of orthodoxy. On the philosophical level, the revitalized holistic vision of Confucianism more closely articulated ethical and political reasoning with a complex thinking capable of competing with Buddhist philosophy: the cosmology of the most abstruse Five Classic, the *Book of Changes*, reinterpreted to define the contours of the Confucian doctrine better. Beyond these general features, the new version of Confucianism was multifaceted (Makeham 2010). Various scholars who organized distinct intellectual lineages in local communities were elaborating on the new orientation, notably around Confucian academies. Song scholars dedicated these privileged places of knowledge and sociability to the ritual worship of selected, old and new, Confucian masters, as well as the study and dissemination of their teachings far from the court.

This new intellectual movement bears various names. Depending on the lineage founders, the localities where the masters were active, or the core notions stressed, the movement is known as, among others, the Confucian Way, the Nature and the Principle, the Principle, the Vital Energy. In Western languages, all are subsumed under, for simplicity, "Neo-Confucianism," which tends to reify a discontinuous reality. The scholars who work on Korea generally refer to Neo-Confucianism as "Learning of the Way" (*Tohak*), "Nature and Principle Learning" (*sŏngnihak*), or "Learning of Master Zhu" (*Chujahak*). The last term highlights the synthesizer, Zhu Xi (1130–1200), and the nature of his teaching, which became the orthodoxy in China and Korea. A term used to underline the philosophical aspect of the tradition taken as a whole is New Confucianism (*sinyuhak*), patterned after Neo-Confucianism in English and more traditional terms such as *yuhak* ("Confucian learning"), *yugyo* ("Confucianism"), or *yugyo sasang* ("Confucian ideology"), all formed from the word meaning "Confucian scholar" (*yu*). In its widest sense, Neo-Confucianism designates the versions of Confucianism that became classical after the first millennium in East Asia. In the narrowest sense, the term designates orthodox Confucianism and even the blind adherence to Zhu Xi, as in the Chosŏn Korean context.

Zhu Xi's impressive synthesis of various trends from the Confucian Renaissance became an orthodoxy long after he died. The texts he emphasized—the *Analects* (*Lunyu*), the *Mencius* (*Mengzi*), the *Great Learning* (*Daxue*), and the *Doctrine of the Mean* (*Zhongyong*)—became known as the Four Books, becoming part of the curriculum for the imperial service examination in China under the Mongol Yuan dynasty (1271–1368). The *Analects* is a collection of sayings by

Confucius and his disciples, as well as their discussions, whereas the *Mencius* is a collection of conversations of Mencius with various rulers. Originally a chapter in the *Book of Rites*, the *Great Learning* consists of a short main text attributed to Confucius and nine commentary chapters by Zengzi (505–435 BCE), one of the disciples of Confucius. The *Doctrine of the Mean*, also a chapter in the *Book of Rites*, is attributed to Zisi (c. 481–402 BCE), the grandson of Confucius. Both the *Great Learning* and the *Doctrine of the Mean* were singled out for their content by Neo-Confucian scholars, especially Cheng Yi (1033–1107) and Zhu Xi, who wrote prefaces and compiled commentaries on the Four Books to form the core of his redefinition of Confucianism. Regarded as an introduction to the Five Classics, the Four Books provided strict reading guidelines for revisiting the Confucian canon.

Neo-Confucianism brought the body of Confucian reference materials to unparalleled sophistication and scale in a relatively short time in Confucianism's history. In the fifteenth century, various prominent Neo-Confucian scholars began working on a voluminous compilation of texts, the *Compendium on Nature and Principle* (*Xingli daquan*), which can be seen as the Neo-Confucian analog of the Buddhist Canon, the Tripitaka. Also, the works of Zhu Xi himself, notably the records of his deeds and sayings, as well as many primers to Neo-Confucianism and historical works written by other Neo-Confucian literati, became compulsory. The Neo-Confucian tradition valued and produced collections of works by individual thinkers. For didactic and edification purposes, comprehensive materials related to their life and work celebrated the moral stature and personal character of great masters in terms of biography, poetical skills, theoretical contribution, political stances, and testimonies from others.

The intellectual position great figures in Neo-Confucianism occupy finds its best expression, in theory, turned into a historical truth: the "transmission of the Way" (Ch. *Daotong*; Ko. *Tot'ong*). According to the theory developed by Zhu Xi (Adler 2015), presenting a genealogy of a unique Confucian tradition, both continuous and discontinuous, Confucius understood, took up, and transmitted the Way of the Sage Kings. After Mencius, historical contingencies and the fallacies preached by heterodox schools interrupted the direct transmission. In a leap of more than a millennium, the direct transmission of the Way resumed with a few Neo-Confucian masters, Zhou Dunyi (1017–73), Cheng Yi, and his disciple Zhu Xi, thanks to the spiritual connection in the "mind-heart" of these exceptional men and Mencius. Zhu Xi designed this epic depiction, mirroring genealogies of Buddhist masters, to clear new ground for the integral tradition of earlier imperial Confucianism and to deny legitimacy to any other competing school of thought discussing political and social matters. Zhu Xi also affirmed the dual nature of the transmission process and highlighted the special role of Confucian masters in history. After the reigns of semi-legendary sage rulers (*shengwang*) of antiquity, the Way was left in the care of human beings and was, hence, subjected to potential loss. Although the political Way of the Sage Kings (*wangdao*) could never be reenacted in human history, exceptional figures—from Confucius to his rightful disciples, who were all scholars, not rulers—successfully passed down its spirit. The Neo-Confucian project of civilization meant the transmission of the Way to set an authoritative argument justifying the special role designed for Confucian scholars, whether in China or beyond.

Neo-Confucianism in Korea: The Primacy of Politics

Neo-Confucianism was known in Korea under the rule of the Koryŏ state (918–1392) since Song but did not replace earlier forms of Confucianism until the Mongol Yuan empire came to dominate Koryŏ. Seen by Koryŏ scholar-officials as a political program of reforms that proved successful in Yuan and defeated the powerful Song, the Neo-Confucian civilizational project contributed to the

Confucianism

Koryŏ–Chosŏn dynastic change (Duncan 2000). Didactic and normative, the Neo-Confucianism introduced from Yuan aimed at implementing an ideal kingship based on one of the Four Books, the *Great Learning*, which the Cheng-Zhu school extracted from the *Book of Rites* for its clear agenda binding politics with ethics, often summed up by the catchy formula "self-cultivation and governance of men" or "self-cultivation for the governance of men" (Ch. *xiuji zhiren*; Ko. *sugi ch'iin*).

In early Chosŏn, the *Great Learning* was not taught per Zhu Xi's interpretation but in the version designed in Yuan emphasizing the ruler's moral training. Chosŏn's interpretation of this "learning for the sovereign" (Ch. *dixue*; Ko. *chehak*) highlighted the balance of power between the king and the bureaucracy due to the Korean context. Chosŏn kings were expected to dedicate themselves to self-cultivation under the supervision of high officials from aristocratic (*yangban*) backgrounds who would scrutinize their actions; the bureaucracy filled itself with talented men recruited on merit through a reformed government service examination system and, at times, by recommendation, to ensure impartiality and loyalty to the king. Whereas the philosophy of the *Great Learning* boosted the compilation of administrative compendia in China under the Ming dynasty (1368–1644) and the Qing dynasty (1616–1912; self-renamed from Later Jin, 1636), it inspired a more intellectual and moral approach of the Confucian political project in Chosŏn Korea. For example, despite its erudite nature and difficult philosophical content, the *Essentials of the Sagely Learning* (*Sŏnghak chibyo*; 1575) Yi I (1536–84) inspired by the *Great Learning* wrote for King Sŏnjo (r. 1567–1608) became compulsory in late Chosŏn for royal lectures (or "Classics Mat Lectures," *kyŏngyŏn*), during which the king and a select group of scholarly officials discussed Neo-Confucian statecraft and ethics through the Classics and histories.

Beyond their pedagogical purpose, royal lectures provided occasions for practicing collegial power by discussing state affairs, and accordingly, official historians diligently recorded each lecture. As new ways of understanding history from a political perspective anchored Neo-Confucianism, the Chosŏn state maintained a systematic writing of official history—commissioned by the king but overseen by officials specifically in charge of historiography. Centered on the king's life, the court, and administrative affairs, Chosŏn's official historiography differed from its Chinese model by its extreme rigor—recording, for example, every meeting between the king and his officials. Upon accession, the king commissioned a compilation of official veritable records (*sillok*) for the previous reign, and the government kept copies under lock at four depositories. No one could consult or alter the veritable records, and historians sanctioned any occasional infringement. For example, officials deposed despotic King Yŏnsan Kun (r. 1495–1506), who launched the first among the four "literati purges" (*sahwa*; 1498, 1504, 1519, and 1545) after consulting the veritable records (Wagner 1974, 51–120). Neo-Confucian historiography in Chosŏn sought to record facts for posterity by placing those destined to make history under the judgment of their offspring and instilling them with a strong sense of moral responsibility.

Zealous propagators of Neo-Confucianism such as Chŏng Tojŏn and Kwŏn Kŭn (1352–1409), who advised the first kings of Chosŏn, carried out the grand project of designing a genuine Confucian kingship in Chosŏn (de Bary and Haboush 1985). The founding of the new state entailed a series of events constituting blatant breaches in Confucian loyalty: the emblematic murder of Koryŏ loyalist Chŏng Mongju (1337–92) in 1392, masterminded by his disciple and Yi Sŏnggye's (King T'aejo; r. 1392–98) son Yi Pangwŏn (King T'aejong; r. 1400–18), with Chŏng Mongju's friend Chŏng Tojŏn's possible consent; Yi Sŏnggye's usurpation three months later; and the Chosŏn court's extermination of the royal Wangs of Koryŏ in 1394 (Park 2018, 11–24). These dramatic events gave rise to the rhetorics of a political and moral division that scholar-officials and historians, in particular, subsequently apply to describing Chosŏn Neo-Confucian tradition.

These rhetorics would apportion blame and shame to individuals or groups and blur the lines between politics and philosophy, turning the intellectual history of Korean Confucianism into an excrescence of Chosŏn's political history. In the case of the founding of Chosŏn, Chŏng Tojŏn, the key advisor to Yi Sŏnggye and radical critic of Buddhism (Muller 2021), is generally cast as the man who sowed the initial discord within late Koryŏ Neo-Confucianism. In contrast, Yi Saek (1328–96)—the influential Neo-Confucian leader who taught both Chŏng Tojŏn and Chŏng Mongju and ultimately refused to serve Chosŏn in moral protest—is considered one founding figure of the Korean Neo-Confucian tradition (Figure 12.1, Figure 12.2). Since then, the history of

Figure 12.1 Portrait of Yi Saek, 1654. Hŏ Ŭi (b. 1601) and Kim Myŏngguk (b. 1600) are said to have painted this version, copying the original portrait, no longer extant. Source: Yi Saek shrine in Sapgyo-eup, Yesan-gun, Chungcheongnam-do, Republic of Korea. Photo credit: Korean Heritage Service.

Figure 12.2 Portrait of Chŏng Mongju, 1555. This is a copy of an earlier version no longer extant. Source: Gyeonggi Province Museum, Republic of Korea. Photo credit: Korean Heritage Service.

Chosŏn Confucianism has been commonly described as driven by a constant dynamic of division opposing, roughly, a pragmatic and bureaucratic trend to a moral and intellectualist trend coexisting within the same tradition, fueling the grand narrative of factionalism in Chosŏn history.

Parties in contention during every reign had to test and negotiate over the Confucian political project. The controversial establishment of Chosŏn preceded the equally controversial reigns of strong monarchs such as T'aejong and King Sejo (r. 1455–68), both usurpers whose efforts to bolster royal power resisted parts of the Neo-Confucian program. Several of their successors also opposed the power of the bureaucracy and aristocracy, using different strategies, including the universally proven divide-and-rule policy that materialized through late Chosŏn partisan strife. Including Yŏnsan Kun, some lost their thrones, as seen above. Others sacrificed on the altar of the political game and for the cause of Confucian monarchy. Thus, for example, King Yŏngjo (r.

1724–76) killed his only son, Prince Sado (1735–62), who failed to live up to the father's expectations but also fell victim to deadly factional struggle (Haboush 1988).

A major problem encountered in implementing the demanding ideals of Neo-Confucian political philosophy lay in the level of commitment and knowledge from kings and officials. Processing all intricacies of Neo-Confucianism based on an extensive textual corpus, written in a sophisticated language in Literary Sinitic (Classical Chinese) and elaborated in a different anthropological and cultural context, required time and effort. For pragmatic reasons, the most knowledgeable scholar-officials tried to keep the Confucian Learning process for kings at a minimum by focusing on the "Learning for the Sovereign" and ritual training. Kings Sejong (r. 1418–50) and Chŏngjo (r. 1776–1800 the iconic exceptions to the general rule that Chosŏn kings might have been knowledgeable enough on Confucianism to rule by playing with its rhetorics—without being true experts of texts, rituals, and regulations (Lovins 2020). Similarly, most of the scholar-officials in the bureaucracy had an average knowledge sufficient to pass the civil examination (*munkwa*) after completing the Confucian Academy (Sŏnggyun'gwan), the highest institution of formal education. Still, they were not necessarily men of deep philosophical knowledge. A recurring problem lay in defining the criteria and curriculum to select competent scholars to meet the needs of an extensive bureaucracy since Confucian merit-based recruitment was an ideal difficult to implement. The main question was whether a command of Literary Sinitic, crucial in diplomacy, should prevail over textual and moral expertise in feeding the higher bureaucracy with genuine Confucian "gentlemen."

Yet, the elite's strategy of educating the kings in Neo-Confucianism was not a failure. An illustration is the royal prerogative to patronize Confucian Learning. Kings attended the palace examination (*chŏnsi*), the final stage of both civil examination and military examination (*mukwa*), with the former selecting the best in the overall ability to apply knowledge of the classics in writing a policy essay following established literary conventions. Monarchs commanded Confucian books' writing, printing, and circulation, especially in basic or abridged versions with a Koreanized presentation (*ŏnhae*), for their officials and the common people. Kings acknowledged and supported many private Confucian academies (*sŏwŏn*), which would benefit from their special status as recipients of royal charter. They enabled promising young civil officials to take a fully funded "royally granted reading leave" (*saga toksŏ*) to continue their Confucian studies. Ultimately, the monarch decided which scholars should be enshrined and paid ritual homage at the State Confucian Shrine (Munmyo). Managed by and located at the Confucian Academy, the shrine consecrated the orthodox lineage of Korean Confucianism.

Confucianization of Korea: Turning towards Society

The project of Chosŏn Confucian kingship relied on a delicate balance that altered the previous political and institutional frameworks and the duties assigned to elites by modifying their social function and self-consciousness. With the reforms implemented in Chosŏn, offspring from aristocratic lineages became more curialized and domesticated. In a regime where prominent families had to foster human resources for the bureaucracy, each generation of a noble descent line had to substantiate the elite status or lose it. Many direct male descendants of early Chosŏn aristocrats found themselves impoverished as the ownership of land and slaves (*nobi*) decreased due to the division of inheritance among legitimate sons of an aristocratic father over generations and as the number of positions in officialdom remained essentially fixed despite the overall growing population. The overall downward social mobility accelerated in mid-Chosŏn when an increasing segment of the aristocratic population as members of losing political parties or factions found themselves locked out of officialdom (Park 2007).

Confucianism

For men of aristocratic descent unable to participate in activities that could produce political power, wealth, or new knowledge, securing marriage ties and earning examination degrees remained important social strategies. The vulnerability of an increasing segment of the aristocratic population from mid-Chosŏn explains why elites focused on maintaining their power, even if purely symbolic. Even if they could no longer pursue official careers, as local elites, they could wield power through the county-level local council (*hyanghoe*), which advised the magistrate, and devoted themselves to their studies. Especially as wealthy commoners began taking over local councils in the eighteenth century (Kim Ingeol 2024), local aristocrats turned towards practicing and disseminating Confucian principles as a strategy of sociopolitical and economic empowerment. The shift was both the effect of a changing social environment and the expression of a new ethos the Neo-Confucian ideology dictated.

Arguably, Korea's Confucian transformation, or the Confucianization, was complete in seventeenth-century Chosŏn. The result of this long impregnation, or indoctrination, of society with Confucian principles was an anthropological shift that transformed the family structures, inheritance and adoption systems (Peterson 2010), and gender dynamics (Ko, Haboush, and Piggot 2003). Rather than blind adoption or adherence, Confucianization consisted of the adaptation and acclimatization of Neo-Confucian ideas in the Korean context. Ideas were molded on, and they exacerbated, in turn, preexisting features of the material context of Korean society, such as slavery, a rigid hierarchy of ascriptive status, and subsistence–agrarian economy. Although based on ideology, Confucianization was a historical process involving non-ideological factors (Deuchler 1992, 2015).

Confucianization generally involved the development of edification literature, comparable with a form of Confucian catechism, targeting the general population to moralize popular manners and customs. Confucian scholars devoted efforts to disseminating moral primers from Chinese Neo-Confucianism, such as Zhu Xi's *Elementary Learning* (*Xiaoxue*; 1187) and *Family Rituals* (*Jiali*). They also compiled new propaedeutic works adapted to the Korean context, such as the *Essential Essentials for Dispelling Folly* (*Kyŏngmong yogyŏl*; 1577) by Yi I, which accommodated the *Great Learning*'s program for beginners (Sancho 2011). Another prominent example is the *Illustrated Guide to the Virtues of the Three Bonds* (*Samgang haengsil to*; 1432), which focused on cardinal virtues for just three of the Five Bonds highlighted in Confucian rites for didactic efficiency: loyalty, filial piety, and female chastity (Oh 2013). Adopting an easy-to-understand format, texts like this employed illustrations for dramatic stories from Korea and China. The recurring use of pictures, diagrams, and synoptic presentations is remarkable in Chosŏn didactic literature. The overwhelming concern for popular education directed toward ordinary people, including women and children, reflects a major characteristic of Chosŏn's appraisal of Neo-Confucianism: a commitment to correct interpretation and application of texts. Mostly, local aristocrats as Confucians and experts in Confucian texts led the educational movement. In their attempts to Confucianize society by following the standards set in China, they showed great concern for a sound understanding and sensible transposition of these rules in Korean culture and society shaped by Buddhist and shamanist worldviews and rituals. As a result of these efforts, some elite women were educated enough to study not only fine arts and literature but also Confucian scriptures (Youngmin Kim and Michael J. Pettid 2011; Ivanhoe and Wang 2023), while some non-*yangban* men and illegitimate sons (*sŏŏl*) could become respected literati in an otherwise discriminatory and status-driven society.

The tendency toward orthodoxy and orthopraxy manifests Chosŏn scholars' keen interest in ritualism and the philosophy of rites in Neo-Confucianism, which had been developing upon cosmological and political premises. The overall intolerant attitude of Chosŏn Neo-Confucian scholar-officials towards Buddhism and Buddhist institutions is related to this overwhelming concern to follow Confucian rites for the sake of the state and society (Evon 2023). Neo-Confucianism conceives Confucian rites as challenging performative self-cultivation exercises, enabling the experimentation and exaltation of humaneness. This Confucian virtue is not so much some mild good intention as a powerful transformative force (Ch. *de;* Ko. *tŏk*), which enables humanity to play a prominent role in the world and, ultimately, transform it (the idea of "civilization," Ch. *wen;* Ko. *mun*). As such, ethical training or "Learning" precisely seeks the correct and vital "transformation" (Ch. *hua;* Ko. *hwa*) of the self by following the laws of the natural universe. It emphasizes the rigorous training of a special organ, the "mind-heart," which is the seat of the emotional and intellectual abilities both subjected to the laws of nature in its substantial, physical dimension and can arouse and drive morality—in the sense of a moral "powerhouse." Being moral in Neo-Confucianism means obeying the laws of nature characterized by constancy through changes and uncertainty (philosophy of the Changes). The ability to remain constantly focused and in full command of one's faculties—regardless of changing circumstances and emotional responses to these changes—is moral and genuinely humane. Confucian rites seek rectitude, balance, and focus, understood as the optimal functioning of human psycho-physical capabilities. Confucian ethical self-cultivation (Ch. *xiuji;* Ko. *sugi*) amounts to the "refinement" and perfection of the raw potential that exists within the very nature of human beings (Ch. *xing;* Ko. *sŏng*), which is consubstantially connected to the natural order. Neo-Confucian ethics are grounded on vitalist, cosmological reasoning, which stands in many ways in sharp contrast with Buddhist metaphysics.

For the most part, Neo-Confucians formulated these intricate speculations on rites, moral self-cultivation, and cosmology in response to the sophisticated Buddhist thinking on several philosophical topics: nature (Buddha-Nature, *sŏng, Pulsŏng*), mind, life, the self, "emptiness" or "voidness" (*hŏ, kong*), "impermanence" (*musang*), and "extinction" (or nirvana, *chimyŏl, yŏlban*). From the outset, Neo-Confucianism defined itself as "plain learning" or "fruit-bearing learning" (*sirhak*) in pointing out its difference from Buddhism, criticized for preaching, literally, "empty learning" (*hŏhak*) since the highest Mahāyāna concept is "true voidness" or "ultimate reality" (*chingong*). Neo-Confucians criticized the latter for propagating "empty" (*hŏ*), fruitless knowledge that was intellectually irrelevant and morally faulty. Since Koryŏ Buddhist tradition was strong when Neo-Confucianism was introduced, the multiple theoretical interfaces between Buddhist and Neo-Confucian philosophies, as well as their commonalities and divergences in vocabulary and themes, helped the acculturation and maturation of Neo-Confucianism in Korea. One such difference lay in the Neo-Confucian ritualist thinking, which, for Chosŏn, consistently connected popular moral education with the institutional, social, and political agenda. Once the Chosŏn state and elites began to satisfy their urge to use Neo-Confucianism as a political ideology and once they had processed the full range of its philosophical reasoning, elaborating further on the rich textual material to contribute to Confucian culture and philosophy awaited.

The Grand Narrative of Korean Confucianism

The Korean contribution to the history of Confucianism is difficult to assess, as the overwhelming historiographical narrative binds Confucianism with "partisan strife" (*tangjaeng*). The overemphasis given to political history and partisan conflicts in the reading of late Chosŏn history (Palais 1996) is correlated with a parallel emphasis intellectual history devotes to the ideological origins of political factions and parties: the division of Korean Neo-Confucianism into competing philosophical schools. More lasting, institutionalized political parties of early modern Korea originated in late sixteenth-century factionalism. Confucian schools grew into political factions that wasted human, economic, and ideological resources by leading elites to ignore the people's struggles and underestimate the country's fundamental challenges. Confucian ideology and its supposed historical avatar, factionalism, caused historical stagnation in Korea while the rest of the world was heading toward modernity, so the narrative goes.

The decades preceding the Imjin War (East Asian War; 1592–98) are regarded as the golden age of Korean Neo-Confucianism, producing two prominent scholars: Yi Hwang (pen name T'oegye; 1501–70) and Yi I (pen name Yulgok; 1536–84). The mainstream discourse in South Korea today celebrates the two towering figures as founders of the Yŏngnam School in Kyŏngsang Province and the Kiho School in the capital and vicinity, respectively: each named after the geographical region where the founding figure fostered disciples and spurred the Confucianization process. According to this scheme of understanding, the history of Korean Confucianism is easy to narrate in terms of the subdivision of these two schools in an endless generative process. From the late sixteenth century, political groups would have formed by superimposition upon diverging philosophical standpoints. They would have enabled, at first, a stimulating culture of "public opinion" (*kongnon*) before turning into raging conflicts plaguing Korean history. Philosophical schools would have become mere interest groups and bastions of political conservatism and radical orthodoxy, leaning towards fundamentalism and reactionary attitudes hindering historical progress.

Such a view is not only teleological but bears a problematic bias. The assumption is that all these schools were distinct social institutions, membership was clearly defined, and philosophical foundations were consistent and unchanging from the seventeenth to the nineteenth century. One of the many ideological reasons this view developed is that since Chosŏn times, specific actors of the implementation of the Confucian project wrote the history of Korean Confucianism. After a major historical turn unfolding over several decades, these actors played a prominent role: the victory of the so-called Sarim ("rusticated literati") in the political scene. The initial moral divide that emerged at the founding of Chosŏn—between scholars who remained loyal to Koryŏ over pragmatism and those who played the game of the new state to carry out reforms or advance their interests—was a first step toward the turning point.

The term "Sarim" generically designates secluded literati who refused to serve in bureaucracy in the early decades of Chosŏn, in the wake of Yi Saek and Chŏng Mongju, but also after Sejo's coup to seize the throne. Disciples of Kil Chae (1353–1419), a disciple of Chŏng Mongju, dedicated themselves to studying Neo-Confucian philosophy in rural areas. When they accepted to take part in the Confucian project by entering officialdom after King Sŏngjong (r. 1470–95) appointed the influent master Kim Chongjik (1431–92), the Sarim began to take over a group of powerful, remonstrance organs in the government, the Three Offices (Samsa). The unfolding political drama in the ensuing decades, including the four literati purges, killed and banished Sarim scholars-officials, as well as shaping the sacred history of Sarim, which became the very history of Korean Neo-Confucianism taken as a whole. It is the history of a special moral community that had fallen victim to persecutions perpetrated by immoral kings and officials. Purges were massive and graphic enough—involving murders, forced suicides, and executions by quartering, among others—to leave strong impressions on witnesses and survivors, as well as descendants who maintained the memory of Sarim's martyrdom. Yŏnsan Kun had the corpse of long-dead Kim Chongjik dug up and beheaded in public during the 1498 purge, and his disciple Kim Koengp'il (1454–1504) suffered execution by beheading during the 1504 purge. The 1519 purge was the most decisive, for it targetted Kim Koengp'il's disciple Cho Kwangjo (1482–1520), who attempted in vain to implement new policies with the initial support of King Chungjong (r. 1506–44) before the latter condoned the purge. Decades later, when the Sarim finally won the battle at Sŏnjo's court, they felt entitled from the sacrifices of their great men earlier to justify their political actions—even bloody ones when factionalism began raging.

The general depiction of late Chosŏn "schools" (*hakp'a*) and "factions" (*tangp'a*) speaks of Sarim as an omnipresent category of scholars, historically constructed. The disciples, descendants, and supporters of Sarim were turned into founding figures of many intellectual schools, organized on the anthropological model of Korean lineages, centered around common ancestors to whom pious rituals would be performed in private academies. These followers, who were the actual drivers of Confucianization, made and wrote the history of Chosŏn Confucianism, both at court and in localities.

Beyond this epic narrative, Yi Hwang and Yi I are undeniably pivotal figures for two reasons. First, they initiated the Korean version of the transmission of the Way. In his genealogy of the Way, Yi Hwang considered himself the direct successor of Zhu Xi and discarded all Chinese scholars after Zhu Xi. As for Yi I, who died prematurely at the height of a meteoric career and exceptional fame, posthumously became a role model of the ideal Korean Neo-Confucian scholar-official self-lessly devoting himself to the country. Second, Yi Hwang and Yi I led the spectacular growth of private academies and the dissemination of community compacts (*hyangyak*) in the countryside. Connecting Confucian scholars with the local elite and common people, both institutions were the actual sites of experimentation for the Confucian social project (Glomb, Lee, and Gehlmann 2020).

This holistic experiment of Confucianization throughout Chosŏn engendered theoretical conflicts, fostered political ambitions, and accentuated regional differences. A major problem was loyalty toward ancestors and masters of increasingly localized scholarly lineages. An expression, those who "live behind the same doors" (*kamun*), designated partisans of Confucian "schools." Considered family, membership in a school as such implied a strong emotional engagement. The main issues causing divisions and power struggles among different groups of scholars, at court and in local society, involved the assessment of Confucian personalities for official recognition as carriers of the Korean version of the transmission of the Way. Criteria were not always based on philosophical and moral excellence. After all, the assessment had to consider the power dynamics within each locality and between conflicting personalities. Even Yi I, whose intellectual caliber cannot be denied, was considered a controversial figure, and his commitment to Confucianism was called into question in raging discussions at court and throughout the country in the seventeenth century. Struggles typically focused on the enshrinement of scholars in the State Confucian Shrine, the ancestor worship to be performed in particular private academies, the collective decision to compile, print, and disseminate the literary anthologies (*munjip*) of individual scholars at great human and material expenses, and the writing of joint petitions that could be potentially damaging.

The grand narrative of Korean Confucianism as the history driven by Sarim scholars is linear, coherent, and lively. It is also myopic, excluding most individuals deserving formal recognition as eminent Confucian scholars. The narrative tends to exclude, for example, the practitioners of "bureaucratic learning" (*kwanhak*), despite their undeniable contributions to the management of Chosŏn's Confucian project at all levels of the bureaucracy. The same goes for all individuals and material resources that created favorable conditions for the project.

The World of Scholars: The Intelligible, the Sensible, and the Material

As discussed below, textual exegesis was integral to the Confucian ethos. Some gifted scholars began articulating their interpretations of various forms of Chinese Neo-Confucianism between the fourteenth and the sixteenth centuries, including non-mainstream trends. The greatest masters of the Chosŏn Confucian tradition would forbid their students from reading "heterodox" (*idan*) texts and anything deemed frivolous literature. Nonetheless, such masters still read and studied

Buddhism, Daoism, or the Chinese Confucian school of Wang Yangming (1472–1529), for example, as they indulged in diverse literary compositions, going from lyrical poetry to fiction. As high-profile experts on texts, many were of mind both sharp and open. Their studies generally covered three main areas: policy-making, moral education, and philosophical erudition. The third area would reveal most clearly the individual virtuosity and panache.

The early Chosŏn reflections on philosophical Confucianism led to what is commonly called "debates" or "controversies," such as the Four-Seven and Horak debates (Back and Ivanhoe 2017). The specificities of Korean Neo-Confucianism may be summed up in the philosophical content and circumstances surrounding these debates, which stage—unsurprisingly—the big names of the Korean tradition, Yi Hwang and Yi I (Chung 1995). Triggered by Chosŏn scholars' unfailing interest in the problem of the "mind-heart" and "human nature" in Neo-Confucian theories on self-cultivation triggered, both debates grappled with explaining the psycho-physiological origins of morality and human nature by focusing on several key notions developed in Neo-Confucianism: the *i* (Ch. *li*; patterning principle) and the qi (Ko. *ki*; psychosomatic energy). The Four-Seven Debate, named after the problem posed by the Four Sprouts of Morality (*sadan*) and the Seven Emotions (*ch'ilchŏng*) in Confucianism (Kalton 1994), engaged with textual inconsistencies that puzzled Korean scholars at the close reading of the works of Neo-Confucian masters, especially Zhu Xi. In general, this and other Chosŏn Confucian debates demonstrate the high level of philosophical technicity reached by Chosŏn scholars in their exegetical reading of the Neo-Confucian canon by the sixteenth century—not much more. After all, these debates were not the most important aspect of the legacy of Korean Confucian masters, according to Confucian standards. A comprehensive and detailed reading of all the writings and biographical materials of major Confucian scholars, all compiled with infinite care in their literary anthologies, presents a different picture since eminent scholars were not so much philosophers in a modern sense as masters in a Confucian sense.

Written records and letters exchanged in the course of ongoing discussions among scholars document the philosophical debates. As partial testimonies of a broader philosophical activity, such discussions are not so much historical "events" than snapshots of intellectual sociability carefully selected and staged. Confucian literati were expected to engage individually with Confucian Learning and hermeneutical labor. All the same, this moral and intellectual undertaking had to be done in a collective setting, which was often public, either at court or in private circles. Confucian studies in both theory and practice required the stimulation and emulation teachers, friends, and disciples provided. Emulation materialized in real-life interactions and epistolary exchanges, all meticulously recorded by participants, witnesses, disciples, and descendants (Cho 2020). The letters were not only copied and circulated but edited for inclusion, along with other types of writing, in literary anthologies (*munjip*). These compilations tended to give equal weight to intellectual productions and biographic materials, as biography was deemed a privileged means for evaluating the moral stature of individual masters. In a Confucian world, this moral evaluation was just as important as, if not more than, any intellectual or scholarly assessment.

Besides the established tradition mostly concerned with assessing orthodoxy and orthopraxy, Chosŏn's adaptation of Neo-Confucianism produced brilliant minds. As exemplified by Kim Sisŭp (1435–93), Sŏ Kyŏngdŏk (1489–1546), and Cho Sik (1501–72), many were free-spirited (Sancho 2022; Glomb and Lowensteinova 2023). All were self-retired or eremitic (*sallim*), whereas some of their later counterparts were forcibly retired as victims of partisan struggle in court. Chŏng Yagyong (1762–1836) was an extreme case: he had to spend 18 years in exile, a house arrest far from his home. Still, as his and his brother's cases illustrate, banishment or exile provided opportunities to deepen studies (Baker 2023) and gain a better insight into society and the natural world. Whether to serve in the government or retire remained an overarching concern for Chosŏn scholars who took Confucianism seriously. The discrepancies between what they studied in Confucian texts—whether by genuine interest or under social pressure—and what they had to experiment with in real life were often difficult to manage. For many, music, literature, calligraphy and painting, travel, drinking, collecting books, and cultivating friendship as acceptable forms of diversion provided escape and solace. Less acceptable forms, certainly not well recorded in literary anthologies or official sources, fueled popular literature with colorful anecdotes and stories. Confucian literati were recurring characters in folk tales and songs, often blending satirical intention with humor and tenderness.

The common thread of Chosŏn Confucian scholars is a strong eagerness to acquire knowledge to act on the world, as summarized in the paradigm of the *Great Learning*. Many late Chosŏn scholars, such as Yi Ik (1681–1763), Pak Chiwŏn (1737–1805), Pak Chega (1750–1805), and Chŏng Yagyong, pursued encyclopedic learning while keeping commenting on Classics and Neo-Confucian reference texts like their predecessors and successors (Figure 12.3). In modern times, Korean scholars have grouped these polymaths too neatly under Sirhak ("Practical Learning"). This classification aimed to prove that Chosŏn Korea produced enlightened minds comparable to Europe's Age of Enlightenment philosophers who challenged orthodoxy and prepared for the advent of modernity well before the Japanese colonization of Korea. However, the celebrated late scholars never constituted a clearly defined philosophical school or a distinct social force.

Figure 12.3 Portrait of Pak Chiwŏn, early nineteenth century. This work by his grandson, Pak Chusu (1816–35), was likely based on an earlier version no longer extant. Source and photo credit: Silhak Museum, Joan-myeon, Namyangju-si, Gyeonggi-do, Republic of Korea.

Rather, they mainly illustrate new aspirations coming from a handful of personalities who, thanks to their social status, interpersonal network, or intellectual predispositions, happened to encounter innovative forms of scholarship coming from Qing China: the so-called Evidential Learning (Ch. *kaozhengxue*; Ko. *kojŭnghak*) and Western Learning (Ch. *xixue*; Ko. *sŏhak*), Catholicism included. Still, these scholars received training in the same principles of Neo-Confucianism as their predecessors and contemporaries, who did not show the same intellectual curiosity. They also saw and reflected upon innovative thinking through Confucian lenses since they had enjoyed the fruits of the Korean maturation of Neo-Confucian philosophy. This process unfolded over almost four centuries, from the late fourteenth to the nineteenth century, producing various stimulating thoughts (Keum 1998).

This rich Korean Confucian tradition, continuously sustained with dedication and conviction for centuries, had been a steady source of inspiration. It enabled a few late Chosŏn historical figures, like Chŏng Yagyong (Choi 2010) but also Ch'oe Namsŏn (1890–1957), as well as a cohort of less known and celebrated scholars from the nineteenth century to envision new ways of adapting their Confucian worldview and scholarly expertise to modern times, when sound reforms were needed (Noh 2016). It also paved the way for the writing of a different history of Korean Confucianism in the early twentieth century, when the plurisecular monarchy came to an end, the Confucian state and institutions collapsed, and the Korean transmission of the Way ceased.

Final Thoughts

Chosŏn Korean scholars were faithful readers of the Confucian moral literature. The best of them tried to live up to their ideals. The Chosŏn state and elites took up their eagerness to learn as exemplars and celebrated the continuous reenactment of the Neo-Confucian project for the society as a whole. This moral spirit was the pride of Chosŏn's *sŏnbi*, a native word designating the Korean version of the ideal Confucian master (Kang 2006). The extent of the Confucian impregnation of Chosŏn society over time and space may be debated. Still, without a doubt, Neo-Confucianism remained the Alpha and the Omega for the learned elite. This small segment of the population would come to embody Korean Confucianism, which they understood as an intellectual and spiritual tradition rather than purely a philosophical tradition.

The Confucianization of Chosŏn Korea was not only a social and anthropological shift in history but also produced a spiritual mutation. Confucian scholars-officials incorporated most parts of Neo-Confucian philosophy's moral and political theories for pragmatic and practical purposes, especially efficient statecraft and social order. They probably retained traces of Buddhist sensitivity that blended into their understanding of the Neo-Confucian ethos. The Confucian legacy in Chosŏn is tangible in many material features characterizing its culture: landscape, architecture, furniture, clothing, cooking, medicine, handicraft, fine arts, music, performing arts, painting, calligraphy, and texts, among others. The legacy is also deeply intangible, arguably a moral tradition testifying to one salient aspect of early modern Korea's sensible and emotional world.

References

Adler, Joseph A. 2015. *Reconstructing the Confucian Dao: Zhu Xi's Appropriation of Zhou Dunyi*. State University of New York Press.

Back, Youngsun, and Philip Ivanhoe, eds. 2017. *Traditional Korean Philosophy: Problems and Debates*. Rowman and Littlefield.

Baker, Don. 2023. *A Korean Confucian's Advice on How to Be Moral: Tasan Chŏng Yagyong's Reading of the Zhongyong*. University of Hawai'i Press.

The Routledge Handbook of Early Modern Korea

de Bary, Wm. Theodore, and JaHyun Kim Haboush, eds. 1985. *The Rise of Neo-Confucianism in Korea*. Columbia University Press.

Cho, Hwisang. 2020. *The Power of the Brush: Epistolary Practices in Chosŏn Korea*. University of Washington Press.

Choi, Byonghyon. 2010. *Admonitions on Governing the People: Manual for All Administrators*. University of California Press.

Chung, Edward Y. J. 1995. *The Korean Neo-Confucianism of Yi T'oegye and Yi Yulgok.* State University of New York Press.

Deuchler, Martina. 1992. *The Confucian Transformation of Korea: A Study of Society and Ideology*. Council on East Asian Studies, Harvard University.

Deuchler, Martina. 2015. *Under the Ancestors' Eyes: Kinship, Status, and Locality in Premodern Korea*. Harvard University Asia Center.

Duncan, John B. 2000. *The Origins of the Chosŏn Dynasty*. University of Washington Press.

Evon, Gregory. 2023. *Salvaging Buddhism to Save Confucianism in Chosŏn Korea (1392–1910)*. Cambria Press.

Glomb, Vladimir, Eun-Jeung Lee, and Martin Gehlmann, eds. 2020. *Confucian Academies in East Asia*. Brill.

Glomb, Vladimir, and Miriam Lowensteinova, eds. 2023. *The Lives and Legacy of Kim Sisŭp (1435–1493): Dissent and Creativity in Chosŏn Korea*. Brill.

Haboush, JaHyun Kim. 1988. *The Confucian Kingship in Korea: Yŏngjo and the Politics of Sagacity*. Columbia University Press.

Ivanhoe, Philip J., and Hwa Yeong Wang. 2023. *Korean Women Philosophers and the Ideal of a Female Sage: Essential Writings of Im Yungjidang and Gang Jeongildang*. Oxford University Press.

Kalton, Michael C. 1994. *The Four-Seven Debate: An Annotated Translation of the Most Famous Controversy in Korean Neo-Confucian Thought*. State University of New York Press.

Kang Jae-eun. 2006. *The Land of Scholars: Two Thousand Years of Korean Confucianism*. Translated by Suzanne Lee. Homa and Sekey Books.

Keum Jang-tae. 1998. *Confucianism and Korean Thoughts*. Jimoondang Publishing Company.

Kim Ingeol. 2024. *Politics of Public Opinion: Local Councils and People's Assemblies in Korea, 1567–1894*. Translated by Eugene Y. Park. Brill.

Kim, Youngmin, and Michael J. Pettid, eds. 2011. *Women and Confucianism in Chosŏn Korea: New Perspectives*. State University of New York Press.

Ko, Dorothy, JaHyun Kim Haboush, and Joan R. Piggot 2003. *Women and Confucian Cultures*. University of California Press.

Lovins, Christopher. 2020. *King Chŏngjo: An Enlightened Despot in Early Modern Korea*. State University of New York Press.

Makeham, John, ed. 2010. *Dao Companion to Neo-Confucian Philosophy*. Springer.

Muller, A. Charles. 2021. *Korea's Great Buddhist–Confucian Debate: The Treatises of Chŏng Tojŏn (Sambong) and Hamhŏ Tŭkt'ong (Kihwa)*. University of Hawai'i Press.

Noh Kwan Bum. 2016. "Academic Trends within Nineteenth-Century Korean Neo-Confucianism." *Seoul Journal of Korean Studies* 29, no. 1 (June): 159–91.

Oh, Young Kyun. 2013. *Engraving Virtue: The Printing History of a Premodern Korean Moral Primer*. Brill.

Palais, James B. 1996. *Confucian Statecraft and Korean Institutions: Yu Hyŏngwŏn and the Late Chosŏn Dynasty*. University of Washington Press.

Park, Eugene Y. 2007. *Between Dreams and Reality: The Military Examination in Late Chosŏn Korea, 1600–1894*. Harvard University Asia Center.

Park, Eugene Y. 2018. *A Genealogy of Dissent: The Progeny of Fallen Royals in Chosŏn Korea*. Stanford University Press.

Peterson, Mark A. 2010. *Korean Adoption and Inheritance. Case Studies in the Creation of a Classic Confucian Society*. East Asia Program, Cornell University.

Sancho, Isabelle. 2011. *Principes essentiels pour éduquer les jeunes gens*. Les Belles Lettres.

Sancho, Isabelle. 2022. *The Master from Mountains and Fields: Prose Writings of Hwadam, Sŏ Kyŏngdŏk*. University of Hawai'i Press.

Wagner, Edward Willett. 1974. *The Literati Purges: Political Conflict in Early Yi Korea*. East Asian Research Center, Harvard University.

13

BUDDHISM

Juhn Y. Ahn

Buddhism has influenced all aspects of life in the Korean Peninsula for some 1,500 years. Like the dynasties that ruled China proper, Korean polities saw much utility in Buddhism. They aspired to follow the Chinese precedent of an agricultural economy that relied on the theoretically predictable taxation of grains, textiles, and corvée—rather than, for example, the progressive taxation of commerce—to cover the government's operational expenses. Naturally, Chinese rulers paid much attention to technologies that could strengthen and protect this economy. For these reasons, Buddhism found a receptive audience in Korea. It introduced new technologies for mitigating the effects of bad weather and reading and controlling the terrestrial force, energy believed to shape the fate of all living in the environment that produced this energy. The power to control weather and the terrestrial force was vital for good harvests and a geopolitical advantage over Korea's neighbors on the continent and the Japanese Archipelago.

In Korea under the rule of the State of Koryŏ (918–1392), if not much earlier, Buddhism became indispensable to the inhabitants of the Korean Peninsula. Rulers liked the Buddhist theory of the universal (Buddhist) monarch—the wheel-turning king (*cakravartin*)—and the religion's access to magic for warding off evil spirits and invaders. Aristocrats found Buddhist theories of causality and rebirth appealing. No less attractive were the opulence, grandiosity, and, hence, tastefulness of its gift-giving practices. For elites, donating wealth to build memorial monasteries where they could expect the best end-of-life hospice care and funerary services became de rigueur. Benefactors gave large endowments of lands and slaves (*nobi*) to private memorial monasteries to perform daily, monthly, and annual rites for the dead and guard the dead's graves in perpetuity. For local society, Buddhism provided such vital services as cremation, burial, and credit-based banking. Monasteries offered seed and grain loans to cultivators and generated income from the interest charged. As local schools, Buddhist monasteries produced valuable commodities such as paper, books, and even tofu. Koryŏ's successor, the State of Chosŏn (1392–1897), parted ways with Buddhism for reasons discussed in this chapter. Patronage became a private affair, and a monastery became less a space for glorification, charisma-building, and miracles than rituals.

Buddhism and the Royal Cult

Less than a month after the founding of Chosŏn, the Privy Council (Todang) urged King T'aejo (Yi Sŏnggye; r. 1392–98) to abolish the Lantern Festival (Yŏndŭnghoe) and the Eight Prohibitions

DOI: 10.4324/9781003262053-18

The Routledge Handbook of Early Modern Korea

Festival (P'algwanhoe). The request is remarkable because the council had to tackle a long list of seemingly more urgent matters. Chosŏn desperately needed, among other things, land reform (despite the Rank Land Law of 1391), an updated administrative structure, a new legal code, and more stable diplomatic relations with Ming dynasty (1368–1644) China. According to scholarly consensus, the emergence of Neo-Confucianism as the new ruling ideology spurred Chosŏn's high officials to prioritize abolishing two festivals. Both were Buddhist, that is, heretical festivals, which had to be banned. Despite the Buddhist link, the reasons for prohibiting them, as shown below, had less to do with religious oppression, as commonly assumed, than with the political jockeying for power that continued to shape the rocky relation between the throne and officialdom.

The Lantern Festival illustrates this point well. The people of Koryŏ regularly lit lanterns twice early in the year. Although similar, the two occasions were far from identical. One was more "public," that is, concerned with the affairs of the state and the throne. Naturally, the government's involvement was heavy at all levels. As for the other, individuals celebrated on a smaller scale on the eighth day of the fourth month. Celebrants lit lanterns to commemorate the Buddha's birthday. In the late fourteenth century, this custom became so popular in Koryŏ's capital, Kaegyŏng (present-day Kaesŏng), that the rich and poor competed to light lanterns (Yi Chongsu 2012, 122). The custom remained popular in Chosŏn despite attempts by the Office of the Censor General (Saganwŏn) to ban it.

The Privy Council's real target in 1392 was the other, more public Lantern Festival. Koryŏ celebrated this festival annually with state support in Kaegyŏng and Sŏgyŏng ("Western Capital"; present-day Pyongyang) on the first full moon of the first month, a special day known as the Upper Primordial (Sangwŏn). Lighting lanterns on this day was in keeping with the Chinese custom of using lanterns and lamps to celebrate the regeneration of life at the beginning of a new year and welcome a new agricultural cycle. In Korea, the Upper Primordial Lantern Festival was also a key event in the ritual calendar of the royal cult (Breuker 2010, 187). For the festival, Koryŏ's king, in full regalia, donned a ceremonial robe of imperial colors (variations of yellow and purple), led an impressive parade of officials to the royal memorial monastery Pongŭn-sa, and offered sacrifices in front of the funerary portrait of Koryŏ's founder, King T'aejo (Wang Kŏn; r. 918–43). At the palace, the monarch received flower offerings, salutations, and prayers from the crown prince and officials for his long life. The festival thus effectively bound the fate of the Koryŏ state, couched in the agricultural terms of bountiful harvests and regeneration of life, to the power of the royal house. This connection between the First Primordial Lantern Festival and the royal cult motivated the Privy Council to act.

Under the same pretense, the Privy Council called to abolish the Eight Prohibitions Festival, celebrated on the full moon of the eleventh month in Kaegyŏng and Sŏgyŏng. Like the Lantern Festival, the Eight Prohibitions Festival publicly displayed the king's cosmic authority as the head of Korea's pantheon of gods and spirits and, thus, protector of the realm. In this capacity, the monarch or his proxy made offerings to Heaven and the Buddha and bestowed new titles upon local mountains, rivers, and dragons. The festival also recognized exceptional loyalty to the throne, honoring ancient Korea's Silla (57 BCE, trad.–935 CE) leaders who defeated Paekche (18 BCE, trad.–660 CE) and Koguryŏ (37 BCE, trad.–668 CE) and Koryŏ merit subjects (kongsin) who assisted in establishing the state. In these and other ways, the Eight Prohibitions Festival ultimately bolstered the authority of the throne, a prerogative the Privy Council did not want the new royal family of Chosŏn to have. After several years, the councilors got what they wanted when King T'aejong (1400–18) ended state support for the festivals. This was a small victory for those who wished to weaken the royal cult.

Buddhism

Reform of the Public Monastery System

Reform-minded officials faced a more significant challenge. Memorial monasteries that housed royal funerary portraits like the Pongŭn-sa mentioned above and the "aid-and-remedy" (*pibo*) monasteries—deemed particularly effective in controlling local spirits, harnessing geomantic powers, or warding off invaders—were critical to the royal cult's smooth functioning. The royal cult retained its authority as long as these public monasteries, receiving state support and thus subject to state control, were allowed to thrive. Naturally, the officials quickly targeted these monasteries.

The process leading to the radical restructuring of state support for public monasteries began a few years before the Koryŏ–Chosŏn regime change. After Yi Sŏnggye marched his army back from Wihwado and gained power through a coup in 1388, the government retrieved all special farmland donated to monasteries if they originally belonged to the royal treasury. Later that year, his key adviser, Cho Chun (1346–1405), proposed that land grants be limited to the aid-and-remedy monasteries supposedly identified by the monk and geomancer Tosŏn (827–98). Had it been adopted, the proposal would have stripped non-aid-and-remedy monasteries of prebends, that is, salaries in grain the state granted. The measure would not have affected the private monasteries and shrines since they retained ownership of land individuals and their families donated. They could also avail themselves of land owned by resident monks.

Contrary to the wishes of the reformists, state support of royal memorial monasteries and aid-and-remedy monasteries did not decrease after the founding of Chosŏn. As king, T'aejo supported, for instance, the restoration of the famed five-story pagoda of Yŏnbok-sa in Kaegyŏng, a project initiated in 1390 by Koryŏ's last king. Officials loyal to T'aejo and scholars at the Confucian Academy (Sŏnggyun'gwan) voiced their objections in vitriolic memorials historians now commonly, but mistakenly, cite as evidence of Chosŏn's adoption of Neo-Confucianism as the official ideology. Notwithstanding such strong (and often customary) opposition, T'aejo chose to see the project's completion. Undoubtedly, as Chosŏn's founder, he sought to demonstrate the vitality of the royal cult and claim its authority and power for himself. Following the example of the Koryŏ kings, he had a copy of the Buddhist canon installed inside the restored pagoda and paid frequent visits to the monastery to offer prayers.

As the Yŏnbok-sa project makes clear, T'aejo was unable and unwilling to deviate from the conventions of past kings. Royal memorial monasteries were sacred spaces where miracles occurred, patrons were glorified as worldly counterparts of the buddhas, and charisma was thus built. Accordingly, in just the third year of his reign, T'aejo transformed his old home into a monastery, hence following the example of Koryŏ's founder. Like Wang Kŏn, T'aejo desired to use the monastery to seek blessings for his ancestors and the kingdom. To the east of his former residence, T'aejo had a new palatial structure built, Tŏganjŏn, which eventually became a monastery, Hŭngdŏk-sa. Another example of T'aejo's reliance on old customs associated with the royal cult is Hŭngch'ŏn-sa, the new memorial monastery he constructed for his wife, the late Queen Sindŏk (1356–96), next to her tomb (Figure 13.1). Investing great care and attention to its construction, he endowed the monastery with a generous land grant of 1,000 standard plots (*kyŏl*; "stacks"). He furnished it with a new reliquary stupa and reliquary hall (Yi Nŭnghwa 1979, 365). Hŭngch'ŏn-sa also received a role befitting its status as the memorial monastery for Chosŏn's first queen consort: the king designated it as the head monastery of the Chogye school of Sŏn Buddhism.

T'aejo's death in 1408 during his son T'aejong's reign presented another opportunity for the throne to invigorate the royal cult. Later that year, T'aejong turned the sacrificial complex next to his father's tomb into a monastery, Kaegyŏng-sa. The gesture was only to be expected since building a memorial monastery for one's parents remained the exemplary expression of filial piety.

Figure 13.1 Hŭngch'ŏn-sa, Donam-dong, Seongbuk-gu, Seoul, Republic of Korea. Photo credit: Korean Heritage Service.

For financial support, T'aejong granted the monastery 150 slaves and 300 hundred standard plots of land. T'aejo's death allowed T'aejong to practice filial piety and political savvy. He used the occasion to honor his birth mother, Queen Sinŭi (1337–91), who had died before the founding of Chosŏn. He granted her memorial monastery Yŏn'gyŏng-sa twenty additional slaves, bringing the total to one hundred, the standard grant for the highest-ranking public monasteries (*T'aejong sillok* 1408/7/29 entry 1). T'aejong justified this donation as a matter that had to be decided hastily, but the circumstances show that the grant was a calculated political move.

T'aejo's favoritism toward his second wife Sindŏk's sons and their murders (1398) during T'aejong's bloody path to the throne threatened the new ruler's legitimacy. Under the circumstances, T'aejong used the royal cult to accord his birth mother Sinŭi privileges commensurate with her status as posthumous queen and king's mother. Not coincidentally, a few months later, the State Council (Ŭijŏngbu), which replaced the Privy Council as the highest-level deliberative body, urged T'aejong to make some noticeable changes to his stepmother Queen Sindŏk's memorial monastery, Hŭngch'ŏn-sa (*T'aejong sillok* 1408/10/21 entry 2). The council argued that the monastery's sectarian affiliation should be changed to the Hwaŏm school. The rationale was deceptively simple: the number of monasteries for each school was set, Kaegyŏng-sa was just named a Chogye school monastery, and another prominent Hwaŏm school monastery, Chich'ŏn-sa, had to be shut down. However, changing Hŭngch'ŏn-sa's sectarian affiliation was not the council's primary objective. The council also wanted the land and cultivators assigned to Chich'ŏn-sa transferred to Hŭngch'ŏn-sa. In exchange, substantially greater land and cultivators Hŭngch'ŏn-sa already owned had to revert to the state. T'aejong, who despised his stepmother, approved the council's recommendation. The council thus rid the state of a grand Buddhist monastery affiliated with the royal cult, and T'aejong bolstered royal legitimacy.

Conventionally portrayed as an anti-Buddhist king, T'aejong maintained a nuanced attitude toward Buddhism. When necessary, he embraced and took advantage of the royal cult. However, he was also willing to trim "excess" resources—land, tax, and labor—off public monasteries and reallocate them to more urgent state-building projects. In 1402, echoing Cho Chun's earlier proposal, the Office of Astronomy and Geomancy (Sŏun'gwan) recommended the confiscation of prebend grants to public monasteries not included on Tosŏn's list of aid-and-remedy monasteries and their reallocation to military expenses (*T'aejong sillok* 1402/4/22 entry 1). The State Council accepted this recommendation but granted exemptions to public monasteries with more than 100 resident monks. The State Council also guaranteed more land and cultivators to monasteries on

Buddhism

Tosŏn's list if they were in financial need. This attempt at monastic reform, however, was short-lived. As the retired king, T'aejo compelled his son T'aejong to reverse the order. T'aejong had to return the confiscated monastic property, safeguard the property of defunct monasteries until its restoration, allow anyone who so desired to receive ordination, not require monks and nuns to have tonsure certificates, and permit women to visit monasteries up to the one hundredth-day anniversary of a parent's death (*T'aejong sillok* 1402/8/2 entry 1).

Three years after this foiled attempt at reform, the State Council sought T'aejong's permission again (*T'aejong sillok* 1405/11/21 entry 2). The council designed a new reform proposal that would limit the number of public monasteries in areas that were significant from a politically administrative standpoint, including the new and old capitals, as well as counties (*kun*, *hyŏn*) of varying administrative standing. The new proposal also limited the number of male slaves that public monasteries could use yearly. Public monasteries could mobilize one slave for every five resident monks. Male slaves not in use were required to perform corvée and transfer their harvests to the state. Female slaves were prohibited from the monastery. To ensure enforcement of this new regulation, a centrally appointed local official was tasked with recording (*chŏk*) all monastic slaves and assigning them land to cultivate near the monastery.

The following year, the State Council submitted an addendum to their reform proposal. The council divided the 12 Buddhist schools in Korea into two broad categories: Sŏn and Kyo (*T'aejong sillok* 1406/3/27 entry 1). The Sŏn schools, generally speaking, are those Buddhist traditions that consider texts produced by enlightened beings and Buddhist saints in China, such as enlightened Chan masters, to have scriptural status. The Kyo schools, in contrast, refer to those traditions that focus on the study of scriptures and texts attributed to the Buddha or Indian Buddhist saints, such as sutras, philosophical treatises, and monastic rules. The council proposed granting one Sŏn and one Kyo monastery in the old capital Kaesŏng (Kaegyŏng as Koryŏ's capital) and the new capital Hansŏng (present-day Seoul) 200 standard plots of land, 100 slaves, and 100 permanent resident monks. Other public monasteries in both Hansŏng and Kaesŏng could have half that amount. Major cities in the countryside could have one public monastery from either Sŏn or Kyo with 100 standard plots of land and 50 slaves (presumably 50 permanent resident monks). Smaller public monasteries in provincial towns known as Chabok-sa each received 20 standard plots of land, 10 slaves, and 10 permanent monks. All the public monasteries on the outskirts of towns were permitted three times that amount.

The State Council's plan intended equal representation of the Sŏn and Kyo schools in the cities, a fixed number of resident monks, and the cultivation of two standard plots of land by a slave for each resident monk at a public monastery. If any of these public monasteries—242 monasteries assigned to twelve schools—lacked land or slaves in their original or present endowments, the council agreed that they should be taken from public monasteries not targeted for further support. These monasteries, however, were not wholly abandoned. T'aejong granted small plots of woodland to those not dilapidated or defunct so they could harvest firewood. He also commanded that land and slaves not be confiscated from Hoeam-sa, P'yohun-sa, and Yujŏm-sa, all monasteries with strong ties to his father T'aejo and the royal cult. Instead, these monasteries each received an additional 100 standard plots of land and 50 slaves.

The court took steps to ensure that public monasteries would maintain high standards. In 1414, T'aejong approved the proposal to implement a monastic examination (*sŭngkwa*) system, according to which only monks of a high caliber could serve as abbots. The government controlled the appointments to the abbacies of public monasteries and the issuance of tonsure certificates through the Central Buddhist Registry (Sŭngnok-sa). To prevent unnecessary competition and lessen the administrative burden, T'aejong reduced the number of recognized Buddhist

The Routledge Handbook of Early Modern Korea

schools from twelve to two, Sŏn and Kyo. However, he rejected the proposal to limit the number of successful candidates. The two schools were to follow their respective customs for testing candidates.

T'aejong's continuing support for the Buddhist establishment and the royal cult in these and other ways was self-serving and manipulative. For instance, he showed no reluctance or hesitation in removing the Palace Chapel (Naewŏndang), which kings since Koryŏ had used. When the state preceptor (*kuksa*), Chogu (d. 1395), died, T'aejo did not appoint a successor, and neither did T'aejong when the royal preceptor (*wangsa*), Muhak (1327–1405), died. He thus broke from an esteemed tradition. Kings had continued to honor state and royal preceptors as their teachers and bow before them for centuries. The same T'aejong restored the monastery Kangnim-sa in Wŏnju, Kangwŏn Province, where he studied in his youth. He claimed the restoration was out of nostalgia, not faith in the Buddha (*T'aejong sillok* 1417/7/5 entry 3). When his estranged wife and devout Buddhist, Queen Wŏn'gyŏng (1365–1420), fell ill in 1413, T'aejong allowed prayers to the Medicine Buddha to be performed in the palace (*T'aejong sillok* 1413/5/6 entry 2). However, when she died seven years later, he allowed no Buddhist protocols.

T'aejong deemed public monasteries the state's obligation worthy of support, but worshiping the Buddha and honoring enlightened monks were a matter of personal choice privately financed. This distinction, though, proved less than clear in the case of his wife Wŏn'gyŏng's death. In keeping with tradition, their son, King Sejong (r. 1418–50), wished to perform his obligation as a filial son by building a graveside memorial monastery for Wŏn'gyŏng and eventually for still-living T'aejong, the retired king, whose adjacent grave was already under construction. T'aejong saw differently. He commanded the State Council to submit their opinions on the matter—stating that if the ministers deemed it righteous to build a memorial monastery, he would cover the expenses with his wealth to not burden the state. Unable to decide whether to side with the king or the retired king, council members voiced conflicting opinions. Chief State Councilor (Yŏngŭijŏng) Yu Chŏnghyŏn (1355–1426) was alone in urging T'aejong not to build a memorial monastery, and the retired king followed Yu's advice, denying him and his wife this privilege (*Sejong sillok* 1420/7/11 entry 5).

T'aejong explored his novel approach to Buddhism at a critical moment when the government's actions were fraught with a risk of financial ruin for the state. With its resources stretched thin, the court decided to gradually withdraw its support for public monasteries, extensions of the government, the throne, and their public authority. Approving the decision was T'aejong, budget-conscious and supposedly agnostic. This shift had an immediate impact on the public monasteries in the countryside. Not only lacking the social networks necessary to attract patrons, they also failed to attract monks willing to serve as abbots. Monks found little incentive to invest in an abbacy or monastery where they could not control its resources. Patrons felt the same. The state, once again, intervened. In 1424, Sejong approved the Ministry of Rites' (Yejo) plan to reduce further state support of public monasteries (*Sejong sillok* 1424/4/5 entry 2). The ministry claimed this action was necessary because public monasteries were being abandoned and falling into disrepair. Given the situation, the ministry advocated reducing the number of state-recognized Buddhist schools to just 2, Sŏn and Kyo, and limiting the number of state-supported monasteries to 36, 18 for each school. The ministry also proposed to abolish the Central Buddhist Registry, reasoning that the monasteries and abbacies for management were too few to warrant a separate government office. In place of the registry, the ministry designated the monasteries Hŭngch'ŏn-sa and Hŭngdŏk-sa as the central administrative offices for the Sŏn and Kyo schools respectively. Although far from oppressed, clearly, by the mid-fifteenth century, Buddhism was no longer the public religion it once used to be.

Buddhism

Weather and Wealth

The early Chosŏn government had many reasons to reduce its investments in the public monastery system. Chief among them, no doubt, was the cost of moving the capital from Kaegyŏng to Hansŏng. Construction projects naturally grew in number, and labor shortages became common. The imposition of corvée duties was the obvious way to meet labor needs. However, fearing its negative impact on farming, the government avoided imposing duties during sowing and harvest seasons. Also, if feasible, laborers were summoned only from areas that enjoyed bountiful harvests the previous year. Given the limits of this solution to labor needs, looking for better solutions was unavoidable. A common alternative utilized was the employment of undocumented monk laborers.

Following the tradition, the early Chosŏn state repeatedly attempted to certify monks with tonsure certificates. The first attempt, made in 1392, eventually saw codification into law, the Six Codes of Governance (Kyŏngje yukchŏn) in 1397. However, especially those who lived outside the capital, as well as kings, commonly ignored the law. As a retired king, T'aejo asked T'aejong not to require tonsure certificates (*T'aejong sillok* 1402/8/4 entry 1). Nevertheless, the officialdom continued to mount pressure against the throne to enforce the law and return monks without tonsure certificates to lay status. Citing many undocumented monks, Sejong refused to bend to the pressure and declared the task unfeasible (*Sejong sillok* 1432/8/2 entry 1). At the time, tonsure certificates were beyond the reach of most people. To receive a certificate, a candidate had to submit one hundred bolts of rough cloth as payment: an amount only sons and daughters of the families of central officials, mostly aristocrats (*yangban*), could afford.

The state intended the prohibitively high cost of a tonsure certificate to be a deterrent against people joining the monastic community as a way to avoid taxation and military service. Even though using tonsure certificates as a kind of payment for undocumented monastic labor thus contravened the objective of reducing the size of the monastic community, the government nonetheless proceeded. As compensation for their labor services to the restoration of the royal memorial monastery Hŭngch'ŏn-sa, monks were promised tonsure certificates in 1429. That same year, the court also rewarded monks who worked on constructing the residence for Chinese envoys with tonsure certificates (*Sejong sillok* 1429/2/3 entry 6, 1429/3/22 entry 1). Despite opposition from his officials, Sejong tried to ensure that the monk laborers received the certificates. Urging him to reconsider, the officialdom complained of a large number of deceitful young men pretending to be monks—among laborers—exploiting the promise of tonsure certificates to secure exemption from corvée (*Sejong sillok* 1429/4/16 entry 3, 1429/8/28 entry 1, 1429/9/30 entry 3). Sejong, however, remained reluctant to enforce the tonsure certificate requirement for all monks.

Sejong's stance reflects his commitment to the royal cult. The monarch clarified this in 1435 when he declared that he would honor his ancestors' legacy and restore the reliquary hall at Hŭngch'ŏn-sa. Anticipating resistance to his plan, Sejong used his wit and expressed his desire to follow the example of T'aejong's restoration of Kangnim-sa: he declared he would use a royal order to gather monks to help with the restoration. Rather than give monks an excuse to wield that kind of power, Chief State Councilor Hwang Hŭi (1363–1452) proposed instead to utilize undocumented monks again (*Sejong sillok* 1435/5/12 entry 1, 1435/5/21 entry 4). Sejong gladly approved Hwang's alternative. This was a favorable outcome for the king, considering that during the reign, the extreme aridity and wetness that continued to trouble Korea had turned construction projects into a source of contention. After all, imposing corvée duties in hardship—floods, droughts, and famines—was taboo. Following the decision, the court issued thousands of tonsure certificates, which increased the number of monks in Hansŏng. In response, the government tried to ban monks from entering the capital.

203

The Routledge Handbook of Early Modern Korea

Continuing bad weather presented Sejong with both a crisis and a political opportunity. For instance, the court deliberated on restoring Hŭngch'ŏn-sa's reliquary hall when another drought came in the same year. Sejong had to negotiate with the officialdom, and bad weather gave him cultural and political grounds to support Buddhism strongly. Subsequently, he obtained consensus for having monks pray for rain at Hŭngch'ŏn-sa. He later decreed that two inspectors of fourth rank or higher (on the nine-rank bureaucratic hierarchy) must examine Hŭngch'ŏn-sa and Hŭngdŏk-sa—both royal memorial monasteries T'aejo established—every three months to check for leaks and signs of deterioration (*Sejong sillok* 1435/5/27 entry 3, 1437/7/18 entry 3). Sejong declared this a permanent rule. When more drought and famine followed in 1445 and 1446, he again turned to Buddhism and the royal cult. The death of his wife, Queen Sohŏn (1395–1446), served as the perfect excuse. To ensure her reincarnation in a desirable state, he ordered a devotional gesture of copying the Buddhist scriptures in gold—with her and the crown prince's wealth covering the expenses (*Sejong sillok* 1446/3/26 entry 6). As part of the memorial rites for the late queen, he used Han'gŭl (Hangul), the phonetic Korean alphabet he and his officials had devised to write such new Buddhist texts as *Songs of the Moon's Reflection on a Thousand Rivers* (*Wŏrin ch'ŏn'gang chi kok*; 1447). In 1448, despite strong objections from the officialdom, Sejong also ordered the restoration of the Palace Chapel (*Sejong sillok* 1448/7/17 entry 1).

The Buddhist Establishment and Sarim

To the dismay of the officialdom, royal support for the Buddhist establishment continued. In 1457, Sejong's second son, King Sejo (r. 1455–68), who took the throne from his young nephew, issued a set of regulations concerning Buddhism (*Sejo sillok* 1457/3/23 entry 3). All women except nuns were forbidden from visiting monasteries. Also, local functionaries (*hyangni*) were prohibited from going to monasteries to investigate crimes committed by monks without the king's permission. Moreover, monks could only be asked to show their tonsure certificates if they committed a crime. Tonsure certificates had to be issued promptly, though monks with official titles, such as "Sŏn master" (*sŏnsa*), were not required to have tonsure certificates. And monasteries were responsible for tribute submission (*kongnap*) but exempt from corvée. These regulations of 1457 reflect a political compromise. Designed to address issues raised by the officialdom, the regulations did so without stripping the Buddhist establishment of too many privileges.

The throne and officialdom continued to compromise on privileges to the Buddhist establishment. In 1461, Sejo had identification tags issued for monks. Although he approved the issuance of the tags based on tonsure certificates, monks of high moral standing and those above 40 could receive tags without a certificate (*Sejo sillok* 1461/8/12 entry 1, 1463/1/12 entry 1, 1464/5/8 entry 1). Sometimes, no compromises were necessary. Continuing his father Sejong's legacy, Sejo established the Superintendency for the Publication of Buddhist Scriptures (Kan'gyŏng togam), which published Buddhist scriptures in the new phonetic alphabet. Other matters, though, required more compromise. Sejo tried to continue issuing tonsure certificates in exchange for public labor services, but eventually, he followed the Ministry of Rites' recommendation and banned the practice in 1462. When monks who participated in constructing the new royal memorial monastery Wŏn'gak-sa in Hansŏng requested tonsure certificates, the Ministry of Rites declined with Sejo's approval (*Sejo sillok* 1462/4/4 entry 2, 1465/1/21 entry 3).

The fortunes of the Buddhist establishment began waning under Sejo's grandson, King Sŏngjong (r. 1470–95), who ascended the throne under precarious circumstances. Sŏngjong's father, Sejo's son and crown prince, died prematurely, and the prince's younger brother, who succeeded Sejo, reigned just fourteen months, also dying prematurely. As the regent, Sejo's widow and powerful officials such as Sŏngjong's father-in-law Han Myŏnghoe (1415–87) chose him as king at age 13. Capitalizing on the situation, in 1471, the officialdom had the king shut down the Superintendency for the Publication of Buddhist Scriptures (*Sŏngjong sillok* 1471/12/5 entry 5). Two years later, Sŏngjong prohibited aristocratic women from becoming nuns (*Sŏngjong sillok* 1473/8/4 entry 6). This measure eventually shut down 23 nunneries in and near Hansŏng, sparing three (*Sŏngjong sillok* 1475/7/19 entry 4). Notably, the court took these measures as Chosŏn—inspired by ideas from *Family Rituals* (*Jiali*) by Zhu Xi (1130–1200) of Song dynasty (960–1279) China—endeavored to create and implement a system wherein *yangban* women would no longer be entitled to an equal share of her family's estate (Deuchler 1992). The effort targeted nunneries, as they served as a convenient loophole for upper-class women to retain control over their inheritance.

Coming of age, Sŏngjong tried to counter his minders by promoting a new generation of scholar-officials, Sarim ("Ruticated Literati"), who employed Neo-Confuain moral rhetoric. Comprising the likes of Kim Chongjik (1431–92) and his disciples, the Sarim claimed to uphold Confucian principles and opposed those who acquired fame and fortune by helping Sejo's usurpation. Gaining ground in the political arena, the Sarim advocated a state governed and managed by worthy officials and a stricter stance against Buddhism and the royal cult. Complying with their request, Sŏngjong, for instance, had provincial governors more thoroughly investigate the certification of monks (*Sŏngjong sillok* 1477/8/20 entry 6). Emboldened, the Sarim began taking daring steps to weaken the royal cult. They even urged him to abolish the Buddhist rite of wishing the king a long life on his birthday (*ch'uksuje*)—a key event in the royal cult's calendar. Although T'aejong had abolished the rite (*T'aejong sillok* 1414/1/3 entry 1), it had been performed for Sejong, Sejo, and Sŏngjong. Nonetheless, Sŏngjong acquiesced and abolished the rite in 1477. At the urging of the officialdom, he also banned the issuing of tonsure certificates in 1492 before the two queen mothers convinced him to retract the ban (*Sŏngjong sillok* 1477/12/4 entry 2, 1492/2/3 entry 3, 1492/11/22 entry 1).

Although Sŏngjong's reign created a hostile environment against the Buddhist establishment, certain protections remained intact. For instance, the court updated and codified regulations concerning monks, nuns, and monasteries in the Great Code of State Administration (Kyŏngguk taejŏn), promulgated in 1485. The new code stipulated the triennial administration of examinations for would-be Sŏn and Kyo monks. The Sŏn and Kyo schools were each allowed to select thirty new ordinands from the examination passers. Kyo candidates had to demonstrate their knowledge of the *Avataṃsaka* and *Daśabhūmika Sūtra*s and Sŏn candidates their understanding of the *Transmission of the Lamp* (*Chŏndŭng*)—presumably referring to the Song Chinese work *Jingde Era Record of the Transmission of the Lamp* (*Jingde chuandeng lu*; sometime 1004–07)— and *Collection of Commentarial Remarks and Verses of the Sŏn Tradition* (*Sŏnmun yŏmsong chip*) attributed to Sŏn master Chin'gak Hyesim (1178–1234) (*Kyŏngguk taejŏn*, 296).

The reign of Sŏngjong's son and successor, King Yŏnsan Kun (r. 1495–1506), proved far less favorable for the Buddhist establishment. In 1503, again, at the urging of Sarim officials, the king ordered the confiscation of land and slaves from monasteries (*Yŏnsan Kun ilgi* 1503/5/9 entry 4), though exempting royal graveside memorial monasteries (*nŭngch'im*) and public monasteries where rites were performed for the royal family (*naewŏndang*). The Confucian Academy received the confiscated property. In 1505, Yŏnsan Kun also ordered the confiscation of land and slaves from royal memorial monasteries and public monasteries (*Yŏnsan Kun ilgi* 1505/12/15 entry 4). After two suspicious fires consumed Hŭngdŏk-sa and Hŭngch'ŏn-sa around this time, they became Yŏnsan Kun's pleasure quarters and royal stable, respectively (*Yŏnsan Kun ilgi* 1504/12/9 entry 1, 1505/2/21 entry 1, 1505/5/29 entry 5). The following year, in 1506, he had monks become either hunters or private slaves of the royal family, and nuns become slaves at

The Routledge Handbook of Early Modern Korea

the royal conservatory (*Yŏnsan Kun ilgi* 1506/3/23 entry 2). How many monks and nuns this order affected is uncertain.

Yŏnsan Kun was deposed that same year, and his half-brother King Chungjong (r. 1506–44), like their father Sŏngjong, sought to counterbalance the powerful officials who enthroned him by promoting the Sarim. Led by Cho Kwangjo (1482–1520), the Sarim pursued a personnel system reform and stripped the merit subjects—those who had enthroned Chungjong—of their privileges. Also, turning their attention to Buddhism, the Sarim convinced the king to enforce the law and laicize undocumented monks. Accordingly, the government issued tags to monks for providing labor. Not only did enforcement prove difficult, the Sarim, who claimed that powerful officials had illegally seized monastic land, ultimately failed to turn fertile land that belonged to provincial monasteries into state property. Nonetheless, in 1516, the government confiscated slaves from both non-public and public monasteries (*Chungjong sillok* 1509/3/21 entry 9, 1509/9/27 entry 1, 1516/11/9 entry 3, 1536/8/8 entry 1, 1537/1/15 entry 1). Only royal graveside memorial monasteries were spared. In 1516, the Sarim also successfully pressured Chungjong to abolish the Buddhist memorial rites for former kings—arguably the most important event in the royal cult's calendar. Later, in 1538, Chungjong approved shutting down monasteries not among approximately 1,650 listed in the *Newly Augmented Geographical Survey of Korea* (*Sinjŭng Tongguk yŏji sŭngnam*; 1530) (Yi Pyŏnghŭi 1997, 34). The order, however, was as ineffective as the attempt to enforce the certification of monks. Executed initially in just two provinces, the court withdrew the order in 1539 (*Chungjong sillok* 1539/5/27 entry 1, 1539/6/3 entry 3).

The Imjin War, Monastic Revival, and Buddhist Genealogies

By the end of Chungjong's reign, the Buddhist establishment faced many obstacles to serving as the privileged vehicle for the royal cult. An officialdom bent on weakening the throne pushed the Buddhist establishment further into the margins of public authority. Some key developments, however, allowed Buddhism to retain strong ties to the royal cult.

First, Queen Munjŏng (1501–65) gained power in 1545 as a dowager. In the name of her young son, King Myŏngjong (r. 1545–67), Munjŏng threw the full weight of the throne behind the Buddhist establishment. Critical to her efforts to revive the royal cult was the role of the abbot of Pongŭn-sa, Pou (pen name Hŏŭng; 1509–65). In 1550, following Pou's advice, Myŏngjong ordered the restoration of the Sŏn and Kyo schools. He had Pongŭn-sa and Pongsŏn-sa serve as their head monasteries. Also, with the dowager's enthusiastic support, the government revived the clerical examination and tonsure certificate systems at Pou's recommendation. The eminent monk Hyujŏng (pen name Ch'ŏnghŏ; 1520–1604) was a beneficiary of this revival. In 1552, he passed the grand selection examination (*taesŏn*) and received an official appointment as director (*p'ansa*) of both the Sŏn and Kyo schools. However, Munjŏng's death in 1565 cut short Hyujŏng's rise to stardom and Pou's efforts to revive the royal cult.

Another critical historical development was the Imjin War (East Asian War; 1592–98). This multi-state conflict was another opportune moment for Hyujŏng and his student Yujŏng (studio name Samyŏngdang; 1544–1610), who passed the revived clerical examination in 1561. At the request of Myŏngjong's nephew and successor, King Sŏnjo (r. 1567–1608), Hyujŏng and Yujŏng assembled a monk militia—"righteous monks" (*ŭisŭng*)—and fought against the invading Japanese forces. In 1604, after the war, Yujŏng traveled to Japan as an official envoy and returned with a peace agreement and thousands of Korean captives. The court handsomely rewarded Hyujŏng and Yujŏng with honorary titles for their services (Figures 13.2 and 13.3).

The third noteworthy historical development is the monk Sŏnsu (pen name Puhyu; 1543–1615) and his disciples' establishment of close connections with Sŏnjo's son and successor, King Kwanghae Kun (r. 1608–23). Born the son of a concubine, Kwanghae Kun spared no time to establish his royal credentials. He constructed Poŭn-sa (later renamed Pongin-sa) as a royal memorial monastery for his mother and installed Sŏnsu as its abbot. For the crown prince, Kwanghae Kun also turned the monastery Ch'ŏnggye-sa into a royal memorial monastery and invited Sŏnsu's disciple Kaksŏng (pen name Pyŏgam; 1575–1660) to oversee the occasion.

Royal patronage of Hyujŏng, Yujŏng, Sŏnsu, and Kaksŏng made it possible for Chosŏn's Buddhist establishment to enjoy a renaissance. Monasteries were eager to invite these eminent Sŏn masters or their disciples as abbots to attract wealthy and influential patrons, which these monasteries could do with their help (Chŏng Pyŏngsam 2017, 157–60). These developments preceded the publication of new genealogical claims and ritual manuals in the seventeenth century (Kim Jong-Myung 2015; Kim Yongt'ae 2016). Sources produced for Hyujŏng, Sŏnsu, and their disciples were the first to advance such genealogical claims. Contrary to earlier customs which traced a monk's lineage through multiple points of contact (for example, tonsure master, precepts master, and dharma masters), the genealogical claims these sources articulated began to emphasize a single line of transmission that connected dharma master and dharma heir (Ahn 2019, 1–32). Since this was not the established custom in Korea, the dharma transmission lineage had to be invented, and competing claims quickly emerged. One claim traced Hyujŏng to the Koryŏ monk Hyegŭn (pen name Naong; 1320–76). Another traced Hyujŏng to Pou (pen name T'aego; 1301–83). Also

Figure 13.2 Portrait of Hyujŏng, early or mid-eighteenth century, 106 cm × 76 cm. Source and photo credit: National Museum of Korea.

Figure 13.3 Portrait of Yujŏng, between 1610 and 1796, 122.9 cm × 78.8 cm. Source: Donghwa-sa (Tonghwa-sa), Daegu, Republic of Korea. Photo credit: Korean Heritage Service.

adopting the Pou theory was the community of monks who traced their lineages back to Sŏnsu and his disciple Pyŏgam Kaksŏng. Eventually, the theory became orthodox in Korean Sŏn Buddhism, but both claims shared the same goal. Their shared, ultimate aim was to trace Hyujŏng and Sŏnsu's lineages to Tang dynasty (618–907) China's Chan master Linji Yixuan (d. 866) and, through him, the Huineng (638–713), the semi-legendary Sixth Patriarch of Chan Buddhism.

As the number of monasteries in their possession grew, abbots who belonged to the lineages of Hyujŏng and Sŏnsu saw the need for more standardization. As each monastery had unique practices, the abbots began to publish ritual manuals for all the monasteries under their control. Some notable examples include Kaksŏng's *Notes on the Funerary Ritual for Buddhists* (*Sŏngmun sangŭi ch'o*; 1636), his disciple Chinil's (pen name Naam; n.d.) *Notes on the Family Rituals for Buddhists* (*Sŏngmun karye ch'o*; 1660), and Yujŏng's student Myŏngjo's (pen name Hŏbaektang; 1593–1661) *Ritual Manual for Buddhist Monastics* (*Sŭngga yeŭi mun*; 1670). Kaksŏng explicitly states in the preface to his *Notes on the Funerary Ritual for Buddhists* that he compiled the manual because Korean monks, lacking a definitive guideline, performed their funerals in various ways. After consulting various Buddhist works of Song China, Kaksŏng decided that producing a funerary manual for monastics was necessary to reflect Korea's indigenous customs better. Myŏngjo similarly explains that he compiled the *Ritual Manual for Buddhist Monastics* to streamline and standardize the various cremation methods among monasteries.

Buddhism

The Korean customs that Kaksŏng and the other abbots wished to preserve in their manuals were the five mourning grades (*obok*) system, a system borrowed from one of the Confucian Five Classics, the *Book of Rites* (Ch. *Liji*; Ko. *Yegi*) (Kim Yongt'ae 2016). The system determined the length of the mourning period and the material of the mourning clothing garment depending on the mourner's relationship to the deceased: three years of mourning in coarse unhemmed sackcloth for first grade, 12 months in coarse hemmed sackcloth for second grade, 9 months in coarse cloth for third grade, 5 months in fine cloth for fourth grade, and 3 months in fine hemp for fifth-grade relatives. Kaksŏng's *Notes on the Funerary Ritual for Buddhists* presents a chart with five grades for mourning fellow monastics. Chinil's *Notes on the Family Rituals for Buddhists* similarly features a chart with five grades for mourning fellow monastics and lay relatives. Myŏngjo's *Ritual Manual for Buddhist Monastics* includes a chart with four grades for mourning fellow monastics. Notably, all three manuals place the tonsure master in the first grade, though Kaksŏng and his disciple also include the dharma master in the same grade.

The heightened appreciation for dharma lineages and mourning grades reflected a deeper concern about economic rights and duties. The Chŏngmyo War (1627) and the Pyŏngja War (1637) left monastic land in ruins, prompting legal battles over land ownership. The increased private ownership of land among monks necessitated legislation concerning the inheritance of such land. In 1657, a new law limited the land inheritance from monks to collateral relatives. In 1674, however, the government amended the law, allowing monastic disciples to inherit half of the land monks owned; the other half had to go to collateral relatives, first cousins, or closer. The deceased monk's monastery received the land as communal property if neither was available. The seventeenth-century ritual manuals adopted the five mourning grade system to address these concerns about private ownership of property and inheritance (Kim Yongt'ae 2016, 188). Also, earlier in Hyŏnjong's reign, in 1660, the state laicized commoners who became monks or nuns to prevent further shrinkage of the tax-paying population (*Hyŏnjong sillok* 1660/12/19 entry 2). This and other measures against Buddhism during the reign prompted the monk Ch'ŏnŭng (pen name Pakekok; 1617–80) to submit his famous "Memorial Remonstrating against the Repression of Buddhism" (Kan p'ye sŏkkyo so) (*Han'guk Pulgyo ch*ŏns*ŏ 8.335b–343a).

Buddhist Ritualism in Chosŏn

Although the Buddhist establishment did not completely sever its ties with the throne and the royal cult, maintaining these ties became increasingly difficult as the government repeatedly issued bans against monks from entering Hansŏng. Fundraising and recruitment from the royal house and families of powerful officials virtually ceased. The state repealed other privileges that once made becoming a monk desirable. In the eighteenth century, ordination, for instance, could no longer exempt one from military service. The authorities used rotations of righteous monks to defend the fortresses near Hansŏng (*Sukchong sillok* 1705/2/6 entry 1, 1714/9/25 entry 3). The righteous monk system, though, evidently fell apart as monks could purchase "nameless appointment certificates" (*kongmyŏngch'ŏp*) that allowed them to write their names in and exempted them from military service. Therefore, King Yŏngjo (r. 1724–76) abolished the righteous monk system in 1725 (*Sukchong sillok* 1718/i8/3 entry 1; *Yŏngjo sillok* 1725/1/11 entry 3, 1745/5/28 entry 1).

Despite these setbacks, the Buddhist establishment continued to thrive by offering vital services such as the water and land ritual (*suryukchae*) performed for the dead. The water and land ritual was designed to divest the dead of bad karma and help them secure a more desirable rebirth and ultimately attain enlightenment. Continuing the Koryŏ tradition, the Chosŏn court used the ritual to appease vengeful spirits believed to cause natural disasters and illnesses. T'aejo, for instance,

The Routledge Handbook of Early Modern Korea

had these rituals performed with state support every spring and autumn for the members of Koryŏ royal house his court massacred in 1394 (Park 2008, 22–29). Although other Buddhist rituals could serve the same purpose, the generic water and land ritual seems to have appealed to the court, especially since the same ritual could be performed for anyone regardless of status. The ritual thus proved to be an effective way to reduce waste and ostentation. After all, for kings and other royals, the court replaced individualized memorial services, prone to unregulated consumption, with a more standardized and hence "frugal" water and land ritual (*Sejong sillok* 1420/8/22 entry 2, 1420/9/22 entry 2, 1420/10/1 entry 1, 1422/5/17 entry 2).

Nonetheless, the water and land ritual was not free from controversy. In one curious instance, a Confucian student (*yusaeng*) caused an uproar at court by performing the water and land ritual for Hyŏnjong's mother and his father King Hyojong's (r. 1649–59) widow, Queen Insŏn (1645–49), at Hwajang-sa, a monastery near the old Koryŏ capital (*Hyŏnjong sillok* 1674/6/3 entry 2). As the queen's death was charged with political significance at the time, the action triggered the so-called second ritual controversy. Court debated how long Insŏn's still-living stepmother-in-law Queen Changnyŏl (1624–88), the widow of Hyŏnjong's grandfather King Injo (r. 1623–49), should mourn Insŏn. One political party, the Southerners (Namin), argued that Changnyŏl should mourn for one full year, which was the recommended duration of mourning for one's first daughter-in-law according to Zhu Xi's *Family Rituals*. The rival Westerners (Sŏin) insisted that she should mourn for nine months, the recommended length for one's second daughter-in-law. Mourning Insŏn for one full year would have made Hyojong's claim to the throne more legitimate. Even as the court fought bitterly over the issue, at least one Confucian scholar still deemed the water and land ritual appropriate for honoring deceased royals.

Indeed, the performance of unsanctioned memorial rites for the royal family continued into the eighteenth century. Upon accession, King Chŏngjo (r. 1776–1800) received a report about the proliferation of monasteries calling themselves royal memorial monasteries and offering sacrifices for the royal family. In response, Chŏngjo forbade the construction and use of such monasteries (*Chŏngjo sillok* 1776/6/14 entry 3). However, the decision did not stop him from constructing the monastery Yongju-sa in 1790 for his father, Prince Sado (1735–62), who was earlier put to death by the king's predecessor and grandfather Yŏngjo (Chŏng Haedŭk 2009). Chŏngjo had been biding his time until his position was strong enough to pursue the project. Establishing Yongju-sa near Sado's tomb, Chŏngjo also began constructing a fortified city, Hwasŏng, with his new military unit—the Robust Brave Division (Changyongyŏng)—to project royal power.

Yongju-sa was the exception to the rule. Earlier, during the reigns of Hyojong and Hyŏnjong, the court had deprived royal graveside memorial monasteries of their right to perform memorial rites. Their role was limited to guarding the tombs and producing goods for memorial rites, such as paper and tofu. They thus came to be known more simply as "tofu-making monasteries" (*chop'osa*) (T'ak Hyojŏng 2020, 142). The decline in status naturally led to deteriorating conditions, and many struggled financially. Accordingly, in 1793, Chŏngjo ordered a thorough inspection of all tofu-making monasteries. The government offered financial support to those struggling by assigning them "subordinate monasteries" (*soksa*), which were required to assist in defraying the cost of producing tribute items. Although not at the scale of Yongju-sa, royal tombs without a tofu-making monastery received one during this period. After Chŏngjo's death, the royal cult entered a moribund state. An oligarchy of consort families and allies wielded power during the three successive reigns as each king ascended the throne either in the minority or unexpectedly (1800–64). During Chŏngjo's reign, a sacred space where the throne could be valorized and glorified in otherworldly terms became unnecessary.

New developments in the seventeenth century had informed the transformation of the monastic space instead. As the influence of Hyujŏng and Sŏnsu's lineages grew, monastic training began to focus on the so-called three gates or three disciplines: Sŏn, Kyo, and *yŏmbul*, recitation of the name of the Buddha Amitābha. Sŏn emphasized using "public cases" (*kongan*), pithy stories of memorable encounters with enlightened Sŏn masters. Chosŏn monks studied these cases by referring to canonical texts such as Hyesin's *Jingde Era Record of the Transmission of the Lamp* and *Collection of Commentarial Remarks and Verses of the Sŏn Tradition*. Kyo training still used texts such as the *Avataṃsaka Sūtra*. This approach was in keeping with the curriculum likely widespread before the seventeenth century. This older curriculum relied on a set number of texts, Four Collections (Sajip) and Four Teachings (Sagyo), as well as the texts mentioned above. What was unique about curricular development in the seventeenth century was the addition of *yŏmbul* as a separate discipline (Kim Yongt'ae 2010, 234). Monasteries built lecture halls (*kangwŏn*) for Kyo, meditation halls (*sŏnwŏn*) for Sŏn, and *yŏmbul* halls for practicing the recitation of the name of the Buddha Amitābha (Chŏng Pyŏngsam 2017, 167).

The monastery as a space also began to undergo subtle transformations, shifting from glorification to rituals. The altar where the icons stood grew larger, placed closer to the back wall of the Buddha hall. Ritual performance, thus, secured more space. Accordingly, wooden floors inside the Buddha hall also became more common. Creating specialized ritual spaces accommodated cults that grew in popularity, centered around the bodhisattva Avalokiteśvara and Kṣitigarbha. During this period, monasteries commissioned large paintings of buddhas, bodhisattvas, and their assemblies known as "hanging buddhas" (*kwaebul*)—up to 50 feet long and 20 feet wide—to accommodate larger ritual gatherings outdoors. Another form of Buddhist painting more commonly used at the time was the "three bodhisattva painting" (*samjangt'aeng*), depicting the bodhisattva of the sky, the earth, and the underworld, Kṣitigarbha. A water and land ritual performance utilized these paintings (Chŏng Pyŏngsam 2017, 163–68).

Lacking public support, monasteries turned to new forms of fundraising, such as financial cooperatives (*kye*), to fund these paintings and the restoration of monasteries (Han Sanggil 1983). The private resources of monks allowed these cooperatives to grow during and after the seventeenth century. Monks and laity began pooling their wealth as a financial cooperative to purchase land for monasteries or commission large paintings or frescos. This practice was widespread in the eighteenth century throughout Chosŏn.

Final Thoughts

Taking what Chosŏn sources say about Buddhism and Neo-Confucianism at face value, modern scholarship tends to overstate radical changes. Inspired by Neo-Confucianism as a new ideology, Korea supposedly escaped its aristocratic, medieval past defined by a blind and irrational adherence to the dark principles of Buddhism in Koryŏ. This change supposedly resulted in religious oppression and the decline of Buddhism in Chosŏn.

To the contrary, as highlighted in this chapter, the continuities and discontinuities coexisted, often uncomfortably, in Chosŏn. Monarchs understood the value of the royal cult and, hence, Buddhism. They were also well aware of the limits of royal power and authority. Efforts to infuse the royal cult with energy often required political finesse and a willingness to compromise. Naturally, Buddhism and the royal cult changed.

New geopolitical realities of the transition from Ming to the Manchu Qing dynasty (1616–1912; Later Jin until 1636) presented unforeseen challenges to Chosŏn kings. They wished to adhere to the cultic practices that allowed the throne to straddle the worldly and otherworldly, reigning over

The Routledge Handbook of Early Modern Korea

both. By the seventeenth century, Buddhism and the royal/imperial cult were no longer an international imperative or cosmopolitan language shared by the ruling elite, *yangban*. Buddhism had become something that kings and the royal house could enjoy in private. The kingdom's fate was no longer at stake in the rituals monasteries performed. Deceased kings and queens were now individuals for whom filial descendants could make offerings so that they may secure a better rebirth or even enlightenment. Such was a privilege—an "old custom," as Chosŏn kings often referred to—that anyone could enjoy.

Works Cited

Ahn, Juhn Y. 2019. "Have a Korean Lineage and Transmit a Chinese One Too: Lineage Practices in Seon Buddhism." *Journal of Chan Buddhism* 1: 1–32.

Breuker, Remco E. 2010. *Establishing a Pluralist Society in Medieval Korea, 918–1170: History, Ideology, and Identity in the Koryŏ Dynasty*. Brill.

Chŏng Haedŭk. 2009. "Chŏngjo ŭi Yongju-sa ch'anggŏn yŏn'gu." *Sahak yŏn'gu* 93: 147–90.

Chŏng Pyŏngsam. 2017. "Chosŏn hugi sawŏn ŭi munhwajŏk t'ŭksŏng." *Pulgyo hakpo* 78: 154–74.

Chŏngjo sillok. In *Chosŏn wangjo sillok*.

Chosŏn wangjo sillok. Available at: https://sillok.history.go.kr/main/main.do.

Chungjong sillok. In *Chosŏn wangjo sillok*.

Deuchler, Martina. 1992. *The Confucian Transformation of Korea: A Study of Society and Ideology*. Council on East Asian Studies, Harvard University.

Han Sanggil. 1983. *Chosŏn hugi pulgyo wa sach'algye*. Kyŏngin munhwasa.

Han'guk Pulgyo chŏnsŏ. 1994. 13 volumes. Tongguk taehakkyo Han'guk Pulgyo chŏnsŏ p'yŏnch'an wiwŏnhoe.

Hyŏnjong sillok. In *Chosŏn wangjo sillok*.

Kim Jong-Myung. 2015. "Sŏn/Zen Monks and Buddhist Funeral Texts in Seventeenth-Century Korea." *Pulgyo hakpo* 73: 227–57.

Kim Yongt'ae. 2010. *Chosŏn hugi pulgyosa yŏn'gu: Imje pŏpt'ong kwa kyohak chŏnt'ong*. Sin'gu munhwasa.

Kim Yongt'ae. 2016. "Yugyo sahoi ŭi Pulgyo ŭirye: 17-segi Pulgyo sangnyejip ŭi obokche suyong ŭl chungsimŭro." *Han'guk munhwa* 76: 169–96.

Kug'yŏk taedong yasŭng. 1971–75. Volume 1. Minjok munhwa ch'ujinhoe.

Kyŏngguk taejŏn. 1934. Reprint. Chōsen sōtokufu Chūsūin.

Park, Eugene Y. 2008. *A Genealogy of Descent: The Progeny of Fallen Royals in Chosŏn Korea*. Stanford University Press.

Sejo sillok. In *Chosŏn wangjo sillok*.

Sejong sillok. In *Chosŏn wangjo sillok*.

Sukchong sillok. In *Chosŏn wangjo sillok*.

T'aejo sillok. In *Chosŏn wangjo sillok*.

T'aejong sillok. In *Chosŏn wangjo sillok*.

T'ak Hyojŏng. 2020. "Chosŏn hugi chop'o soksa yŏn'gu: P'aju samnŭng ŭi Mihwang-sa sarye rŭl chungsim ŭro." *Namdo munhwa yŏn'gu*: 137–67.

Tongmun sŏn. 1994. Reprint. Minjok munhwasa.

Yi Chongsu. 2012. "Chosŏn sidae yŏndŭnghoe ŭi chonp'ye wa pulgyosajŏk ŭimi." *Pulgyo yŏn'gu* 37: 113–45.

Yi Nŭnghwa. 1979. *Chosŏn Pulgyo t'ongsa*. Reprint. Poryŏn'gak.

Yi Pyŏnghŭi. 1997. "Chosŏn sigi sach'al ŭi sujŏk ch'ui." *Yŏksa kyoyuk* 61: 31–67.

Yongjae ch'onghwa. Miscellanae by Sŏng Hyŏn. In *Kug'yŏk taedong yasŭng*.

Yŏnsan Kun ilgi. In *Chosŏn wangjo sillok*.

14

POPULAR RELIGION

Boudewijn Walraven

Popular religion is not an easily defined category. Roughly, it comprises religious beliefs and practices that do not belong to institutionalized religions with their own institutional structures and canonized scriptures that are the object of explicit hermeneutical traditions (Yi Yong Bhum 2015, 1–14). To a large extent, the practices aim to secure this-worldly benefits thanks to the force of prayer and ritual. From an alternative perspective, popular religion may denote beliefs that the government or the elite do not condone. In more positive terms, it is the religion of the ordinary people, roughly defined, and closely linked to daily life and the social occasions and units of everyday life, such as the household, the site of residence and its natural and social surroundings, or to the workplace; rather than to institutionalized, exclusively sacred sites such as churches, Confucian shrines or Buddhist monasteries. The shamans, who may be regarded as the religious specialists of popular religion, are not appointed by a formal institutional hierarchy but tend to rely on personal charisma or a more personal, inherited pedigree that lends them authority. On the other hand, popular religion tends to adopt and adapt elements of institutional religions, sometimes making it difficult to discern where one begins and the other ends.

In this way, Korean shamans have borrowed many elements from Buddhism. In a shaman song relating the myth of Pari kongju ("the Abandoned Princess"), who became the first shaman, she receives aid from the Buddha in her struggle to overcome all the obstacles (Seo Dae-seok 2000, 116–52). Conversely, Buddhist monks have taken up roles that also were assumed by shamans (such as that of the fortune-teller) and incorporated earlier, popular forms of worship, like the veneration of the constellation of the Great Dipper (Ursa Major; Ko. Ch'ilsŏng), which goes back to prehistoric times. Some Buddhist practices performed by laypeople may be deemed part of popular religion. A good example is the custom that in intercalary months, elderly women would throng to Buddhist monasteries around the country to make offerings to the Buddha to ensure rebirth in the Pure Land of Amitābha (Sasse 2022, 63).

Between popular religion and institutional religion, there are not a few shared deities. Thus, mountain gods were (and are) worshipped in Buddhist monasteries and by shamans, while Confucians, too, would recognize the numinous aspects of mountains. There is also overlap in terms of practice. The practices of popular religion largely concern direct human needs in the here and now, related to birth, death, and people's livelihood, which are also important to institutional religion. Nevertheless, although a specific worldview undergirded them, no theology or metaphys-

DOI: 10.4324/9781003262053-19

ics somewhat distanced popular religion's practices from the believers' immediate needs, of the kind that the elitist specialists of the institutional religions formulated. In the case of childlessness or illness, for instance, staunch Confucians might judge that this was due to the will of Heaven and not to be changed by prayers or sacrifices. In actual life, however, the practices of popular religion, although spurned by religious elites, often remained part of the daily lives of members of all classes, from poor peasants to those who dwelt in the royal palaces. On the whole, women of all classes tended to rely on such practices to a much greater degree. Including certain Buddhist practices, it was arguably the most common form of religion in Korea under the rule of the Chosŏn state (1392–1897). However, the ubiquity of the manifold manifestations of popular religion, less often described in written sources, has been overlooked.

From the above description of popular religion, it follows that something that deserves to be called popular religion, despite its ancient roots, was not present from the dawn of history (Walraven 2015). There first had to be a measure of social differentiation and, above all, the emergence of religious forms based on scriptures, canonization, and hierarchical priesthood, creating a divergence between the religious practices of the elite and those of the ordinary people. Popular religion, though, does not merely consist of traditions from a hoary past. Popular practices may have roots in ancient beliefs, but they still had to adapt to changing circumstances to survive. Upon the appearance of institutional religions such as Confucianism (which certainly has religious elements in the way it functioned in Chosŏn, besides such other elements as a political philosophy and social ethics), these influenced ancient practices that flourished among all layers of society. The influence gave rise to the more or less separate realm of popular religion, which adopted some elements of the newly introduced beliefs while maintaining its own identity.

Popular Religion and Shamanism

In Korea, the acceptance of scripture-based religions and worldviews involved a gradual pushing of shamanism toward the status of popular religion, a phenomenon that started at an early date. The institutional religion that enjoyed the favor of the elite was Buddhism in, among others, Silla (57 BCE, trad.–935 CE) and Koryŏ (918–1392), and Confucianism in Chosŏn. As described in more detail below, Chosŏn ultimately excluded shamanism from any form of state ritual (at least at the level of the central government). Accordingly, there is a general tendency to equate popular religion in Chosŏn with shamanism. On the contrary, one of the main points made in this chapter is that popular religion encompassed more than the rituals of the shamans alone. Nonetheless, at least roughly defining what a shaman is in the context of Korean popular religion will be helpful. As used here, the term refers to religious specialists who, without being appointed by an institutional hierarchy and without needing a literate tradition, possess a very personal, charismatic ability to act as an intermediary between the realm of gods and spirits and the human world. Ecstasy and trance are not decisive factors in this concept of shamanism (Hamayon 1993; Walraven 2009, 75–76). Crucial, however, is the performance of traditional rituals during which the shamans are assumed to lend their voice to gods or spirits and directly enunciate messages or oracles from the invisible realm (Kendall 1985).

The functions of the shamans were manifold. Their ability to commune with the invisible world enabled them to divine the causes of all kinds of misfortune, from illness and childlessness to unnatural death and natural disasters such as the unseasonal drought that seemed to augur famine. Most importantly, it enabled them to do something about it. Also, they were supposed to have the ability to commune with the dead and lead them to a "good place," where they would be at peace and no longer pose a danger to the wellbeing of the living because of their frustration with

Figure 14.1 Female shaman performing a ritual. This depiction is by a late nineteenth-century artist, Kisan Kim Chun'gŭn. Photo © NRICH/Museum am Rothenbaum (MARKK), Hamburg.

their miserable fate in the hereafter. Their rituals would involve music, singing, and dancing, which might also serve as entertainment (Figure 14.1). For instance, King Kojong (r. 1864–1907; emperor from 1897) enjoyed watching the dancing and singing of shamans who had been called to the palace by his wife, Queen Myŏngsŏng (Hwang Hyŏn 1980, vol. 1, 293).

Because Korean shamans are not thought to travel to celestial or underworldly regions in a state of ecstasy and instead are supposed to be possessed by deities or spirits that "descend" into them, some might prefer to call them mediums. However, the fact that they remain in complete control of their contacts with the spirit world and are not just passive vehicles for transmitting the intentions and desires of that world makes them more similar to figures elsewhere, usually referred to as shamans. Therefore, the term shaman is justifiable because of its use in comparative studies, though in Korea, the term was not used before the modern era. In Korean, there are various designations for the persons we call shamans, the most common being *mudang* and—in pre-modern records—*munyŏ*. Both terms are used specifically for female shamans, who for a long time have outnumbered male shamans, while for male shamans, the most common term is *paksu*, or in old documents, *mugyŏk*.

The preponderance of female shamans corresponded with the predominance of female clients, who were much more numerous than the men, who were more deeply influenced by Confucianism and Confucian ritual styles, even if they performed rituals that should be considered to belong to popular religion. Women consistently formed the core of the clientele of the shamans. They were less exposed to the elite literate culture, which had less to offer them and hardly addressed their particular needs. Shamans, for instance, were called when children were sick, when mothers did not have enough milk to feed their babies, or when infants were unusually naughty (Walraven 1999, 186).

Outline of the Universe as Seen in Popular Religion

Before surveying the specific rituals and practices of popular religion, considering the view of the universe that roughly determined its structure in Chosŏn will be helpful. All aspects of human life were thought to be influenced by the invisible force of numerous deities and spirits. These were almost all imagined to be anthropomorphic or at least to act according to emotions that were quite like those of human beings. Rituals would be needed to placate their anger and dissatisfaction and move them to bestow blessings rather than venting their anger. Of particular importance were ancestral spirits and the unquiet dead, the spirits of persons who had died an unnatural death before they had completed their natural lifespan, such as victims of war, famine, pestilence, or accidents. The frustrations of these spirits were held to be the cause of all kinds of human misfortune, as was the wrath of deities whose sacrifices had been neglected or who had otherwise been offended. Taking away these frustrations and resolving the wrath of the gods, thereby ensuring the well-being of the living, was the aim of the practices of popular religion. This was generally done by placating the invisible forces rather than by exorcism (although that, too, had a minor place in the array of practices). Spatially, spirits and gods could be found in any place, but mountains, seen in many cultures as a connection between heaven and earth, were held to be highly numinous. People everywhere in Chosŏn venerated mountain gods (*sansin* or *sansillyŏng*) as the tutelary deities of particular localities.

Such was the worldview behind popular religious practices and specific shamanic rituals. Not only found among ordinary people, it was present, to some degree, among all social layers. The way of dealing with it varied, and a salient example is the treatment of the unquiet dead, which was a concern of shamans as well as of Buddhist priests and Confucian officials. In the capital, Hansŏng (present-day Seoul), shamans refer to these spirits as *yŏngsan* (Kim Hŏnsŏn 2020, 70). To deal with the nefarious consequences of the accumulated wrath of war dead not properly buried, causing epidemics and inauspicious events such as a fire in a royal palace, the Chosŏn government in 1401 decided to institute the *yŏje* ritual, which continued to be performed by Confucian officials until the early twentieth century, for the benefit of fifteen categories of restless spirits that were very similar to the *yŏngsan* (Walraven 1993, 71–75). For the same kind of spirits, Buddhist priests would perform the *suryukchae* ritual, literally the ritual for [the spirits] of water and land (Mihwa Choi 2009; Teiser 1983). Their death was vividly depicted in the Nectar Ritual Paintings (*kamnot'aeng*) produced from the mid-sixteenth century and often commissioned by palace ladies. These paintings depicted the Buddhist ritual needed to placate the dead and shamans performing their rites (Kang Woo-bang 1993). Earlier, the government had the ritual performed for more than a century for the hundreds of members of the previous royal house, the Wangs, whom it had killed *en masse* to prevent Koryŏ's restoration (Eugene Y. Park 2018, chapter 1; Mihwa Choi 2009). In the centuries that followed; however, the government instead had the ritual performed to assuage unrest among the population caused by raging epidemics.

The Elimination of Shamans from State Rituals and Their Relegation to the Private Sphere

Already in Koryŏ, the literate elite started to distance itself from the activities of the shamans (although the latter continued to serve the government in an official capacity). One example should suffice. The eminent statesman Yi Kyubo (1168–1241) wrote a poem called "An Old Shaman" (*Nomu p'yŏn*) about a *mudang* living near his house (*Tongguk Yi Sangguk chip, kwŏn* 2, 2b–4a; Yi Nŭnghwa 2008, 110–15). He ridiculed that, with her lined face and greying hair, she dared to claim that Indra, the supreme Buddhist celestial deity, descended in her body and that she had adorned the walls of her house with garish paintings of gods and pictures of star constellations. All this would lead simple, innocent people astray. He also objected to the ungodly din of the rituals, with their insistent drumming, and to the "bizarre" songs the shaman sang. Fortunately, he

Popular Religion

noted, the government had issued an order expelling all shamans from the capital, and he admiringly mentioned Ham Yuil (1106–85), who, as a local magistrate, had taken firm (and violent) action against shamanic practices. Together with its prose introduction, this poem contains several themes that remained relevant almost until the end of Chosŏn. Elite scholars like Yi Kyubo could not accept that the shamans upset the social order, with uneducated women arrogating to themselves the authority of mighty deities or former monarchs whose messages they claimed to transmit. Moreover, their rituals suggested that the common people could obtain blessings while neglecting the (Confucian) morality that encouraged them to know their station and accept hardship due to Heaven's Will. The style of the rituals, with loud music and colorful depictions of deities and spirits, also conflicted with the serene decorum Confucians thought proper. As confirmed by Pierre Bourdieu, taste is one element that sets social classes apart and contributes to defining popular religion (Bourdieu 1987).

In Chosŏn, the shamans increasingly lost their role in state rituals and official recognition of their activities. The government made concerted efforts to outlaw all kinds of rituals that did not conform to ritual handbooks, labeling them "illicit rituals" (*ŭmsa*). In particular, the term referred to rituals performed for officially recognized spirits by persons who did not possess the proper status to do so. At times, Confucian scholars (*yusaeng*) without official functions initiated the suppression of such cults, and they did not hesitate to use extreme violence, burning down shrines deemed improper. Thus, in 1566, Confucian scholars incensed by the sight of men and women in mixed company and in large numbers praying for luck at a shrine on Mount Songak near Kaesŏng set it ablaze (Yi Nŭnghwa 2008, 384). Such persecution, based on the perception that shamanic ritual was a waste of resources and did not accord with proper morality, substantially changed Chosŏn's ceremonial landscape but never led to the complete eradication of popular religion and shamanism.

Strident condemnation of illicit worship by Confucian scholars and officials should not create the impression that they were wholly opposed to any form of the veneration of invisible forces. Ritual codes specified such worship at the altar for the deities of Land and Grain (Sajik, who were metonymically identified with the nation), for Wind and Clouds, Thunder and Rain, at a special Rain Altar, for Mount Samgak, the mountain that protected Hansŏng in the north, for the Han River that ran south of the capital, for mountains and rivers across the land, and at the Sŏnnongdan (an altar for the promotion of agriculture), Sŏnjamdan (for the promotion of sericulture), and at the Chongmyo, the royal ancestral shrine (*Sinbo sugyo chimnok*, 238). In the palace grounds and elsewhere, there were countless shrines (*myo*), ancestral shrines (*kung*), and ceremonial halls (*chŏn*) for the spirits (*hon*) of dead royals, including many women (*Tongguk yŏji pigo*, *kwŏn* 1, 116–24). The existence, at least for a limited period, of spirits of the dead was not categorically denied, although the preferred way of dealing with them differed from that of the shamans. Unless they were of persons to whom the living owed deference or were close family members like princesses, such spirits were not deemed worthy of veneration and were best ignored—certainly not to be feared. Government worship of the unquiet dead in the *yŏje* ritual was, for most of the period, the limit of what was admissible, and that, too, was at least in part performed to reassure popular sentiment at times when epidemics raged. Still, the continued performance of this ritual until the first decade of the twentieth century contributed to the blurring of the exact borderline between official ideology and popular religion.

Despite the negative attitude toward shamans of thirteenth-century literati such as Yi Kyubo, the *yangban* class still trusted shamans in the early fifteenth century. Reflecting such an attitude is the fact that *yangban* households did not immediately abandon the tradition of keeping the ancestral tablets of their forebears, the most sacred objects in the Confucian veneration of ancestors, in

The Routledge Handbook of Early Modern Korea

the shrines of shamans or Buddhist monasteries (Han Ugŭn 1976). Of course, this, too, became taboo in due time. After about a century, urged by the government, elite families started creating their own ancestral shrines.

In the first decades following the founding of Chosŏn, the government still regularly employed shamans. Most prominent was the *kungmu*, which may be translated as state or royal shaman. In 1426, the Censorate urged abolishing the *kungmu*'s function and dismissing other shamans of lower status. However, 17 years later, in 1443, according to the veritable records (*sillok*), there still was a *kungmu* in the capital (Ch'oe Chongsŏng 2002). In due time, the office of *kungmu* disappeared, but the use of the term continued for shamans who, in a private capacity, served the court, particularly the ladies of the court. Such continuity is but one instance of a general trend: rituals that did not conform to Confucian standards, not only those of the shamans but also Buddhist ceremonies, were still performed and sometimes flourished—but as private events no longer on behalf of the state. A prime example is King Chŏngjo's (r. 1776–1800) dedicating a Buddhist monastery to his father, Prince Sado (1735–62), who suffered a tragic death. Chŏngjo's gesture was "private" in the sense that he had become the posthumously adopted son of his uncle, Sado's uncle, and in the veritable records, the monastery appears only in the context of the uniforms of its monks, who also performed military duties. Indeed, shamans continued to visit the royal palaces. Queen Myŏngsŏng (1851–95), the first wife of King Kojong, was famous as a patron of the shamans. Even after her murder by the Japanese, shamans were frequent visitors to royal palaces at least until 1907, that is two years after Japan turned Korea into a protectorate (Walraven 1995).

Not only forbidding shamans from entering the sacred confines of Hansŏng, but laws also prohibited sacrifices to any deity of popular religion (*sinsa*) in a radius of five *li* (about two kilometers) from the capital (*Sinbo sugyo chimnok*, 409). There was a concerted striving to spatially separate manifestations of popular religion from the court. The Chosŏn state never completely suppressed popular religion as long as it knew its place. Thus, in 1730, court ladies and *mudang* were punished with banishment because they had dared to hold a ritual near the king's route to a royal tomb (*Sinbo sugyo chimnok*, 422). Such rituals would remain unpunished only if they kept a proper distance from the monarch and his court.

Chosŏn was predominantly an agricultural society much dependent on timely rainfall. Any threat of severe drought compelled the government to take some ritual action, and early Chosŏn delegated this to shamans, properly rewarding them when their intervention was successful. Such a role of shamans invoked the ire of Confucian scholar-officials who ensured this ceased in due time. Although the regular participation of shamans probably ended much earlier, the last instance of them performing a rain ritual for the central government dates to 1638 (Ch'oe Chongsŏng 2002). In the countryside, however, shamans took part in rain rituals throughout Chosŏn, sometimes with the connivance of local magistrates (Walraven 1999, 174). At the same time, the government continued to have rain rituals performed in an unassailable Confucian style (Choi Byonghyon 2010, 452–59).

Although what happened in the provinces was of less concern than what transpired in Hansŏng, the central site of royal authority, the government made a serious attempt to bring the worship of local guardian deities in the provinces under control. These deities were generally mountain gods but often known as Sŏnghwang, the Korean pronunciation of Chinese *chenghuang*, literally the gods of the city walls and moats. In Korea, the term became a general appellation for local guardian deities venerated by the entire population of particular localities. To the government, the practice was *ŭmsa* that should be stopped. Instead, the Chosŏn state devised a bureaucratic structure, codified in the ritual handbooks, in which the *sŏnghwang* was the spiritual counterpart of the local magistrate; no one else should worship them (Walraven 1999, 174–77). This move

Popular Religion

was only partly successful. Local people and shamans continued to worship local guardian deities they called *sŏnghwang*, usually simplified to *sŏnang*. These deities received veneration not at the official *sŏnghwang* altar but at places called *sŏnangdang*. Despite the suffix *-dang* (hall, shrine), these were generally more natural places of worship, such as an imposing tree or a stone cairn.

Local guardians were sometimes also identified with historical persons, ideally martial figures, who had met with an untimely end, leaving them with a residue of spiritual power that might be marshaled to protect the living. The government attempted to undo the anthropomorphizing of deities worshipped as local guardians with images of the gods and their spouses. One example of a historical hero worshipped as a tutelary deity was the general and Meritorious Subject Sin Sunggyŏm (d. 927), who had sacrificed his own life to save King T'aejo (Wang Kŏn; r. 918–43), the founder of Koryŏ. He enjoyed popular worship as the *sŏnghwang* of Koksŏng, his native place. This custom created some ambiguity because the official *sŏnghwang* was not supposed to have such a personal character. The government nonetheless supported Sin Sunggyŏm's veneration at a special shrine, Tŏgyangsa (not the regular Sŏnghwang Altar of the ritual handbooks), which presented him as a paragon of the Confucian virtue of loyalty (*Chodurok*, 27a). His continued popular veneration was testimony to the resilience of popular beliefs.

The government did not condemn the veneration of images in all cases. In the eighteenth century, the government attempted to curb the tendency of lineages to create new shrines where a likeness of a famous forebear was venerated (*Sinbo sugyo chimnok*, 232). However, the practice might be condoned if done by persons whose status entitled them to it. As the case of Sin Sunggyŏm also suggests, this might create ambiguity and sometimes misunderstandings. In 1904, a campaign to root out *ŭmsa* destroyed an image of the celebrated scholar Yi Saek (1328–96). His portrait, however, was enshrined in a small shrine (still in existence, on prime land in the very heart of Seoul) maintained for centuries by the Hansan Yi descent group to which Yi belonged (*Han'gyŏng chiryak* 1956, 283–84) and therefore fully authorized to pay homage to his likeness. Thus, destroying his image caused the person responsible great embarrassment (Walraven 1995, 112).

Another ambiguous case was the worship of the Chinese God of War Guan Yu (Ko. Kwan U), also venerated as a paragon of loyalty. The worship began at the instigation of the Chinese, who had come to the aid of the Koreans during the Imjin War (East Asian War; 1592–98) and argued that Guan Yu had lent supernatural support in battles—therefore meriting worship by the Koreans. Official worship was conducted at the Tongmyo (Eastern Shrine) and the Nammyo (Southern Shrine) in the capital area, while homage was also paid to Kwan U at military events. But as true in China (ter Haar 2017), the worship of Kwan U spread among the general population, and the nature of the deity changed, turning him, among other things, into a god of wealth and a moral example. Accordingly, by the end of the nineteenth century, merchants would visit the Nammyo in great numbers in the tenth lunar month of the year, whereas at the capital's Six Markets (Yugŭijŏn), they worshipped a clay image of Kwan U in a small shrine next to the Posin'gak, the site of the City Bell (Yi Nŭnghwa 1981, 314, 487). Kwan U had at the time garnered a great following in a morality cult that supported Confucian values and also enjoyed the court's support (Walraven 2000, 191–95; Jihyun Kim 2020).

But this did not mean that the authorities encouraged all and sundry to worship Kwan U in any way they liked. In 1761, King Yŏngjo (r. 1724–76) noted that lately, at the Tongmyo and Nammyo, there had been "illicit worship" of "King Kwan" (Kwan-wang, Kwan U's official title) and ordered to put an end to it (*Yŏngjo sillok* 1761/12/13 entry 3). Yet much later, in 1904, to stamp out illicit cults, the police impounded 3,000 images of Kwan U in Hansŏng. This suggests that, at the time, this popular cult in the city of roughly 200,000 inhabitants was very widespread and had only grown in the intervening years. That Kwan U deserved to be venerated in the eyes of government

The Routledge Handbook of Early Modern Korea

officials is confirmed by the fact that the confiscated images were respectfully deposited in the official shrines (Walraven 1995, 127).

Evidence that shamans, too, venerated Kwan U comes from an unexpected corner. Queen Myŏngsŏng put great trust in two shamans, who both claimed to be possessed by Kwan U, and thanks to their protection by the queen resided in shrines that were called Pungmyo (Northern Shrine) and Sŏmyo (Western Shrine), suggesting equivalence with the Tongmyo and Nammyo (Yi Nŭnghwa 2008, 140–41). This shows, once again, that popular religion and officially recognized religion were not entirely separate universes, even though the authorities might forcefully suppress the former.

It is tempting to describe official efforts to suppress shamanic rituals as the marginalization of shamanism, but this would be misleading. Shaman rituals and popular religion generally remained meaningful to most of the population, including the court women (Ch'oe Kilsŏng 1981, 83–90). In the eighteenth century, the encyclopaedist Yi Ik (1681–1763) noted that shamans still frequented royal palaces and provincial offices (Yi Nŭnghwa 2008, 139).

Popular Rituals Performed by Others than the Shamans

Important as the shamans were for popular religion, they were not the only persons who could commune with the invisible world and conduct rituals. Ordinary women would also address prayers to higher forces accompanied by simple offerings like a bowl of pure water. During shaman rituals for the dead, female relatives of the deceased might also become possessed by his or her spirit and transmit messages specifying the desires and complaints of the dead. Children who suffered from smallpox were supposed to be possessed by the much-feared and much-respected smallpox deities. Dallet wrote in his nineteenth-century history of the Catholic Church in Chosŏn, which was based on the reports of missionaries who had illegally entered the country: "Everyone is convinced that during the illness the afflicted children are in communication with the spirits, that they have the gift of second sight, and that they perceive through the walls what goes on, even if it is at a great distance" (Dallet 1874, vol. 1, cxlviii). Dallet incidentally was convinced that some of the spirits were real: "[T]hat there are true sorcerers, and especially sorceresses [*mudang*], who by magical rituals establish contact with infernal powers, that is an absolutely incontrovertible fact" (Dallet 1874, vol. 1, cl).

Rituals similar to those of the shamans were also conducted by blind exorcists, who had their roots in Daoist traditions. Although Daoism in Korea never developed into a full-fledged institutionalized religion the way it did in China, its influence was not negligible, and practices of Daoist derivation cannot be ignored in a survey of popular religion. One of the most prominent scholars of Chinese Daoism, the late Kristofer Schipper, held that Korean shamanism was nothing but a form of popular Daoism (personal communication). In Koryŏ, the government frequently had Daoist rituals performed.

In Chosŏn, there still existed blind exorcists with Daoist roots. They drove away or prevented calamities by reciting scriptures of both Buddhist and Daoist origin, sometimes in rituals in which *mudang*, who tended to approach the invisible world in a more placatory way, also participated. The exorcists were blind and accordingly called *maengin, changnim* (both meaning blind person), or *p'ansu* (Figure 14.2). Although they offered services such as praying for good luck or rain and healing, which also were part of the tasks of the *mudang*, they were treated differently. They were allowed entrance to the capital and were famous for knowing their way everywhere in Hansŏng without the benefit of eyesight. Also, they would always be addressed in polite language by *yangban*, as if they were *chungin* (members of the status group comprising government-employed professionals). Typically, *maengin* were male, although some women were also among them (Yi

Figure 14.2 Blind exorcist (*p'ansu*) at work, as depicted by Kisan Kim Chun'gŭn. Photo © NRICH/ Museum am Rothenbaum (MARKK), Hamburg.

Nŭnghwa 1981, 262). It is doubtful, however, that they were shown the same deference as the men. Over the centuries, the male *maengin*, too, gradually declined in status. In 1745, Yŏngjo had *maengin* rituals (*maengje*), scripture reciting rituals, *maengin* rituals to pray for rain (*maengin kiuje*), and *maengin* scripture rituals held when the king changed residence (but had not been performed for a long time) struck from the roster of the Ritual Office, the T'aesangsi (Yi Nŭnghwa 1981, 265, 463). This does not mean, though, that the *yangban* no longer sought the services of *maengin*. Rather, the status of the *maengin* ritual as a form of popular religion was secure.

Thus, a popular ritual of Daoist derivation survived in the pursuit of private goals, also of the members of the *yangban* class. The constellation of Ch'ilsŏng, literally the "Seven Stars" (of Ursa Major), was worshipped as an astral deity in Daoism. In early Chosŏn, a Daoist government office, Sogyŏksŏ oversaw the veneration of Ch'ilsŏng before being discontinued after the Imjin War (Yi Nŭnghwa 1981, 142–43, 410). Even in the early nineteenth century, though, encyclopaedist Yi Kyugyŏng (1788–1856) mentioned that literati would privately go to a Ch'ilsŏng shrine on Mount Inwang located at the northwestern periphery of Hansŏng to pray that they would come first in the government examination to recruit new officials (Yi Nŭnghwa 1981, 293, 477). Apart from that, Ch'ilsŏng received worship by shamans and in Buddhist monasteries.

The House as a Sacred Space

Unsurprisingly, the house, as the fundamental environment where daily life takes place, occupied a central place in popular religious rituals, partly performed by household members and partly by shamans. The god of the house itself and, by extension, the guardian of the male head of the house and the household as a whole was Sŏngju. He was worshipped as a piece of paper with rice affixed to the main beam of the house, the latter the metonymical representation of the desired sturdiness of the house and family (Walraven 1994, 143–200). Every tenth lunar month, a shaman should invite the god again to the house and renew the representation of the deity (Sasse 2022, 54). The women's quarters maintained a paper envelope covered by a paper monk's cap (*kokkal*), identified with the Buddhist heavenly deity Indra (Ko. Chesŏk), whom Korean shamans had fully integrated into their pantheon as a deity in charge of childbearing, children's health, and health and fertility in general. Likewise venerated in the women's quarters was the Birth Grandmother (Samsin halmŏni). Outside, in a corner of the courtyard, there would be a representation of the god of the site of the house in the form of a sheaf of straw. Around the house, there were also a female deity of the toilet, sometimes called Puch'ul kaksi, "Miss Squatting Board," and many other lesser spirits, including the kitchen god (Chowang) and the gate god (Walraven 1994, 192; Choi Jong Seong 2015). Taking care of all these spirits was as much the task of the women of the household as of the *mudang* called in on special occasions. As Laurel Kendall wrote of the twentieth century, "Shaman and housewife perform analogous tasks and deal with the same spirits (Kendall 1985, 166), which undoubtedly also applied to earlier periods.

Village and District Rituals

The village was one of the primary forms of communal life, cemented by the cult of village guardian deities. Written sources from Chosŏn rarely mention this form of popular religion, but village rituals and beliefs—of which evidence from the first half of the twentieth century abounds—had existed in a quite similar form for centuries. A very early description of a "Five Dragons Shrine" (Oryongmyo) in a book written about Korea by a Chinese envoy who visited Koryŏ in 1123 still broadly fits the current state of that village shrine on the island Sŏnyudo in North Chŏlla Province (Lee Kyung Yup 2015, 20–21; Vermeersch 2016, 140). What changed was that in Chosŏn, men increasingly adopted Confucian-style worship to honor village deities, although *mudang*, too, continued to venerate them in the community festivals. In most cases, the village guardian deity was the god of the mountain near the village. These deities were sometimes identified with historical figures, particularly generals who had died a violent death, and also with the *sŏnghwang*, who, as noted above, were mountain deities rather than true city gods as they were in China.

One of the relatively rare sources from Chosŏn describing local rituals is the nineteenth-century *Tongguk sesigi* (Record of the Seasonal Customs of Korea) by Hong Sŏngmo (Hong Sŏk-mo), who frequently quotes older sources. (Hong's work is available in an English translation, Sasse 2022.) Doing so, Hong describes customs in Kunwi, Kyŏngsang Province, where at the West Mount Peak outside the town was a shrine devoted to the Silla general Kim Yusin (595–673). For the Tano Festival (fifth day of the fifth lunar month), the county's head clerks would lead the people to welcome the deity to the town (Sasse 2022, 48–49; *Sinjŭng Tongguk yŏji sŭngnam, kwŏn* 25). This custom was typical in several respects. A tutelary deity who was not the officially recognized *sŏnghwang* (whom only the magistrate appointed by the central government could worship at a special altar reserved for the purpose) received veneration by the population led by the local clerks—a common pattern throughout Chosŏn.

According to Hong, in Kosŏng, Kangwŏn Province, sacrifices would be offered at the local shrine by persons from the local magistracy (probably the clerks) on the first and fifteenth day of each lunar month. The representation of the deity was a satin mask kept in the shrine. From the twentieth day of the lunar month, the deity would descend in a person from the town, who wearing the mask would dance in the public offices and the streets of the town to be welcomed and entertained in every house. Only on the fifteenth day of the first lunar month would the deity, who was supposed to protect against misfortune, return to the shrine (Sasse 2022, 63). Clearly, the ritual was popular (the form alone in which the deity was represented suffices for that conclusion), with the local clerks playing an important role condoned by the authorities. That a spirit or deity descends in a person who is not a shaman is not unusual. It has often been witnessed in the twentieth century,

Popular Religion

and in the nineteenth century, Dallet observed that people treated children suffering from smallpox as if they were smallpox deities themselves, as mentioned earlier.

In Ch'ŏngan in Ch'ungch'ŏng Province, the head of the local clerks would lead the people of the town to bring down two guardian deities (Kuksa, literally the National Preceptor, originally a Buddhist title, and his spouse) from a tree on a nearby mountain in the third lunar month. They would be fêted for 20 days by shamans, and rituals were held for them with loud music "in the county office and at every government office building" (Sasse 2022, 42). The pattern seen here was similar to that seen in other places. The tutelary deity was a mountain god (in this case worshipped in the form of a tree, although the deity was anthropomorphic) and from time to time (once every year or once in two years) escorted down from the mountain by the people from the town and local clerks, assisted by shamans, who would fête them in a raucous fashion that ran counter to Confucian decorum. Yet, the highest authority in place, the magistrate sent by the central government, would condone this, though, at the same time, he kept some distance from forms of worship that might invoke the ire of Confucian stalwarts.

To get a picture of the ubiquity of community rituals, one may also look at rituals of this kind that survived into the twentieth century, as these undoubtedly have roots in the nineteenth century or earlier. A study devoted to the popular beliefs of twentieth-century Seoul counted in 1990 no less than 35 community shrines (Yi Chaegon 1996, 189–97). Many of these shrines were called Pugun-dang. None of the shrines was within the old city walls, the area that the Chosŏn state intended to constitute a kind of Confucian sacred city, free of Buddhist monasteries and *ŭmsa* (Walraven 2000). All this undoubtedly represented forms of popular worship, with a variety of deities that would have no place in Confucian rituals performed in the Munmyo, the national Confucian shrine within the old city walls, or the *hyanggyo* (the local schools in the provinces that were small-scale replicas of the Munmyo). Although part of the rituals performed might be Confucian in style, in most cases, shamans would also be involved in the rituals, and the spirits would not be on the roster of official worship.

Rituals Conducted by Occupational Groups with or without the Aid of Shamans

One form of occupational worship has already been alluded to, involving the provincial government clerks, and those in Hansŏng were no different. One example is the worship of Im Kyŏngŏp (1594–1646), venerated at the Kyosŏgwan, the government agency in the capital charged with printing books. A historical general, Im was the Kyosŏgwan's subject of veneration not so much for any involvement in printing books as his residence in the neighborhood (*Han'gyŏng chiryak* 1956, 291; Walraven 2000, 197).

Rituals were particularly important to people whose work was potentially dangerous or involved an element of chance. A shaman song about the god of the house recorded in the 1920s or 1930s describes some occupational rituals performed by the woodcutters who felled trees for building a house and those who bound together the timber to form rafts before setting them afloat downstream on the Han River to the capital. These rituals were undoubtedly conducted in Chosŏn, as the song mentions the tax payment to a government bureau abolished in 1883. The song provides a good description of what would be involved in popular rituals (Walraven 1994, 165–66):

When they wanted to cut wood,
Would there not be a sacrifice?
Three *mal* and three *toe* of rice cake
Three *toe* and three *hop* of sacrificial rice [they sacrificed].

The Routledge Handbook of Early Modern Korea

They slaughtered a whole ox and cut it in pieces.
Clear rice wine and cloudy rice wine [they offered]
And dried pollack complete with the head.
They lit two pairs of yellow wax candles,
And three sheets of paper they burned.
The thirty-three workmen
Washed their hands and feet in the lower pool.
They washed their bodies in the middle pool
And they washed their hair in the upper pool.
[and they prayed]
"We pray, we pray
To the sun- and moon-gods of far-away mountains and nearby mountains
We pray to the Mountain God and to the Spirit of the Earth
That even though we enter these mountains
And cut trees,
You will annoy nor harm us,
That you will help us [to ensure]
That the thirty-three workmen
Will have no diseases of the body or the feet.

The song shows that the work crew conducted a quite elaborate ritual and took care to ritually purify themselves for the sacrifice—without the aid of ritual specialists. When the raft was set afloat, a simpler ritual was also performed, again without the intervention of shamans. Once the construction work for the house began, moreover, another ritual had to be performed by the builders, with prayers for the wealth and fame of the occupants of the house and also for the safety of the workers: "Please assist us, so that the carpenters will not hurt themselves with their tools" (Walraven 1994, 180).

Part of the ritual conducted by the woodcutters was motivated by the belief that their work constituted an invasion of the numinous realm of the mountains and might invoke the ire of the mountain deities (or perhaps attract tigers, who sometimes were identified with the mountain god). This belief also applied to the men who would go into the mountains to dig the roots of wild ginseng—men because the occupation emphatically excluded women. Every year in spring, before the ginseng diggers would enter the mountains for the first time, they would have a small ritual (*kosa*) with the usual offerings: a pig's head, rice cake, and rice wine.

The danger and hardship involved in their job performance prompted the boatmen who steered the rafts of timber down the Han River to pray for safety. Similarly, the sailors who ventured out to the open sea as merchants or fishermen had recourse to ritual to ensure safe passage and profit. They might do this simply, by themselves, but also with the help of shamans. There is a description of the latter in a Chinese poem by Yi Kŏnch'ang (1852–98), in which the deity worshipped speaks through the mouth of the shaman and promises the sailors the "treasures of the water palace [of the dragon king]," that is an abundant catch of fish (Im Hyŏngt'aek 1992, 308). Rituals for merchant ships' safe sailing were also considered indispensable (Tsuruya 1908, 55). Rituals for success in fishing were not only devoted to dragon deities (water gods) but also to the aforementioned Im Kyŏngŏp, the guardian deity of the Kyosŏgwan. For remaining loyal to China proper's Ming dynasty (1368–1644) when the rising Manchu Qing dynasty (1616–1912; Later Jin until 1636) forced Chosŏn's capitulation and allegiance, he paid for it with his life. For his loyalty, in the centuries that followed, Im remained the subject of worship at government-approved shrines (Saeyoung Park 2014): the Ch'ungnyŏlsa in his home county, Ch'ungju, Ch'ungch'ong Province (*Chodurok*, 15a); the Sungŭijŏn in Majŏn, Kyŏnggi Province (*Chodurok*, 14a); and the

Hyŏnch'ungsa in Ŭiju, P'yongan Province (*Chodurok*, 32b). The fishermen venerated Im because while serving as a naval commander, he supposedly discovered a better way to catch yellow corvina, a popular fish in Korean cuisine. The various forms of his worship show that at times, popular and elite worship shaded into one another.

Final Thoughts

The rituals of popular religion were often suppressed by the government or at least regarded negatively by the literati. Nevertheless, they survived in many forms, sometimes disguised by a light Confucian veneer. The blurring of the borderline between popular practices and the worldview of the elite that sometimes occurred contributed to this. Popular religion remained part of the warp and woof of Chosŏn society. Shamans continued to visit the houses of the *yangban* and the royal palaces, although primarily catering to the women. Moreover, despite official condemnation of their beliefs and rituals, shamans can be said to have supported the state and elite ideology. The prayers of the shamans were for the birth of children who would become loyal subjects (*ch'ungsin*), filial sons (*hyoja*), and virtuous women (*yŏllyŏ*), asserting essential Confucian virtues. The vernacular shaman songs (*muga*) also affirmed and propagated the elite view of the history, territory, and culture of Chosŏn, thus contributing to the emergence of national consciousness among all layers of the population (Walraven 2010).

It should be evident from the above discussion that Chosŏn's popular religion encompassed much more than only shamanism. At almost every level of society, there existed forms of ritual and worship, some of which were part of daily routines, especially in the case of women, and performed without the intervention of shamans. The latter were only called in on special days or when people had to deal with crises. When the totality of Chosŏn's popular religious practices is considered, including the popular rituals in which shamans did not take part, some popular Buddhist practices, and popular rituals of Daoist derivation, it becomes clear that the still limited body of scholarship in no way reflects the importance popular religion had in the daily goings-on of life in Chosŏn.

References

Bourdieu, Pierre. 1987. *Distinction: A Social Critique of the Judgement of Taste*. Translated by Richard Nice. Harvard University Press.

Ch'oe Chongsŏng [Jong Seong Choi]. 2002. *Chosŏnjo musok kukhaeng ŭirye yŏn'gu*. Ilchisa.

Ch'oe Kilsŏng. 1981. *Han'guk musok non*. Hyŏngsŏl ch'ulp'ansa.

Chodurok. Undated woodblock print. Referenced in *Bibliographie coréenne*. By Maurice Courant, 1894–1901, no. 1156. Ernest Leroux.

Choi Byonghyon. 2010. *Admonitions on Governing the People: Manual for All Administrators*. University of California Press.

Choi, Jong Seong [Ch'oe Chongsŏng]. 2015. "Family Popular Beliefs." In *Korean Popular Beliefs*, edited by Yong Bhum Yi, Kyung Yup Lee, Jong Seong Choi, and Boudewijn Walraven, 55–80. Jimoondang.

Choi, Mihwa. 2009. "State Suppression of Buddhism and Royal Patronage of the Ritual of Water and Land in the Early Chosŏn Dynasty." *Seoul Journal of Korean Studies* 22, no. 2: 181–214.

Dallet, Charles. 1874. *Histoire de l'église de Corée*. Victor Palmé.

ter Haar, B. J. 2017. *Guan Yu: The Religious Afterlife of a Failed Hero*. Oxford University Press.

Hamayon, Roberte N. 1993. "Are 'Trance,' 'Ecstasy' and Similar Concepts Appropriate in the Study of Shamanism?" In *Shamanism in Performing Arts*, edited by Tae-gon Kim and Mihály Hoppál with Otto J. von Sandovszky, 17–34. Akademiai Kiado.

Han Ugŭn. 1976. "Chosŏn wangjo ch'ogi e issŏsŏ ŭi yugyo inyŏm ŭi silch'ŏn kwa sinang chonggyo: saje munje rŭl chungsim ŭro." *Han'guk saron* 3: 147–228.

Han'gyŏng chiryak. 1956. Reprint. Seoul t'ŭkpyŏlsi sa p'yŏnch'an wiwŏnhoe.

Hwang Hyŏn. 1980. *(Chŏnyŏk) Maech'ŏn yarok, kwŏn chi sang*. Translated by Im Pyŏngju. Ch'ŏnggu munusa.

Im Hyŏngt'aek. 1992. *Yijo sidae sŏsasi, sang*. Ch'angjak kwa pip'yŏngsa.

Kang, Woo-bang. 1993. "Ritual and Art During the Eighteenth Century." In *Korean Arts of the Eighteenth Century: Splendor and Simplicity*, edited by Hongnam Kim, 79–98. Weatherhill.

Kendall, Laurel. 1985. *Shamans, Housewives, and Other Restless Spirits: Women in Korean Ritual Life*. University of Hawaii Press.

Kim Hŏnsŏn. 2020. *Chŏnt'ong Hanyang kut sin'ga chip*. Pogosa.

Kim, Jihyun. 2020. "Enlightenment on the Spirit-Altar: Eschatology and Restoration of Morality at the King Kwan Shrine in *Fin de Siècle* Seoul." *Religions* 11, no. 6: 273.

Lee, Kyung Yup. 2015. "Village Beliefs." In *Korean Popular Beliefs*, by Yong Bhum Yi, Kyung Yup Lee, Jong Seong Choi, and Boudewijn Walraven, 17–53. Jimoondang.

Park, Eugene Y. 2018. *A Genealogy of Dissent: The Progeny of Fallen Royals in Chosŏn Korea*. Stanford University Press.

Park, Saeyoung. 2014. "Memory, Counternarrative, and the Body Politic in Post-Imjin War Chosŏn Korea." *Journal of Korean Studies* 19, no. 1: 153–78.

Sasse, Werner. 2022. *Record of the Seasonal Customs of Korea: Tongguk sesigi by Toae Hong Sŏk-mo*. University of Hawai'i Press.

Seo, Dae-seok. 2000. *Myths of Korea*. Edited by Peter H. Lee. Jimoondang International.

Sinbo sugyo chimnok: Chosŏn hugi sae pŏmnyŏng moŭm. 2000. With translations and annotations by the Han'guk yŏksa yŏn'guhoe. Ch'ŏngnyŏnsa.

Sinjŭng Tongguk yŏji sŭngnam. Available at: https://shorturl.at/bZSPD.

Teiser, Stephen F. 1983. *The Ghost Festival in Medieval China*. Princeton University Press.

Tongguk Yi Sangguk chip. 1958. By Yi Kyubo. Reprint. Tongguk munhwasa.

Tongguk yŏji pigo. 1956. Seoul t'ŭkpyŏlsi sa p'yŏnch'an wiwŏnhoe.

Tsuruya Kairyū. 1908. *Chōsen no shūkyō*. Shūkyō kenkyūkai.

Vermeersch, Sem. 2016. *A Chinese Traveler in Medieval Korea: Xu Jing's Illustrated Account of the Xuanhe Embassy to Koryŏ*. University of Hawai'i Press.

Walraven, Boudewijn. 1993. "Confucians and Restless Spirits." In *Conflict and Accommodation in Early Modern East Asia: Essays in Honour of Erik Zürcher*, edited by Leonard Blussé and Harriet Zurndorfer, 71–93. Brill.

Walraven, Boudewijn. 1994. *Songs of the Shaman: The Ritual Chants of the Korean Mudang*. Kegan Paul International.

Walraven, Boudewijn. 1995. "Shamans and Popular Religion around 1900." In *Religions in Traditional Korea*, edited by Henrik H. Sørensen, 107–30. The Seminar for Buddhist Studies.

Walraven, Boudewijn. 1999. "Popular Religion in a Confucianized State." In *Culture and the State in Late Chosŏn Korea*, edited by JaHyun Kim Haboush and Martina Deuchler, 160–98. Harvard University Asia Center.

Walraven, Boudewijn. 2000. "Religion and the City: Seoul in the Nineteenth Century." *Review of Korean Studies* 3, no 1: 178–206.

Walraven, Boudewijn. 2009. "National Pantheon, Regional Deities, Personal Spirits? *Mushindo, Sŏngsu*, and the Nature of Korean Shamanism." *Asian Ethnology* 68, no. 1: 55–80.

Walraven, Boudewijn. 2010. "Divine Territory: Shaman Songs, Elite Culture and the Nation." *Korean Histories* 2, no. 2: 42–57. Available at: https://koreanhistorieswebsite.files.wordpress.com/2017/04/kh2 _2_walraven_divine_territory.pdf.

Walraven, Boudewijn. 2015. "The History of Korean Folk Beliefs and Popular Religion." In *Korean Popular Beliefs*, edited by Yong Bhum Yi, Kyung Yup Lee, Jong Seong Choi, and Boudewijn Walraven, 201–19. Jimoondang.

Yi Chaegon. 1996. *Sŏul ŭi min'gan sinang*. Paeksan ch'ulp'ansa.

Yi Nŭnghwa. 1981. *Chosŏn Togyosa*. With Korean translation by Yi Chongŭn. Posŏng munhwasa.

Yi Nŭnghwa. 2008. *Chosŏn musok ko*. With Korean translation and annotations by Sŏ Yŏngdae. Ch'angbi.

Yi, Yong Bhum. 2015. "Understanding Korean Popular Beliefs." In *Korean Popular Beliefs*, by Yong Bhum Yi, Kyung Yup Lee, Jong Seong Choi, and Boudewijn Walraven, 1–14. Jimoondang.

Yŏngjo sillok. In *Chosŏn wangjo sillok*. Available at: https://sillok.history.go.kr/main/main.do.

15

CATHOLICISM

Franklin D. Rausch

Catholicism and modernity are more likely to be seen as being in conflict than complementary.[1] This is particularly true in the case of the French Catholic Church. Its missionaries played a central role in the growth of Catholicism in Korea under the rule of the Chosŏn state (1392–1897) and produced much of the extant knowledge about that church. Catholicism, as such, attracted and won converts with a promise of salvation through articles of faith centered around the Savior, the Son of God, and how the church interpreted them.

All the same, the Korean Catholic community at the time embodied certain aspects of modernity, particularly a growing sense of critical reflection towards previous modes of thought, a commiserate openness to new ideas, a greater emphasis on individual and human equality, and, to an extent, acceptance of pluralism. Also, when we consider the perspective of Chosŏn Koreans, we gain a greater sense of their own lives and perspectives, of their experience of suffering and joy as they struggled to support each other and maintain a tiny community whose members the government was quite willing to devote significant resources to torture and kill. This chapter, therefore, provides an overview of the Korean Catholic Church, focusing on the experience of Chosŏn's Catholics themselves, highlighting aspects that reveal how a small, persecuted Catholic community on the margins of Chosŏn society could possess limited but recognizably modern characteristics.

Founding, Growth, and Development of the Korean Catholic Church: 1784–1801

Two founders, in particular, are noteworthy for understanding the birth of a continuous Catholic community on the Korean Peninsula: Yi Pyŏk (1754–85), who would take the name John the Baptist, and Yi Sŭnghun (1756–1801), who would be baptized Peter. In his *Silk Letter*, Alexius Hwang Sayŏng (1775–1801) wrote how Yi Sŭnghun was politically well-connected and impressed Yi Pyŏk, a formidable scholar "secretly reading Catholic books." Learning that Yi Sŭnghun would accompany his father on a 1784 tribute mission to Beijing, Yi Pyŏk approached him and told him to ask the Western missionaries there for "religious books" and to be "baptized." These actions would please them, and they would consequently give him "a lot of interesting and enjoyable things." Since Yi Sŭnghun was not particularly interested in religion then, this last statement implied that he would acquire books with valuable secular knowledge (Baker

DOI: 10.4324/9781003262053-20

227

The Routledge Handbook of Early Modern Korea

with Rausch 2017, 171). Hwang then described how Yi Sŭnghun did just as he was told and received baptism. After his return to Chosŏn, Yi began to convert family and friends, becoming the leader of the Catholic community.

The authorities soon discovered Yi Sŭnghun's activities, leading to criticism from his peers and his father to order him to leave the Catholic community (Baker with Rausch 2017, 172–73). He would vacillate, leaving and returning to the community. His final apostasy during the 1801 persecution could not prevent his execution. Likewise, Yi Pyŏk would give in to similar pressure, dying of disease shortly after Yi Sŭnghun's return. Thus, Catholicism was already under attack with familial pressure even *before* Koreans learned of the religion's stricture against ancestor rites. Once that became known in 1790, some began to leave the Catholic community, while others would redouble their loyalty to it.

Despite their fates, Yi Sŭnghun and Yi Pyŏk played central roles in establishing and growing the Catholic Church in Chosŏn. Converting to Catholicism in 1790, Alexius Hwang and Yi Sŭnghun became connected after Yi Pyŏk's death. Both were related by marriage to the prominent Southerner (Namin) aristocratic (*yangban*) Chŏng family, including Augustine Chŏng Yakchong (1760–1801), who wrote the first Korean language Catholic catechism and would die a martyr, and his brother and celebrated Practical Learning (Sirhak) scholar, Chŏng Yagyong (1762–1836). Moreover, Yi Sŭnghun, whose relationship with Yi Pyŏk had already been established, provided Hwang Sayŏng with books. Yi Pyŏk also played an essential role in the conversion of Paul Yun Chich'ung (1759–91), who, along with his cousin James Kwŏn Sangyŏn (1751–91), would be executed for not only refusing to conduct ancestor rites but also burning the tablets in their possession. While Catholic knowledge spread through books, often family and scholarly networks gave access to them.

Alexius Hwang is a complex figure. He had worked with another *yangban* Catholic, Augustine Yu Hanggŏm (1756–1801), hoping to invite a Western ship to Korea. Augustine Yu's brother, Yu Kwan'gŏm (1768–1801), argued that Western warships were so powerful that they could protect Catholics and bring Western technology and wealth for building churches, implying, at the very least, legal tolerance for the new religion. In fact, in addition to providing a record of the Korean Catholics who had died as martyrs, one of the critical reasons Hwang wrote the *Silk Letter* imploring the pope to call upon Western countries to assemble a Catholic armada to force the Chosŏn state to stop persecuting Catholics was to bring a priest into the country. The death of the only priest in Korea, James Zhou Wenmo (1752–1801), who had come from Qing dynasty (1616–1912; Later Jin until 1636) China, compelled Hwang to write the letter, and its section on martyrs presents Father Zhou's death as the climax. Hwang draws clear parallels between the priest's death and Christ's Passion (Rausch 2009; Baker with Rausch 2017).

Alexius Hwang's request for an armada to transport a priest to Korea reflects James Zhou's critical importance to the Korean Catholic community. Not only had he promoted theological education that could help Chosŏn's Catholics understand their faith more deeply than books, Father Zhou, more importantly, performed the sacraments vital in the faithful's spiritual life. His stature is evident in the case of Luthgarde Yi Suni (1782–1801). She participated in the first Easter Mass Zhou performed in Chosŏn in 1795. After receiving communion, Yi had a profound spiritual experience in which she promised to live her life as a virgin dedicated to God. As refusal to marry would only bring unwanted attention to the Catholic community as she aged, Zhou married her to a young Catholic man with the same desire: John Yu Chungch'ŏl (1779–1801), the son of Augustine Yu. The couple lived together as brother and sister until their arrest and separation. Yi was sentenced to enslavement as punishment for the actions of her father-in-law. Subsequently, however,

228

Catholicism

she demanded treatment as a Catholic and suffered execution, thus following her husband–spiritual brother to death (Rausch 2019).

As seen in Luthgarde Yi's case, Catholicism could provide a space for strong-willed women, and in such a context, Columba Kang Wansuk (1761–1801), in particular, is remarkable. Divorced by her husband following her conversion to Catholicism, she would travel to Hansŏng (present-day Seoul) and establish a community of women who wished to live celibate lives. She enjoyed certain legal protections as a *yangban* woman, particularly immunity from a government official entering her quarters. Kang used the privilege to provide a safe base of operations for Father Zhou. Noting how the priest recognized and supported Kang in her missionary work among women, Alexius Hwang praised her for caring for and protecting him. Hwang expressed admiration: "She had a clear understanding of Catholic teachings and was very good at explaining them, so she converted more people than anyone else did. In managing church matters, she was firm, decisive, and stern, and the people all stood in awe of her" (Baker with Rausch 2017, 181–82). He would also record that after her arrest, the guards, impressed by her fortitude during torture, wondered if she was divine (Baker with Rausch 2017, 182). There would be other women leaders, but none would have the same stature as Kang nor wield the power she did, making her both remarkable and unique. All the same, despite the recognition of a kind of spiritual equality between the sexes, thanks to the likes of Kang, the Korean Catholic Church remained primarily male in leadership. Also, despite her strength, she, like others mentioned, save Yi Pyŏk, would fall victim to the 1801 persecution. As the result of both partisan strife and a conviction that Catholicism was a severe moral, even existential, threat to Chosŏn, the persecution would kill hundreds of Catholics (Rausch 2012).

Rebuilding the Church, 1801–39

The 1801 persecution devastated the Korean Catholic Church, killing many, including its only priest and other leaders. Deprived of most sacraments, many members apostatized, and far more fled their homes only to find harsh lives on the margins of society. Considering that Catholics numbered only around 10,000 just before the persecution, the community would have collapsed without survivors dedicated to rebuilding the church. Indeed, that fear motivated Alexius Hwang's attempt to invite a Western armada to the peninsula. Among the survivors, Paul Yi Kyŏngŏn (1792–1827) and Paul Chŏng Hasang (1795–1839) tirelessly rebuilt the church, as examined in this section.

Both survived, perhaps because they were children, but the thoroughness of the Chosŏn government's attempts to suppress Catholicism had left them almost without any adult family members. Paul Yi and Paul Chŏng attempted to restore the faith as a family tradition and to continue it. The following discussion first considers Yi, the younger brother of two elder siblings who died as martyrs, Luthgarde Yi and Charles Yi Kyŏngdo (1780–1801). Their mother somehow survived (their father, who had led the family to conversion to Catholicism, had died of illness before the persecutions), and likely under her care and with the aforementioned family models, Paul Yi grew into a devout Catholic who would become a community leader.

Much of the surviving information on Paul Yi comes from his letters and prison journal, as he was arrested during a regional persecution in 1827. As recorded in the writings, his ordeal reveals how Korean Catholics understood and practiced their faith. For instance, in a letter to his mother and family, he expressed how happy he was to follow in the footsteps of his "martyred brother and sisters" (Richard T. Chang with Perry D. Chang 2017, 235). His spiritual models included not only Jesus and European saints but also his beloved older sister, whose martyrdom mirrored his suffer-

229

The Routledge Handbook of Early Modern Korea

ing. The contrast between his virtuous siblings and his failings, as Yi saw, also reveals the tensions that marked the Korean Catholic worldview—the "glory" of martyrdom that inspired one to die for Christ and the sense of sinfulness that could lead believers to doubt their ability to do so. Belief in the benevolence of God and his mother resolved this tension somewhat, as an excerpt from a letter he wrote to his family illustrates: "But I believe in the unlimited mercy of the Lord of Heaven and the Blessed Virgin Mary. How could they abandon me?" (Richard T. Chang with Perry D. Chang 2017, 233).

Hopes for union with God and the family drove this zeal for martyrdom. In a way similar to his sister, Paul Yi wrote in that same letter: "How glorious it would be for our mother, brothers, and sisters to gather together in the eternal country in order to praise the grace of our impartial Father" (Richard T. Chang with Perry D. Chang 2017, 234). Likewise, in another letter to his wife, Yi wrote that after his martyrdom, "I will become an envoy of the Lord who will transmit the happiness that he has decided to grant you, so that I may come to you, stand face to face with you, and take you hand in hand to the place where we shall enjoy eternal blessing" (Richard T. Chang with Perry D. Chang 2017, 236). This sentiment echoed his sister's letter to their mother, in which she promised to take her by the hand and lead her to heaven (Richard T. Chang with Perry D. Chang 2017, 192).

Though martyrdom might be glorious, suffering marked the road to that destination, and Paul Yi's journal is replete with the harsh beatings that he endured. Interrogations that sought to convince him to apostatize interspersed such torture. One interrogator played to his vanity, asking him why a handsome descendent of *yangban* who was so different "from ignorant commoners" could follow a wicked teaching like Catholicism. His response was that appearance and status were unimportant and that it was, in fact, one's knowledge of the truth that mattered (Richard T. Chang with Perry D. Chang 2017, 223). Though, in one sense, this asserted a new kind of hierarchy in terms of knowledge, it was a knowledge equally available to all human beings. That knowledge was attainable through talking to Catholics or reading books. The interrogation addressed both approaches, pressuring Yi to reveal the names of his fellow Catholics, particularly those who had taught him (he was careful only to provide the names of those he knew to be long dead), and to confess where his Catholic books were. When he claimed that he did not have any books, the interrogator did not believe him, retorting that even ignorant Catholics had many books. When shown many Catholic paintings he had created and asked if they were his, Yi responded in the affirmative. Korean Catholics were then practicing a religion of not only the written word but also visual images, likely used in private devotion or communal prayer services (Richard T. Chang with Perry D. Chang 2017, 220–21).

Besides Catholic material culture and theology, Paul Yi's writings reveal the organizational structure of the Korean Catholic Church and the emotional ties within it. According to a letter he wrote to members of the Myŏngdohoe (Association for Illuminating the Way), the association comprised cells established by Father Zhou and modeled itself on similar associations in China. The Myŏngdohoe's secretive nature, which enabled its survival, has left little information about the organization. Yi's letter nonetheless shows that it played an essential role in spreading Catholicism and facilitating communal worship. Mentioning that two catechists were connected to his cell, the letter recognizes the existence of others outside it.

Paul Yi's missive to the Myŏngdohoe also reflects a degree of tension between this world and the next Catholic faced. Anticipating martyrdom, he was somewhat optimistic. Though deeming himself weak, he was confident that God and the Virgin Mary would not forsake him. All the same, he feared for the future of the Catholic Church. Thus, after noting that the news of his arrest must have surprised and worried other members of the church, the letter states that they all "know the

Catholicism

history of how the true religion of our Lord Jesus Christ has grown" and that after working hard and with the help of the Lord of Heaven, they had been able to build a "small house" in Chosŏn. However, he would write, "Owing to harsh rains and winds that house is about to collapse." This was not simply a theoretical concern. The letter observed: "Even though here we once gathered more than 200 brethren, there were very few who endured perpetually and almost all of them apostatized" (Richard T. Chang with Perry D. Chang 2017, 244).

Paul Yi sought hope in God's power and the community's faith. He wrote that "by virtue of the protection of the kind Blessed Virgin Mary" and by their efforts, they could "preserve the small house ... and without failure ... reach the large house of the Lord of Heaven to rejoice together" (Richard T. Chang with Perry D. Chang 2017, 243). He felt especially close to one community member, Charles Hyŏn Sŏngmun (1799–1846). Their relationship had "gone beyond ordinary friendship" partly because Hyŏn was "brave enough to tell me my faults." The friendship allowed Yi to beseech Hyŏn: "[T]ake care of my wife and children" (Richard T. Chang with Perry D. Chang 2017, 244). Thus, though glorious, the death of the martyr rent asunder, if only temporarily, the bonds of affection that existed within the Catholic community. Yi hoped that the church on earth would see to the needs of those dependent upon the martyr.

While Paul Yi Kyŏngŏn focused, through the Myŏngdohoe, on sustaining a Catholic community led by Koreans, Paul Chŏng looked to Beijing, where he could contact Catholic missionaries. This was mainly because there was no priest in Korea, no one to hear confessions or offer Mass—an abnormal situation that needed urgent remedy from Chŏng's perspective. The search for priests and the sacraments that they offered shaped his life. The son of Augustine Chŏng Yakchong and his second wife, Cecilia Yu Sosa (1761–1839), Paul Chŏng, ten in 1801, must have remembered his father and the time he and his mother spent in prison before their release, as well as the martyrdom of his father and older brother Charles Chŏng Ch'ŏlsang (d. 1801). Paul Chŏng would also have remembered their wandering life, looking for a place to live as they had lost their livelihood as punishment for Augustine Chŏng's faith. Ultimately, fellow Catholics took care of them. It would seem that Paul Chŏng, like Paul Yi, chose to follow in the footsteps of his martyred family members, devote himself to the church, and marry. In 1816, he began accompanying tribute missions from Korea to China. His contact with missionaries and his direct petitioning of the pope with a letter written in 1825 ultimately resulted in the dispatch of priests to Korea in the 1830s. Yi played an essential role in guiding them successfully into the country (Rausch 2021).

The arrival of clerics and the consequent increase in the number of Catholics, combined with a new government that saw Catholicism as a serious threat, led to the persecution of 1839. The state quickly arrested Paul Chŏng. He had prepared for that day, writing a defense of Catholicism, which he would submit to the government after being taken into custody. His apologia offers a glimpse of the Korean Catholic understanding of their faith at the time, at least among educated believers such as Chŏng. Citing some notable Confucian figures, he argued that a teaching should be examined carefully before being rejected. He then offered several classical arguments for the existence of God. Then, declaring that having demonstrated God's existence and His creation of the universe, Chŏng argued that humanity owed God a debt that must be repaid by obeying God's moral law comprising two categories: the love one owed God and the love one owed to one's neighbor. After stressing that a person's eternal fate—joy in heaven or suffering in hell—depended on their response to this moral law, Chŏng emphasized that Catholicism was both true and fair: all people, whatever their status, level of education, sex, or age, were called to practice the faith. The government should, therefore, stop punishing Catholicism and end its prohibition of the religion (Kim 2005). Ultimately, his letter failed to change the government's policy. Chŏng would be

The Routledge Handbook of Early Modern Korea

killed, along with the two priests and one bishop in Chosŏn, as well as other Catholic community leaders.

Picking up the Pieces, 1839–60

Following the 1839 persecution, the Catholic Church in Korea faced a situation similar to 1801 in that its members had suffered a great deal, and the community was devasted. Nevertheless, as before, a core group of Catholics would pick up the pieces and begin to rebuild, setting the stage for significant expansion despite another persecution in 1846 that would take the life of the first Korean Catholic priest, Andrew Kim Taegŏn (1821–46). Had it not been for the persecution of 1839, Paul Chŏng, who had been studying Latin, might have been the first. As it turned out, he played a crucial role in Kim becoming Korea's first Catholic priest. Chŏng introduced him to Pierre Maubant (1803–39), the first French missionary priest to reach Korea. Looking for promising young Catholics to be sent abroad for theological training, Father Maubant sent Kim to Shanghai. He would not stay there long, though, having to seek shelter in the Philippines due to the fallout of the First Opium War (1839–42). Kim would also take breaks from his preparation for the priesthood, exploring overland and sea routes that could be used to smuggle priests onto the peninsula (Yang Insŏng 2010, 105–46). Such trips could involve braving sea voyages in a tiny boat nearly destroyed by a storm (the crew being saved by the intercession of the Holy Mother, according to Kim) and bluffing his way past Chinese border guards, if not outrunning them (Anthony and Han-Yol 2021, 87, seventh letter; 140, sixteenth letter). Excited and perhaps even exhilarated, he knew the stakes were high. Once, while returning to Chosŏn, he would, with the help of Charles Hyŏn, gather material on the persecution of 1839, which had claimed the life of his father and forced his mother from her home into a life of poverty.

Andrew Kim was well aware of the suffering Catholics could endure. In the report on the 1839 persecution, he wrote glowingly of Father Maubant and other French clerics, men whom he admired and hoped to emulate (Anthony and Han-Yol 2021, "A Report on the History of the Korean Martyrs," 181–85). He would also write an entry on Chŏng Hasang. Noting the failure of Chŏng's apology for Catholicism to sway the hearts of government officials, Kim described how the apologist tortured so badly was covered in blood with his cracked bones protruding and the marrow oozing. Like the priests, Chŏng died bravely as a martyr (Anthony and Han-Yol 2021, "A Report on the History of the Korean Martyrs," 207–10). In the same work, Kim included the hagiography of one Lucy Kim (d. 1839), who, like him, had vowed celibacy. He praised her for her good work, particularly her attention to the poor. Upon arrest, Lucy Kim ignored her interrogator's praises of her beauty and grace, making the interrogator change tactics and attempt to argue her out of her faith. Just over 20, the young woman quite easily responded to his arguments. Infuriated, he had her tortured terribly, but she met it with joy, confounding her enemies, who told one another that she must be possessed. As further efforts failed to convince her to apostatize, she suffered execution (Anthony and Han-Yol 2021, "A Report on the History of the Korean Martyrs," 204–06).

In the end, Andrew Kim, ordained as a priest in 1845, would be captured during one of his scouting missions and martyred in 1846. Like the martyrs he described, Father Kim would meet his death bravely and even exhort those watching his execution to embrace the faith. Emphasizing that he had not betrayed his country, Kim asserted that he had only sought contact with foreigners so Koreans could better learn about Catholicism and obtain salvation (Han'guk Kyohoesa 2021, "Ex Processu 1857," 287).

While exalting in his international connections, they also challenged Andrew Kim with conflicting attitudes toward the relationship between Chosŏn Korea and the outside world. As much

Catholicism

as he was a proud subject of Chosŏn, what he deemed the government's irrational persecution of Catholicism, claiming the lives of many he held dear, frustrated him. Also, he was ashamed of what he saw as the ignorance of his country. When Father Kim's interrogators confronted him with letters he and a bishop had written in Latin, they could not read them but could still see that they were products of a different hand. Wishing to protect the bishop, Kim claimed that he had written both and could not recreate the writing without a proper Western pen. He then showed how he could write in different ways using a quill, thus convincing the interrogators that both letters belonged to him, even though one was his and the other was from the bishop. He understood this as showing the comparative ignorance of the representatives of the Chosŏn state. Kim recalled the incident in the letter to a French priest: "You will understand, Monsignor, that our Korean scholars are not up to the level of European scholars" (Anthony and Han-Yol 2021, twentieth letter, 240–41). All the same, he noted that Europeans seemed unwilling to do anything significant to help Catholics in Korea and that the French tendency to sail ships ineffectually around the peninsula without taking any consequential action only emboldened the Chosŏn government to persecute Catholics (Anthony and Han-Yol 2021, twentieth letter, 242).

Thomas Ch'oe Yangŏp (1821–61), the second Korean priest, would leave behind many important letters providing insight into Chosŏn's Catholic Church. These could differ in tone from Andrew Kim, for instance, revealing more spiritual conflict. For instance, in a letter written in 1849 after failing to enter Chosŏn, Father Ch'oe expressed his frustration that he was "writing again from this land of exile," by which he meant Shanghai, and that he had accomplished nothing after an attempt to enter the country via a sea route (Ch'oe Yangŏp 1995, sixth letter, 46). Such statements reflected his difficult situation and the theological dilemmas it had raised. After all, he, his fellow priests, and some lay Korean Catholics had been striving to enter Chosŏn to spread the Gospel—yet God had permitted the Catholic community to suffer multiple persecutions and the martyrdom of the first Korean priest. In a letter written in 1854, this time after finally entering Chosŏn, he would lament that a French missionary priest, whom they had assisted in entering the country, had fallen ill and died after a short time (Ch'oe Yangŏp 1995, tenth letter, 110). Why would God allow such things to happen? In that 1849 letter written from "exile," Ch'oe answered the question by arguing that although their plans had been unsuccessful thus far, they did not consider themselves as having failed. They should follow Jesus by willingly accepting their suffering in the knowledge that many saints might have had to pray and perform acts of sacrifice for decades before God responded, Ch'oe wrote.

Believing that God might have allowed this suffering for their reliance on the help of humans rather than God's angels, Thomas Ch'oe included a plaintive prayer asking that he may do God's will, even if it meant "being cast into the deep sea." Such prayers seemed to have consoled him. In the same letter, Father Ch'oe also described his reaction to his ordination. While describing it as a great burden for someone as "lowly" and "weak" as him, Ch'oe was grateful that he would be able to offer Mass (Ch'oe Yangŏp 1995, sixth letter, 46–52). In another letter, he stated that despite his difficulties, he was happy to live an "apostolic life," for which he obtained special graces from God (Ch'oe Yangŏp 1995, seventeenth letter, 162).

Thomas Ch'oe would need such consolation, as he would suffer greatly following his successful entry into Chosŏn in 1850. Historiography of Korean Catholicism tends to focus on the years of great persecution and refers to persecutions by the years in which they took place, for example, the persecution of 1801. However, outside of these years, Catholics could still suffer for their faith, even if it was only from the ever-present fear that persecution would break out again. For example, Father Ch'oe noted in one letter that a decade had passed since the persecution of 1839, the "scars" remained and that the stories of those who survived tore at his heart. Lamenting that "it is as if all

233

The Routledge Handbook of Early Modern Korea

of the laws, conventions, and customs only seek to prevent the people of Chosŏn from following the commandments of Catholicism," Ch'oe described how Catholics had to flee to mountains to keep their faith and survive by growing tobacco and living poor lives in mud huts. Even then, they could not stay long because eventually, non-Catholics would learn about them, and they would have to move again out of fear of being apprehended (Ch'oe Yangŏp 1995, eighth letter, 87–89).

Thus, Thomas Ch'oe could lament in one letter that "though there is no serious persecution, there is also no freedom to spread Catholicism." As the proclamation forbidding the religion was still in effect, people could do whatever they liked to Catholics. Corrupt officials would take advantage of the law to seize Catholic property. Later, in the same letter but written at a different time, a testament to how quickly the situation could change, he described a more systematic persecution, noting that Catholics were being driven from their homes, losing their lands and goods. Officials and their underlings even went after non-Catholics who had ties to Catholics, leading fearful villagers to expel Catholics from their settlements. Realizing that it could not possibly apprehend all Catholics, the government sought to sew chaos and stir the people up against them. Such a slow, grinding persecution was even worse for Catholics, forcing many to drift away from the faith, Father Ch'oe explained. Although many people likely believed that they could not become Catholics under such circumstances, if the situation were more similar to China, where Catholics enjoyed more freedom to work following the First Opium War, Catholics in Korea could expect better results, he observed (Ch'oe Yangŏp 1995, eighth letter, 90).

Considering these circumstances, Thomas Ch'oe greatly admired the suffering people endured to practice Catholicism or to learn more about it. He mentioned a 15-year-old *yangban* girl fleeing home to learn about Catholicism despite her father's disapproval. However, on the road, she was kidnapped by a non-Catholic who forced her to marry him. She wanted to run away again but had nowhere to go and was afraid she would be kidnapped again. Thus, for more than a decade, she could not learn more about Catholicism until a chance meeting with a Catholic gave her access to books on the religion. Even so, Father Ch'oe could not meet her to offer the sacraments (Ch'oe Yangŏp 1995, seventh letter, 57–58). In another case showing the additional vulnerability of female Catholics because of their sex, a mixed group of Catholic men, women, and girls on their way to meet him to receive the sacraments encountered a group of armed men intent on raping the females. Rather miraculously, an elderly man shamed them into retreating, allowing the faithful to continue their journey (Ch'oe Yangŏp 1995, thirteenth letter, 132–33). Likewise, a group of avowed perpetual virgins—led by one Agatha known and respected in the Catholic community—suffered arrest by constables, even though they had been ordered not to take females into custody. Sensing the risk of being violated, the women entreated their captors to let them go. According to Ch'oe, this calmed those constables' "beast-like lust," and they let the women go. Their leader Agatha would be forced to wander until she found him. Though obtaining refuge, her suffering led her to take ill and die (Ch'oe Yangŏp 1995, nineteenth letter, 172–73).

Thomas Ch'oe did his best to aid such women. For instance, a mixed household would sometimes consist of non-Catholic men and Catholic women. In such a case, word would be delivered to him when the family patriarch left his home to care for some matter. He would then visit, posing as a simple guest. The Catholic women would then need to provide for his needs in the name of offering hospitality, allowing him to administer the sacraments to them (Ch'oe Yangŏp 1995, eighth letter, 82–83). If the patriarch was only absent for a short time, Father Thomas might simply be secreted into the house, quickly offer absolution and give communion without saying Mass, and then make his escape (Ch'oe Yangŏp 1995, seventh letter, 59). He seems to have come to a deep understanding of the difficulties faced by women, writing sensitively about them, as seen in his description of the death of one Barbara, a young Catholic woman who desired to live as a perpetual

Catholicism

virgin. The French Catholic bishop, though, had refused permission to do so and insisted that she marry, fearful that living conspicuously as a single woman would bring unwanted attention to the community. When Barbara refused this command, the cleric denied her communion. Church law nonetheless allowed someone in her situation to receive communion if she was in danger of death. She fell ill, and as she lay dying, Ch'oe visited her and administered the sacrament before her death. His sensitive description of the situation and respect for Barbara's piety reveals the tensions within the persecuted Catholic community, which celebrated celibacy but also emphasized clerical authority (Ch'oe Yangŏp 1995, seventh letter 63–74; Torrey 2018).

Undoubtedly, Thomas Ch'oe experienced many difficulties. While visiting a village to give the sacraments, a non-Catholic headman heard he was there and, from the early afternoon to night, insulted and threatened Father Ch'oe, calling him a "dirty Westerner" and a bandit. Though the headman finally relented and Ch'oe could get some sleep, in the middle of the night, he fled after the local catechist warned him that he should do so (Ch'oe Yangŏp 1995, seventh letter, 56–57). Things could be worse. On one occasion, constables surrounded the house where he was offering the sacraments. The Catholics resisted their attempts at entry, allowing the priest to escape through the back gate with his accoutrements needed to say Mass but without his shoes. Several Catholics would be arrested, their fate seemingly unknown (Ch'oe Yangŏp 1995, twelfth letter, 120–22). In another case, he had to brave knee-deep snow to escape his pursuers (Ch'oe Yangŏp 1995, seventeenth letter, 161–62). Not surprisingly, he noted in a letter written a year before he died that he was too weak to walk his pastoral circuit anymore and had to ride a horse—a significant expense for the impoverished Catholic community (Ch'oe Yangŏp 1995, eighteenth letter, 167).

Nonetheless, Thomas Ch'oe saw in these adversities rays of hope that consoled him. The ability of Catholics to maintain their faith amidst such difficulties impressed him, as well as the gratitude they showed him. One isolated Catholic woman he visited stated that having "heard the word of God from the mouth of a priest," she could now die at peace (Ch'oe Yangŏp 1995, thirteenth letter, 130). Similarly, Father Ch'oe described how Catholics would turn out to greet him when he entered their village in their new clothes and would begin to cry "an ocean's worth of tears" when he put on his traveling clothes. Many grabbed his sleeves to prevent him from leaving; others climbed mountain peaks to watch his departure for as long as possible (Ch'oe Yangŏp 1995, seventh letter, 62–63). On another occasion, he found particularly moving the story of a young man who, having learned of Catholicism, pestered a suspicious catechist until he agreed to teach him more, hand-copied Catholic books, and then went off to convince friends and relatives to join the new religion (Ch'oe Yangŏp 1995, thirteenth letter, 134–35). Ch'oe would react joyfully at the news that in 1857, the pope had declared eighty-two martyrs of Korea venerable and that they could one day be canonized saints (Ch'oe Yangŏp 1995, seventeenth letter, 158–59). His careful recording of the martyrdom of his parents during the persecution of 1839 in these letters was likely not only inspiring to him but also might have led him to hope that they would one day count among that number (Ch'oe Yangŏp 1995, eighth letter, 96–109). Moreover, he found hope in the supernatural power Catholicism seemingly offered—such as when those who believed they were accosted by demons reported being delivered from them upon conversion to the faith (Ch'oe Yangŏp 1995, thirteenth letter, 135–36).

Though happy with the support of the Korean faithful, Thomas Ch'oe was frustrated with the French government's inaction. He firmly believed that if France were to act with resolve and dispatch a fleet, it could compel the Chosŏn government to tolerate Catholicism. After all, France only made empty threats, thus emboldening Chosŏn's officials to persecute Catholics with impunity. He seems to have been aware that pressure from Western governments had given Catholicism more space in China and likely wanted the same for Korea. He also recognized that non-Catholic

The Routledge Handbook of Early Modern Korea

Koreans were critical of Catholicism owing to its secrecy and saw the French as pirates (Ch'oe Yangŏp 1995, nineteenth letter, 175–76). Perhaps he hoped that if French pressure could force the Chosŏn state to tolerate Catholicism, that would allow Catholic mission work to proceed in the open, allowing more Koreans to learn the truth about the religion and convert. Such a hypothesis would be proven incorrect: anti-Christian movements would expand in China and emerge in Korea following Western pressure for toleration.

What Thomas Ch'oe thought about Western imperialism or modernity is hard to assess, but he certainly was critical of the Chosŏn state and society, even in areas not directly touching on religion. For instance, he deplored the limitations on *yangban* women's freedom of movement and the demands of chaste widowhood. Likewise, he spoke against the overall paramount position of *yangban* and rampant corruption among government officials that amounted to the "extortion" of burdensome taxes and surcharges from the general population. At one point, he referred to the "Republic of France"—indicating his interest in an alternative to the monarchy—and tantalizingly noted that he had many things to say about changes that could be made in Korea but would not provide them. Instead, he limited himself to describing an illness afflicting Koreans and noting that he believed it came from drinking dirty water. He wondered if the priest he was writing to knew of any water purification method (Ch'oe Yangŏp 1995, seventh letter, 77). Father Ch'oe was circumspect in his letters, for instance, not providing the full names of any living Korean Catholics. He likely wanted to avoid saying anything the authorities could take as treasonous and thus see Catholicism in a bad light. Had he lived to 1886, the year the treaty between Chosŏn Korea and France effectively brought toleration of Catholicism, Ch'oe would have had the freedom to pontificate on themes of modernity and reform. As it was, however, the hard life he lived would eventually cause him to fall ill and die to the great regret of the Korean Catholic community and the missionary priests who served it. The Korean Catholic community would have to wait for another Korean priest until 1897, when Paul Han Kigŭn (1868–1939) received ordination.

Highs and Lows, 1860–66

Although Thomas Ch'oe's death was a devasting loss for Korean Catholics, their church was still quite healthy in many ways. By 1865, a dozen French priests (though several suffered from severe illness), a small seminary, and printing press served more than twenty thousand Catholics (Rausch 2021). Also, such Korean Catholics as John the Baptist Nam Chongsam (1817–66) were developing political connections that some Catholics hoped would grant them the freedom to practice their religion without fear of persecution. John the Baptist Nam was the adopted son of Augustine Nam Sanggyo (1784–1866), who had been a high-ranking government official before resigning, an act he took partly because state service would require him to engage in rituals forbidden by Catholicism. John the Baptist Nam would face a similar situation and find making a lasting choice difficult. Under the influence of his adopted father, his reading of Confucianism, and his meeting with Catholics, including Bishop Siméon-François Berneux (1814–66), he would come to believe that Catholicism was true (Yi Wŏnsun 2009, 80–83). At the same time, as a scholar who had to support a large family, he would also seek to be an official. Conflicted, he thus moved back and forth between the Catholic and official worlds.

John the Baptist Nam would eventually find himself fatally drawn into politics. In late 1865, Russian forces would encroach on Korean territory, causing great concern in the Chosŏn government. Some Korean Catholics believed that if the good offices of their French clergy could involve the French government in resolving the issue, that could lead to freedom for their reli-

Catholicism

gion. They were not without reasons for hope. By then, Nam was a tutor to King Kojong (r. 1864–1907; emperor from 1897), still a minor, and one of his former wet nurses was a Catholic, Martha Pak (d. 1868). Also, Kojong's mother was sympathetic to Catholicism—and would receive baptism in 1897. Eventually, Nam, who had learned much about the world beyond East Asia from the French clergy he had been in contact with, was drawn into the idea of seeking the good offices of the French government. He wrote to Kojong's father and de facto regent, Hŭngsŏn Taewŏn'gun (1821–98), proposing to arrange treaties in Nagasaki with Britain and France with the help of the French missionaries (Figure 15.1). A cordial meeting followed, despite the Taewŏn'gun's inquiry about the Catholic refusal to conduct ancestor rites. When the Taewŏn'gun asked him to arrange a meeting with Bishop Berneux, Nam presented a plan in

Figure 15.1 Portrait of Hŭngsŏn Taewŏn'gun painted by Yi Hanch'ŏl (b. 1808), 1869. Introduced to Catholicism by Martha Pak, the regent's wife, Lady Yŏhŭng Min (1818–98), would later receive baptism (1896). Source: Seoul Museum of History. Photo credit: Korean Heritage Service.

The Routledge Handbook of Early Modern Korea

traditional Sino–Korean terms: "using barbarians to control barbarians" (*i I che I*). Regardless, the proposal was a major shift away from a policy of isolation and rejecting Western ideas (Yi Wŏnsun 2009, 103–10).

The meeting, however, did not take place. Bishop Berneux was away on his circuit, visiting Catholics to provide the sacraments, and before any meeting could take place, Russian forces withdrew. Also, conservative forces within the Chosŏn government seem to have learned of the Taewŏn'gun's meetings with John the Baptist Nam and other Catholics, possibly thanks to the imprudent spreading of rumors by Catholics that religious freedom would soon come. The Taewŏn'gun feared that he might not only lose the support of conservative officials but also elicit challenges to his position as the de facto regent—which had no precedent in Chosŏn history. Thus, when Nam sought a follow-up meeting with the Taewŏn'gun, he received a cold shoulder, leading him to flee Hansŏng in fear. Several weeks later, he decided to return to the city, but not before stopping in Paeron, Chech'ŏn, where the Catholic seminary was located, so that he could make his confession. He was preparing to die (Yi Wŏnsun 2009, 110–18).

John the Baptist Nam was arrested shortly after returning to Hansŏng, where he would be interrogated and tortured. Responding to accusations of betraying the country, he asserted that had he not spoken up and made an effort to deal with the Russian threat by utilizing the means at hand, his French connections, it risked the country's fate. On the contrary, he only risked his life by taking action, thus acting for the good of his country. At the same time, he asserted that Catholicism was the true way. Moreover, upon reaching Hansŏng city wall's southwestern gate, Sŏsomun, the place of his execution, Nam proclaimed he had by no means sold out his country and that he would suffer gladly for eternal joy in heaven (Yi Wŏnsun 2009, 118–35).

The persecution that would take the life of John the Baptist Nam in 1866 was not so much the climax of violence against Catholics at the time as only the beginning. Of the 12 French clerics in Korea, 2 bishops and 7 priests died in 1866, whereas 3 others escaped. Violence would continue against Catholics, flaring up in the autumn of that year when one priest served as a guide for a French incursion; in 1868, when another priest did the same for Ernst Oppert (1832–1903), a German businessman-adventurer whose crew sought to break into the tomb of the Taewŏn'gun's father to steal his remains for negotiation for trade and the end of anti-Catholic persecution; and in 1871, when an American incursion briefly seized the fortifications on Kanghwado, a strategic island at the mouth of the Han River, which flows through Hansŏng. The actualization of foreign threats and perceived Catholic connections to them led to the persecution taking thousands of lives rather than the hundreds, as they had done in the past.

Final Thoughts

Change awaited. The end of the Taewŏn'gun's rule in 1873 led to an increasingly open foreign policy. French priests would secretly enter the country in May 1876, a few months after Chosŏn Korea and Japan's Treaty of Kanghwado stipulated relations and the opening of ports for trade. While Chosŏn's Catholics would continue to die at the hands of the government in small numbers, no more foreign clerics would suffer death. Moreover, though it would not end all the difficulties faced by Catholics, the 1886 treaty between Korea and France gave the community enough protection that Catholics could gather and worship publicly.

As seen from the lives and words of the Catholics examined above, Chosŏn Korea's acceptance of Catholicism was unfeasible without an openness to new ideas that conflicted with traditional modes of thought. This openness could move beyond simply religious ideas to a knowledge of radically different forms of political authority, such as the republic and science and technology, as well as a greater belief in the positive nature of interactions with the outside world. In a society governed by a state hostile to Catholicism, the very act of becoming Catholic or maintaining the faith in the face of persecution could, in many cases, reflect a critical reflection on traditional modes of thought and assertion of the individual will against traditional authority. Also, while gender and status hierarchies certainly existed within Chosŏn's Catholic Church, a willingness to die for this faith led to the celebration of men and women, elites and nonelites, as martyrs, equality in death that led them to the same glory in heaven. A celibate man, Thomas Ch'oe, wrote critically about *yangban* society and movingly about the plight of women, recording how they could, in their quest for Catholic knowledge and the sacraments, assert their equal individuality. Moreover, while earlier Catholics seemed to have dreamed of a Catholic dynastic state, their descendants were more open to a pluralistic society where Catholics were free to practice and spread their religion. Sadly, Chosŏn's Catholic movement towards modernity made them enemies of the state.

As seen in this overview, the conflict that arose between Catholics and the Chosŏn state, in part because of the former's arguably modern character, led to their misery as humans. In addition to martyrdom, Catholics faced humiliation, exile, and sexual assault. Even when not facing active persecution, a gnawing fear that one could break out at any time lingered. In the face of suffering, they sought to find hope through their community; in the priests, whom they welcomed joyously and parted from sadly, climbing a mountain to catch at least one last glimpse; in reflection on the sufferings of Jesus; in the help they believed came from the Holy Mother, the saints, and angels; and in a heaven in which they would find joy with God and be reunified with their family, made whole and healed from their wounds. The small victories—be it a narrow escape, the delivery of the sacraments to a person cut off from the community, or recognition by the pope of the glory of Chosŏn's martyrs—inspired the courage to stay faithful. This way, this community would survive and play its role in early modern Korea.

Note

1. This work was supported by the Fostering a New Wave of K-Academics Program of the Ministry of Education of the Republic of Korea and the Korean Studies Promotion Service (KSPS) at the Academy of Korean Studies (AKS-2021-KDA-1250010).

References

Anthony and Han-Yol, of the Community of Taizé. 2021. *The Letters of Saint Andrew Kim Dae-geon*. The Research Foundation of Church History.

Baker, Don, with Franklin Rausch. 2017. *Catholics and Anti-Catholicism in Chosŏn Korea*. University of Hawai'i Press.

Chang, Richard T., with Perry D. Chang. 2017. *Be Faithful Until Death: The Study of the Jail Letters of the Blessed Martyr Lutgarda Yi Suni and Her Brothers*. Martyr's Pulse Publishing Co.

Ch'oe Yangŏp. 1995. *Nŏ nŭn chuch'u nok'o na nŭn seugo*. Translated by Chŏng Chinsŏk. Paoro ttal.

Han'guk kyohoesa yŏn'guso. 2021. *Sŏng Kim Taegŏn Andŭrea: Sinbu ŭi ch'ep'o wa sun'gyo*. Han'guk kyohoesa yŏn'guso.

Kim, Jae-Hyun. 2005. "Sang-jaesang-seo." By Paul Chong Ha-sang. Translated by Won Jae-Hur. *KIATS Theological Journal* 1, no. 2 (Fall): 133–47.

Rausch, Franklin. 2009. "Wicked Officials and Virtuous Martyrs: An Analysis of the Martyr Biographies in Alexius Hwang Sayŏng's *Silk Letter*." *Kyohoesa yŏn'gu*, no. 32 (July): 5–30.

Rausch, Franklin. 2012. "Like Birds and Beasts: Justifying Violence against Catholics in Late Chosŏn Dynasty Korea." *Acta Koreana* 15, no. 1 (June): 43–71.

The Routledge Handbook of Early Modern Korea

Rausch, Franklin. 2019. "Choosing to Die: Catholic Voluntary Martyrdom in Late Chosŏn Korea." In *Beyond Death: The Politics of Suicide and Martyrdom in Korea*, edited by Charles Kim, Jungwon Kim, Hwasook Nam, Serk-Bae Suh, and Clark Sorenson, 87–111. University of Washington Press.

Rausch, Franklin. 2021. "Foreign Missionaries in Korea in the Nineteenth Century." In *The Palgrave Handbook of the Catholic Church in East Asia*, edited by Cindy Yik-yi Chu and Beatrice Leung. Palgrave Macmillan, Singapore. https://doi.org/10.1007/978-981-15-9365-9_17-1.

Torrey, Deberniere. 2018. "Young Barbara's Devotion and Death: Reading Father Ch'oe's Field Report of 1850." *Korean Studies* 42: 17–40.

Yang Insŏng. 2010. "Chosŏnin saje ŭi tŭngjang." In *Han'guk Ch'ŏnju kyohoesa* 3, edited by Han'guk kyohoesa yŏn'guso, 105–46. Kyohoesa yŏn'guso.

Yi Wŏnsun. 2009. *Sŏngin Nam Chongsam kwa kŭ ilga ŭi Ch'ŏnju sinang*. Kippŭn sosik.

PART V

Language, Learning, and Knowledge

16
LANGUAGE

Ross King

Discussions of "*kŭndae*" (modern) Korean present an array of challenges in terms of linguistic periodization. According to the standard nomenclature of South Korean historical linguistics, the term *kŭndae kugŏ* ("national language of the modern era") refers to the language found in texts of Korea ruled by the Chosŏn state (1392–1897), dating from the years after the Imjin War (East Asian War; 1592–98) until the Kabo Reform (1894–96). That is, *kŭndae kugŏ* typically refers to the language of the early seventeenth to late nineteenth centuries. Thus, it is differentiated from the language of texts from the immediately preceding mid-fifteenth to late sixteenth centuries, which is referred to as *chungse kugŏ* ("national language of the middle ages"); *kŭndae kugŏ* is usually treated as a transition period between *chungse kugŏ* and the contemporary language. Following now classic treatments of Korean linguistic history by scholars like Yi Kimun (1972), most South Korean periodizations look like this:

- *Chŏn'gi chungse kugŏ* (Early Middle Korean): late fourteenth century–1446 (the promulgation of the indigenous Korean script).
- *Hugi chungse kugŏ* (Late Middle Korean; LMK): mid-fifteenth century–Imjin War.
- *Kŭndae kugŏ* (Modern Korean): early seventeenth century–late nineteenth century.
- *Hyŏndae kugŏ* (Contemporary Korean): since the late nineteenth century.

Of course, the term *kŭndae* is usually rendered as "modern" in English, but in the case of linguistic periodizations, this creates a problem. Lee and Ramsey (2011) equate *kŭndae kugŏ* with "Early Modern Korean" and refer to everything thereafter as "Contemporary Korean." To make matters more confusing, some South Korean researchers like Hong Chongsŏn (1998) would prefer to subdivide *kŭndae kugŏ* into early and late periods, a classification which necessitates distinguishing in English between "Early Early Modern Korean" (closer to LMK) and "Late Early Modern Korean" (closer to Contemporary Korean). Some researchers have advocated for distinguishing a separate "Enlightenment Period Korean" (*kaehwagi kugŏ*) for a short period from the 1890s until the Japanese annexation of Korea in 1910. The problem is that language change "does not have to follow other historical developments" (Kopaczyk 2012, 234).

But what is the basis for the Korean periodization, and what does *kŭndae* mean here? Can we speak of an "early modern" form of Korean? If so, what are its distinguishing characteristics? The

DOI: 10.4324/9781003262053-22

243

The Routledge Handbook of Early Modern Korea

following pages address these questions before discussing alternatives to the fundamental disconnect between the periodizations used in Korean historical linguistics and those used in Korean history and literature.

Early Modern Korean (EMK) According to Language-Internal Criteria

The references above to the Imjin War and the Kabo Reform suggest some role for language-external criteria in periodizing Korean linguistic history, but strictly speaking, clusters of significant linguistic changes should guide linguistic periodization. Hong Chongsŏn (1998), Hong Yunp'yo (2009), and Lee and Ramsey (2011) outline the main sources for and features of this stage of the language. In terms of textual sources for EMK, whereas sources for LMK are almost exclusively *ŏnhae* texts: vernacular exegeses of or cribs to classical (mostly Buddhist) texts in Literary Sinitic (Ko. *hanmun*). In contrast, EMK texts include both *ŏnhae* versions of a considerably wider variety of Literary Sinitic texts, reprinted but revised versions of LMK *ŏnhae* texts, as well as translations (mainly from Literary Sinitic but also from Mongolian, Manchu, Japanese, English, and French, among others), and texts composed directly in vernacular Korean.[1]

EMK Phonological Changes[2]

Consonants

1. The LMK voiced fricatives ㅸ /W/, ㅿ /z/, and what Martin (1992) calls "big *G*" (presumably a voiced velar fricative pronounced [ɣ]) drop out of the language, as does the letter for ㆁ /ng/. In EMK, -ㄹㄹ- –*ll*- or (especially in later EMK) -ㄹㄴ- –*ln*- replaced earlier orthographic sequences of -*lG*-.
2. The series of tense unaspirated/reinforced consonants (*kk, tt, pp, cc*, but with varying spellings; the spelling ㅺ *sc* was new to EMK) resulting from earlier LMK consonant clusters becomes established. Early seventeenth-century texts confuse the spellings of *psk-, sk-*, and *pk-*. All such consonant cluster spellings presumably reflected the new reinforced consonant series by the mid-seventeenth century. Lee and Ramsey (2011) note a general spread of reinforcement and aspiration in EMK.

Vowels

1. The "arae a" vowel · *o* had already started to merge with ㅡ *u* in non-initial syllables in the sixteenth century but remained distinctive in first syllables in the seventeenth century before merging with ㅏ *a* in the eighteenth century. This dephonologization of · *o* led to chaos in spelling, as it continued to be (mis-) spelled and confused with ㅏ *a* and ㅡ *u* well into the twentieth century.
2. Sometime after the change of earlier ·ㅣ *oy* to ㅐ *ay*, the LMK diphthongs ㅐ [ay] and ㅔ [əy] were monophthongized as /æ/ and /e/, respectively, yielding the following new eight-monophthong vowel system sometime between the seventeenth and eighteenth centuries:

   a. ㅣ *i* [i]   ㅡ *u* [ɨ]   ㅜ *wu* [u]
   b. ㅔ *ey* [e]   ㅓ *e* [ə]   ㅗ *wo* [o]
   c. ㅐ *ay* [æ]   ㅏ *a* [a]

   Monophthongization is supposed to have occurred after losing the "arae a" vowel · *o*.

244

Language

3. Later in the EMK period, the diphthongs ㅚ *woy* and ㅟ *wuy* became monophthongized in some dialects as [ö] and [ü], respectively (but mostly reverted to diphthongs in the contemporary language).
4. The various changes in the abovementioned vowel system weakened the formerly more robust LMK vowel harmony system. Whereas in LMK, the vowels — *u* and ㆍ *o* were vowel harmonic opposites, in EMK, — *u* became a neutral vowel with respect to vowel harmony (like ㅣ *i*). Another change that contributed to an erosion of vowel harmony was the raising of ㅗ *wo* to ㅜ *wu* in non-initial syllables (for example, LMK *poyhwo-* "learn, study" → EMK *poywu-*).

Prosody

The pitch accent dots (one to the left for High, two to the left for Rising, unmarked for Low) dropped out of the language. Thus, whereas LMK was in some sense a "tone language," EMK lost this feature. Distinctive pitch accent, however, remains in northeastern and southeastern dialects to this day. One reflex of the Rising pitch in initial syllables was vowel length. Though never reflected in spelling, this feature sometimes surfaces in EMK texts in the case of long versus short ㅓ *e*: long ㅓ *e* shows up in some late nineteenth-century texts as — *u*, reflecting a difference in not only quantity but quality for this long vowel.

Sound Changes

1. *T*-palatalization (and *k*- and *h*-palatalization in some dialects): along with the dephonologization of the "arae a" vowel, this was probably the most distinctive sound change in EMK. According to Lee and Ramsey (2011), "palatalization must have occurred during the latter half of the seventeenth or in the eighteenth century." The first significant shift was the change in the pronunciation of ㅈ *c* (and ㅊ *ch*, ㅉ *cc*) from [ʦ] → [ʧ] /__*i, y* (before *i* or *y*). After this change, ㄷ *t* (and ㅌ *th*, ㄸ *tt*) affricated and palatalized in the same environment: from [t] → ㅈ [ʦ] / __*i, y*, after which ㅈ [ʦ] → [ʧ] /__*i, y*. The only dialects to escape these developments were P'yŏngan in the northwest and Yukchin in the far northeast tip of Hamgyŏng. At the beginning of the nineteenth century, 듸 *tuy*, 틔 *thuy*, 띄 *ttuy* changed to 디 *ti*, 티 *thi*, 띠 *tti*, giving rise to those consonant-vowel combinations anew.
2. Fronting caused by the vowel ㅣ *i* (often, somewhat misleadingly, referred to as "umlaut" in South Korean scholarship). Thus, we find changes like /*api*/ → /*aypi*/ → [æbi].
3. Loss of ㄴ *n* before *i, y*, as in the word for "tooth": 니 *ni* → 이 *i*. The spellings for Sino–Korean pronunciations tended to be more conservative about this rule than those for native Korean words. In general, spellings treated Sino–Korean readings more conservatively than native Korean words.
4. Fronting of — [ɨ] to ㅣ [i] after ㅈ *c* (ㅊ *ch*, ㅉ *cc*) and ㅅ *s* (primarily a nineteenth-century phenomenon, and only in certain regions). This change began in non-initial syllables but soon spread to initial syllables.
5. Vowel rounding/labialization. For example, 믈 *mul* → 물 *mwul*, 주근 *cwukun* → 주군 *cwuk-wun*. Examples of regressive assimilation are also found: 기름 *kilum* → 기룸 *kilwum*.
6. Loss of *h* in voiced environments, including, by the end of EMK, the loss of final ...ㅎ ...*h* in the eighty or so nouns that ended in this consonant in LMK.
7. The earlier rule whereby the final ㄹ *l* deleted before following ㄷ *t* disappears at the end of the nineteenth century (and deleted ㄹ *l* is reinstated).

The Routledge Handbook of Early Modern Korea

8. Noun-final consonants were simplified (restructured) and streamlined for the most part to just seven in spelling: ㄱ *k*, ㄴ *n*, ㅁ *m*, ㅂ *p*, ㅅ *s*, ㅇ *ng*, ㄹ *l*). This entailed the change of many earlier LMK *t*-final nouns to -*s* and posed challenges to the representation of underlying final ...*t* and ...*c* as well as final aspirates. Of particular interest are cases that involve palatalization and affrication like LMK 벋이 *pet i* "friend-Nominative" → 벚이 *pec i* → Modern 벗 *pes*. Also: 뜯 *ptut* ("meaning, sense, intention") → Modern 뜻 **ttus**, 곧 *kwot* ("place") → Modern 곳 **kos**.

EMK Grammatical Changes

Lee and Ramsey (2011, 267) note a "tendency toward simplification" in EMK grammar compared to LMK but also remark that "it is undeniably difficult ⋯ to ascertain through the textual record which grammatical changes took place in the Early Modern period and not before." Research on newly discovered epistolary sources (*ŏn'gan*, that is, letters written in Han'gŭl) over the past two decades has revealed many forms and phenomena not previously seen in *kanbon* (printed, dated texts) and has also shown that many changes thought to have originated in EMK were already well underway before the seventeenth century:

1. The LMK morpheme ㅅ *s* that attached to a noun when it modified a following noun (in compounds) gradually fell out of the language.
2. The LMK adnominal ㅅ *s* for inanimate and honorific nouns dropped out of the language by the mid-seventeenth century. By the early nineteenth century, the genitive 의 *uy* had mostly pushed out its vowel harmonic alter ego 이 *oy*.
3. Whereas nominalizations in LMK were created overwhelmingly with -옴/ -움 -*wom/-wum*, in the seventeenth century, the innovating ending in -기 -*ki* began to replace them. Indeed, -기 -*ki* is a typical diagnostic form for EMK.
4. Changes in the inventory of particles and endings: nominative particle 가 *ka* is clearly in evidence in the seventeenth century, occurring in restricted cases after forms (usually pronouns) ending in *y*. However, like many other forms now prevalent in Contemporary Korean, foreign missionaries first reported it in the late nineteenth century. Honorific nominative 씌셔 *skuysye*; comparative 도곤 *twokwon*, replaced in later EMK by comparative 보다가 *pwotaka*, the direct ancestor of Contemporary 보다 **pota**; loss of honorific vocative 하 *ha*.
5. The verbal morpheme -오/우- -*wo/wu*- (called the "volitive" by South Korean linguists) fell out of the language.
6. The LMK tripartite system of honorifics (subject honorification), deferentials (object honorification), and politeness changed to just honorifics and politeness, as the LMK deferential/object honorific in -숳- -*zoW*- became incorporated into a new politeness system. Thus, the EMK polite endings -옵닝이다 -*opnoyng.ita*, -옵니이다 -*opnoyita*, -옵ᄂ이다 -*opnoita* all trace back to the Middle Korean form -숩ᄂ이다 -*zopno.ngita*.
7. The LMK system that distinguished Yes–No interrogatives in -가 -*ka* from WH-interrogatives in -고 -*kwo* was seriously eroded in favor of -가 -*ka*, and the earlier system of nominal interrogatives in just Noun + -가 -*ka* or Noun + -고 -*kwo* changed to a copular structure in Noun + -인가 -*i-n ka* or Noun + -인고 -*i-n kwo*.
8. Verb stems could appear in isolation in LMK but not so in EMK. Thus, combining verb stems directly into compounds was no longer possible.
9. Nominalizing suffix -*i* became unproductive.
10. LMK honorific plural 내 *nay* lost its honorific function as it morphed into 네 *ney*.

Language

11. In LMK, the causative form of the verb ᄒᆞ- *ho-* "do" had been :히 *:hoy-*. In the sixteenth century, we find examples of this rendered as ᄒᆞ이- *hoi-*; This latter form gave way to 시기- *siki-* (direct ancestor of Modern 시키- **sikhi-**) later in EMK.

12. The earlier alternation between 이시- *isi-* and 잇- *is-* in the verb stem "be, exist" was reduced to just 잇- *is-* in EMK and then restructured to 있- *iss-* late in EMK.

13. EMK developed two new tense-aspect markers: past tense -앗/엇- *-as/es-* and future-presumptive -겟- *-keyss-*, which latter form, like nominative particle 가 *ka*, rarely appeared in texts. Foreign missionaries first noticed them.

14. Of the four LMK modifiers -ᄂᆞᆫ *-non*, -던 *-ten*, -건 *-ken*, and -린 *-lin*, only the first two survived (the first as -는 *-nun*).

15. LMK conjunctive endings -곤 *-kwon*, -곡 *-kwok*, -곰 *-kwom*, -ᆞ(♀/으)며셔 *-⁽ᵒ/ᵘ⁾myesye*, -ᆞ(♀/으)명 *-⁽ᵒ/ᵘ⁾myeng*, -악 *-ak*, and -암 *–am* all disappeared (-ᆞ(♀/으)며셔 *-⁽ᵒ/ᵘ⁾myesye* morphed into -(으)면서 *-(u)myense*).

16. LMK -ᆞ(♀/우) 디 *-⁽ʷᵒ/ʷᵘ⁾toy*, which comprised the volitive *-wo/wu-* plus accessive *-toy*, became restructured as the one-shape ending -되 *-twoy* in EMK.

17. LMK forms like -더이다 *-te.ngita*, -ᄂᆞ이다 *-no.ngita*, -노이다 *-nwo.ngita*, -노소이다 *-nwoswo.ngita*, and -도소이다 *-twoswo.ngita* generally gave way to shorter forms such as -데 *-tey*, -늬 *-noy*, -뇌 *-nwoy*, -노쇠 *-nwoswoy*, and -도쇠 *-twoswoy* (following the copula, -로쇠 *-lwoswoy*) by eliding the final declarative -다 *-ta*.

18. The LMK deferential imperative in -ᆞ(♀/으)쇼셔 *-⁽ᵒ/ᵘ⁾sywosye* was replaced by -소 *-swo*.

19. LMK interrogative forms in -녀 *-nye* and -려 *-lye* changed to -냐 *-nya* and -랴 *-lya*.

EMK Lexical Changes

1. Hong (2009) cites as one of the most striking changes in the EMK lexicon the incorporation of large numbers of loans from spoken Chinese. For example, 자디 *cati* 紫的 "purple," 비단 匹段 *pitan* "silk," 토슈 套袖 *thwosywu* "sleevelet," 무명 木綿 *mwumyeng* "cotton," 보리 玻璨 *pwoli* "glass."

2. Additionally, numerous (graphic) Sino-Korean loans and innovations—some imported via Sinitic texts and others coined in Chosŏn—continued to enter the Korean language, often pushing out native vocabulary like 뫼 *mwoy* "mountain," ᄀᆞ룸 *kolom* "river, lake," and 오래 *wolay* "gate." It is dangerous to assume that any words written in sinographs were somehow "Chinese," as many would have been unknown in China. For example, 원졍 *wencyeng* 原情 in the meaning of "petition, appeal," 인졍 *incyeng* 人情 in the meaning of "bribe" instead of "human feelings," 방송 *pangswong* 放送 in the meaning of "set free" ("broadcast" is a later Meiji Japanese import), 하옥 *hawok* 下獄 "imprison," 등디 *tungtoy* 等待 "prepare in advance and wait," 발명 *palmyeng* 發明 "pretext" ("invention" is another Meiji-period Japanese import), and 졍체 *cyengchyey* 政體 "governing conditions" (not "system of government").

3. A related feature of EMK with regard to sinography was the growing interest in the vernacular and attempts to incorporate vernacular Korean and vernacular Sinitic words into otherwise sinographic texts, using arbitrary sinographs as phonograms—rather than use the Korean script, which most elites considered beneath their dignity until the end of the EMK period. For example, 보리 *pwoli* for "glass," a loan from spoken Sinitic 玻璨 *boli*, was rendered as 菩里 (the Sino–Korean pronunciation of 玻璨 would have been 파려 *phalye*).

4. In the last decades of the nineteenth century, increasing numbers of loanwords from Western languages (mostly English), but especially—and overwhelmingly—from Japanese, began to enter the Korean vocabulary.

The Routledge Handbook of Early Modern Korea

EMK Spelling

The spelling in LMK texts from the fifteenth and sixteenth centuries is generally regular and disciplined. This is one reason the leading South Korean grammar of LMK is titled *A Theory of Standard Middle Korean Grammar* (Ko 2020), but there were no grammars or official spelling guides. Also, of course, no textbooks or nationwide system of education in the new script and its orthography, making the word "standard" here anachronistic at best. Still, the earliest texts are astonishingly reliable and consistent in their spelling. This reliability and consistency deteriorate after the sixteenth century, and spelling becomes increasingly chaotic toward the end of Chosŏn. One early Western observer, the brilliant German linguist Georg von der Gabelentz (1892, 587), characterized the situation as "an anarchy in the orthography and even in certain parts of the declension system which is well understandable if one recalls the contempt in which the Korean language is held in its own country."

In principle, LMK could be spelled either morphophonemically (analytically, ignoring regular sound changes and writing nouns and verb stems consistently in the same shape, separated from following particles and endings, as in modern standard Korean) or phonemically (all run together "like it sounds"). The former type is *punch'ŏl* (analytic spelling), and the latter *yŏnch'ŏl* (sequential spelling). In terms of the contemporary Korean language, the difference between spelling 먹어 **mek.e** versus 머거 **me.ke** for "eat" illustrates the two types of spelling.

The overwhelming majority of LMK texts were spelled phonemically, using a system that restricted the number of possible syllable-final consonants to eight: ㄱ *k*, ㄴ *n*, ㄷ *t*, ㄹ *l*, ㅁ *m*, ㅂ *p*, ㅅ *s*, ㅇ *ng*. However, with the neutralization of syllable-final /ㅅ *s*/ and /ㄷ *t*/ as (pronounced) [t] at the end of LMK, ㄷ *t* was no longer spelled in coda position, and a spelling system with seven syllable-final consonants instead of eight characterized EMK: ㄱ *k*, ㄴ *n*, ㄹ *l*, ㅁ *m*, ㅂ *p*, ㅅ *s*, ㅇ *ng*. This placed intense pressure on orthographic ㅅ *s* to represent a number of different underlying consonants and introduced complications into the orthography—on top of other sound changes, the usual lag behind sound change and spelling, and the general lack of any state-wide official cultivation or education efforts.

A consensus has formed among South Korean linguists, starting with Yi Iksŏp (1992), that the overall historical trajectory of Korean spelling has been a gradual drift from the LMK *yŏnch'ŏl*-type sequential spelling to more analytical *punch'ŏl*-type spelling, eventually institutionalized in its most radical form in the *Han'gŭl Unified Orthography* of 1933 that is still in use today. Certain sixteenth-century texts already show some analytically spelled forms, but the incidence of such forms gradually increases across the three centuries of EMK. Moreover, the inherent tension between these two approaches to orthography gave rise to another type of compromise spelling found in numerous EMK texts: *chungch'ŏl* (over-spelling or duplicate/redundant spelling). Over-spelling was of two types. In the first type, ㄱ *k*, ㄴ *n*, ㄷ *t*, ㄹ *l*, ㅁ *m*, ㅂ *p*, ㅅ *s* appear both as coda in the preceding syllable and again as the first letter of the following syllable. This phenomenon appears in three LMK texts from 1517 and 1518 already and in EMK, where it is mostly confined to ㅅ *s*.

The second type concerns underlying forms ending in aspirated ㅊ *ch*, ㅋ *kh*, ㅌ *th*, and ㅍ *ph*, where the tension between *yŏnch'ŏl* and *punch'ŏl* was especially acute. Hong (1986, 128–129) describes the problem as follows: whereas in LMK, the locative of 밭 *path* "field" was spelled 바테 *path oy* (*yŏnch'ŏl*), in EMK, the analytic spelling 밭이 *path oy* was not an option, and they did not write 밧이. Instead, two different solutions are found (Table 16.1).

A form like 겨틔 *kyeth uy* in Type (1) was the usual LMK *yŏnch'ŏl* spelling, which continued into EMK. In the early seventeenth century, 겻틔 *kyesth uy* in Type (2) (which could also manifest as 곁틔 *kyetth uy* or 곧투니 *kotthoni*, although technically this violated the new "Seven Codas Rule") began to sideline Type (1). Type (3) is usually described as "re-phonologization" because

Language

Table 16.1 Early Modern Korean chungch'ŏl Over-Spelling in Aspirates

Type	Declension				Conjugation	
1	겨틔	비체	알픠	녀크로	ᄀᆞ투니	자피다
(LMK)	*kyeth uy*	*pich ey*	*alph oy*	*nyekh ulwo*	*kothoni*	*caphita*
	beside	in the light	in front	to the side	is like	get caught
2	겻틔	빗체	앒픠	녁크로	ᄀᆞᆺ투니	잡피다
	kyesth uy	*pisch ey*	*alpph oy*	*nyekk ulwo*	*kosthoni*	*capphita*
3	겻희	빗헤	앒히	녁흐로	ᄀᆞᆺ후니	잡히다
	kyesh uy	*pish ey*	*alp.h oy*	*nyek.h ulwo*	*koshoni*	*cap.hita*

it deconstructs the aspirates ㅊ *ch*, ㅋ *kh*, ㅌ *th*, and ㅍ *ph* into just ㅈ *c*, ㄱ *k*, ㄷ *t*, and ㅂ *p* + ㅎ *h*. Type (3) became especially prominent from the end of the eighteenth century through the nineteenth century. In any case, all three types likely were a compromise between *yŏnch'ŏl* and *punch'ŏl* and are interpreted as part of the orthographic drift from the former to the latter.

Summary

The list of different characteristic linguistic features of EMK above could be augmented but nonetheless gives a general outline of what to expect from EMK texts. More than 40 years ago, Skillend (1979, 119) complained that it was "virtually impossible to date any literary work within this period [seventeenth-nineteenth cc.] by its language," but research in the intervening decades now enables the use of diagnostics like those given above to guesstimate within a half-century or so the dates of otherwise undated texts. Because features like these are always best appreciated with concrete examples, the following section presents a series of excerpts from representative EMK texts, both print and manuscript, along with a barebones annotative apparatus and English translations.

Annotated Excerpts from Representative EMK Texts

Excerpt 1: New Sequel to the Illustrated Exemplars of the Three Moral Relationships from Korea *(*Tongguk sinsok Samgang haengsilto*; 1617)*[3]

"Kaebaek Slices off a Digit" (*Filial Son* 7.19; Figures 16.1 and 16.2).

유혹 니[4]개빅은 양셩현 사롬이니 져머셔브터 효힝이 잇더니

Private scholar Yi Kaebaek was from Yangsŏng prefecture. Ever since he was little, he was filial in his conduct.

ᄌᆞ라매 미처 부뫼 다 오래 병드럿거롤[5] 개빅이 겨틔 떠나디 아니ᄒᆞ야

When he reached adulthood, both his parents were ill for long periods, and Kaebaek never left their side;

안ᄌᆞ며 누우며 음식기며[6] 오줌쏭 눌 제 반ᄃᆞ시 븓자바

he never neglected to support them day and night with their meals or when they went to the toilet

닐곱 히예 니르도록 게올리[7] 아니 ᄒᆞ더니 어미 죽거놀 슬허ᄒᆞᆷᅟᅵᆯ 녜예 넘게

Figure 16.1 Illustration for "Kaebaek Slices Off a Digit." Source: Sejong taewang kinyŏm saŏphoe, *Yŏkchu Tongguk sinsok Samgang haengsilto* [Annotated translation of *New Sequel to the Illustrated Exemplars of the Three Moral Relationships from Korea*] (n.d.). Photo credit: King Sejong the Great Memorial Society.

for seven years. When his mother died, Kaebaek grieved above and beyond the call of propriety,

ᄒᆞ고 영장ᄒᆞ매 미처 시묘 사라 쥭만 먹더라 아비 병이 듕커놀[8]

and upon laying her to rest, he kept vigil by her grave, eating only gruel. When his father's illness grew severe,

똥을 맏보고[9] 손가락 베혀[10] 약애 빠[11] 밧ᄌᆞ온대[12] 병이 즉제 됴ᄒᆞ니라

Kaebaek tasted his feces and cut off a digit to mix into medicine, which he gave his father, whereupon his sickness improved immediately.

아븨 거상을 ᄒᆞ골ᄀᆞ티[13] 젼상대로 ᄒᆞ니 젼후 여ᄉᆞ 히로 ᄒᆞᆫ 번도 지븨

Kaebaek mourned his father just as with his previous bereavement, and during those six years, never once

니ᄅᆞ디 아니ᄒᆞ니라 탈상ᄒᆞ고 미일 새배 어을메[14] ᄉᆞ당의 뵈ᅀᆞᆸ고 나며 들 제 …

went home. After completing his mourning, he would pay his respects every day at dawn and dusk at the family's shrine, and every time he left or returned home …

250

Language

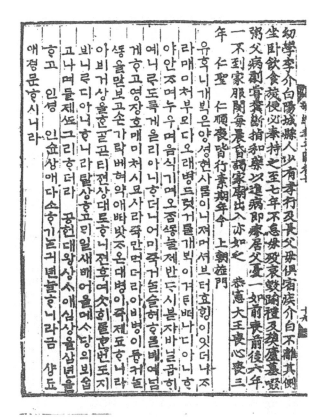

Figure 16.2 Text page for "Kaebaek Slices Off a Digit." Source: Sejong taewang kinyŏm saŏphoe, *Yŏkchu Tongguk sinsok Samgang haengsilto* [Annotated translation of *New Sequel to the Illustrated Exemplars of the Three Moral Relationships from Korea*] (n.d.). Photo credit: King Sejong the Great Memorial Society.

인성 인순 샹애 다 소ᄒᆞ거늘 긔년늘[15] ᄒᆞ니라 금샹됴애 졍문 ᄒᆞ시니라

when Queens Insŏng and Insun died, he refrained from meat for one year. The reigning king erected a memorial gate in his honor.

Excerpt 2: **A Mountain Fortress Diary (Sansŏng ilgi**; *Sometime between 1636 and 1647)*

만녁 십칠 년 긔튝 구월의 노라치란 오랑캐로 뇽호쟝군을 ᄒᆞ이다[16] ⋯

In the ninth month of the *kich'uk* year [1595], in the seventeenth year of the Wanli era, they made the Jurchen called Nurhaci Dragon Tiger General ⋯

븍녁희[17] 모든 오랑캐롤 침노ᄒᆞ야 긔셰 졈졈 듕ᄒᆞ고 잇다감

He invaded all the Jurchens to the north, and as his power gradually grew, he would sometimes

노략한 한인을 도로 보내여 듕됴에 헌튱ᄒᆞ더니 다른 오랑캐 ⋯

The Routledge Handbook of Early Modern Korea

send marauding Chinese back [to the Ming court] and [thereby] show his fealty to the Chinese court. When another Jurchen ⋯

ᄃ라나거ᄂᆞᆯ 노라치 즉시 근오십의 머리를 버혀[18]

fled to Jianzhou, Nurhaci immediately cut off Kŭgosip's head

Excerpt 3: **The Kasa Verses of Songgang Chŏng Ch'ŏl** *(Songgang kasa; 1690–96)*

Introductory Verse

江강湖호애 病병이 깁퍼[19] 竹듁林님의 누엇더니[20]

Reclined in the bamboo grove,[21] victim of my love for rivers and streams.

關관東동 八팔百빅里리에 方방面면을 맛디시니[22]

Big news! I am to be Governor of Kwandong, all eight hundred *li.*

어와 聖셩恩은이야 가디록 罔망極극ᄒᆞ다

The king's favor knows no limits!

延연秋츄門문 드리ᄃᆞ라

I race on horseback through Long Autumn Gate,

慶경會회南남門문 ᄇᆞ라보며 下하直직고 믈너나니[23]

take my leave of the king and set out on my way, eyes trained on the Gate of Feasts,

玉옥節졀이 알픠 셧다[24]

the king's jade tally my standard.

平평丘구驛역 몰을 ᄀᆞ라 黑흑水슈로 도라ᄃᆞ니

Change horses at P'yonggu Post Station, follow the Black River.

蟾셤江강은 어듸메오[25] 雉티岳악은 여긔로다

Where is Toad River? That is Pheasant Ridge.

Excerpt 4: **Illustrated Exemplars of the Two Moral Imperatives** *(Iryun haengsilto; 1727)*

"Ji and Shou join each other in death" (Zhou)

윗[26]나라 공ᄌᆞ 슈ᄂᆞᆫ 션공이란 님금의 아ᄃᆞ리니 태ᄌᆞ 급비[27]

Young Master Shou of the state of Wei was the son of a ruler called Duke Xuan. The Crown Prince Ji

다문어믜게 난 아이오 공ᄌᆞ삭이와 ᄒᆞᆫ 어믜게 난 형이라 그 어미 삭이와

was a child born unto his stepmother, and Shou was his elder brother, born unto the same mother as Young Master Shuo. His mother plotted with Shuo.

Language

몬쏘 젯나라히[28] 태ᄌ룰 보내고 도적 ᄒ야 길헤[29] 가

On another occasion, they dispatched the Crown Prince to the state of Qi and had bandits take to the road,

태ᄌ의 기룰 가거든 보고 주기라 ᄒᆫ대 쉬 가디 말라 ᄒ야놀 태지 닐오디[30] 아비 명을 더디면[31]

telling them to kill him when they saw his standard pass by. Shou told him, "Do not go," but the Crown Prince said, "To disobey one's father's order

ᄌ식의 되 아니라 ᄒᆫ대 쉬 ᄯ 조차가더니 그 어미 말리디 몯ᄒ야 경계ᄒ야 닐오디

is not the Way of a child." Shou once again accompanied him; his mother could not dissuade him but warned:

앏셔디 말나[32] ᄒ더니 ⋯

"Do not go in the lead." ⋯

Excerpt 5: Diary of a Journey to Tongmyŏng *(Tongmyŏng ilgi; 1772)*

괴튝년 팔월의 낙을 써나 구월 초싱의 함흥으로 오니 다 니ᄅ기롤

Departing the capital in the eighth month of the *kich'uk* year [1769], we arrived in Hamhŭng early in the ninth month. Everybody had told me

일월츌이 보암죽다 하디[33] ᄆ옴 듕난ᄒ디

that the moon- and sunrises were well worth seeing, so I was giddy with anticipation, and

기싱들이[34] 못내[35] 칭찬ᄒ여 거록ᄒ믈 일ᄏᄅ니 내 ᄆ옴이 들셕여

the *kisaeng* girls could not stop praising [Tongmyŏng] and raving about how divine a place it is. My restless excitement tempted me

원님긔 청ᄒᆫ대 ᄉ군이 ᄒ시디 녀ᄌ의 출입이 엇디 경이 ᄒ리오 ᄒ여

to ask the magistrate for permission [to go], but my husband told me: "How can you, a woman, think so casually of excursions?" and

뇌거불허ᄒ니 홀일업서 그첫더니[36]

dismissed the idea out of hand. So I had no choice but to give up on the idea.

Excerpt 6: Memoirs Written in Silence I *(Hanjung mallok il; 1795–1805)*

니[37] 유시의 궐니의 드러와 셔찰 왕복이 됴셕의 이시니[38] 니 집의

From the time I came to the palace as a child, each morning and evening, I exchanged letters of greeting with my parents, and many

니 슈젹이 만히 이실 거시로디 입궐 후 선인겨오셔 경계하[39]오시디

of those letters should have remained with my family. Upon my departure, however, my father cautioned me,

The Routledge Handbook of Early Modern Korea

외간 셔찰이 궁듕의 드러가 흘릴 거시 아니오

"It is not right that letters from the outside should be scattered about the palace.

문후훈 의외[40]예 수연이 만키가[41] 공경ᄒᆞᄂᆞᆫ 도리의[42] 가치[43] 아니ᄒᆞ니

Nor would it be proper for you to write of anything at length aside from simple words of greeting.

됴셕봉셔 회답의 쇼식만 알고 그 죠희의 뻐[44] 보니라[45] ᄒᆞ시기

It would be best if, after reading the news from home, you wrote us on the same sheet of paper."

션비겨오셔 아참 져역[46] 승후ᄒᆞ오시ᄂᆞᆫ 봉셔의 션인 경계디로 됴희 머리의 써[47] 보내옵고[48]

As he instructed, I wrote to them on the top margin of the letters Mother faithfully sent twice daily.

Excerpt 7: **An Encyclopedia for the Inner Quarters** *(Kyuhap ch'ongsŏ; 1809)*[49]

긔을ᄉᆞᆨ[50]의 늬[51] 도호[52] 힝뎡의 집 ᄒᆞ야 듕궤훈 결을의 우연이

In the fall of the *kisa* year [1809], we were staying at the Haeng Pavilion at the Eastern Lake. In my spare time between

군ᄌᆞ의 쇼롤 죠차[53] 녯[54] 글이 인싱일용의 졀훈 것과 산야 모든 문자을 어더 보고 신슈피열ᄒᆞ니 …

cooking rice and preparing side dishes, I went to my husband's quarters and read the desperately needed writings of practical use in our daily lives; I read everything my hands could reach …

홀연 싱각ᄒᆞ니 고인이 왈, 춍명이 둔필만 굿디[55] 못ᄒᆞ다 ᄒᆞ니,

Suddenly, it came to mind that people in the old days said a good memory is not as good as poor writing.

뻐[56] 긔록ᄒᆞ미[57] 잇디[58] 아니족[59] 엇디 유망을 굿쵸아[60] 인의 조ᄒᆞ리오[61].

How could this knowledge be helpful if not recorded for the time when I will [inevitably] forget?

Other Ways to Define (Early) Modern Korean

As noted in the introduction, traditional approaches to periodizing Korean linguistic history try to adhere strictly to language-internal criteria and eschew language-external factors. Where does this leave us when broaching the question of "Early Modern Korean?" A good place to start would be with some of the rationales for the term "early modern" in adjacent historical fields. For example, Berry (2012, 42) lists the following hallmarks of the "early modern" from the perspective of Japanese history: "urbanization; the specialization and integration of labor; the redistribution of income to a nascent middle class; the growth of popular consumption; the spread of schooling, literacy, and commercial printing; and the improvement in standards of well-being, from nutrition to life expectancy." In a similar vein, Clements (2015, 6) picks out "the growth of cities, spread of secular thought, the expansion of mercantile capitalism and the development of a commercial publishing industry."

None of these have any direct bearing on linguistic change, save perhaps those related to schooling and commercial printing, which were virtually undeveloped in Chosŏn. But Clements (2015, 7) adds: "a growing awareness of language as an abstract concept … accompanied by

Language

debates about the nature of language, reading practices, and translation that had not been observed in Japan before …" This begs the question of what sociolinguistic factors and contexts beyond technical questions of linguistic change at the levels of phonology, grammar, and orthography might usefully be mobilized to think about "linguistic modernity."

Here, we find some useful analogs from early modern Europe. For example, in her stimulating rethinking of the traditional periodization of Scots, Kopaczyk (2012, 234) calls for attention to "the interfaces between language, literature, society and the general mindset of a given era" and asks why sixteenth-century Scots is labeled as "middle" while English of the same period is labeled uncontroversially as "early modern." She then notes that the term "Middle Polish" is assigned to the language of Poland well into the eighteenth century "because of the persistence of Latin in the public sphere and the inadequacy of the vernacular to render all types of discourse" (Kopaczyk 2012, 240). As this leads her to question the relative status of Latin vis-à-vis the vernacular in Scotland, she opines that "the use of Latin in the public domain would support the label 'middle' for the vernacular until Latin ceases to be the major vehicle of formal communication" (Kopaczyk 2012, 245).

The relationship between a superposed cosmopolitan language like Latin or Literary Sinitic and the vernacular beneath it is thus one important factor to consider. But Kopaczyk highlights three other sociolinguistic features: (1) the standardization of spelling, which "can in itself be treated as a token of early modernity"; (2) the lexicon, where, in the case of Scots, "the impact of French and Scandinavian vocabulary" "changed the Anglo-Saxon character of the English lexicon into a less homogenous inventory"; and (3) elaboration of function, that is, the development of "a variety which could be used in more than one register" and serve as the principle literary and record language of the nation (Kopaczyk 2012, 246, 248, 251). Peter Burke's influential *Languages and Communities in Early Modern Europe* (2004) makes similar points about standardized language as a part of the Eliasian "civilizing process" and also notes vocabulary enlargement as a feature of European early modernity. For example, some 38,000 new words entered the English vocabulary between 1450 and 1750.

Where do Chosŏn Korea and the Korean language stand if we apply such sociolinguistic criteria to the periodization of Korean? Would it be Eurocentric of us to do so? Some recent South Korean research suggests not. Unhappy with the conventional periodization of *kŭndae* Korean, Hŏ (2011) notes that literary historians typically locate the beginnings of the modern Korean literary language in the last decade of the nineteenth century and asks: "If we take the seventeenth century as the starting point, how can we harmonize the characteristic features of Early Modern Korean with other academic fields?" Hŏ calls for an approach that looks not only to sound change but also to the lexicon and to *ŏmun saenghwalsa* (the history of linguistic and literary life) more generally when defining modernity in Korean. Thus, he proposes to label the period from the opening of Korea's ports in the 1870s until the March First Movement of 1919 as "*kŭndae* Korean," and within that period sees the years between the Kabo Reform and Japan's annexation of Korea in 1910 as a distinct subperiod. Kim (2011) takes a similar tack and calls for a prioritization of the written language over spoken language, with a focus on the eradication of inequality in linguistic and literary life—the achievement of *ŏnmunilch'i* or congruity between speech and writing—as the main criterion. Thus, his preferred periodization looks like this (the suggested English equivalents are mine):

kŭnse kugŏ (Early Modern Korean?): early seventeenth century–1894
kŭndae kugŏ (Modern Korean): 1894–1945 or 1910–45
hyŏndae kugŏ (Contemporary Korean): 1945–present

Finally, Ko (2013) also calls for a sociolinguistic perspective in defining *kŭndae* Korean and similarly proposes to locate the origins of Korean linguistic modernity in the 1890s around the time of

The Routledge Handbook of Early Modern Korea

the Kabo Reform. For Ko, we can only really speak of Contemporary Korean from 1957, when the publication of the monumental *Great Dictionary* (*K'ŭn sajŏn*) saw completion. He insists—citing an important paper by I Yonsuku from 1987—that for linguistic modernity, "allowing even the lowest members of the relevant linguistic community to participate in the world of reading and writing as indispensable constituent members of the 'nation' is an essential condition for the creation of a centralized nation state."

Final Thoughts

In many ways, the question of "Early Modern Korean"—in English at least—is bedeviled by the translation problem. Should we render *kŭndae* as "modern" or "early modern?" Does it really matter? However we translate it, South Korean research agrees that the language in texts stretching from the early seventeenth century to the end of the nineteenth century can be treated as a more or less discrete stage in the development of the language, separate from both the language of the texts of the preceding fifteenth and sixteenth centuries and different again from the language found in texts from the Enlightenment Period and later.

Recent challenges to this periodization seek not to push *kŭndae* Korean further back in time to incorporate what is usually referred to as "(Late) Middle Korean" but rather to deny modernity to the Korean language of Chosŏn at all. In addition to the reasons adduced by Hŏ, Kim, and Ko above, following the analogs in Poland and Scotland mentioned above (and others could be adduced) we must remember that Literary Sinitic was the official language of Chosŏn until 1894. Second, spelling did not become standardized until the colonial period. Third, Korean was severely constricted in terms of the elaboration of functions and registers, as well as the language's use in the public domain. Fourth, the most intense, concentrated, and massive shock to the Korean lexical system came through contact with modern Japanese from the 1880s onward. And fifth, modern Korean writers did not settle on a modern Korean literary language until the 1920s. All things considered, justifying the label "modern" for the language of Korean texts before the last decade of the nineteenth century and even the label "Early Modern" for the language of the seventeenth through nineteenth centuries may need additional justification.

Notes

1 Features below are summarized from Hong Chŏngsŏn (1998), Hong (2009), and Lee and Ramsey (2011).
2 One of the challenges in writing about LMK and EMK in English is that of romanization. Because the McCune–Reischauer (MR) system was designed as a transcription system focused on rendering modern pronunciation, rather than as a transliteration system designed to aid in foregrounding linguistic structure or reconstructing the orthography of a Korean text, linguists use the Yale romanization. MR is particularly unsuited to romanizing Korean texts from before 1933 (when the obsolete vowel · *o* called "arae a" was finally abolished) that include letter- and syllable shapes alien to the contemporary language. Thus, all LMK and EMK forms here are rendered in Yale romanization following Martin (1992), which requires *italics* for premodern forms and bold for modern reflexes. But where helpful, we also give the Han'gŭl (Hangul) forms.
3 For all of the following excerpts I have relied on Na (2013). For reasons of space, I omit romanizations in the body of the main text.
4 Spelling of Sino–Korean pronunciations was usually more conservative than that of native words, but the treatment of syllables with underlying initial ㄹ *l* varied in EMK. Sometimes the initial ㄹ *l* was retained as such (though almost certainly pronounced as ㄴ *n*). In cases like this where the following vowel was *i* or y, the initial ㄴ *n* was retained in spelling, even at a time when we can assume that initial ㄴ *n* in this environment had otherwise dropped in speech. North Korean spelling to this day retains both initial Sino-Korean ㄴ *n* and initial Sino-Korean ㄹ *l*—as an orthographic policy choice, not a dialect fact.

Language

5 Note the new past tense morpheme in -엇- -*es*-. The ending -거롤 -*kelol* is a mistake for -거놀 -*kenol*: itself a confused spelling for what was pronounced -거늘 -*kenul* by now.

6 The extra ㄱ *k* here is an example of EMK *chungch'ŏl* over-spelling, seen as a compromise between 음시기 (*yŏnch'ŏl*) and 음식이 (*punch'ŏl*).

7 For expected *게을리 *keyulli* "lazily": an example of the confusion in spelling between · *o* and — *u* in non-initial syllables, reflecting the merger of these two vowels in favor of the latter in this environment.

8 For expected *듕커늘 *tywungkhenul* (contracted from 듕ᄒ거늘 *tywunghokenul*): another example of the confusion in spelling between · *o* and — *u* in non-initial syllables.

9 맏 *mat* here for "taste" is an archaism reflecting the earlier LMK spelling system of eight codas (ㄱ *k*, ㄴ *n*, ㄷ *t*, ㄹ *l*, ㅁ *m*, ㅂ *p*, ㅅ *s*, ㅇ *ng*), but reflecting the actual EMK pronunciation of what underlyingly was still 맛 *mas*.

10 A good example of the vowel-fronting (umlaut) rule that was characteristic of most EMK texts: 베히- *peyhi*- "chop off; cut down" was fronted from earlier LMK 버·히- *pe·hi*-.

11 A good example of an EMK orthographic *p*-cluster that nonetheless would have been pronounced as just 타 *tha*. The spelling here continues LMK ᄩ- *ptho*-.

12 Unlike the example above with 맏 *mat*, this example spells according to the newer EMK spelling system of seven codas (ㄱ *k*, ㄴ *n*, ㄹ *l*, ㅁ *m*, ㅂ *p*, ㅅ *s*, ㅇ *ng*)—minus ㄷ *t*. The stem is 받- *pat*- "render up; offer up" but spelled with ...ㅅ ...*s* in coda position.

13 곧티 *kotthi* is a good example of EMK over-spelling (*chungch'ŏl*) of intervocalic aspirates for what underlyingly is 그티 *kothi*. Here the coda is rendered in the older eight-coda spelling rather than as *긋티 *kosthi*.

14 A good example of the loss of intervocalic LMK -*z*- coming into EMK. The LMK form was *ezulum ~ ezulm*.

15 Another example of EMK *chungch'ŏl* over-spelling: a compromise between 긔녀늘 (*yŏnch'ŏl*) and 긔년을 (*punch'ŏl*).

16 A good example of the new EMK causative in ᄒ이- *hoi*- of ᄒ- *ho*- "do" as compared to LMK :히- :*hoy*- ⟨ *ho·Gi*-.

17 A nice example of EMK rephonologized spelling of intervocalic aspirates: the underlying form is 북녁 *puknyekh* + locative 의 *uy*, but the aspirated ㅋ *kh* has been deconstructed/rephonologized as ㄱ *k* + ㅎ *h*.

18 An unfronted (un-umlauted) and thus older version of the verb "slice off; cut down" seen in the previous excerpt.

19 A good example of *chungch'ŏl* over-spelling of intervocalic aspirates: the underlying form is just 기퍼 *kiphe* "deep."

20 Note the new EMK past tense morpheme in -엇- -*es*-.

21 English translation from O'Rourke (2014, 97).

22 Verb stem 맛디- *masti*- "entrust to/with" here continues LMK 맛·디- *mas·ti*-, the causative of 맛- *mast*- "take over; take charge of." Modern 맡기- *mathki*- is quite a late (and mysterious) development.

23 Recall that spelling of underlying intervocalic -ㄹㄹ- -*ll*- as -ㄹㄴ- -*ln*- is common in EMK texts.

24 An example of the new past tense morpheme -엇- -*es*-, here in what underlyingly is 셔엇다 *sye-es-ta*, although by now the LMK distinction between 셔 *sye* and 서 *se* was moribund.

25 A continuation of the LMK nominal interrogative pattern in NOUN + *kwo* for WH-questions but with interrogative particle 고 *kwo* lenited to 오 *wo* (via earlier LMK *Gwo*) after *y*. In EMK, these gradually gave way to copular structures: 어듸메인고 *etuymey inkwo*.

26 By EMK, the function of ㅅ *s* as compounding element between nouns (*wuy s nala* "the state of Wei") was moribund.

27 A good example of EMK *chungch'ŏl* over-spelling, seen as a compromise between 그비 (*yŏnch'ŏl*) and 급이 (*punch'ŏl*).

28 For the ㅅ *s*, see two notes above. Whereas final ...*h* in LMK nouns tended to disappear in most nouns in EMK, it held on more tenaciously in 나랗 *nalah* "nation; state" and 낳 *nah* "age."

29 Another example of LMK final ...*h* retained in EMK (LMK 긿 *kilh* "road; way"). In this particular text, a contributing factor to the retention was that it was a reprint of a text first printed in the early sixteenth century.

30 By the time this text was printed in the early eighteenth century, the LMK accessive ending in -오/우듸 -*wo/utoy* had been restructured as just -되 -*twoy*. However, the conservative shape here (mirroring exactly LMK 닐오듸 *nilGwotoy*) is again due to the fact that this text is a reprint.

The Routledge Handbook of Early Modern Korea

31 The shape 더디- *teti-* here is conservative: we would expect palatalization and affrication by now, leading to 더지- *teci-*. This affrication was the prerequisite for another EMK innovation: nasal insertion → *tenci-*. Also compare with *incey* ⟨ *icey* "now."

32 Spelling of underlying intervocalic -ㄹㄹ- *-ll-* as -ㄹㄴ- *-ln-* is common in EMK texts.

33 A good example of the spelling confusion between ㆍ *o* and ㅏ *a* indicative of the EMK dephonologization of the "arae a," here in the initial syllable—where the second stage of this dephonologization took place.

34 The LMK plural suffix 둟 *tolh* ~ 듏 *tulh*, like most LMK nominal forms in final …*h*, lost the *h* in EMK.

35 The LMK form of this adverb was :몯:내 *:mwot:nay*, but here we see the new EMK seven-coda spelling system in play, with final orthographic …*s* replacing earlier …*t* even while it was pronounced as *t*.

36 The LMK stem for "finish; stop" was just 궂- *kuch-*, but in EMK was restructured to 그치- *kuchi-*. With the loss of the distinction, for example, between 처 *che* and 쳐 *chye* and between 저 *ce* and 져 *cye* in EMK, speakers must have been tempted to reanalyze an innovating past-tense form like 그첫다 "finished" (stem 궂- *kuch-* + -엇- *-es-* + -다 *-ta*) as 그첫다—as if from stem 그치- *kuchi-*.

37 The LMK first-person pronoun had the shape 나 *na*: another good example of the spelling confusion between ㆍ *o* and ㅏ *a* indicative of the EMK dephonologization of the "arae a."

38 The LMK double 이시-/잇- *isi-/is-* for "be" survived in EMK mostly as 이시- *isi-*. Note, though, that the Karam copy of this memoir has 잇시니 *issini* here, suggesting it was copied much later in EMK when the verb had already assumed the shape 잇- *iss-*.

39 Another good example of the spelling confusion between ㆍ *o* and ㅏ *a* indicative of the EMK dephonologization of the "arae a"—the traditional shape and spelling for "do" was 호- *ho-*.

40 Mistake for 이외 *ioe* "outside of, besides."

41 A good example of two innovating forms typical of EMK: the nominalizer in -기 *-ki* and the subject particle 가 *ka*.

42 Whereas the locative/directional particle in LMK had five different shapes (·의/·이 *·uy/·oy*, ·에/·애 *·ey/·ay*, and (after *i, y,* and Sino-Korean *YWU*) ·예 *·yey*), earlier EMK had a strong tendency to standardize these as just 의 *uy*, and then later as 에 *ey*. Like most palace texts, Lady Hong's memoir is conservative in much of its spelling. For an English translation of the memoir, see Haboush (2013).

43 Contracted from *kahoci anihoni* = 가(可) 호지 아니호니. Note also the palatalization of earlier 가티 *kathi* to 가치 *kachi*.

44 The *p*-cluster here is historically inaccurate (LMK had ㅅ-/ㅆ- *su-/ssu-* "write"), indicating that in fact these *p*-clusters were simply representing the newly formed series of tense unaspirated consonants (된소리 *toensori*).

45 Another example of the spelling confusion between ㆍ *o* and ㅏ *a* indicative of the EMK dephonologization of the "arae a"—the LMK shape for "send" was 보·내- *pwo·nay-*.

46 Mistake for 져녁 *cyenyek*.

47 The alternate spelling for "write" (compare with 써 three notes above). Alternations (that is, confusion) like this in spellings indicate that a sound change is in progress, if not that the change has already run its course.

48 The historically correct shape for "send," spelled 보내- *pwonoy-* in the proceeding sentence.

49 English translation cited from that by Pettid and Cha (2021, 37).

50 Mistake for 그ᄉᆞᆯ *kuyso koul*, with the latter form showing loss of both LMK ㅿ *z* and final …*h* from earlier *kozolh* "autumn."

51 The LMK first-person pronoun was always 나 *na*, so a good example of the spelling confusion between ㆍ *o* and ㅏ *a* indicative of the EMK dephonologization of the "arae a."

52 Mistake for 동호 (東湖) *twonghwo*.

53 By EMK, the LMK distinction, for example, between 서 *se* versus 셔 *sye* and between 조 *cwo* versus 죠 *cywo* had fallen away in most dialects because of ongoing palatalization. The LMK stem for "follow" was always 좇- *cwoch-* so the spelling here suggests a breakdown in these distinctions.

54 A spelling archaism: by now, initial *n* would have dropped before *i, y.*

55 The spelling of 굿 for underlying 곹 *koth-* exemplifies the EMK transition to a spelling system with seven codas instead of eight as in LMK. In other words, this exemplifies the orthographic neutralization of …*s* and …*t* in favor of the former.

56 A calque from *hanmun* 以 (써 이) in its sense of "therefore; thus" and a good example of EMK orthographic cluster *ps-* representing tense unaspirated *ss*.

57 An example of the EMK transition from LMK nominalizer in *-wo-m/wu-m* to just *–(u)m*. LMK would have had 호미 *hwomi*.

Language

58 The 잇- *is-* is the innovating EMK form from LMK doublet 이시- *isi-* ~ 잇- *is-*, while the -디 *-ti* is conservative for what by now was pronounced -지 *-ci* in the spoken language.

59 Mistake for 아닌죡 (= 아닌즉) and a good example of the confusion between ᆞ *o* and ㅡ *u* in non-initial syllables long after these had neutralized in favor of the latter.

60 An example of over-spelling (*chungch'ŏl*) of intervocalic aspirates: the underlying stem is just ᄀ초-. Also another example of the loss of distinction between 셔 *se* versus 셔 *sye* and between 쵸 *chwo* versus 쵸 *chywo*.

61 The LMK stem for "good; nice; get better" was *:tywoh-*. By EMK, this had undergone the change *tywoh- → cywoh- → cwoh-*, with the LMK Rising tone reflected as vowel length but unnoted in writing.

References

Berry, Mary Elizabeth. 2012. Defining "Early Modern." In *Japan Emerging: Premodern History to 1850*, edited by Karl F. Friday, 42–52. Westview Press.

Burke, Peter. 2004. *Languages and Communities in Early Modern Europe*. Cambridge University Press.

Clements, Rebekah. 2015. *A Cultural History of Translation in Early Modern Japan*. Cambridge University Press.

Gabelentz, Georg von der. 1892. "Zur Beurteilung des koreanischen Schrift-und Lautwesens." *Sitzungsberichte der Königlich Preussischen Akademie der Wissenschaften zu Berlin* 23 (June–December): 587–600. Königlich Preussische Akademie der Wissenschaften zu Berlin.

Haboush, JaHyun Kim. 2013. *The Memoirs of Lady Hyegyŏng: The Autobiographical Writings of a Crown Princess of Eighteenth-Century Korea*. University of California Press.

Hŏ Chaeyŏng. 2011. "Kundae kugŏ ŭi sŏlchŏng kwa kundaeŏ sajŏn ŭi p'iryosŏng." In *Han'guk sajŏnhakhoe che 18 ch'a chŏn'guk haksul taehoe charyojip*, edited by Han'guk sajŏnhakhoe che 18 ch'a chŏn'guk haksul taehoe, 105–17. Han'guk sajŏnhakhoe.

Hong Chongsŏn. 1998. "Kŭndae kugŏ ŭi hyŏngt'ae wa t'ongsa." In *Kŭndae kugŏ munpŏp ŭi ihae*, edited by Hong Chongsŏn, 13–77. Pagijŏng.

Hong Yunp'yo. 2009. "Kŭndae kugŏ ŭi kugŏsajŏk sŏngkyŏk." *Kugŏsa yŏn'gu* 9: 153–72.

I Yonsuku [Yi Yŏnsuk]. 1987. "Chōsen ni okeru gengoteki kindai." *Hitotsubashi kenkyū* 12, no. 2: 81–96.

Kim Sŭrong. 2011. "Kugŏ kyoyuk ŭl wihan kŭndae kugŏ sidae kubunnon." *Sahoe ŏnŏhak* 19, no. 2: 85–106.

Ko Yŏnggŭn. 2020. *P'yojun chungse kugŏ munpŏmnon*. Fourth edition. Chimmundang.

Ko Yŏngjin. 2013. "Kŭndae Han'gugŏ yŏn'gu ŭi sŏngkwa wa kwaje: 'Kŭndae kugŏ' ŭi kichŏm munje wa kwallyŏnhayŏ." In *Han-Il kŭndae ŏmunhak yŏn'gu ŭi chaengchŏm*, edited by Yŏnse taehakkyo Kundae Han'gukhak yŏn'guso, 199–240. Somyŏng ch'ulp'an.

Kopaczyk, Joanna. 2012. "Rethinking the Traditional Periodization of the Scots Language." In *After the Storm: Papers from the Forum for Research on the Languages of Scotland and Ulster Triennial Meeting, Aberdeen 2012*, edited by Janet Cruickshank and Robert McColl Millar, 233–60. Forum for Research on the Languages of Scotland and Ireland.

Lee, Ki-moon [Yi Kimun], and S. Robert Ramsey. 2011. *A History of the Korean Language*. Cambridge University Press.

Martin, Samuel E. 1992. *A Reference Grammar of Korean*. Tuttle Publishing Co.

Na Ch'anyŏn. 2013. *Kŭndae kugŏ munpŏp ŭi ihae: Kangdok p'yŏn*. Wŏrin.

O'Rourke, Kevin. 2014. *The Book of Korean Poetry: Chosŏn Dynasty*. Stallion Press.

Pettid, Michael J., and Kil Cha. 2021. *The Encyclopedia of Daily Life: A Woman's Guide to Living in Late-Chosŏn Korea*. University of Hawai'i Press.

Skillend, William 1979. "The Expression of the Subject in *Imjin nok*." In *Mélanges de Coréanologie offerts à M. Charles Haguenauer*, edited by Collège de France, Centre d'Études Coréennes, 119–38. Collège de France, Centre d'Études Coréennes.

Yi Iksŏp. 1992. *Kugŏ p'yogipŏp yŏn'gu*. Sŏul taehakkyo ch'ulp'anbu.

Yi Kimun [Ki-moon Lee]. 1972. *Kugŏsa kaesŏl*. Revised edition. Minjung sŏgwan.

Yi Yŏnsuk. See I Yonsuku.

17

EDUCATION

Diana Yuksel

This chapter takes a syncretic approach to education in early modern Korea by examining the historical development of educational institutions and surveying understandings of education's purpose and scholars' roles. Beginning with an overview of the tradition of Confucian education and its core ideas on learning and teaching, the chapter explores the dual aspect of Confucian education—the purpose of self-cultivation for individuals and the social aim of creating a public servant—as reflected in the works of iconic scholars in Korea ruled by the State of Chosŏn (1392–1897). The discussion also critiques various approaches to "study" (*hak*) and the methods they imply, the importance of educational institutions and their transformations, and the fundamental texts constituting formal education's core. A consideration of the role of formal education highlights two unique aspects of Chosŏn's political institutions: the official recognition of Confucian moral training through the royal lectures and the tradition of remonstrance, a privilege and duty of Confucian scholars. While the chapter acknowledges the crucial role played by the state educational institutions of Chosŏn and the private academies in educating the elite and transmitting Confucian ideas throughout society, it also points out that women had limited opportunities for formal education since Confucianism reinforced traditional gender roles.

By analyzing the educational landscape from various angles, this chapter offers insights into the complex interplay between education, governance, and societal norms in Chosŏn. This approach contributes to a better understanding of its historical trajectory and cultural dynamics. The aim is to underscore that, despite the apparent limitations, Confucian studies and education made significant contributions to Korean society, providing a foundation for ethical conduct and social stability, and that the socio-political implications of formal, semiformal, or informal education in Chosŏn reflected and shaped power dynamics within the society.

Confucianism was a dominant force shaping political, social, and cultural life in Chosŏn. As the revised body of Confucian teachings, Neo-Confucianism became the official ideology and the basis for social and cultural life. Governed by a bureaucratic state, those of education, especially Confucian scholars, formed the driving force behind all matters of state. Chosŏn emerged from the need for a reform in government and society that arose toward the end of its predecessor, the State of Koryŏ (918–1392). A vital element of this reform was selecting the state officials based on merits rather than recommendations or family ties. The rationale was that the country's best minds

260

DOI: 10.4324/9781003262053-23

Education

should handle matters of the state. From this perspective, the Chosŏn state and the elite, *yangban*, assigned education a crucial role in reforming the state through meritocracy.

The Role of Education

Education in Chosŏn was inherently Confucian, encompassing both social and philosophical dimensions. Shaping them was the classical notion of education's purpose: preparing individuals to fulfill their social roles. Shaped by the traditional Confucian philosophy, which posits a universe composed of interconnected concentric circles and a worldview that emphasizes a system of life correspondences, Chosŏn's education system upheld Five Cardinal Bonds: monarch–minister, father–son, husband–wife, elder brother–younger brother, and friends. This system aimed to instill the values and responsibilities associated with these bonds, ensuring individuals could contribute effectively to the Confucian social hierarchy. These were, in turn, defined by Five Moral Imperatives per *Mencius*, a collection of conversations of Mencius (372–289 BCE) with various rulers of his time: rightness (Ch. *yi*; Ko. *ŭi*) between sovereign and subject; care (Ch. *qin*; Ko. *ch'in*) between father and son; differentiation (Ch. *bie*; Ko. *pyŏl*) between husband and wife, birth order (Ch. *xu*; Ko. *sŏ*) between elder and younger brothers, and trust (Ch. *xin*; Ko. *sin*) between friends (Deuchler 1992, 110).

Fulfilling one's role in this intricate social system is vital for maintaining the harmony required for a society to prosper, but fulfillment requires training and self-cultivation. Clearly articulating this idea, the first chapter of the *Great Learning* (*Daxue*)—comprising a short main text attributed to Confucius (c. 551–c. 479 BCE) and nine commentary chapters by one of his disciples, Zengzi (505–435 BCE)—presents all beings, things, and phenomena in the world as part of a concentric system of interconnected stages:

> The ancients who wished to illustrate illustrious virtue throughout the kingdom, first ordered well their own states. Wishing to order well their states, they first regulated their families. Wishing to regulate their families, they first cultivated their persons. Wishing to cultivate their persons, they first rectified their hearts. Wishing to rectify their hearts, they first sought to be sincere in their thoughts. Wishing to be sincere in their thoughts, they first extended to the utmost their knowledge. Such extension of knowledge lay in the investigation of things. Things being investigated, knowledge became complete. Their knowledge being complete, their thoughts were sincere. Their thoughts being sincere, their hearts were then rectified. Their hearts being rectified, their persons were cultivated. Their persons being cultivated, their families were regulated. Their families being regulated, their states were rightly governed. Their states being rightly governed, the whole kingdom was made tranquil and happy. From the Son of Heaven down to the mass of the people, all must consider the cultivation of the person the root of everything besides (Legge 1960, 357–58).

Confucian scholars underlined the intrinsic relationship between an individual's ethical integrity and the broader sociopolitical equilibrium. Confucian educational philosophy situated the underpinning of social order in harmonious familial relationships—perceiving the family as a microcosm of political structures and a pivotal arena for an individual's moral growth. The family served as a crucial preparatory space where the individual acquired qualifications for governing the more extensive societal framework. Consequently, the concept of "learning" (Ch. *xue*; Ko. *hak*) as described in the *Analects* (*Lunyu*)—comprising sayings attributed to Confucius and his disciples—emphasized a duty to oneself and a source of personal fulfillment. Through learning, individuals gained profound insights into the world, cultivating their innate moral qualities and

The Routledge Handbook of Early Modern Korea

striving for social propriety and adequacy. Hence, learning "connotes a complex path of instruction, study, practice, and reflection" (Ivanhoe 2016).

Many scholars in Chosŏn adeptly traversed this path, embodying a "love for learning" (Ch. *haoxue*; Ko. *hohak*) as a way of life. They pursued self-improvement with little regard for seeking public recognition, securing prominent positions in the government, or accruing personal benefits. Despite this pronounced emphasis on the individual's engagement with education as a means for moral development, Confucian teachings consistently associated education with a broader societal role. Although the primary objective of education remained the cultivation of personal moral character, the effectiveness of this moral development was contingent upon its lucrative manifestation in a social context.

Confucianism emphasizes, thus, self-cultivation as a form of moral education at an individual, personal, and intimate level. Simultaneously, Confucian education holds a pragmatic and social purpose, as individuals are duty-bound to utilize their talents to serve the state and its people. In Chosŏn, education aimed to cultivate scholar-officials (*sadaebu*). As highly knowledgeable scholars with strong moral principles, they could also serve the government and guide the people through exemplary behavior. Chosŏn's education also sought to disseminate Confucian ethics widely, enlightening the people to fulfill their assigned societal roles, akin to scholar-officials' responsibilities. In this context, three types of educational processes in Chosŏn are noteworthy: personal education as continuous self-cultivation not only moral but also in terms of acquired knowledge; state education, formal, based on government-maintained schools; and semiformal education through Confucian private academies (*sŏwŏn*). These three educational approaches shaped three interrelated roles that a true scholar was to fulfill: to achieve sagehood, to serve the people, and to teach and transmit the Way (Ch. *Dao*; Ko. *To*).

A Scholar's Path

Elementary Learning (*Xiaoxue*; 1187) by Zhu Xi (1130–1200) of Song dynasty (960–1279) China stated the guidelines for the proper path of a Confucian scholar. Based on Confucian ethical teachings, the text became a primer for education in China and Korea. As a manual for a code of conduct befitting a gentleman-scholar, *Elementary Learning* underlines the importance of putting one's knowledge into practice and paints a clear image of the life of a proper Confucian scholar. From the age of one to nine, the future scholar trains at home, becoming proficient not only in reading and writing but also in the ways of the world—including proper behavior while eating, dressing, talking, and studying. Whereas this is the time spent at home, in a personal, private space, the scholar's life in public, outside the personal, secluded family space, begins at the age of ten. Until turning 20, the scholar completes his training by studying with a master and at an academy. One establishes his family and relationships with fellow scholars between 20 and 30. At 40, he accepts serious appointments as a government official and acts with caution. If he can act following the Way, he should continue an official career; otherwise, he should retreat from public office. By 50, the scholar should be a high official and do important things for the people. Finally, at 70, the scholar may give up his official duties and retire, returning home. Ultimately, the path of a scholar is cyclical, emerging from private life, entering public life, and then returning to private life (Ch'oe Pongyŏng 1983).

The path the *Elementary Learning* outlines for Confucian scholars aligns with the prevailing principles in a society founded on interconnectedness. In such a society, individuals derive their worth from their impact on the community, transforming them into "role bearers" with a moral responsibility to themselves and others. This ethos underscores the Confucian emphasis on the

Education

harmonious integration of individuals into the broader social fabric. Their actions and contributions foster a morally responsible and interconnected community. The process of fulfilling one's role and of following one's designated path in life begins for every worthy Confucian with self-cultivation (Ch. *xiushen*; Ko. *susin*) or (Ch. *xiuji*; Ko. *sugi*) or self-betterment, the scope of which is not limited to the individual. Self-training enables the individual to, among others, perform the role appropriately. The role of a servant of the state might seem like the outer social duty of the scholar, but it has individual and inner value as well. By being a good public official, one also grows as an individual. The experience of the social role forms the self in the process of self-becoming and, in turn, the self-models the outer world. Consequently, self-cultivation was a deliberate process focused on developing personal ethics in alignment with Confucian cardinal values, including benevolence (Ch. *ren*; Ko. *in*), propriety (Ch. *li*; Ko. *ye*), rightness (Ch. *yi*; Ko. *ŭi*), and wisdom (Ch. *zhi*; Ko. *chi*). This transformative journey aimed to instill virtues such as compassion, respect, reciprocity, loyalty, and filial devotion in interpersonal interactions.

Chosŏn scholars perceived self-cultivation as an intellectual endeavor intricately connected to the concept of sage learning (*sŏnghak*) and the continuous pursuit of sagehood. Emphasizing the adage of governing the self to rule others (*chasu ch'iin*), these scholars stressed introspection and self-reflection as integral components of projecting Confucian values outwardly, as seen in numerous works of prominent Confucian scholars. Two of the best-known were Yi I's (pen name Yulgok; 1536–84) *Essentials for Dispelling Folly* (*Kyŏngmong yogyŏl*) and Yi Hwang's (pen name T'oegye; 1501–70) *Ten Diagrams for Sage Learning* (*Sŏnghak sipto*).

Formal Education: The Confucian Academy

The iconic educational institution in Chosŏn was the Confucian Academy (Sŏnggyun'gwan), the seat of "bureaucratic learning" (*kwanhak*) at the highest level. Established in 1397 in the capital, Hansŏng (present-day Seoul), by Chosŏn's founder, King T'aejo (r. 1392–98), the Confucian Academy was the official institution for grooming prospective scholar-officials. As recorded in the *Analects*, it played a pivotal role in actualizing the Confucian ideal to "learn and then have occasion to practice what you have learned" (Slingerland 2003, 1). Admission to the academy required passing either the classical licentiate examination (*saengwŏnsi*) or the literary licentiate examination (*chinsasi*). The former entailed demonstrating a candidate's knowledge of the contents of specific classics, whereas the literary licentiate examination required the composition of a rhyme-poem on the model of Chinese odes (Ch. *fu*; Ko. *pu*) and an old-style poem (Ch. *gushi*; Ko. *kosi*), based on a standard poetic form from Han dynasty (202 BCE–220 CE) China. Some candidates passed both licentiate examinations. Once enrolled in the academy, the licentiates pursued a rigorous study to prepare for the civil examination (*munkwa*), the most prestigious competition for aspiring government officials (Park 2007, 26).

Chosŏn society emphasized the centrality of the examination system in shaping the political and social landscape. For aspiring officials, the licentiate examinations and the civil examination functioned as *sokwa* ("lesser examinations") and *taekwa* ("great examination"), respectively. Both levels of competition featured two stages: the preliminary examination (*ch'osi*) or local examination (*hyangsi*) and the "re-examination" (*poksi*) or metropolitan examination (*hoesi*). The civil examination also featured a third stage, the palace examination (*chŏnsi*), during which the candidates competed for final ranking in the king's presence. Both *sokwa* and *taekwa* featured competitions held triennially and others administered on various special occasions involving the king or the royal house (Park 2007, 25–26).

Three types of examinations tested candidates for official appointment. The civil examination, the military examination (*mukwa*), and the technical examinations (*chapkwa*, "miscellaneous examinations") recruited potential civil, military, and technical officials, respectively. Civil examination candidates had to write two interpretative essays utilizing their orthodox Confucian understanding of the topics. The first essay provided a commentary on a fragment from one of the Five Classics: the *Classic of Poetry* (*Shijing*), the *Book of Documents* (*Shujing*), the *Book of Rites* (*Liji*), the *Book of Changes* (*Yijing*), and the *Spring and Autumn Annals* (*Chunqiu*). The second essay covered a particular topic from one of the Four Books: the *Great Learning*, the *Doctrine of the Mean* (*Zhongyong*), which is a chapter in the *Book of Rites* attributed to Confucius's grandson Zisi (481–402 BCE), the *Analects*, and the *Mencius* (Song Mu Lee 2009, 77–80). Less highly regarded by elites, the military examination assessed each candidate's knowledge of classics related to governance and military affairs, including Sunzi's (c. 544–c. 496 BCE) *Art of War*, and athletic skills linked to combat, including archery, horseback lance-wielding, and polo (Park 2007, 26–27). Regarded even more lowly, the technical examinations recruited specialists: foreign language interpreters, jurists, physicians, astronomers, and accountants. Vital to the state were interpreters—trained in Mandarin Chinese, Japanese, or Mongolian (later replaced by Manchu)—as they placed vital roles in diplomacy (Kim Yangsu 1999, 174–75, 180–96).

In theory, state examinations and education were open to the vast majority of the male population, but many factors limited the granting of degrees to a small segment. For sure, provincial quotas aimed at geographic diversity and triennial civil and military examinations each capped the number of successful candidates at 33 and 28, respectively. The civil examination, particularly triennial and special competitions, shaped political elites and reinforced the status hierarchy. In early Chosŏn, the civil examination and, to a lesser extent, various other types of examination excluded those deemed ineligible on legal or moral grounds (for example, children of remarried women) and the "lowborn" (*ch'ŏnmin*), most of whom were slaves (*nobi*). Even among those eligible, financial constraints kept a degree out of reach for most, as only those well-to-do could afford examination preparation. Unsurprisingly, Chosŏn's ostensibly meritocratic system of official recruitment did not affect the overall continuity in aristocratic membership from Koryŏ to Chosŏn (Duncan 2000, 151). Subsequently, by the seventeenth century, families still producing civil, military, and technical examination passers typically specialized in one of the three types and marrying others like them. In contrast, licentiate examinations became increasingly dissociated from official careers— instead appealing to anyone of education as a status symbol (Park 2007, 68–78).

Since licentiate examinations tested candidates for admission into the Confucian Academy, the state maintained interest and invested in government schools. From the beginning of the Confucian Academy, T'aejo supported it with land grants and newly constructed buildings, including a study hall and a food granary (Yanghyŏn'go). Then, in 1398, the academy saw the completion of the State Confucian Shrine (Munmyo) within the compound. The new edifice functioned as the venue for performing rituals in honor of great Confucian masters of the past. Given the central role of ancestral rites in Confucianism, honoring and venerating the eminent figures representing the Way was only befitting for the academy.

The State Confucian Shrine underwent a complex historical evolution. Flourishing during the reigns of early Chosŏn kings, the shrine experienced a series of destructions and reconstructions. Following the reconstruction after the devastations of the Imjin War (East Asian War; 1592–98), the shrine maintained the Hall of Great Achievement (Taesŏngjŏn) dedicated to Confucius and other Confucian worthies, the Hall of Bright Morality (Myŏngnyundang) serving as the lecture hall, and two dormitories, the East and West Dormitories (Tongjae, Sŏjae), among others. The Hall of Great Achievement housed at least the spirit tablet of Confucius, alongside those of "Four Sages" (Ch. Sipei; Ko. Sabae), who were his disciples or renowned later Confucians: Yan Hui (521–481 BCE), Zengzi, Zisi, and Mencius. When more worthies were enshrined, they were

Education

known as "Ten Wise Disciples" (Ch. Shizhe; Ko. Sipch'ŏl)—Yan Hui, Min Sun (536–487 BCE), Ran Geng (b. 544 BCE), Ran Yong (b. 522 BCE), Ran Qiu (552–489 BCE), Zhong You (542–480 BCE), Zai Yu (522–458 BCE), Duanmu Ci (520–456 BCE), Yan Yan (b. 506 BCE), and Bu Shang (507–400 BCE)—and Neo-Confucian scholars, the "Six Sage Masters of Song Dynasty" (Ch. Songchao liuxian; Ko. Songjo yukhyŏn): Zhou Dunyi (1017–73), Cheng Hao (1032–85), Cheng Yi (1033–1107), Shao Yong (1012–77), Zhang Zai (1020–77), and Zhu Xi. Alongside the Chinese masters were the "Eighteen Sages of the East" (Ko. Tongbang sipp'arhyŏn), the scholars representing Korea's orthodox Confucian lineage: Ch'oe Chi'wŏn (857–908?), Sŏl Ch'ong (650–730), An Hyang (1243–1306), Chŏng Mongju (1338–92), Kim Koengp'il (1454–1504), Chŏng Yŏch'ang (1450–1504), Cho Kwangjo (1482–1520), Yi Ŏnjŏk (1491–1553), Yi Hwang, Cho Hŏn (1544–92), Yi I, Sŏng Hon (1535–98), Kim Changsaeng (1548–1631), Song Siyŏl (1607–89), Song Chun'gil (1606–72), Pak Sech'ae (1631–95), Kim Inhu (1510–60), and Kim Chip (1574–1656).

The proximity of the Hall of Bright Morality and the State Confucian Shrine at the Confucian Academy was not arbitrary. After all, self-cultivation, as part of the life-long education process, rites, and the connection between the two were at the core of the classical Confucian teachings. Since "the one who does not understand the rites cannot find his place [in the world]," the ritual's primary function is to tame the individual and mediate the assumption of one's proper (Ch. *zheng*; Ko. *chŏng*) place among others. Thus, the ritual has the meaning of a fundamental cultural act. Huang Kan (488–545), the author of the *Meaning of the Analects* (*Lunyu yishu*), declared: "Ritual governs reverence, dignity, temperance, and respectfulness, and thus is the root of establishing oneself" (Slingerland 2003, 235). The educational process at the Confucian Academy had as its final goal the cultivation of the moral consciousness of the potential servants of the state and the people through the study and practice of Confucian core values. Accordingly, a series of rules of conduct strictly regulated the routine at the Confucian Academy. Reflected in the rules were various recommendations on how a scholar should behave in society, such as those found in the *Revised and Expanded Reference Compilation* (*Chŭngbo munhŏn pigo*; 1908) that strictly set the curriculum and clearly define the order of the readings—allowing no others, deemed heterodox (Glomb 2020b). In its section, "On Education" (Hakkyo ko), the *Revised and Expanded Reference Compilation* offers a stern admonition:

> The students must first brighten their righteousness and master the whole of everything. They should not get caught up in phrases and paragraphs. They should always read the Four Books, the Five Classics and general history, and are forbidden to walk around holding books such as *Laozi*, *Zhuangzi* or Buddhist sutras, as well as other obscure texts and compilations. Those who fail to obey will be punished.
>
> *(Sin and Chang 2012, 147)*

Hierarchically organized, the Confucian Academy regulated student conduct with a set of rules. They defined everything from manners, conduct, and speech to socializing and interacting with teachers and other students; and from the daily schedule to studying and preparing for the examinations. Failure to respect any of these prescriptions led to punishment:

> When meeting a master (*sajang*), the students must show courtesy (*ye*) by showing themselves and standing on the left side of the road. If the master is passing by on horse, the students should conceal themselves or hide their faces. Those who are unwilling to pay their respect will be punished. Everyday, before the daybreak, at the first beat of the drum, the students should rise up. At the second beat of the drum, they should clean their desks,

sit properly and study. At the third beat of the drums, the students should go in order to the dining hall, take their places facing the East side or the West side and after having finished their meal, they go out in order. Those who do not respect the order or are noisy will be punished.

(Gehlmann 2020, 149)

Sanctions for violating regulations ranged from reprimands to any combination of suspension, expulsion, prohibition from participating in government service examinations, and loss of exemption from military service. The expulsion, in particular, brought social disgrace to the entire extended family of the student.

The reigns of King Yŏngjo (r. 1724–76) and King Chŏngjo (r. 1776–1800) saw a renewed focus on cultural development, prompting the government and Confucian scholars to redirect their attention towards education and its institutions. A scholarly monarch, Yŏngjo increased land grants to educational establishments, including the Confucian Academy, and supported extensive intellectual projects like *Reference Compilation of Documents on Korea* (*Tonguk munhŏn pigo*; 1770), which covered categorized Chosŏn's encyclopedic knowledge covering government, politics, geography, society, and government. Subsequently, in 1776, Yŏngjo's grandson and successor, Chŏngjo, who too was scholarly, established a royal library and archive, Kyujanggak. During the era, the scale of production of historical and literary works entailed a rapid accumulation of books that outgrew the capacity of the Kyujanggak. Consequently, in 1782, Chŏngjo established the "Outer Kyujanggak" (Oe Kyujanggak) on the island, Kanghwado, to accommodate additional holdings. Besides Confucian books, the Kyujanggak housed government documents, private letters from the court, maps, and historical records, including the veritable records (*sillok*), *Daily Records of the Royal Secretariat* (*Sŭngjŏngwŏn ilgi*), and *Royal Protocols* (*Ŭigwe*).

Apart from the Confucian Academy, the government maintained four additional educational institutions in Hansŏng, the Learning Halls of Four Districts (Sabu haktang), also known as the Four Schools (Sahak). Although less prestigious than the Confucian Academy, their curriculum closely mirrored the academy's, encompassing the study of the Four Books, the Five Classics, and the writings of Song Confucian scholars. Studying at one of the Four Schools was the preparatory stage in a student's educational journey toward gaining admission to the Confucian Academy. Analogous to the capital's Four Schools were county schools (*hyanggyo*), one in each of some 300 counties or comparable levels of administrative jurisdiction. The Chosŏn state maintained county schools with the ambitious objective of nurturing a corps of erudite individuals prepared to contribute to the governance and aware of their moral duty to the self and others. County schools, too, provided a foundational Confucian education for anyone with intellectual and political aspirations, though over time, eclipsed by private academies among elites.

Semiformal Education: The Private Academies in the Countryside

In the sixteenth century, the Confucian private academies (*sŏwŏn*) and village schools (*sŏdang*) began appearing in the countryside as a new educational institution. Just as it had happened in Koryŏ, the private schools began to flourish as the state institutions declined in popularity (Edward Y. J. Chung 1995, 4). Village schools offered elementary education for village youth, while the private academies attracted local elites who were increasingly shunning county schools. Private academies were new to Korea, following a tradition that emerged in China, where private schools of Confucian studies had grown. Especially under Song China, such private institutions "developed in ways that were to have an enduring, yet intermittent, legacy" (Tillman 2020, 23) extending

Education

beyond China and inspiring the emergence of private academies in Chosŏn Korea. They also presaged the Confucian Academy by educating young men to become scholars.

The rise of private academies in Chosŏn reflects the historical and political shifts within the society, influenced by various interconnected factors. Above all, the waning effectiveness of the state's educational infrastructure prompted private initiatives. Concurrently, promoting Confucian principles in society involved establishing local shrines attached to academies, emphasizing the veneration of scholar-officials of high moral standing. Additionally, political events, rather than societal demands, played a pivotal role in the emergence of private academies. The four "literati purges" (*sahwa*; 1498, 1504, 1519, and 1545) dissuaded many Confucian scholars from pursuing public office. Instead, they chose a more contemplative existence in rural settings, where they could dedicate themselves to studying and teaching Confucian ideas. However, such a decision did not mean they had severed all ties with officialdom or lost political influence. On the contrary, prominent scholars established private academies to advance their ideological and political agendas (Yŏng-ho Ch'oe 1999, 15–45).

Korea's earliest known private academy was established in 1541 by the scholar Chu Sebung (1495–1554) in Yŏngju on the model of White Deer Grotto Academy re-established by Zhu Xi in 1179 in Song China (Chung Soon-noo 2013, 29–30; Gehlmann 2020, 252–81). Starting from the premise that ensuring the well-being of the people required education more than any other measures, Chu Sebung initially called his school the White Cloud Grotto Academy. By venerating An Hyang, a renowned Neo-Confucian scholar of late Koryŏ, this institution served as a pioneering model for the subsequent establishment of other private academies in Chosŏn. Building upon the initiative of Yi Hwang to obtain governmental support for the school while safeguarding its autonomy, the White Cloud Grotto Academy underwent a significant transformation. Officially renamed Sosu Academy in 1550, the school received a royal charter from King Myŏngjong (r. 1545–67), entailing a grant of books, land, and slaves.

Following this new paradigm established by the Sosu Academy, private academies proliferated in the ensuing years in Chosŏn, especially in the southeast. As the epicenter of Neo-Confucianism, Kyŏngsang Province emerged as the location preferred by prominent scholars for establishing their schools. The Imgo Academy (1553; Yongch'on), the Todong Academy (1564; Hyŏnp'ung), the Oksan Academy (1573; Kyŏngju), and Yi Hwang's Tosan Academy (1574; Yean) were especially famous among them (Figure 17.1). The primary role of these private academies resided in the instruction of students in classical studies and the philosophical elucidation of Confucian principles, alongside their engagement in the tasks of gathering, organizing, and disseminating literary works (Glomb and Eun-Jeung Lee 2021, 175–98).

This intellectual effervescence, soon doubled by increased support from the local communities aiming at enshrining local personalities in their private academies, did not escape criticism, particularly in places where more than one private academy appeared. Besides more immediate concerns, such as the cost of maintaining a private academy burdening the local people and the government, some scholars were unhappy with the selection of personalities for enshrinement or the quality of education compromised by the *yangban* youth enrolling in the academies to avoid military duty. As the stringent criteria for enshrining individuals solely based on outstanding academic accomplishments gradually relaxed, private academies began to favor former government officials, irrespective of their scholarly achievements. Simultaneously, as the student population swelled, many private academies were losing their reputation as bastions of high morality and Confucian scholarship by the reign of King Sukchong (r. 1674–1720). In 1792, the criticism went as far as the likes of a mid-level official, Yi Pokhyu (1729–1800), accusing these institutions of being used as "places of drinking and eating by loafers" (*Chŏngjo sillok* 1792/10/1 entry 1).

Figure 17.1 Looking out from the Tosan Academy's main hall, Chŏn'gyodang. Photo credit: Korean Heritage Service.

Despite the continuing criticism, private academies proliferated throughout Chosŏn, symbolizing intellectual fervor and expressing pride for local communities. By the eighteenth century, more than eight hundred had been established (Yi Man'gyu 1991; Yŏng-ho Ch'oe 1999).

Many private academies were wealthy, had extensive book collections, and could set the tone for defining the curriculum and the rules of private education. These characteristics were common among those established earlier and associated with prominent scholarly figures, including the Tosan Academy in Yean, the Pyŏngsan Academy (1613) in Andong, the Sosu Academy and the Isan Academy (1573) in Yŏngju, and the Oksan Academy in Kyŏngju, all in Kyŏngsang Province, as well as the P'iram Academy (1590) in Changsŏng, Chŏlla Province, and the Tonam Academy (1634) in Nonsan, Ch'ungch'ŏng Province. With a few variations, their basic curricula coincided with those of county schools in that all students studied the *Four Books*, the *Five Classics*, and such Song Neo-Confucian works as Zhu Xi's *Reflections on Things at Hand* (*Jinsilu*; 1175) and Zhen Dexiu's (1178–1235) *Classic of the Mind* (*Xinjing*; 1234). Some academies also used Zhu Xi's *Elementary Learning* and *Family Rituals* (*Jiali*) to foster further personal development and continuous cultivation. Books dealing with history, poetry, or Chinese literary works were allowed but not mandatory.

Although the fundamental readings were the same among all private academies, the hierarchy of the essential texts and, subsequently, the order suggested for reading varied. Whereas the schools following Yi Hwang's prescriptions placed the Chinese canonical texts at the beginning of the study, those following the rules Yi I had set for the Munhŏn Academy (1549) and the Sohyŏn Academy (1578; renamed from Ŭnbyŏng Study Hall, 1610) in Haeju area, Hwanghae Province, favored studying the Five Classics. These were to be followed by the philosophical writings of the Song masters, also hierarchically arranged: Zhu Xi's *Reflections on Things at Hand*, *Family Rituals*, the *Classic of the Mind*, and the *Complete Writings of the Two Cheng Brothers* (*Er Cheng quanshu*); the *Complete Works of Master Zhu* (*Zhuzi daquan*); *Classified Conversations of Master Zhu* (*Zhuzi yulei*); and lastly, other Song philosophical texts (*Yulgok chŏnsŏ* 27.8a). In the fourth chapter of his work *Essentials for Dispelling Folly*, "Reading Books" (Toksŏ), Yi I insisted on this particular order of study for a deep understanding of the metaphysical and moral principles at work in the world (Yŏng-ho Ch'oe, Lee, and de Bary 2000, 35–36).

Education

Despite variations in the reading order or the emphasis on specific texts, the curriculum remained relatively consistent among private academies. Not fundamentally different from state institutions, the curriculum showed little regional variation. A stringent rule maintained by the founders of private academies explicitly prohibited non-Confucian writings, including Daoist and Buddhist texts perceived as promoting "false learning" (Glomb 2020b, 89–112; Glomb and Eun-Jeung Lee 2021, 175–98). Also forbidden were historical, literary, technical, and medical texts and those containing licentious contents.

Each private academy drafted a set of rules (*wŏn'gyu*) concerned not only with the curricula or the academy's general organization but also the general objectives and practical matters. Such rules included guidelines governing students' daily lives, admission criteria, learning sessions, and examinations. Inspiring much of the corpus of rules was the *Study Regulations of Master Zhu* (*Zhuzi xuegui*) and the rules of the leading private academies of the sixteenth century. Some academies took as inspiration Yi I's works, such as the *Rules for the Munhŏn Academy* (*Munhŏn sŏwŏn hakkyu*), the *Rules for the Ŭnbyŏng Study Hall* (*Ŭnbyŏng chŏngsa hakkyu*), *A Model for Schools* (*Hakkyo mobŏm*), or *Essentials for Dispelling Folly*. Others adopted Yi Hwang's *Rules for the White Cloud Grotto Academy* (*Paegundong sŏwŏn kyu*), *Rules of the Isan Academy* (*Isan sŏwŏn kyu*), or prescriptions of moral training from his *Ten Diagrams for Sage Learning*.

Private academy students generally adhered to a disciplined daily routine. They began their day at daybreak by tidying their beddings, with younger members responsible for cleaning the sleeping quarters. Upon washing, the students donned formal caps and gowns, proceeding to the shrine to pay respects to the enshrined figures. Afterward, they returned to their rooms to study. Seniority guided student interactions, from seating arrangements to housecleaning duties. Students primarily engaged in individual study, emphasizing wholehearted dedication and proper posture. Talking during study hours was prohibited. During leisure, students could discuss moral and principled issues, compose prose and poetry, practice calligraphy, explore the library, or stroll in the courtyard. After supper, studies continued late into the night. Their academic progress, which included debates and discussions, among other things, was periodically evaluated by the academy faculty (Yŏng-ho Ch'oe 1999).

Although, in principle, open to all males with a love for learning, most private academies sought to attract scholars from elite families. As such, some academies would prefer civil examination passers, or at least licentiates, to enhance their prestige. For the same reason, other academies aimed at attracting potential Confucian prodigies, regardless of whether they passed the civil examination. Despite variations in admission criteria, academies continued to stress a high moral character regardless of a candidate's social standing (Yŏng-ho Ch'oe 1999).

A private academy's stated mission and the realities of its student body often clashed. Whether admitting seasoned scholars or novices, *yangban* or commoners, a frequently articulated desideratum of the private academies was to guide individuals towards the diligent and proper study of the Confucian texts and to cultivate their wholehearted commitment to the teachings of Confucian sages, prioritizing this over preparing them specifically for success in civil examinations. The mission as such led to the dissatisfaction of some Confucian masters, who often lamented—as recorded in *Essentials for Dispelling Folly*—the lack of seriousness and dedication among the academy students:

People say that they cannot dedicate themselves to the study because they have to prepare for the civil service examination. These excuses betray a non-sincere mind. [...] Nowadays, people pretend to be preparing for exams, but they do not make any effort. They pretend to study the patterning principle [Ch. *li*; Ko. *i*], but they do not even have a basic understanding of it.

(Sancho 2011, 62)

Ideally, the Confucian study and service to the state should have complemented each other, but many perceived the two as incompatible. Deepening this divergence were the efforts of many private academies to delineate their scholarly identity by differentiating themselves from county schools or even the Confucian Academy. As such, their measures against being seen as centers for training for future scholar-officials cemented their autonomy and detachment from the state ideology and politics.

Indeed, many scholars championed the distinctiveness of private academies from the state educational institutions. Among others, Yi Hwang actively emphasized the academic and moral superiority of the private academies as places of transmission of pure knowledge—in contrast to the perceived corruption and obsolescence of the county schools. All the same, his rhetoric urged the state to provide more support for private academies and acknowledge their contributions. The rationale was that Confucian scholars who retired in the countryside and established academies preferred to teach the Way instead of serving the government, thus replacing one moral duty with another. Unlike Yi Hwang, Yi I diverged from a preoccupation with the autonomy of Confucian academies or state intervention in private school affairs. His primary concern was to ensure proper education, placing greater emphasis on its quality. Instead of pivoting private academies against county schools, Yi I viewed the academies as integral components of an ideal educational system. He actively worked towards enhancing their functionality for the betterment of the literati community and the state (Glomb 2020a, 323). Despite the efforts of some scholars to establish a distinct separation between the Confucian academies and the state, private academies began identifying themselves with particular intellectual lineages, facilitating the transmission of distinct interpretations of the Confucian canon through master–disciple relationships. After all, private academies taught students in a structured format featuring lectures by renowned scholars, especially in the seventeenth century.

In and outside the court, the continuing evolution of and divisions among the intellectual lineages of Yi Hwang and Yi I shaped factional strife into institutionalized partisan politics. As of the turn of the seventeenth century, the Southerners (Namin) and the Westerners (Sŏin) asserted themselves as disciples and intellectual heirs of Yi Hwang and Yi I, respectively. Private academies assumed roles as sociopolitical hubs, actively engaging in contemporary debates, both philosophical and political, despite their proclaimed autonomy. The challenges arising from the political engagements of the scholars associated with the rapidly growing number of academies—coupled with the economic burden they imposed on the government and the people—prompted the state to intervene and more strictly regulate the establishment of a new private academy. The efforts culminated in 1868 when Hŭngsŏn Taewŏn'gun (1821–98), the regent for his son and king, who was a minor at the time, abolished academies and shrines without a royal charter (Lee Byoung-Hoon 2020, 197). The measure spared just 47 out of nearly 700 academies. Today, anyone doing a quick web search on a Chosŏn private academy would most likely learn that the Taewŏn'gun shut it down.

In addition to the private academies, the growing number of village schools provided education to the general population. In contrast to private academies, which became documented in such sources as the *Register of Private Academies* (*Sŏwŏn tŭngnok*), village schools did not receive as much attention. Accordingly, far less information about their modus operandi is available. Nonetheless, village schools undoubtedly provided elementary education for students aged seven to fifteen in reading, prose, poetry, and calligraphy. The curriculum mainly comprised the *Thousand Character Classic* (Ch. *Qianzi wen*; Ko. *Ch'ŏnja mun*); Pak Semu's (1487–1564) *Primer for Youth* (*Tongmong sŏnsŭp*), Zhu Xi's *Outline and Details of the Comprehensive Mirror in Aid of Government* (*Zizhi tongjian gangmu*; 1172), the *Elementary Learning*, and *Reflections on Things at Hand*; the Four Books; the *Three Character Classic* (*Sanzijing*) attributed to Song China's Wang Yinglin (1223–96); and *Spring and Autumn Annals*, among others. Depending on the erudition of the teacher, the educational guidance that village schools offered occasionally enabled a commoner to enter a private academy dominated by *yangban*.

Other Types of Education

Royal Education

Drawing inspiration from the Chinese system, Chosŏn monarchs embraced and supported the royal lectures for the king (*kyŏngyŏn*) and the crown prince (*sŏyŏn*). Managed by the Tutorial Office for the Crown Prince (Seja sigangwŏn), royal lectures for the prince ensured that the heir apparent received his education distinct from that of other royal offspring. As Chosŏn deemed Confucian training indispensable (Haboush 1985), distinguished Confucian scholars assumed the responsibility of imparting to the monarch the essential knowledge for governing the people through the power of moral exemplification. Royal lectures aligned with the principles of *Great Learning*, which posits a natural order functioning in concentric circles where every being, including the monarch, must fulfill their designated roles impeccably.

Thus, the royal lectures aimed to educate the ruler on self-cultivation so that he could perform his role optimally. The curriculum generally paralleled that of the Confucian Academy and the private academies across the country. Over time, this academic institution underwent politicization (Daeyeol Kim 2009, 1). As high officials and censors began attending lectures, discussions evolved to encompass political ideas and state policies. Consequently, royal lectures became a "forum for the reconciliation of principle and practice" (Haboush 1985, 164).

Women's Education

Extant sources on women's education in Chosŏn predominantly pertain to *yangban*, but the available information suggests that women were not a uniform mass of illiterates. Although women likely were not deeply involved in the culture of writing and knowledge reproduction, they made some noteworthy contributions beginning in the sixteenth century. A notable figure is Hŏ Ch'ohŭi (pen name Nansŏrhŏn; 1563–89), a celebrated poet and painter. After her death, her family compiled and published Nansŏrhŏn's work in the volume *Collected Works of Nansŏrhŏn* (*Nansŏrhŏn chip*; 1606). During subsequent centuries, notable women of erudition emerged, following in Nansŏrhŏn's footsteps. A Confucian writer, Lady P'ungch'ŏn Im (studio name Yunjidang; 1721–93), advocated for recognizing Chosŏn women as scholars. Lady Chinju Kang (pen name Chŏngiltang; 1772–1832), a poet, left behind a remarkable collection of letters, contributing to the cultural and intellectual landscape of women in Chosŏn society.

Preserving a woman's complete works for posterity was rare, as the prevailing social ideology did not prioritize writing as a woman's primary duty. Confining women to the private sphere, societal norms expected women to remain unseen in the public space and thus linked their education to the inner quarters. Their primary duties were "being obedient to their husbands and in-laws, providing for their children, and refraining from becoming learned ladies" (Cawley 2023, 556). Accordingly, women's education encompassed didactic teachings, exemplified by works like

The Routledge Handbook of Early Modern Korea

Instructions for the Inner Chambers (*Naehun*; 1475), attributed to King Sŏngjong's (r. 1470–95) mother, Queen Sohye (1437–1504). These teachings reiterated moral principles from the *Family Rituals*, underscoring patriarchal authority and the prescribed gender roles. The women mentioned above stand out, given that this framework did not recognize the concept of women pursuing education or aspiring to become scholars.

Self-Taught Scholars with Disdain for Formality

Although the Chosŏn state pursued the ideal of Confucian society and actively advocated Confucian education, the political landscape occasionally produced renowned scholars who achieved erudition solely without external support. Such individuals were recluses: Confucian scholars who declined to serve the state or engage in official education. This tradition solidified in the fourteenth century, particularly when King Sejo (r. 1455–68) ascended the throne upon deposing his young nephew, and the usurpation impassioned many scholars' sense of loyalty to the ruler.

Several distinct categories of such scholars emerged. Protesting the usurpation, some out of power spent the rest of their lives wandering (Chong 1983, 52–59), including the famous Kim Sisŭp (1435–93). His contemporaries, Kim Chongjik (1431–92) and Kim Koengp'il, too, refused government posts, believing they inherited the true tradition of scholars known as Yŏngnam School, so named as the representative scholars—including Chŏng Mongju—hailed from Kyŏngsang (also known as Yŏngnam). After successive literati purges, another group of scholars emerged, regarding authority and honor as detestable, and chose scholarly talks and refinement. Notable examples include Sŏ Kyŏngdŏk (pen name Hwadam; 1498–1546) and Cho Sik (pen name Nammyŏng; 1501–72). All lived in seclusion, dedicating their time to an in-depth study of Confucian books, leaving an impressive literary legacy. Other scholars, including Yi Hwang and Yi I, had episodes of escapism in the countryside away from state politics. The scholars mentioned above adhered to the Confucian dictum of learning for its own sake, believing there was no need for formal education. In particular, the likes of Kim Sisŭp, Sŏ Kyŏngdŏk, and Cho Sik fulfilled their moral duty by not serving the state—or, in Yi Hwang's case, at least refusing to do so for the most part. Although intellectual heirs of Cho Sik, Yi Hwang, and Yi I fought bloody political battles among themselves as Northerners, Southerners, and Westerners, respectively, in mid-Chosŏn, the earlier Chosŏn scholars' disdain for formal education and government service continued to inspire independent pursuit of scholarly ideals, making a lasting impact on Confucian scholarship.

Final Thoughts

The educational landscape in early modern Korea was diverse, with intricate connections to societal and political realms, despite official attempts to maintain a degree of separation. The interplay of personal, the state's, and semiformal educational processes reflected the multifaceted nature of education. All pursuing scholarship had to contribute to the nuanced roles expected of scholars. Whether through the Confucian Academy or private academies, Chosŏn's educational system aimed at cultivating scholar-officials dedicated to ethical governance. However, though intended to be inclusive, the state examinations became increasingly exclusive, leading to a preponderance of aristocratic officials.

Private initiatives made significant cultural contributions in times of challenges and sporadic declines in state-sponsored education. These private academies in the countryside supplemented the state-sponsored educational system, fostering alternative intellectual and political perspectives and contributing to the spread of Confucian ideology. Increased activism of private academies did not always align with the interests of the state, but the phenomenon enriched public discourse,

Education

both political and intellectual. Other practices, such as the Royal lectures for the monarch and heir, served as platforms for discussing statecraft and governance, intertwining Confucian principles with practical policy. On the other hand, by withdrawing from officialdom, recluses challenged the established educational structure and pursued scholarly endeavors outside its constraints, showcasing the diversity of Confucian thought.

Increasingly, the dynamics of educational philosophies and practices added to the complexity of the educational landscape. By the late nineteenth century, Chosŏn Korea was weathering the external challenges of imperialism and the growing internal demand for social change. In 1894, the Kabo Reform (1894–96) government abolished the status hierarchy and the examination system buttressing it. However, before becoming obsolete, the lengthy existence of this complex and dynamic education system shaped the intellectual, social, and political landscape of Chosŏn while providing the moral and philosophical framework for governing the state and perpetuating Confucian values within society.

References

Cawley, Kevin N. 2023. "Christian Pyrexia and Education Fever: Female Empowerment in the Late Chosŏn Dynasty." *History of Education* 52, no. 4: 553–70.

Ch'oe Pongyŏng. 1983. "'Chosŏn sidae sŏnbi chŏngsin yŏn'gu." *Chŏngsin munhwa yŏn'gu* 18: 120–45.

Ch'oe, Yŏng-ho. 1999. "Private Academies and the State in Late Chosŏn Korea." In *Culture and State in Late Chosŏn Korea*, edited by JaHyun Kim Haboush and Martina Deuchler, 15–45. Harvard University Asia Center.

Ch'oe, Yŏng-ho, Peter H. Lee, and Wm. Theodore de Bary, eds. 2000. *Sources of Korean Tradition*. Volume 2, *From the Sixteenth to the Twentieth Centuries*. Columbia University Press.

Chong, Chong-bok. 1983. "The Life and Thought of So Kyong-dok." In *Main Currents of Korean Thought*, edited by Korean National Commission for UNESCO, 52–59. Si-sa-yong-o-sa Publishers, Inc.

Chŏngjo sillok. In *Chosŏn wangjo sillok*. Available at: https://sillok.history.go.kr/main/main.do.

Chung, Edward Y. J. 1995. *The Korean Neo-Confucianism of Yi T'oegye and Yi Yulgok*. State University of New York Press.

Chung Soon-noo. 2013. *Sŏwŏn ŭi sahoesa*. T'aehaksa.

Deuchler, Martina. 1992. *The Confucian Transformation of Korea: A Study of Society and Ideology*. Council on East Asian Studies, Harvard University.

Duncan, John B. 2000. *The Origins of the Chosŏn Dynasty*. University of Washington Press.

Gehlmann, Martin. 2020. "Transmissions of the White Deer Grotto Academy Articles of Learning in Korea." In *Confucian Academies in East Asia*, edited by Vladimír Glomb, Eun-Jeung Lee, and Martin Gehlmann, 252–81. Brill.

Glomb, Vladimír. 2020a. "Shrines, Sceneries, and Granary: The Constitutive Elements of the Confucian Academy in 16th-Century Korea." In *Confucian Academies in East Asia*, edited by Vladimír Glomb, Eun-Jeung Lee, and Martin Gehlmann, 319–58. Brill.

Glomb, Vladimír. 2020b. "Toegye's Appraisal of Daoism." *Review of Korean Studies* 23, no. 1 (June): 89–112.

Glomb, Vladimír, and Eun-Jeung Lee. 2021. "'No Books to Leave, No Women to Enter': Confucian Academies in Pre-Modern Korea and Their Book Collections." In *Collect and Preserve: Institutional Contexts of Epistemic Knowledge in Pre-modern Societies*, edited by Eun-Jeung Lee, Eva Cancik-Kirschbaum, and Jochem Kahl, 175–98. Harrassowits Verlag.

Haboush, JaHyun Kim. 1985. "The Education of the Yi Crown Prince: A Study in Confucian Pedagogy." In *The Rise of Neo-Confucianism in Korea*, edited by Wm. Theodore de Bary and JaHyun Kim Haboush, 161–222. Columbia University Press.

Ivanhoe, Philip J. 2016. *Three Streams: Confucian Reflections on Learning and the Moral Heart-Mind in China, Korea, and Japan*. Oxford University Press.

Kim, Daeyeol. 2009. "King Chŏngjo's Political Strategy around the Royal Lecture on the Confucian Classics." Paper presented at the Association for Korean Studies in Europe Conference, June.

Kim Yangsu. 1999. "Chosŏn hugi sahoe pyŏndong kwa chŏnmunjik chungin ŭi hwaltong." In *Han'guk kŭndae ihaenggi chungin yŏn'gu*, edited by Yŏnse taehakkyo Kukhak yŏn'guwŏn, 171–298. Sinsŏwŏn.

Lee Byoung-Hoon. 2020. "Books and Book Culture in Oksan Academy." In *Confucian Academies in East Asia*, edited by Vladimír Glomb, Eun-Jeung Lee, and Martin Gehlmann, 197–225. Brill.

Lee, Song Mu. 2009. "The Government Service Examinations of the Chosŏn Dynasty." In *The Institutional Basis of Civil Governance in the Chosŏn Dynasty*, compiled and translated by John B. Duncan, Jung Chul Lee, Jeong-il Lee, Michael Ahn, and Jack A. Davey, 63–100. Seoul Selection.

Legge, James. 1960. *The Chinese Classics: With a Translation, Critical and Exegetical Notes, Prolegomena, and Copious Indexes*. Volume 1, *Confucian Analects, the Great Learning, and the Doctrine of the Mean*. Hong Kong University Press.

Park, Eugene Y. 2007. *Between Dreams and Reality: The Military Examination in Late Chosŏn Korea, 1600–1894*. Harvard University Asia Center.

Sancho, Isabelle. 2011. *Principes essentiels pour éduquer les jeunes gens*. Les Belles Lettres.

Sin Changho and Chang Chiwŏn. 2012. *Tongyang kyoyuk sasangsa*. Sŏhyŏnsa.

Slingerland, Edward. 2003. *Analects of Confucius: With Selections from Traditional Commentaries*. Hackett Publishing Company.

Tillman, Hoyt Cleveland. 2020. "Some Reflections on the Confucian Academies in China." In *Confucian Academies in East Asia*, edited by Vladimír Glomb, Eun-Jeung Lee, and Martin Gehlmann, 21–44. Brill.

Yi Man'gyu. 1991. *Chosŏn kyoyuksa*. Volume Sang [1]. Kŏrŭm. Reprint of the 1947 original.

Yulgok chŏnsŏ. Collected writings of Yi I. Available at: http://db.itkc.or.kr.

18

SCIENCE AND TECHNOLOGY

Don Baker

"Science" and "technology" had different connotations in Korea under the rule of the Chosŏn state (1392–1897) than they do presently. Presently, science is the systematic observation, analysis, and manipulation of objects, events, and processes in the natural world using the tools of mathematics and experimentation. Mathematics is an essential component of modern science as a tool for measuring and predicting natural phenomena and explaining why nature does what it does. In modern science, such explanations utilize quantifiable terms. Another important element of modern science is rigorous experimentation, with the expectation that the accuracy of the results of that experiment can be verified either by repeating it in a laboratory or by checking its results through mathematical calculations. Moreover, the modern fields of science and technology overlap. Technicians draw on scientific discoveries to create new technologies, and scientists use new technologies provided by technicians to uncover more of the secrets of nature.

Such an approach to the natural world is a relatively recent historical phenomenon. Many in Chosŏn closely observed natural phenomena to understand them better. Some also used the tools of mathematics to predict some natural phenomena. However, they generally did not rely on mathematics to go beyond prediction and explain natural events. Also, they did not tend to use replicable experiments to test their hypotheses about natural phenomena. Experiments in Chosŏn were usually thought experiments done in the heads of philosophers rather than in a lab. Therefore, these "experiments" were not amenable to empirical verification.

Those who studied nature in Chosŏn were not so much scientists as natural philosophers. This does not mean that before the advent of modern science, Chosŏn intellectuals did not improve their understanding of how nature behaved or did not learn better ways to take advantage of what nature provided. On the contrary, they made significant progress toward making it easier for humans to live healthy and productive lives. They also made substantial progress in observing and predicting natural events. Even though such progress did not occur at the rapid pace expected in the modern world, if "science" means nothing more than the systematic search for ways to explain, manipulate, and predict natural phenomena without recourse to supernatural actors or forces, then Chosŏn arguably had science.

Chosŏn also had the technology, of course. No organized society could function without the tools technology provides. Chosŏn technology, however, was not intertwined with Chosŏn science. Rather, science and technology occupied separate realms. Today's developments in scientific

DOI: 10.4324/9781003262053-24

275

The Routledge Handbook of Early Modern Korea

theories often stimulate technological advances, and, at the same time, technological advances frequently lead to new, more accurate, and precise scientific hypotheses. Not so in Chosŏn. Technicians and natural philosophers lived in two different worlds. Technicians built tools, and philosophers theorized about the natural world. The separation between science and technology was such that technicians normally would not seek the insights of those who carefully observed nature to help them improve old technologies or create new ones. Nor did those interested in investigating natural phenomena usually expect technical experts to provide them with better tools. There was little cross-fertilization between those who observed nature and those who created tools for monitoring or manipulating nature.

The gap between those who thought about nature and those who worked with and on nature may have been wider in Chosŏn Korea than in China and Japan. In Chosŏn, philosophers and technicians stood on different rungs of a social ladder. Philosophers were aristocrats, *yangban*, at the top of the social hierarchy. They usually did not think they could learn anything worthwhile from those beneath them. By the early seventeenth century, the distinction between the *yangban* and another group of educated males, who came to occupy the rung on the social ladder just beneath them, hardened. The latter were lower-level civil servants, known as *chungin* ("middle people"), for residence in the central part of the capital, Hansŏng (present-day Seoul).

The government certified the technical expertise of *chungin* with "miscellaneous examinations" (*chapkwa*), deemed not as prestigious as the civil examination (*munkwa*) on Confucian philosophy, history, and literature the *yangban* privileged. Passing a technical examination earned *chungin* access to such government posts as interpreters, physicians, jurists, astronomers, and mathematicians—all denigrated by *yangban* as narrowly trained technicians. By the early seventeenth century, *chungin* families, all based in Hansŏng, married among themselves, thus forming a distinct hereditary status group below *yangban* but above commoners. *Chungin* would not dare to offer advice on philosophical matters to *yangban*, who ostensibly exhibited a command of philosophical questions. *Chungin* did not enjoy the respect or status engineers and other technical experts enjoy today (Kim Yŏngsik 2021, 130–50).

Despite their differences in social status, philosophers and technical experts shared the same basic Neo-Confucian assumptions about how the natural world was formed and operated. They both assumed that everything in the universe comprises qi (Ko. *ki*; psychosomatic energy). Moreover, they both thought that qi is given shape and direction by *i* (Ch. *li*), the patterns of appropriate interactions that provide the structure that brings order to the universe.

Analytically distinguishable, qi and *i* are inseparable in the real world. Without *i*, Qi would be disorganized and unrecognizable as forming specific objects or operating regularly. *I* shapes qi into objects and direct them to operate so that they form normal patterns reflected in appropriate interactions. As the patterning force in the universe, *i* is neither conscious nor external to that which it directs. Nor is *i* a thing. It is simply the innate tendency of things to act and interact the way they should and do. Also, *i*, as written in Literary Sinitic (Classical Chinese), the language of Chosŏn elites, is both a singular and a plural noun. Every individual thing, process, and event is directed by its *i*. Still, all those *i* are intertwined through their direct interactions to create one universal network of interactions, also called *i* (Yung Sik Kim 2019, 169). This network of interactions constantly constructs and reconstructs the universe.

This Neo-Confucian vision of the universe features no external creator or creation occurring at one point in time. Neo-Confucians believed that creation was an ongoing process. They drew on the example of lice to support their assumption of unending spontaneous creation. They had noticed that lice often got into their clothes and bit them. They could wash those clothes in hot water and kill all those lice. When they put on clean, lice-free clothes, lice again bit them after a

276

Science and Technology

few days. According to An Chŏngbok (1712–91), a prominent Neo-Confucian scholar and historian, this proved that "things come into existence naturally, through the fertile [*i*-directed] intermingling and coalescing of *ki*" (Baker with Rausch 2017, 135–36).

Besides *i* and qi, Chosŏn thinkers utilized yin and yang (Ko. *ŭm* and *yang*), too, as formative forces in the universe to explain the order and change in the natural world. Yin and yang are labels for two complementary ways things interact or processes unfold. Sometimes explained as yang being bright, active, masculine, and hard contrasted with yin being dark, passive, feminine, and soft, the two would be better described as brighter compared to darker, more active compared to more passive, more masculine compared to more feminine, and as harder and softer. Yin and yang have no meaning apart from their contrasts, which emerge in the different stages of various natural processes or the roles played in any interaction. Also, yin and yang must balance each other—or there will be chaos in the universe. Regularity and stability, highly valued in Confucianism, occur when yin and yang interact harmoniously.

All the same, Chosŏn intellectuals realized that the universe, in all its complexity, could not be explained with two contrasting concepts alone. That is why they argued that yin and yang, through their interactions, produce the Five Phases. Those Five Phases are named wood, fire, earth, metal, and water, respectively, but they are not substances. Instead, they each represented a stage in an endless cycle of growth and decline. Wood stood for slow increase and growth, fire for peak growth and activity, earth for balance and neutrality, metal for slow decrease and decline, and water for maximum decrease and inactivity.

Moreover, those Five Phases do not exist in isolation. They get their designations by comparison with what preceded them and what will follow them. Like yin and yang, the Five Phases should play their assigned interactive roles, emerging from what preceded them at the right moment and receding in time for what follows them to appear. When they do not play their assigned roles, chaos can ensue. For example, traditional Korean medicine often explains disease as caused by one of the organs associated with one of the Five Phases acting inappropriately, such as a kidney not producing enough water. Only when the Five Major Organs are linked to one of the Five Phases—with each playing its proper role so that all Five Major Organs interact appropriately— can a person, or nonhuman animal, be healthy. Any attempt to understand the roles of yin, yang, and the Five Phrases only in terms of what they do would be incomplete. They also have to be understood in terms of what they *should* do in the interactive roles assigned to them.

This Neo-Confucian vision of the natural world as one of the constant interactions producing never-ending but orderly change informs the Chosŏn approach to investigating things. The "investigation of things" (Ch. *gewu*; Ko. *kyŏngmul*) was an important imperative for the educated Chosŏn elite. They wanted to "investigate things" to understand better the patterns revealed in how things interacted with each other. Understanding patterns would, they believed, make it possible for them to align with those patterns and, therefore, interact with those things appropriately. Chosŏn science was predominantly a practical endeavor, driven by a need to uncover correlations and patterns of interaction within the natural world, such as those between heaven and earth, between the human body and the rest of the material world, and between energy within the earth and energy and fortune above it. Chosŏn Koreans believed humans needed to know such correlations and patterns to interact appropriately with and within their physical environment. These patterns manifest in specific correlational correspondences, such as the Five Phases linking the human body with seasonal changes and dragon and tiger mountains connecting human fortune with geographic features. Such patterns of interaction attracted more attention and were studied, discussed, and analyzed more intensively than the physical objects interacting (Yung Sik Kim 2000, 42–69; Kim Yŏngsik 2021, 34–34).

The Routledge Handbook of Early Modern Korea

Since Chosŏn intellectuals wanted to understand how things interacted with one another so that they could know how they should interact with those things, they focused on the material world in terms of its interactive complementary forces, such as the aforementioned yin, yang, and the Five Phases. Such core elements of their pattern perspective are hard to quantify, since they operate primarily as descriptions of complementarity and correlations revealed in patterns of interactions. That makes it difficult to view them as scientific concepts, in the modern sense. They are not amenable to easy mathematical analysis. Chosŏn intellectuals, however, knew that to understand how to interact with the natural world, they had to consider that it was also a world of quantities. They knew they needed specific ways to point out that something is faster or larger than something else is, for example. For that, they naturally turned to mathematics.

Mathematics

Mathematics in Chosŏn was Chinese-style mathematics with some Korean variations. Chosŏn learned basic mathematical techniques from books originally produced in China, many of them from ancient China, such as the *Nine Chapters on the Mathematical Art* (*Jiuzhang suanshu*), which dates back at least to Han dynasty (202 BCE–220 CE) China. During the reign of King Sejong (r. 1418–50), Chosŏn also acquired copies of books providing information about advances in mathematics during China's Song (960–1279) and Yuan (1271–1368) dynasties (Kim Yŏnguk et al. 2022, 202). All those books used the inductive approach to mathematics that East Asians had long preferred.

Mathematics in East Asia tended to focus on concrete solutions to specific problems rather than on general rules governing a class of problems. A method that produced a correct answer to a problem would be applied to several similar issues rather than abstracted into the form of a rule framed in universal symbolic terms. If that method turned out to have wide applicability, then that applicability would be shown, not by restating it as a theoretical principle but by providing several concrete examples of that method in operation. This is inductive reasoning, based more on the recognition of patterns than on logic. It differs from the deductive approach long favored in the West in which formulas are logically deduced from abstract axioms and then applied to specific mathematical problems. Koreans shared this inductive approach with the Chinese and Japanese. Drawing on this inductive tradition, Chosŏn Koreans could add, subtract, multiply, divide, and extract square roots and solve equations with more than one unknown integer.

Despite this shared foundation, Koreans did mathematics in distinct ways. For example, they used counting rod notation long after the Chinese had come to prefer the abacus. Koreans wrote numbers in Sinographs and, after the first half-century of Chosŏn, also in Han'gŭl (Hangul). However, when writing down mathematical problems on paper, they generally chose to replicate the placement of counting rods to make it easier to visualize the numbers with which they worked. In the fifteenth century, the Chinese began replacing counting rods with the abacus (Li and Du 1987, 184). The abacus also came to be widely used in early modern Japan. Korea, however, stayed with the counting rods until almost the end of Chosŏn (Kim Yong Woon 1986, 37).

In counting rod notation, numbers were written like they were counting rods placed on a page. For example, four could be written as ≡ or ||||, depending on its place value. To avoid having too many lines next to each other, for the number six, they would put one horizontal line for "five" and then add a vertical line to make it represent six: T or ⊥. They used place values when they went beyond nine. Moving from right to left, they would change the orientations of the lines to show that they now represented a number in the 10s, 100s, 1,000s, and beyond, alternating the direction of the lines as they moved through the decimal places. For example, 6,446 would be written ⊥≡||||⊤. By Chosŏn, Koreans also have a zero they could use as a placeholder.

Using counting rods notation, even algebraic equations could be expressed as visualizations of the placement of counting rods on a counting board. With such concrete conceptualization of numeral relations, Korean mathematicians, working within their East Asian tradition, were able to attack complex algebraic problems so successfully that they often approached geometrical problems with algebraic tools—in contrast to the traditional European method, which often reformulated algebraic problems in geometric terms (Needham 1959, 112–39). Chosŏn Koreans, like the Chinese they learned mathematics from, were more inclined to algebraic than geometric formulations anyway since they were more interested in the specific patterns that governed relations between particular numbers than in the abstract properties of generic lines, planes, and solids (Needham 1959, 23–24).

All male members of the educated elite in Chosŏn were expected to have some familiarity with techniques for mathematical calculations, even though schools they attended as children did not formally teach mathematics. After all, China's ancient Western Zhou dynasty (c. 1046–771 BCE), which Chosŏn Confucians revered, had listed mathematics, along with ritual, music, archery, charioteering, and calligraphy, as one of the six arts which all educated men were supposed to be familiar with (*Shisanjing zhushu fu jiaokanji*, 707. [Vol X, 69]). However, Chosŏn Confucian scholars, who hoped to serve as high-level government officials, did not make mathematics the focus of their academic endeavors (Kim Yŏngsik 2021, 75–76). That was left for the professional *chungin* mathematicians to handle.

The existence of a status group of professional mathematicians was another way Korea's mathematical culture differed from neighboring China or Japan. Those serving as mathematicians for the government had to pass a mathematics examination (*sankwa*), testing their knowledge of Chinese mathematics texts and their application. They were not a hereditary status group since they did not inherit their positions. However, since schools did not teach basic mathematics, they tended to learn enough from their fathers, grandfathers, or other relatives, who were mathematicians, to pass the examination. Of the 1,627 men who passed the mathematics examination between 1498 and 1888, the vast majority came from mathematician families (Kim Yong Woon 1986, 31–36).

In early Chosŏn, some *yangban* took up posts as mathematicians, but after about 1600, the government mathematicians came from *chungin* families. This change reflected how Chosŏn's social hierarchy grew more rigid. All the same, the government recognized a need for more mathematicians. The number of people passing a qualifying examination and becoming accepted for further training and appointment as official mathematicians at the Board of Taxation grew substantially (Kim Yong Woon 1986, 33). Many *chungin* mathematicians had *yangban* ancestors but belonged to descent lines that had failed to do well on the civil service examination. Among them were 169 Chŏnju Yi, many among whom were of royal descent, albeit usually through an illegitimate son somewhere in the intervening generations before 1600.

Among such *chungin* mathematicians is Hong Chŏngha (1684–1727), whose methods reveal a third way regarding how Chosŏn mathematics differed from mathematics in Qing China (1644–1912) at the time. Hailing from a family of mathematicians going back several generations, Hong was an expert on a method for solving equations with one or more unknowns. His "celestial element" method entered early Chosŏn from Ming China (1368–1644) but then was forgotten in China itself (Hong Sung Sa et al. 2014, 155–56). We are told that, in 1713, Hong met a well-respected Chinese mathematician who had traveled to Hansŏng on a diplomatic mission. Having heard that Hong was respected for his calculating skills, the Chinese mathematician decided to contest with Hong to see if one could stump the other with a problem. Hong won with a complex

The Routledge Handbook of Early Modern Korea

issue that could only be solved with the celestial element method, unknown to the Chinese visitor (Kim Ho 2003, 198–203; Kim Yŏnguk et al. 2022, 294). The continued use of the celestial element method for solving complex equations was another way Chosŏn's mathematical culture differed from China's, along with the Korean use of counting rod notation and the existence of a status group of professional mathematicians.

One aspect of mathematics Koreans shared with the Chinese was a fascination with magic squares. Earlier in 1275, Yang Hui (fl. 1261–75) in Song China had constructed nine magic squares. Four centuries later, Ch'oe Sŏkchŏng (1646–1715) in Chosŏn Korea constructed several magic squares of his own. Ch'oe was a *yangban* official, advancing to the post of chief state councilor (Yŏngŭijŏng). Ch'oe would have been insulted to have been called a professional mathematician, but he liked what mathematics could tell him about the universe's structure. He even constructed and wrote about magic squares so others could see what he saw in them.

Like all magic squares, a set of integers placed within a square in vertical columns and horizontal rows form Ch'oe Sŏkchŏng's magic squares. Every number from the lowest to the highest is used once, but only once. When one adds up the numbers forming lines in every direction, horizontal, vertical, or a central diagonal, they all add up to the same sum (Kim Ho 2003, 190–97). One of his magic squares uses numbers 1 to 25; the sum is always 65 (Figure 18.1).

For Ch'oe Sŏkchŏng, this magic square was more than a mathematical curiosity. It was a graphic representation of the interconnected nature of the universe, as Neo-Confucians understood. Each number in the magic square was unique in that it was different from every other number in that magic square. Yet it had its identity as a number in a magic square only as part of the total pattern that constituted the magic square. This is an example of a core Neo-Confucian assumption: the

1	23	16	4	21
15	14	7	18	11
24	17	13	9	2
20	8	19	12	6
5	3	10	22	25

Figure 18.1 Magic square. At the time, Koreans were not using Arabic numerals, which are shown here only for ready recognition by the readers of this chapter. Illustration © Don Baker.

Science and Technology

Neo-Confucian universe comprises individual entities whose existence is defined by the roles they play in the patterns of which they are formative elements.

What shows the importance of playing assigned roles is that, in this magic square pattern, if even just two numbers switch places, no matter which numbers they are, the magic square loses its entire coherent pattern. Its lines will no longer produce the same sum and be a magic square. A magic square is only if each digit is properly placed (plays its role). Ch'oe Sŏkchŏng's magic squares illustrate the Neo-Confucian assumption that each component of the universal pattern, which constitutes reality, must play its assigned role, or disorder will result.

In the second half of Chosŏn, Koreans began learning about the Western approach to mathematics through books imported from Qing China. They were impressed with some formulae found in those books published in China by European missionaries and their disciples, particularly formulae used in calendrical calculation. Koreans, however, did not begin changing their basic approach to mathematics until Chosŏn's final decades. To begin with, the fundamental assumptions of Western mathematics differed from the fundamental assumptions underlying Korean mathematics. Also, the fact that Korean mathematics already gave them most of the tools they needed to solve the problems they needed to solve meant that as long as Neo-Confucianism dominated the educated elite's worldview, they saw no need to abandon tradition and embrace the alien mathematical traditions of the West (Kim Yong Woon 1986, 46; Baker 2012, 227–56).

Astronomy

The same confidence in their tradition is evident in how Chosŏn Koreans dealt with Western astronomy's challenge. Koreans adopted Western tools they believed they could utilize to serve their ends. However, until the last decades of Chosŏn, Koreans did not abandon their basic approach to studying the heavens. That basic approach was the Neo-Confucian emphasis on focusing more on patterns than individual objects. One name for astronomy in Chosŏn was *ch'ŏnmun*, meaning "celestial patterns."

Despite the lack of the tools of modern astronomy, Chosŏn was fairly advanced in its ability to predict movement in the sky. However, *chungin* astronomers did not worry about the exact nature of the celestial objects they were tracking. Instead, they focused on discerning the patterns that those objects moving across the sky revealed. On the other hand, Confucian scholars sometimes discussed the nature of the universe, such as whether the traditional Chinese view that the earth was flat and the sky was round was correct or if the planet might also be rounded. However, they did not test such hypotheses against the data astronomers collected. Philosophers and technical experts largely remained in separate worlds.

Astronomy might not be quite the right word for the study of the heavens in Chosŏn since the goals of that science were more like the goals of astrology than the reasons for astronomical investigations today. The Chosŏn government assigned three primary tasks to the *chungin* it appointed as astronomers. First, they had to find a way to align the calendar Chosŏn, as a tributary state, received every year from the emperor in China with the astronomical phenomena observed from the Korean Peninsula. Given the distance between China and Korea's capitals, that was not always easy (Chŏn 2021, 176, 246–66). Second, Chosŏn astronomers had to align the movements of the stars and planets above with their king's actions below, ensuring that the court performed important rituals on the appropriate date and time (Park 1998; Mun 2010, 49). That is the reason the Ministry of Ritual (Yejo) oversaw the Office for Observation of Natural Phenomena (Kwansanggam) (Mun 2010, 56). Third, they had to read movements in the skies, especially unusual movements, as reflections of the king's behavior below. Chong Tojŏn (1342–98), an important figure in laying the

The Routledge Handbook of Early Modern Korea

foundations for Chosŏn, observed: "Heaven, earth, and all the things therein are intertwined such that when the heart-minds of human beings are as they should be, all is right in heaven as well … . When natural anomalies exist, humans have not acted as they should" (*Sambong chip*, X.18a; Park 1998, 185).

To be appointed official astronomers, candidates had to pass the astronomy examination (*ŭmyangkwa, unkwa*). Those who passed served in the Office for Observation of Natural Phenomena alongside experts in geomancy (feng shui; Ko. *p'ungsu*) and divination. They would work together to advise the king of what nature was telling them about when it was appropriate to engage in certain actions and when it was inappropriate. They would also warn the monarch if he needed to improve his conduct to restore harmonious interactions with the natural world.

Despite what may appear to modern eyes as a superstitious orientation, Chosŏn nonetheless made significant progress in predicting events and movements in the sky. One Western expert on the history of science in East Asia noted that early in Chosŏn, "in 1450, the Korean Royal Observatory [Kwansanggam] possessed one of the finest and most complete sets of astronomical instruments in the world" (Needham et al. 1986, 94). Two men are responsible for that achievement: King Sejong and Chang Yŏngsil (1380?–1450?).

Chang Yŏngsil was a craftsman, not an astronomer. He began life as a slave (*nobi*) in a government office in the countryside. Sejong's father and predecessor, King T'aejong (r. 1400–18), had him transferred to Hansŏng because of his skill at making tools. Sejong recognized how exceptionally skilled Chang was, emancipated him, and told him to improve the accuracy of Chosŏn's equipment for observing celestial phenomena. Sejong was a master at recognizing talent and taking advantage of the skills and talents of others for the betterment of his kingdom. Sending Chang to China to observe the instruments Chinese astronomers were using and then having him create new instruments for the Office for Observation of Natural Phenomena by improving on what he had seen in China is one example of Sejong's managerial genius (Nam 2012).

Though Chang Yŏngsil had no experience in astronomy before he was brought up to Hansŏng, he devised several innovative tools for the Office for Observation of Natural Phenomena. The most remarkable was a water-powered automatic clock that announced not only the 12 hours in a day (a day then was divided into 12 units twice as long as our hours today) but also the five divisions of the time between dusk and dawn, which, of course, varied according to the seasons. The water clock announced the correct time despite those seasonal variations. Those announcements of the time were made by a wooden figure stepping out of the device and hitting either a bell, a drum, or a gong. Chang also constructed sundials and armillary spheres. Armillary spheres are devices used to pinpoint, via connected metal rings, where celestial bodies are in the sky even when it is too cloudy to see. When one object on one ring is moved, the other rings move as well, putting the models of the celestial objects on them in proper relationship to the model of the object the first ring represents. Chang's armillary sphere may have been water-powered, so it needed no human intervention to show the changing spatial relationships of various celestial objects (Needham et al. 1986, 16–93).

The purpose of these complicated machines was to confirm the accuracy—in a Korean context—of the calendars Chosŏn received from Ming China (Chŏn 2021, 188–88). Two factors made that more difficult. First, those calendars were not just lists of days, weeks, and months. Rather, they were ephemerides, giving the predicted positions of various visible objects in the sky and predicted times for important events such as eclipses. Second, the capitals of Ming and Chosŏn, Beijing and Hansŏng, respectively, were so distant from each other that the positions and times on the ephemerides did not always coincide with what could be seen from Hansŏng.

Science and Technology

To complicate matters further, upon Chosŏn's founding and recognition of it as a tributary state, Ming told Chosŏn to use Ming's *Datong-li* calendar, based on Sino–Islamic calendrical mathematics (Lee et al. 2020). When Qing replaced Ming, Qing made Chosŏn use a new calendar based on the European calendrical calculation method. Chosŏn needed quite a while to understand how to fit the Ming calendar to Chosŏn time. It took it even longer to figure out how to adapt the Qing calendar, known as the *Shixian-li*, especially since Qing did not want a tributary state to learn how to make its calendar and therefore tried to withhold from Chosŏn the mathematical formulae necessary to do so. Nevertheless, Chosŏn had created a calendar reflecting the skies above the Korean Peninsula by the late eighteenth century. This was an important achievement, not so much because of concern for astronomical accuracy but because Chosŏn needed a local calendar that made it easier to coordinate its activities with those of Qing (Lim 2012).

Calculating a calendar was the job of *chungin*. Accordingly, the Chosŏn court dispatched many *chungin* astronomers to Beijing in the seventeenth and eighteenth centuries to try to (illegally) obtain the information they needed to produce a more workable calendar. Quite a few *yangban*, too, were interested in discussing celestial phenomena, including Hong Taeyong (1731–83). On a trip to Beijing from 1765 through 1766, Hong met with some missionary astronomers in Beijing. He sought to learn more about astronomy and told them, "Stupidly and without consideration of the difficulties I presumed to build an armillary sphere by myself, but when I checked it with the actual heavenly phenomena, there were many errors" (*Tamhŏn sŏ,* Oeji, VII.13b).

Hong Taeyong is best known not for his clumsy attempts at creating his astronomical observatory but for his assertion that the earth was round and rotated on its axis. Hong did not say the earth revolved around the sun. Instead, he challenged only the traditional notion that the world was a stationary square. He insisted that since nature creating any other square objects cannot be seen, the earth cannot be an exception. He also pointed out that round things naturally are not stationary but rotate instead. Again, how could the earth be an exception? He does not prove his challenge to tradition through mathematical analysis. Instead, Hong's radical claim was grounded in philosophy rather than what we today would consider scientific argumentation (Park 1980). That is what we should expect from a typical Confucian in Chosŏn.

Geography

The skies above were not the only part of the natural world that attracted attention in Chosŏn. Chosŏn also had geographers, not just geomancy experts but also men who could draw maps of the Korean Peninsula and the world beyond. The men assigned to the Office for Observation of Natural Phenomena as geographers were not usually those who drew important maps. Those who drew the most comprehensive maps were not *yangban* or even *chungin*. Some were commoners.

Chosŏn produced three kinds of terrestrial maps. First, maps of the world as Koreans knew it then were almost always Sinocentric. They positioned China in the center, with the Korean Peninsula on the right side. Second, maps of Chosŏn alone grew more detailed over time but still maintained a traditional geomantic focus on mountains and waterways. Third, geomantic maps of small areas showed the details of the best sites for tapping into what were deemed to be invisible channels of energy coursing underground. *Chungin* geographers might be asked to draw such maps to identify an auspicious place for a royal burial or the construction of a royal dwelling.

Just as astronomy and astrology were intertwined in Chosŏn, so were cartography and geomancy. Chosŏn maps usually had a geomantic component except for maps of the world. Geomancy assumes invisible channels of energy (*ki*) flowing underground. Human beings can benefit in two ways if they tap into those channels. If they place a dwelling on a site on low

The Routledge Handbook of Early Modern Korea

ground where that energy is concentrated, they will live long and prosper. If they bury their parents and grandparents on a site on high ground where that energy is concentrated, they and their descendants will prosper (Hong-key Yoon 2006, 67–135). According to the approach to geomancy most popular in Chosŏn, the patterns of hills, dales, and waterways determine where such beneficial energy is more likely to be concentrated. In particular, mountains are believed to play a key role in directing where that energy will flow and also in determining where high concentrations of that energy are most likely to be found. It is not the mountains per se but the patterns formed with waterways that determine the best spot to benefit from the invisible qi underground. Geomancy is why maps of the Korean Peninsula paid more attention to the patterns formed by mountain ranges than is usually seen in maps produced by other countries (Hong-key Yoon 2006, 163–75).

In Chosŏn, Koreans increasingly voiced criticism against the geomantic belief that the resting place of ancestors' bones would affect the lives of descendants. Nevertheless, the demands of filial piety still led people to try to find the most auspicious sites for their parents' graves. Using the geomantic principles of having mountains behind a housing site and slow-moving water in front remained a respectable practice (Oh 2010). This is the principle behind Korea's first cultural geography, *A Place to Live* (*T'aengni chi*), by the unemployed *yangban* scholar Yi Chunghwan (1690–1756) (Inshil Choe Yoon 2019).

At the same time, Chosŏn maps of the Korean Peninsula grew more detailed and more accurate. Historians tend to date the beginning of Korea's greater geographical accuracy to the work of Chŏng Sangi (1678–1752) in the eighteenth century (Ledyard 1994, 305–10; Oh Sang-hak 2015, 246–57). Chŏng created a scale for his maps based on the traditional measure of distance known as *ri* (Ch. *li*), which varied depending on how long it took someone to go from one point on that map to another. For flat terrain, one unit on his map would represent a distance of 100 *ri,* but for more rugged terrain that might require going up over hills and down into valleys, that same unit would mean 120 to 130 *ri* traveled (Ledyard 1994, 307–09; Han 2008, 49). This allowed Chŏng to consider how long it would take people to go from one place to another while still producing a remarkably accurate map of the mountainous terrain of the Korean Peninsula.

In the nineteenth century, Kim Chŏngho (1804?–1866?) created an even more precise and detailed map of Chosŏn. Kim was a printer, not a professional geographer. Nevertheless, in 1861, he drew and published the *Complete Map of the Territory of Korea* (*Taedong yŏjido*). That map was so detailed that it had to be printed on multiple sheets of paper, though he also printed a one-sheet simplified version (Ledyard 1994, 323–29; Oh Sang-hak 2015, 297–331). The original version is seven meters long and three meters wide when all its component sheets are put together. This was the first map to accurately show the contours of all of Chosŏn, including the northern border region (Jeon 2011, 320–30).

Chosŏn maps of the broader world were not as detailed nor as accurate. As early as 1402, Chosŏn produced a world map that included not only Ming China and Japan but also the rest of Asia and Africa. However, it was not very accurate, with even its close neighbor Japan placed in the wrong location and made to look smaller than Korea (Ledyard 1994, 244–49; Oh Sang-hak 2015, 133–46). Nevertheless, that map from so long ago tells us that Koreans already had a well-established cartographic tradition in early Chosŏn (Jeon 2011, 282–89).

Sometime in the seventeenth century, Chosŏn began creating "wheel maps," positioning the Asian continent in the center. They show both China and Korea disproportionally large as parts of the Asian continent, an island surrounded by an inland sea. On the other side of that inland sea was another land mass, a thin ribbon of land spotted with the names of mostly imaginary countries. It, in turn, is encircled by an outer sea.

Science and Technology

Such wheel maps are unique to Korea and unknown in China or Japan (Oh 2008, 10), but they follow East Asian tradition in that they are Sinocentric. China is always in the center, much bigger than any other. Korea's landmass is also exaggerated, making it look disproportionate to Japan's. (Present-day China, Japan, and Korea North and South are roughly the same landmass as the United States, Germany, and Britain.) Chosŏn wheel maps did not attempt to reflect the actual relative sizes of various countries because, if they were drawn to scale, that would mean that China's cultural superiority would not be apparent in those maps (Ledyard 1994, 256–67; Oh Sang-hak 2015, 227–41). Instead, Chosŏn cartographers designed their wheels maps to show the patterns of cultural geography, indicating which people Chosŏn should interact with respectfully, above all the Confucianized Chinese, and those they should look down on, such as the non-Confucianized Japanese. They were less concerned about cartographical accuracy and geographical reality than they were with representing graphically their vision of the patterns defining the cultural geography of the earth.

Medicine

The fourth major scientific and technological tradition of Chosŏn Korea was medicine. Just as in the focus we saw on mathematical, astronomical, and terrestrial patterns, Chosŏn medicine focused on physiological patterns and how the various parts of the human body should interact. Moreover, just as Chosŏn mathematics, astronomy, and geography rose from a Chinese foundation but had significant Chosŏn variations, so did medicine in Chosŏn rise from a Chinese foundation but added significant indigenous variations.

Chosŏn Korea had three types of medical practitioners. First, government physicians, *chungin*, who passed the physician examination (*ŭikwa*) on mostly Chinese medical texts, performed their duties at government clinics. Second, some female entertainers (*kisaeng*), who were employed by the government and were of the same social status, the "lowborn" (*ch'ŏnmin*), as slaves, acquired enough medical knowledge to apply pulse diagnosis and administer acupuncture to higher-status women, whom male physicians were not allowed to touch (Yŏ et. al. 2012, 114–17). Third, many who were not formally recognized as physicians had acquired enough knowledge of medical theory and practice to provide advice and even treatment to people who did not have access to the limited number of government medical clinics. This last group grew in number in the second half of Chosŏn as the population increased, but growth in the number of official physicians did not keep up (Shin 2010).

These medical practitioners resembled astronomers, geomancers, and mathematicians in that they were more interested in patterns of interaction than in the actual material entities interacting. In traditional medicine, function preceded structure, and physiology preceded anatomy. People in Chosŏn recognized the existence of bodily organs, of course. They knew, for example, that the heart, the lungs, the kidneys, the liver, and the spleen were major organs responsible for the most important bodily functions. Those terms mean something quite different in Chosŏn Korea than in modern biomedicine. It would be more accurate to refer to them as "visceral systems of function" than as organs since the Sino-Korean names for those organs refer more to interactive physiological functions than anatomical structures (Sivin 1987, 68, 124–33).

This was another example of Chosŏn's pattern perspective. It meant that Chosŏn had no surgeons. Instead of removing or refashioning a specific dysfunctional organ within a patient's body, medical treatment relied on pharmaceuticals, acupuncture needles, or moxibustion (the burning of small amounts of the moxa herb on acupuncture points on the body) to restore the entire body to proper physiological harmony. The goal was to preserve and promote a harmonious interaction

285

The Routledge Handbook of Early Modern Korea

of all the body's physiological and psychological activities and between its internal operations and external environment. Chosŏn medicine is often expressed in terms of the harmonious flow of qi within the body and the various organs interacting by the proper pairings of the Five Phases. While defining health in those ways, Chosŏn medicine understood disease as disharmony: in the interactions among the various internal activities of the body and between those processes within the body and processes outside the world at large. In other words, the disease was a body failing to operate by its proper pattern of interactions.

Working within this framework, Chosŏn medicine developed a comprehensive approach to treating the body. The best example of this approach, and also an example of how Koreans in Chosŏn could take what they learned from China and improve on it, is *Exemplar of Korean Medicine* (*Tongŭi pogam*) of Hŏ Chun (1539–1615), a *chungin* physician. *Exemplar of Korean Medicine* shows three significant components. First, Hŏ introduced to Chosŏn the latest medical theories from China (Yŏ et al., 136–37). Second, he integrated the concepts and practices of Daoism, particularly its school of internal alchemy, into a mainstream medical theory. Hŏ wrote that those who wish to remain healthy and enjoy a long life should focus first on Daoist techniques for strengthening the production and harmonious circulation of qi within their bodies so that they will not need the healing methods of medicine. Prescribing medications and needles would be unnecessary unless those Daoist techniques failed. Third, he argued for incorporating native Korean ingredients and folk prescriptions into Chinese-style treatment. Accordingly, he rewrote Chinese prescriptions to replace expensive Chinese *materia medica* with Korean equivalents. Also, he provided simple prescriptions for those who could not afford the many ingredients many Chinese prescriptions demand (Sin 2015, 234–41, 320–21).

Exemplar of Korean Medicine gained its persuasive power from how Hŏ Chun wove those three strands together. Previous medical encyclopedias in Korea were primarily compilations of medical texts that did not evaluate the relative effectiveness of the various prescriptions and other medical strategies those texts recommended. Hŏ provided an interpretative framework for understanding which healing and health-enhancing techniques were likely to work better than others. He also evaluated which medicines or procedures were likely the most effective in specific situations. His comprehensive approach won him readers, not only in Chosŏn but beyond. When Hong Taeyong was in Beijing in 1765, he learned that local publishers had reprinted it (*Tamhŏn sŏ*, Oeji, VIII.21b). Reprints also circulated in Japan (Sin 2015, 335–53). In the twenty-first century, an English translation of the entire massive text would appear (An et al. 2013).

Final Thoughts

Science and technology in Korea today are very different from what they were in Chosŏn. They began to change in the final decades of Chosŏn, when new schools began teaching modern mathematics, geography, astronomy, and medicine, among other subjects such as English. Science in Korea today is based on mathematical analysis and experimental verification, not philosophy. *I*, qi, yin, yang, and the Five Phases have disappeared from scientific and technological discourse. The pattern perspective no longer dominates.

Moreover, due to the introduction of modern science, scientists and technicians talk to each other much more than they did in Chosŏn. A hereditary status group of technical experts denigrated by *yangban* with a philosophical education no longer exists. Koreans no longer practice traditional mathematics and astronomy. Geomancy is still practiced, and geomantic maps are still produced, but other maps follow modern rather than traditional formats. Chosŏn medicine is one

Science and Technology

traditional science that still flourishes in Korea today, North and South. However, it exists alongside modern biomedicine and is no longer the only recourse for Koreans falling ill.

Korea's tremendous changes since the late nineteenth century should not overshadow how much the people of Chosŏn accomplished using traditional tools and concepts. They calculated most of what they needed to calculate. They produced useful maps, predicted celestial events, and cured illnesses. When compared to how other societies dealt with the natural world before the advent of modern science and technology, Chosŏn has no reason for shame. Chosŏn science and technology are much recognized today as ahead of its time.

References

An Sangu, Kwŏn Omin, and Jeong Hwa Lee. 2013. *Dongui Bogam: Treasured Mirror of Eastern Medicine.* Translated by Kim Namil and Wung Seok Cha. Ministry of Health and Welfare.

Baker, Don. 2012. "Impotent Numbers: Korean Confucian Reactions to Jesuit Mathematics." *Korean Journal for the History of Science* 34, no. 2: 227–56.

Baker, Don, with Franklin Rausch. 2017. *Catholics and Anti-Catholicism in Chosŏn Korea.* University of Hawai'i Press.

Chŏn Yonghun. 2021. *Han'guk ch'ŏnmunhaksa.* Tŭllyŏk.

Han Young-woo. 2008. "The Historical Development of Korean Cartography." In *The Artistry of Early Korean Cartography*, edited by Han Young-woo, Ahn Hwi-joon, and Bae Woo Sung, translated by Choi Byonghyon, 1–90. Tamal Vista Publications.

Hong Sung Sa, Hong Young Hee, and Kim Young Wook. 2014. "Hong Jeongha's Tianyuanshu and Zhengcheng Kaifangfa." *Journal of the History of Mathematics* 27, no. 3: 155–64.

Jeon, Sang-Woon. 2011. *A History of Korean Science and Technology.* NUS Press.

Kim Ho. 2003. *Chosŏn kwahak inmul yŏlchŏn.* Hyumŏnisŭt'ŭ.

Kim Yong Woon. 1986. "Pan-Paradigm and Korean Mathematics in the Chosŏn Dynasty." *Korea Journal* 26, no. 3: 25–46.

Kim Yŏngsik [Yung Sik Kim]. 2021. *Han'guk chŏnt'ong kwahak ŭi paegyŏng.* Tŭllyŏk.

Kim Yŏnguk, Yi Changju, and Chang Hyewŏn. 2022. *Han'guk suhak munmyŏngsa.* Tŭllyŏk.

Kim, Yung Sik [Kim Yŏngsik]. 2000. *The Natural Philosophy of Chu Hsi, 1130–1200.* American Philosophical Society.

Kim, Yung Sik [Kim Yŏngsik], trans. 2019. "Science and Natural Philosophy." In *Zhu Xi: Selected Writings*, edited by Philip J. Ivanhoe, 162–86. Oxford University Press.

Ledyard, Gari. 1994. "Cartography in Korea." In *Cartography in the Traditional East and Southeast Asian Societies*, edited by J. B. Harley and David Woodward, 235–345. University of Chicago Press.

Lee, Ki-won, Young-Sook Ahn, Byeong-Hee Min, and Young-Ryan Lim. 2020. "Study on the Period of the Use of Datong-li in Korea." *Journal of Astronomy and Space Science* 27, no. 1: 55–68.

Li Yan and Du Shiran. 1987. *Chinese Mathematics: A Concise History.* Translated by John N. Crossley and Anthony W. C. Lun. Clarendon Press.

Lim Jongtae. 2012. "Learning 'Western' Astronomy from 'China': Another Look at the Introduction of the Shixianli Calendrical System into Late Joseon Korea." *Korean Journal for the History of Science* 34, no. 2: 205–25.

Mun Chungyang. 2010. "Wang ŭi hŏrak ŭl ŏdŏ hanŭl ŭl kwanch'al hada." In *Chosŏn chŏnmun'ga ŭi ilsaeng*, edited by Kyujanggak Han'gukhak yŏn'guwŏn, 47–74. Kŭlhangari.

Nam Moon-hyon. 2012. "Jang Yeong-sil: Inventor of the Striking Clepsydra during the Reign of King Sejong in Joseon." In *Explorations in the History of Machines and Mechanisms*, edited by Teun Koetsier and Marco Ceccarelli, 83–105. Springer.

Needham, Joseph. 1959. *Science and Civilization in China.* Vol. 3. Cambridge University Press.

Needham, Joseph, Lu Gwei-Djen, John Combridge, and John Major. 1986. *The Hall of Heavenly Records: Korean Astronomical Instruments and Clocks, 1380–1780.* Cambridge University Press.

O Sanghak [Oh Sang-hak]. 2015. *Han'guk chŏnt'ong chirihaksa.* Tŭllyŏk.

Oh Sang-hak [O Sanghak]. 2008. "Circular World Maps of the Joseon Dynasty: Their Characteristics and Worldview." *Korea Journal* 48, no. 1: 8–45.

The Routledge Handbook of Early Modern Korea

Oh Sang-hak [O Sanghak]. 2010. "The Recognition of Geomancy by Intellectuals during the Joseon Period." *Review of Korean Studies* 13, no. 1: 121–47.

Park Seong-rae. 1980. "Hong Tae-yong's Idea of the Rotating Earth." *Korea Journal* 20, no. 8: 21–29.

Park Seong-rae. 1998. *Portents and Politics in Korean History*. Jimoondang.

Sambong chip. Collected works of Chŏng Tojŏn. Available at: https://db.itkc.or.kr.

Shin, Dongwon [Sin Tongwon]. 2010. "How Commoners Became Consumers of Naturalistic Medicine in Korea, 1600–1800." *East Asian Science, Technology and Society: An International Journal* 4, no. 2: 275–301.

Sin Tongwŏn [Dongwon Shin]. 2015. *Tongŭi pogam kwa Tong Asia ŭihaksa*. Tŭllyŏk.

Shisanjing zhushu fu jiaokanji. 1980. Reprint. Zhonghwa shuju.

Sivin, Nathan. 1987. *Traditional Medicine in Contemporary China*. Center for Chinese Studies, University of Michigan.

Tamhŏn sŏ. 2023. Collected works of Hong Taeyong. Available at: https://db.itkc.or.kr.

Yŏ Insŏk, Yi Hyŏnsuk, Kim Sŏngsu, Sin Kyuhwan, Pak Yunhyŏn, and Pak Yunje. 2012. *Han'guk ŭihaksa*. Taehan ŭisa hyŏphoe ŭiryo chŏngch'aek yŏn'guso.

Yoon, Hong-key. 2006. *The Culture of Fengshui in Korea: An Exploration of East Asian Geomancy*. Lexington Books.

Yoon, Inshil Choe. 2019. *A Place to Live: A New Translation of Yi Chung-hwan's T'aengniji, the Korean Classic for Choosing Settlements*. University of Hawai'i Press.

PART VI

Creative Genres

19

LITERATURE

Gregory N. Evon

The assumption that Korean literature is necessarily written in Korean is a relatively recent innovation. By the founding of the State of Chosŏn (1392–1897), Koreans had been using Literary Sinitic (classical Chinese) for roughly a millennium. To be sure, not many extant works date back so far. However, Buddhist historical sources show that by Chosŏn's founding, Korean monks had been engaged for centuries in scholarship requiring high literacy levels in Literary Sinitic. The early-to-mid-sixth century is a convenient date, marking Korean monks' introduction of Buddhism to Japan. Likewise, extant materials from Chosŏn's predecessor, the State of Koryŏ (918–1392), show how Korean intellectuals saw themselves as part of a larger literary community bonded by a shared use of Literary Sinitic rather than divided by various spoken languages.

An exception that affirms this general rule is the small body of *hyangga* ("native songs") or local songs Koryŏ recorded. *Hyangga* used Sinographs (Chinese characters) to represent Korean vernacular songs. This genre inadvertently illuminates key features of Chosŏn literary history. First, something written in the vernacular was not necessarily easier to understand than Literary Sinitic. Modern scholars have relied on Literary Sinitic translations to interpret *hyangga*. Second, various scripts can be more or less useful for writing a given language. Theoretically, one can write English using Sinographs, but it would be unwieldy. By contrast, one can use the Korean alphabet, Han'gŭl (Hangul), to record the English language, not as a matter of translation but of transcription (that is, by recording the sounds of words). As discussed later, the Korean alphabet's strength is its ability to represent sound.

The central question is the relationship between a given script and the oral sounds of a given language. The Japanese used Sinographs early on to represent the sounds of the Japanese language, a practice stimulated by Korean scribes and enabled by the fact that Japanese is not as phonologically complex as Korean (Takayama 1995, 483). Therefore, matching a given Sinograph to a given syllable in Japanese was more straightforward. Finally, there is the question of educational curricula. Those who left examples of *hyangga* were, first and foremost, literate in Literary Sinitic, which formed the basis for formal education and literary training until the end of Chosŏn. The most critical feature of Literary Sinitic is that it differs from everyday speech and is thus "unsayable" (Mair 1994, 708). The gap underpinned literary development because mastery of Literary Sinitic required much time and formal education. Such difficulty, in turn, explains the utility of the alphabet and the fierce resistance to it.

DOI: 10.4324/9781003262053-26

The Routledge Handbook of Early Modern Korea

The Significance of Writing

The founding of Chosŏn initially resulted in a lull in literary production, partly due to the fear that Koryŏ's education system emphasized writing at the expense of Confucian moral cultivation. Leading figures such as Kwŏn Kŭn (1352–1409) decided to deemphasize writing and institute oral examinations. The experiment failed. Chosŏn reinstated written examinations as it became clear that students could still take shortcuts in their studies, albeit without attaining command of Literary Sinitic essential to the government (Kalton 1985, 92–93). Moreover, literary skills were crucial in diplomacy—an issue highlighted when Ming (1368–1644) Chinese officials took offense to what they deemed poorly written Korean documents in 1396 and 1397. An exchange of Literary Sinitic poetry between China's Hongwu emperor (r. 1368–98) and Kwŏn Kŭn partly ameliorated the diplomatic tensions (Alston 2009, 104–05).

A burst of intellectual and literary activity followed the early lull. Among the new works were the *History of Koryŏ* (*Koryŏ sa*; 1451), the *Essentials of Koryŏ History* (*Koryŏ sa chŏryo*; 1452), and the *Anthology of Korean Writings* (*Tongmun sŏn*; 1478), which contained pieces in various Literary Sinitic genres by Koreans from the seventh through fifteenth centuries. The *Anthology* was a political and literary statement. Its compilers, led by Kwŏn Kŭn's grandson Sŏ Kŏjŏng (1420–88), recounted through their selections the importance of Chosŏn's founding in cultural terms anchored in Literary Sinitic writing. Sŏ Kŏjŏng judged that Chosŏn, at his historical moment, marked the culmination of literary culture and Confucian civilization in Korean history (Wei and Lewis 2019, 5). The compilation included selections from Chosŏn figures (many still alive at the compilation's completion) that reflect the failure of the early educational reforms. The majority of the Chosŏn selections were by those who, like Kwŏn Kŭn, were educated during the waning years of Koryŏ. The works by those who, like Sŏ Kŏjŏng, came of age after the early educational reforms were abandoned.

One of the most critical literary developments of Chosŏn occurred with the invention of Han'gŭl under the leadership of King Sejong (r. 1418–50) in the mid-1440s. The alphabet immediately came under attack at court for degrading Chosŏn's Confucian culture by adopting barbarous practices of peoples like the Mongols and the Japanese, who had unique scripts to write their vernacular languages. This confrontation revolved around a point at the forefront of the compilation of the *Anthology of Korean Writings* three decades later, namely, the centrality of Sinographs and Literary Sinitic writing in Confucian civilization (Ledyard 1998, 127–60).

Han'gŭl laid the groundwork for popular literacy because it captures a wide range of sounds, enabling true vernacular Korean writing. Moreover, the alphabet can represent pronunciations of Sinographs. Sejong's critics were most fearful about popular literacy, and it seems that he emphasized the practical uses of the alphabet to enhance education in Sinographs (Ledyard 1998, 133). These fears make sense in their historical context and mark Sejong as a maverick. The acquisition of Literary Sinitic through mastery of the Confucian classics necessarily drew a link between Literary Sinitic literacy and Confucian morality. No such link existed for vernacular literacy, which, in principle, was readily available to anyone who spoke Korean. Over time, these fears would be borne out in popular vernacular fiction that recounted tales of adventure and love.

Vernacular writing in Han'gŭl did not supplant Literary Sinitic, which remained the dominant written language for literature, intellectual work, and government until the end of the nineteenth century. Likewise, the Confucian distaste for fiction and emphasis on the importance of poetry shaped subsequent literary developments. Instead, vernacular Korean and Literary Sinitic writings had a complex relationship that was evident in early poetic writings and became more prominent over the following centuries. To illustrate these features concisely, the following discussion pre-

Literature

sents the context of the earliest literary applications of Han'gŭl, highlights the two earliest Korean novels, one each in Literary Sinitic and vernacular Korean, and then turns to common poetic genres.

Key Developments in Literary Sinitic and Vernacular Literature

One of the earliest literary applications of the alphabet is the *Songs of Flying Dragons* (*Yongbi ŏch'ŏn ka*; 1447), a collection that praised Chosŏn's Yi royal house (Lee 2008, 151–64). It shows how vernacular writing in the earliest instance was dependent upon Literary Sinitic. This dependency is evident throughout the work, and the title partly illustrates the basic principle. Not vernacular Korean, the title is a transcription of the Korean pronunciations of a string of Sinographs that mean "dragon/s flying to heaven song/s." The discussion below further addresses the issue.

Court officials' utilization of the *Songs of Flying Dragons* to attack Sejong highlighted the relationship between Chosŏn's Confucian moral foundations and literature. The king had overseen harsh anti-Buddhist policies early in his reign, following the lead of his officials in fortifying policies his father, King T'aejong (r. 1400–18), had inaugurated. Sejong, however, subsequently grew wary of his officials' anti-Buddhist views and began actively antagonizing them with demonstrations of his Buddhist faith. In 1448, Sejong's critics framed his stubbornness over Buddhism as a failure to live up to the Confucian ideals enshrined in the *Songs of Flying Dragons* and embodied by his father (*Sejong sillok* 1448/7/22 entry 2).

This conflict had another literary dimension. At roughly the same time that work on the *Songs of Flying Dragons* was underway, Sejong and his son, future King Sejo (r. 1455–68), were using the alphabet for Buddhist literary purposes (Mair 1994, 734–736; Lee 2008, 165–67). That body of work remains poorly understood and highly contested (King 2018, 1–8). Nonetheless, it was immediately evident that if Han'gŭl could be used for purposes championed by Confucian moralists, the script could also be utilized for purposes that the critical officials found reprehensible.

Experimentation and a burst of activity in the production of Literary Sinitic texts superseded the Confucian literary conservatism seen in the disputes around the alphabet. Two prominent figures were Sŏ Kŏjŏng and Kim Sisŭp (1435–93). As Kwŏn Kŭn's grandson, Sŏ Kŏjŏng had an illustrious pedigree, and he enjoyed an enviable career in the central government spanning four decades. By contrast, Kim Sisŭp abandoned his hopes for a career in government in protest against Sejo's usurpation of the throne and became an itinerant Buddhist monk. Each would establish himself as a writer of the first order (Figure 19.1).

Sŏ Kŏjŏng's role in the compilation of the *Anthology of Korean Writings* was one of many government-sponsored undertakings in which he was involved. These included works on literature, history, and law, and his reputation as a writer—specifically, as a poet—was a crucial factor in his involvement in the *Anthology of Korean Writings*. Nevertheless, his literary interests and activities were far-ranging. Such works included a compilation of anecdotes entitled *Humorous Accounts Leisurely Recounted in a Time of Great Peace* (*T'aep'yŏng hanhwa kolgye chŏn*), a collection of unofficial historical accounts under the title the *Brush Garden Miscellany* (*P'irwŏn chapki*), and a collection of poetry criticism and poetic anecdotes entitled *Poetry Talks by a Man from the East* (*Tongin sihwa*). The last of these three is especially significant because it marked a resurgence of the poetry talks (*sihwa*) genre that had taken shape in Koryŏ under Chinese literary influence. As discussed above, early Chosŏn suffered a hiatus in literary production, but Sŏ Kŏjŏng's writings marked a renewed confidence and vigor reflected in his insistence in the *Anthology of Korean Writings* that literary quality in Korean history had reached an apex in his lifetime.

Figure 19.1 Portrait of Kim Sisŭp, late seventeenth or early eighteen century, 71.8 cm × 48.1cm. Source: Central Buddhist Museum, Seoul, Republic of Korea. Photo credit: Korean Heritage Service.

Like Sŏ Kŏjŏng, Kim Sisŭp was an esteemed poet, and the *Anthology of Korean Writings* includes a significant number of his poems. Nevertheless, in literary-historical terms, Kim Sisŭp's primary significance rests on the fact that he wrote the *New Tales of the Golden Turtle* (*Kŭmo sinhwa*), generally regarded as the first novel in Korean history (Wuerthner 2012, 166, 168). The question of genre is problematic. It was not a novel per se but a collection of individual ghost stories. The work was nonetheless innovative in that it used a longer-form fictional format, albeit with a considerable amount of Literary Sinitic poetry embedded throughout and functioning as a vital part of the stories.

Written in Literary Sinitic, Kim Sisŭp modeled the collection on the *New Tales Written While Trimming the Wick* (or *New Tales Told by Lamplight*; *Jiandeng Xinhua*) by Qu You (1347–1433), a Ming Chinese author (Chang 2010, 7–10). Due to Qu You's influence, the earliest examinations of Kim Sisŭp's collection paradoxically emphasized its derivativeness and embodiment of the Korean national spirit. However, the more significant point of historical importance is how the employment of ghost stories allowed Kim to offer a veiled critique of contemporary politics. Qu You had done the same, but Kim Sisŭp went further by aiming at the brutal and immoral conduct of identifiable figures, which is to say, Sejo and his enablers who had usurped the throne (Wuerthner 2012, 165–69, 178–79, 180–81).

The collection is also important for reasons apart from genre, and these illustrate crucial features of the development of Chosŏn literature. First, Qu You's influence on Kim shows that there

Literature

was an interest in literary developments in China. But counterbalancing that interest was a literary and intellectual conservatism that viewed contemporary literary Chinese influence with suspicion. As discussed below, this was an early instance of a theme that would become increasingly pronounced. Second, Kim's collection had little impact on Chosŏn writers, mainly because the Japanese looted the collection during the Imjin War (East Asian War; 1592–98). Subsequently reprinted and published commercially several times in Japan, the collection exerted some influence on Japanese literature. The collection was thus lost in Korea until it was famously rediscovered in Japan and reintroduced to Korea in the early twentieth century (Wuerthner 2012, 165).

Theft by the Japanese, though, is not the only explanation. Attitudes towards printing and publication reflected the conservatism in the debates about the alphabet. In the early sixteenth century, conservative views were prominent in debates over attempts to make books more freely available in a manner similar to what existed in China. These attempts failed, however, and several decades later, an official at the royal court, Yun Ch'unnyŏn (1514–67), began pushing once again for the establishment of bookstores. Eccentric and widely reviled due to his wide-ranging interests, Yun Ch'unnyŏn was intensely interested in literature in general and Kim Sisŭp and Qu You in particular. The central problem was that he was dissatisfied with the Confucian orthodox approach to literature, and this dissatisfaction was prominent in his interest in fiction. (The question of genre receives a more detailed treatment further below.) Apart from failed agitations over making books more freely available, Yun collected and printed Kim's writings, including *New Tales of the Golden Turtle*, and working with a translator-interpreter, he produced a gloss of Qu You's *New Tales Written While Trimming the Wick* (Evon 2009, 14–16).

Clearly, at least some within the ranks of the elite were dissatisfied with dominant conservative views of literature. The earliest example of Korean vernacular fiction, the *Tale of Hong Kiltong* (*Hong Kiltong chŏn*), was written around the turn of the seventeenth century, not long after Yun's death—if the traditional view that the official Hŏ Kyun (1569–1618) wrote it is valid. However, most discussions of authorship of premodern fiction require a degree of caution. After all, authors did not put their names on such writings, nor was fiction (in Literary Sinitic or the vernacular) included in individuals' collected writings (*munjip*). These collections, typically compiled after one's death, maintained genre and linguistic distinctions that affirmed elite literary values. Such collections thus preserved writings in Literary Sinitic (with a heavy emphasis on Literary Sinitic poetry) but excluded works of fiction and vernacular writings that circulated independently.

There are other reasons to question Hŏ Kyun's authorship of the *Tale of Hong Kiltong*, but these entail textual and historical comparisons that are too complex to be addressed here (Kang 2019, 32–42, 71–84). Suffice it to emphasize that difficulties in authorial attribution derive partly from how texts were unstable as they circulated, and were copied and recopied, allowing for subsequent additions and alterations. For the sake of simplicity, I, therefore, follow the commonplace assumption that Hŏ Kyun was the author. This assumption has a solid foundation in the writings of Hŏ Kyun's contemporary, Yi Sik (1584–1647), which inadvertently highlight commonplace difficulties in confirming basic information about novels and authors. Guesswork based on limited information is the result. These difficulties, moreover, are exacerbated by the ravages of war in Korea in the centuries following Hŏ Kyun's death and, we can assume, the loss of texts. Whatever the case, it is problematic to view Hŏ Kyun as the author of any extant versions of the *Tale of Hong Kiltong* (Kang 2019, xiv, 38, 39).

The collected works of Yi Sik illustrate how scholars might discuss a piece of literature, such as the *Tale of Hong Kiltong*, in an acceptable literary format that would subsequently be included in their collected works. Such acceptable literary formats can allow a better understanding of writings outside the bounds of respectability. In the case of the *Tale of Hong Kiltong*, a collection of

The Routledge Handbook of Early Modern Korea

miscellaneous essays by Yi Sik recorded comments on authorship, context, and literary inspiration. Discussing the *Water Margin* (Ch. *Shui hu zhuan*), a famous Chinese vernacular novel that recounts the exploits of bandits, Yi Sik noted that the author's family was struck deaf and dumb for three generations as cosmic retribution for writing a work that celebrated banditry. He then explained how the work inspired Hŏ Kyun to write the *Tale of Hong Kiltong* and concluded that Hŏ Kyun's malign influence resulted in a punishment that exceeded that of the author of the *Water Margin*. The basis for Yi Sik's judgment was that Hŏ Kyun was executed for plotting against the state ("Sallok").

Hŏ Kyun is a fascinating figure whose career has significant parallels with Yun Ch'unnyŏn's that illuminate Chosŏn literary history. First and foremost, Hŏ Kyun was, like Yun Ch'unnyŏn, drawn to the relatively less restrained intellectual and literary culture found in Ming China. In addition, his wide-ranging interests ran against the prevailing orthodox Confucian conservatism but did so in a far more provocative way. The *Tale of Hong Kiltong* challenged prevailing norms, as did its literary model, the *Water Margin*. Nevertheless, the story's core also had a real-life counterpart in the career of a bandit named Hong Kiltong, who was apprehended by the Chosŏn authorities in 1500 and most likely died in jail not long thereafter. The *Tale of Hong Kiltong* took the side of its protagonist against the ruling elite and its emphasis on social hierarchy, which preserved wealth and stability for the few at the expense of the many. The general thrust of the *Tale of Hong Kiltong* had parallels with Hŏ Kyun's other writings and, most importantly, with contemporary views by his peers that he was a traitor to his class and the values espoused by the state. Allegations of that type plagued his career and were prominent in the charges that led to his execution in 1618.

In the broader context of Chosŏn literature, the *Tale of Hong Kiltong* is significant on linguistic, literary, and social grounds. To begin with, assessing premodern literacy rates is an unresolvable problem, but nothing indicates a phenomenon resembling mass literacy even in the vernacular throughout Chosŏn's history. Even so, the fact that the novel circulated in vernacular Korean suggests a potential readership among those who did not belong to the elite educated class. The question of literacy rates in the vernacular is misleading in and of itself. The Korean alphabet and the use of vernacular Korean could have a multiplier effect on disseminating written content because those who could read the vernacular could read to those who were illiterate. In this respect, the novel's theme and linguistic format were perfectly matched in a fashion that appears at once like a distorted version of Sejong's ambition for his alphabetic script and a validation of his critics' worst fears.

Yi Sik alluded to these linguistic and social implications in conjunction with his overview of the *Water Margin*. This raises the second point. In Yi Sik's account, Chinese bandits revered the *Water Margin* and took it as a model or justification for their activities. This depiction seems odd, but it makes much more sense given that the *Water Margin* was, as noted above, a Chinese vernacular novel. Distinctions between Literary Sinitic and vernacular Chinese writing are often unclear in Korean scholarship due to the Korean focus on script, by which script serves as a stand-in for language. The result is a commonplace conceptual confusion that can be easily illustrated through the notion that knowing the Korean alphabet is the same as knowing Korean. That notion is, of course, false but common. That is to say, the average foreign learner can master the Korean script within a matter of days without substantial knowledge of the Korean language.

Knowledge of Chinese vernacular writing among the Chosŏn elite is another vexing question in the debates over creating the Korean script. In addition, even popular Chinese writings in Literary Sinitic could pose difficulties for Chosŏn Korean readers educated in Literary Sinitic. That is why Yun Ch'unnyŏn produced a gloss for Qu You's *New Tales Written While Trimming the Wick*. The point of interest here is that the *Tale of Hong Kiltong* took the linguistic format of the *Water*

Margin to its logical conclusion in the Chosŏn Korean context by employing the Korean script and vernacular language. In stark contrast, Literary Sinitic and vernacular Chinese writing in the Chinese context employed Sinographs.

For these reasons, the *Tale of Hong Kiltong* was more innovative than the *New Tales of the Golden Turtle*. This assessment does not estimate their respective literary worth, nor is it a species of Korean linguistic nationalism that prioritizes writings in the Korean language. Kim Sisŭp's collection was far more artfully constructed. Nevertheless, Kim's *New Tales of the Golden Turtle* existed within a linguistic and literary field that had a prominent precursor in the writings of Qu You and other predecessors in the Literary Sinitic idiom. The *New Tales* was a product of high literacy in Literary Sinitic. Above all else, it required skill in Literary Sinitic poetics since lengthy poetic exchanges between characters convey much of the content of the stories in the collection. Those literary skills, in turn, reflected a deep knowledge of Literary Sinitic texts. These characteristics are best appreciated through translation, requiring copious footnotes to understand what is contained within the collection fully. The idea of giving a meaningful rendition of Kim's *New Tales* through an oral vernacular retelling—that is, reading it aloud in translation—is therefore unimaginable. One could, of course, give a paraphrase, but much would necessarily be lost. The collection is meant to be read, and its intricacies can only be fully understood through reading.

The *Tale of Hong Kiltong* is radically different as there is little difficulty in imagining it read aloud as written. To be sure, premodern texts like it are modernized for contemporary readers by specialists, and modern readers who examine premodern print and manuscript versions of vernacular texts confront a range of difficulties that encompass everything from spelling to word spacing. These difficulties are apparent in even a relatively recent manuscript copy dating from 1901 that was, it seems, produced to be lent out for a fee from a lending library in Seoul (*Hong Kiltong chŏn*, 1901). Despite all that, however, it is easy to envision someone reading the work aloud to others. Indeed, one can intuit unease over that fact in Yi Sik's comments.

Therefore, the most significant innovation in the *Tale of Hong Kiltong* is also the most difficult to appreciate. Whereas the fundamental literary building blocks for the *New Tales of the Golden Turtle* had been in use for centuries and were common tools for those who were educated throughout East Asia, the composition of the *Tale of Hong Kiltong* required the use of the Korean script to articulate a vernacular tale with no obvious domestic literary precursors. This innovation is particularly striking in light of the *Songs of Flying Dragons*, in which the vernacular elements are minimal compared to the Literary Sinitic components. Indeed, the vernacular elements serve, in effect, to help parse the text, and these portions, in turn, are supported by lengthy explanations in Literary Sinitic (*Songs of Flying Dragons*). The *Tale of Hong Kiltong* is radically different.

The fact that the *Water Margin* was composed in vernacular Chinese could thus serve as a general guide for producing a Korean vernacular tale about bandits, nothing else. The *New Tales of the Golden Turtle* and the *Tale of Hong Kiltong* were both "firsts" in Korean literary history. However, the *New Tales Written While Trimming the Wick* and the *New Tales of the Golden Turtle* were written in the same language. In contrast, the *Water Margin* and the *Tale of Hong Kiltong* were written in radically different vernacular languages. The *Tale of Hong Kiltong*, therefore, required a degree of innovation that is difficult to appreciate if we think of vernacular writing as easy.

Poetic Genres

The *New Tales of the Golden Turtle* and *The Tale of Hong Kiltong* illustrate some of the essential characteristics of Chosŏn literature evident from the turn of the seventeenth century onward. The first and most important was what can be loosely called Chinese influence. This influence was, in many respects, paradoxical. On the one hand, Literary Sinitic remained the dominant, esteemed literary language until the end of the nineteenth century, and Confucian literary ideas served as a bedrock for much vernacular poetic production. On the other hand, Chosŏn's intellectual and political elite had a high degree of self-confidence in the quality of their Confucian civilization, and they typically took a dim view of contemporary Ming and then Qing dynasty (1616–1912; Later Jin until 1636) China for failing to maintain proper orthodox Confucian standards.

China was not a single thing, and Chosŏn thinkers instead thought in terms of China's dynastic succession. The commonplace view was that the quality of Confucian civilization in China began to degenerate in the aftermath of the death of the Neo-Confucian reformer Zhu Xi (1130–1200). To question that attitude was one of the crucial reasons for the negative views toward Yun Ch'unnyŏn and Hŏ Kyun, as outlined earlier, and the critique set the stage for a literary-cultural tumult that erupted at the end of the eighteenth century.

The cornerstone Confucian idea in the *Anthology of Korean Writing* equated political, moral, and civilizational excellence with literary production. This idea came from the reputed role of Confucius (c. 551–c. 479 BCE) in compiling the *Classic of Songs* (Ch. *Shijing*; Ko. *Sigyŏng*). That emphasis profoundly affected views on literature. It meant that poetry or song, in general, was affirmed as a literary genre, which also applied to vernacular poetry and songs. Likewise, it meant that fiction—whether in Literary Sinitic or the vernacular—was necessarily suspect since Confucius had nothing to say about fiction per se. Instead, Confucius is famously supposed to have refused to speak of disorder and spirits.

Moreover, the question of romantic love was necessarily problematic insofar as the marriage bond was to be decided by families rather than individuals. The net result was that the topics that might serve as the basis for fiction—and indeed, that did serve as the basis for fiction as seen earlier—were typically seen as offensive from a rigorous Confucian literary perspective. At the same time, the *Classic of Songs* dealt with romantic love. That fact was essential to the development of the complex commentarial tradition on the collection's treatment of sexual desire (Chin 2006, 71). Moral and political concerns nonetheless dominated in the commentarial tradition that exerted the greatest influence in Chosŏn through the work of Zhu Xi, who acknowledged the sexual elements in the collection and drew a sharp distinction between its morally "proper" and "improper" poems (Chin 2006, 57).

As a result of these essential features drawn from the larger Confucian tradition, poetic genres were a favored literary medium throughout Chosŏn's history. Furthermore, elite education in the Chinese classics, which aimed at mastery of Literary Sinitic, was largely the domain of men. There were notable exceptions, but these nonetheless highlight how status determined education. For example, Lady Sin (studio name Saimdang; 1504–51) was an artist with a remarkably good education and composed Literary Sinitic verse. The memory of her abilities was preserved primarily because she was the mother of Yi I (pen name Yulgok; 1536–84), one of the most important Neo-Confucian thinkers and revered as a founding figure among the Patriarchs (Noron) who triumphed as the hegemonic political party by the mid-eighteenth century.

Likewise, Lady Hŏ (pen name Nansŏrhŏn; 1563–89) garnered esteem as a Literary Sinitic poet. Her family played a crucial role in fostering her intellectual and literary attainments, and her pedigree, in turn, helped to ensure the preservation of her memory as well as complicate it. She was the sister of Hŏ Kyun and Hŏ Pong (1551–88), both regarded as fine poets in Literary Sinitic. The Chosŏn official Sim Sugyŏng (1516–99), however, judged that she was a better poet than either brother (*Kyŏnhan chamnok*). A woodblock print Hŏ Kyun prepared in 1608, several years after Sim Sugyŏng's death, preserved a selection of Lady Hŏ's poems (*Nansŏrhŏn sijip*). This collection is problematic because Hŏ Kyun compiled it by memory after her death. This even led to charges

Literature

that it contained plagiarism and poems forged by Hŏ Kyun. However, judging by Sim Sugyŏng's comments, one would have no reason to anticipate the subsequent controversy over the collection. I will return to the implications of this question.

Those problems to the side, the collection is nonetheless instructive because it highlights what the elite at the time deemed the pinnacle of literary achievement. The main sections of the collection were devoted to Literary Sinitic poetry in several distinct styles: five-syllable ancient style verse, seven-syllable ancient style verse, five-syllable regulated verse, seven-syllable regulated verse, five-syllable quatrains, and seven-syllable quatrains. Literary collections by male writers typically contained writings related to their professional lives as officials and scholars, including memorials, policy pieces, and philosophical analyses. However, the inclusion of poems, as organized in the collection of Hŏ Nansŏrhŏn's works, was commonplace.

At the conceptual level, the importance of poetry derived from the broader Confucian literary tradition as sketched earlier, but there was also a practical consideration. Mastery of poetry served as an index for one's literary skills more generally, and poetry was of fundamental importance in this respect. The reason was implicit in the categories found in the collection of Hŏ Nansŏrhŏn's works. All those genres had a minimal common requirement of end rhyme at the ends of even-numbered lines, and poets could also introduce the rhyme at the end of the first line. The demands of regulated verse were far greater. In addition to end rhyme, regulated verse also required syntactic parallelism/antithesis and the alteration of tones at specific points throughout the poem. Quatrains required rhyme but could be composed in an ancient or regulated style, with or without parallelism/antithesis and tonal alteration. Apart from quatrains, poems typically consisted of eight lines, but adventurous poets could write much longer poems. Poems in Literary Sinitic nonetheless typically followed the basic genre requirements of the anthology of Hŏ Nansŏrhŏn's poems. There were variations, but these constituted a small fraction of Chosŏn's overall poetic output.

The formal requirements of Literary Sinitic poetry entailed technical knowledge of the tonal and rhyme categories of individual Sinographs established centuries earlier in China. This linguistic divide between the vernacular and Literary Sinitic also existed in China, as in Japan and Vietnam, where Literary Sinitic was employed. The use of a written language with set, learnable requirements helped to make it a powerful common medium for people who spoke different vernacular languages. That was one of the elements in Hŏ Kyun's eagerness to introduce his sister's writings to Ming Chinese ambassadors and solicit praise from them so her works could be included in the woodblock print. None of that would have been possible or have made any sense had she written in Korean.

Due to the importance placed on poetry and song in the larger Confucian tradition, male scholars and officials practiced vernacular verse forms in addition to their customary use of Literary Sinitic poems. The two main genres were *kasa* and *sijo*, and while practiced far less than Literary Sinitic genres, such vernacular literature could be the object of praise among the educated male elite. This marked a sharp contrast with *p'ansori*, a type of vernacular popular narrative performance practiced and enjoyed by the people at large. Insofar as *p'ansori* was essentially an orally transmitted musical tradition rooted in popular practices, detailed examination falls outside the scope of this discussion. But it is helpful to consider it as a point of contrast with *kasa* and *sijo*. At issue is the blurred line between a song as something sung (which can be recorded in writing) and a poem as something fundamentally reliant on writing. Oral performance, for example, played a role in court life, but prior to the creation of Han'gŭl, such songs were transmitted orally or through Sinographs. The Korean alphabet made it possible to record existing vernacular songs far more accurately and enabled the written composition of vernacular songs and poems.

The Routledge Handbook of Early Modern Korea

Nonetheless, extant collections have complicated linguistic features and variations in approach. The central point is that this body of vernacular written work was not uniformly transmitted solely using Han'gŭl. A famous example of *kasa* composed by the statesman Chŏng Ch'ŏl (pen name Songgang; 1536–93) while touring scenic sites of Kwandong (Kangwŏn Province) illustrates this. A copy of his "Song of Kwandong" (Kwandong pyŏlgok) from 1747 contains pure Korean words and words of Chinese origin that functioned in the Korean lexicon. The Korean alphabetic script here serves two functions: writing pure Korean elements in the poem and transcribing the sounds or readings of Sinographs. For instance, the number "eight hundred" occurs in the poem, and this is given first in Sinographs and followed by *p'albaek*, a transcription of those graphs in the Korean alphabet. *P'albaek*, however, functions as a Korean word and, on the face of it, does not require the addition of Chinese graphs in this specific context where the meaning is obvious ("Kwandong pyŏlgok").

Chŏng Ch'ŏl's "Song of Kwandong" highlights the overlay of the larger tradition and influence of Chinese writing and literature on even a vernacular Chosŏn poem after the invention of the Korean alphabet. The larger Chinese literary and intellectual tradition belonged to males such as Chŏng Ch'ŏl, and they used its tropes and ethos (for example, celebrations of nature and moral rectitude) in their vernacular poems. Therefore, the distinction between vernacular Korean and Literary Sinitic literature is often blurry in the context of vernacular literary forms (Rutt 1971, 14). To put the matter starkly, vernacular poems are, in many instances, fully understandable only to those who know Literary Sinitic; therefore, the term vernacular can be misleading. At the same time, such vernacular poems cannot be understood by those who only know Literary Sinitic. Literary Sinitic translations of Chosŏn vernacular verse illustrate this characteristic (McCann 1993, 100).

Textual Transmission: A Sketch of Core Issues

The writings of Hŏ Nansŏrhŏn and Chŏng Ch'ŏl exemplify key features of Chosŏn's literary tradition that center on the transmission of written works in general (for a detailed examination of the main issues, see Kim 2004, 1–31). For example, the distinction between printing and publication is problematic because printing did not necessarily mean that a given text had wide circulation. Throughout Chosŏn's existence, handwritten manuscripts remained essential for textual transmission. Printed works and manuscripts, in turn, interacted in various complex ways. A manuscript, for example, might be printed at some point, and that printed version might circulate along with a handwritten one. Alternatively, someone might make a handwritten copy of a handwritten or printed source text. Translation was an additional factor. A work composed in vernacular Korean might be translated into Literary Sinitic or vice versa. As these works circulated, they might be translated yet again and then printed or hand-copied, with those versions entering circulation. The result is a profusion of varying versions of texts that occupy considerable attention among those who specialize in Chosŏn literature.

These questions are an area in which the digital humanities play a crucial role as South Korean scholarly organizations make an increasing number of texts freely available online. These online materials include photographic reproductions of premodern printed books and manuscripts as well as digitized premodern works. The effects of these efforts are enhanced by the production of annotated Korean vernacular translations of Literary Sinitic works and detailed bibliographic information dealing with the works' formats and provenance. The range and quality are astonishing. Therefore, scholars of premodern literature can uncover information and linkages among that information in a fashion unimaginable in the past.

Literature

The observations of Sim Sugyŏng and Yi Sik on Hŏ Nansŏrhŏn and Hŏ Kyun discussed above provide a straightforward example. Precisely how Sim Sugyŏng made his judgment on Hŏ Nansŏrhŏn's poetic skill is unclear, but this account leaves no doubt that Hŏ Nansŏrhŏn's fame as a poet existed even though her writings were not in circulation in Sim Sugyŏng's lifetime. Moreover, Hŏ Kyun's subsequent printing of his sister's poems and execution all occurred after Sim Sugyŏng's death. Read against Yi Sik's later comments, Hŏ Kyun's eventual infamy likely tarnished his sister's reputation.

The Crisis over Literature: Foundations and Intimations of Looming Change

To all appearances, literary production and textual transmission increased over the seventeenth century (Kim 2004, 4). Many of the core features of Chosŏn literature, as outlined above, are evident in the *Tale of Unyŏng* (*Unyŏng chŏn*). This love story was innovative in adopting a female perspective and was originally composed in Literary Sinitic, most likely between 1616 and 1641, before being translated into vernacular Korean (Cha and Pettid 2009, 26–34; Pieper 2021, 562–65). That a woman wrote this novel is a possibility. Whether composed by a man or a woman, its concerns with love, freedom, and the tensions between individual autonomy and a strict Confucian social hierarchy betray unhappiness with the status quo.

The *Tale of Unyŏng* points to a heightened degree of complexity in the literary imagination that comes into sharp focus at the end of the seventeenth century in two novels, *A Nine Cloud Dream* (*Kuunmong*) and *Lady Sa's Journey to the South* (*Sassi namjŏng ki*). These two works are unique in several respects. First, their authorship is known: the scholar-official Kim Manjung (1637–92) wrote them over the final decade of his life. Second, Kim Manjung employed the two available literary languages. Although numerous Literary Sinitic and Korean vernacular texts of *A Nine Cloud Dream* have led to complex debates about the original language of composition, the evidence suggests that *A Nine Cloud Dream* was written in Literary Sinitic and subsequently translated into vernacular Korean. By contrast, the situation with *Lady Sa's Journey to the South* is precisely known due to records left by Kim Manjung's grandnephew, Kim Ch'unt'aek (1670–1717).

According to Kim Ch'untaek, *Lady Sa's Journey to the South* was composed in vernacular Korean and then translated by him into Literary Sinitic. Kim Ch'unt'aek's comments on the novel and his decision to translate it show how Confucian poetics and the emphasis on the link between writing and morality provided the overarching structure for thinking about literature, at least among the educated male elite (Bouchez 1979, 27–32). Kim Ch'unt'aek translated it because he regarded its depiction of its protagonist Lady Sa's Confucian moral virtue as exemplary for even educated men who would not read a vernacular novel. Finally, we have concrete information about the circumstances of this translation through a note Kim Ch'unt'aek appended to his introduction. It is dated 1709 and refers to the fact that Kim Ch'unt'aek was then in exile.

Kim Ch'unt'aek undertook this translation as an intellectual diversion during a difficult period in his life, but the crucial fact is that he did the translation and took credit. His justification for this work, moreover, at once affirmed conservative Confucian literary values and challenged conservative literary practices. This is a variation of the complexity seen in the *Tale of Unyŏng*. Although it is impossible to provide a full account of what cultural factors were in play, it is clear there was an inventiveness in literary culture seen as threatening by some among the male elite. This threat underpinned a political crisis at the court of King Chŏngjo (r. 1776–1800) and later provided the framework for a defense of proper literary values by Chŏng Yagyong (1762–1836) (Evon 2006/2007, 57–82). Due to the complexity of these questions, the following discussion considers features that are most significant in relation to the vast changes that followed.

The Routledge Handbook of Early Modern Korea

During Chŏngjo's reign, concerns over literature erupted in a political crisis. Domestic and international factors were equally important, each exacerbating the other in a vicious cycle. The main domestic factor was filicide in the royal house. Chŏngjo's father was mentally ill and prone to bouts of erratic behavior before being put to death by his father, Chŏngjo's grandfather. This trauma played a crucial role in shaping Chŏngjo's personality. Chŏngjo was a tireless champion of Zhu Xi's orthodox Confucian teachings, and his grand project was to show, through his discipline and leadership, that Chosŏn guarded those teachings China had lost. This historical interpretation had precursors but was particularly conspicuous in his thinking. The central idea was that lax standards among Ming scholars had weakened China, thus enabling the establishment of Qing by the barbaric Manchus. The Manchus were an inescapable annoyance. They had invaded Chosŏn and forced it to become a vassal state in 1637, and after the Ming–Qing transition, Chosŏn kings had to dispatch embassies to the Qing court. But in roughly the middle of the eighteenth century, a shift in views among some Chosŏn scholars became strikingly obvious. This international factor led to a crisis at the royal court. Literature was central.

Some who went on embassies to Qing China began to question Chosŏn's civilizational superiority. This attitude was an intensification of views evident in Yun Ch'unnyŏn and Hŏ Kyun. This growing phenomenon had two main consequences. First, it marked an interest in Qing's intellectual and literary atmosphere. Through written accounts and word of mouth, this interest spread among those who were educated but could not visit China. Second, this growing interest in Qing threatened Chŏngjo's great project. The result was a crackdown on heterodox literature, typically called the "rectification of literary styles" (*munch'e panjŏng*). Although anachronistic, this term adequately captures the main features of what occurred as Chŏngjo attempted to force those under his control to write properly and embrace orthodox Confucian literary and cultural values. The linguistic features of this literary-political tumult are too complex for discussion here (for sustained treatment, see Wang 2019, 29–62). Instead, what follows focuses on the implications of this historical moment and how it foreshadowed changes that would follow when Korea's modern age began.

Final Thoughts

Chŏngjo's rectification took shape as he read, with mounting horror, a variety of materials, including—but not limited to—court documents and essays produced by students at the State Confucian Academy (Sŏnggyun'gwan). The people responsible for maintaining the highest standards were actively undercutting those standards, incorporating words from Ming and Qing Chinese fiction. Chŏngjo's various pronouncements on this problem, as found in the court documents and his writings, are dizzying and beyond the scope of this discussion. The essential point is that he knew what was afoot, most likely because he knew those Chinese works firsthand. Whatever the case, Chinese fiction became a cultural and political problem at the end of the eighteenth century, as Chŏngjo sought to stanch the flow of Chinese texts into Chosŏn.

However, this was not an isolated phenomenon. Contemporary figures also criticized the popularity of vernacular Korean fiction (Cha and Pettid 2009, 58–59). As outlined earlier, works circulated in Literary Sinic and vernacular Korean, and due to translation, there is no reason to think that the works in question had all been produced in Chosŏn by those writing in vernacular Korean. Instead, these complaints show how vernacular Korean as a literary medium was becoming commonplace, whether for the composition of original works or translation of Literary Sinic works by Korean or Chinese writers. These complaints thus seem to mark an incipient stage in Korea's literary modernity that soon took shape as writers and thinkers explored new notions of literature during a moment of great cultural change.

302

Literature

Hong Hŭibok (1794–1859) provides strong evidence for this conclusion and the connection between Chŏngjo's crackdown and a growing audience for Korean vernacular fiction. Hong's preface to his Korean vernacular translation of a Chinese vernacular novel contains this evidence. Hong argued that Korean vernacular fiction was worthy of literary and historical analysis. Furthermore, he wrote his defense in vernacular Korean (Pastreich 2005, 1–3, 10–11). Hong demonstrated that the vernacular could be used for purposes customarily reserved for Literary Sinitic and thus hinted at the massive cultural changes that would accelerate at the end of the nineteenth century.

For these reasons, Hong's work reflected the core characteristics of Chosŏn literature and its evolution, as sketched above. Chinese influence was crucial but one element in developments that became increasingly complex after the invention of Han'gŭl. Although the educated elites of China and Korea shared a common written medium of Literary Sinitic, they spoke vastly different languages. For Koreans, vernacular literary production entailed not merely a different language but a different script, and the examples surveyed above suggest that the application of Han'gŭl for literary purposes developed slowly due to a widespread antagonism toward it among the male elite. Moreover, overarching ideas to conceptualize literature were rooted in the Confucian intellectual tradition and antagonistic toward fiction, especially vernacular fiction. At the same time, it was perfectly acceptable for educated males to compose vernacular verse. Questions of genre and literary language were related but not identical. Over time, however, the elite monopoly on literacy weakened, and this, in turn, challenged Confucian preoccupations with the moral foundations of literature. Chŏngjo's fears were rooted in a reality he could not alter no matter how hard he tried.

Several decades later, Hong Hŭibok underscored that reality. The fact that Hong used the vernacular to examine vernacular fiction seems unremarkable, but it was, in fact, a striking innovation. In emphasizing that vernacular fiction was a meaningful topic, Hong challenged fundamental elite assumptions. His use of the vernacular to mount that challenge suggested that Korean vernacular writing could be employed as a tool of intellectual inquiry. In the decades after Hong's death, growing awareness of Korea's parlous international position and external threats led to an awareness of the need for mass literacy.

Shifting attitudes toward the Korean alphabet were crucial in marking both the start of literary modernity and the birth of modern Korean nationalism that took shape at the turn of the twentieth century. This shift can be traced to the 1870s when the Chosŏn court confronted vexing international political conditions due to China's defeat in 1860 by the British and French in the Second Opium War (1856–60) and the civil war in Japan that ended the Tokugawa shogunate (1603–1868). The result was a growing recognition of the need to employ the vernacular for widespread education and literacy, and it marked a fundamental shift from the longstanding emphasis on Literary Sinitic as the prestige medium.

References

Alston, Dane. 2009. "Emperor and Emissary: The Hongwu Emperor, Kwŏn Kŭn, and the Poetry of Late Fourteenth Century Diplomacy." *Korean Studies* 32: 104–47.

Bouchez, Daniel. 1979. "A Neo-Confucian View of Literature: Kim Ch'unt'aek's Comments on the 'Namjŏng-ki.'" *Korea Journal* 19, no. 5 (May): 27–32.

Cha, Kil, and Michael J. Pettid. 2009. *Unyŏng-jŏn: A Love Affair at the Royal Palace of Chosŏn Korea.* Center for Korean Studies, Institute of East Asian Studies, University of California.

Chang, Kang-I Sun. 2010. "Literature of the Early Ming to Mid-Ming (1375–1572)." In *The Cambridge History of Chinese Literature*, edited by Kang-I Sun Chang and Stephen Owen, 1–62. Cambridge University Press.

Chin, Tamara. 2006. "Orienting Mimesis: Marriage and the *Book of Songs*." *Representations* 94, no. 1: 53–79.

The Routledge Handbook of Early Modern Korea

Evon, Gregory N. 2006/2007. "Chinese Contexts, Korean Realities: The Politics of Literary Genre in Late-Chosŏn Korea (1725–1863)." *East Asian History* 32 (December)/33 (June): 57–82.

Evon, Gregory N . 2009. "The Conservation of Knowledge and Technology of the Word in Korea." *Asian Studies Review* 33: 1–19.

Hong Kiltong chŏn. 1901. Available at: https://kostma.aks.ac.kr/.

Kalton, Michael C. 1985. "The Writings of Kwŏn Kŭn: The Context and Shape of Early Yi Dynasty Neo-Confucianism." In *The Rise of Neo-Confucianism in Korea,* edited by Wm. Theodore de Bary and JaHyun Kim Haboush, 89–123. Columbia University Press.

Kang, Minsoo. 2019. *Invincible and Righteous Outlaw: The Korean Hero Hong Gildong in Literature, History, and Culture.* University of Hawai'i Press.

Kim, Michael. 2004. "Literary Production, Circulating Libraries, and Private Publishing: The Popular Reception of Vernacular Fiction Texts in the Late Chosŏn Dynasty." *Journal of Korean Studies* 9, no. 1: 1–31.

King, Ross. 2018. "The Moon Reflected in a Thousand Rivers: Literary and Linguistic Problems in the *Wŏrinch'ŏn'gang chi kok.*" *Sungkyun Journal of East Asian Studies* 18, no. 1: 1–42.

"Kwandong pyŏlgok." By Chŏng Ch'ŏl. Excerpted from and listed under "Songgang kasa." Anthology of Chŏng Ch'ŏl's poems. Available at: https://www.hangeul.go.kr/main.do.

Kyŏnhan chamnok. Miscellanea by Sim Sugyŏng. Available at: https://db.itkc.or.kr/.

Ledyard, Gari K. 1998. *The Korean Language Reform of 1446.* Sin'gu munhwasa.

Lee, Peter H. 2008. *A History of Korean Literature.* Cambridge University Press.

Mair, Victor H. 1994. "Buddhism and the Rise of the Written Vernacular in East Asia: The Making of National Languages." *Journal of Asian Studies* 53, no. 3: 707–51.

McCann, David R. 1993. "Chinese Diction in Korean *Shijo* Verse." *Korean Studies* 17: 92–104.

Nansŏrhŏn sijip. Anthology of Hŏ Nansŏrhŏn's poems. Available at: https://db.itkc.or.kr/.

Pastreich, Emanuel. 2005. "Making the Vernacular Visible: How Hong Hŭi-bok Redefined the Korean Popular Novel by Translating the Chinese Novel *Jinghuayuan.*" *Sungkyun Journal of East Asian Studies* 5, no. 1: 1–25.

Pieper, Daniel. 2021. *Redemption and Regret: Modernizing the Writings of James Scarth Gale.* University of Toronto Press.

Rutt, Richard. 1971. *The Bamboo Grove: An Introduction to Sijo.* University of California Press.

"Sallok." By Yi Sik. In *T'aektang chip.* Collected writings of Yi Sik. Available at: https://db.itkc.or.kr/.

Sejong sillok. In *Chosŏn wangjo sillok.* Available at: https://sillok.history.go.kr/main/main.do.

Takayama, K. Peter. 1995. "Adaptation and Resistance to Chinese Literary Hegemony: Korea and Japan." *International Journal of Politics, Culture and Society* 8, no. 3: 467–88.

Wang, Xixiang. 2019. "*Story of the Eastern Chamber*: Dilemmas of Vernacular Language and Political Authority in Eighteenth-Century Chosŏn." *Journal of Korean Studies* 24, no. 1: 29–62.

Wei, Xin, and James B. Lewis. 2019. *Korea's Premier Collection of Classical Literature: Selections from Sŏ Kŏjŏng's Tongmunsŏn.* University of Hawai'i Press.

Wuerthner, Dennis. 2012. "The *Kŭmo sinhwa*: Product of a Cross-Border Diffusion of Knowledge between Ming China and Chosŏn Korea during the Fifteenth Century." *Sungkyun Journal of East Asian Studies* 12, no. 2: 165–85.

Yongbi ŏch'ŏn ka. Epic poem by Chŏng Inji, An Chi, and Kwŏn Che. Available at: https://kostma.aks.ac.kr/classic/gojun.aspx.

20

VISUAL ARTS

Yoonjung Seo

In the scholarly exploration of East Asian art, early modern Korea ruled by the Chosŏn state (1392–1897) is significant not only for artistic flourishing but also pivotal for the development of distinct Korean aesthetic values within the broader regional context. This chapter delves into the rich visual art and visual culture of Chosŏn, where the robust adoption of Neo-Confucianism profoundly influenced artistic practices, tastes, and production. This chapter offers a historical overview of Chosŏn art and its sociopolitical, cultural, and religious context by examining key themes such as the evolution of landscape painting styles and the emergence of "true-view" (*chin'gyŏng*) landscape painting, court paintings for state rituals and events, the development of genre painting, Buddhist art under royal patronage, the aesthetics and technical development of porcelain, and palace architecture and garden.

During the reign of King Sejong (r. 1418–50), for instance, An Kyŏn (c. 1400–64+) painted landscapes inspired by native and Chinese traditions, reflecting Chosŏn's open engagement with cross-cultural influences. An's works, alongside other genres such as figure painting and Buddhist art sponsored by royalty, highlight the integration of art into the daily and spiritual lives of the people of Chosŏn. This chapter analyzes how these artistic endeavors expressed aesthetic preference and manifested the era's philosophical and religious ideologies.

Furthermore, this investigation extends to the role of art in reinforcing the social hierarchy and Confucian values that characterized Chosŏn Korea. Through a detailed study of various art forms, including painting, calligraphy, and ceramics, the following discussion explores how Chosŏn's art served as a conduit for cultural transmission and as a reflection of Chosŏn's interaction with its neighboring cultures. By doing so, it aims to provide a comprehensive overview of how art in Chosŏn functioned as a dynamic element of both statecraft and personal expression, thereby offering insights into the cultural landscape of early modern Korea.

Landscape Painting in Chosŏn: From Ideal to True-View Landscape

During Sejong's reign, An Kyŏn emerged as a prominent court painter with a unique style drawing inspiration from Guo Xi (c. 1020–c. 1090) of Song dynasty (960–1279) China and his followers. An's masterpiece, *Dream Journey to the Peach Blossom Land* (*Mongyu towŏndo*; 1447), depicts a poetic landscape inspired by an earlier Chinese masterpiece, Tao Yuanming's (365–427) *The*

DOI: 10.4324/9781003262053-27

Peach Blossom Spring (*Taohua yuanji*; 421)—drawing from a Chinese tale of a fisherman's accidental discovery of an ethereal utopia hidden behind a mountain adorned with peach blossoms. An painted his work for Sejong's third son, Anp'yŏng Taegun (1418–53), an avid art collector and aesthete (Jungmann 2011, 107–26). Illustrating the prince's dream of visiting the Peach Blossom Land, An's painting incorporates the stylistic features of Guo Xi, such as cloud-like rock formations, the dramatic interplay between solids and voids, effective use of vapor and mist, twisting and turning brushstrokes, subtle use of ink, and perspectives employing "three distances": high distance (looking up from the bottom of the mountains), level distance (foreground of the mountains), and deep distance (the distant background beyond the mountains) (Ahn 1980, 60–71). Subsequently, many Chosŏn artists emulated An's style and landscape paintings. Sixteenth-century works inspired by him include *Eight Views of Xiao and Xiang Rivers* (*Sosang p'algyŏngdo*) and *Eight Views of Four Seasons* (*Sasi p'algyŏngdo*), as well as paintings depicting literati gatherings.

A genre of Chosŏn paintings that depicts such gatherings, *kyehoedo*, was popular among scholar-officials. These paintings served as a record of actual gatherings and emphasized the camaraderie among participants. A *kyehoedo* comprises three elements: (1) the title at the top, (2) the depiction of the gathering in the middle, and (3) a list of participants at the bottom. Commissioned to commemorate the event, multiple copies were produced for attendees. The oldest extant work of this genre, *Gathering of Officials of the Censorate General* (*Miwŏn kyehoedo*; 1540), reflects the typical style of An Kyŏn prevalent in the early sixteenth century: the asymmetrical composition slanted to the right, with short and jagged brushwork, and dotted textured strokes applied to the mountains (Ahn 1995, 85–106). While paintings of literati gatherings in early Chosŏn tend to present idealized landscapes, *Gathering of Scholars at the Book Reading Hall* (*Toksŏdang kyehoedo*; c. 1531) depicts a rather realistic view of the Eastern Lake of the Han River where the event took place in 1531 (Figure 20.1). With a panoramic view encompassing the Han River area from present-day Ttuksŏm to Oksu-dong, this painting shows rocky hills in the foreground topped with trees rendered with washes and short strokes, an extensive middle ground with a boat full of scholars enjoying wine, and the Book Reading Hall (Toksŏdang) nestled in the misty background against Mount Ŭngbong (present-day Mount Maebong).

In the mid-sixteenth century, a new style of painting inspired by the Zhe School of Ming dynasty (1368–1644) China emerged in Chosŏn Korea, exemplified by works such as *A Boy Pulling Donkey* (*Tongja kyŏnnyŏdo*) by Kim Si (1524–93). This painting depicts, in a playful manner, a stubborn donkey resisting a boy's efforts to lead it across a small stream. This work pioneered the Korean Zhe School style, characterized by a fragmentary, additive approach (rather than a subtle, unified composition) and vivid plays of ink and color. Reflecting such tendencies, Korea's Zhe School favored a diagonal composition emphasizing one side and using axe-cut strokes on the rocks, strong contrast between light and dark ink tones, and shimmering mountains in the distance. A flat pictorial space, bold and rough brushwork, and subtle use of ink washes are all unique to the Korean Zhe School (Jungmann 2014, 72–75).

Generations later, in the eighteenth century, "true-view" landscape and genre paintings, both emerging new styles, featured artists focused on their homeland, people, customs, and culture. Departing from the long-prevalent styles that pursued conceptual and idealized depictions of imaginary landscapes, true-view landscapes depicted mountains, rivers, trees, and other natural elements—emphasizing topographical accuracy and the beauty of Korea. Among such true-view landscapists was Chŏng Sŏn (1679–1759), renowned for depicting Mount Kŭmgang, a celebrated landmark on Korea's northern central coast. As seen in his mature works such as *Complete View of Mount Kŭmgang* (*Kŭmgang chŏndo*; 1734) and *After Rain at Mount Inwang* (*Inwang chesaekto*; 1751), Chŏng employed a bird's eye perspective, contrasting between soft and sharp brushwork,

Visual Arts

Figure 20.1 Gathering of Scholars at the Book Reading Hall, c. 1531, hanging scroll, ink and light color on silk, 62.2 cm × 91.3 cm. Source and photo credit: National Palace Museum of Korea.

and juxtaposing hemp-fiber texture strokes with axe-cut strokes. Hemp-fiber texture strokes use fine, parallel lines to create the texture of rugged rock surfaces and mountains, resembling the long, straight fibers of hemp, whereas axe-cut strokes are characterized by their sharp, chiseled appearance similar to the textures left by an axe-splitting wood (Figure 20.2). In contrast to both works widely admired as examples of Chŏng's later style, *Album of Autumn Mount Kŭmgang in the Year 1711* (*Sinmyo nyŏn p'ungak toch'ŏp*; 1711) is an important work showing the early development of his style from the Chinese Southern School of painting—by scholar-bureaucrat ("literati") artists as distinct from the Northern School's professional painters. Chŏng's album portrays various scenic sites he and his company visited on their journey to Mount Kŭmgang. Despite the lively depiction of 'their activities during their travels, the painter portrays the rocks and trees in a somewhat tentative and stiff manner, lacking the spontaneous, rhythmical brushwork and the bold, dynamic compositions that are trademarks of his late style.

Genre Paintings: Everyday Life, Work, and Leisure

Besides true-view landscapes, genre paintings depicting scenes from the daily lives of commoners and native customs flourished in the eighteenth century. Leading court painters of the era, Kim

Figure 20.2 Chŏng Sŏn, *After Rain at Mount Inwang*, 1751, hanging scroll, ink on paper, 79.2 cm × 138.2 cm. Source and photo credit: National Museum of Korea.

Hongdo (1745–1806?) and Sin Yunbok (1758–1814) were the pinnacles of genre painting. Born into a family of *chungin* ("middle people"), who lived and worked in the capital, Hansŏng (present-day Seoul), as semihereditary, government-employed experts in various fields, Kim became the most distinguished court painter under King Chŏngjo's (r. 1776–1800) auspices (Kumja Paik Kim 2016, 51–80). He was a versatile painter excelling in virtually all types of painting at the time in Chosŏn, including Daoist and Buddhist figures, birds and flowers, animals, and landscapes, though genre paintings were what truly distinguished him. Kim skillfully portrayed people's daily lives, thoughts, and emotions with wit and humor. His teacher, Kang Sehwang (1713–91), the eminent literati painter, praised his talent in genre painting: "He was also good at depicting daily lives and common customs. When his brush drew streets, ferries, shops and open markets, exam centers, and playgrounds, everyone clapped their hands and marveled at the paintings' realism" (Oh 2005, 52–54).

The ingenuity of Kim Hongdo's genre paintings showcases dynamic composition, vivid expression of figures' emotions, and powerful brushwork. His mastery is evident in *Screen of Genre Scenes* (*Haengnyŏ p'ungsokto pyŏng*; 1778), which portrays the work and leisure of ordinary people, including scenes where a local official encounters litigants on the street, farmers thresh in the yard, peddlers head to market, travelers arrive on horseback, and a blacksmith hammers steel (Figure 20.3). Kim's skillful portrayal of genre scenes is also evident in his most famous work, the *Album of Genre Painting* (*P'ungsokto ch'ŏp*). The thick and robust brushstrokes, immaculate composition based on circular or X-shaped designs, and depiction of figures with wit all invigorate the paintings and bring to life the people Kim observed around him.

In contrast, Sin Yunbok, a *chungin* descendant of a brother of Chief State Councilor (Yŏngŭijŏng) Sin Sukchu (1417–75) through an illegitimate son (*sŏŏl*), depicted the hedonistic lifestyle of the nouveau riche and *kisaeng*, female entertainers. Sin's paintings feature delicate renditions of figures with thin and fine brushstrokes, sensual use of colors, and carefully constructed compositions that evoke a poetic atmosphere. His *Album of Genre Painting* (*P'ungsokto hwach'ŏp*) offers a compelling glimpse into the customs, fashions, and pastimes of the well-to-do. Some thirty paintings in the album feature such scenes as an amorous couple's midnight tryst, a festive party on a

Figure 20.3 Kim Hongdo, *Screen of Genre Scenes*, 1778, eight-fold screen, ink and light color on silk, each 90.9 cm × 42.7 cm. Source and photo credit: National Museum of Korea.

barge over the river, *kisaeng* sword dancers performing, spring outings, women laundering at a stream, and women hair-washing on the Double Fifth Festival (Tano) day, which brought all outdoors for polo, swinging (*kŭne*), and wrestling (*ssirŭm*). Most paintings depict seduction, flirting, and leisurely activities of the nobility, appealing to the capital's middle class. Sin also produced many erotic paintings (*ch'unhwa*) depicting a more sensual and private aspect of life, rarely portrayed in traditional Korean art. His delicately refined style, combined with sophisticated colors and intricate details, allows his paintings to convey nuanced emotional and sexual expression subtly. These elements underscore the tension between rigid Confucian social norms and personal freedoms in late Chosŏn.

Portraiture in Confucian Society: Ancestral Ritual and Expression of Selfhood

Considerations of Confucian values such as filial piety, ancestral worship, and loyalty to the king heavily influenced the official portraiture the Chosŏn court sponsored. The court commissioned portraits of the king as well as "merit subjects" (*kongsin*)—whom the state honored as such for extraordinary service to the throne and enshrined them in the Hall of Portraiture (*chinjŏn*), family ancestral shrines (*sau*), county schools (*hyanggyo*), and private academies (*sŏwŏn*). Given the monarch's symbolic and political importance, the most skillful court painters produced his portrait. Additionally, literati painters, who were knowledgeable about art, often took on supervisory roles in the creation process. The production demanded the utmost care, from the recruitment of painters to the drawing, coloring, and enshrinement to the documentation of the entire process with an *ŭigwe* (royal protocol manual).

Exemplifying the tradition of royal portraiture in early Chosŏn, the *Portrait of King T'aejo* is a full-length painting depicting Chosŏn's founding monarch (r. 1392–98) seated (Figure 20.4). Although the extant version was a copy commissioned in 1872 to replace the worn original, the portrait retained the early Chosŏn style while incorporating styles from the late nineteenth century. The frontal, symmetrical posture, simple outlines of a voluminous blue robe, and facial features reflect early Chosŏn conventions. In contrast, the subtle shading on the face and the detailed rendering of the winged cap demonstrate late nineteenth-century techniques (Insoo Cho 2020, 267–70).

Besides royal portraits, the court produced portraits of merit subjects each time they were honored following significant events such as the founding of Chosŏn, the suppression of a rebellion, repelling a foreign invasion, and royal accession after dethroning the predecessor. The throne commissioned these portraits and bestowed them upon the merit subjects as tokens of royal favor and privilege. The recipient's family typically preserved such portraits in their ancestral shrines

Figure 20.4 Cho Chungmuk, Pak Kijun, Paek Ŭnbae, Pak Yonggi, Yu Suk, Yi Ch'angok, Pak Yonghun, An Kŏnyŏng, Cho Chaehŭng, and Sŏ Tup'yo, *Portrait of King T'aejo*, 1872, hanging scroll, color on silk, 150 cm × 218 cm. Source and photo credit: Royal Portrait Museum, Jeonju, Jeollabuk-do, Republic of Korea.

for generations and displayed them during ancestral rites to commemorate the achievements of the portrait's subject in perpetuity (Sunmie Cho 2007, 112–15). One of the earliest surviving examples of this tradition depicts Sin Sukchu, a four-time merit subject, and attests to the portraiture of early Chosŏn's key political players (Hong and Chang 2009, 67–69).

Likewise, literati occupied a central position in Chosŏn's portraiture. Unlike portraits of merit subjects in official attire, literati often portrayed themselves as carefree recluses, as scholars and nestled in nature while pursuing learning. The self-portraits of two eminent scholar-painters, Yun Tusŏ (1668–1715) and Kang Sehwang, exemplify how literati utilized portraiture to express their self-identity and artistic excellence. Yun's self-portrait showcases a stunning appearance with a dazzling facial expression and penetrating gaze. The full frontal face that occupies the entire canvas appears suspended in the air, as the rest of the body remains invisible. His realistic depiction of the eye contours, pupils, wrinkles under the eyes, and creases around the mouth not only conveys the notion of "conveying the spirit," a fundamental principle of portraiture in East Asian tradition, but also heralds a new trend of Western painting techniques introduced into Chosŏn through Qing dynasty (1616–1912; Later Jin until 1636) China (Lee Tae Ho 2005, 112–15). Also employing realism in his *Self Portrait*, Kang Sehwang alludes to his dual identity as a reclusive scholar and a government official by adorning himself with a black official's hat and a scholar's robe (Figure 20.5). Receiving an official appointment only at sixty-one after decades of study, Kang imbues

Figure 20.5 Kang Sehwang, *Self Portrait,* 1782, hanging scroll, color on silk, 88.7 cm × 51.0 cm. Source and photo credit: National Museum of Korea.

The Routledge Handbook of Early Modern Korea

the portrait with his internal mentality and spirit. Reflecting on the twists and turns of his life, his writing on the portrait attests to a self-awareness and inner conflict: "While my heart lay outside the government, I held an official post. Thus, I portrayed myself wearing a black official hat and a scholar's attire" (Kang 2005, 207–09). Emphasizing texture and depth, the portrait pays great attention to his face's minute creases and curves, as well as applying elaborate shading to his voluminous attire and his face's concave and convex areas.

Incorporating shading techniques derived from Western painting styles was a significant development in late Chosŏn portraiture. Yi Myŏnggi (1756–1813), a prominent court painter during Chŏngjo's reign, effectively employed such techniques to create naturalistic depictions of his sitters. One of his most famous works, a portrait of Kang Sehwang, presents his mastery of brushstrokes and inspiration from European paintings (Chang 2020, 306–11). The delicate lines used to render subtle creases, the skillful use of shading for the subject's facial wrinkles, and the reddish pupils dilated behind the eyelids all contribute to the liveliness and realism.

Court Painting: Royal Authority and Symbols of Auspiciousness

Chosŏn's court painters performed a crucial ideological function by promoting the moral values of Confucian society by adorning palace buildings and embellishing state rituals with decorative paintings replete with auspicious symbols. Affiliated with the Bureau of Royal Painting (Tohwasŏ), court painters produced portraits of the king and merit subjects, documentary paintings of court events, maps and topographical landscapes for military and administrative functions, *ŭigwe* illustrations, designs of ritual objects and palace architecture, didactic images for a royal audience, and decorative and seasonal paintings for the royal household and the aristocracy. In addition, court painters played a significant role in cultural exchanges in early modern East Asia. While accompanying envoys dispatched to China and Japan, they painted for foreign audiences and acquired or copied Chinese and Japanese paintings (Jungmann 2014, 207–39).

Court painters created numerous documentary paintings under the auspices of the throne and high officials. As vivid pictorial records of the state rituals and courtly life, court painters' works depict the court ceremonies, public projects, palace banquets, royal processions, and birthday celebrations for the royal family. For example, Chŏngjo's political acumen as the monarch commissioned an eight-panel folding screen to depict his visit to Hwasŏng, the site of his father Prince Sado's (1735–62) relocated tomb, in 1795 (Yoo 2020, 371–406). The visit celebrated the sixtieth birthday of his mother, Lady Hyegyŏng-gung Hong (1735–1816), and honored his late father, who had suffered a tragic, disgraceful death. The monarch's procession put on a full display of royal power and featured ceremonies in Hwasŏng intended to rehabilitate his father as a posthumous king. The screen illustrates various events during Chŏngjo's eight-day trip between Hwasŏng and Hansŏng: visits to the Confucian Shrine (Sŏngmyo) in Hwasŏng; the degree ceremony for candidates who passed the special civil and military examinations (*munkwa, mukwa*) at Nangnam Pavilion; a birthday banquet for his mother at Pongsu Hall; a reception for the local elders at Nangnam Pavilion; and a night military drill at Sŏjang Fort; royal archery at Tŭkchung Pavilion; the procession returning to the palace; and the procession crossing the Han River over a pontoon bridge (Figure 20.6). Participating in producing the screen paintings were the most distinguished painters-in-waiting of the Kyujanggak, Chŏngjo's newly built royal archive (1776). They created multiple copies for the king and high officials. The symmetrical composition, distorted space, simultaneous portrayal of consecutive events, and meticulously rendered blue-and-green landscape typify late Chosŏn's documentary paintings.

Much more costly to produce than other paintings, such as hanging scrolls or albums, a screen effectively provided a conspicuous backdrop for the person seated before it, lending a monumen-

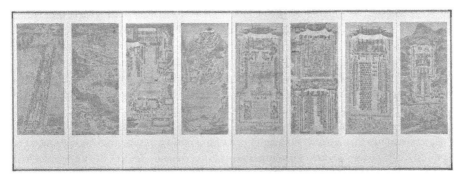

Figure 20.6 King Chŏngjo's Visit to the Royal Tomb in Hwasŏng, 1795–96, eight-fold screen, ink and color on silk, each panel 151.5 cm × 66.4 cm. Source and photo credit: National Museum of Korea.

tal yet festive air to the occasion. In particular, the large-scale, multi-panel folding screen was an ideal format for maximizing the magnificence of the motifs and projecting the sitter's political stature—depicting the king in an aniconic form (Jungmann 2007, 106–07). One example is the *Screens of the Sun, Moon, and Five Peaks* (*Irwŏl obongdo*), with rigidly symmetrical compositions, bold stylized design, and intense colors. The orderly configured pictorial elements, such as the pine trees, blue-and-green mountains, streams, the sun, and the moon, all resonate with the harmonious universe and evoke the balance between heaven and earth. These screens positioned behind the throne manifested the ruler's legitimacy and authority. Not only were the screens used in the throne hall, but they were also placed behind the king's portrait in the ancestral shrine and his coffin during the funeral.

Depicted on screens, Ten Symbols of Longevity (Sip changsaeng) adorned palaces and celebrated such auspicious occasions as the New Year, royal wedding, the queen dowager's birthday, and the crown prince's recovery from illness. Rooted in the Daoist cult of immortality, the combination of ten symbols rendered in rich colors is unique to Korea. The meticulously executed blue-and-green mountains, sun, pines, waterfalls, clouds, and waves are symbols of eternal youth. Tortoises and lingzhi (*yŏngji*) mushrooms symbolize longevity, deer are Daoist immortals' companions, and peaches nourish the immortals with their magical power of conferring longevity. All ten symbols are depicted in even numbers to convey their connotation with conjugal harmony. The *Ten Symbols of Longevity* (*Sip changsaengdo*), completed in 1880 during the reign of King Kojong (r. 1864–1907; emperor from 1897), is one of the few court paintings on this theme, and its production date and circumstances are known (Lachman and Gehrke 2006, 11–23). This screen was a commemorative painting celebrating Kojong's son and crown prince's (future Emperor Sunjong; r. 1907–10) recovery from smallpox. The last two panels on the left list the names and ranks of 14 officials of the Royal Department of Pharmacy (Ŭiyakch'ŏng) responsible for curing the prince's illness. The pharmaceutical officers commissioned the screen of *Ten Symbols of Longevity* to wish for his health and long life, as well as to celebrate their successful treatment.

In the nineteenth century, Chinese historical figures and Daoist lore became popular subjects of court painting in Chosŏn. Two popular themes of multi-panel folding screens reflect the trend: the banquet of Guo Ziyi (697–781) and the banquet of the Queen Mother of the West. Guo Ziyi, a prominent general and statesman of Tang dynasty (618–907) China, symbolized abundant blessings of wealth, longevity, and numerous progeny. Accordingly, depictions of Guo's banquet show him surrounded by his multiple offspring in a magnificent mansion and enjoying dancing and musical performances. Enhancing the auspiciousness of the occasion is the presence of trees, deer, birds, cranes, and peonies. *The Banquet of the Queen Mother of the West* portrays a festive scene of Daoist immortals gathering at the Turquoise Pond (Figure 20.7). The Queen Mother of the West—an important deity, the earliest historical mention of whom dates to a fifteenth-century BCE oracle bone inscription—occupies the center of the painting with King Mu (r. 976–922 BCE) of the Zhou dynasty (c. 1046–256 BCE) welcoming a large group of Daoist immortals and Buddhist figures as they approach the banquet from sky, sea, and road. The joyful atmosphere of the banquet is enhanced by musicians and dancers entertaining the guests while jade maidens prepare food and drinks. Highly sought in Chosŏn by anyone wishing for a long and prosperous life, the folding screens depicting either theme were frequently used for wedding ceremonies and produced to commemorate festive occasions such as the enthronement of a crown prince or the birth of an heir to the throne. For instance, the Office of the Herald (Sŏnjŏn'gwanch'ŏng) commissioned a screen depicting the banquet of the Queen Mother of the West to mark the investiture of Chŏngjo's son as crown prince, eventual King Sunjo (r. 1800–34), in 1800. Similarly, officials from the Delivery Room Office (Sansilch'ŏng) ordered a screen featuring the same theme to celebrate the birth of Sunjo's son, Prince Hyomyŏng (1809–30), upon his investiture as crown prince in 1812 (Seo 2014, 169–241).

Among the objects adorning an auspicious occasion, peonies were a favorite in Chosŏn art for the beauty of their large blossoms and brilliant colors and their symbolic association with prosperity and nobility. Painters often depicted the intertwining branches of peonies, ranging from buds to half-open blossoms to full blossoms, surrounded by verdant leaves and groups of oddly shaped rocks, creating a magnificent and stately atmosphere. The court used large-scale folding screens of peonies for various purposes, including ritualistic and practical applications (Woo 2014, 53–67). Besides the female quarters, royal funerals, weddings, ancestral shrine rituals, and banquets all utilized such screens.

Outside the royal house, well-to-do aristocrats and *chungin* increasingly collected antiques, and the pictorial genre of *ch'aekkŏri* (scholar's accoutrements) became popular (Sunglim Kim 2018, 53–109). Flourishing at the court in the late eighteenth century, the genre gained a wider audience through the nineteenth century. Chŏngjo, who was especially fond of books, is an ardent patron of this genre and ordered a court painter to create screens of *ch'aekkŏri* motif for installation behind the royal throne. His favorite artist, Kim Hongdo, gained renown for his skillful use of European painting techniques in creating illusionistic effects in *ch'aekkŏri* screens. Such works showcase various scholarly accoutrements such as stacks of books, brushes, ink stones, scrolls, and seals, as well as luxurious antiques such as bronze vessels and burners, porcelain vases, a jade-carved fish ornament, a coral

Figure 20.7 The Banquet of the Queen Mother of the West, 1800, eight-fold screen, ink and color on silk, each panel 145.0 × 54.0 cm. Source and photo credit: National Museum of Korea.

branch with pendants, and a Western alarm clock. These motifs connote the owner's knowledge, social distinction, and wealth. Extant *ch'aekkŏri* screens reflect such European painting techniques as *trompe l'oeil* and *chiaroscuro* to create the illusions of three-dimensional space and accentuate the sense of volume in the modeling of objects (Jungmann 2014, 277–89). Another famous court painter, Yi Hyŏngnok (1808–83), created several *ch'aekkŏri* screens featuring playfully hidden names in the screens' seals (Black 2020, 1–25, 61–63). His screens tend to be well organized in composition, with radiant colors and refined details. Yi Hyŏngnok often combines Western perspectives with East Asian isometric views in his depictions of the interiors of bookshelves (Figure 20.8).

Buddhist Art and Royal Patronage

In Chosŏn, Confucianism gradually replaced Buddhism as the dominant ideology, as the state's anti-Buddhist policies diminished the resources and influence of Buddhism. By the first half of the sixteenth century, Buddhism's role had become limited to personal religious life. Even as Buddhism lost ground in public spaces, court painters and monk painters continued to produce Buddhist paintings commissioned by royals. One of the most powerful royal patrons of Buddhism in Chosŏn history is Queen Munjŏng (1501–65), the third wife of King Chungjong (r. 1506–44) and mother of their son King Myŏngjong (r. 1545–67). Revitalizing Buddhism, Munjŏng, as queen dowager, ordered the reconstruction of Hoeamsa, a magnificent monastery in Yangju. In 1565, she also commissioned four hundred paintings of Shakyamuni (historical Buddha; c. 563/480–c. 483/400 BCE), Maitreya (Buddha of the Future), Bhaishajyaguru (Buddha of Medicine), and Amitabha (Buddha of the Pure Land Paradise), 50 of each in gold and 50 of each in colors with gold, to wish for Myŏngjong's health and longevity, benevolent rule, and numerous offspring. Only six of these paintings have survived: four of Bhaisajyaguru and two of Shakyamuni. As illustrated in two versions of the *Bhaisajyaguru Triad* in the National Museum of Korea, this genre of paintings follows the tradition of Chosŏn's predecessor, Koryŏ (918–1392), which divides the composition into upper and lower registers for the Buddha and accompanying bodhisattvas (Figure 20.9). Compared to Koryŏ works, they show a more simplified iconography, a less naturalistic rendition of the body, and a more restricted use of gold pigments. New features include wider faces with smaller facial features and pointed, jeweled *ushnisha* (Song 2014, 57–59).

Some two centuries later, Chŏngjo commissioned the construction of a Buddhist monastery in honor of his father, Sado. As an act of filial piety, the king ordered the construction of Yongjusa

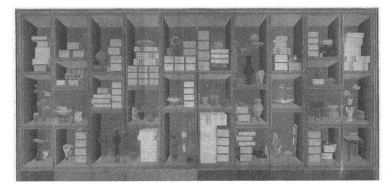

Figure 20.8 Yi Hyŏngnok, *Ch'aekkŏri*, nineteenth century, ten-fold screen, color on silk, 153.0 cm × 352.0 cm. Source and photo credit: National Museum of Korea.

Figure 20.9 The *Bhaisajyaguru Triad*, 1565, hanging scroll, gold on silk, 54.2 cm × 29.7 cm. Source and photo credit: National Museum of Korea.

near his father's tomb in Hwasŏng as a mortuary monastery. Chŏngjo also composed a prayer for the Buddha's virtue and commissioned the printing of woodblocks of the *Sutra of Shakyamuni's Teaching on Parental Love* (*Pulsŏl pumo ŭnjunggyŏng*). Furthermore, he commissioned Kim Hongdo and other court painters, such as Kim Tŭksin (1754–1822) and Yi Myŏnggi, to paint Buddhist images for enshrinement in the monastery. The painting, measuring 440 by 350 centimeters, depicts the Shakyamuni in the center, accompanied by Bhaishajyaguru to the right and Amitabha to the left. Two attendant bodhisattvas of each Buddha and ten disciples, along with four guardian kings appear with the three Buddhas. The painting's vivid coloring, chiaroscuro, and illusionistic representation of space were unprecedented among Chosŏn's Buddhist paintings. The new features strongly allude to European techniques of shading and linear perspectives.

In the nineteenth century, royal house members continued to commission Buddhist paintings, statues, and monasteries. For example, a large-scale banner painting in Hŭngch'ŏnsa, *The Buddhas of the Three Bodies* (*Pirojana samsin kwaebulto*), was commissioned in 1832 by Kim Chosun (1765–1832), who was not only Sunjo's father-in-law but also a significant political figure in his own right. Also commissioning such works were Sunjo's daughters and sons-in-law, including Myŏngon Kongju (1810–32) and her husband Kim Hyŏn'gŭn (1810–68); Pogon Kongju (1818–32) and her husband Kim Pyŏngju (1819–53); and Tŏgon Kongju (1822–44). Likewise, decades later, Kojong and his wife, Queen Myŏngsŏng (1851–95), sponsored *Amitabha Buddha with Assembly* (*Amitabul hoedo*; 1867) and *Nine Levels of Buddhist Paradise* (*Kŭngnak kup'umdo*; 1885). These large-scale paintings feature the dazzling use of gold pigment and elaborately decorative style characteristic of Buddhist paintings commissioned by the royal house (Song 2020, 388). Despite the decline of Buddhism's public roles, a tacit acceptance of Buddhism and royal patronage of Buddhist monasteries and images in personal realms persisted until the end of Chosŏn.

Royal Kilns and Production of *Buncheong* Ware and White Porcelain

Chosŏn produced two main types of ceramics, *buncheong* (*punch'ŏng*) ware and porcelain, serving purposes ranging from daily uses to ceremonial events. *Buncheong* is a gray-bodied stoneware with white slip designs under a green-tinted translucent glaze, forming a distinctive style of early Chosŏn ceramics. Whereas *buncheong* wares existed for about two centuries, white porcelain emerged in early Chosŏn, and its production continued until the end of Chosŏn. The unpainted surface or simple porcelain designs reflect the Confucian ideal of frugality and austere aesthetics. Blue-and-white porcelain (*ch'ŏnghwa paekcha*), embellished with cobalt-blue pigment, was an extravagance catering to the demands of the royal family and the upper class.

In the first two centuries of Chosŏn, private local kilns across the kingdom produced *buncheong* ware. The state levied these ceramics as tribute from the provinces to satisfy the government and court's demands. As an official tribute, *buncheong* ware was systematically and strictly managed by marking the vessels with the name of the production site and the government offices among which they were to be distributed. Various designs and techniques decorated *buncheong* ware, including incised, stamped, carved, and sgraffito designs. Slips of brush adorning the ceramics or the vessels were dipped entirely in white slips and decorated with free-style iron-brown images (Soyoung Lee 2020, 321–30). Among such works, *Buncheong Flat Bottle with Incised Fish Design* (*Punch'ŏng sagi chohwa ŏmun p'yŏnbyŏng*) has a unique shape with various decorative techniques, including dynamic, spontaneous, playful drawings and bold patterns created by scratching the white slip background.

In the mid-sixteenth century, porcelain gradually replaced *buncheong* ware in popularity. Throughout Chosŏn's history, undecorated white porcelain mainly was favored, and porcelains with cobalt-blue decoration also emerged in the early fifteenth century. *White Porcelain Jar with Plum and Bamboo Design in Underglaze Cobalt Blue* (*Ch'ŏnghwa paekcha maejuk munho*) in the Leeum Museum of Art showcases the skillful depiction of plums and bamboo on the body, along with other decorative flower motifs on the lip and bottom. The composition of the pattern, color, and shape of this porcelain is similar to its Ming Chinese equivalent. The lustrous glaze on the thick body, light-blue clay, and fine sand on the bottom indicate that the kilns in Kwangju, Kyŏnggi Province produced this type of vessel in the mid-fifteenth century. Trained painters of the Bureau of Royal Painting, whom the court dispatched to the kilns, executed the deftly applied design on the porcelain. The official court kilns established in Kwangju around 1466 produced most of the high-quality porcelains commissioned by the court and governmental offices (Soyoung Lee 2009, 43–60). Overseeing the operation for the court was the Bureau of the Royal Kitchen (Saongwŏn), which sent a supervisor to manage the kilns' overall management and daily operations. Not only the Bureau of the Royal Kitchen but also the Bureau of the Royal Painting dispatched court painters to decorate the surface of porcelains.

As Chosŏn became more conscious of its culture and customs distinct from others, art forms such as the emergence of true-view landscapes and genre painting began to flourish in the eighteenth century. A quintessential characteristic of this trend is evident in the "moon jar" (*tal hangari*): the name comes from the jar's round shape and milky white color, evoking the moon. Typically made by joining two bowl-shaped halves, the jar has a discernible horizontal seam at the center of its body. During the drying and firing process, the two joined halves of the moon jar sag and shrink, resulting in an asymmetrical and unique shape. This slightly slanted body and the subdued contours of white tones embody Chosŏn's aesthetic values of naturalism and spontaneity, favoring a gentle imperfection over rigid perfection.

During the reigns of Kings Yŏngjo (r. 1724–76) and Chŏngjo, blue-and-white porcelain experienced its golden age and became increasingly popular as tableware for royal banquets and ceremonies. The shapes and decorations of these wares became more varied, incorporating auspicious symbols such as mythical animals and plants: images of dragons and tigers, Daoist immortals, bird-and-flower designs, floral designs, "Four Gentlemen" (Sa kunja), and mountains and rivers. *The Porcelain Jar with Cloud and Dragon Design in Underglaze Cobalt Blue (Paekcha ch'ŏnghwa ullyongmun chun)* is an impressive example of this type of porcelain, often used for court banquets, royal rites, and receptions for foreign envoys (Figure 20.10). This tall jar features a bulging shoulder and swirling dragons in clouds, representing the king's authority and power

Figure 20.10 The Porcelain Jar with Cloud and Dragon Design in Underglaze Cobalt Blue, late eighteenth century, porcelain with cobalt-blue decoration, height 57.5 cm. Source and photo credit: National Palace Museum of Korea.

(Kwon 2014, 41–43). A five-clawed dragon with elaborately rendered scale and fin plays with a *cintamani* at the center. Other motifs, including flowers, foliage-scroll patterns, and fret designs, decorate the rim and shoulder. Over time, the refined rendition of dragon faces and scales in earlier porcelains gave way to a looser and more spontaneous expression.

While blue-and-white porcelain was prevalent in middle and late Chosŏn, potters also produced ceramics decorated with copper-oxidized red and iron-brown painted images and ornaments (Soyoung Lee 2020, 334). The *White Porcelain Jar with Plum and Bamboo Design in Underglaze Iron Brown* (*Paekcha ch'ŏrhwa maejungmun ho*) is a magnificent example. The elegant design with iron-brown underglaze features a highly realistic rendering of bamboo, alternating dark and light hues, and plum trees with a gnarled, curved trunk, likely painted by court painters. The porcelain's bluish powdery white glaze and imposing body with an everted mouth rim of this porcelain resembles a late sixteenth-century vessel from the official kiln in Kwangju. A later work, *White Porcelain Jar with Grapevine Design Painted in Underglaze Copper Red (Paekcha tonghwa p'odomun ho)* in the collection of the Metropolitan Museum, exemplifies mid-eighteenth-century porcelains crafted by private kilns. In contrast to court-manufactured porcelain, this work features more liberated, dynamic, and free-style brushwork, revealing diverse esthetic spectrums of late Chosŏn.

Chŏngjo's Vision of Nature and Confucian Kingship: The Rear Garden of Ch'angdŏk Palace

The construction of garden landscapes and architecture significantly enhanced royal authority in late Chosŏn by visualizing the monarch's political ideologies. Chŏngjo's restoration of Ch'angdŏk Palace's Rear Garden (Huwŏn) and his gathering there with his subjects are significant for illustrating how the Chosŏn elite engaged with the venue both ideologically and aesthetically. Cultural activities and artistic exchanges between the monarch and subjects in the garden enhanced its social and political functions. Ultimately, the communal experience of those enjoying the royal garden together helped to augment royal authority and shape the Confucian rulership in Chosŏn society.

A duality of *pŏpkung* (the king's main palace as his permanent residence) and *igung* (the king's temporary domicile) informed Chosŏn's palace administration. Among the various palaces in Hansŏng, Kyŏngbok Palace, constructed in 1394 upon T'aejo's order, functioned as the *pŏpkung*. In the seventeenth century, Ch'angdŏk Palace, originally built as a secondary palace in 1405, became the primary palace since Kyŏngbok Palace suffered destruction during the Imjin War (East Asian War; 1592–98). Unlike Kyŏngbok Palace, which featured a bifurcated arrangement of a dominant front palace and a rear garden, Ch'angdŏk Palace features an asymmetrical layout of buildings by the topographical characteristics. The Rear Garden, which covers an area of approximately 434,877 square meters, is located in the northwest part of Ch'angdŏk Palace. Ten pavilions grace the garden, to which King Injo (r. 1623–49) added Ongnyu, an artificial water channel for floating wine cups with a waterfall (1636). The architecture in the Rear Garden features four bodies of water: Ongnyu, T'aeak Pond, Aeryŏn Pond, and Pando Pond.

Upon his accession, Chŏngjo ordered the construction of the Kyujanggak to store royal portraits, books, documents, and calligraphic works. More than a royal archive, Kyujanggak also functioned as a political institution for policy and academic research, an educational institution for young scholar-officials, and the center for government publication (Jeong 2002, 4–11). Whether working at or visiting the archive, anyone approaching the Kyujanggak—a two-story structure located atop a hill that allowed the best view of the rear garden—had to walk through Ŏsu Gate

The Routledge Handbook of Early Modern Korea

and encounter the Puyong Pond of square shape with a round island at the center, featuring a pine tree. The design reflects the yin-and-yang theory of garden construction ("the heaven is round, and the earth is square") and symbolizes the islands of Daoist immortals. Passing through Pullo Gate, a stone structure, one can access Aeryŏn Pond and a pavilion. Farther north, several pavilions and halls are grouped around Panwŏl Pond. Nearby, Ongnyu is nestled in the innermost part of the garden. The name of the artificial stream in Injo's calligraphy was carved on a rock named Soyo (1636). Later, King Sukchong's (r. 1674–1720) poem in his calligraph was engraved on the rock, reading: "The artificial waterfall is 300 *cha* [90 meters] in height and looks like it is falling from the Milky Way. It looks as though a white rainbow arches over it and sounds as though thunder resounds in a valley" (1670).

The construction and renovation of the Puyong Pond area and Ongnyu can be understood in the political context of Chŏngjo's efforts to consolidate his power and take the initiative in the power struggles at court. Departing from precedents, Chŏngjo invited junior scholars affiliated with the Kyujanggak to visit the palace garden, previously deemed the royal family's private space. The gesture aimed to strengthen the king's bond with his subjects, as pursued through his frequent excursions with the same scholars from 1781 to 1795. The Rear Garden gatherings fostered their loyalty to the throne through exchanging ideas in a less formal setting and, thus, more personal interactions with the king.

Two works commemorate the occasions when the monarch and his attending scholar-officials exchanged poems near Puyong Pavilion and Ongnyu. As documented in *Compilation of Poems Composed at the Flower-Viewing Event in the Inner Garden in 1792* (*Naewŏn sanghwa imja kaengjae ch'uk*), Chŏngjo and the Kyujanggak officials gathered at Nongsan Pavilion to view spring blossoms, fish at Puyong Pond, and perform archery at Ch'undang Terrace. Offering an abundance of wine and food to the officials present, Chŏngjo improvised a poem before them, who then composed their poems using his rhymes. The gathering the following year, as documented in the *Compilation of Poems Composed at the Flower-Viewing Event in the Inner Garden in 1793* (*Naewŏn sanghwa kyech'uk kaengjae ch'uk*), marked a special occasion: the fiftieth year of the sexagenary cycle, which had circulated 24 times since the year 353 when, in Eastern Jin dynasty (317–420) China, Wang Xizhi (303–61)—a prominent statesman and one of the best calligraphers in East Asian history—and his 41 guests, all literati, held the celebrated Orchid Pavilion Gathering (Kameda-Madar 2011). In commemoration, Chŏngjo hosted a banquet at Ongnyu on the twentieth day of the third month in 1793 and invited 40 guests. Following the legendary gathering of the Orchid Pavilion, Chŏngjo floated wine cups down the winding stream at the Soyo Rock with the scholars of Kyujaggak, drinking and reciting poetry. The *Veritable Records of King Chŏngjo* (*Chŏngjo sillok*) describes the occasion in spring as a great achievement of the peaceful era and notes that the poetry scroll comprising the attendees' contributions measured 25 meters long. The poems reflect how each composer appreciated the scenery visually, aurally, and olfactorily, associating their activities with the refined cultural achievements of ancient Chinese gatherings. Additionally, the poems extol what their creators see as a reign of peace and prosperity.

Poems Chŏngjo wrote before ascending the throne, *Ten Views of the Royal Garden* (1767), reflects his artistic perception and aesthetic of landscape gardening. Describing the rich and various views of nature and landscape in the Rear Garden through the seasons, these works offer the prince's poetic, lyrical, and ethical interpretations of nature. The poems culminate in an expression of the necessity of self-cultivation. Through the ten poems, the future king guides readers on a visionary journey through the Rear Garden. After ascending to the throne, his excursions to the garden finally realized this imaginary journey. The choice of sites in the poems reveals his aesthetic preference and

Visual Arts

perception of nature, which continued to influence his later visits to the Rear Garden, which became a venue where the monarch and officials together compose poems, practice calligraphy, drink wine, and appreciate nature. This highly sophisticated structure incorporated rocks, ponds, trees, pathways, architecture, and historical and literary references, reflecting the king's vision, morality, and values.

Final Thoughts

The comprehensive examination of art and visual culture in Chosŏn elucidates the profound interplay between art, society, and politics in early modern Korea. The development of various art forms—landscape painting to portraiture and genre paintings—reflects the underlying Confucian values and Chosŏn's interactions with internal sociopolitical dynamics and external influences. The flourishing of true-view landscape painting, emphasizing realistic and native scenery, along with the detailed depiction of daily life in genre paintings, underscored a cultural identity that was distinctly Korean yet open to external influences. This era of artistic vibrancy was a reflection of aesthetic evolution and an integral part of the social fabric, embodying the philosophies, spiritual beliefs, and hierarchical structures of the time.

The role of art in reinforcing social hierarchies and Confucian ideology was particularly evident in the use of art for royal patronage and state rituals. Large-scale projects like the construction and adornment of palaces, the production of portraiture to immortalize monarchs and merit subjects, and the integration of auspicious symbols in decorative arts were all ways the Chosŏn state propagated and strengthened both the royal authority and Confucian ethos. Art served as a conduit for reinforcing the moral values of society, playing a crucial role in governance and personal expression. These endeavors highlight the dual function of art in Chosŏn society—as tools of statecraft and as mediums of individual or collective expression.

In conclusion, the art of Chosŏn offers profound insights into the cultural landscape of Korea during one of its most pivotal eras. By examining the intricate relationship between art and its broader cultural and political contexts, we can appreciate how art functioned as an aesthetic expression and a vital component of Chosŏn's identity and legacy. The legacy of Chosŏn art continues to influence contemporary Korean culture, reminding us of the enduring power of visual culture to shape and reflect societal values and transformations. Through this historical lens, we gain a deeper understanding of Korean art and the dynamic interplay between culture, politics, and society in shaping Korea's heritage.

Confucianism exerted a profound influence on art and visual culture in Chosŏn. At elite levels, royal patrons commissioned large-scale paintings, devotional images, magnificent construction projects, and the management of official kilns. Literati painting and the white porcelain produced at the royal kilns reflect Confucian aesthetics, emphasizing purity, austerity, and frugality. Also, the delicately rendered screens of auspicious symbols, blue-and-white porcelain replete with splendid patterns, and lavishly executed paintings and sculptures commissioned for Buddhist monasteries reveal the sumptuous and elegant taste of the royal house and the aristocracy. Various shapes of ceramics produced at local kilns and genre paintings depicting the everyday life of ordinary people attest to Chosŏn's aesthetic sensibility, which appreciated the bold, vigorous, spontaneous qualities and untrammeled naturalistic manner. At times, these various aesthetic standards and values encountered and mutually interacted to transcend the class, regional, philosophical, and religious boundaries, resulting in a splendid amalgamation of styles and art forms in Chosŏn. In addition to this internal stimulation, inspiration from and exchanges with China, Japan, and Europe contributed to the colorful development of art in Chosŏn.

References

Ahn, Hwi-joon. 1980. "An Kyon and *A Dream Visit to the Peach Blossom Land*." *Oriental Art* 26, no. 1 (Spring): 60–71.

Ahn, Hwi-joon. 1995. "Literary Gatherings and Their Paintings in Korea." *Seoul Journal of Korean Studies* 8 (1995): 85–106.

Black, Kay E. 2020. *Ch'aekkŏri Painting: A Korean Jigsaw Puzzle*. Sahoipyoungnon Publishing.

Chang, Chin-Sung. 2020. "Transformation: Three Centuries of Chang in Late Chosŏn Painting." In *A Companion to Korean Art*, edited by J. P. Park, Burglind Jungmann, and Juhyung Rhi, 291–320. John Wiley & Sons.

Cho, Insoo. 2020. "The Emergence of Confucian Culture: Early Chosŏn Painting." In *A Companion to Korean Art*, edited by J. P. Park, Burglind Jungmann, and Juhyung Rhi, 263–90. John Wiley & Sons.

Cho, Sunmie. 2007. "A Perspective on the History of Korean Portrait Painting." *International Journal of Korean Art and Archaeology* 1: 112–15.

Hong, Sunpyo, and Chang Chin-Sung. 2009. "Peace under Heaven: Confucianism and Painting in Early Joseon Korea." In *Art of the Korean Renaissance, 1400–1600*, edited by Soyoung Lee, 65–92. Metropolitan Museum of Art.

Jeong, Ok-ja. 2002. "Gyujanggak: Heart of Joseon Dynasty Learning and Ideology." *Koreana* 16, no. 3: 4–11.

Jungmann, Burglind. 2007. "Documentary Record versus Decorative Representation: A Queen's Birthday Celebration at the Korean Court." *Arts Asiatiques* 62: 106–07.

Jungmann, Burglind. 2011. "Sin Sukju's Record on the Painting Collection of Prince Anpyeong and Early Joseon Antiquarianism." *Archives of Asian Art* 61: 107–26.

Jungmann, Burglind. 2014. *Pathways to Korean Culture: Paintings of the Joseon Dynasty, 1392–1910*. Reaktion Books.

Kameda-Madar, Kazuko. 2011. "Pictures of Social Networks: Transforming Visual Representations of the Orchid Pavilion Gathering in the Tokugawa Period (1615–1868)." Ph.D. dissertation, University of British Columbia.

Kang Kwan-shik. 2005. "Self-Cultivation in the Portraits of Joseon Literati Scholars." *Korea Journal* 45, no. 2: 182–215.

Kim, Kumja Paik. 2016. "King Jeongjo's Patronage of Kim Hong-Do." *Archives of Asian Art* 66, no. 1: 51–80.

Kim, Sunglim. 2018. *Flowering Plums and Curio Cabinets: The Culture of Objects in Late Chosŏn Koren Art*. University of Washington Press.

Kwon, So-hyun. 2014. "Ceramics and Ritual Vessels of the Royal Household." In *Treasures from Korea: Arts and Culture of the Joseon Dynasty*, edited by Hyunsoo Woo, 36–43. Philadelphia Museum of Art.

Lachman, Charles H., and Richard Gehrke. 2006. *The Ten Symbols of Longevity, Shipjangsaengdo: An Important Korean Folding Screen in the Collection of the Jordan Schnitzer Museum of Art at the University of Oregon*. Seattle: Jordan Schnitzer Museum of Art.

Lee, Soyoung. 2009. "Art and Patronage in the Early Joseon." In *Art of the Korean Renaissance, 1400–1600*, edited by Soyoung Lee, 15–64. Metropolitan Museum of Art.

Lee, Soyoung. 2020. "Ceramics and Culture in Chosŏn Korea." In *A Companion to Korean Art*, edited by J. P. Park, Burglind Jungmann, and Juhyung Rhi, 321–42. John Wiley & Sons.

Lee Tae Ho. 2005. "Portrait Paintings in the Joseon Dynasty: With a Focus on Their Style of Expression and Pursuit of Realism." *Korea Journal* 45, no. 2: 107–50.

Oh, Ju-seok. 2005. *The Art of Kim Hong-do: A Great Court Painter of 18th-Century Korea*. Sol.

Seo, Yoonjung. 2014. "Connecting Across Boundaries: The Use of Chinese Images in Late Chosŏn Court Art from Transcultural and Interdisciplinary Perspectives." Ph.D. dissertation, University of California, Los Angeles.

Song, Unsok. 2014. "Buddhism and Art in the Joseon Royal House: Buddhist Sculpture and Painting." In *Treasures from Korea: Arts and Culture of the Joseon Dynasty*, edited by Hyunsoo Woo, 53–67. Philadelphia Museum of Art.

Song, Unsok. 2020. "Faith, Ritual, and the Arts: Chosŏn Buddhist Art and Architecture." In *A Companion to Korean Art*, edited by J. P. Park, Burglind Jungmann, and Juhyung Rhi, 371–402. John Wiley & Sons.

Woo, Hyunsoo. 2014. "Screen Paintings of the Joseon Court." In *Treasures from Korea: Arts and Culture of the Joseon Dynasty*, edited by Hyunsoo Woo, 25–35. Philadelphia Museum of Art.

Yoo, Jaebin. 2020. "Political Implications of Court Art Under King Jeongjo: Aesthetics and Production of King Jeongjo's Visit to Hwaseong." *Korea Journal* 60, no. 3: 371–406.

21

PERFORMING ARTS

CedarBough T. Saeji

Many today, even those who live in Korea, have had little exposure to the performing arts of Chosŏn (1392–1897). The average audience member at traditional performances typically knows little about what they are watching. Even the names of standard instruments or how to tell them apart is often beyond their knowledge (Saeji 2016). Traditional performances emerged for different audiences in the past and under very different conditions. Unsurprisingly, a contemporary Korean, raised on a musical diet of Western classical music, as well as Western and Korean songs from diverse popular genres, would be challenged by the unfamiliar tonal qualities, meters, timbres, and lyrical content in premodern Korean music.

Some of these Chosŏn genres, particularly those created for court rituals, are different precisely because the context for which they were developed and performed is disconnected from contemporary aesthetic decision-making. The creation of the performance may have been guided less by aesthetic desires and more by the sense of performance as a musical manifestation of Confucian philosophical ideas. Contemporary audiences are constantly seeking something more spectacular. For example, ballet dance increasingly demands dramatic lifts and high jumps, whereas Chosŏn court dance is sedate, ordered, and slow, repeating the same motions. Other genres, such as *kagok*, are so highly elaborated that the sung lyrics are not intelligible to the listener unless they have memorized the same poem. For performance scholars, these genres manifest the governing ideology of a different time, an ideology so pervasive that performance for the elite was not for entertainment but rather an enactment of philosophy.

On the other hand, the performances for commoner and slave class audiences were both rollickingly fun and irreverent. Although Korean culture has changed, and certain aspects of past stories and their humor may read differently today—such as the comedic treatment of drama characters who are hunchbacked, mentally disabled, blind, or suffering from Hansen's disease—folk performances also featured faster music, freer dance, and jokes about flatulence. Such crowd-pleasing performances may command a smaller audience today, but they can still charm audiences who seek out or encounter traditional shows.

DOI: 10.4324/9781003262053-28

The Routledge Handbook of Early Modern Korea

Performance for the Royal Court

Neo-Confucianism and Performing Arts

From the outset, the Chosŏn state began removing Buddhism from court rituals and performances. Replacing them were rituals and performances that fell within Confucian parameters. The process of revising rituals and music in the context of Confucianizing society continued throughout Chosŏn's history, especially the first few decades until the end of the fourth monarch, King Sejong (r. 1418–50), which saw the most changes. To begin with, the state stopped sponsoring two important Buddhist festivals, P'algwanhoe and Yŏndŭnghoe. Instead, Confucian performances at the Royal Ancestral Shrine (Chongmyo) and State Confucian Shrine (Munmyo) became important court rituals. Accordingly, the court reorganized the bureaus for performance and performers, instituting the Confucian Ritual Music Agency (Aaksŏ) for music performed at the Royal Ancestral Shrine and the State Confucian Shrine and the Court Music Agency (Chŏnaksŏ) for other types of music for the court. The three principal types of court music were *aak*, the Confucian ritual music adopted earlier by Chosŏn's predecessor state, Koryŏ (918–1392), from Song dynasty (960–1279) China in 1116 and revised under the direction of Sejong; *tangak,* the music Koryŏ's predecessor, Silla (57 BCE, trad.–935 CE), had imported from Tang dynasty (618–907) China and had undergone much change over time; and *hyangak*, the indigenous Korean court music.

The Confucian *Book of Rites* (*Liji*) includes a music chapter, the "Record of Music" (Yueji), which articulates the understanding that *ye* (Ch. *li*; rites, rituals) and *ak* (Ch. *yue*; music) must be in balance for people to behave properly (Jiwon Song 201, 8). In this vein, the "royal court ensembles throughout Chosŏn's history represented the ideal of *yeak* (rite and music), the harmonious balance between the ruling class and the people as well as between the king and his officials, in a discursive space made meaningful by notions of both morality and politics." According to the Confucian texts, "only when the two stay in perfect balance can *yeak* function well with life-giving energy" (Hee-sun Kim 2012, 83).

The Chosŏn court took this seriously in its management of music and rites. State rites comprised five categories: *killye* (auspicious rites), *karye* (festive rites), *pillye* (envoy rites), *kullye* (military rites), and *hyungnye* (funeral rites for the royal family). Collectively, the five could be performed as the *kukka chŏllye* (state rites), also called *orye* (five rites). Conducted in accordance with Confucian understandings of *ye* and *ak*, each rite featured song, dance, and music. In early Chosŏn, as the Confucian influence reshaped court institutions, various offices and officials created guidelines for the performance of the rites, including important historical documentation of song, dance, and music. The rites were divided into six different grades, and the grade determined the number of performers involved and how elaborate the rites would be (Jiwon Song 2015, 10–11). The largest and most important were two *killye*: rites performed at the Royal Ancestral Shrine and the Altar of Earth and Grain (Sajik). Although the two most extensive always saw performance, there was also a large variety of other *killye*. The number and type performed each year varied, with records showing forty-one varieties of *killye* performed throughout Chosŏn's history. Because the "music for sacrificial rites was considered the most important in court music" (Lim 2021, 21), the court maintained detailed records, and the music has survived to the present. Since *killye* is only one of the five types of rites, the court was staging rites and ceremonies, large or small, throughout the year.

The Chosŏn state deemed *aak* the most important type of music. "Since its principles and systematic order were established in the period of the Zhou [d]ynasty [c. 1046–256 BCE] and recorded in the *Rites of Zhou* (*Zhouli*), this music came to be perceived as the reflection of a Golden Age and so was handed down as the ideal music for the Confucian state" (Byeon 2022, 216). All the same, despite the perceived importance of ritual music, the court emphasized *ye* over *ak* (Jiwon Song 2015, 27). Such perception ran counter to Confucian philosophy: "If there were ceremonies but no music, people and society would lose their harmony and become fragmented; if there were music but no ceremonies, there would be disorder" (Hye-jin Song 2008, 24). Indeed, Confucian ideology was ever-present in the performance of *ak*. Such presence, for example, required instruments used for ritual music performances to be made from all the materials of East Asian cosmology: metal, stone, silk, bamboo, gourd, earth, leather, and wood (Jongsu Kim 2015, 50). According to the concept, *p'arŭm kŭkhae sinin ihwa*, the gods and people can be in harmony only if the eight materials are well matched (Hye-jin Song 2008, 15). The performances symbolized heaven, earth, and humanity in the ritual context. Some texts conceived of the two *aak* ensembles as heaven (or yang) and earth (or yin; Ko. *ŭm*), with the dancers representing humanity (Hye-jin Song 2008, 33). Nothing was random: the ritual manuals categorized even the food offerings into 12 types for the 12 months, handled by 63 different ceremonial utensils (Hye-jin Song 2008, 40).

The more elevated the rite, the more musicians and instruments were used, but regardless, the performances were a balance of *ka* (song), *mu* (dance), and *ak* (music). Discussion of the Korean performing arts rarely omits the term *kamuak*—suggesting that all types of performances were deemed part of a balanced whole. The songs for the Royal Ancestral Shrine rites, *akchang*, typically featured lyrics describing the ritual actions and addressing the person to whom a rite was dedicated. The dance for these rites, *ilmu*, was performed by lines of dancers who turned, raised their legs, and gestured but did not move forward, back, or to the sides throughout the entire dance. Sejong used six lines of six dancers for *ilmu*, but King Sejo (r. 1455–68) expanded it to eight lines of eight dancers (Jongsu Kim 2015, 60). The dance had two parts—a civil dance and a military dance—and the performers would hold representative objects in their hands during the performance (Jongsu Kim 2015, 53, 64).

Extant records about the types of rites and how they were performed are abundant, and the record-keeping was impressive. In the past few decades, Korean scholars of music and dance have experimented with reconstructing pieces in Chosŏn records that fell out of active performance because the records include the notated music, spell out the number of performers for each instrument, and even provide illustrations of the performers in the act (Table 21.1).

The Kings and Court Music

According to Chosŏn philosophy, only virtuous people could understand music; therefore, understanding music showed one's aptitude for governing the country (Hye-jin Song 2008, 25). No one better demonstrated this than Sejong, who had a tremendous influence on the Chosŏn performing arts. Seeing the deterioration of *aak* as a danger to the state, the king studied the musical theories from the *New Volume of Standard Musical Sounds* (*Lulu xinshu*). Sejong and his scholar-officials sought to restore "the authentic *aak*" in line with "the orthodoxy" of Zhou (Byeon 2022, 217). For example, the monarch composed the two pieces, "Preserving the Grand Peace" (Po t'aep'yŏng) and "Founding of the [Chosŏn] State" (Chŏng taeŏp). Subsequently, in 1464, Sejo designated both as the music for the Royal Ancestral Shrine rites (Jongsu Kim 2015, 62; Jiwon Song 2015, 11). Two groups of musicians, the "upper terrace" and "lower terrace" orchestras, performed these complex works (Figure 21.1).

Sejong implemented other measures for court rituals. In 1430, he changed the music for the Altar of Earth and Grain rites based on his reading of the *Rites of Zhou* (Jiwon Song 2015, 12). The rites performed for the Royal Ancestral Shrine and the Altar of Earth and Grain were long. Each entailed numerous ritual activities, as well as sections with only music or with music and dance but

The Routledge Handbook of Early Modern Korea

Table 21.1 Important performance-related texts and commissioning monarchs.

Reign	Text
Munjong (r. 1450–52)	*Veritable Records of King Sejong* (*Sejong sillok orye*): Treatise on the Five Rites (Orye)
	Veritable Records of King Sejong: Treatise on Musical Scores (Akpo)
Sŏngjong (r. 1470–95)	*Veritable Records of King Sejo* (*Sejo sillok*): Treatise on Musical Scores (Akpo)
	Manual for the Five Categories of State Rites (*Kukcho orye ŭi*)
	Canon of Music (*Akhak kwebŏm*)
	Great Code of Administration (Kyŏngguk taejŏn): sections on rites
Yŏngjo (r. 1724–76)	*Amended Manual for the Five Categories of State Rites* (*Kukcho sok orye ŭi*)
	State Music Text (*Kukcho akchang*)
	Reference Compilation of Documents on Korea (*Tongguk munhŏn pigo*): On Music (Akko)
	Amended Great Code (Sok taejŏn): sections on rites
Chŏngjo (r. 1776–1800)	*Comprehensive Five Rites of State* (*Kukcho orye t'ongp'yŏn*)
	Compendium on the Ministry of Rites (*Ch'un'gwan t'onggo*)
	Book of Standard Music Theory (*Siak hwasŏng*)
	Comprehensive Great Code (Taejŏn t'ongp'yŏn): sections on rites

The veritable records for a monarch were completed after his reign. Some were initiated by the successor and completed by the latter's successor.

without simultaneous ritual. The king also revised the music for the State Confucian Shrine rites, based on a reading of the Music Score for Confucius (*Sŏkchŏn akpo*) by Pak Yŏn (1378–1458). Generally emphasizing *hyangak* over the imported musical forms, Sejong developed the earliest mensural notation format in Asia (Jeonghui Yi 2015, 201–02).

Sejong's successors made some changes to the court music. Sejo combined various musical institutions of the court into the Bureau of Court Music (Changagwŏn), as he did not believe *hyangak, tangak*, and *aak* to be so distinct (So 201, 162). Subsequently, under Sŏngjong's command, the scholar-official Sŏng Hyŏn (1439–1504) "rewrote the lyrics of songs from the Goryeo [Koryŏ] Dynasty … which were considered lewd" (So 2015, 166). Two centuries later, in 1690. King Sukchong (r. 1674–1720) further reorganized court music, adding singing to the music of the lower terrace orchestra (Jongsu Kim 2015, 52). A century later, Chŏngjo made musical contributions that included new rites for his ill-fated father, Prince Sado (1735–62). Chŏngjo also created the texts for songs used in *Kwanwang myoje*, which honored a deified Chinese general, Guan Yu (d. 220), from 1786 (Jongsu Kim 2015, 66–67). Notably, unlike Sejong and Pak Yŏn, who evidently were confident enough to revise *aak*, earlier introduced to Koryŏ in 1116 from Song instead of deferring to Chinese sources, Sejong's heirs were more conservative. In fact, throughout Chosŏn's history, the majority of performance-related projects spearheaded by the throne occurred under only 5 out of 27 monarchs: Sejong, Sejo, Sukchong, Yŏngjo, and Chŏngjo.

Court Music Organizations and Performers

In 1466, the court performers began working mainly for the Bureau of Court Music (So 2015, 163). This government office was a third-grade government office, equivalent to the Royal Secretariat (Sŭngjŏngwŏn), the Office of the Censor General (Saganwŏn), and the Office of Royal Decrees

Figure 21.1 A screen painting of a royal court banquet with performers. Source and photo credit: National Museum of Korea.

(Yemun'gwan). The court musicians, known as *akkong* or *aksaeng* (*kwanhyŏn maengin*, if blind), performed all types of works, especially for sacrificial rites, banquets, and military ceremonies (Jiwon Song 2015, 18). Overseeing all aspects of the performance was the director (*chejo*) of the Bureau of Court Music. Perhaps the most famous among those who held the position is Sŏng Hyŏn, who wrote the *Canon of Music* (So 2015, 166). Some directors, such as Sŏng, thrived and achieved recognition; others even suffered chastisements by kings for problems with performances (Jeonghui Yi 205, 187). Other officials working under the director had roles such as compiling scores or preparing official records of the Bureau's activities (So 2015, 167).

Career trajectories and duties of court musicians varied. In the Bureau of Court Music, under the director, who often was not a performance specialist, was the *chŏnak*, the highest-ranked performer. A *chŏnak* would train other performers in music, song, and dance, arrange songs, and determine how to stage performances, as well as accompanying envoys to China and Japan. Below *chŏnak* was *kajŏnak*, the rank some musicians held until retirement or death without ever becoming the *chŏnak*. The court sometimes rehired experienced, retired *chŏnak* to perform other performance-related tasks. Otherwise, they could devote themselves to teaching youth or writing their own compositions. Among court musicians, the *aksaeng* were usually *chungin* ("middle peo-

The Routledge Handbook of Early Modern Korea

ple")—the status group just below aristocrats (*yangban*) and comprising government-employed experts in various fields—or children born into the families of *aksaeng*. In contrast, the *akkong* were "lowborn" (*ch'ŏnmin*), the status group mainly consisting of slaves (*nobi*) but also some entertainers and others holding socially denigrated occupations. Whereas *aksaeng* performed *aak* and *ilmu*, the *akkong* played *tangak and hyangak*. Since these positions did not pay well and were not well regarded, *aksaeng and akkong* were part of the corvée system (Jiwon Song 2015, 22). Even though they might not be willing workers, they were still forced to audition and were tested four times a year (Jeonghui Yi 2015, 192).

Every year, the court staged seven performances at the Royal Ancestral Shrine and three at the Altar of Earth and Grain, and each occasion demanded almost all *aak* performers. Not all performances required every instrument, and the scale of performances varied. Nonetheless, the performers were busy throughout the year, particularly since they had mandatory rehearsal twice every ten-day cycle in addition to performances (So 2015, 172; Jeonghui Yi 2015, 191). Due to the low pay, they would perform at private events when not on duty, and such occasions exposed more people to court performance genres. Sometimes, the throne sent court musicians elsewhere to perform "royally bestowed music" (*saak*) (Lim 2021, 28).

Besides the musicians, *mudong* (or *namak*) and *yŏgi* (or *yŏak*) performed as boy and female dancers, respectively. The *mudong* and *yŏgi* did not perform the same repertoire. Each province had to recruit a certain number of 8- to 15-year-old boys as *mudong*. When the boys had completed training, they had a limited span of performance life before they were deemed too old. At that point, they were either sent home or, if musically talented, could become *akkong*. Upon Chosŏn's founding, *yŏgi* were similarly recruited. When no longer working for the Bureau of Court Music, they assumed other palace roles, such as maids at the Office of the Royal Physicians (Naeŭiwŏn) or sewing maids (*ch'imsŏnbi*) at the Office of Royal Attire (Sangŭiwŏn) (Lim 201, 17). As increasingly conservative Confucian social norms forbade men and women from sitting in the same place, in 1623, the court banned women's performances except in women's quarters of the palace (Jiwon Song 2015, 27). Court banquets continued to use boy dancers unless the banquet was an "inner banquet" (*naeyŏn*). In that case, female dancers accompanied by blind musicians could perform for the queen and court ladies. If the inner palace banquet was particularly grand, regular *akkong* could perform with a screen separating them from female dancers and court women (Lim 2021, 17). As of a record in the Great Code of Administration, completed in Sŏngjŏng's reign, the court maintained 1,068 performers, including trainees. However, in the course of the Imjin War (East Asian War; 1592–98), the Chŏngmyo War (1627), and the Pyŏngja War (1637), the number decreased. In 1778, during Chŏngjo's reign, the number was down to 258 (So 2015, 168).

Among the performances accompanying banquets, the court took special care in entertaining Chinese envoys. One of six official categories of banquet entertained an official diplomatic visit from China, generally lasting ten days in Hansŏng (present-day Seoul). According to the *Canon of Music*, a one- or two-day tour of the Han River to the south of the city wall for the envoy involved the Bureau of Court Music director, 10 musicians, and 20 female entertainers (Jiwon Song 2015, 17). Such banquets were more than background music with powerful individuals eating and drinking: in the etiquette-bound Chosŏn court, "dance was performed every time the king raised a cup of wine" (Lim 2021, 25).

Over time, entertainment performances at the court lost ground. The growing cultural conservatism of the *yangban* elite and the financial woes during the mid-Chosŏn wars led to the abolition of the Directorate-General of Entertainment (Sandae togam) in 1634. Decades later, Sukchong's reign saw another reorganization of entertainment at the palace that further reduced the sizes of orchestras. The court also eliminated some of the pieces of its performance repertoire (Lim 2021, 19).

Performances for (and by) the Literati

Genres the elite patronized were musically distinct from court genres and often from one another. Although frequently performed by professionals with *yangban* patronage, in some cases, the *yangban* demonstrated their own cultivation of *yeak* by practicing, composing, and performing music. What follows is an overview of: (1) the literati ensemble for playing salon music, *p'ungnyu*, (2) the sung poetry of *chŏngga*, and (3) professional female performers, *kisaeng*.

Ensemble Music: P'ungnyu

P'ungnyu was performed in three different contexts: at festivals, regular practices, and when aristocrats invited professionals to play with them (Howard 2007, 141). Ensembles performing *p'ungnyu* were part of a particular culture of the Chosŏn aristocracy that centered on the *p'ungnyu pang*, the salon room in an aristocrat's home (Hee-sun Kim 2012, 8). *P'ungnyu* shares many characteristics with other Korean instrumental music (Hee-sun Kim 2007, 56):

1) instrumental music derived from vocal music; 2) new pieces as variants of one prototype or old melody; 3) long performances due to suite form; 4) single repertoire that can be several depending on its instrumentation as solo, ensemble or duet; 5) tempo changes within the piece that follow the same pattern from slow to fast; 6) no conductor and drum player or bak player lead the ensemble; 7) musicians are able to perform more than one instrument; and 8) rhythmic patterns are the most important musical element.

Although "originally performed at the court," the *p'ungnyu* music was developed mainly by professional *chungin* whose social status was just below the literati, yet were raised with the tastes and education of the literati, if not the same opportunities. Such *chungin* were just as interested in "cultivating one's culture as suggested by Confucian teaching" (Hee-sun Kim 2007, 49) as the literati were, through the "refined and stylish recreation, intrinsic to a tasteful lifestyle, and relevant to Korean collective and individual entertainment culture" of *p'ungnyu* (Hee-sun Kim 2007, 50). As a more economically driven culture emerged in late Chosŏn, many *chungin* amassed wealth, expanding their influence in such areas as culture and becoming important art patrons. Besides such *chungin*, the Sarim—who were Neo-Confucian scholar-officials advocating the dissemination of knowledge and culture in their communities—were also instrumental in promoting *p'ungnyu* music (Hee-sun Kim 2007, 52).

P'ungnyu has attracted much research because "many old scores have survived that allow scholars to explore and document its history" (Howard 2007, 141). Among *p'ungnyu* music pieces, the best known and most performed today is "Yŏngsanghoesang," a suite comprising various tunes (Hee-sun Kim 2007, 53), and three versions of the suite are extant. The patrons played *p'ungnyu* in the salon, typically on the dignified *kŏmun'go* ("black zither"), with professional musicians on other instruments and other artists such as poets and painters in attendance.

Sung Poetry: Chŏngga

Besides enjoying the instrumental *p'ungnyu* music, salon gatherings appreciated *chŏngga*. The genre comprises three types: *Sijo*, *kasa*, and *kagok*. The elite penned many *chŏngga* texts, as appre-

The Routledge Handbook of Early Modern Korea

ciating poetry through song was a mark of aristocratic refinement. *Kasa* was based on prose poetry, whereas both *sijo* and *kagok* drew from *sijo* poetry sung in distinctively different ways. Among the three forms of *chŏngga*, *kagok* is "the most formalized and elaborate" in "vocal techniques, performance styles, expression, forms, gender classification, musical features, and accompanying instrumentation" (Hee-sun Kim 2018, 8). Some *kagok* are for male voice, others for female. Men use the "chest voice or *yuksŏng* 'natural voice' with wide, slow vibrato," whereas women use "both the chest voice and the head voice, known as *sokch'ŏng* 'inner voice' or *sesŏng* 'fine voice' with relatively narrow vibrato." Also characterized by a high pitch and a nasal quality, the female voice shifts back and forth from chest to head so often that it can sound similar to yodeling (Um 2002, 88). Amateurs could perform *sijo*, sometimes without any accompaniment—a preferred performance format of literati. Still extant are 26 male and 15 female *kagok*, approximately 100 *sijo*, and 12 *kasa*. Contemporary singers generally are registered heritage performers of one genre, though they typically train in all three.

Kisaeng

As women trained in various arts, the most accomplished *kisaeng* (or *kinyŏ*) engaged in intellectual and artistic pursuits, including poetry and performing arts. A *kinyŏ* combined "artistic excellence, beauty, and sex appeal, all of which were officially forbidden to the ladies of the yangban class" (Suh 2008, 144). At the bottom of Chosŏn status hierarchy as the "lowborn," some *kisaeng* were government-registered entertainers (*kwan'gi*), whereas the rest comprised three skill groups (*samp'ae*) of "folk musicians" (Ha 2021, 110). Among the former, in the 1700s, a famed *kisaeng*, Kyesŏm (b. 1736), was even asked to perform at a banquet in front of Yŏngjo (Jeonghui Yi 2015, 208). Legally no different from slaves, who constituted the majority of the lowborn, for most of her life, Kyesŏm had little control over her performance patron and venue. However, as a free woman late in her life, she performed at the *hwan'gap* (sixtieth birthday) celebration of Lady Hyegyŏng-gung Hong (1735–1816), the mother of Chŏngjo, when Kyesŏm was also 60 (Jeonghui Yi 2015, 209). Women had few opportunities to concentrate on acquiring and refining performing arts skills, and *kisaeng* were unique in this regard. Their expertise produced women's versions of popular performances. For example, *kisaeng* often performed the women's *kagok* repertoire (Hee-sun Kim 2018, 9).

Professional Performers: *Ch'angu*

Most professional performers in Chosŏn were *ch'angu*, who were the "major folk entertainers" (Bo-hyung Lee 2009, 54), and those who lived in Hansŏng were *panin*, who were slaves owned by the Confucian Academy (Sŏnggyun'gwan). Depending on one's training, *panin* performed in a wide range of genres, including *p'ansori* (epic storytelling), acrobatics, dance, and instrumental music (Bo-hyung Lee 2009, 55). As professional entertainers performing outside the court, *ch'angu* bridged literati music and the music of the commoners in terms of repertoire and audience.

Kwangdae

Sometimes glossed as "clowns," *kwangdae* (or *chaein*) were professional, sometimes itinerant, performers. Generally performing multiple genres, including mask dance drama, puppetry, tightrope acts, and tumbling, *kwangdae* were also skillful drummers. In late Chosŏn, many played various instruments professionally, became the main *p'ansori* vocalists, or sang *kagok*. While some *kwang-*

dae would be rooted in a location and performed *p'ansori* or other specialized genres, either when invited by literati or in the market, others traveled around Korea performing. Among a wide variety of traveling acts was one type, *sadangp'ae*, which were groups of itinerant female performers managed by men who focused on dance, singing, and tightrope acts. The *namsadangp'ae* were groups of male performers whose standard repertoire was "dish spinning, acrobatics on the ground and tightrope walking" *p'ungmul* drumming, a type of mask dance drama, and puppet plays (Jeon 2008, 142–43).

Shamanic Music

The increasingly conservative Confucian Chosŏn society marginalized shamans, who, along with *kisaeng* and slaves, were the lowborn on the rigid status hierarchy. At least two distinct types of shamans coexisted: the hereditary shamans (primarily south of the Han River) and the "spirit-descended" shamans. In general, the hereditary shamanic tradition developed and nurtured advanced performing arts. In such traditions, the men of the families would be trained in music and ritual from early childhood, whereas women who married into shamanic families (and tended to be from similar families) learned singing, dancing, and ritual. In contrast, the spirit-descended shamans mastered performance techniques on their own (Yong-shik Lee 2007, 164) after becoming "infected" with a spirit or spirits. Accordingly, their rituals, centered on the presence of a spirit or spirits, were less artistically ornate—but no less spectacular.

The musical accompaniment for shamanic rituals could be a small *sinawi* ensemble or a percussion ensemble using the same instruments as *p'ungmul*. Groups of *ch'angu* performers often provided the *sinawi* for shamans (Bo-hyung Lee 2009, 7). Because *sinawi* can also mean non-shamanic music, it can be confusing. The simple explanation is that "any sacred/secular divide has routinely been breached by professional musicians. They may have worked as ritual accompanists, perhaps living as the spouses of female shamans, but many also taught and performed in secular contexts" (Howard 2007, 139). Shamanic ceremonial vocalizations vary from short, repetitive ritual prayers to *p'ansori* excerpts to extended shamanic songs. Excellent examples are the early folklorist Im Sŏkchae's (Im Sok-jae; 1903–98) collection of shamanic songs (See Im 2003). Although we have few specific records about the performances of shamans in Chosŏn, the symbolic importance of ritual content and the frequency of rituals by popular shamans drove the arts to be highly articulated.

Performances of and by the People

In Chosŏn society, a wide range of performance genres entertained nonelites. Either the commoner (*yangin*) or the lowborn on the status hierarchy, nonelites vastly outnumbered *yangban* elites and *chungin*. A survey of Buddhist ritual performance, *p'ungmul*, *minyo* (folk song), *sanjo* (solo instrumental music), *p'ansori*, and the fascinating mask dance dramas follows.

Ritual Performances in Buddhism

Among the many genres of Chosŏn performance were religious works, Buddhist, shamanic, or both. Chosŏn became more broadly Confucian over the centuries, with the state and the elite upholding Neo-Confucianism as the official ideology. Nonetheless, the religious landscape remained pluralistic and syncretic. Both Buddhism and shamanism continued to serve especially nonelites and women whose needs the heavily text-based, philosophical Neo-Confucianism could not fully address.

The Routledge Handbook of Early Modern Korea

Although the founders of Chosŏn officially rejected Buddhism and its ritual performing arts gradually declined, some early kings, including Sejong, encouraged reforms and advancement in Buddhist performance (Byong Won Lee 2007, 18). Nonetheless, opportunities to perform the Buddhist rites decreased. By the 1850s, monks had forgotten the intonation of the chants, and surviving chant musicians were precious few. Buddhist performances were even staged as evening banquet entertainment, particularly in the form of dances like *sŭngmu* and *ogomu* adapted from the Buddhist Ritual Drum Dance (*pŏpko ch'um*) (Byong Won Lee 2007, 149). The Buddhist ritual performances included dance (*chakpŏp*); *ch'wit'a*, which is a percussive band-type music and is similar to royal marching music; *p'ungmul*; *samhyŏn yukkak*, which is a dance music ensemble; and two types of chants, *yŏmbul* and *pŏmp'ae*. *Yŏmbul* are chanted sutras that can be heard daily, whereas *pŏmp'ae* serve more special ceremonies. A soloist or a chorus could perform *pŏmp'ae*, with or without optional solo interpolations or as call-and-response. Highly melismatic in musical style, *pŏmp'ae* "makes such extensive use of vocables that the original text syllables are difficult to locate during an actual performance" (Byong Won Lee 2007, 152). Unlike China or Japan, at some point, Korea's Buddhist rituals began to include dance. Since the "choreography of the ritual dances is quite different from that of Korean traditional dances" (Byong Won Lee 2007, 156), it may reflect the influence of Tibetan Buddhist ritual introduced to Koryŏ under Mongol domination (1259–1356). Four types of Korean Buddhist ritual dances are known: the Butterfly Dance, the Cymbal Dance, the Ritual Drum Dance, and the Stick Dance.

In addition to various ritual performances, some poor monks who struggled to survive in Confucian Chosŏn performed in itinerant groups (*chungmaegu*, *kutchung*). They traveled from house to house, playing instruments, dancing, telling fortunes, and chanting prayers before collecting donations (Jeon 2008, 140). Those giving alms tended to be nonelites in general and women across status boundaries.

Group Drumming Music: **P'ungmul**

The drumming music, *p'ungmul*, would come to be called *nongak* ("farmers music") in colonial Korea (1910–45), but the older term still favored by the performers reflects the genre's presence in both farming and fishing communities. The drumming music best known today, *samulnori* ("four-object play"), can be deemed extractions of *p'ungmul* and other folk music for a concert stage, stripped of traditional context yet preserving key musical elements. The traditional context for *p'ungmul* varied widely, but it was the soundtrack of celebration and community work. "Typically performed in the past by an ensemble of (male) villagers playing on gongs and drums with little or no distinctions made between performers and onlookers" (Hesselink 2007, 93), *p'ungmul* could be used in all sorts of village rituals, for shaman's rituals, to accompany a mask dance drama or other types of performance (including itinerant performances), or to encourage group work such as mending nets or transplanting rice. Regional varieties of *p'ungmul* are distinctive. Rhythms can be different, common rhythms vary, and the accompanying aerophone can shift from the *nabal* (a horn) to the *t'aep'yŏngso* (a reed instrument). A festival performance often had a theatrical or visual component, such as *chapsaek* (comedic character) dancers or hand-drum-wielding dancers creating eye-catching displays with the *sangmo* (ribbon or feather-tufted hat). Regardless, in every region, *p'ungmul* revolved around rhythm played on the barrel drum (*puk*) and hourglass drum (*changgu*) and on a large and small gong. The most experienced players on small gongs and hourglass drums were essential to leading rhythms for other players, who could be less experienced or skilled yet still fruitfully participate in the music-making.

Performing Arts

Folk Songs

Although the term *minyo* is widely used to mean folk songs or traditional songs in Korea, it has both amateur and professionalized variants. One of the two main types of *minyo* were songs anyone could sing easily while working, playing, or even carrying the deceased to the tomb. The professionalized type of *minyo* was often sung by singers who also sang *chapka* ("miscellaneous songs") and *sŏnsori*, two other types of professionalized song. These songs were generally sung with the verse and refrain alternating, where strong singers sang verses, and the group collectively sang the refrain. Talented singers could elaborate on the structure and localize lyrics or compose verses on the spot.

Folk songs feature widely ranging lyrical content. Love songs were prevalent, but those sung by those performing group labor depicted the activities of the farmers or fishers. Other songs wished for abundance. Unsurprisingly so, given the paramount position of Confucianism in the society, "Confucian obedience and the preservation of order also appear as one of the major themes ..., expressing the three bonds and moral rules in human relations based on loyalty and filial piety" (Paek 2007, 68). Many of these songs were well-known and enjoyed popularity throughout Chosŏn's history. Four or five regional styles of singing emerged: Namdo (south), Sŏdo (west), Kyŏnggido (central), Tongbu (east), and Cheju (island Chejudo).

Both *chapka* and *sŏnsori* drew from an increasingly diverse pool of singers. *Chapka* appeared in the eighteenth century, deriving from other popular singing forms such as *kasa, sijo, p'ansori,* and *minyo* (Paek 2007, 80), and popularity increased. At first sung primarily by those of low social status, who probably sang anything to please an audience, *chapka* became more distinct—attracting *kisaeng* and singers of *chŏngga* like *sijo*, all of whom could also see the advantage in dipping into other complementary repertoires. Likewise, itinerant groups originally sang *sŏnsori*, arguably a subcategory of *chapka*, but other professional vocalists mined the repertoire over time.

Solo Instrumental Music: Sanjo

Sanjo is a solo genre performed on an instrument with an hourglass drum player for accompaniment. Musicologists link *sanjo* to a sort of proto-*sanjo* called *simbanggok,* which was a name for female performers who accompanied shamans on the *gayageum* zither (Yun 2018, 247), to shamanic *sinawi,* and also to the vocal genre of *p'ansori* (Bo-hyung Lee 2009, 7). Specifically, the "aspect of *sanjo* that relates most closely to pansori is mode" (Howard 2007, 13). An extension of other professionalized music-making, *sanjo* seems to have emerged around the same time as *p'ansori* (Bo-hyung Lee 2009, 8). Unlike *p'ansori*, however, *sanjo* was an "invention": as the earlier music became more formalized and less improvisatory, in the late nineteenth century, Kim Ch'angjo (1865–1919)—a *kŏmun'go* virtuoso also adept in many other instruments—created *sanjo* for the 12-string zither, *kayagŭm* (Hee-sun Kim 2009, 13). Subsequently, *sanjo* developed in ways accommodating other chordophone and aerophone instruments. A full-length *sanjo* performance lasts approximately an hour, if not longer.

P'ansori

One of the most well-known types of vocal music, *p'ansori*, is performed by a professional singer showcasing a wide range of challenging techniques, accompanied by a drummer on the barrel drum. A full-length performance of a *p'ansori* epic can require three to eight hours, but this would not become the norm until the mid-twentieth century (Creutzenberg 2022). In Chosŏn, featuring only the highlights or performing *p'ansori* in serialized fashion over several days was common.

The Routledge Handbook of Early Modern Korea

Besides staging "open-air performances" for an audience mostly of ordinary people, *p'ansori* performers began to entertain *yangban* by the mid-eighteenth century. The elites, though, continued to consider the genre vulgar (Um 2007, 107). *P'ansori* was perhaps the most popular type of performance in late Chosŏn. Singers switched between spoken narration in plain language that would move the story along and bring the audience to a moment of key action and singing in more flowery language, including references to Chinese history and literature. The names of the most popular *p'ansori* performers appear in many written records of the time to such an extent that "discussion of the history of pansori is ultimately a description of the performers" (Willoughby 2008, 7).

The history of *p'ansori* is somewhat unclear. Consistent use of the term *p'ansori* only begins in the twentieth century, but the genre seems to have emerged in the seventeenth century, drawing from "traditional tales, shamanic epics, professional entertainers (also known as *ch'angu* or *kwangdae*) and *kangch'ang* (storytelling) literature." From what was probably an "impromptu play performed by street entertainers" (Kee-hyung Kim 2008, 3), *p'ansori* developed until it had a standard repertoire of twelve epic works. In the 1870s and '80s, a *chungin p'ansori* singer, Sin Chaehyo (1812–84) not only wrote down the stories, he refined and removed "vulgar" elements frowned upon by the elites.

Due to Sin's editorializing, only five of these epic story-songs are extant. Each maps onto a different Confucian relationship in ways that subtly challenge the restrictions of Confucianism. *Song of Ch'unhyang* (*Ch'unhyang ka*) is a morality tale that exposes government corruption and celebrates the loyalty between husband and wife. A poem by Yu Chinhan (1711–91) from 1754, during Yŏngjo's reign, already recorded the whole *Song of Ch'unhyang*, suggesting that elites were already fascinated with *p'ansori* (Jeon 208, 122). *Song of Simch'ŏng* (*Simch'ŏng ka*) extols the filial love of a daughter who sacrifices herself so that her blind father can see again. *Song of the Red Cliffs* (*Chŏkpyŏk ka*) celebrates an epic battle, after which a victorious general, Guan Yu, reflects on the hospitality once extended to him by his sworn elder brother's defeated archenemy and lets him go. *Song of the Underwater Palace* (*Sugung ka*) depicts benevolent rule and an ideal relationship between a king and his subject. And *Song of Hŭngbo* (*Hŭngbo ka*) narrates the relationship between a selfish, mean elder brother and a kind, generous younger brother.

The penetration of Confucianism even into a performing art for the general populace outside the court reflects the widespread dissemination of Confucian moral rhetoric in late Chosŏn. All the same, the *p'ansori* texts present themes speaking for ordinary people while poking fun at the follies and failings of aristocrats. Such dualism can be explained as "two types of audiences, namely, the upper and lower classes, and pansori musicians had to meet the needs and tastes of both groups" (Um 2007, 110).

Mask Dance Dramas

Among the most exciting performances of Chosŏn were the mask dance dramas. Like other folk performing arts, few records related to mask dance dramas exist. The current understanding of the dramas in Chosŏn is based on some poems and mentions in literati writing (Saeji 2012, 150), as well as the speculations in folklore texts produced during that colonial era that became accepted as knowledge over the years. Hahoe *pyŏlsin kut t'alnori* (the mask dance drama of Hahoe Village's shamanic ritual) claims a history of over 800 years, and records of mask dance drama competitions in Hwanghae Province show the vibrancy of the performance form in late Chosŏn. Nonetheless, the dramas likely grew more popular and became widespread only near the end of Chosŏn.

Performing Arts

By then, mask drama was a genre that featured a wide range of styles but still generally fell under two categories. Many were village ritual dramas, such as Hahoe *pyŏlsin kut t'alnori*. Others were *sandae*-descended dramas, including Pongsan *t'alchum* (Hwanghae Province), Yangju Pyŏlsandae (Kyŏnggi Province), and T'ongyŏng Ogwangdae (Kyŏngsang Province) (Jeon 2009). When the Directorate-General of Entertainment stopped supporting mask dance drama performances for local entertainment, performers who lost their jobs presumably dispersed around the peninsula and kept the dramas alive.

Over time, these dramas diverged from the earlier model shaped and managed by the Directorate-General. Between the early 1600s and the end of Chosŏn, the mask dance dramas' primary performers were amateurs, usually holding one production per year for a village festival. Accordingly, many performed at the first full moon after the Lunar New Year, the Double Fifth Festival (Tano), Buddhist All Souls' Day (Paekjung), and the Autumn Harvest Festival (Ch'usŏk). In the case of the drama in Hahoe, though, performances were much less frequent—perhaps just once in ten years. In addition, itinerant troupes roving the Korean Peninsula brought varied routines, including mask dance drama, to dispersed localities. On the south coast, where entertainers performed many mask dance dramas in late Chosŏn, local dramas emerged when itinerant troupes reneged on commitments, disappointing local villagers waiting for the show.

The *sandae* origins of the dramas explain similarities in stories, with a core repertoire that includes a story about a foolish literati, a monk chasing one or more women, and a literati gentleman amidst a conflict between his old wife and his young concubine. The various scenes in mask dance dramas stand alone, and accordingly, they could be performed in any order. With a notable exception of Kangnŭng on the central east coast, the dramas do not depict a single narrative from beginning to end. Today, the Hwanghae and Kyŏnggi dramas run three to four hours, but most other dramas can be performed in approximately one hour. This may also reflect the proximity of Hwanghae and Kyŏnggi Province to important government offices where the Directorate-General of Entertainment performances were held, whereas mask dance drama content in other regions preserved the most popular highlights of the *sandae* shows but lost much of the detailed and extensive dialogue in plays from Hwanghae and Kyŏnggi provinces.

All the same, the mask dance dramas can differ significantly from one another, especially those not rooted in the *sandae* pattern. Not all the dramas include all three stories just sketched. Some dramas are rich in references to Chinese history and literary works, whereas others, such as Kangnŭng Government Slave Mask Drama (Kangnŭng *kwanno kamyŏn'gŭk*), are entirely nonverbal. Either a *p'ungmul* drumming team or, for dramas from Kyŏnggi and Hwanghae Provinces, a small dance ensemble (*samyŏn yukkak*) accompanies every mask drama—except Pukch'ŏng Lion Play (Pukch'ŏng *saja norŭm*) features vertical flutes (*t'ungso*) and the barrel drum. The Pukch'ŏng drama has few masked characters, unlike most dramas where nearly all characters wear masks. The masks were burned after a show, except in the case of Hahoe's drama, where they were ritually kept in the village shrine. Dramas on the south coast often include one or more characters with Hansen's Disease—as there were leper colonies on some of the small islands in the region. And although almost every drama features a clever servant, in Hahoe's drama the servants are rather dim-witted.

The mask dance dramas probably provided a carnivalesque Bakhtinian leveling effect on Chosŏn society—by temporarily allowing criticism and expression of resentment against the elite and thus keeping society more stable (Saeji 2012, 156). To that end, the characters in mask dance dramas do not have names. Rather, they hold such generic titles as Horse Servant, Old Grandmother, Blue Yangban, Young Master, Old Monk, Police Inspector, and Shoe Salesman (Saeji 2012, 154). The dramas present the literati gentlemen lampooned, with pointed criticism

The Routledge Handbook of Early Modern Korea

related to the capriciousness of the rigid hereditary status hierarchy. In Kosŏng Ogwangdae, a servant hailing from a lineage stripped of rank in a factional purge demonstrates his superiority to his master, and the master even compares his own son to a tapeworm or washed kimchi. The *yangban* in the dramas are boastful, idle, and pleasure-seeking. Buddhist monks are reprimanded for amoral acts, but considering the origin of the stories in the Directorate-General of Entertainment, at least some such scenes may have been a form of Confucian government propaganda. They may also reflect a massive purge of Buddhist monasteries in early Chosŏn, leaving many former monks with only the clothing (robes) on their backs to their name (Saeji 2012, 157–58).

In the late nineteenth century, mask dance dramas began to be performed in commercial contexts, such as the five-day market at the Han River port of Songp'a (now a district of Seoul). The Pongsan Mask Dance, notably, began to professionalize (Tuhyon Yi 1975, 52):

> It is said that the man who revived the Bongsan mask dance was An Chomok, a low-ranking official who lived in Bongsan about two hundred years ago. After he had been exiled ... he returned and instituted many innovations into the drama, changing the wooden masks that had been in use to paper [papier-mâché] ones, and later, together with other low-grade officials, taking principal command over the play altogether.

After An Ch'omok (n.d.) changed the heavy wooden masks to paper (Cho 1988, 203), Yi Sŏnggu (fl. late nineteenth century), a servant employed by the local magistracy, made Pongsan's mask dance drama more professional. Spicing up the genre, he made the dances faster with the motions bigger and showier (Jeon 2005, 4). Another change from the era was the inclusion, at times, of a prominent local *kisaeng* as Aesadang, the singing maiden character. Aesadang was the first female performer in any of Korea's mask dance dramas, and since the attraction was her beautiful face, her mask remained perched atop her head.

In the modern era, early folklorists would begin to write down mask dance drama dialogues in the 1930s, but in the climate of Japanese colonization, where many yearly festivals were canceled for years on end, only a few dramas continued to be irregularly performed, generally in a more commercialized format (Janelli 1986). Although most dramas fell out of active performance, they remain regional, national, and, since 2022, UNESCO-certified heritage, providing a window into Chosŏn Korea's artistic humor.

Final Thoughts

This overview of the performing arts in Chosŏn Korea focused on explaining the performing arts and their place in society, as well as the connection between them and sociopolitical changes. To a considerable extent, the discussion above reflects that research on the subject has benefitted from the principles of historical musicology and salvage anthropology, together seeking to preserve a heritage. Such an approach was inevitable as Korea's engagement with imperialism in the late nineteenth century impacted the arts. Under the subsequent Japanese colonial rule, recorded music from around the world began to influence Korean arts, causing shifts through inspiration and the necessity of matching such requirements as the length of vinyl records and competing for an expanding audience. Chosŏn's performing arts, which the colonizers enjoyed, had an easier time, but the overall sociocultural context was changing—making it difficult for performances to continue.

Once colonial rule ended, the division of Korea and the establishment of mutually antagonistic regimes introduced new challenges for the performing arts. In the early 1960s, as the South Korean government began certifying "intangible cultural heritage," genres received legitimizing titles and performance opportunities. While in the South, the preservation of arts usually tried to roll back changes to preserve a late Chosŏn format, North Korea used the arts to showcase Kim Il-sung's ideology. Musicologists collected folk songs in the 1950s, editing and preserving them according to their correspondence with the northern regime (Howard 2020, 34–36). Instruments were also "improved" to be more "suitable for the socialist state" (Howard 2020, 43). Indeed, many traditional performances only exist today because of governmental patronage, North and South, and unsurprisingly, issues with reconstruction and authenticity plague some arts. This is a continuation of the Chosŏn pattern, where the art forms that found wealthy (or the state's) patronage fared better. Thus, among the performing arts this chapter surveyed that still exist in the South, some survive as a recreation offered free to onlookers rather than an artistic form that can draw an audience naturally.

References

Byeon, Gyewon. 2022. "Intertwining Influences on the Musical Achievements of 15th Century Korea." *Review of Korean Studies* 25, no. 2: 215–42.

Cho, Oh-Kon. 1988. *Traditional Korean Theatre*. Asian Humanities Press.

Creutzenberg, Jan. 2022. "Making Masters, Staging Genealogy: Full-Length Pansori as an Invented Tradition." In *Invented Traditions in North and South Korea*, edited by Andrew David Jackson, Codruta Sintionean, Remco E. Breuker, and CedarBough T. Saeji, 279–303. University of Hawai'i Press.

Ha, JuYong. 2021. "Female Masculinity and Cultural Symbolism: A History of Yeoseong Gukgeuk, the All-Female Cast Theatrical Genre." *Review of Korean Studies* 24, no. 2: 107–44.

Hesselink, Nathan. 2007. "Folk Music: Instrumental." In *Music of Korea*, edited by Byong Won Lee and Yong-shik Lee, 93–104. Gugakwon.

Howard, Keith. 2007. "Professional Music: Instrumental." In *Music of Korea*, edited by Byong Won Lee and Yong-shik Lee, 127–43. Gugakwon.

Howard, Keith. 2020. *Songs for 'Great Leaders': Ideology and Creativity in North Korean Music and Dance.* Oxford University Press.

Im, Sok-jae. 2003. *Mu-ga: The Ritual Songs of Korean Mudangs.* Translated by Alan C. Heyman. Asian Humanities Press.

Janelli, Roger. 1986. "The Origins of Korean Folklore Scholarship." *Journal of American Folklore* 99, no. 391: 24–49.

Jeon, Kyungwook. 2005. *Korean Mask Dance Dramas: Their History and Structural Principles.* Youlhwadang.

Jeon, Kyungwook. 2008. *Traditional Performing Arts of Korea.* Korea Foundation.

Jeon, Kyungwook. 2009. "Han'guk kamyŏn'gŭk ŭi kyet'ong ŭl ponŭn sigak chaeron." *Han'guk minsokhak* 50: 513–75.

Kim, Hee-sun. 2007. "Classical Music: Instrumental." In *Music of Korea*, edited by Byong Won Lee and Yong-shik Lee, 49–63. Gugakwon.

Kim, Hee-sun. 2009. "Music of Sanjo." In *Sanjo*, edited by The Gugakwon, 13–43. Gugakwon.

Kim, Hee-sun. 2012. "Performing History and Imagining the Past: Re-Contextualization of Court Ensembles in Contemporary South Korea." *World of Music* 1: 81–102.

Kim, Hee-sun. 2018. "Introduction." In *Gagok, Gasa, Sijo: Classical Vocal Music of Korea*, edited by The Gugakwon, 7–10. Gugakwon.

Kim, Jongsu. 2015. "Sacrificial Rituals and Music." In *Ritual Music of the Korean Court*, edited by The Gugakwon, 29–71. Gugakwon.

Kim, Kee-hyung. 2008. "History of Pansori." In *Pansori*, edited by The Gugakwon. Gugakwon.

Lee, Bo-hyung. 2009. "Social History of Sanjo." In *Sanjo*, edited by The Gugakwon, 3–12. Gugakwon.

Lee, Byong Won. 2007. "Religious Music: Buddhism." In *Music of Korea*, edited by Byong Won Lee and Yong-shik Lee, 145–57. Gugakwon.

Lee, Yong-shik. 2007. "Religious Music: Shamanism." In *Music of Korea*, edited by Byong Won Lee and Yong-shik Lee, 159–70. Gugakwon.

Lim, Misun. 2021. "The Symbols and Cultural Implications of the Court Music of the Joseon Dynasty." *Review of Korean Studies* 24, no. 2: 11–44.

Paek, Inok. 2007. "Folk Music: Vocal." In *Music of Korea*, edited by Byong Won Lee and Yong-shik Lee, 65–91. Gugakwon.

Saeji, CedarBough T. 2012. "The Bawdy, Brawling, Boisterous World of Korean Mask Dance Dramas." *Cross Currents: East Asian History and Culture Review* 4: 146–68.

Saeji, CedarBough T. 2016. "The Audience as a Force for Preservation: A Typology of Audiences for the Traditional Performing Arts." *Korea Journal* 56, no. 2: 5–31.

So, Inhwa. 2015. "Court Music Institutions." In *Ritual Music of the Korean Court*, edited by The Gugakwon, 161–78. Gugakwon.

Song, Hye-jin. 2008. *Confucian Ritual Music of Korea: Tribute to Confucius and Royal Ancestors.* Translated by Inok Paek. Korea Foundation.

Song, Jiwon. 2015. "Introduction." In *Ritual Music of the Korean Court*, edited by The Gugakwon, 7–28. Gugakwon.

Suh, Ji-young. 2008. "Women on the Borders of the Ladies' Quarters and the *Ginyeo* House: The Mixed Self-Conciousness of *Ginyeo* in Late Joseon." *Korean Journal* 48, no. 1: 136–59.

Um, Hae-kyung. 2002. "Korean Vocal Techniques." In *Garland Encyclopedia of World Music East Asia: China, Japan, and Korea*, edited by Robert Provine, Yosihiko Tokumaru, and J. Lawrence Witzleben, 817–20. Routledge.

Um, Hae-kyung. 2007. "Professional Music: Vocal." In *Music of Korea*, edited by Byong Won Lee and Yong-shik Lee, 105–26. The Gugakwon.

Willoughby, Heather A. 2008. "Pansori Master Singers." In *Pansori*, edited by The Gugakwon, 70–96. Gugakwon.

Yi, Jeonghui. 2015. "Court Musicians." In *Ritual Music of the Korean Court*, edited by The Gugakwon, 179–221. Gugakwon.

Yi, Tuhyon. 1975. "Mask Dance Dramas." In *Traditional Performing Arts of Korea*, edited by Korean National Commission for Unesco, 35–80. Korean National Commission for Unesco.

Yun, Ayeong. 2018. "Kiak simbanggok ŭi kungjung kyoryu palsaengsŏl e kwanhan ch'uron." *Kugagwŏn nonmunjip* 37: 247–65.

EPILOGUE
Korea since 1873

Mark E. Caprio

December 1873 was a turning point in Korean history. King Kojong (r. 1864–1907; emperor from 1897) began ruling in person as the twenty-sixth monarch of the State of Chosŏn (Chosŏn kuk; 1392–1897) with his father Hŭngsŏn Taewŏn'gun's (1821–98) "retirement." Kojong is remembered for opening Chosŏn to the global community, a change from his father's isolationist policy. Kojong, however, is also a controversial figure, as he was remembered as a weak leader until recently.

Efforts to "preserve the social and political status quo based on the traditional formula of a dominant aristocracy combined with weak monarchial and central authority" prevented Korea from effecting essential reforms (Palais 1975, 285). The damage this would inflict on Korea would outlast World War II (1939–45). It continues to the present with the division of the Korean Peninsula into the Republic of Korea (ROK; since 1948) in the south and the Democratic People's Republic of Korea (DPRK; since 1948) in the north.

Both states succeeded in establishing the strong central administrations that Korea arguably needed in the nineteenth century. The South has evolved into a vibrant, dynamic society supported by a thriving economy and a globally popular culture; the North has been dominated for much of the post–Korean War (1950–53) period by a strong central government that has isolated its society from global trends. Reaching these levels has taken a roller coaster ride over its modern history. Indeed, only in the past few decades have the two states assumed these reputations. Since the late nineteenth century, Korea's history endured competition from neighboring powers, foreign occupation, and a bloody war before rivalries forged dictatorships. The postwar fate of a divided peninsula determined the path that the two Koreas would tread over the past eight decades. The ROK's success in breaking through this trying history to reach a position of being able to brag of responsible political and economic institutions is a story of miraculous development, but one also intrinsically tied to its being placed in the capitalist Western bloc since 1945. The DPRK in the rival communist bloc has struggled through virtual isolation from the US-dominated political and economic mainstream of the global community, faced devastating famines, and endured crippling sanctions, particularly from its late twentieth-century decision to develop a nuclear arsenal in what the regime perceived as a post–Cold War environment dominated by the United States as the only superpower.

DOI: 10.4324/9781003262053-29

The Routledge Handbook of Early Modern Korea

Foreign Relations, 1873–1910

Korea's transition to modernity was complicated primarily by its geographic position, late "opening" to the Western world, and conservative politics. Indeed, intruding forces from Europe and the United States in the nineteenth century challenged Chosŏn. To further complicate the situation, the Koreans also had to contend with a waning empire in its traditional partner, China, and a waxing threat from the east, Japan. In 1874, a new delegation of Meiji Japan's (1868–1912) envoys led by Moriyama Shigeru (1842–1919) initiated a second attempt—the first failed in 1869—to change their diplomatic relationship. Some Korean officials, such as Pak Kyusu (1807–77), argued that Chosŏn should negotiate a deal with Japan in the name of peace. Chosŏn's military, being weaker than that of the Japanese, would not be able to defend the country against a Japanese invasion. Thus, it would be better in the long run for the Koreans to accept the Japanese demands and establish closer relations with them. Kojong was initially convinced that this provided the better option. Still, a more conservative position won the day on the ground that opening to Japan would invite others unwelcome to Korea's door (Deuchler 1977, 17–23).

Soon thereafter, the Japanese instigated an incident to draw it into confrontation with the Koreans. Designated to chart the Korean coastline, in May 1875, the Japanese dispatched warships for the task. In an effort or a ruse to get water, one of the ships, the *Unyō*, attempted to dock ashore, only to be rebuffed by the Koreans. The Japanese engaged the Koreans in a battle, with both sides claiming to have been victimized by the other's initial shot. The Japanese got the better of the two and managed to get ashore to obtain the requested water. The Japanese retreated across the East Sea (Sea of Japan) to organize a second expedition, which boarded warships to force upon the Koreans the Japan–Korea Treaty of 1876. The treaty's resemblance to those that the Japanese had forged with the United States in 1854 and 1858 is striking—unsurprising given that the leader of the diplomatic core heading the expedition, Kuroda Kiyotaka (1840–1900), brought with him a copy of Matthew Perry's (1794–1858) *Narratives of a Voyage* (to Japan) as a reference for his mission to Korea. Using similar tactics to gain entrance to Korea, the Japanese borrowed various terms the United States had forced on Japan, then ruled by the Tokugawa shogunate (1603–1868). The 1876 treaty allowed the Japanese to establish more modern trade relations with the Koreans. It also forced the Koreans to open three settlement ports for the Japanese to reside and secured the Japanese the right of extraterritoriality that the United States had secured from Japan.

Within a decade after being forced to upgrade these relations, Chosŏn entered into treaty relations with Western powers. The Chinese advised the Koreans to work toward developing these relations as they would serve to counter Japan's influence. Thus, Chosŏn signed treaties with the United States (1882), Britain and Germany (1883), Italy and Russia (1884), France (1886), and Austria-Hungary (1892). The first Article of the treaty with the United States would generate controversy by stipulating that the two states commit their "good office" to resolve problems with a third country if necessary. Did the United States renege on this Article by not aiding Korea against Japan, allowing Korea to become a protectorate in 1905? The then-US president, Theodore Roosevelt (1858–1919), issued statements that suggested the United States support of Japanese aggression as inevitable due to Korea's weakness as a state.

When Japan's attempt to take over Korea began is debatable. Even though the 1876 treaty "opened" Korea, the country remained subservient to the Chinese until 1894. One study of this period likens the Chinese influence over Korea to an imperial-like relationship (Larsen 2008). Chinese envoy Yuan Shikai (1859–1916) arrived in Korea in October 1885 and oversaw Korea's foreign affairs, as evident in his interference in the first attempt by the Koreans to establish a presence in Washington, DC, in September 1887. At the time, the Korean envoy violated his instruc-

Epilogue

tions to first visit the Chinese embassy to allow Chinese diplomats to introduce them to the US State Department. The missionary-turned-diplomat Horace N. Allen (1858–1932) warned the head Korean diplomat, Pak Chŏngyang (1842–1905), that to do so would be interpreted as an insult by the United States. Pak's decision to follow Allen's advice and go himself directly to the US offices resulted in Kojong ordering the diplomat's immediate recall and demotion (Harrington 1944).

One major problem at the time was the strong support the Chinese received from the natal family of Queen Myŏngsŏng (1851–95), and the Japanese attempted to weaken the ties several times. For example, Korea's 1876 treaty with Japan worded Korea's status as "independent" in English but "sovereign" in Chinese. This aimed to placate Japanese needs: to suggest a break in the traditional Sino–Korean relations while appeasing the Chinese. The 1885 Convention of Tianjin placed Japan on a near-equal balance with China, allowing the Japanese to match Chinese troops in numbers should they be dispatched to the peninsula. The First Sino–Japanese War (1894–95) gave a victorious Japan an upper hand over the Chinese in Korean matters, although Russia replaced China as Japan's rival in Korea. The advent of the Japan-influenced Kabo Reform (1894–96) in Korea followed, as well as their brutal murder of Myŏngsong in October 1895. In February of the following year, Kojong escaped his virtual confinement in the Japanese-controlled palace by fleeing to the Russian legation and disbanding the Kabo government.

In October 1897, Kojong launched the Kwangmu Reform (1897–1904), which demonstrated—contrary to what the Japanese continued to claim—that now the Empire of Korea (Taehan cheguk; 1897–1910) could modernize on its own. Non-Koreans residing or traveling to Korea at this time marveled over the advancements that it was now making. Isabella Bird (1831–1904), for one, left Korea in 1895 with the impression that its capital city, Hansŏng (present-day Seoul), was one of the two "foulest" in Asia, Peking (Beijing) being worse (Bird 1985, 40). Yet, when she returned in 1897, she saw the city as "unrecognizable" due to the advancements that Hansŏng had made in her absence (Bird 1985, 435). However, with the Japanese defeat of Russia (Russo–Japanese War; 1904–05), the door toward Korea stood ajar, ripe for conquest. Japan duly accomplished what other great powers expected: incorporating Korea into its expanding empire as a protectorate, stripping it of diplomatic representation (November 1905). Seeking help from other countries, Kojong dispatched secret emissaries to The Hague Convention of 1907, which took place in the Netherlands. Not only were the emissaries denied participation by the Dutch government, but the infuriated Japanese dethroned him and propped up his son and crown prince, Emperor Sunjong (reign name Yunghŭi; r. 1907–10). As a gradualist, Itō Hirobumi (1841–1909), as the first Resident General of Korea, attempted to recreate the Japanese government's earlier utilization of the young Meiji emperor (r. 1867–1912) by leading Sunjong around Korea to meet his subjects and by making his birthday a holiday. Itō's failure to convince the Korean people of the merits of his efforts led to his abrupt resignation. Did this decision signal his acceptance of Japan's annexation of the peninsula? We may never know, as An Chunggŭn's (1879–1910) killing of Itō left this question unanswered. His death did clear the way for Japan's hardliners to proceed with Korea's outright annexation into the Japanese empire, thus ending Korea's autonomous, united monarchy since 936 in August 1910.

Internal Developments, 1873–1910

Before the Japanese take-over, Chosŏn Korea also suffered from internal division and turmoil. A viable threat to its existence could have forced the central government into reforming at a revolutionary level, if not succumbing to a new regime such as that which occurred in Japan with the collapse of the Tokugawa shogunate. Instead, the Chosŏn government and reformers attempted

The Routledge Handbook of Early Modern Korea

to survive the crisis by strengthening the center when more drastic measures were required. With China's aid, the leadership quashed the Imo Mutiny (1882) and the Kapsin Coup (1884). Tonghak ("Eastern Learning") was a much bigger challenge a decade later. As a socio-religious movement, the Tonghak had been gaining a following since the authorities had executed the founder, Ch'oe Cheu (1824–64), who had developed a following from his eclectic teachings that drew from Confucianism, Buddhism, Daoism, shamanism, and even Christianity. Despite ongoing harassment by the government, the Tonghak had grown in strength, even organizing themselves militarily in 1892 under Chŏn Pongjun (1855–95) and others. The subsequent Tonghak Uprising (1894) gave pretexts for both China and Japan to send troops, sparking the First Sino–Japanese War. The Japanese immediately set up a pro-Japanese government, collaborated with Korean troops to crush the rebellion, and drove the Chinese off the peninsula.

The Tonghak Uprising and other movements advocated reforms. The Tonghak put forth their reformist ideas during the uprising, some of which the ensuing Kabo Reform measures reflected, including abolishing the hereditary status hierarchy. Following the Kabo Reform, the Independence Club (1896–98) advocated ideas and institutions inspired mainly by Britain, the United States, and Japan until disbanded by the Kwangmu government, which had come to conclude that the Club was advocating republicanism. Subsequently, until Japan turned Korea into a protectorate, many "patriotic enlightenment" (*aeguk kyemong*) groups continued to advocate reform in politics, economics, and society to avoid what was perhaps inevitable—Korea's colonization. Their overlapping demands articulated what the Korean society saw as lacking. Ubiquitous was a call for a reflection on how its political elite was selected and the purging of "corrupt" leaders. They were also united in demanding reforms in a corrupt tax system, which overburdened subsistence farmers, and other unfair practices that mistreated the people. In 1898, a leading member of the Independence Club and the founder of its mouthpiece, *The Independent*, Philip Jaisohn (Ko. Sŏ Chaep'il; 1864–1951), who had become a naturalized American citizen while in exile, argued in a November 16–17 editorial, "People are the Masters," the need for the "masters" to claim their position above the "servants":

> If the masters (the people) were to unite and prod their servants to carry out useful projects that would augment the nation's honor and glory, even the wicked servants would surely be transformed into trustworthy servants. As the masters, having been suddenly awakened after several hundred years of slavery, attempt to regain their rightful power, the servants who have usurped their masters' status will naturally oppose the change and try to continue the previous practices by any means … . It is up to the people to transform the officials.
>
> *(Lee 1996, 397)*

At the turn of the twentieth century, the Koreans did succeed in implementing some reforms thanks to favorable internal and external circumstances. Above all, the conclusion of the First Sino–Japanese War barely allowed Japan to celebrate its victory as the Triple Intervention (April 1895)—by Germany, France, and Russia—stripped Japan of China's Liadong Peninsula that it had gained per the peace treaty. Also, both the Japanese government's subsequent involvement in the brutal murder of Myŏngsŏng and Kojong's escape to the Russian legation tarnished Japan's reputation among the imperialist powers, and Russia effectively held Japan back. Amidst a mounting domestic call for Kojong to assert the nation's independence and to lead modernization, he made a triumphant comeback. Ending his year-long sojourn at the Russian legation, the king declared himself the emperor with a new era name, Kwangmu ("resplendent martial prowess"), and renamed the State of Chosŏn the Empire of Korea. In support, the Independence Club pursued projects that

Epilogue

further distanced the Koreans from the Chinese—such as constructing the Independence Arch at the spot where the monarch would greet Chinese embassies. The Club also published a Korean–English bilingual newspaper, *The Independent*. For a broader domestic readership, the Korean section used Han'gŭl (Hangul) only, with no Chinese characters, while the newspaper also used English to inform foreigners of Korea's progress with reform.

The Independence Club and other reform movements insisted on lessening or removing foreign influence without resorting to violence, as the Japanese did in the shogunate's final years. The arrival of Protestant missionaries in the late nineteenth century introduced not only the Protestant form of Christianity but also modern Western medical practices, science, and technology by educating Korean youth, male and female. Distinct from the Catholic form that had begun spreading in Korea a century earlier, Protestant Christianity began growing to its present level. South Korea—with about a quarter of its population as either Protestant or Catholic—has become the most Christian country in contemporary East Asia.

Yet, none of the reform movements demanded the dethronement of Kojong or the overthrow of the monarchy, as seen in Japan, where the Tokugawa shogunate had ended. This is not to judge Kojong in any way as a weak or strong leader but rather to suggest the revolutionary measures needed to truly reform Korea's politics, economy, and society at the time demanded a regime change. To what extent did the Japanese movement benefit from having a young, inexperienced, but legitimate monarch in the Meiji emperor being brought into the new government, a figurehead around which the new regime could enact the necessary reforms? To what extent did Koreans prolonging the more than five centuries of rule by the Chosŏn state prevent the country from effecting the reforms modernization required? At this time, the Korean government found it difficult to introduce any reform that clashed with the traditional Confucian values that had served as a foundation of Chosŏn for centuries—the kind of radical changes necessary for convincing the "great powers" at the time that the Korean people had the tools to self-strengthen.

The years leading up to Japan's colonization were turbulent, with Korean society making some advancements to modernize but also having to form militias, the "righteous armies" (*ŭibyŏng*), to resist the Japanese. These righteous armies grew in size from 1907 when the Japanese, learning of Kojong's efforts to gain a seat at the table of The Hague Convention of 1907, disbanded the Imperial Korean Army and forced him to abdicate. In doing so, Resident General Itō dispelled the notion that Japan was assisting Korea to remain a sovereign nation. The Japanese were calling the shots, foreign and domestic matters alike.

In October 1909, An Chunggŭn shot Itō to death when the Japanese diplomat arrived in Harbin, Northeast China (then Manchuria), to meet with Russians on issues stemming from the conclusion of the Russo–Japanese War. They would never meet due to Itō's death, and thus, his true intentions toward Korea are left to speculation. Ample evidence suggests that he was against complete annexation until his residency generalship in Korea ended in June. Beginning to doubt Korea's ability to develop into a modern state unless placed entirely under Japanese control, Itō joined those calling for Korea's full incorporation into the Japanese empire. His death, though, prevents us from understanding completely his views on this issue.

The Japanese Colonial Rule, 1910–45

Present-day Korean disputes with Japan stem from Japan's treatment of the Koreans during the colonial period. Any claims that the era was the most brutal example of colonial subjugation in history are exaggerated. Still, it was undeniably brutal, particularly over the initial 14 years following Japan's turning Korea into a protectorate, then a colony (1905–19), and again during the

The Routledge Handbook of Early Modern Korea

Pacific War (1941–45). Japan used Koreans for forced labor and as "comfort women" during this wartime period. In between, the Japanese exercised subtle control policies. The post–March First Movement (1919) reforms that the Government General of Korea (1910–45) instituted look relatively progressive on paper: indigenous Korean newspapers, right of assembly, and the like. Japanese were encouraged to study the Korean language and become more familiar with things Korean. At the same time, it can also be said—and some Japanese claimed—that these reforms allowed the Japanese to understand the Korean people better and thus exercise better control, therefore avoiding anything like mass protests throughout the colony during the March First Movement. Though the new policy helped to boost Korean culture, particularly its print culture, it also made the Koreans more transparent to the Japanese but the Japanese less so to the Koreans. The encouragement of the Japanese to learn the Korean language entailed the annual tests held to measure Korean competence among the Japanese, and the police, who were in charge of censoring Korean newspapers, typically received the top scores.

The anti-Japanese demonstrations that began on March 1, 1919, were the most powerful articulation of Korean resentment toward the Japanese colonial rule. The event was inspired by a January 1918 speech by US President Woodrow Wilson (1856–1924) that called for people worldwide to be granted "self-determination" in choosing the form of government that would guide them. The speech encouraged anti-colonial demonstrations around the world, including Korea, where nationalist organizers sought to maximize the scale of the demonstrations on the day of the Japanese Shinto-style funeral of Kojong. On January 21, the healthy former emperor died suddenly under suspicious circumstances, likely of poisoning (Ch'oe and Yi 2011). A declaration of independence, a draft of which had first been written in Tokyo, Japan by Korean students and smuggled into Korea, was read in T'apkol Park in central Kyŏngsŏng (Ja. Keijō; present-day Seoul), sending the people in attendance into the streets to initiate peaceful demonstration against Japanese rule. Panicked Japanese soldiers began firing on the Korean demonstrators, killing many. An even greater number were arrested and tortured. Japan's harsh response drew criticism from around the world. The immediate consequences of the March First Movement compelled the Japanese to usher in a new administrative policy of Cultural Rule (1919–31), which replaced a strict period of Military Rule (1910–19), and to introduce the ambitious reform package mentioned as mentioned. The Korean people took advantage of the opportunities that the Cultural Rule presented by expanding their cultural base, particularly in print culture: magazines, newspapers, and books.

The Korean people continued to demonstrate their anti-Japanese sentiment in various ways. Besides forming organizations that promoted Korean culture, such as the Korean Language Society, students boycotted classes or took other less formal actions in reaction to what they interpreted as Japanese prejudicial treatment toward them. For example, Korean students protested the more severe disciplinary measures that schools took against them, particularly when the Japanese students were equally, or even more, deserving of punishment. For instance, in 1929, in the city of Kwangju, when Korean students came to the rescue of Korean girls whom Japanese boys were teasing, the Koreans involved in the ensuing fight—with some Japanese students ending up in the hospital—were heavily disciplined by the authorities while the Japanese students' actions went unpunished. The injustice resulted in the biggest anti-Japanese demonstrations since the March First Movement as students across the colony joined the Kwangju students in protest.

In the meantime, some Korean independence leaders chose a life in exile to continue their nationalist activities unfeasible in Korea. During the 35-year Japanese occupation of Korea, independence movements of various ideological orientations flourished in China, the Soviet Union, the United States, and several Latin American countries, among others. These groups attempted to overcome their ideological differences, as seen in the original cabinet of the Provisional

Epilogue

Government of the Republic of Korea (1919–48) headquartered in Shanghai. Still, these efforts soon failed due to differences in their ideas on the most effective way to achieve independence. For example, many conservatives rallied around the future first president of South Korea, Syngman Rhee (Yi Sŭngman; 1875–1965), who prioritized diplomacy vis-à-vis Western political leaders and the public. In contrast, some progressives eventually followed the future first leader of North Korea, Kim Il-sung (Kim Ilsŏng; 1912–94), who pursued guerrilla tactics against the Japanese.

Other Koreans left their homeland for different parts of the Japanese empire. A large number migrated across Korea's northern border and into Manchuria. Yet an even larger number crossed over to the Japanese Archipelago. By the end of World War II, an estimated 2 to 2.5 million Koreans were residing primarily in the Archipelago's urban centers, including perhaps the most populous communities of Koreans in the Kansai area around Osaka. Over the decades before the Second Sino–Japanese War (1937–45), which eventually merged with World War II when Japan attacked America's Pearl Harbor and sparked the Pacific War (1941–45), a large number of Koreans, driven by higher wages and more advanced opportunity, sought work in Japan to better their lives. While their decisions to move were not forced at first, their situations in Korea limited their options—thus spurring relocation, mainly to Japan but to a large extent to the Japanese puppet state in Manchuria, Manchukuo (1932–45). In addition to Korean laborers, a smaller but significant number of Koreans traveled to Japan to attend its schools. Life overseas could be harsh. In the 1920s, for example, an abundance of employment opportunities available during World War I (1914–18) dried up as the Japanese economy slowed. The Korean population in the Tokyo–Yokohama Kanto area suffered a massacre in the aftermath of the 1923 Great Kanto Earthquake when baseless rumors that the Koreans were committing acts of sabotage, such as poisoning the wells of drinking water, spurred Japanese to target and kill thousands of Koreans in the region.

Those who stayed in Korea generally stayed clear of any nationalist activity, while some collaborated with their colonizers. The degree to which Koreans had to assist the Japanese to be considered "guilty" of collaboration is a question that Koreans following liberation grappled with through such efforts as South Korea's legislation drafted to punish the most notorious collaborators. Nearly every Korean during the colonial period collaborated to some extent, as one had to survive. Then where should the line be drawn to establish a person's guilt as a traitor to their people? Was a Korean sending their child to a Japanese school, using Japanese money for their business, being employed by the colonial police force, or assisting the Japanese in their war effort going too far? The problem here involved intention, a near-impossible criterion to measure. For example, was the Korean policeman who broke up a pro-independence meeting by Koreans battling against his people, and thus anti-Korean, or was he doing his job? Was the Korean pressured by the Japanese into giving speeches on behalf of the Japanese military doing so because he supported the Japanese war effort or because he felt that he had no other choice?

The American-educated Christian educator Yun Ch'iho (1865–1945) may be a case in point. Yun had been arrested in 1911 on suspicion of being part of a plot to assassinate Governor General Terauchi Masatake (1852–1919), where his "confession," he claimed, had been forced by torture. He later entered in his extensive diary—kept mostly in English—that he performed many of his subsequent actions out of fear that the Japanese would further harass him if he did not participate. Seeing no signs that the Japanese were preparing to withdraw from Korea and unaware of their impending defeat even into August 1945, Yun and other "collaborators" wanted to carry on with their lives as best they could under the trying circumstances—a stance arguably excusable. The line separating the collaborator from the patriot was razor-thin.

Many issues plaguing Japan–Korea relations trace back to the 15 years of war leading up to Korea's liberation. Problems began in the late 1930s when the Japanese decided to limit the

The Routledge Handbook of Early Modern Korea

avenues available to Koreans in their native language. The colonial government shut down the Korean-language newspapers it had begun allowing in 1920, leaving only the government-friendly *Maeil sinbo* [Daily news]. Also, the Korean language classes offered to Koreans and Japanese in school were discontinued, making the curriculum Japanese only. Moreover, Koreans were pressed to change their family and given names to make them sound more Japanese and to adopt a wartime mentality in daily life. As the war progressed, Korean males who had initially been encouraged to volunteer for military service in 1938 were, by 1944, being conscripted. An estimated 600,000 Korean men were forced to labor in mines and factories throughout the Japanese empire. Young women were "recruited" as comfort women: sex slaves for military bases.

Imperial Japan's wartime mobilization of Koreans was discriminatory. A wartime regime tends to demand all potential assets of the country, including its people, to prosecute the war. For example, men (and women in some countries) are expected to join the military to serve the nation. The subway, used for public transportation, can transport troops and supplies during a war. In Japan's case, the state and its agents enslaved females as comfort women to serve its military for carnal pleasures—arguably a military purpose but most certainly a socially unacceptable activity, if not a human rights crime. Thus, the argument that the institution of comfort duty allowed these women the opportunity to serve in the war as national subjects and that the service furthered their assimilation into Japanese society is faulty. After all, the practice amounted to abusive discrimination, one that disproportionately used women from Korea and other parts of its empire over the Japanese. Some contend that the Korean population during the years of colonial rule had become Japanese subjects or even citizens, a status they lost with Japan's defeat in the Pacific War. Even if the Korean people had become Japanese legally, much evidence demonstrates that the Japanese did not recognize their new status socially.

The colonial state's promises of equality for Koreans belied the harsh, discriminatory treatment of Koreans during the wartime years, but the Koreans made some gains. Japanese men from Korea being transferred to the battlefield allowed faster Korean promotion, particularly in industry. The wartime situation also compelled the Japanese to think more about and finetune their rhetoric of assimilating Koreans. The colonial state, for example, promised Koreans compulsory education and suffrage, both slated to begin in 1946. It is fair to question whether the Japanese saw these ambitions as the result of the Korean people's advancement toward civilization or whether the dismal war news forced the Japanese to make them, hoping to appease the Korean people. For some three decades of colonial rule, the Japanese had been big on rhetoric yet small on policy to advance the assimilation goal upon which they had based their colonial policies.

Liberation, Division, and the Korean War, 1945–53

Inserting a break to separate modern Korean history from August 1945, when the Japanese surrender gave Koreans their liberation, may seem natural. Still, it is also problematic on several grounds. Korea's former colonizer maintained influence in the southern half of the peninsula and participated in many ways in the Korean War. The decades that followed the establishment of two rival, sovereign states were trying for Koreans. Ideological and other differences that emerged among Koreans during the colonial era, primarily over the means that they employed to drive the Japanese from their homeland, persisted even after the colonial rule ended, to a large extent thanks to a divided postwar occupation scheme proposed by the United States and accepted by the Soviet Union. Originally meant to be temporary, the division of Korea gained strength from the Cold War (1947–91) conflict and continues to this day.

Epilogue

A fundamental difference emerged when the Soviet Union and the United States began establishing institutions and supporting extremists that reflected their ideological bases. At the core of this was their differences over the concept of democracy, which both ostensibly introduced to the Korean people. The United States envisioned a process of presenting fundamental rights such as freedom of speech and assembly to the Korean people. In contrast, the Soviet Union's analog was to establish equality at the base in terms of economic status, labor-gender relations, and the like before granting Koreans the rights emphasized in the American-occupied South. The Soviet Union's thinking was that prematurely giving these rights to Koreans would result in a few loud voices dominating the society.

Plans for post-liberation land reform presented a telltale example of the differences between the two. Both the United States and the Soviet Union acknowledged the reform as necessary for building a democratic society. The North, however, gained the advantage by introducing a land reform plan in March 1946, ahead of attempts by the United States to do the same. The primary problem that the United States saw in the North's plan was not that it proposed distributing land to former sharecroppers but that the land was to be redistributed without requiring the new landlords to compensate the former landlords. The plan the Americans proposed had the new landowners paying for the land as an annual share of their harvest. The North enacting their land redistribution plan first empowered Southern leftists who made similar demands on the United States, while in the South, the occupiers confronted objections from the large landowners, many of whom had fled from the North.

Japanese influence remained strong, particularly in southern Korea. Even though the United States and Japan had fought close to four years of bloody war, relations between the two rebounded quickly while the US–Soviet relations deteriorated. Koreans began to see signs that the United States was softening its stance toward Japan even before the conclusion of the Pacific War. Even before the war's end, Americans considered the possible advantage of protecting the Japanese emperor from postwar military trials and the possibility of offering Japan conditions to gain their early surrender—ostensibly to save American lives but also to contain the Soviet Union and communism from extending their influence. Upon Japan's surrender, Koreans realized that the United States favored the Japanese over the Koreans. For instance, at the plush Chosŏn Hotel in Seoul in early September 1945, U.S military personnel—who arrived to prepare for the occupation to commence in a week—held a party in their suite that lasted for several days and invited Japanese officials to join while refusing admittance by Koreans who had come to welcome them. Even before the American occupation began, General Douglas MacArthur (1880–1964) issued from Tokyo his Proclamation No. 1. Here, the Supreme Commander of the Allied Powers directed that the colonial bureaucracy, including Governor General Abe Nobuyuki (1875–1953), remain at their posts until Koreans could be trained to replace them. While directives from Washington days later ordered that the top brass of the colonial government be purged—Abe would be arrested for war crimes though subsequently released before going to trial—the Japanese-trained Korean members of the colonial police force would form the core of the postwar police force and brutally demonstrate their anti-leftist prejudices to the approval and support of the United States Army Military Government in Korea (USAMGK; 1945–48).

The two Koreas would engage in battle less than five years after their liberation from colonial rule. The "textbook" version of the origins of the Korean War, the one generally accepted by ROK, the United States, and Japan's historiography, concludes that the war erupted suddenly, like a clap of thunder against a blue sky, at 4 a.m. on Sunday, June 25, 1950, when DPRK soldiers, backed with Soviet arms, crossed the thirty-eighth parallel north that divided the Korean Peninsula into Soviet and US occupation zones. The DPRK contends that this infiltration was a "counterattack"

The Routledge Handbook of Early Modern Korea

in response to a southern attack. Some, however, have begun to trace the war's origins to an earlier time to disturbances that broke out soon after liberation. As the majority of US and Soviet troops had withdrawn by 1949, leaving behind only advisors, arguably, who attacked first cannot be ascertained. Both Korean leaders, Kim Il-sung in the North and Syngman Rhee in the South, were determined to unify the peninsula by force if necessary. While the United Sates had refused to give Rhee the hardware he needed to carry out an attack, the Soviets eventually provided Kim with the arms that he would need to conduct such an operation. The Chinese communists, as victors of the Chinese Civil War (1927–49) and as leaders of the new People's Republic of China (since 1949), had released their battle-hardened Korean communist comrades in China to reinforce the DPRK army.

Several theories have evolved to contest the "suddenness" that started the war. In 1951, while the war was still raging, the journalist I. F. Stone (1907–89) raised questions in his book, *Hidden History of the Korean War*. Decades later, the historian Bruce Cumings (b. 1943) traced the origins back to the Japanese colonial rule that engendered divisions among the Korean people that sparked a civil war once Korea was liberated. The internal conflicts then turned international once the Korean War drew in foreign actors (Cumings 1981, 1990). A common counter-argument against Cumings's thinking is that the war, from the outset, was an international war; such a conflict could not have been carried out between the two Koreas without international assistance (Stueck 1995).

Soon after the full-scale commencement of the Korean War, various concerned nations intervened. The United States immediately formed a 16-nation United Nations Command that dispatched troops in aid of the ROK, followed in October by Chinese entry into the war in support of DPRK after the UN Command had driven back the DPRK forces and had crossed into DPRK territory to continue the war. America's top circles discussed whether nuclear weapons could be employed, ultimately deciding against using them. While the United States voiced fear that such a deployment would draw in the Soviet Union and spark World War III, officials also lamented that the thorough conventional bombing of the north had left few, if any, suitable sites to employ the weapons. The fighting ceased in July 1953 when the United Nations Command, the DPRK, and China, but not the ROK, signed an armistice agreement, which created a Demilitarized Zone (DMZ)—with a North–South demarcation line running through it—as an adjustment of the thirty-eighth parallel earlier separating the two Koreas.

Democracy eluded postwar Korea. In DPRK, Kim Il-sung claimed the non-victory as a victory and used it to purge his rivals and solidify his ground as the supreme leader, a position he retained until he died in 1994. His son Kim Jong-il (Kim Chŏngil 1941–2011) and then grandson Kim Jong-un (Kim Chŏngŭn, b. 1983) have held the position up to the present. In the ROK, Syngman Rhee remained in power through increasingly heavy-handed legislative maneuvers and even election-rigging until pro-democracy student demonstrations forced him out in April 1960. After a democratic interlude, two military coups—first in May 1961 by Major General Park Chung-hee (Pak Chŏnghŭi; 1917–79), then in December 1979 by Major General Chun Doo-hwan (Chŏn Tuhwan; 1931–2021)—subjected ROK to close to three decades of de facto military rule before the triumph of democracy in June 1987.

ROK Democratization and DPRK Totalitarianism

The end of the Korean War allowed both Korean regimes to use the threat from across the DMZ to bolster one-person rule in their countries. This threat—in tandem with the urge to sustain their respective capitalist and communist bases to demonstrate the superiority of one system over the other—ensured the two Korea's support from their superpower patrons, at least through the Cold

Epilogue

War. This history has put the two Koreas on different political trajectories, which has produced vastly different results.

Many trace the beginnings of the ROK's democratization to the 1919 March First Movement and other anti-Japanese incidents during the colonial period, when the peninsula was still a whole. Following liberation, division, and war, the ongoing democratization movement ousted Rhee from office and ushered in intense activity among many students who opposed corrupt governments. The rule of Park Chung-hee (1961–79; president from 1963) introduced long-term prison sentences and even death penalties to those Koreans who opposed his 1972 Yushin Constitution that made Park president for life. Park's reign ended in October 1979 when he was assassinated by his Korean Central Intelligence Agency chief, Kim Jae-kyu (Kim Chaegyu; 1924–80), amidst a power struggle among the members of Park's inner circle. In the resulting power vacuum, another military man, Chun Doo-hwan, gained de facto supreme power through a coup, setting off larger-scale pro-democracy demonstrations—culminating with the deadly uprising in the southwestern city of Kwangju. Protests continued during Chun's presidency (1980–88) even though he promised to step down after completing a single seven-year-term presidency per the new constitution he devised in 1981. His virtual appointment of his former military colleague and successor, General Roh Tae-woo (No T'aeu; 1932–2021), escalated demonstrations in June 1987 as the people demanded the right to make this choice. Before the month's end, this forced No to issue a statement promising that the next presidential election would be by popular vote, a method Park had replaced with a system of electors in 1972. Roh won the December 1987 presidential election by plurality, gaining 36 percent of the vote, with two long-time liberal opposition leaders and Park's former military colleague splitting most of the rest. Nonetheless, from this time, South Korea's restored democracy has featured a presidency of a single five-year term with a conservative party and a liberal party competing.

In stark contrast, Kim Il-sung and his direct male descendants have headed a totalitarian regime in the DPRK. Since the end of the Korean War, the state has prioritized protecting its political system controlled by the Kim family and, accordingly, national defense. The state has been able to achieve both by citing potential threats of attack by the United States and its "puppet," the ROK, to control its people and to justify a totalitarian government centered around a leadership cult. How the regime has minimized, if not suppressed, discontent is unclear due to strict control of information flow to and from the outside world. To some degree, the famines that the people suffered in the 1990s—caused by weather-related issues and exacerbated by failures of the regime's economic policy emphasizing self-reliance and the reduced financial support from former Eastern Bloc countries—aroused widespread resentment against the central government. Responding to the DPRK's ongoing development of nuclear, international sanctions have become a choke-hold on the economy.

Many of the DPRK's problems surfaced in the 1990s after both of its two most important allies, Russia, as the Soviet Union's successor state, and China established relations with the ROK. The DPRK, from the 1990s, embarked on a two-card policy of developing nuclear capabilities and securing good relations with the United States, maintaining the option of discarding the former if the latter materialized to meet the critical needs that China and the Soviet Union had provided for long—food, defense, and energy—while protecting the Kim family rule. The DPRK's failure to make progress in terms of relations with the United States has spurred the development of dual-use nuclear technology. This partly led the country to accept occasional assistance from international NGOs such as the World Food Organization. The DPRK's pursuit of weapons of mass destruction elicited sanctions by the United Nations, amounting to a chokehold on the country's economy. At the same time, the ROK joined the ranks of advanced economies.

The Routledge Handbook of Early Modern Korea

ROK Economic Recovery versus DPRK Economic Stagnation

Just when the ROK's economy "took off" is debatable. One argument emphasizes late Chosŏn's "sprouts of capitalism" germinated by a more liberalized economy of the eighteenth century, increasingly centered around commerce. The opposing viewpoint counters that "colonial modernity" engendered the ROK's success as a global economic powerhouse. For example, the development of a major Korean business, the Kyŏngbang Spinning and Weaving Company, relied on Japanese capital (Eckert 1991). In comparison, what happened after the Japanese colonial rule is clear. Following Korea's liberation and division in 1945, the more industrialized North initially outpaced the more agricultural-centered South in economic development. The disparity persisted into the early 1970s when the ROK was able to surpass the DPRK. Today, the ROK maintains an advanced economy with a GDP (Purchasing Power Parity) per capita higher than Japan and many Western countries, while the DPRK remains impoverished.

Regarding the post-1945 economic development of the ROK, a debate rages over whether Syngman Rhee's emphasis on import substitution or Park Chung-hee's export substitution triggered the ROK's "economic miracle." One economist argues that the ROK succeeded by getting things "wrong," that is, by not following the accepted order of economic advancement (Amsden 1989). The ROK benefitted from the 1965 Treaty on Basic Relations Between Japan and the Republic of Korea, according to which the two countries established full diplomatic relations and Japan provided economic assistance instead of reparations for colonial rule. The Treaty, which the United States unofficially but vigorously brokered, also helped the ROK gain access to open markets in the United States, initiating the ROK's export-led growth. The economic development benefited many at the top but also spurred labor protests against low wages and harsh working conditions.

Less known is the labor situation in the north. The DPRK, too, benefitted from its superpower partners, China and the Soviet Union, as both supplied fuel, foodstuffs, and other goods at reduced prices. The Chollima ("flying horse") Movement launched in December 1956 mobilized the population to increase industrial production, even at the household level, and to meet a series of quotas per multi-year plans instituted by the central government. However, after stagnation in the 1970s and '80s, the DPRK's economy began shrinking in the early 1990s when its superpower patrons reduced the assistance amidst the global collapse of most communist regimes. Also, the DPRK's failure to come to terms with the United States, Japan, and other capitalist states, international sanctions designed to punish the regime for its pursuit of weapons of mass destruction, and insistence on self-reliance based on unwavering loyalty to the Kim family has increased its dependence, primarily on neighboring China.

The present-day Korean Peninsula, divided from 1945 for the first time since 936, appears on the surface to differ from the mid-nineteenth-century Korea. Destruction across the peninsula during the Korean War entirely transformed the region and at least sent the South on a long and winding path toward political and economic success. The DPRK has sought to build a military that can deter outside threats—countering US President Theodore Roosevelt's claim in 1905 that Korea "has shown its utter inability to stand by itself" (Esthus 1967, 61). In both Koreas, gender relations have changed to give women more educational and professional opportunities.

As the saying goes, the more things change, the more they stay the same. In many areas, this is the case with Korea. Throughout the last decades of the nineteenth century, the peninsula faced pressures from its neighbors trying to expand its presence in Korea. Modernizing Korea succumbed to Japan, becoming its protectorate and then a colony. Toward the end of the Pacific War, the Allied powers led by the United States proposed a five-year trusteeship for post-liberation

Epilogue

Korea, an unwelcome plan rejected by most Koreans eager for sovereignty. Throughout the Cold War, the divided Korea was able to determine its allies and economic partners to some degree. Still, it once again negotiated the constraints of its powerful neighbors and the United States. Even Japan's influence continued to haunt the Koreas after the liberation. Nonetheless, contemporary Korea, while still divided, comprises two states with more sovereignty than precolonial Korea.

Both Koreas face an enduring question today as they contemplate their futures: whether they will reunite as one nation. Recently, with sharper differences once again dividing the concerned actors in East Asia, the possibility of a second wave of Cold War–like antagonism between a northern triangle (Russia, China, and the DPRK) and a southern triangle (United States, Japan, and the ROK) has re-emerged. Neither China nor the United States—and Russia to a lesser extent—would ever allow the "other" Korea on its terms to control the entire peninsula. In this sense, the dynamics of international relations for the Korean Peninsula share a degree of similarity with Chosŏn Korea of 1873.

References

Amsden, Alice H. 1989. *Asia's Next Giant: South Korea and Late Industrialization*. Oxford University Press.

Bird, Isabella. 1985. *Korea and Her Neighbors*. Pacific Basin Books. Reprint of the 1897 original.

Ch'oe, Yŏng-ho, and Tae-jin Yi. 2011. "The Mystery of Emperor Kojong's Sudden Death in 1919: Were the Highest Japanese Officials Responsible?" *Korean Studies* 35: 122–51.

Cumings, Bruce. 1981. *The Origins of the Korean War*. Volume 1, *Liberation and the Emergence of Separate Regimes, 1945–1947*. Princeton University Press.

Cumings, Bruce. 1990. *The Origins of the Korean War*. Volume 2, *The Roaring of the Cataract, 1947–1950*. Princeton University Press.

Deuchler, Martina. 1977. *Confucian Gentlemen and Barbarian Envoys: The Opening of Korea, 1875–1885*. University of Washington Press.

Eckert, Carter J. 1991. *Offspring of Empire: The Koch'ang Kims and the Colonial Origins of Korean Capitalism, 1878–1945*. University of Washington Press.

Esthus, Raymond A. 1967. *Theodore Roosevelt and Japan*. University of Washington Press.

Harrington, Fred H. 1944. *God, Mammon, and the Japanese: Dr. Horace N. Allen and Korean-American Relations, 1884–1905*. University of Wisconsin Press.

Larsen, Kirk W. 2008. *Tradition, Treaties, and Trade: Qing Imperialism and Chosŏn Korea, 1850–1910*. Harvard University Asia Center.

Lee, Peter H., ed. 1996. *Sourcebook of Korean Civilization*. Volume II, *From the Seventeenth Century to the Modern Period*. Columbia University Press.

Palais, James B. 1975. *Politics and Policy in Traditional Korea*. Council on East Asian Studies, Harvard University.

Stueck, William. 1995. *The Korean War: An International History*. Princeton University Press.

INDEX

aak 324–325, 328
adoption *see* patrilineal descent
Agreement of 1547 33
agriculture, economy (up to 1873) 120–121
ak 324–325
akkong 327–328
aksaeng 327–328
Allen, Horace N. 341
Altan Khan 29
Altar of Earth and Grain (Sajik) 324, 325
Altar of Great Requital (Taebodan) 36, 159–160
Amitābha 211, 315
Amitabha Buddha with Assembly (Amitabul hoedo) 317
An Ch'omok 336
An Hyang 267
An Iksin Rebellion 107
An Kyŏn 305
An Yongbok 157
Analects (Lunyu) 183–184
ancestral rites, Confucianism 264
Andong Kim, Lady 172
Andong Kwŏn genealogy 139
Ankokuji Eiji 65
Anp'yŏng Taegun 306
Arai Hakuseki 67
archery contests 96
aristocracy (*yangban*) 134–140
armored soldiers (*kapsa*) 94
art 305; ceramics 62; Korea–Japan relationship 61–64; *see also* performing arts; visual art
artisans 133
Ashikaga shogunate 28, 32, 58–59
Ashikaga Yoshimitsu 59
Ashikaga Yoshimochi 65
Asian backwardness 15
astronomy 281–283

bandits 106
The Banquet of the Queen Mother of the West 314
"barbarians" (*hu*) 37
Battle of Sarhu 156
Benevolence *see* Humaneness
Berneux, Siméon François 159, 237–238
Bhaishajyaguru 315–316
The Bhaisajyaguru Triad 316
bilaterality *see* lineage
Bird, Isabella 341
Black Satsuma 62
blind exorcists (*p'ansu*) 220–221
Book of Changes (Yijing) 183
Book of Rites (Liji) 184–185
books: Japan-Korea relationship 64–66; morality books 166–167; *see also* literature
Border Defense Council (Pibyŏnsa) 94
The Buddhas of the Three Bodies (Pirojana samsin kwaebulto) 316–317
Buddhism 6, 183, 197–198, 211–212; art 315–317; Buddhist establishment 204–209; Buddhist genealogies 206–209; ceremonies 218; Hwaŏm school monastery 200; Kyo Buddhism 201–202, 205–206, 211; monasteries 199–210; monks 206–209, 213; nuns 168; reform of public monastery system 199–202; ritual performances 331–332; ritualism 209–211; royal memorial monasteries 199, 205; Sŏn Buddhism 199; subordinate monasteries 210; Tibetan Buddhists 22; tonsure certificates 203–204
buncheong (punch'ŏng) ware 317–319
Buncheong Flat Bottle with Incised Fish Design (Punch'ŏng sagi chohwa ŏmun p'yŏnbyŏng) 317
Bureau of Court Music (Changagwŏn) 326
Bureau of Royal Painting (Tohwasŏ) 312
Bureau of the Royal Kitchen (Saongwŏn) 317–318
Butterfly Dance 332

Index

calendar 50–52, 282–283; *Shixian-li* 283
Catholicism 7, 55, 195, 227, 238–239;
anti-Catholic persecution 159; Catholic
community 84, 158–159, 220, 227;
Korean church (1784–1801) 227–229;
Korean church (1801–39) 229–232; Korean
church (1839–60) 232–236; Korean church
(1860–66) 236–238; missionaries 158–159;
persecution 159
"Central State" (Ch. Zhongguo; Ko.
Chungguk) 45–46
ceramics 62
ch'aekkŏri 314–315
Chang Pogo 21
Chang Yŏngsil 18, 136, 282
Ch'angdŏk Palace 319–321
changnim 220–221; *see also maengin*
Changnyŏl (Queen) 210
ch'angu 330
chaogong see chogong
chapka 333
chapkwa see technical examinations
Cheng Yi 184
Chich'ŏn-sa 200
Chikamatsu Monzaemon 64
Chikchi 18
Ch'ilsŏng 213, 221
Chinese characters *see* Sinographs
Chingbirok (The Book of Corrections) 65
Chinju Kang, Lady 271
Chinju Rebellion 113–114
chinoserie 39
Cho Chongun 135
Cho Chun 152, 199–200
Cho Kwangjo 76, 82, 139, 191, 206
Cho Saŭi 105
Cho Sik 193, 272
Ch'oe Musŏn 97
Ch'oe Namsŏn 195
Ch'oe Sŏkchŏng 280
Ch'oe Yangŏp, Thomas 233–236
chogong (Ch. *chaogong*) 44, 51; *see also* tribute
system
Ch'ŏlchong (King) 55
chŏnak 327
Chŏng Ch'ŏl 300
Chŏng Hasang, Paul 229–231
Chŏng Inhong 155
Chŏng Mongju 185, 187, 272
Chŏng Sangi 284
Chŏng Sŏn 307–308
Chŏng Tojŏn 185–186, 281
Chŏng Yagyong 86, 193–195, 301
Chŏng Yakchong, Augustine 228, 231
chŏngbyŏn 103
chŏngga 329–330

Chŏngjo (King) 37, 54, 83, 91, 96, 98, 110–111,
119, 143, 159, 169, 188, 210, 266, 301–302, 316,
320, 326
Chŏngmyo War 46, 75, 154
Chŏnju Yi, Lady 172
Chŏnju Yi males 76, 137–138
Chōsen gunki monogatari 64–65
Christianity 40; Protestantism 343; *see also*
Catholicism
Chu Non'gae *see* Non'gae
Chu Sebung 267
Chun Doo-hwan (Chŏn Tuhwan) 348–349
Ch'ungch'ŏng Province 108, 224
chungin 2, 5, 8, 19–20, 78, 118, 133–140, 276, 327;
geography 283; mathematicians 279; medicine
285–286
Chungjong (King) 33, 82, 139, 191, 315
Ch'ungnyŏlsa 224
chungse kugŏ 243
civil examination (*munkwa*) 76, 90, 113, 136, 188,
263–264, 276, 312
civil society 16–17
class 133–140, 146–147
Classic of Songs (Ch. *Shijing*; Ko. *Sigyŏng*) 298
colonialism 14
commerce, economy (up to 1873) 126–127;
merchants 126–127, 133; unlicensed
merchants 127
commoners (*yangin*) 133–140, 145; stabilization of
local society (1567–1724) 141–142
concubines 140
Confucian Academy (Sŏnggyun'gwan) 205,
263–266
Confucianism 66, 85, 164, 181–182, 187, 214, 260,
262; ancestral rites 264; Confucian education
260–261; Confucian lineages and schools
190–191, 265; Confucian scholars 192–195,
261–262, 279; Korean Confucianism 190–192;
Neo-Confucianism 183–184; performing arts
334; Yŏngnam School 191
Confucianization 22, 80, 188–190
Confucius 181–182
Contemporary Korean 243
Convention of Tianjin 341
copper seals, trade 60
Corea, Antonio 40
corvée 203
cosmopolitanism 22
coups 103, 107
court ladies 168; homosexuality 173
court music 324–329; Court Music Agency
(Chŏnaksŏ) 324; musicians 327; organizations
326–329
court paintings 312–315
craftspeople 126–127
"Credential Letter Incident" (Ko. Sŏgye sakkŏn) 68

Index

Cultural Rule 344
Cymbal Dance 332

dances 325, 328; Buddhist Ritual Drum Dance 332; Cymbal Dance 332; mask dance dramas 334–336
Daoism 220, 286
Daveluy, Marie-Nicolas-Antoine 158–159
Dayan Khan 29
decolonization 14
Defend Orthodoxy–Reject Heterodoxy (Wijŏng ch'ŏksa) 84
deities 218–223
Democratic People's Republic of Korea (DPRK) 339, 347–348; economic stagnation 350–351; totalitarianism 348–349
descent groups 160–161
Disciples (Soron) 85
discontent 103–104; An Iksin Rebellion 107; challengers from the north (1392–1583) 104–106; Chinju Rebellion (1862) 113–114; eighteenth-century court politics 108–110; food scarcity 112; forms of protest 111; geopolitical changes (1583–1728) 106–108; Hong Kyŏngnae Rebellion 112–113; peasant uprisings in Tokugawa Japan 115; political turmoil (1583–1728) 106–108; popular uprising 103; ritualized protest and popular unrest (1729–1873) 110–112; taxation 104
discrimination 104, 346
district rituals 222–223
divorce 165
dramas 334–336; Hwanghae 335; Kyŏnggi 335; mask dance 9, 334–336
drumming music *see p'ungmul*
Du Shizhong 155
Dutch East India Company 156–157

Early Early Modern Korean 243
Early Modern Korean 243–244, 254–256; consonants 244; excerpts from representative texts 249–254; grammatical changes 246–247; lexical changes 247; phonological changes 244–246; spelling 248–249; vowels 244–245
early modernity *see* historiography
East Asian War *see* Imjin War
Eastern Jin dynasty 320
Eastern Learning *see* Tonghak
Easterners (Tongin) 84
economy (up to 1873) 117; agriculture 120–121; commerce 126–127; development 16; gift economy 119; money 127–128; population 118–119; prices 121–123; slavery 123–124; state finance 119–120; stature 125–126; wages 124–125
education 260; Confucian Academy (Sŏnggyun'gwan) 113, 188, 199, 263, 302, 330;

Confucian education 260–261; *Elementary Learning* (*Xiaoxue*) 262–263; formal education 263–266; Learning Halls of Four Districts (Sabu haktang) 266; moral education for women 167; morality books 166–167; private academies (*sŏwŏn*) 266–271; role of 261–262; royal education 271; self-taught scholars 272; village schools (*sŏdang*) 266; women's education 271–272
Eight Prohibitions Festival (P'algwanhoe) 197–198
Elementary Learning (*Xiaoxue*) 262–263
elimination of shamans from state rituals 216–220
embroidery 171
Enlightenment Party (Kaehwadang) 84, 147
Enlightenment Period Korean 243
ensemble music *see p'ungnyu*
envoy missions 37–39
Esen Khan 29
Ever-Normal Circulating Treasure 127–128
Evidential Learning (Ch. Kaozhengxue; Ko. Kojŭnghak) 195
examination system *see* government service examination (*kwagŏ*)
exorcists 220
Extreme Disciples (Chunso) 109

Faction of Principle (*Pyŏkp'a*) 96
family structure 164–165
farmer soldiers 94
farmers 126–127, 141
female chastity (*yŏl*) 6, 165
female virtue 167
femininity 174–175
Fighting Males at a Kisaeng House (*Yugwak chaengung*) 144
finance, economy (up to 1873) 127–128
firearms 97–99
First Opium War 55
First Sino–Japanese War 17, 21, 342
fishermen 224–225
Five Bonds (Ch. *wulun*; Ko. *oryun*) 182
Five Cardinal Bonds 261
Five Classics 209, 264; *Book of Changes* 183; Confucianism 182
Five Dragons Shrine (Oryongmyo) 222
Five Guards (Owi) 94
Five Major Organs 277
Five Moral Imperatives 261
Five Phases 277–278, 285
folk songs 333
food scarcity 112
foreign relations: 1392–1521 28–32; 1521–1624 32–35; 1644–1850 35–40; 1873–1910 340–343; 1910–45 343–346; 1945–53 346–348
foreigners 151–153; continuities in 158–161; defectors 153–154; deserters 155–156;

Index

disruptions 158–161; *hyanghwa* status 151; *hyanghwain* 38, 151, 153; impact of mid-Chosŏn wars 153–158

fortifications 29; mountain fortresses 96; Namhan Fortress 95

"Founding of the [Chosŏn] State" (Chŏng taeŏp) 325

"Four Outposts" (Sagun) 29

"Four Sages" (Ch. Sipei; Ko. Sabae) 264

Four Schools (Sahak) 266

Four Sprouts of Morality (*sadan*) 193

Four-Seven Debate 193

fubing system 94

Fujiwara Seika 66–67

functionary surnames 136

furs 32

GDP *see* Gross Domestic Product (GDP)

gender 164; hierarchy 166; ideology 6; love relationships 175–176; norms 164–167; perfect femininity 174–175; sex segregation 165; sexuality 172–174; social life 167–174; transgender 172–174

genre paintings 307–309

geography 283–285; maps 283–285; wheel maps 284–285

geomancy 283–284

gift economy 119

ginseng 39; wild ginseng 32

globalizing world 32–35

government service examinations (*kwagŏ*) 90, 165, 264; local examination (*hyangsi*) 263; preliminary examination (*ch'osi*) 263; "re-examination" (*poksi*) 263

Go-Yōzei (Emperor) 66

grain submission (*napsok*) 123

Grand Ritual Protocols (*Taesarye ŭigwe*) 96–100

Great Code of Administration (Kyŏngguk taejŏn) 80, 139, 205, 328

Great East Asian War *see* Imjin War

Great Learning (*Daxue*) 184–185, 261, 271

Great Ming Code (Da Ming lu) 80

Great Northerners (Taebuk) 85

Gross Domestic Product (GDP) 125

group drumming music *see p'ungmul*

Guan Yu *see* Kwan U (Ch. Guan Yu)

gun powder 23, 97

Guo Xi 305

Guo Ziyi 313

Gutenberg, Johannes 18

Hague Convention of 1907 341

Hall of Bright Morality (Myŏngnyundang) 265

Hamel, Hendrik 40, 156

Han Chinese 53

Han Hyosun 98

Han Kigŭn, Paul 236

Han Myŏnghoe 205

Han River 126–127

"hanging buddhas" (*kwaebul*) 211

Han'gŭl (Hangul) 292–293, 303, 343

Hangul *see* Han'gŭl (Hangul)

hat-licensing system 39

Hayashi Razan 66

height data 125

hereditary elites 133

Hermit Kingdom 3, 150

Hideyoshi Invasion *see* Imjin War

hired-soldier system 94

Hishikawa Moronobu 64

historiography: connected history 21; of Chosŏn 14–15; disconnections 22–24; early modernity 3, 13, 15, 20–21, 24; global periodization 3; Hermit Kingdom 3, 150; *kŭndae* 14, 243, 255; *kŭnse* 14–15; modernist view 17; modernity 7, 15, 20; Pax Mongolica 22; political modernity 16–17; Weberian approach 15

Hŏ Ch'ohŭi *see* Hŏ Nansŏrhŏn

Hŏ Chun 8, 286

Hŏ Kyun 172, 295–296, 298–299

Hŏ, Lady *see* Hŏ Nansŏrhŏn

Hŏ Mok 85

Hŏ Nansŏrhŏn 172, 271, 298, 300

hoesi 263–264

homosexuality 172–174

Hong Chŏngha 279

Hong Hŭibok 303

Hong, Hyegyŏng-gung, Lady 172, 312, 330

Hong Kugyŏng 76

Hong Kyŏngnae 93

Hong Kyŏngnae Rebellion 21, 93, 112–113

Hong, Lady *see* Hong, Hyegyŏng-gung, Lady

Hong Sŏngmo 222

Hong Taeyong 18, 37, 283

Hong Taiji 34, 46, 93

Hong Yangho 100

Hongwu (Emperor) 28–30, 159

Hŏnjong (King) 55

hop'ae system 105

house, as a sacred place 221–222

Huang Kan 265

Huineng 208

human tribute 32

Humaneness (Ch. *ren*; Ko. *in*) 182, 190

Hundred-Cash Coin (*Tangbaekchŏn*) 120, 128

Hŭngch'ŏn-sa 200, 203–204

Hŭngsŏn Taewŏn'gun 55, 84, 159, 237

Hun'gu 134

Hwang Hŭi 203

Hwang Sayŏng, Alexius 40, 51, 228–229

hwanyangnyŏn 165

Hwaŏm school monastery 200

Index

Hwarang 88
hyangak 324, 328
hyangga 291
hyanghwa status 151
hyanghwain 38, 151, 153
Hyojong (King) 48, 83, 85, 210
Hyomyŏng (Prince) 314
Hyŏnch'ungsa 225
Hyŏnjong (King) 36, 83, 209
Hyujŏng 206
hyungnye 324

i (Ch. *li*) 276–277
identity 18, 63, 155
ilmu 325, 328
Im Kkŏkchŏng 106, 137
Im Kyŏngŏp 223–224
Imagawa Ryōshun 65
Imgo Academy 267
Imjin War 23, 33, 35, 45, 60–61, 64–65, 75, 88, 91–92, 139, 153, 155, 206–209
Imo Mutiny 342
Independence Club 342–343
Indra (Ko. Chesŏk) 221–222
Injo (King) 34, 45, 83, 155, 210
Injong (King) 82
Inner Sea 152
Insŏn (Queen) 210
"internal development theory" (*Naejaejŏk palchŏn non*) 14
Isan Academy 268
Itō Hirobumi 341
Iwakura Tomomi 68

Jaisohn, Philip (Ko. Sŏ Chaep'il) 342
Japan 4, 55, 58; art 61–64; books 64–66; colonial rule in Korea 343–346; First Sino–Japanese War 342; Imjin War 34–35; Imperial Japan 3; Korea's trade with 39; *kyorin* 44; male homosexuality 173–174; medicine 66–67; Meiji Japan 41, 58, 68, 86, 340; Muromachi Japan 59; nineteenth-century politics 67–68; peasant uprisings 115; philosophy 66–67; pirates 31; raiders 152; relations with 33–34, 37–38, 58–68, 340–341, 345–346; Three Ports 31; Tokugawa Japan 21, 37, 67–68; Wakō raids 60, 88, 90; Warring States (Sengoku) Japan 58, 60
Japan House (Waegwan) 37–38
Japanese Red Seal Ships 21
Jianwen (Emperor) 31
Jin dynasty (Jurchens) 45
Jingū (Empress) 59
"Jiubian" 31
Jurchens 33–34, 45–46, 75, 91–92, 105–107, 151–153; relations with 92; *see also* Later Jin; Manchus; Qing dynasty

Kabo Reform 21, 273, 342
Kaegyŏng-sa 199
kagok 330
kajŏnak 327
Kaksŏng 208–209
Kang Ch'ŏm 171
Kang Hang 66, 153–154
Kang Hongnip 92
Kang Paengnyŏn 175
Kang Sehwang 308, 311
Kang Shijue 156
Kang Wansuk, Columba 229
Kanghwado 266; Treaty of 68, 86, 340
Kangxi (Emperor) 36, 53
Kanō Tan'yū 64
Kapsin Coup 342
karye 324
kasa 299–300
Katō Kiyomasa 64, 68
Katsushika Hokusai 64
Khitans 45, 89; *see also* Liao dynasty
ki see qi
Kigye Yu, Lady 167
Kija (Ch. Jizi) 52, 155
Killye 324
Kim Ch'angjip 37
Kim Ch'angŏp 37, 49
Kim Chinam 99
Kim Chŏngho 284
Kim Chongjik 191, 272
Kim Chosun 317
Kim Ch'ungsŏn 35, 154
Kim Ch'unt'aek 301
Kim Hongdo 307–309
Kim Hyŏn'gŭn 317
Kim Hyowŏn 84
Kim Igyo 174
Kim Jae-kyu (Kim Chaegyu) 349
Kim Jong-il (Kim Chŏngil) 348
Kim Koengp'il 191, 272
Kim, Lucy 232
Kim Mandŏk 169
Kim Myŏngguk 186
Kim Pyŏngju 317
Kim Si 306
Kim Sik 108
Kim Sisŭp 176, 193, 272, 293–295
Kim Sŏkchu 98
Kim Suhang 166
Kim Taegŏn, Andrew 158, 232
Kim Yusin 222
"King-Ki-Tao" 40
kisaeng 134, 137, 168–169, 330–331, 333, 336; Kyesŏm 330; Kyewŏrhyang 169–170; Non'gae 169
Kojong: Emperor 17–18, 55, 342–344; King 17, 55, 58, 68, 84, 159, 215, 237, 313, 317, 339–342

357

Index

kokatsujiban 66
kongnon *see* public opinion (*kongnon*)
Kōrai chawan 62
Korean language: *chungse kugŏ* 243; Early Modern
   Korean 244–256; experts from representative
   texts, Early Modern Korean 249–254; *kŭndae
   kugŏ* 243; South Korean periodization 243;
   spelling, Early Modern Korean 248–249
Korean Royal Observatory *see* Office for
   Observation of Natural Phenomena
   (Kwansanggam)
Korean War 346–348
Koryŏ–Chosŏn transition 104–106, 135
kukka chŏllye 324
kullye 324
Kŭmgang, Mount 306–307
kŭndae kugŏ 243
kungmu 218
Kunlun, Mount 54
Kuroda Kiyotaka 340
Kwan U (Ch. Guan Yu) 219–220; *Kwanwang
   myoje* 326
kwangdae 330–331
Kwanghae Kun (King) 45–46, 82, 92, 107, 155, 207
Kwangmu Reform 341, 342
Kwanwang myoje 326
Kwŏn Kŭn 66, 185, 292
Kwŏn Sangha 175
Kwŏn Sangyŏn, James 228
kyehoedo 306
Kyesŏm 330
Kyewŏrhyang 169–170
Kyo Buddhism 201–202, 205–206, 211
Kyŏngbang Spinning and Weaving Company 350
Kyŏngbok Palace 319
Kyŏngjong (King) 83
Kyŏngsang Province 38
kyorin 44
Kyujanggak 83, 266; "Outer Kyujanggak" (Oe
   Kyujanggak) 266
Kyushu 59–60; *tandai* 33

Lady Sa's Journey to the South (*Sassi namjŏng
   ki*) 301
land: grants 199; landlord–tenant relationship
   124–125; ownership 120–121
landscape painting 305–307
Lantern Festival (Yŏndŭnghoe) 197–198; Upper
   Primordial (Sangwŏn) Lantern Festival 198
Late Early Modern Korean 243
Late Middle Korean 256
Later Jin 34, 46; *see also* Jurchens; Manchus; Qing
   dynasty
Law of Avoidance (*sangp'ije*) 77
Learning (Ch. *xue*; Ko. *hak*) 182
Learning Halls of Four Districts (Sabu haktang) 266

lèse-majesté 77
Lesser Northerners (Sobuk) 85
LGBTQ *see* gender; homosexuality
Li Rumei 160
Li Rusong 160
Liao dynasty 45, 89; *see also* Khitans
Liaodong Peninsula 153
lice 276
lineage 136–140; bilaterality 164; lineage
   consciousness 143; lineage heir 142; patrilineal
   descent 138; posthumous adoptions 143
Linji Yixuan 208
literary arts *see* literature
Literary Sinitic (Classical Chinese) 168, 172,
   291–297; poetry 299
literati: performing arts 329–330; portraiture 311;
   purges 80, 82, 267
literature 291; literary arts 171–172; poetry 297–
   300; significance of writing 292–293; textual
   transmission 300–301; vernacular literature
   293–297
Little China *see So Chunghwa* (Little China)
Little Ice Age 28, 32
local council roster (*hyangan*) 78, 138, 140, 144
local councils (*hyanghoe*) 78–79, 138–140,
   144–147
local elites 139
local government 77–78
"local punishment" (*hyangbŏl*) 78
local society, stabilization of (1567–1724) 140–142
love: relationships 175–176; songs 333
"lowborn" (*ch'ŏnmin*) 134–140, 142; women 168

Ma Shunshang 160
maengin 220–221; *see also changnim*
magic square 280–281
Maitreya 315
Manase Shōrin 65
Manchuria 89
Manchus 17, 35, 37–38, 46, 48, 53, 151, 211 302;
   Chŏngmyo War 46, 75, 154; Manchu invasions
   209; Pyŏngja War 75; *see also* Jurchens; Later
   Jin; Qing dynasty
Mandate of Heaven 35, 52, 103
Mao Wenlong 154
maps 283–285; wheel maps 284–285
March First Movement 344, 349
market prices 122
marriage: to foreigners 155; remarriage ban 165;
   uxorilocal marriage 142
mask dance dramas 9, 334–336
mathematics 275, 278–281; counting rod notation
   278–279
Maubant, Pierre 232
medicine 285–286; Japan–Korea relationship 66–67
Meiji Restoration 58

358

Index

Mencius 181, 183–184, 261
Mengtemu *see* Möngke Temür (Mengtemu)
merchants 126–127, 133; Muslim merchants 22; peddlers 126–127, 137, 145; unlicensed merchants 127
migration: migrants 151–153, 159–161; policy 157–158
military 88–90, 152; firearms 97–99; gun powder 23, 97; leadership 90–91; militia 94–95; monk militia 206; organization of 93–96; peasant–soldier system 94; "righteous armies" (*ŭibyŏng*) 34, 155, 343; "righteous monks" (*ŭisŭng*) 82, 206; security threats 91–93; *sogo* army 95; technology 96–100; texts of military tactics 96–100
military examination (*mukwa*) 5, 77, 90–91, 96–97, 136, 140, 141, 159, 188, 263–264, 312
military registers, height data 125
Military Training Agency (Hullyŏn togam) 94–95
militia 94–95; "righteous armies" (*ŭibyŏng*) 34, 155, 343; "righteous monks" (*ŭisŭng*) 82, 206
millan 103
Ming dynasty 1, 15, 19, 28, 32–35, 38, 44, 59–60, 75, 90, 92, 104–107, 150, 152, 155–156, 185, 198, 279; clashes with Yuan 104–106; emperors 29; merchant pirates 21; migrants to Chosŏn 159–161; relations with 29, 32–33; Southern Ming 156; war with Later Jin 45
Ming loyalism 36
Ming–Qing transition 38, 53, 93, 106
Ministry of Rites (Yejo) 77, 158
Ministry of War (Pyŏngjo) 77
minjung movements 17
minyo 333
Miryang Pak, Lady 146
Moderate Disciples (Wanso) 109
modernity *see* historiography
money: "coin drought" (*chŏnhwang*) 127; copper coins 128; economy (up to 1873) 127–128
Möngke Temür (Mengtemu) 152
Mongols 22, 28–32, 89; *see also* Yuan dynasty
monk militia *see* "righteous monks" (*ŭisŭng*)
"moon jar" (*tal hangari*) 318
moral education, for women 167
morality books 166–167
Moriyama Shigeru 340
Motoori Norinaga 67
mountain gods (*sansin, sansillyŏng*) 213, 223
Mu (King) 314
mudang 215–216, 220–222; *see also munyŏ*; shamans
mudong 328
Mukedeng 36
Munhwa Yu genealogy 139
Munjong (King) 173, 206, 315, 326
Munjŏng (Queen) 82, 206, 315

munyŏ 215; *see also mudang*; shamans
music: court music 325–326; Court Music Agency (Chŏnaksŏ) 324; ensemble music 329; folk songs 333; group drumming music 332; *kagok* 330; *kajŏnak* 327; love songs 333; *minyo* 333; organizations 326–329; *orye* 324; for royal courts 324–325; shamanic music 331; *tangak* 324, 328
musicians 327–329
Musin Rebellion 93
mutual assistance societies (*kye*) 122
Myŏngjong (King) 82, 137, 206, 208, 315
Myŏngon Kongju 317
Myŏngsŏng (Queen) 218, 317, 341
Myung-sul-lu 48

Naeshirogawa kilns 62
Nagasaki 157
Nam Chongsam, John the Baptist 236–238
namak see mudong
Namhan Fortress 95
namsadangp'ae 331
Nanboku Tsuruya 64–65
nationalism 17–18; "primordialist" view 17; proto-nationalism 17
Nature and Principle Learning (Sŏngnihak) *see* Neo-Confucianism
Nectar Ritual Paintings (*kamnot'aeng*) 216
Neo-Confucianism 8, 18, 66, 75, 82, 85, 172, 183–184, 189–190, 195, 276–277, 331; Korean Neo-Confucianism 193; mathematics 279–281; Nature and Principle Learning (Sŏngnihak) 183; Neo-Confucian vision 277; performing arts 324–325; politics 184–188; self-cultivation 262–263; self-improvement 262; self-reflection 263; self-taught scholars 272; self-training 263; Seven Emotions (*ch'ilchŏng*) 193
New Tales of the Golden Turtle (*Kŭmo sinhwa*) 296–297
A Nine Cloud Dream (*Kuunmong*) 301
Nine Levels of Buddhist Paradise (*Kŭngnak kup'umdo*) 317
"Nine Righteous Scholars" (*Kuŭisa*) 156, 158
Nit'anggae Rebellion 106
Non'gae 169
nongak 332; *see also p'ungmul*
North Korea *see* Democratic People's Republic of Korea
Northern Expedition (*Pukpŏl*) 93
Northerners (Pugin) 84
Nurhaci 34, 45, 92, 153

O Toil 36
O Wŏn 174
occupational groups, rituals 223–225
"ocean barbarians" (*Yangi*) 55
Oda Nobunaga 60

359

Index

Office for Observation of Natural Phenomena (Kwansanggam) 281–282
officials in government 76–77
Oksan Academy 267–268
Ōkubo Toshimichi 68
Oppert, Ernst 238
oral performance 299
orye 324
Ōshima 60
Ōtomo family 60
Ōuchi: clan 33; daimyo family 60, 153

Pacific War 344
paekchŏng 104
Paektu, Mount 53–54, 153
Paektu-taegan 53–54, 56
painting: court paintings 64, 312–315; genre paintings 307–309; landscape painting 305–307; portraiture 309–312; women 171; *see also* visual arts
Pak Chega 37, 194
Pak Chiwŏn 37, 51, 194
Pak Chonggyŏng 100
Pak Chŏngyang 341
Pak Chusu 194
Pak Kyusu 340
Pak, Martha 236–237
Pak Sedang 86
Palace Chapel (Naewŏndang) 203
p'albaek 300
panin 330
p'ansori 9, 299–331, 333–334
Pari kongju 213
Park Chung-hee (Pak Chŏnghŭi) 348–350
partisan strife 190; *see also* political parties
Patriarchs (Noron) 85, 91, 93, 96, 109–110, 145
patrilineal descent *see* lineage
Pax Mongolica 22
peasant–soldier system 94
peddlers 126–127, 137, 145
people's assemblies (*minhoe*) 79, 145–147
performing arts 323; *ch'angu* 330; court music 325–326; dances 325, 328; ensemble music 329; folk songs 333; group drumming music 332; *kisaeng* 330; *kwangdae* 330–331; literati 329–330; mask dance dramas 334–336; music 324; Neo-Confucianism 324–325; *p'ansori* 333–334; performance for royal courts 324–329; performance-related texts 326; performers 326–329; ritual performances in Buddhism 331–332; shamanic music 331; solo instrumental music 333; sung poetry 329–330
periodization *see* historiography
"personal tribute" (*sin'gong*) 135
petitions 111
philosophy: Japan-Korea relationship 66–67; philosophers 276

pillye 324
P'iram Academy 268
pirates 21–22, 31, 32, 35; raiders 152; Wakō raids 30–31, 60, 88, 90
"plank-structure ships" (*p'anoksŏn*) 97
poetry 67, 297–300; poetry parties 64; sung poetry 329–330
political parties 84–85; *see also* partisan strife
politics: kings 76; local government 77–78; Neo-Confucianism 184–188; officials 76–77; overview of 79–84; partisan strife 190; political parties 84–85; political turmoil (1583–1728) 106–108; public opinion 78–79
Pongsan Mask Dance 336
popular religion 213–214; deities 218–223; elimination of shamans from state rituals 216–220; house as a sacred place 221–222; outline of the universe 215–216; rituals 220–221; rituals conducted by occupational groups 223–225; shamanism 214–215; universe in 215–216; village and district rituals 222–223
popular unrest *see* discontent
popular uprising *see* discontent
population 140; economy (up to 1873) 118–119
porcelain 317–319
Porcelain Jar with Cloud and Dragon Design in Underglaze Cobalt Blue (*Paekcha ch'ŏnghwa ullyongmun chun*) 318–319
portraiture 309–312
Pou 206
Poŭn-sa 207
Practical Learning (Sirhak) 96
"Preserving the Grand Peace" (Po t'aep'yŏng) 325
prices, economy (up to 1873) 121–123
primogeniture 142
printing press 18
private academies (*sŏwŏn*) 266–271; curriculum 267–271
Privy Council (Todang) 197–198
prosody, Early Modern Korean 245
proto-nationalism 17; *see also* nationalism
public opinion (*kongnon*) 78–79, 133, 145, 191
public sphere 16–17
Puch'ul kaksi ("Miss Squatting Board") 222
Pugun-dang 223
P'ungch'ŏn Im, Lady 172, 271
p'ungmul 331–332; *see also* nongak
Pungmyo 220
p'ungnyu 329
Pyŏngja War 46, 75, 83, 154
Pyŏngsan Academy 268
P'yŏngsan Sin, Lady *see* Sin Saimdang

qi (Ch. *qi*; Ko. *ki*) 276–277
Qi Jiguang 95, 97–98, 100
Qianlong (Emperor) 35–36

Index

Qing dynasty 15, 17, 35–37, 45–46, 48, 50, 75, 92, 107, 151, 156, 185, 211, 228, 279, 302; anti-Qing sentiment 107; relations with 36, 39, 341; *see also* Jurchens; Later Jin; Manchus
Qu You 294–295
quatrains 299

Rank Land Law (*Kwajŏn pŏp*) 120–121
Red Turban invasions 21, 28
remonstrance 260
Republic of Korea 339, 345, 347; democratization 348–349; economic recovery 350–351
Rhee, Syngman (Yi Sŭngman) 345, 348
rice 119–120; prices 123
"righteous armies" (*ŭibyŏng*) 34, 155, 343
"righteous bandits" (*ŭijŏk*) 106
"righteous monks" (*ŭisŭng*) 82, 206
rites 182, 325; Neo-Confucianism 189–190; practicing 182; state rites 324
Rites Controversy 85
Ritual Drum Dance (*pŏpko ch'um*) 332
ritualized protest and popular unrest (1729–1873) 110–112
rituals: conducted by occupational groups 223–225; court music 325; district rituals 222–223; popular religion 215–216, 220–221; village rituals 222–223; *see also* Buddhism; shamanism
Robust and Brave Division (Changyongyŏng) 83–84, 96
Roh Tae-woo (No T'aeu) 349
Royal Ancestral Shrine (Chongmyo) 324, 328
royal cult 203, 210
Royal Defense Command (Suŏch'ŏng) 95
royal education 271
royal kilns 317–319
royal kin (*chongch'in*) 137
royal land 120
royal memorial monasteries 199, 205
royal patronage 315–317
Rubens, Peter Paul 40
Russia 55
Ryukyu Islands: Kingdom 22; *kyorin* 44; Ryukyuans 32

sacrifices 222–223
sadae (Ch. *shida*) 43–46, 51, 55
sadae chuŭi 4, 56
Sado (Prince) 188, 210
Saigō Takamori 68
sajok 133; *see also yangban*
samulnori 332
sandae 335
sanjo 333
Sarim 134, 139, 191, 204–206
Satsuma 63

science 275–278; astronomy 281–283; geography 283–285; mathematics 278–281; medicine 285–286; physical anthropology 125–126; scientific progress 18–19
Screens of the Sun, Moon, and Five Peaks (*Irwŏl obongdo*) 313
Second Sino–Japanese War 345
secret inspectors (*amhaeng ŏsa*) 76
security threats 91–93
Sejo (King) 80, 105, 138, 204, 293, 325
Sejong (King) 8, 29, 80, 104–105, 119, 136, 152, 188, 202–204, 278, 292–293, 305, 324–326
self-determination 344
Seno no Rikyū 62
Seven Emotions (*ch'ilchŏng*) 193
"Seven Stars" *see* Ch'ilsŏng
sexuality 172–174
Shakyamuni 315
shamanism 214–215, 331; music 331
shamans 168, 213; elimination from state rituals 216–220; *kungmu* 218; *see also mudang*; *munyŏ*
Shi Wenyong 155
Shi Xing 160
Shixian-li 283
shrines 36–37, 217, 219–220, 223–225, 265; Royal Ancestral Shrine 324, 328; State Confucian Shrine 264; State Shrine to Confucius 324
sijo 299, 330
Silk Letter 228
Silla 59, 61, 88–89, 214
silver 39
Sim Kiwŏn 107–108
Sim Saju 175
Sim Sugyŏng 298–299, 301
Sim Uigyŏm 84
Sin Hŏn 100
Sin, Lady *see* Sin Saimdang
Sin Saimdang 171–172, 298
Sin Sunggyŏm 219
Sin Yunbok 308
Sindŏk (Queen) 199–200
Sinocentrism 44; Sinocentric worldview 44–45
Sinographs 291
Sino–Japanese–Korean War *see* Imjin War
Sinŭi (Queen) 200
Sirhak *see* Practical Learning
Six Codes of Governance (Kyŏngje yukchŏn) 203
"Six Garrison Fortresses" (Yukchin) 29
Six Markets (Yugŭijŏn) 219
Six Ministries (Yukcho) 77, 80
"Six Sage Masters of Song Dynasty" (Ch. Songchao liuxian; Ko. Songjo yukhyŏn) 265
slavery 40, 134–135, 137, 145, 167; economy (up to 1873) 123–124; monasteries 201; private slaves 145; public slaves 145; "tribute-submitting" slaves (*napkong nobi*) 123

Index

smallpox 220
Sŏ Chaep'il *see* Jaisohn, Philip (Sŏ Chaep'il)
So Chunghwa (Little China) 4, 43–45, 47, 49–52,
54–55, 83; national unity 52–54; space 52–54;
time 50–52
Sŏ family 33–34, 60
Sŏ Kŏjŏng 292–293
Sŏ Kyŏngdŏk 193, 272
Sŏ Yoshitoshi 60
social discrimination 104
social disintegration 47
social status *see* status
sogo army 95
Sŏhak *see* Western Learning (Sŏhak)
Sohŏn (Queen) 204
Sohye (Queen) 272
Sohyŏn (Prince) 40
sokwa 263
Sŏl Changsu 151
Sŏmyo 220
Sŏn Buddhism 199, 211; Sŏn schools 201–202,
205–206
Song dynasty 4, 45, 75, 139, 183, 278, 280
Song Hŭigyŏng 30
Sŏng Hyŏn 327
Song Iyŏng 19
Song Kyubin 98
Song of Ch'unhyang (*Ch'unhyang ka*) 334
"Song of Kwandong" (Kwandong pyŏlgok) 300
Song of Simch'ŏng (*Simch'ŏng ka*) 334
Song of the Red Cliffs (*Chŏkpyŏk ka*) 28
Song Siyŏl 17, 49, 76, 85–86
sŏnghwang (Ch. *chenghuang*) 218–219, 222
Sŏngjong (King) 29, 80, 139, 204–205, 326
Sŏngju 221
Songs of Flying Dragons (*Yongbi ŏch'ŏn ka*) 30,
293, 297
Sŏnjo (King) 34, 45, 63–64, 82, 140, 185
Sŏnnongdan 217
sŏnsori 333
Sŏnsu 207–208
Sosu Academy 268
South Korea *see* Republic of Korea
Southern Ming 156
Southerners (Namin) 85–86, 109
Soviet Union, occupation of Korea 346–348
stabilization of local society (1567–1724) 140–142
state 16–17
State Confucian Shrine (Munmyo) 188, 223,
264–265, 324, 326
State Council (Ŭijŏngbu) 77, 200
state examinations *see* government service
examinations (*kwagŏ*)
state finance, economy (up to 1873) 119–120
state rites 324
stature 125–126

status 133–140, 146–147; accelerating mobility
143–146; *see also chungin*; commoners (*yangin*);
"lowborn" (*ch'ŏnmin*); slavery; *yangban*
Stick Dance 332
Sui dynasty 30
Sukchong (King) 83, 109, 159, 267, 328
sung poetry 329–330
Sungŭijŏn 224
Sunjo (King) 55, 84, 145, 314
Sunjong (Emperor) 341
Sunzi 264
Superintendency for the Publication of Buddhist
Scriptures (Kan'gyŏng togam) 204–205
surnames 136, 151; functionary surnames 136
suryukchae 216
Sutra of Shakyamuni's Teaching on Parental Love
(*Pulsŏl pumo ŭnjunggyŏng*) 316

T'aejo (King of Chosŏn) 103–104, 152, 197–199,
203, 209–210, 263, 309–310; *see also* Yi
Sŏnggye
T'aejo (King of Koryŏ) 89
T'aejong (King) 31, 52, 79–80, 90, 136, 200–
203, 293
taekwa 263
taesik 173
Taiwan *see* Tungning, Kingdom of
Tale of Hong Kiltong (*Hong Kiltong chŏn*) 295–297
Tale of Unyŏng (*Unyŏng chŏn*) 301
Tang dynasty 75, 88, 183, 313
tangak 324, 328
Tano Festival 222
Tao Yuanming 305–306
tax system 104, 118; tribute price 122; tribute
system 29; tribute tax (*kongnap*) 119; Uniform
Land Tax Law (Taedongpŏp) 82
tea bowls 62
tea ceremony 62
technical examinations (*chapkwa*) 276
technology 275–278; firearms 97–99; gun powder
23, 97; military 96–100; "plank-structure ships"
(*p'anoksŏn*) 97
Ten Symbols of Longevity (*Sip changsaengdo*) 313
Ten Views of the Royal Garden 320
"Ten Wise Disciples" (Ch. Shizhe; Ko.
Sipch'ŏl) 265
Terauchi Masatake 345
Three Ports (Samp'o) 31
Three-Lake Pavillion Poetry Society (Samhojŏng
sisa) 172
Tibetan monks 22
titles for Japanese and Jurchen leaders 152
Tō Teikan 67
Tōdō Takatora 66
Todong Academy 267
Tŏganjŏn 199

Index

Tǒgon Kongju 317
Tokugawa Iemitsu 64
Tokugawa Ieyasu 34, 66
Tokugawa shogunate 58, 151, 158, 340
Tokugawa Yoshinobu 67–68
Tonam Academy 268
Tonghak ("Eastern Learning") 21, 342
Tonghak Uprising 342
tonsure certificates 203, 204
Tosan Academy 267–268
Tosǒn 199
Toyotomi Hideyoshi 33, 60–61, 68
trade 22–23, 32, 39–40, 127; economy (up to 1873) 127–128; ginseng 39; with Japan 59–61; late fifteenth century 35; resources for 39–40; silver 39
tributary system 44, 152; human tribute 32
tribute system *see* tax system
Tripitaka Koreana 60
true-view (*chin'gyǒng*) landscapes 306
Tsushima 59–60
Tumu Crisis 29
Tungning, Kingdom of 108
Tungusic peoples 89
ture 141

Ubong Ch'oe 89
ŭinyǒ 169
Ukita Hideie 65
Ullŭngdo 157–158
ŭm and *yang see* yin and yang
Uniform Land Tax Law (Taedongpǒp) 82
United States 340–341; Korean War 346–348
universal state 46–48, 51

vernacular literature 293–297
visual arts: Buddhist art 315–317; *buncheong* ware and porcelain 317–319; *ch'aekkǒri* 314–315; Ch'angdǒk Palace 319–321; court paintings 312–315; genre paintings 307–309; landscape paintings 305–307; portraiture 309–312; royal patronage 315–317
von Bell, Johann Adam Schall 40

wages, economy (up to 1873) 124–125
Wakō 28, 30–31, 60, 88, 90
Wang Kǒn 89; *see also* T'aejo (King of Koryǒ)
Wang Tǒkku 160
Wang Yangming 193
Wang Zhi 21
Wanli (Emperor) 36
Water Margin (Ch. *Shui hu zhuan*) 296
Way of the Sage Kings 184
Weltevree, Jans Janse 40, 156
Western Learning (Sǒhak) 195
Western Zhou dynasty 279

Westerners (Sǒin) 84
wheel maps 284–285
White Cloud Grotto Academy 267
white porcelain 317–319
White Porcelain Jar with Grapevine Design Painted in Underglaze Copper Red (*Paekcha tonghwa p'odomun ho*) 319
White Porcelain Jar with Plum and Bamboo Design in Underglaze Cobalt Blue (*Ch'ǒnghwa paekcha maejuk munho*) 317
White Porcelain Jar with Plum and Bamboo Designs in Underglaze Iron Brown (*Paekcha ch'ǒrhwa maejungmun ho*) 319
White Satsuma 62
Willow Palisade 53
wives, perfect femininity 174–175
women: concubines 140; court ladies 168; cultural activities of 169–172; divorce 165; economic activity 167–169; education 271–272; female chastity 6, 165; female virtue 167; femininity 174–175; gender roles 165; literary arts 171–172; moral education 167; perfect femininity 174–175; professions for 168; religion 214; rituals 220; rules for 165; sexuality 172–174; as shamans 215; wives 174–175
Wǒn'gak-sa 204
woodblock printing 18
woodcutters 223–224
writing, significance of 292–293

Xunzi 181

Yalu River 53, 156
Yamanoue no Sōji 62
Yanagawa clan 34
Yang (Emperor) 30
Yang Hui 280
yangban 2, 5, 8, 75–77, 90–91, 96, 118, 133, 134, 136, 140, 146, 276; hereditary elites 133; lineage 138; literary arts 171–172; local elites 139; mathematicians 279; rules for women 165; *sajok* 133; shamans 217–218; wives 167; *see also* local council roster (*hyangan*); local councils (*hyanghoe*); public opinion (*kongnon*)
Yangi see "ocean barbarians" (*Yangi*)
ye 324
Yi Ch'anghyǒn 136
Yi Chingok 105
Yi Chiran 151
Yi Chunghwan 52–53
Yi Hwang 154, 191–192, 268–270, 272
Yi Hyǒngnok 315
Yi Hyorip 107
Yi I 185, 191–192, 268–270, 272
Yi Ik 54, 171, 194
Yi In'gǒ 107

Index

Yi Injwa 93, 109
Yi Injwa Rebellion 109–110
Yi Kwal 35, 92, 107
Yi Kyŏngdo, Charles 231
Yi Kyŏngŏn, Paul 229–231
Yi Kyubo 216–217
Yi Kyugyŏng 173–174
Yi Myŏnggi 312
Yi Pangwŏn 79, 185; *see also* T'aejong (King)
Yi Pokhyu 267
Yi Pyŏk 227–229
Yi Saek 186, 219
Yi Siae 105
Yi Sibal 155
Yi Sik 295–296
Yi Sŏnggye 44, 48, 79, 90–91, 103, 105, 150–151, 185–186; *see also* T'aejo (King of Chosŏn)
Yi Sŭnghun 40, 227–228
Yi Sŭngman *see* Rhee, Syngman (Yi Sŭngman)
Yi Suni, Luthgarde 228
Yi Sunsin 82
Yi Taenyŏn 173
yin and yang 166, 277
yŏgi 328
yŏje 217
yŏmbul 211
Yŏnbok-sa 199
Yŏngch'ang Taegun 45
Yŏngjo (King) 53–54, 83, 93, 95, 108–109, 143, 159, 187–188, 209, 219, 266, 318, 326
Yongju-sa 210

Yongle (Emperor) 29
Yŏngnam School 191
yŏngsan 216
"Yŏngsanghoesang" 329
Yŏn'gyŏng-sa 200
Yŏnsan Kun (King) 33, 80–82, 168, 191, 205–206
Yu Chinhan 334
Yu Hanggŏm, Augustine 228
Yu Hyŏngwŏn 76
Yu Sŏngnyong 65
Yuan dynasty 28, 89, 104–106, 150, 278; *see also* Mongols
Yuan Shikai 340
Yujŏng 208
Yun Ch'iho 345
Yun Ch'unnyŏn 295
Yun Hyu 85–86
Yun Tusŏ 311

Zen *see* Sŏn Buddhism
Zengzi 184, 261
Zhang Yu 100
Zhe School 306
Zheng Zhilong 21
Zhou dynasty 52, 181
Zhou Wenmo, James 158, 228–229
Zhu Xi 75, 85–86, 139, 166, 183–185, 192–193, 210, 262–263, 268, 298
Zisi 184, 264
zongfan 44